RECIPE FOR A LIVABLE PLANET

AGRICULTURE AND FOOD SERIES

A strong food and agriculture system is fundamental to economic growth, poverty reduction, environmental sustainability, and human health. The Agriculture and Food Series is intended to prompt public discussion and inform policies that will deliver higher incomes, reduce hunger, improve sustainability, and generate better health and nutrition from the food we grow and eat. It expands on the former Agriculture and Rural Development series by considering issues from farm to fork, in both rural and urban settings. Titles in this series undergo internal and external review under the management of the World Bank's Agriculture and Food Global Practice.

Titles in this series

Recipe for a Livable Planet: Achieving Net Zero Emissions in the Agrifood System (2024) by William R. Sutton, Alexander Lotsch, and Ashesh Prasann

Insect and Hydroponic Farming in Africa: The New Circular Food Economy (2021) by Dorte Verner, Nanna Roos, Afton Halloran, Glenn Surabian, Edinaldo Tebaldi, Maximillian Ashwill, Saleema Vellani, and Yasuo Konishi

What's Cooking: Digital Transformation of the Agrifood System (2021) by Kateryna Schroeder, Julian Lampietti, and Ghada Elabed

The Safe Food Imperative: Accelerating Progress in Low- and Middle-Income Countries (2019) by Steven Jaffee, Spencer Henson, Laurian Unnevehr, Delia Grace, and Emilie Cassou

The Land Governance Assessment Framework: Identifying and Monitoring Good Practice in the Land Sector (2012) by Klaus Deininger and Harris Selod

Agricultural Innovation Systems: An Investment Sourcebook (2012), by World Bank

Rising Global Interest in Farmland: Can It Yield Sustainable and Equitable Benefits? (2011) by Klaus Deininger, Jonathan Lindsay, Andrew Norton, and Harris Selod

Gender and Governance in Rural Services: Insights from India, Ghana, and Ethiopia (2010) by World Bank

Building Competitiveness in Africa's Agriculture: A Guide to Value Chain Concepts and Applications (2010) by C. Martin Webber and Patrick Labaste

Bioenergy Development: Issues and Impacts for Poverty and Natural Resource Management (2010) by Elizabeth Cushion, Adrian Whiteman, and Gerhard Dieterle

The Sunken Billions: The Economic Justification for Fisheries Reform (2009) by World Bank and the Food and Agriculture Organization

Agribusiness and Innovation Systems in Africa (2009) by Kurt Larsen and Florian Theus

Agricultural Land Redistribution: Toward Greater Consensus (2009) by Hans P. Binswanger-Mkhize, Camille Bourguignon, and Rogier van den Brink (eds.)

Organization and Performance of Cotton Sectors in Africa: Learning from Reform Experience (2009) by David Tschirley, Colin Poulton, and Patrick Labaste

Forests Sourcebook: Practical Guidance for Sustaining Forests in Development Cooperation (2008) by World Bank

Gender in Agriculture Sourcebook (2008) by World Bank and Food and Agriculture Organization

Sustainable Land Management Sourcebook (2008) by World Bank

Changing the Face of the Waters: The Promise and Challenge of Sustainable Aquaculture (2007) by World Bank

Reforming Agricultural Trade for Developing Countries, Volume 2: Quantifying the Impact of Multilateral Trade Reform (2006) by Alex F. McCalla and John Nash

Enhancing Agricultural Innovation: How to Go Beyond the Strengthening of Research Systems (2006) by World Bank

Reforming Agricultural Trade for Developing Countries, Volume 1: Key Issues for a Pro-Development Outcome of the Doha Round (2006) by Alex F. McCalla and John Nash

Sustainable Land Management: Challenges, Opportunities, and Trade-offs (2006) by World Bank

Agriculture Investment Sourcebook (2005) by World Bank

Shaping the Future of Water for Agriculture: A Sourcebook for Investment in Agricultural Water Management (2005) by World Bank

All books in the Agriculture and Food Series are available free at
https://hdl.handle.net/10986/2151

AGRICULTURE AND FOOD SERIES

RECIPE FOR A LIVABLE PLANET
Achieving Net Zero Emissions in the Agrifood System

William R. Sutton, Alexander Lotsch, and Ashesh Prasann

 **WORLD BANK GROUP**

CONTENTS

Boxes

Figures

Tables

FOREWORD

We are faced with a startling and largely misunderstood reality: the system that feeds us is also feeding the planet's climate crisis. The world's agrifood system emits about 16 gigatons of greenhouse gasses per year, about a third of all global emissions, and is projected to keep growing. At this rate, the Paris Agreement's goal of limiting global heating to 1.5°C by 2050 becomes impossible. The narrative is clear: to protect our planet, we need to transform the way we produce and consume food.

The good news? The ingredients that comprise the *Recipe for a Livable Planet* are already in the pantry.

This report lays out a recipe for transforming the agrifood system from an adversary to an ally in the fight against climate change. The authors show that there are affordable and practical measures currently available to get agrifood system emissions to net zero.

Every country possesses unique opportunities to reduce agrifood emissions tailored to its economy and natural environment. High-income countries can help the developing world reduce agrifood emissions through technology and climate finance and reflect environmental costs in the price of domestically produced, high-emitting foods to drive demand toward sustainable alternatives. Middle-income countries, where most of the cost-effective mitigation opportunities are to be found, can slow down the conversion of forests to pasture and take steps to cut methane in livestock and rice. Meanwhile, low-emitting developing countries have the chance to go straight to green technologies, leading the way toward a new development model and healthier planet.

Governments need to create the legal and economic conditions to facilitate this transformation. The mobilization of finance is essential, both through increased investment and the repurposing of subsidies that encourage environmentally harmful practices. This unified action must be inclusive, safeguarding the most vulnerable people on the frontlines of climate change and food insecurity.

The report underscores the necessity for innovation, bolstered by rigorous research and development, to unlock new methods of sustainable production. This comprehensive recipe is both possible and pragmatic—it promises an agrifood system that is secure and resilient to climate pressures while improving livelihoods and generating sources of employment. By uniting around this strategic and humane approach, we can cultivate an agrifood system that nourishes the planet and its people, ensuring the well-being of current and future generations.

Axel van Trotsenburg
Senior Managing Director for Development Policy and Partnerships
World Bank

ACKNOWLEDGMENTS

This report was prepared by a World Bank Agriculture and Food Global Practice team led by William R. Sutton, Alexander Lotsch, and Ashesh Prasann under the strategic guidance and general direction of Juergen Voegele, Martien Van Nieuwkoop, Renaud Seligmann, and Julian Lampietti. Core World Bank team members from the Climate-Smart Agriculture Team include (in alphabetical order) Malte Paul Plewa, Fatma Rekik, and Ioannis Vasileiou.

Additional World Bank contributors include (in alphabetical order) Margaret Arnold, Cecilia Borgia, Cristina Elizabeth Coirolo, Timila Dhakhwa, Santiago Escobar, Nafiseh Jafarzadeh, Pierre Jean Gerber, Joshua Gill, Kayenat Kabir, Chaerin Lim, Ghazala Mansuri, Anil Markandya, Ana Maria Rojas Mendez, Roy Parizat, Joseph Pryor, Loraine Ronchi, Parmesh Shah, Ahmed Slaibi, Amal Talbi, Janna Dakini Tenzing, Ailin Tomio, Renos Vakis, Mitik Zegeye, Alemayehu Zeleke, and Nkulumo Zinyengere. Ilyun Koh and Michael Norton provided data analytics and visualizations.

Background inputs to the report were provided by a team from the Food and Agriculture Organization of the United Nations (FAO) that included (in alphabetical order) Nancy Aburto, Astrid Agostini, Lorenzo Giovanni Bellù, Martial Bernoux, Hugo Bourhis, Ronnie Brathwaite, Mohamed Eida, Patrizia Fracassi, Fatima Hachem, Jim Hancock, Yenory Hernandez, Israel Klug, Ana Kojakovic, Irini Maltsoglou, Cecilia Nardi, Giulia Palma, Isabel Parras, Manas Puri, Luis Rincon, Nuno Santos, Laure-Sophie Schiettecatte, Jacopo Monzini Taccone di Sitizano, Pedro Morais de Sousa, Francesco Tubiello, Dietmar Ueberbacher, Melissa Vargas, Tancrède Voituriez, and Thomas Zandanel.

The following provided additional data, data analysis, or advice on data: from the World Bank, Luc Christiaensen, Gianluigi Nico, Euijin Jung, and Maryla Maliszewska; externally, Christopher Marcius, Tek Sapkota, and Lou Verchot (Consortium of International Agriculture Research Centres); Daniela Chiriac and Harsha Vishnumolakala (Climate Policy Initiative); Caterina Ruggeri Laderchi (Systemiq); Matthew Jones (University of East Anglia); Alessandro Flammini, Kevin Karl, and Francesco Tubiello (FAOSTAT); Krystal

Crumpler (FAO Agrifood Economics and Policy Division); Philip Thornton (Clim-Eat); Monica Crippa and Efisio Solazzo (European Union Joint Research Centre); Stefan Frank and Petr Havlik (International Institute for Applied Systems Analysis); Francesco Brusaporco and Lorenzo Marelli (World Farmers' Organization); Stefanie Roe (World Wildlife Foundation); Nancy Harris (World Resources Institute); and Keith Fuglie (US Department of Agriculture, Economic Research Service).

Invaluable feedback and advice were received from the following peer reviewers: Richard Damania, Stephane Hallegatte, Andy Jarvis (Bezos Earth Fund), and Dina Umali-Deininger. Additional helpful advice or feedback was provided by World Bank colleagues Alan David Lee, Jason Daniel Russ, Samuel Fargher, and Francisna Christmarine Fernando.

Maximillian Ashwill was the report's primary editor. Alexander A. Ferguson helped draft the Main Messages. Communications and outreach support were provided by Nicolas Douillet, Clare Murphy-McGreevey, and Nugroho Sunjoyo. Venkatakrishnan Ramachandran provided administrative support.

This work was made possible by the generous financial support of Food Systems 2030, an umbrella multi-donor trust fund that helps countries build better food systems by 2030, progressing toward development and climate goals.

ABOUT THE AUTHORS

Alexander Lotsch is a senior climate finance specialist with the World Bank's Agriculture and Food Global Practice, where he shapes strategic engagement on climate finance, climate analytics, and food system transformation. Previously, he led work on nature-based solutions, forests, and land use for the World Bank's Climate Change Group and—while based in Hanoi, Viet Nam—he led the World Bank Environment, Natural Resources and Blue Economy Global Practice's engagement on innovative jurisdiction-wide programs to reduce emissions from deforestation and forest degradation. His earlier work for the World Bank focused on the economics of adaptation, climate risk management, agricultural weather insurance, and decision-making under climate uncertainty. Prior to joining the World Bank in 2004, he worked at the National Aeronautics and Space Administration (United States) and the Environmental Systems Research Institute. He holds a PhD in earth system science and an MA in geography from Boston University and undergraduate degrees in physical geography from Free University Berlin and in agricultural sciences from Humboldt University Berlin.

Ashesh Prasann is a senior agriculture economist in the World Bank's Office of Global Director for the Agriculture and Food Global Practice. He is currently working on climate mitigation through the agrifood system and repurposing of agriculture support policies and programs. Previously, he has authored major analytical pieces, including the World Bank's flagship reports *Future of Food: Shaping the Food System to Deliver Jobs* and *Scaling Up Disruptive Agricultural Technologies in Africa*. He has also led World Bank investment and advisory projects in Latin America and the Caribbean and Sub-Saharan Africa. He holds a PhD in agricultural, food, and resource economics from Michigan State University, an MPP from the University of Chicago, and undergraduate degrees in economics and international studies from Trinity College, Hartford, Conn.

William R. Sutton is the global lead for the World Bank's Climate-Smart Agriculture program and lead agricultural economist in the Agriculture and Food Global Practice. He has worked for more than 25 years to promote sustainable development by integrating across disciplines—including agriculture, the environment, and climate change—and leading investment and analytical projects in East Asia and the Pacific, Europe and Central Asia, the Middle East and North Africa, and Sub-Saharan Africa. Previously, he coordinated the World Bank's climate-smart and sustainable agriculture program in China, including preparing the innovative Hubei Smart and Sustainable Agriculture Project. He has authored and coauthored dozens of journal articles, reports, and books, including the pioneering World Bank report *Looking Beyond the Horizon: How Climate Change Impacts and Adaptation Responses Will Reshape Agriculture in Eastern Europe and Central Asia,* and received the World Bank Green Award in 2011 in recognition of his innovative work on climate change and agriculture. He holds a PhD and MS in agricultural and resource economics from the University of California, Davis.

MAIN MESSAGES

Introduction

Recipe for a Livable Planet is the first comprehensive global strategic framework for mitigating the agrifood system's contributions to climate change. It shows how the system that produces the world's food can cut greenhouse gas (GHG) emissions while continuing to feed the world. The report's main messages are

- The global agrifood system presents a huge opportunity to cut almost a one-third of the world's GHG emissions through affordable and readily available actions.
- These actions will also have three key benefits: they will make food supplies more secure, help our food system better withstand climate change, and ensure that vulnerable people are not harmed by this transition.

The Challenges

Agrifood is a bigger contributor to climate change than many think. It generates almost a third of GHG emissions, averaging around 16 gigatons annually. This is about one-sixth more than all of the world's heat and electricity emissions.

Three-quarters of agrifood emissions come from developing countries, including two-thirds from middle-income countries. Mitigation action has to happen in these countries as well as in high-income countries to make a difference. It is also necessary to take a food systems approach, including emissions from relevant value chains and land use change as well as those from the farm, because more than half of agrifood emissions come from those sources.

Emissions from agrifood must be cut to net zero by 2050. This is needed for the world to achieve its goal of keeping global average temperatures from rising above 1.5°C from pre-industrial levels. Emissions from agrifood alone are so high that they could by themselves make the world miss this target.

Too little money is invested in cutting agrifood emissions, and agrifood lags other sectors in financing for climate action. Finance for reducing or removing emissions in the agrifood system is anemic at 2.4 percent of total mitigation finance.

Agrifood emissions must be cut carefully to avoid job losses and food supply disruptions. The risks of inaction, though, are even greater. Not only would inaction bring job losses and disrupt food supplies. It would also make our planet unlivable.

The Big Opportunities

The agrifood system is a huge, untapped source of low-cost climate change action. Unlike other sectors, it can have an outsize impact on climate change by drawing carbon from the atmosphere through ecosystems and soils.

The payoffs for investing in cutting agrifood emissions are estimated to be much bigger than the costs. Annual investments will need to increase by an estimated 18 times, to $260 billion a year, to halve current agrifood emissions by 2030 and put the world on track for net zero emissions by 2050. Previous estimates show that the benefits in health, economic, and environmental terms could be as much as $4.3 trillion in 2030, a 16-to-1 return on investment costs.

Some of the cost can be paid for by shifting money away from wasteful subsidies, but substantial additional resources are needed to cover the rest. The costs are estimated at less than half the amount the world spends every year on agricultural subsidies, many of them wasteful and harmful for the environment.

Mitigation action in agrifood brings with it many other benefits for people and the planet. Among the benefits are increased food security and resilience, better nutrition for consumers, improved access to finance for farmers, and conservation of biodiversity.

Mitigation in the agrifood system can contribute in many ways to a just transition. This could secure jobs, good health, livelihoods, and food security for vulnerable groups and smallholder farmers.

The Opportunities for Action in Countries and Globally

With their access to resources and technological know-how, high-income countries can play a central role in helping the world cut emissions in agrifood.

- Energy demands by agrifood are the highest in high-income countries, so such countries should do more to promote renewable energy.

- High-income countries should give more financial and technical support to low- and middle-income countries to help them adopt low-emission agrifood practices and build their capacity to effectively use new technologies.
- High-income countries should decrease their own consumer demand for emissions-intensive, animal-source foods. They can influence consumption by ensuring that the environmental and health costs borne by society are fully included in food prices. These countries can also shift subsidies for red meat and dairy toward lower-emission foods, such as poultry, pulses, or fruits and vegetables.

Middle-income countries have great opportunities to cut their agrifood emissions. These countries are where three-quarters of the opportunities exist for emissions to be cut in a cost-effective way. Fifteen large, mostly middle-income countries account for almost two-thirds of the world's cost-effective mitigation potential.

- One-third of the world's opportunities to reduce agrifood emissions in a cost-effective way relate to land use in middle-income countries. Reducing the conversion of forests to croplands or pastures and promoting reforestation or agroforestry can bring big emissions cuts and store carbon in biomass and soils.
- Other opportunities exist in cutting methane in livestock and rice paddies, as well as using sustainable soil management to store carbon and boost agricultural yields and climate resilience.
- Middle-income countries easily emit the most pre- and post-food production emissions, particularly from fertilizer production, food loss and waste, and household food consumption. However, there are cost-effective options for emissions cuts in each of these areas.

Low-income countries should focus on green and competitive growth and avoid building the high-emissions infrastructure that high-income countries must now replace.

- More than half of the agrifood emissions in low-income countries come from converting forests to croplands or pastures; thus, preserving and restoring forests can be a cost-effective way to reduce emissions and promote sustainable economic development.
- Carbon credits and emissions trading can put a value on forests' standing that preserves them as carbon sinks, a refuge for animals and plants, and a source of sustainable jobs for Indigenous peoples and others.
- Improved agricultural practices such as agroforestry, which integrates trees in croplands, could not only store carbon but also make the land more productive, offer job opportunities, and provide more diversified diets. Likewise, climate-smart agriculture techniques could lower emissions while offering economic gains and more resilience to climate change.

Actions at the country and global levels can create more favorable conditions for reducing agrifood emissions. Governments, businesses, farmers, consumers, and international organizations must work together to:

- Make private investments in agrifood mitigation less risky and more possible, while repurposing wasteful subsidies and introducing public policies to encourage low emissions and productivity-enhancing technologies;

- Capitalize on emerging digital technologies to improve information for measurement, reporting, and verification of GHG emissions reductions, while investing in innovation to drive the agrifood system transformation into the future; and
- Leverage institutions at the international, national, and subnational levels to facilitate these opportunities while ensuring a just transition through the inclusion of stakeholders like smallholder farmers, women, and Indigenous groups, who are at the front lines of climate change.

Conclusion

The food system must be fixed because it is making the planet ill and is a big slice of the climate change pie. There is action that can be taken now to make agrifood a bigger contributor to overcoming climate change and healing the planet. These actions are readily available and affordable.

Overview

Introduction

The global agrifood system's top priority is ensuring food and nutrition security for everyone, but it also has an increasingly large role to play in protecting the planet. The Paris Agreement on climate change explicitly states that "the fundamental priority" of the agrifood system is "safeguarding food security and ending hunger" and to "foster climate resilience and low greenhouse gas emissions." Society also relies on the agrifood system to provide jobs and development while protecting the environment and promoting human health (Willett et al. 2019). However, conventional agriculture and food production often degrade soils and natural ecosystems and contribute to deforestation, biodiversity loss, ocean acidification, and air and water pollution (IPCC 2022c; UNCCD 2022). Likewise, common diets can undermine nutrition and human development. It has also become increasingly clear that the agrifood system is one of the biggest contributors to greenhouse gas (GHG) emissions and the world's worsening climate crisis. These conditions are set to deteriorate even further as the world attempts to feed a global population that will grow by 2 billion by 2050. More food means accelerating food production, land use changes, and related emissions, which exacerbate global heating. In turn, global heating will affect future agricultural yields and food security (Bajželj and Richards 2014). To compensate, food producers will intensify activities even further, causing even higher GHG emissions in a vicious circle (figure O.1).

All dollar amounts are US dollars unless otherwise indicated.

FIGURE O.1 Positive Feedback Loops between Agrifood Activities and the Climate Have Created a Vicious Circle That Precludes Adaptation Alone as a Solution to the Crisis

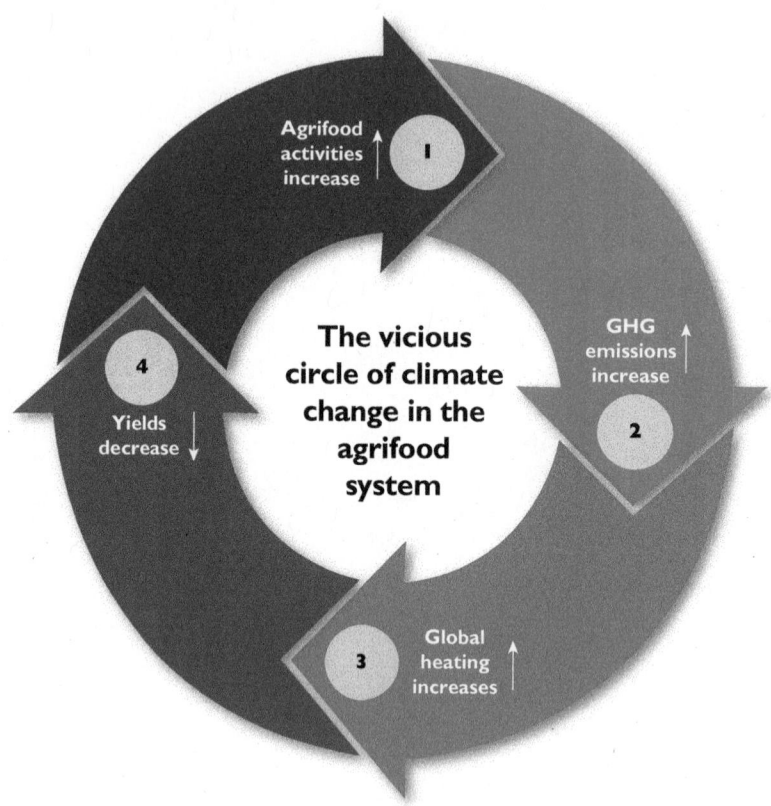

Source: Original figure for this publication.
Note: GHG = greenhouse gas.

Most of the world's action to limit GHG emissions has not targeted the agrifood system, but this must change to achieve net zero emissions and limit global heating. Until now, efforts to reduce GHG emissions have focused elsewhere—on sectors like energy, transport, and manufacturing, where scaling up a few key technologies has made an important difference in reducing emissions. However, these low-hanging fruits have mostly been harvested, and emissions levels are still far from where they need to be to avert climate catastrophe. The world has avoided confronting agrifood system emissions for as long as it could because of the scope and complexity of the task, instead focusing on helping people and businesses adapt to the problem. But, according to scientists, "we cannot adapt our way out of the climate crisis" (Harvey 2022), and now is the time to put agriculture and food at the top of the mitigation agenda. If not, the world will be unable to ensure a livable planet for future generations (IPCC 2023, 21–22).

This report, *Recipe for a Livable Planet: Achieving Net Zero Emissions in the Agrifood System*, is the first comprehensive global strategic framework for mitigating the agrifood system's contributions to climate change. It identifies solutions that cost-effectively limit agrifood GHG emissions to net zero while maintaining global food security, building climate resilience, and ensuring a just transition for vulnerable groups. It identifies mitigation areas with the greatest potential for reducing agrifood system emissions for each World Bank country income category (high-, middle-, and low-income). The logic is that by focusing on the biggest emissions sources and the most cost-effective mitigation options, countries will be able to most quickly and cheaply diminish or prevent agrifood GHGs from reaching the atmosphere. This is not to say that these solutions are mutually exclusive: ideally, all countries would apply all cost-effective mitigation options immediately and concurrently. It is simply recognizing that countries have different opportunities to combat climate change through the agrifood system. The report also illuminates a path for strengthening the enabling environment for transforming the agrifood system to a net zero model through six I's: investments, incentives, information, innovation, institutions, and inclusion. Collaborative efforts among governments, businesses, citizens, and international organizations and frameworks to bolster this environment will give the world its best chance to meet the Paris Agreement's emissions targets.

This report is timely for several reasons. First, there is much more knowledge today about the global agrifood system and its growing climate footprint than there was even a few years ago. Second, it has become clear that virtually all pathways to limiting global heating to 1.5°C by 2050 will require net zero emissions from the agrifood system. Third, now is the time to drastically reorient the agrifood system, as its current form is pushing the planet beyond its operating limits. Fourth, despite the urgency, the agriculture negotiations under the United Nations Framework Convention on Climate Change (UNFCCC) have stalled, with a particular divide between countries from the global north and south over the issue of mitigation (Puko 2023). Fifth, the World Bank, under the leadership of its new president, has announced a new vision that puts climate change mitigation and other global public goods at the center of everything it does, with a mandate to create a world free from poverty "on a livable planet" (World Bank 2023).

The Agrifood System Has a Big Climate Problem

GHG emissions from the agrifood system are significantly higher than previously thought. Previous calculations estimated that agriculture, forestry, and other land use (AFOLU) have generated about one-fifth of global GHGs (IPCC 2022b). However, more recent and holistic measurements that include pre- and post-production emissions show that the global agrifood system is responsible for significantly higher GHG emissions than previously thought: on average, 16 billion metric tons of carbon dioxide equivalent (CO_2eq) per year, or about 31 percent of the world's total GHG emissions (figure O.2) (Crippa et al. 2021; Tubiello et al. 2022). To put that into perspective, that is 2.24 billion tons, or 14 percent, more than all of the world's heat and electricity emissions.[1] However, reducing GHG emissions from the global agrifood system has received scant attention. For example, only about half of the Paris Agreement countries originally included agriculture-related GHG targets in their Nationally Determined Contributions (NDCs) (Fransen et al. 2022). The biggest contributions to agrifood system emissions come from eight key emissions sources: (1) livestock-related emissions, 25.9 percent; (2) net forest conversion, 18.4 percent; (3) food system waste, 7.9 percent; (4) household food consumption patterns, 7.3 percent; (5) fertilizer production and use, 6.9 percent; (6) soil-related emissions, 5.7 percent; (7) on-farm energy use and supply, 5.4 percent; and (8) rice production–related emissions, 4.3 percent. These categories represent the supply side of emissions, or the sources from which GHGs are emitted. It is worth noting that an examination of agrifood emissions from the demand side would paint a different picture.

FIGURE O.2 Greenhouse Gas Emissions from the Agrifood System Are Significantly Higher Than Previously Thought

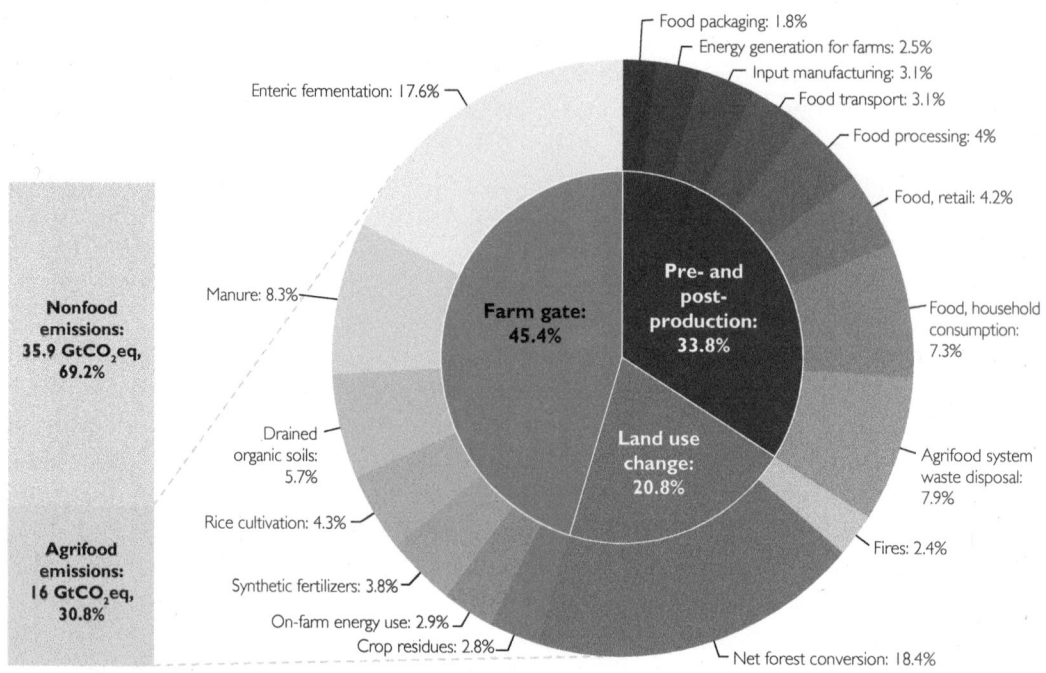

Source: World Bank analysis based on data from FAOSTAT 2023a.
Note: Left: Mean annual global greenhouse gas (GHG) emissions from the agrifood system as a share of total GHG emissions, 2018–20. Right: Emissions broken down by the three main subcategories and their individual components. $GtCO_2eq$ = gigatons of carbon dioxide equivalent.

Middle-income countries (MICs) are the biggest contributors to cumulative agrifood system emissions, while high-income countries (HICs) have the highest per capita emissions. This report analyzes agrifood system emissions by World Bank–defined country income levels—specifically, HICs, MICs, and LICs. It reveals widely diverse emissions profiles, with MICs generating most agrifood emissions both today and historically, HICs having the highest per capita emissions, and low-income countries (LICs) having the highest rates of emissions increases. Today, MICs contribute 68 percent of global agrifood emissions, compared with 21 percent from HICs and 11 percent from LICs. Note that the MIC category has the most countries, 108 worldwide, compared with 77 HICs and just 28 LICs. In that sense, it should be no surprise that MICs and their larger populations emit the most.[2] However, splitting the MIC group into lower-middle-income countries (LMICs) and upper-middle-income countries (UMICs) results in 55 LMICs and 53 UMICs but does not change the result, with agrifood emissions from each MIC sub-group far outstripping emissions from HICs and LICs (figure O.3). HICs' high per capita emissions are driven largely by the heavy consumption of meat and dairy and the increase in food transport, processing, packaging, and waste (FAO 2018). That said, HICs' share of agrifood emissions has declined as their population growth has decelerated, their economies have shifted from agriculture to manufacturing and services, they have outsourced food production to MICs and LICs, and they have invested in food sector productivity and renewable energy (Crippa et al. 2021). LICs produce the fewest overall GHG emissions from the agrifood system but have had

FIGURE O.3 Upper-Middle-Income Countries Generate the Highest Agrifood Emissions, Both Today and 30 Years Ago

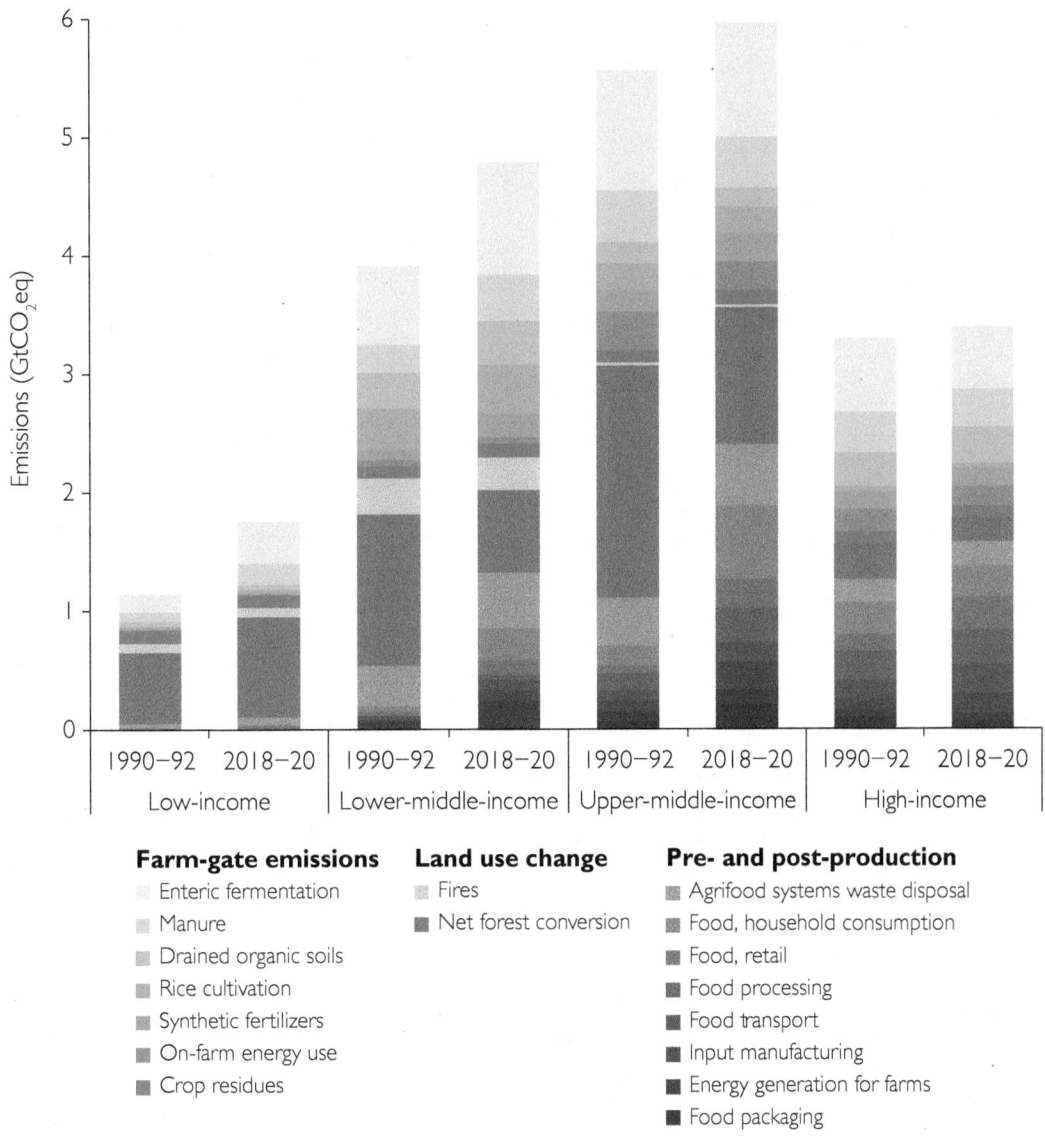

Sources: World Bank analysis based on data from World Bank 2024 and FAOSTAT 2023a.
Note: Panel shows mean annual agrifood emissions for 1990–92 and 2018–20 by source category and country income group. Categories are grouped to reduce those with small values. "Manure" consists of manure left on pasture, manure management, and manure applied to soils. "Crop residues" consists of savanna fires, crop residues, and burning crop residues. "Fires" consists of fires in organic soils and fires in humid tropical forests. "Input manufacturing" consists of fertilizer manufacturing and pesticide manufacturing. "On-farm energy use" consists of on-farm heat use and on-farm electricity use. GtCO$_2$eq = gigatons of carbon dioxide equivalent; HICs = high-income countries; LICs = low-income countries; LMICs = lower-middle-income countries; UMICs = upper-middle-income countries.

the highest rate of increase since the early 1990s: a 53 percent increase, compared with a 12.3 percent increase for MICs and a 3 percent increase for HICs. Digging deeper into these profiles shows that the bulk of agrifood emissions are concentrated in a handful of countries, mostly MICs (figure O.4). This trend is likely to continue because MICs are largely following the same emissions-heavy development path that HICs (Jones et al. 2023) historically followed but with much larger and growing populations.

FIGURE O.4 Seven of the Top 10 Agrifood System Emitters Are Middle-Income Countries, and One Is a Low-Income Country

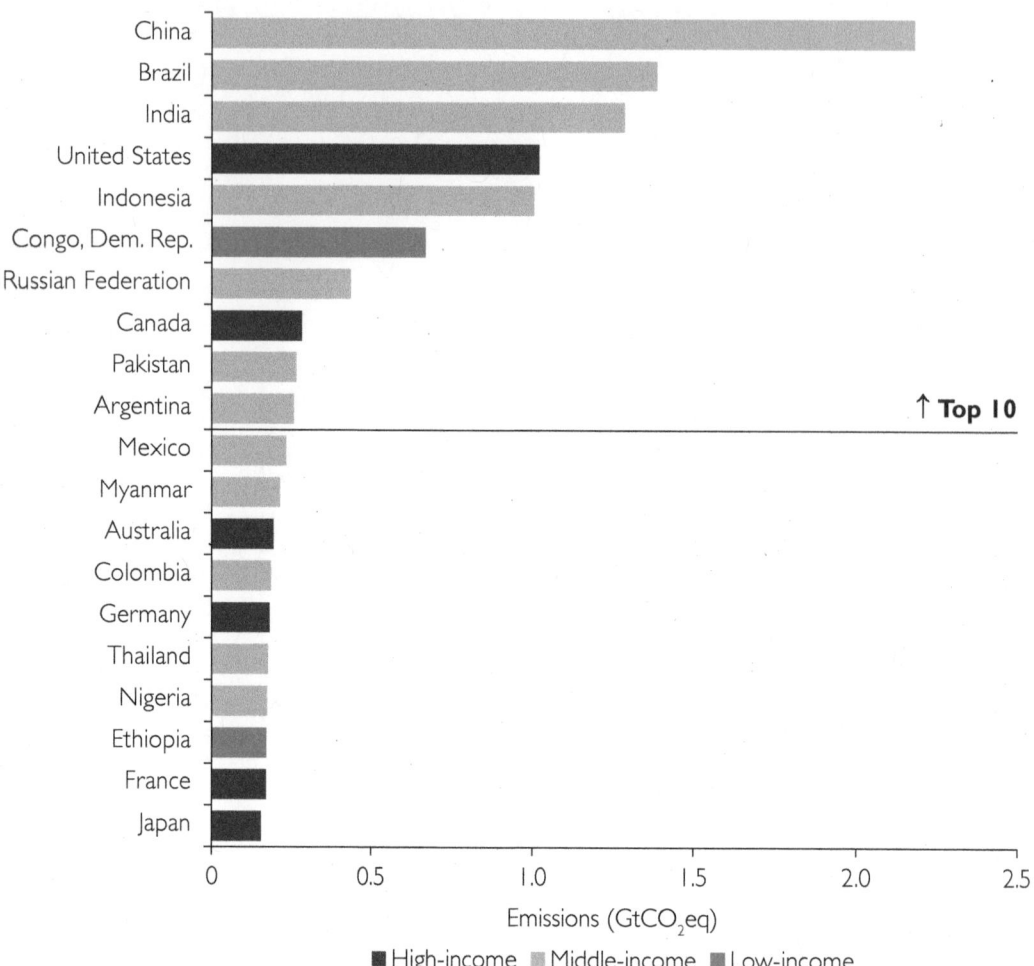

Sources: World Bank analysis based on data from World Bank 2024 and FAOSTAT 2023a.
Note: Figure shows average annual agrifood system emissions for 2018–20. GtCO₂eq = gigatons of carbon dioxide equivalent.

The world cannot achieve the Paris Agreement targets without achieving net zero emissions in the agrifood system. The temperature targets enshrined in the Paris Agreement reflect the scientific consensus that warming above 1.5°C from preindustrial levels threatens the most exposed countries and that warming above 2°C would lead to wide-ranging and catastrophic impacts, such as food shortages and more-destructive storms (IPCC 2018). To meet the 1.5°C target, the world would effectively need to reduce global GHG emissions from 52 gigatons per year to zero annually by 2050, with any unavoidable emissions offset by GHG-capturing activities. However, current projections, with policies in place as of 2020 and no additional action, or "business as usual," suggest that global warming would reach 3.2°C by 2100 (IPCC 2023). Moreover, recent research finds that even if all fossil fuel emissions are eliminated from every other sector, the emissions from the agrifood system alone would be enough to drive the planet past the 1.5°C threshold and even put the 2.0°C goal at serious risk (Clark et al. 2020). Therefore, the world would need to reduce net agrifood

GHG emissions from 16 gigatons annually to zero by 2050 to have any hope of meeting the 1.5°C Paris Agreement target.

There is a major financing shortfall for agrifood system mitigation. Overall, climate finance has almost doubled over the past decade (Naran et al. 2022), but project-level climate financing for the agrifood system stands at only 4.3 percent, or $28 billion, of global climate finance for mitigation and adaptation in all sectors (figure O.5). Mitigation finance for the agrifood sector was even more anemic, reaching only $14.4 billion in 2019–20, or 2.2 percent of total climate finance and 2.4 percent of total mitigation finance (CPI 2023; Naran et al. 2022). Instead, most climate finance is dedicated to other sectors, such as renewable energy, which receives 51 percent of financing, or low-carbon transportation, which receives 26 percent of financing (Naran et al. 2022). This report estimates that annual investments in reducing agrifood emissions will need to increase by 18 times, to $260 billion, to reduce current food system emissions by half by 2030.

If not done carefully, there could be short-term social and economic trade-offs in converting to a low-emission agrifood system. Some studies predict that agrifood system reforms, if not designed carefully, could lead to less agricultural production and higher food prices (Hasegawa et al. 2021). For example, reducing fertilizer or adopting organic farming would reduce emissions by 15 percent but could also reduce agricultural production by

FIGURE O.5 Finance for Mitigation in the Agrifood System Is Strikingly Low Relative to Its Importance

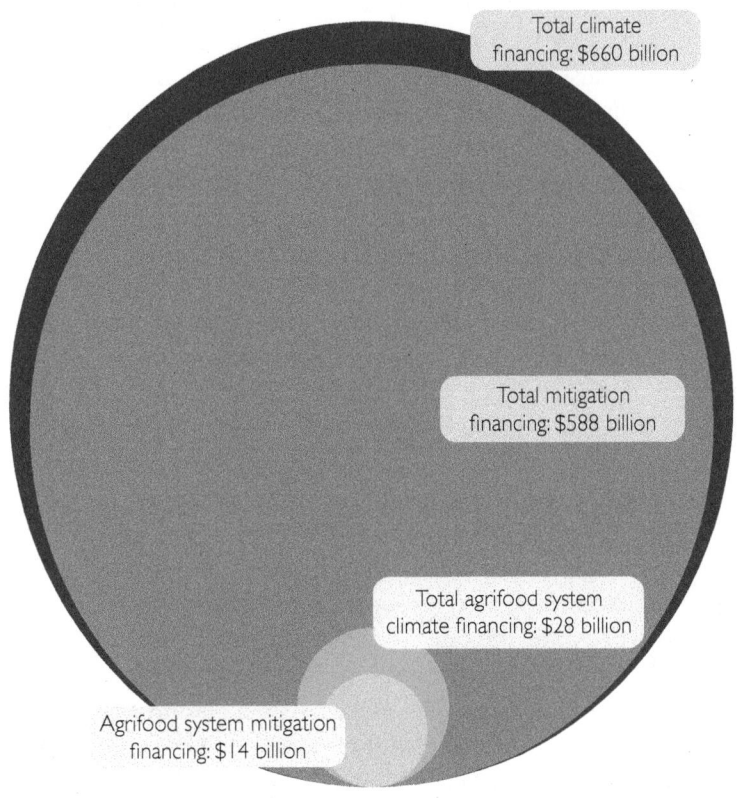

Sources: World Bank analysis based on data from CPI 2023 and Naran et al. 2022.
Note: Figure shows for 2019/20 global tracked project-level climate finance ($, billions) for adaptation, mitigation, and dual-purpose action economywide and for the agrifood system.

5 percent, increase world food prices by 13 percent, and raise the cost of healthy diets by 10 percent (European Commission 2020). Other studies have been even gloomier, projecting that afforestation measures could put 40 million people at risk of food insecurity by 2050 (Fujimori et al. 2022). Likewise, emissions pricing schemes would inherently increase prices for high-emitting foods, disproportionately affecting low-income families. Other studies predict that lowering agrifood emissions could lead to competition over land, water, and energy resources and affect jobs in LICs, where the agrifood sector accounts for 64 percent of total employment, compared with 39 percent in MICs and 11 percent in HICs. Because of these potential trade-offs, the transition to a net zero agrifood system is likely to encounter political and cultural obstacles.

The costs of inaction are even higher than the potential trade-offs. The world's food system has successfully fed a growing population but has fallen short of promoting optimal health and nutrition goals. Starting in 2014, human health outcomes began to decline because the agrifood system's simple focus on increasing calorie availability meant that there was less attention to producing healthier foods (Ambikapathi et al. 2022). Partly as a result, adult and child obesity keeps rising (FAO et al. 2021), and 6 of the top 10 risk factors for death and disease in both men and women are diet related (Abbafati et al. 2020). However, by 2020, healthy diets were unaffordable for 3 billion people, an increase of 119 million from 2019. Likewise, the global agrifood system disproportionately and detrimentally affects poor communities and smallholder farmers who cannot compete with industrial agriculture, thereby exacerbating rural poverty and increasing landlessness (Clapp, Newell, and Brent 2017).

In addition, the globalized nature of the agrifood system entails food price volatility. For example, over 122 million more people faced hunger since 2019 because of supply chain disruptions caused by COVID-19 (coronavirus) and repeated weather shocks and conflicts, including the Russian Federation's invasion of Ukraine (FAO et al. 2023). Besides these human costs, today's food system also causes trillions of dollars' worth of negative externalities every year. *Externalities*, in this case, refers to indirect costs that arise from the agrifood system that are felt not by the actor that creates the cost but by society. These global food system externalities are estimated to cause around $20 trillion in costs per year, or nearly 20 percent of gross world product (Hendriks et al. 2021). These externalities are already pushing the planet beyond its operational boundaries (figure O.6) (Roson 2017).

Transformation of the agrifood system can deliver multiple benefits without any of these trade-offs if coupled with resilience building. Investing in low-emission agriculture and transforming food and land use could generate health, economic, and environmental benefits totaling $4.3 trillion in 2030,[3] a 16-to-1 return on investment costs. Likewise, new research (Damania, Polasky, et al. 2023) shows that climate-smart practices that combine adaptation and mitigation measures could increase cropland, livestock, and forestry incomes by approximately $329 billion annually while at the same time increasing global food production by enough to feed the world until 2050, without losses in biodiversity or carbon storage levels. According to one study, more-efficient land use could sequester an additional 85 gigatons of carbon dioxide—equivalent to over a year and a half of total global GHG emissions—with no adverse economic impacts (Damania, Polasky, et al. 2023). In addition, better production strategies and smarter spatial planning can improve crop yields and reduce agriculture's land footprint while limiting its GHG footprint and increasing global calorie production by more than 150 percent. This translates to an 82 percent increase in net value from the world's current crop, livestock, and timber production. Over the long term (2080–2100), the benefits are much clearer. Early mitigation action is projected to lower

FIGURE O.6 Environmental Pressures Are Surpassing Many Planetary Boundaries

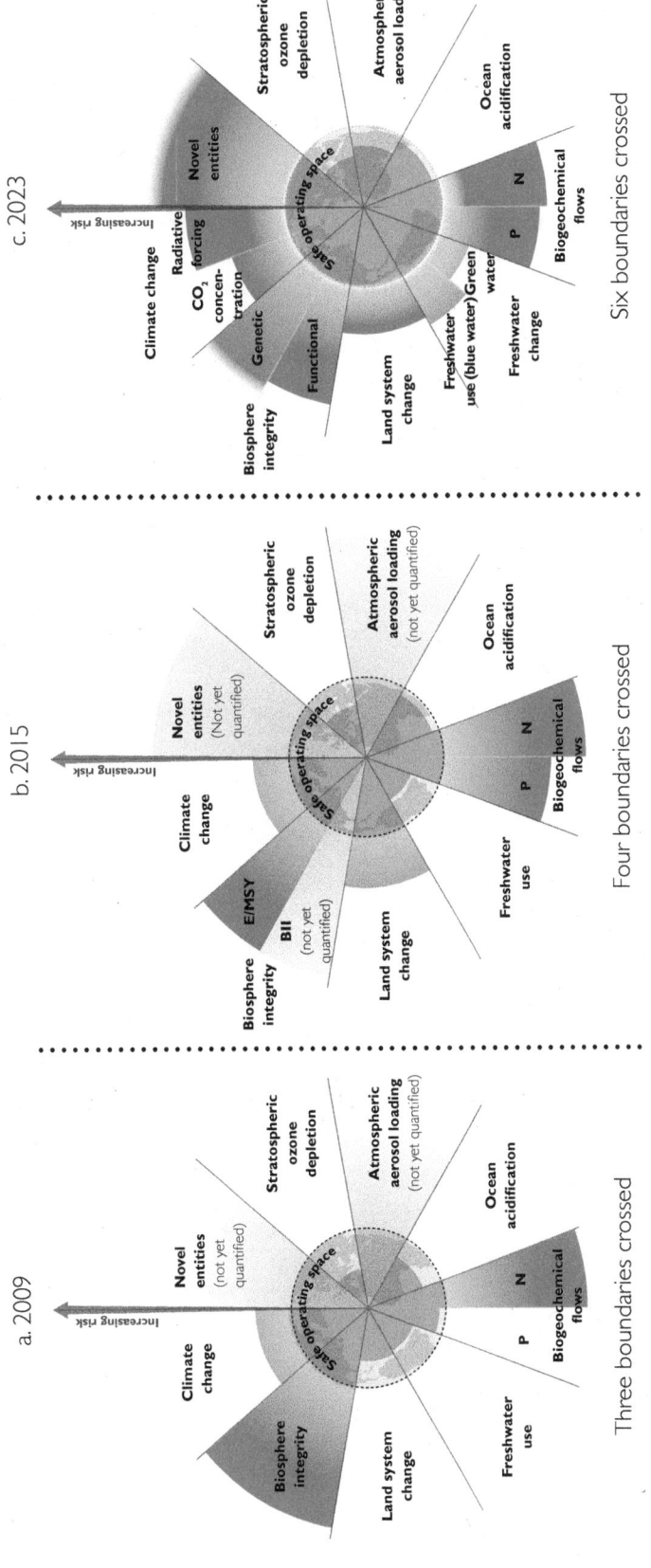

a. 2009

Three boundaries crossed

b. 2015

Four boundaries crossed

c. 2023

Six boundaries crossed

Source: Azote for Stockholm Resilience Centre, Stockholm University. Based on Richardson et al. 2023, Steffen et al. 2015, and Rockström et al. 2009.

Note: BII = Biodiversity Intactness Index; CO_2 = carbon dioxide; E/MSY = extinctions per million species-years; N = nitrogen; P = phosphorus.

long-term food prices by 4.2 percent, hunger risk for 4.8 million people, and water demand for irrigation by 7.2 cubic kilometers (km^3) per year (Hasegawa et al. 2021).

Country Mitigation Potential: Every Country Can Harness Priority Opportunities to Achieve Net Zero Agrifood Emissions While Advancing Development

There are cost-effective mitigation opportunities for all countries, but they depend on each country's relative circumstances. Fifteen large countries account for 62 percent of the world's cost-effective mitigation potential (figure O.7). Eleven of these countries are MICs. Cost-effective mitigation potential is the technical mitigation potential that is available and costs less than $100 per ton of CO_2eq reductions.[4] Among country categories, 73 percent of cost-effective AFOLU mitigation opportunities are in MICs, 18 percent are in HICs, and 9 percent are in LICs. The Intergovernmental Panel on Climate Control (IPCC) estimates that 39 percent (5.3 gigatons of CO_2eq [$GtCO_2$eq]) of the cost-effective mitigation potential is achievable at costs below $50 per ton of CO_2eq, including 28 percent (3.8 $GtCO_2$eq)

FIGURE O.7 The Most Cost-Effective Mitigation Potential Is in Middle-Income Countries

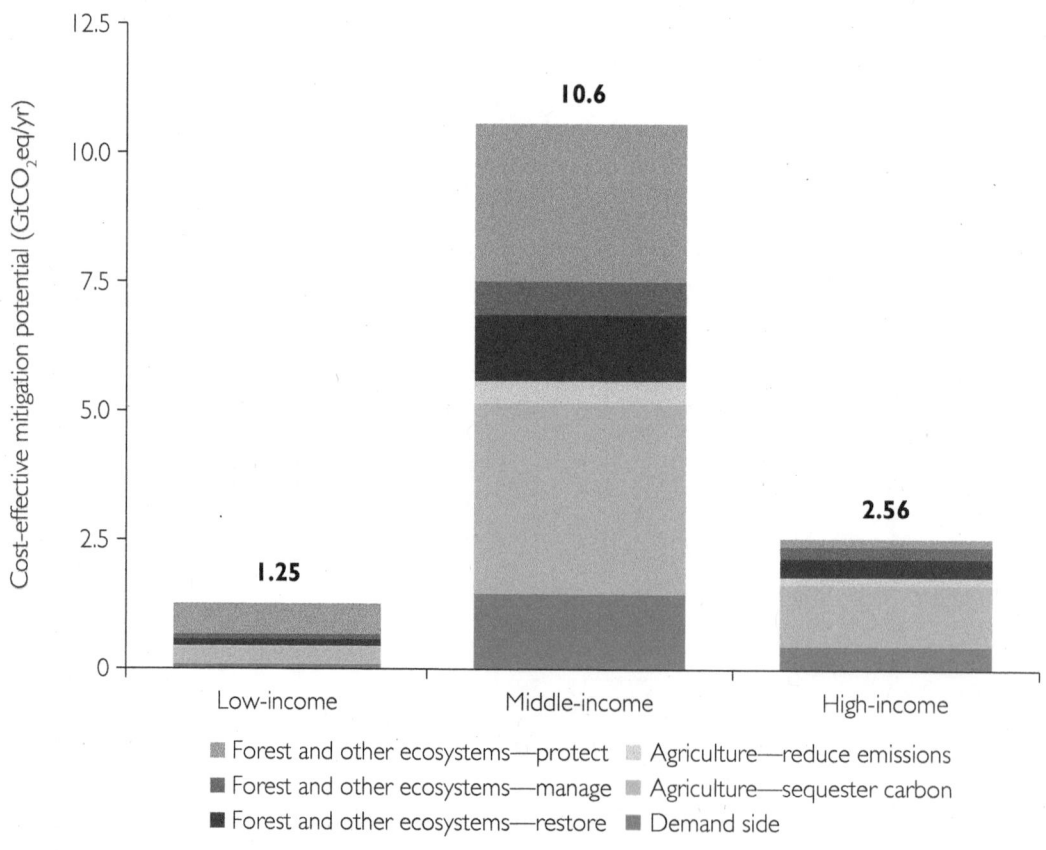

Sources: World Bank analysis based on data from Roe et al. 2021 and World Bank 2024.
Note: Figure shows for 2020–50 the average annual cost-effective mitigation potential by country income group and measure. $GtCO_2$eq/yr = gigatons of carbon dioxide equivalent per year.

Recipe for a Livable Planet

at less than $20 per ton of CO_2eq (Nabuurs et al. 2022). Moreover, some countries have mitigation options with negative costs (less than $0 per ton of CO_2eq), suggesting that these options can both reduce emissions and increase farm profitability. For example, 40 percent of current methane emissions could be avoided at no net cost when co-benefits are accounted for (IEA 2023b). Such cost-saving mitigation options account for more than a third of technical mitigation potential in China's agriculture sector, half in India's, and three-quarters in Bangladesh's. A country's pathway to cost-effective emissions reductions is shaped by its natural endowments and other factors. For example, Brazil is a large, heavily forested, meat-producing and -consuming MIC that has the highest cost-effective mitigation potential in Latin America and the Caribbean. This is because many cost-effective measures are available for the country to take to reduce food system emissions, from protecting and restoring forests to shifting to healthy and sustainable diets and sequestering carbon in agriculture (figure O.8) (Roe et al. 2021).[5] In contrast, the pathway to cost-effective decarbonization is much narrower for the Democratic Republic of Congo, which is also heavily forested but has significantly less income per capita and less meat production and consumption.

FIGURE O.8 **Countries Have Specific Pathways to Reducing Their Agrifood System Emissions**

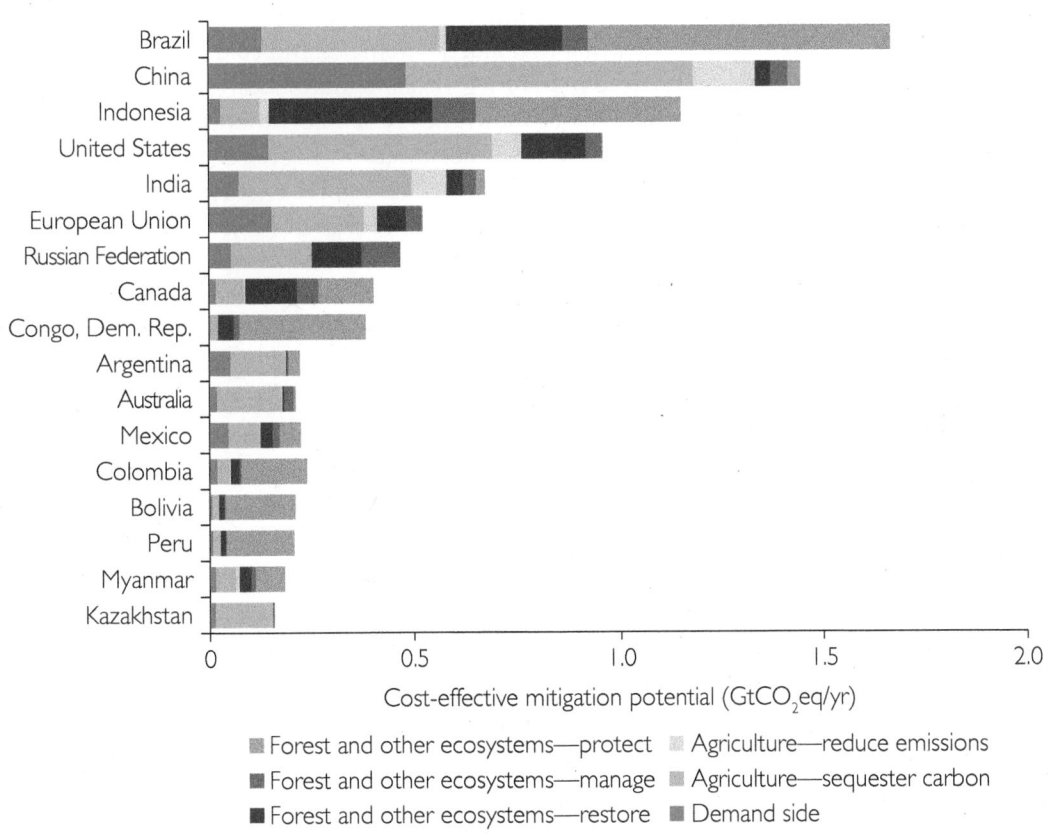

Cost-effective mitigation potential (GtCO$_2$eq/yr)

- Forest and other ecosystems—protect
- Forest and other ecosystems—manage
- Forest and other ecosystems—restore
- Agriculture—reduce emissions
- Agriculture—sequester carbon
- Demand side

Source: World Bank analysis based on data from Roe et al. 2021.
Note: Figure shows for top 16 countries and the European Union the total cost-effective mitigation potential by mitigation category and measure. GtCO$_2$eq/yr = gigatons of carbon dioxide equivalent per year.

HICs' Greatest Opportunities for Reducing Agrifood System Emissions Are From Curbing Energy Emissions, Aiding Developing Nations in Their Shift to Low-Emissions Pathways, and Fully Pricing High-Emissions Foods

The global agrifood system's energy demands are highest in HICs and are on the rise globally, but alternative low-emission energy sources provide a counterbalance. Today, energy use accounts for a third of all agrifood system emissions (Crippa et al. 2021), with most of these energy needs being met by fossil fuel–based energy. The doubling of energy-intensive pre- and post-production emissions, especially in HICs (Tubiello et al. 2022), led to a 17 percent increase of agrifood systems emissions between 1990 and 2015 (Crippa et al. 2021). Indeed, 46 percent of agrifood system emissions in HICs come from pre- and post-production processes. For comparison, 35 percent of agrifood system emissions in MICs and only 6 percent in LICs come from these processes. In fact, the food industry has the slowest progress in energy efficiency among economic sectors (IEA 2022). Partly as a result, the world is off track to meet the sustainable development goal of doubling the global energy efficiency rate by 2030.[6] Renewable energy production is helping to change this situation. In 2022 alone, renewable energy–generated electricity avoided 600 million tons of CO_2 emissions (IEA 2022) compared to if that electricity had come from fossil fuels (Wiatros-Motyka 2023). This has impacts on the agrifood system as well. For instance, replacing one-quarter of India's 8.8 million diesel irrigation pumps with solar ones would reduce emissions by 11.5 million tons per year. This amount is more than twice as much as the 5 million tons in global emissions that electric vehicles and solar panels prevented in 2020.[7] Deploying renewables leads to other positive outcomes, such as increased employment and reduced pollution (IRENA and ILO 2022). Fortunately, the adoption of renewable energy sources is growing, with renewables accounting for 83 percent of all new electricity capacity (IRENA 2023). Most importantly, renewable energy is a cost-effective mitigation strategy, with abatement costs of only $20 to $50 per ton of carbon dioxide (Elshurafa et al. 2021).

HICs are positioned to transfer financial and technical support to LICs and MICs for agrifood system mitigation. This financial support could be in the form of grants, concessional loans, or climate finance. Such financial support is in everyone's interest, because climate change mitigation is the ultimate global public good. Moreover, many HICs are at the forefront of technological advancements. As such, they can leverage their expertise to transfer advanced technologies to LICs and MICs, empowering them to adopt low-emission agrifood system practices. However, merely transferring technology is not enough. HICs and their international partners could also lead comprehensive capacity-building initiatives to ensure that LICs and MICs can effectively utilize these technologies. That said, MICs must continue to recognize their own agrifood system contributions to GHG emissions by continuing to invest in and implement policies for climate action.

HICs can decrease consumer demand for emissions-intensive, animal-source foods by fully pricing environmental and health externalities, repurposing subsidies, and promoting sustainable food options. As global populations become wealthier, they consume more emissions-intensive foods, like meat and dairy (Ranganathan et al. 2016). HICs have the highest per capita incomes, so demand for and consumption of high-emitting, animal-source foods are greatest in those countries (Vranken et al. 2014). For example, in North America, the average citizen consumes 36 kilograms (kg) of bovine meat per year, whereas the global average is 9 kg per person per year (FAO 2023a; FAOSTAT 2023b). This trend of increased meat consumption is also occurring in MICs and LICs as their populations graduate out of poverty (Clark and Tilman 2017; Clark et al. 2020). For example, as poverty declined from 1990 to 2020, cattle meat production grew from 53 to 68 million tons, a 30 percent increase, and added close to 0.25 $GtCO_2eq$ to the atmosphere.

Currently, the demand for animal-source diets accounts for almost 60 percent of total agrifood emissions across all emissions categories (Xu et al. 2021). Thus, the cost-effective mitigation potential from shifting diets away from meat is about twice as high as that from reducing enteric fermentation and other livestock production mitigation methods. Full-cost pricing of animal-source food to reflect its true planetary costs would make low-emission food options more competitive. Globally, one-third of agricultural subsidies were directed toward meat and milk products in 2016 (Springmann and Freund 2022). Indeed, studies have shown that if prices were to reflect the true health, climate, and environmental costs of meat, meat prices would be 20–60 percent higher, depending on the type of meat (Funke et al. 2022). As a result, repurposing red meat and dairy subsidies toward low-emission foods, like poultry, pulses, or fruits and vegetables, could lead to significant changes in consumption patterns and large emissions reductions. Likewise, governments, businesses, and citizens can expand low-emission food options through (1) financial measures, (2) choice architecture strategies, (3) food labeling, and (4) education and communication campaigns. Consumer changes to healthy, low-emission diets would reduce diet-related emissions by up to 80 percent and reduce land and water use by 50 percent (Aleksandrowicz et al. 2016).

MICs Have the Opportunity to Curb Up to Two-Thirds of Global Agrifood Emissions through Sustainable Land Use, Low-Emission Farming Practices, and Cleaner Pre- and Post-production Processes

A shift to more sustainable land use in MICs could reduce a third of global agrifood emissions cost-effectively. Cropland expansion and deforestation leave a massive carbon footprint in MIC economies. Globally, deforestation contributes 11 percent of total CO_2eq emissions (IPCC 2022c), with 90 percent of that caused by expanding croplands and livestock pastures (FAO 2020). Since 2001, a few MICs with extensive forests have caused over 80 percent of commodity-driven deforestation emissions (WRI 2023). A quarter to a third of permanent forest loss is linked to the production of seven agricultural commodities: cattle, palm oil, soy, cocoa, rubber, coffee, and plantation wood fiber. A similar amount of forest loss is driven by shifting agriculture (figure O.9) (Goldman et al. 2020). The largest share of global cost-effective agrifood mitigation options comes from the conservation, improved management, and restoration of forests and other ecosystems, with reduced deforestation in tropical regions being particularly effective (IPCC 2022b). Cost-effective land use mitigation measures could avoid 5 $GtCO_2eq$ emissions per year in MICs alone (6.5 $GtCO_2eq$ globally). By some estimates, the cost of protecting 30 percent of the world's forests and mangroves would require an annual investment of just $140 billion (Waldron et al. 2020), which is equal to only about one-quarter of global annual government support for agriculture. In response, a growing number of commodity producers in these countries have introduced programs to reduce their deforestation footprint, but results are limited. There is still a lack of transparency about where many commodities come from and whether they contribute to deforestation (zu Ermgassen et al. 2022).

FIGURE O.9 Emissions from Converting Forests to Agriculture Have Increased Since 2001

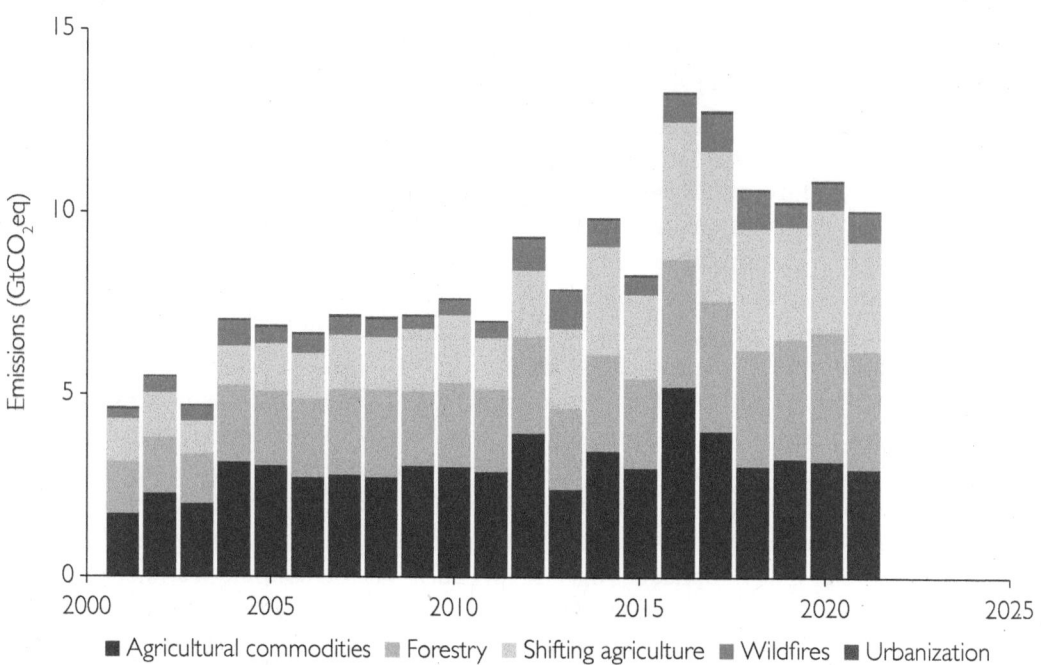

■ Agricultural commodities ■ Forestry ■ Shifting agriculture ■ Wildfires ■ Urbanization

Source: World Bank analysis based on data from Harris et al. 2021.
Note: Figure shows for 2001–21 the annual global greenhouse gas emissions by driver. Emissions—carbon dioxide (CO_2), nitrous oxide (N_2O), and methane (CH_4)—from the gross forest loss globally are disaggregated by drivers. Forest clearing for agricultural commodities such as oil palm or cattle and shifting cultivation make up more than half of deforestation emissions. $GtCO_2eq$ = gigatons of carbon dioxide equivalent.

More than a quarter of MICs' agrifood system emissions are in the livestock sector. As of 2019, MICs caused 67 percent of GHG direct emissions from livestock, including 34 percent for LMICs and 33 percent for UMICs (FAOSTAT 2023a). By comparison, LICs contributed only 11 percent of livestock emissions in 2019. Moreover, MIC livestock emissions are on the rise. Between 2010 and 2019, MIC livestock emissions grew by 6 percent, compared with a decrease of 2 percent for HICs and an astounding 64 percent increase for LICs, although from a much lower level of initial emissions (Delgado et al. 1999). MICs also have high emissions intensity in livestock production. For example, producing 1 kg of livestock protein in MICs generated 121 kg of CO_2eq, compared with only 79 kg of CO_2eq per kg of proteins in HICs (FAO 2023d). That said, this high-emission intensity also means that livestock mitigation potential is greatest in MICs. Therefore, supply-side solutions such as reducing animal-source food loss and waste, increasing livestock productivity, limiting pasture expansion, and adopting innovative technical solutions could go a long way toward reducing agrifood system emissions to zero. However, as previously stated, demand-side measures to curb meat demand are much more cost-effective than these supply-side measures.

There are multiple avenues for mitigating emissions, particularly methane, in rice production in Asian MICs. Rice supplies around 20 percent of the world's calories (Fukagawa and Ziska 2019), but the warm, waterlogged soil of flooded rice paddies provides ideal conditions for bacterial processes that produce methane—most of which is released into the atmosphere (Schimel 2000). As a result, paddy rice production is responsible, on average, for 16 percent of agricultural methane emissions, or 1.5 percent of total anthropogenic GHG emissions (Searchinger et al. 2021). The high methane content of rice emissions means that rice's yield-scaled global warming potential is about four times higher than that of wheat or maize (Linquist et al. 2012). Notably, virtually all rice-related GHG emissions, which also include carbon dioxide and nitrous oxide, originate in MICs, and the vast majority originate in Asian countries. That said, intermittent water application and aerobic rice production methods have great potential for reducing rice-related GHG emissions while saving water. Indeed, 70 percent of the technical mitigation potential of improved rice cultivation can be achieved cost-effectively. Therefore, governments must apply policy and financing incentives and share technical knowledge with rice farmers to accelerate their adoption of these low-emission practices.

Soils could sequester about 1 billion tons of solid carbon, or 3.8 billion tons of CO_2eq, per year cost-effectively. Terrestrial ecosystems (such as forests, grasslands, deserts, and others) absorb around 30 percent of total anthropogenic CO_2 emissions (Terrer, Phillips, and Hungate 2021). The top meter of soil stores approximately 2,500 billion tons of carbon, which is almost three times the amount of carbon found in the atmosphere (Lal et al. 2021) and 80 percent of all terrestrial carbon (Ontl and Schulte 2012). This easily makes soils the biggest terrestrial carbon sink. Moreover, 12 of the 15 countries with the greatest organic carbon sequestration potential in the top 30 centimeters of soils are MICs. However, unsustainable land management practices associated with conventional agriculture have released large amounts of soil carbon into the atmosphere (Lal 2011). For example, soil organic carbon stocks in croplands and grazed grasslands are 25–75 percent lower than they are in undisturbed soil ecosystems (Lal 1999). Today, 52 percent of the world's agricultural soils are considered carbon depleted (UNCCD 2022). This issue provides an opportunity to reduce GHG emissions by restoring and sustainably managing soils. According to the IPCC, around half of the soil organic carbon sequestration potential would cost less than $100 per ton of CO_2eq (IPCC 2022b), and about a quarter would cost less than $10 per ton of CO_2eq (Bossio et al. 2020). Our estimates show that soil sequestration can store 3.8 $GtCO_2$eq annually for less than $100 per ton of CO_2eq, equal to just over 1 gigaton of solid carbon.

Pre- and post-production processes are a significant and growing source of agrifood system emissions in MICs. Globally, pre- and post-production emissions account for a third of all agrifood system–related emissions and increase as countries become wealthier. In HICs, pre- and post-production emissions make up 46 percent of agrifood system emissions; in MICs, they make up 35 percent; and in LICs, they make up only 6 percent (FAOSTAT 2023a). That said, when excluding emissions from the processing-to-consumption stages of the agrifood system, which are mostly HIC energy emissions, MICs easily generate the most pre- and post-production emissions, particularly from fertilizer production and use, food loss and waste, and household food consumption. Overall, 80 percent of the world's fertilizer is consumed in MICs (International Fertilizer Association 2022). Moreover, fertilizer application in these countries is often wasteful: on average, MICs apply 168 kg of fertilizer per hectare, compared to 141 kg for HICs and 12 kg for LICs (FAOSTAT 2023c). Overall, fertilizer production and use cause 6.4 percent of total agrifood emissions. Fortunately, research shows that a combination of interventions could reduce emissions from nitrogen fertilizer production and use by up to 84 percent (Gao and Cabrera Serrenho 2023).

Another major emissions source of pre- and post-production stages is food loss and waste, which equals 30 percent of the world's food supply (World Bank 2020). In fact, 28 percent of the world's agricultural area is used to produce food that is wasted (FAO 2013; World Bank 2020). Waste reduction, especially of rice and meats, is highly cost-effective and can reduce methane at a negative cost (UNEP and Climate and Clean Air Coalition 2021). Estimates indicate that cost-effective measures to reduce food waste could reduce emissions by about nearly a half a gigaton of CO_2eq per year by 2030 (Thornton et al. 2023). Household food consumption, for its part, is the largest emissions category within pre- and post-production processes. It makes up 7.3 percent of all agrifood emissions, including 8.2 percent of MIC emissions and 7.8 percent of HIC emissions but only a fraction of a percent of LIC emissions. Most of the emissions in this category come from running household kitchen appliances. Renewable energy and clean cooking are two cost-effective measures for limiting this growing emissions category.

LICs Can Bypass a High-Emission Development Path, Seizing Climate-Smart Opportunities for Greener, More Competitive Economies

LICs contribute the least to climate change but suffer the most. Historically, LICs bear a negligible responsibility for GHG emissions and global warming, accounting for just 3.65 percent of cumulative historical emissions since 1850 (Evans 2021; Jones et al. 2023). Today, LICs contribute 4.2 percent to global GHG emissions (Climate Watch 2023) and 11 percent to global agrifood system emissions (World Bank 2024, FAOSTAT 2023a). This suggests that LICs are not yet locked into a high-emission trajectory. Currently, 53 percent of agrifood system emissions in HICs comes from the energy-intensive postharvest stages, whereas the emissions from these stages are negligible in LICs. However, this is starting to change. As countries industrialize and move up the income ladder, energy-consuming technology, such as refrigeration or food-processing machinery, tends to enter the food value chain and increase energy demand. Also, 82 percent of LIC emissions come from the agrifood system, well above the global average of 31 percent (Crippa et al. 2021), and half of LICs' agrifood emissions comes from land use, land use change, and forestry (Climate Watch 2022; Crippa et al. 2021). That said, climate change disproportionately affects agrifood systems in LICs, which are highly dependent on agriculture and have low adaptive capacity (IPCC 2022a). Moreover, the human toll in developing countries from extreme weather events is much costlier than that in developed countries, with a staggering 91 percent of disaster-related deaths occurring in poorer countries (United Nations 2021).

Preserving and restoring forests is a cost-effective way to promote development and limit the growth of LICs' emissions. Forest conversion contributes over half of LICs' agrifood system emissions, compared with 17 percent in MICs and 6 percent in HICs. Apart from Brazil, Sub-Saharan Africa has the largest block of primary forest in the world. However, the demand for agricultural commodities has been increasing the pressure on forests in LICs, and in response the forest area is shrinking—from 31.3 percent in 1990 to 26.3 percent in 2020.[8] For instance, in Congo Basin countries, there has been a 40 percent increase in land allocated for oil palm from 1990 to 2017 (Ordway et al. 2019).

In addition to conservation, forest restoration can achieve climate objectives and drive development. By one estimate, forest restoration could deliver a net benefit of $7 to $30 for every dollar invested through ecosystem services (Verdone and Seidl 2017). Agroforestry— the practice of integrating trees in croplands—produces benefits in LICs (FAO 2023b) beyond carbon storage, such as greater land productivity, livelihood opportunities, diversified diets, and greater ecosystem resilience and services (FAO 2023b). Emerging economies are beginning to monetize their forest cover and agrifood emission reductions through carbon credits and emissions trading. A global study of all country types shows that LICs can earn the highest potential income from carbon sequestration.

LICs can avoid GHG lock-in by improving agrifood system efficiency and marketing sustainable products. This GHG lock-in occurs when a country's investments or policies hinder the transition to lower-emission practices even when they are technically feasible and economically viable. Lock-in has already largely occurred in HICs and MICs, where high-emitting infrastructure and other long-lived assets are costly to decommission (Rozenberg and Fay 2019). By contrast, these and other barriers are less entrenched in LICs. One way to avoid lock-in is for LICs to improve their food system efficiency and productivity. Agriculture value added in LICs is only $210 per hectare, whereas in MICs it is five times that at $1,100 per hectare.[9] In fact, most LICs and MICs are achieving less than half of their potential agricultural output, whereas HICs are achieving 70 percent. Another way for LICs to avoid lock-in would be to orient their agrifood systems toward low-emission food options. Such options cater to potential emissions trading schemes that tax GHG emissions and favor emerging retail markets for healthy foods. For example, global markets for certified organic products have grown by 102 percent between 2009 and 2019 (Willer et al. 2021). Still, only 1.5 percent of all agricultural land in 2019 was geared toward producing such foods (Willer et al. 2021).

Climate-smart agriculture (CSA) provides LICs an avenue to low-emission rural development. CSA is an integrated approach to managing agricultural production that can achieve the "triple win" (World Bank 2021) of the following: (1) economic gains, (2) climate resilience, and (3) lower GHG emissions. There are 1,700 combinations of production systems and technology that could be classified as CSA, with two-thirds pertaining to cropping systems for maize, wheat, rice, and cash crops. Only 18 percent of CSA technologies are for livestock systems, and just 2 percent are for aquaculture systems (Sova et al. 2018). Adopting CSA practices reduces emissions and contributes to economic development, a particularly helpful outcome in LICs. For example, in Zambia, the economic rate of return for such practices was 27–35 percent (World Bank 2019). CSA practices can also help LICs access carbon markets and benefit from emissions trading schemes. Furthermore, CSA can improve rural development. For example, developing renewable energy sources in agrifood systems has been shown to contribute to rural electrification and increased incomes in LICs (Christiaensen, Rutledge, and Taylor 2021).

Enabling Environment: The World Must Strengthen the Enabling Environment for the Agrifood System Transformation through Global and Country-Level Actions

Investments

Governments and businesses can remove barriers to agrifood sector climate investments through improved targeting, de-risking, accountability, and carbon markets. New business opportunities linked to agrifood systems transformation will likely be worth $4.5 trillion per year by 2030. However, investment risks and the high transaction costs of dealing with many small producers and small and medium enterprises pose challenges to investors and financial service providers. To facilitate the private sector's risk acceptance for decarbonization projects requires embracing higher risk-return profiles (Guarnaschelli et al. 2018; Santos et al. 2022) and building a pipeline of bankable projects that can secure financing (Apampa et al. 2021; IFC 2017). Part of the problem is that investors find short-term loans with immediate returns appealing but shy away from offering medium- and longer-term financial solutions (Apampa et al. 2021), which are necessary for food system transformation. Blended finance can overcome these concerns by leveraging public finance to reduce credit risks for private investments in climate action (OECD 2021). Increased corporate accountability can also make investments more effective (Santos et al. 2022) through government policies and business standards. Further, there are opportunities to expand innovative financing mechanisms, such as results-based climate finance and climate bonds. Incentivizing carbon credits and carbon taxes also offers opportunities to control the agrifood system's GHG emissions. At present, however, a relatively small share of the world's carbon markets and carbon pricing schemes apply to nonenergy agricultural emissions (despite covering a quarter of economy-wide emissions) (World Bank 2022). That said, carbon markets offer growing opportunities for carbon finance. The voluntary carbon market has grown considerably over the past five years, reaching approximately $2 billion in 2022 (Shell and BCG 2023), with expectations of further growth of from $5 billion to $50 billion by 2030, depending on many factors (Blaufelder et al. 2021). However, carbon markets and carbon pricing still suffer from several flaws. They are subject to "carbon panics," emissions exemptions are common, carbon markets are very complex, and emissions are difficult to measure. Carbon markets can overcome these flaws through greater transparency and carbon credit integrity.

Incentives

Policy measures that could accelerate the transformation to a net zero argifood system are emerging. Two decades ago, HICs pioneered the development of mitigation policies for the agrifood sector, and in recent years, several MICs have followed suit. This movement toward agrifood sector mitigation is increasingly reflected in countries' NDCs. Currently, 147 of 167 second-round NDCs include AFOLU or agrifood systems in their mitigation commitments. This is a 20 percentage point increase from first- to second-round NDCs (figure O.10) (Crumpler et al., forthcoming).[10] The quality of these commitments has also improved: the share of NDCs with agriculture sector–specific GHG targets nearly doubled from 20 to 38 percent, and the share with specific agriculture-related mitigation actions increased from 63 to 78 percent (Crumpler et al., forthcoming). However, most NDC commitments are conditional on international support, including 92 percent of MIC NDC commitments in the AFOLU sector (Crumpler et al., forthcoming). This share is 100 percent for LICs but only 54 percent for HICs. Therefore, unfulfilled financial pledges have limited NDC implementation. Further, a lack of national policy coherence across sectors and within the agrifood sector also inhibits policy effectiveness. Improving this coherence and repurposing harmful subsidies toward agrifood system mitigation can deliver emissions reduction and multiple other benefits. A recent World Bank report shows that repurposing $70 billion of the world's approximately $638 billion in annual agriculture support during 2016–18 (Gautam et al. 2022; Voegele 2023) toward technologies that reduce emissions and improve productivity will boost crop production by 16 percent and livestock production by 11 percent. This would also increase national incomes by 1.6 percent, reduce the cost of healthy diets by 18 percent, and decrease overall agricultural emissions by 40 percent compared with business-as-usual 2020–40 levels (Gautam et al. 2022).

Information

Improving GHG monitoring can unlock climate finance. The measurement, reporting, and verification (MRV) of GHG emissions reductions is a complex, and often inaccurate, process

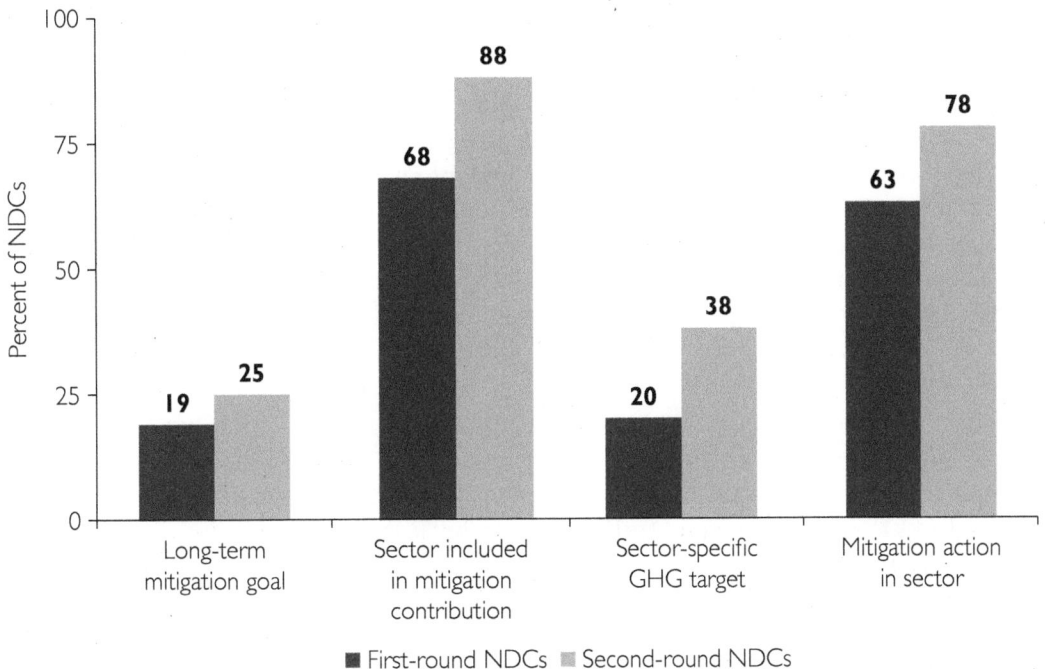

FIGURE O.10 Agrifood Systems Have Become a Stronger Component of Nationally Determined Contributions

Source: World Bank based on data and original analysis carried out by the Food and Agriculture Organization for this report.
Note: Figure compares NDC mitigation contributions to the agrifood sector in first-round and second-round NDCs. GHG = greenhouse gas; NDCs = Nationally Determined Contributions.

(Toman et al. 2022). Nevertheless, MRV is important for accessing carbon markets, assessing emissions reduction progress, and tracking project performance, among other reasons. However, several constraints are holding back the development of robust MRV systems. They include limited budgets, data availability, technical capacity among practitioners, and infrastructure to monitor emissions. That said, a growing number of international organizations are helping countries build MRV capacity to track Paris Agreement targets (WRI 2024). There are three main technologies that assist practitioners in measuring agricultural emissions: (1) remote-sensing technologies, (2) ground-based sensors, and (3) ecosystem carbon flux measurements (Dhakhwa et al. 2021). Likewise, emerging digital technologies offer new opportunities to improve MRV and lower its costs. Digital technologies enable faster and easier access to information for all players in the agrifood value chain. This information flow incentivizes farmers to adopt production tools and systems that can mitigate climate change, contribute to environmental sustainability, and optimize productivity (Schroeder, Lampietti, and Elabed 2021).

Innovation

Innovative practices for reducing agrifood emissions are expanding and becoming cost-effective, though there is a desperate need for more research and development (R&D) to continue this trend. Nascent, innovative mitigation technologies could greatly contribute to emissions reductions and improved productivity in the agrifood system (Alston et al. 2011). These technologies include using chemical methane inhibitors, feed additives from red seaweed, crop roots to sequester carbon, indoor farming methods, precision machinery, plant-based meats, lab-grown protein, and other protein sources. Moreover, some of these technologies are already providing viable solutions that are affordable. A conservative estimate is that innovative agrifood technologies that are cost-effective in the near term could reduce 2 $GtCO_2eq$ per year. R&D can drive many of these innovative technologies by further reducing costs and making them competitive with fossil fuel options (Bosetti et al. 2009). The Paris Agreement specifically recognizes the importance of R&D and calls for "collaborative approaches" to enhance and produce climate-related technologies.[11] Returns from R&D expenditures are high for both developing and developed countries: a 1 percent increase in R&D investment yields internal rates of return of 46 percent in developed countries and 43 percent in developing countries (Alston et al. 2000). However, R&D spending in the agrifood sector remains minimal.

Institutions

Climate institutions will govern the agrifood system's transformation to a net zero model. The global institutional architecture supporting climate action in the agrifood system is complex and operates at various levels (figure O.11). This architecture includes international frameworks to aid developing countries in acquiring finance, technologies, and knowledge to address climate change challenges. For example, one of UNFCCC's mandates is to promote and facilitate environmentally sound technology transfers to these nations, ensuring effective climate change mitigation and adaptation. Likewise, at the UN Climate Change Conference in 2009 (COP15), HICs pledged to mobilize $100 billion annually to support developing countries in their climate actions. Growing steadily since 2015, HICs provided $89.6 billion in total climate finance in 2021. This was a 7.5 percent increase from 2020 but still $10.4 billion short of the goal (OECD 2023). Nearly half of this total went to the energy and transport sectors, and only 8 percent went to agriculture, forestry, and fishing. Similarly, multilateral and bilateral donors are positioning themselves to lead in climate action but still lag in the agrifood transformation. For example, multilateral development banks reached a record of nearly $100 billion of climate financing in 2022 but allocated only $2.3 billion to mitigation in agrifood-related sectors. That said, agrifood mitigation has increasingly become a part of climate negotiations and NDCs, with a full day dedicated to food, agriculture, and water for the first time at the UN Climate Change Conference in 2023 (COP28). National and subnational institutions also have important roles to play in agrifood system mitigation, but this theme is often fragmented across various institutions that lack policy coherence, making coordinated action difficult. Creating "green jurisdictions," where subnational jurisdictions come together around climate action, can help overcome many subnational divisions. However, in many cases, these jurisdictions are also fragmented or focus on competing or parallel issues (Khan, Gao, and Abid 2020).

Inclusion

Governments and civil society must work together to ensure that the agrifood system transformation is equitable, inclusive, and just. Poorly targeted mitigation policies could raise production costs and food prices in the short term, which accounts for a larger share of household budgets for poor people than for the well-off, leading to unequal burden sharing. Therefore, a just transition in the agrifood system means reducing emissions while ensuring jobs, good health, livelihoods, and food security to vulnerable groups and smallholder farmers (Baldock and Buckwell 2022; Tribaldos and Kortetmäki 2022). The transition must

FIGURE O.11 **Governments, Businesses, Civil Society Groups, and International Organizations All Have Roles to Play in Scaling Climate Action**

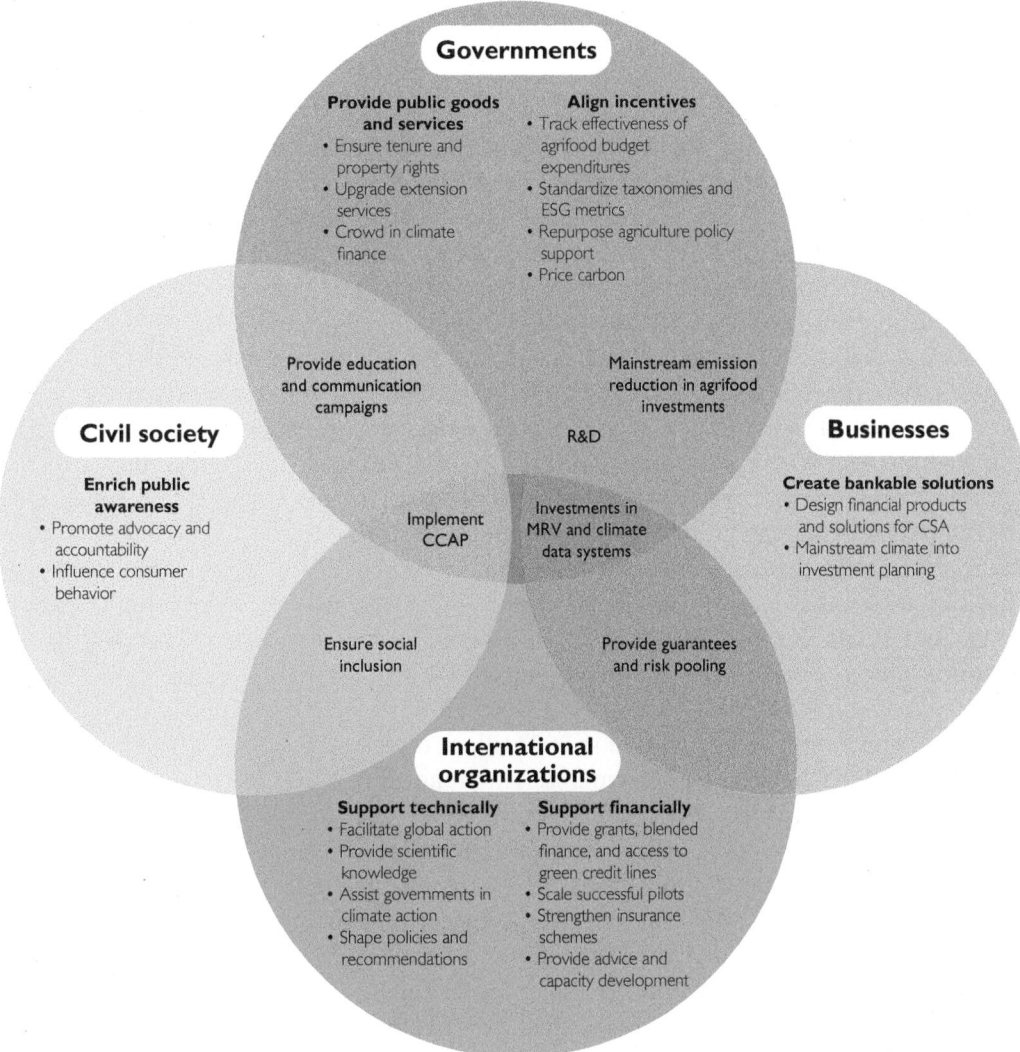

Source: Original figure for this publication.
Note: CCAP = Climate Change Action Plan; CSA = Climate-Smart Agriculture; ESG = environmental, social, and governance; MRV = measurement, reporting, and verification; R&D = research and development.

achieve procedural, distributive, and restorative justice to avoid the adverse health, social, economic, and environmental impacts from previous food system changes (Tribaldos and Kortetmäki 2022). Ample stakeholder engagement can help guarantee procedural justice or process legitimacy. Meanwhile, benefit sharing, especially in agrifood sector employment, can ensure distributive justice. For example, the agrifood system transformation will likely create new types of employment, and it is important for governments to facilitate this transition from farm work to higher-quality nonfarm jobs through skills training (Rotz et al. 2019) and mobility assistance (Fuglie et al. 2020). Likewise, the informal jobs sector can buffer the agrifood sector from job losses and food insecurity and assist with short-term job placement. The transformation must also ensure restorative justice by supporting groups that historically have not benefited from the agrifood system, such as smallholder farmers. To do so, governments should partner with affected communities and local governments to deliver local social empowerment through the agrifood system.

The Recipe Is Doable

Solutions for transforming the agrifood system to net zero emissions are available and affordable. Over the past three decades, the food system has witnessed remarkable successes. Agricultural producers have dramatically increased their output through more efficient resource use and superior technologies and practices. Moreover, conditions to propel the transformation into the future are in place. There are new technologies, an engaged private sector, heightened consumer awareness, and advanced digital tools. Moreover, there are no intrinsic trade-offs between climate action and the goals of income generation or food security. With the right adaptation and mitigation measures, it is entirely possible to diminish agrifood system emissions while simultaneously bolstering economies, supporting farmers, and feeding the planet. From a pragmatic perspective, the most compelling aspect is that an agrifood system transformation is affordable now and can improve the trade competitiveness of countries specializing in low-emission agrifood practices. Figure O.12 shows that there are many cost-effective or cost-saving mitigation options available for the agrifood system that can cover all 16 gigatons of the agrifood system's annual GHG emissions, which is about four times Europe's total annual emissions. Consequently, the estimated costs of mitigating the agrifood system's climate impact are just a fraction—roughly one-tenth—of the projected global energy investments for 2023 and less than 5 percent of fossil fuel subsidies, which reached $7.1 trillion in 2022 (Black et al. 2023).

The recipe for achieving net zero emissions in the agrifood system entails country-specific and global enabling efforts. HICs should lead the way. They can do this by curbing energy emissions, aiding developing nations in their shift to low-emission development pathways, and repurposing subsidies away from high-emission and environmentally destructive foods to curb their demand. Likewise, MICs have an outsize role to play. They generate two-thirds of global agrifood emissions and could cut most of them by focusing on lowering methane emissions from rice and livestock production, harnessing the potential of soils to sequester carbon, and shifting to cleaner, more efficient, and circular approaches to the agrifood system's pre- and post-production activities. LICs can bypass the high-emissions development path taken by HICs and MICs for a greener, more competitive development path. LICs have an opportunity to make smart choices now that will benefit them in the long term by avoiding a high-emissions development path that would be costly to reverse later. They should prioritize and monetize the protection and restoration of carbon-rich forests and other ecosystems, improve agrifood systems' efficiency, and promote climate-smart practices, thereby achieving a triple win of increased productivity, climate resilience, and reduced emissions. Empowering countries to take these actions at scale requires a conducive enabling environment, both globally and within countries. Governments, businesses, consumers, and international organizations must work together to (1) generate investments and create incentives through policy, (2) improve information and innovation to drive the agrifood system transformation into the future, and (3) leverage institutions to facilitate these opportunities while ensuring the inclusion of stakeholders and marginalized groups (figure O.13).

FIGURE O.12 By 2050, Cost-Effective Mitigation Action in the Agrifood System Transformation Can Reduce Greenhouse Gases by Over 16 Gigatons a Year, Achieving Net Zero Emissions

a. All countries can reduce emissions cost-effectively now, and the largest potential is in MICs

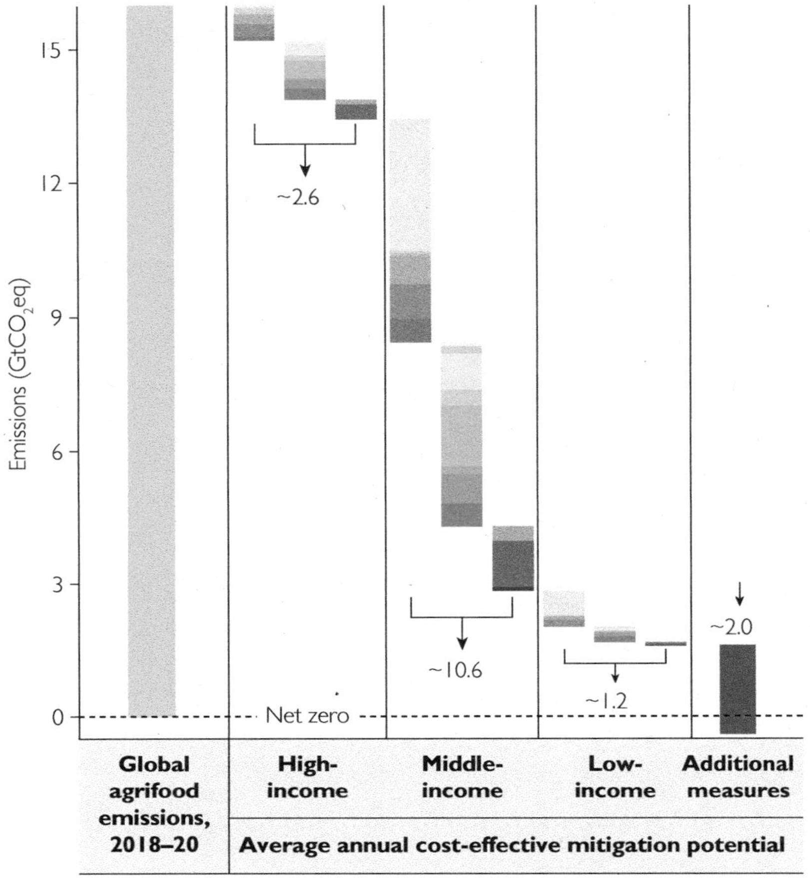

b. HICs, MICs, and LICs can follow different pathways to reduce their emissions

	Mitigation action	High-income	Middle-income	Low-income
	Land use			
Protect	Reduced deforestation	1.8	28.0	45.0
Protect	Reduced peatland degradation	5.5	0.5	0.7
Protect	Reduced mangrove conversion	0.3	0.6	0.2
Manage	Forest management	8.5	5.8	6.0
Manage	Grassland, fire management	0.1	0.1	1.4
Restore	Afforestation, reforestation	11.2	7.3	11.4
Restore	Peatland, mangrove restoration	3.2	4.8	0.2
	Total	**30.6%**	**47.1%**	**64.8%**
	On-farm			
Livestock	Enteric fermentation	1.0	0.6	0.7
Livestock	Manure management	2.5	0.3	0.1
Rice	Rice cultivation	0.2	1.5	0.3
Integrated production	Agroforestry	9.5	7.5	6.4
Integrated production	Bioenergy	4.7	3.5	1.0
Soils	Biochar from crop residues	15.5	13.0	2.9
Soils	Nutrient management	1.7	1.7	0.1
Soils	Soils in croplands	7.4	6.1	6.6
Soils	Soils in grasslands	9.8	5.0	10.3
	Total	**52.1%**	**39.2%**	**28.4%**
	Pre- and post- production			
Demand side	Reduced food waste	4.2	3.1	1.2
Demand side	Shift diets	13.1	9.8	4.3
Demand side	Clean cooking	—	0.8	1.3
	Total	**17.3%**	**13.7%**	**6.8%**

Sources: World Bank based on data from Roe et al. 2021 and World Bank 2024.

Note: Panel a shows by country income group the cost-effective annual mitigation potential for reducing emissions from land use, on-farm, and pre- and post-production process. Additional measures include technologies and innovations that can deliver cost-effective emissions reductions by 2030. These include: nitrous oxide abatement in fertilizer production; plant-based proteins; low-emission energy sources for on-farm machinery; improved on-farm energy-efficiency; improved livestock feed digestibility and feed additives; and increased use of renewable energy in cold chains. Details on these measures are described in chapter 4. Average annual mitigation potential for land-based mitigation measures for high-, middle-, and low-income countries are based on 2020–2050 scenarios. $GtCO_2eq$ = gigatons of carbon dioxide equivalent. HICs = high-income countries; LICs = low-income countries; MICs = middle-income countries; — = not available.

FIGURE O.13 The Recipe for Creating an Enabling Environment Allows Countries in All Income Groups to Contribute to Transforming Agrifood Systems to Achieve Net Zero Emissions

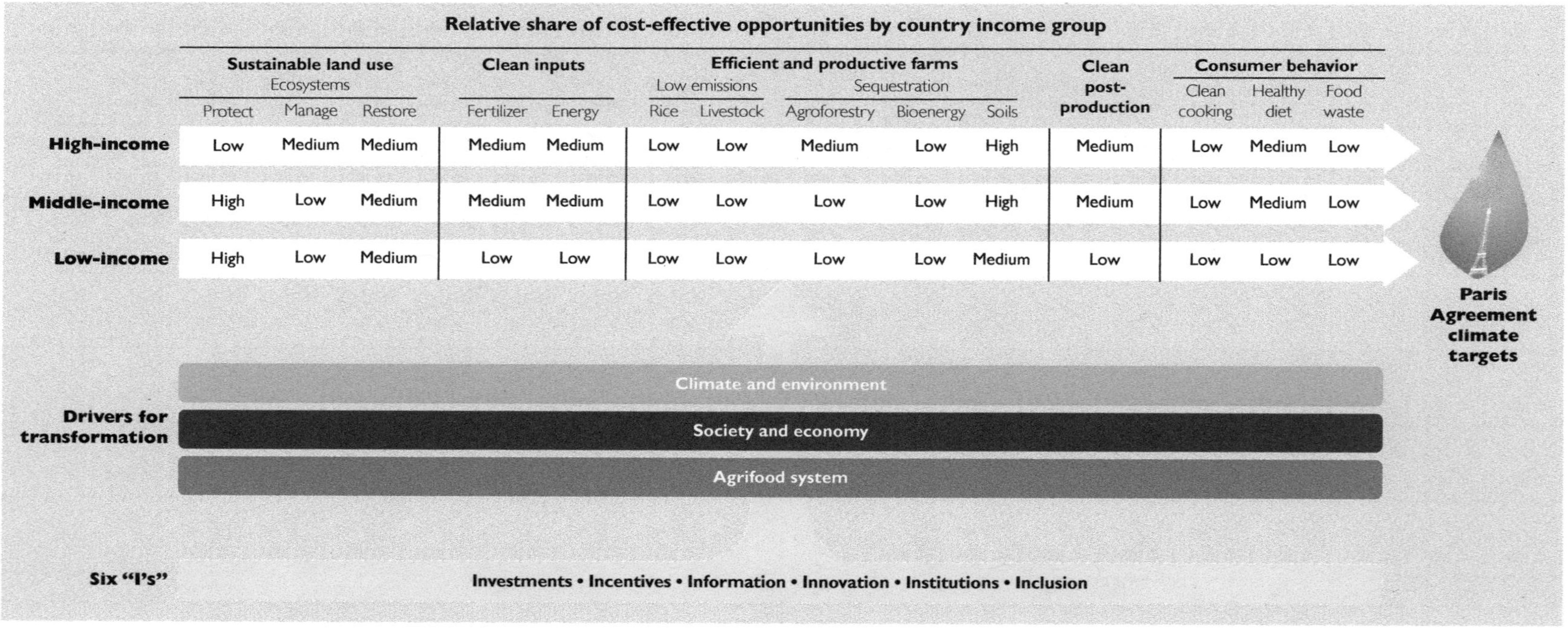

Relative share of cost-effective opportunities by country income group

| | Sustainable land use (Ecosystems) | | | Clean inputs | | Efficient and productive farms | | | | | Clean post-production | Consumer behavior | | |
	Protect	Manage	Restore	Fertilizer	Energy	Rice (Low emissions)	Livestock (Low emissions)	Agroforestry (Sequestration)	Bioenergy (Sequestration)	Soils (Sequestration)		Clean cooking	Healthy diet	Food waste
High-income	Low	Medium	Medium	Medium	Medium	Low	Low	Medium	Low	High	Medium	Low	Medium	Low
Middle-income	High	Low	Medium	Medium	Medium	Low	Low	Low	Low	High	Medium	Low	Medium	Low
Low-income	High	Low	Medium	Low	Low	Low	Low	Low	Low	Medium	Low	Low	Low	Low

Paris Agreement climate targets

Drivers for transformation
- Climate and environment
- Society and economy
- Agrifood system

Six "I's"   Investments • Incentives • Information • Innovation • Institutions • Inclusion

Source: Original figure for this publication.
Note: Figure summarizes the distribution of cost-effective mitigation potential by income group across 14 key areas of intervention related to sustainable land use, clean inputs, efficient and productive farms, clean post-production, and consumer behavior (top part of the table). The relative share of cost-effective mitigation potential is indicated as follows: low: <8 percent; medium: 8–16 percent; high: >16 percent.

Moving Forward

This recipe lists the required ingredients for transforming the global agrifood system to achieve net zero emissions. These cost-effective mitigation practices and enabling actions should be implemented immediately and concurrently by all countries. That said, this report has shown where different countries—high-, middle-, and low-income countries—have the greatest opportunities to reduce global agrifood emissions. This potential was determined on the basis of where emissions concentrations were highest or fastest growing and the relative costs of mitigating those concentrations. Put simply, this report guides countries toward agrifood system mitigation efforts that give the most bang for the buck. Consequently, this should be a country-driven approach in which HICs, the World Bank, and other bilateral or multilateral donors provide the knowledge and finance to enable public and private national actors to contribute to this transformation. More immediately, the World Bank and its development partners can build on this report by filling remaining knowledge gaps and carrying out similar analyses at the country level.

Notes

1. World Bank calculations using IEA and FAOSTAT data covering 2018–20. Accessed in 2023.

2. World Bank/FAOSTAT 2023 databases.

3. Authors' estimates, calculated using benefits corresponding to 6 of the 10 critical transformations that directly contribute to agrifood mitigation, as identified in FOLU 2020.

4. This is the selected threshold for economic mitigation potential in the IPCC's AR6 Chapter on AFOLU (Nabuurs et al. 2022) and is the high estimate for the World Bank's shadow price of carbon in 2030. It is also policy relevant, given that it falls within the 2030 carbon price corridor based on the recommendations of the High-Level Commission on Carbon Prices, adjusted for inflation.

5. Shift to sustainable health diets is defined in Roe et al. 2021 as emissions reductions from diverted agricultural production (excluding land-use change) from the adoption of sustainable healthy diets: (1) maintain a 2,250 calorie per day nutritional regime; (2) converge to healthy daily protein requirement, limiting meat-based protein consumption to 57 grams per day; and (3) purchase locally produced food when available. Carbon sequestration in agriculture includes (1) agroforestry, (2) biochar from crop residues, (3) soil organic carbon in croplands, and (4) soil organic carbon in grasslands.

6. In the decade 2010–19, energy efficiency increased by 1.9 percent, far lower than 3.2 percent, the rate needed to achieve the Sustainable Development Goal 7.3 target.

7. See calculations for this example at https://energyaccess.duke.edu/catalyzing-climate-finance (The James E. Rogers Energy Access Project at Duke).

8. World Bank, Development Indicators, "Forest area (% of land area)—Sub-Saharan Africa (accessed 2023), https://databank.worldbank.org/source/world-development-indicators.

9. World Bank, World Development Indicators (accessed 2023), https://data.worldbank.org/indicator.

10. First-round NDCs refer to intended nationally determined contributions and NDCs submitted by Parties to the UNFCCC as of July 29, 2016. Second-round NDCs refer to the latest NDCs submitted by Parties to the UNFCCC as of June 30, 2023. This includes new/updated NDCs as well as first NDCs (if new/updated NDCs were not submitted).

11. In accordance with Article 10, Paragraph 5, of the Paris Agreement.

References

Abbafati, Cristiana, et al. 2020. "Global Burden of 369 Diseases and Injuries in 204 Countries and Territories, 1990–2019: A Systematic Analysis for the Global Burden of Disease Study 2019." *Lancet* 396: 1204–22. https://doi.org/10.1016/S0140-6736(20)30925-9.

Aleksandrowicz, L., R. Green, E. J. M. Joy, P. Smith, and A. Haines. 2016. "The Impacts of Dietary Change on Greenhouse Gas Emissions, Land Use, Water Use, and Health: A Systematic Review." *PLoS ONE* 11 (11): e0165797. https://doi.org/10.1371/journal.pone.0165797.

Alston, J. M., M. A. Andersen, J. S. James, and P. G. Pardey. 2011. "The Economic Returns to U.S. Public Agricultural Research." *American Journal of Agricultural Economics* 93 (5): 1257–77. https://doi.org/10.1093/ajae/aar044.

Alston, J. M., M. C. Marra, P. G. Pardey, and T. J. Wyatt. 2000. "Research Returns Redux: A Meta-analysis of the Returns to Agricultural R&D." *Australian Journal of Agricultural and Resource Economics* 44 (2): 185–215. https://doi.org/10.1111/1467-8489.00108.

Ambikapathi, Ramya, Keri R. Schneider, Blake Davis, et al. 2022. "Global Food Systems Transitions Have Enabled Affordable Diets but Had Less Favourable Outcomes for Nutrition, Environmental Health, Inclusion and Equity." *Nature Food* 3: 764–79. https://doi.org/10.1038/s43016-022-00588-7.

Apampa, A., C. Clubb, B. E. Cosgrove, G. Gambarelli, H. Loth, R. Newman, V. Rodriguez Osuna, J. Oudelaar, and A. Tasse. 2021. "Scaling Up Critical Finance for Sustainable Food Systems through Blended Finance." CCAFS Discussion Paper, CGIAR Research Program on Climate Change, Agriculture and Food Security (CCAFS), CGIAR, Montpellier, France. https://financeincommon.org/sites/default/files/2021-11/Scaling%20up%20critical%20finance%20for%20sustainable%20food%20systems%20through%20blended%20finance.pdf.

Bajželj, Bojana, and Keith S. Richards. 2014. "The Positive Feedback Loop between the Impacts of Climate Change and Agricultural Expansion and Relocation." *Land* (3): 898–916. https://doi.org/10.3390/land3030898.

Baldock, D., and A. Buckwell. 2022. *Just Transition in the EU Agriculture and Land Use Sector.* Brussels: Institute for European Environmental Policy. https://ieep.eu/publications/just-transition-in-the-eu-agriculture-and-land-use-sector.

Black, Simon, Antung A. Liu, Ian Parry, and Nate Vernon. 2023. "IMF Fossil Fuel Subsidies Data: 2023 Update." Working Paper 23/169, International Monetary Fund, Washington, DC. https://www.imf.org/en/Publications/WP/Issues/2023/08/22/IMF-Fossil-Fuel-Subsidies-Data-2023-Update-537281.

Blaufelder, Christopher, Cindy Levy, Peter Mannion, and Dickon Pinner. 2021. "A Blueprint for Scaling Voluntary Carbon Markets to Meet the Climate Challenge." January 29, 2021. Report. McKinsey & Company. https://www.mckinsey.com/capabilities/sustainability/our-insights/a-blueprint-for-scaling-voluntary-carbon-markets-to-meet-the-climate-challenge#/.

Bosetti, Valentina, Carlo Carraro, Romain Duval, Alessandra Sgobbi, and Massimo Tavoni. 2009. "The Role of R&D and Technology Diffusion in Climate Change Mitigation: New Perspectives Using the WITCH Model." Unpublished manuscript, Stanford University, Stanford, CA. http://stanford.edu/dept/france-stanford/Conferences/Climate/Carraro.pdf. PDF file.

Bossio, D. A., S. C. Cook-Patton, P. W. Ellis, J. Fargione, J. Sanderman, P. Smith, S. Wood, et al. 2020. "The Role of Soil Carbon in Natural Climate Solutions." *Nature Sustainability* 3: 391–98. https://doi.org/10.1038/s41893-020-0491-z.

Christiaensen, L., Z. Rutledge, and J. E. Taylor. 2021. "Viewpoint: The Future of Work in Agri-food." *Food Policy* 99:101963. https://doi.org/10.1016/j.foodpol.2020.101963.

Clapp, J., P. Newell, and Z. Brent. 2017. "The Global Political Economy of Climate Change, Agriculture, and Food Systems." *Journal of Peasant Studies* 45 (1): 60–66. https://doi.org/10.1080/03066150.2017.1381602.

Clark, Michael A., Nina G. G. Domingo, Kimberly Colgan, Sumil K. Thakrar, David Tilman, John Lynch, Inés L. Azevedo, and Jason D. Hill. 2020. "Global Food System Emissions Could Preclude Achieving the 1.5° and 2°C Climate Change Targets." *Science* 370: 705–08. https://doi.org/10.1126/science.aba7357.

Clark, Michael, and David Tilman. 2017. "Comparative Analysis of Environmental Impacts of Agricultural Production Systems, Agricultural Input Efficiency, and Food Choice." *Environmental Research Letters* 12 (6): 064016. https://doi.org/10.1088/1748-9326/aa6cd5.

Climate Watch. 2022. World Resources Institute, Washington, DC. Accessed March 30, 2024. https://www.climatewatchdata.org.

Climate Watch. 2023. "Historical GHG Emissions: Global Historical Emissions" (web page). 2023. Accessed March 30, 2024. https://www.climatewatchdata.org/ghg-emissions.

CPI (Climate Policy Institute). 2023. "Global Landscape of Climate Finance 2023." CPI, San Francisco, CA. https://www.climatepolicyinitiative.org/publication/global-landscape-of-climate-finance-2023/.

Crippa, M., E. Solazzo, D. Guizzardi, F. Monforti-Ferrario, F. N. Tubiello, and A. Leip. 2021. "Food Systems Are Responsible for a Third of Global Anthropogenic GHG Emissions." *Nature Food* 2: 198–209. https://doi.org/10.1038/s43016-021-00225-9.

Crumpler, K., C. Angioni, P. Prosperi, L. Roffredi, M. Salvatore, E. Tanganelli, V. Umulisa, A. Wybieralska, I. Brierley, N. Rai, G. Dahlet, G. Bhalla, M. Knowles, J. Wolf, and M. Bernoux. Forthcoming. *Agrifood Systems in Nationally Determined Contributions: Global Analysis*. Rome: Food and Agriculture Organization of the United Nations.

Damania, Richard, Stephen Polasky, Mary Ruckelshaus, Jason Russ, Markus Amann, Rebecca Chaplin-Kramer, James Gerber, Peter Hawthorne, Martin Philipp Heger, Saleh Mamun, Giovanni Ruta, Rafael Schmitt, Jeffrey Smith, Adrian Vogl, Fabian Wagner, and Esha Zaveri. 2023. *Nature's Frontiers: Achieving Sustainability, Efficiency, and Prosperity with Natural Capital*. Environment and Sustainable Development series. Washington, DC: World Bank. https://doi.org/10.1596/978-1-4648-1923-0.

Delgado, C., M. Rosegrant, H. Steinfeld, S. Ehui, and C. Courbois. 1999. "Livestock to 2020: The Next Food Revolution." Food, Agriculture, and the Environment Discussion Paper 28, International Food Policy Research Institute, Washington, DC. https://hdl.handle.net/10568/333.

Dhakhwa, Timila, Nkulumo Zinyengere, Bethany Joy Linton, Erick C. M. Fernandes, Chandra Shekhar Sinha, Timothy R. H. Pearson, Blanca Bernal, Sophia Simon, and Meyru Bhanti. 2021. *Soil Organic Carbon MRV Sourcebook for Agricultural Landscapes*. Washington, DC: World Bank Group. http://documents.worldbank.org/curated/en/948041625049766862/Soil-Organic-Carbon-MRV-Sourcebook-for-Agricultural-Landscapes.

Elshurafa, Amro M., Hatem Alatawi, Salaheddine Soummane, and Frank A. Felder. 2021. "Assessing Effects of Renewable Deployment on Emissions in the Saudi Power Sector until 2040 Using Integer Optimization." *Electricity Journal* 34 (6): 106973. https://doi.org/10.1016/j.tej.2021.106973.

European Commission. 2020. "Factsheet: How the Future CAP Will Contribute to the EU Green Deal" (web page). Accessed March 30, 2024. https://ec.europa.eu/commission/presscorner/detail/en/fs_20_910.

Evans, Simon. 2021. "Analysis: Which Countries Are Historically Responsible for Climate Change?" (article). Carbon Brief, May 10. https://www.carbonbrief.org/analysis-which-countries-are-historically-responsible-for-climate-change/.

FAO (Food and Agriculture Organization of the United Nations). 2013. *Food Wastage Footprint: Impacts on Natural Resources*. Summary Report. Rome: FAO. https://www.fao.org/3/i3347e/i3347e.pdf.

FAO (Food and Agriculture Organization of the United Nations). 2018. *The Future of Food and Agriculture: Alternative Pathways to 2050*. Rome: FAO. https://www.fao.org/global-perspectives-studies/resources/detail/en/c/1157074/.

FAO (Food and Agriculture Organization of the United Nations). 2020. *Global Forest Resources Assessment 2020: Main Report*. Rome: FAO. https://doi.org/10.4060/ca9825en.

FAO (Food and Agriculture Organization of the United Nations). 2023a. "Global Livestock Environmental Assessment Model (GLEAM)" (web page). Accessed March 30, 2024. https://www.fao.org/gleam/en/.

FAO (Food and Agriculture Organization of the United Nations). 2023b. "Integrated Production Systems." In *Climate Smart Agriculture Sourcebook*. Rome: FAO. https://www.fao.org/climate-smart-agriculture-sourcebook/production-resources/module-b5-integrated-production-systems/chapter-b5-1/en/.

FAO (Food and Agriculture Organization of the United Nations), IFAD (International Fund for Agricultural Development), UNICEF (United Nations Children's Fund), WFP (World Food Programme), and WHO (World Health Organization). 2021. *The State of Food Security and Nutrition in the World 2021: Transforming Food Systems for Food Security, Improved Nutrition and Affordable Healthy Diets for All*. Rome: FAO. https://doi.org/10.4060/cb4474en.

FAO (Food and Agriculture Organization of the United Nations), IFAD (International Fund for Agricultural Development), UNICEF (United Nations Children's Fund), WFP (World Food Programme), and WHO (World Health Organization). 2023. *The State of Food Security and Nutrition in the World 2023: Urbanization, Agrifood Systems Transformation and Healthy Diets across the Rural-Urban Continuum.* Rome: FAO. https://doi.org/10.4060/cc3017en.

FAOSTAT. 2023a. "Emissions totals" (data set). Accessed March 30, 2024. https://www.fao.org/faostat/en/#data/Gt.

FAOSTAT. 2023b. "Food Balance Sheets 2010–" (data set). Accessed April 12, 2024. https://www.fao.org/faostat/en/#data/FBS.

FAOSTAT. 2023c. "Fertilizer indicators (National-Global-Annual)" (data set). Accessed December 15, 2023. https://data.apps.fao.org/catalog/dataset/fertilizers-indicators-national-global-annual-faostat.

FAOSTAT. 2023d. "Emission Intensities" (data set). Accessed April 14, 2024. https://www.fao.org/faostat/en/#data/EI.

FOLU (Food and Land Use Coalition). 2020. "Food and Land Use Transformation Pyramid" (web page). https://www.foodandlandusecoalition.org/interactive-pyramid/#:~:text=The%20Food%20and%20Land%20Use,all%20while%20unlocking%20%244.5%20trillion.

Fransen, T., C. Henderson, R. O'Connor, N. Alayza, M. Caldwell, S. Chakrabarty, A. Dixit, et al. 2022. *The State of Nationally Determined Contributions: 2022.* Washington, DC: World Resources Institute. https://doi.org/10.46830/wrirpt.22.00043.

Fuglie, Keith, Madhur Gautam, Aparajita Goyal, and William F. Maloney. 2020. *Harvesting Prosperity: Technology and Productivity Growth in Agriculture.* Washington, DC: World Bank. https://openknowledge.worldbank.org/server/api/core/bitstreams/3621191c-15f3-5ede-a89c-f7190d7e1dba/content.

Fujimori, S., W. Wu, J. Doelman, S. Frank, J. Hristov, P. Kyle, R. Sands, et al. 2022. "Land-Based Climate Change Mitigation Measures Can Affect Agricultural Markets and Food Security." *Nature Food* 3: 110–21. https://doi.org/10.1038/s43016-022-00464-4.

Fukagawa, N. K., and L. H. Ziska. 2019. "Rice: Importance for Global Nutrition." Supplement, *Journal of Nutritional Science and Vitaminology* (Tokyo) 65: S2–S3. https://doi.org/10.3177/jnsv.65.S2.

Funke, Franziska, Linus Mattauch, Inge van den Bijgaart, H. Charles J. Godfray, Cameron Hepburn, David Klenert, Marco Springmann, and Nicolas Treich. 2022. "Toward Optimal Meat Pricing: Is It Time to Tax Meat Consumption?" *Review of Environmental Economics and Policy* 16 (2): 219–40.

Gao, Y., and A. Cabrera Serrenho. 2023. "Greenhouse Gas Emissions from Nitrogen Fertilizers Could Be Reduced by up to One-Fifth of Current Levels by 2050 with Combined Interventions." *Nature Food* 4: 170–78. doi:10.1038/s43016-023-00698-w.

Gautam, Madhur, David Laborde, Abdullah Mamun, Will Martin, Valeria Pineiro, and Rob Vos. 2022. *Repurposing Agricultural Policies and Support: Options to Transform Agriculture and Food Systems to Better Serve the Health of People, Economies, and the Planet.* Washington, DC: World Bank. https://openknowledge.worldbank.org/handle/10986/36875; http://hdl.handle.net/10986/36875.

Goldman, E., M. J. Weisse, N. Harris, and M. Schneider. 2020. "Estimating the Role of Seven Commodities in Agriculture-Linked Deforestation: Oil Palm, Soy, Cattle, Wood Fiber, Cocoa, Coffee, and Rubber." Technical note, World Resources Institute, Washington, DC. https://www.wri.org/research/estimating-role-seven-commodities-agriculture-linked-deforestation-oil-palm-soy-cattle.

Guarnaschelli, Serena, Benhan Limketkai, Pauline Vandeputte, Lieke Homminga, Anisa Khadem Nwachuku, and Malika Mehta. 2018. "Financing Sustainable Land Use: Unlocking Business Opportunities in Sustainable Land Use with Blended Finance." Brussels: Kois Invest. Accessed March 30, 2024. https://koisinvest.com/wp-content/uploads/2020/04/Financing-sustainable-land-use-report.pdf.

Harris, N. L., D. A. Gibbs, A. Baccini, R. A. Birdsey, S. de Bruin, M. Farina, L. Fatoyinbo, et al. 2021. "Global Maps of Twenty-First Century Forest Carbon Fluxes." *Nature Climate Change* 11: 234–40. https://doi.org/10.1038/s41558-020-00976-6.

Harvey, Fiona. 2022. "We Cannot Adapt Our Way out of Climate Crisis, Warns Leading Scientist." *Guardian*, June 1, 2022. https://www.theguardian.com/environment/2022/jun/01/we-cannot-adapt-our-way-out-of-climate-crisis-warns-leading-scientist.

Hasegawa, T., S. Fujimori, S. Frank, F. Humpenöder, C. Bertram, J. Després, L. Drouet, et al. 2021. "Land-Based Implications of Early Climate Actions without Global Net-Negative Emissions." *Nature Sustainability* 4: 1052–59. https://doi.org/10.1038/s41893-021-00772-w.

Hendriks, S., A. D. G. Ruiz, M. H. Acosta, H. Baumers, P. Galgani, D. Mason-D'Croz, Ç. Godde, et al. 2021. "The True Cost and True Price of Food." Paper prepared for the UN Food Systems Summit 2021, New York, September 23. https://sc-fss2021.org/wp-content/uploads/2021/06/UNFSS_true_cost_of_food.pdf.

IEA (International Energy Agency). 2022. *Energy Efficiency 2022*. Paris: IEA. https://www.iea.org/reports/energy-efficiency-2022.

IEA (International Energy Agency). 2023a. *Fossil Fuels Consumption Subsidies 2022*. Paris: IEA. https://www.iea.org/reports/fossil-fuels-consumption-subsidies-2022.

IEA (International Energy Agency). 2023b. *Global Methane Tracker 2023*. Paris: IEA. https://www.iea.org/reports/global-methane-tracker-2023.

International Fertilizer Association. 2022. "IFASTAT: Consumption" (web page). Accessed March 30, 2024. https://www.ifastat.org/databases/plant-nutrition.

IPCC (Intergovernmental Panel on Climate Change). 2018. "Summary for Policymakers." In *Global Warming of 1.5°C: An IPCC Special Report on the Impacts of Global Warming of 1.5°C above Pre-industrial Levels and Related Global Greenhouse Gas Emission Pathways, in the Context of Strengthening the Global Response to the Threat of Climate Change, Sustainable Development, and Efforts to Eradicate Poverty*, edited by V. Masson-Delmotte, P. Zhai, H.-O. Pörtner, D. Roberts, J. Skea, P. R. Shukla, A. Pirani, et al., 3–24. Cambridge: Cambridge University Press. https://doi.org/10.1017/9781009157940.001.

IPCC (Intergovernmental Panel on Climate Change). 2022a. *Climate Change 2022: Impacts, Adaptation and Vulnerability; Contribution of Working Group II to the Sixth Assessment Report of the Intergovernmental Panel on Climate Change*, edited by H.-O. Pörtner, D. C. Roberts, M. Tignor, E. S. Poloczanska, K. Mintenbeck, A. Alegría, M. Craig, et al. Cambridge: Cambridge University Press. https://doi.org/10.1017/9781009325844.

IPCC (Intergovernmental Panel on Climate Change). 2022b. "Summary for Policymakers." In *Climate Change 2022: Mitigation of Climate Change. Contribution of Working Group III to the Sixth Assessment Report of the Intergovernmental Panel on Climate Change*, edited by P. R. Shukla, J. Skea, R. Slade, A. Al Khourdajie, R. van Diemen, D. McCollum, M. Pathak, et al. Cambridge: Cambridge University Press. https://doi.org/10.1017/9781009157926.001.

IPCC (Intergovernmental Panel on Climate Change). 2022c. *Climate Change and Land: IPCC Special Report on Climate Change, Desertification, Land Degradation, Sustainable Land Management, Food Security, and Greenhouse Gas Fluxes in Terrestrial Ecosystems*. Cambridge: Cambridge University Press. https://doi.org/10.1017/9781009157988.

IPCC (Intergovernmental Panel on Climate Change). 2023. *Climate Change 2023: Synthesis Report; Contribution of Working Groups I, II and III to the Sixth Assessment Report of the Intergovernmental Panel on Climate Change*, edited by H. Lee and J. Romero. Geneva: IPCC. https://doi.org/10.59327/IPCC/AR6-9789291691647.

IRENA (International Renewable Energy Agency). 2023. *Renewable Capacity Statistics 2023*. Abu Dhabi: IRENA. https://www.irena.org/Publications/2023/Mar/Renewable-capacity-statistics-2023.

IRENA (International Renewable Energy Agency) and ILO (International Labour Organization). 2022. *Renewable Energy and Jobs: Annual Review 2022*. Abu Dhabi: IRENA and Geneva: ILO. https://www.ilo.org/wcmsp5/groups/public/---dgreports/---dcomm/documents/publication/wcms_856649.pdf.

Jones, M. W., G. P. Peters, T. Gasser, R. M. Andrew, C. Schwingshackl, J. Gütschow, R. A. Houghton, P. Friedlingstein, J. Pongratz, and C. Le Quéré. 2023. "National Contributions to Climate Change Due to Historical Emissions of Carbon Dioxide, Methane, and Nitrous Oxide since 1850." *Scientific Data* 10: 155. https://doi.org/10.1038/s41597-023-02041-1.

Khan, N. A., Q. Gao, and M. Abid. 2020. "Public Institutions' Capacities Regarding Climate Change Adaptation and Risk Management Support in Agriculture: The Case of Punjab Province, Pakistan." *Scientific Reports* 10 (1): 14111. https://doi.org/10.1038/s41598-020-71011-z.

Lal, R. 1999. "Soil Management and Restoration for C Sequestration to Mitigate the Accelerated Greenhouse Effect." *Progress in Environmental Science* 1 (4): 307–26.

Lal, R. 2011. "Soil Carbon Sequestration." SOLAW Background Thematic Report TR04B, Food and Agriculture Organization of the United Nations, Rome. https://www.fao.org/fileadmin/templates/solaw /files/thematic_reports/TR_04b_web.pdf.

Lal, R., C. Monger, L. Nave, and P. Smith. 2021. "The Role of Soil in Regulation of Climate." *Philosophical Transactions of the Royal Society* 376 (1834): 20210084. https://doi.org/10.1098/rstb.2021.0084.

Linquist, B., K. J. Van Groenigen, M. A. Adviento-Borbe, C. Pittelkow, and C. Van Kessel. 2012. "An Agronomic Assessment of Greenhouse Gas Emissions from Major Cereal Crops." *Global Change Biology* 18 (1): 194–209. https://doi.org/10.1111/j.1365-2486.2011.02502.x.

Nabuurs, G.-J., R. Mrabet, A. Abu Hatab, M. Bustamante, H. Clark, P. Havlík, J. House, et al. 2022. "Agriculture, Forestry and Other Land Uses (AFOLU)." In *Climate Change 2022: Mitigation of Climate Change; Contribution of Working Group III to the Sixth Assessment Report of the Intergovernmental Panel on Climate Change,* edited by P. R. Shukla, J. Skea, R. Slade, A. Al Khourdajie, R. van Diemen, D. McCollum, M. Pathak, et al., chap. 7. Cambridge, UK: Cambridge University Press. https://doi .org/10.1017/9781009157926.009.

Naran, Baysa, Jake Connolly, Paul Rosane, Dharshan Wignarajah, and Githungo Wakaba. 2022. *Global Landscape of Climate Finance: A Decade of Data; 2011–2020.* Washington, DC: Climate Policy Initiative. https://www.climatepolicyinitiative.org/wp-content/uploads/2022/10/Global-Landscape-of-Climate -Finance-A-Decade-of-Data.pdf.

OECD (Organisation for Economic Co-operation and Development). 2021. "A Global Analysis of the Cost-Efficiency of Forest Carbon Sequestration." Working Paper 185, OECD, Paris.

OECD (Organisation for Economic Co-operation and Development). 2023. "Climate Finance Provided and Mobilised by Developed Countries in 2013–2021: Aggregate Trends and Opportunities for Scaling Up Adaptation and Mobilised Private Finance, Climate Finance and the USD 100 Billion Goal." OECD Publishing, Paris. https://doi.org/10.1787/e20d2bc7-en.

Ontl, T. A., and L. A. Schulte. 2012. "Soil Carbon Storage." *Nature Education Knowledge* 3 (10): 35. https:// www.nature.com/scitable/knowledge/library/soil-carbon-storage-84223790/?_amp=true.

Ordway, E. M., R. L. Naylor, R. N. Nkongho, and E. F. Lambin. 2019. "Oil Palm Expansion and Deforestation in Southwest Cameroon Associated with Proliferation of Informal Mills." *Nature Communications* 10: 114. https://doi.org/10.1038/s41467-018-07915-2.

Puko, Timothy. 2023. "Rich Countries Promised Poor Nations Billions for Climate Change. They Aren't Paying." *Washington Post*, October 9, 2023. https://www.washingtonpost.com/climate -environment/2023/10/09/rich-nations-pledged-poor-ones-billions-climate-damages-they-arent-paying/.

Ranganathan, Janet, et al. 2016. "Shifting Diets for a Sustainable Food Future." Working paper, Installment 11 of *Creating a Sustainable Food Future.* Washington, DC: World Resources Institute. https://www.wri .org/research/shifting-diets-sustainable-food-future.

Richardson, J., W. Steffen, W. Lucht, J. Bendtsen, S. E. Cornell, et al. 2023. "Earth beyond Six of Nine Planetary Boundaries." *Science Advances* 9 (37).

Rockström, J., W. Steffen, K. Noone, Å Persson, et al. 2009. "A Safe Operating Space for Humanity." *Nature* 461: 472–75. https://doi.org/10.1038/461472a.

Roe, S., C. Streck, R. Beach, J. Busch, M. Chapman, V. Daioglou, A. Deppermann, et al. 2021. "Land-Based Measures to Mitigate Climate Change: Potential and Feasibility by Country." *Global Change Biology* 27 (23): 6025–58. https://doi.org/10.1111/gcb.15873.

Roson, Roberto. 2017. "Simulating the Macroeconomic Impact of Future Water Scarcity." Discussion paper, World Bank, Washington, DC. https://doi.org/10.1596/26027.

Rotz, S., E. Gravely, I. Mosby, E. Duncan, E. Finnis, M. Horgan, J. LeBlanc, et al. 2019. "Automated Pastures and the Digital Divide: How Agricultural Technologies Are Shaping Labor and Rural Communities." *Journal of Rural Studies* 68: 112–22. https://doi.org/10.1016/j.jrurstud.2019.01.023.

Rozenberg, Julie, and Marianne Fay, eds. 2019. *Beyond the Gap: How Countries Can Afford the Infrastructure They Need while Protecting the Planet.* Sustainable Infrastructure Series. Washington, DC: World Bank. https://doi.org/10.1596/978-1-4648-1363-4.

Santos, N., J. Monzini Taccone di Sitizano, E. Pedersen, and E. Borgomeo. 2022. *Investing in Carbon Neutrality—Utopia or the New Green Wave? Challenges and Opportunities for Agrifood Systems.* Rome: Food and Agriculture Organization of the United Nations. https://doi.org/10.4060/cc0011en.

Schimel, J. 2000. "Rice, Microbes and Methane." *Nature* 403 (6768): 375, 377. https://doi.org /10.1038/35000325.

Schroeder, Kateryna , Julian Lampietti, and Ghada Elabed. 2021. *What's Cooking: Digital Transformation of the Agrifood System.* Agriculture and Food Series. Washington, DC: World Bank. http://hdl.handle .net/10986/35216.

Searchinger, T., M. Herrero, X. Yan, J. Wang, P. Dumas, K. Beauchemin, and E. Kebreab. 2021. "Opportunities to Reduce Methane Emissions from Global Agriculture." Unpublished manuscript. https://searchinger.princeton.edu/publications/opportunities-reducemethane-emissions -fromglobal-agriculture.

Shell Energy and BCG. 2023. "Carbon Market Reports: Exploring the Future of the Voluntary Carbon Market." 2022. Shell Energy. Accessed March 30, 2024. https://www.shell.com/shellenergy /othersolutions/carbonmarketreports.html.

Sova, C. A., G. Grosjean, T. Baedeker, T. N. Nguyen, M. Wallner, A. Jarvis, A. Nowak, C. Corner-Dolloff, E. Girvetz, P. Laderach, and M. Lizarazo. 2018. *Bringing the Concept of Climate-Smart Agriculture to Life: Insights from CSA Country Profiles across Africa, Asia, and Latin America.* Washington, DC: World Bank and International Centre for Tropical Agriculture.

Springmann, Marco, and Florian Freund. 2022. "Options for Reforming Agricultural Subsidies from Health, Climate, and Economic Perspectives." *Nature Communications* 13 (1): 82. https://doi.org/10.1038/s41467 -021-27645-2.

Steffen, W., K. Richardson, J. Rockström, S. E. Cornell, et al. 2015. "Planetary Boundaries: Guiding Human Development on a Changing Planet." *Science* 347 (6223).

Terrer, C., R. P. Phillips, and B. A. Hungate. 2021. "A Trade-Off between Plant and Soil Carbon Storage under Elevated CO_2." *Nature* 591: 599–603. https://doi.org/10.1038/s41586-021-03306-8.

Thornton, Philip, Yuling Chang, Ana Maria Loboguerrero, and Bruce Campbell. 2023. "Perspective: What Might It Cost to Reconfigure Food Systems?" *Global Food Security* 36: 100669. https://doi.org/10.1016/j .gfs.2022.100669.

Toman, M. J. Baker, R. Beach, H. Feng, E. McLellan, and E. Joiner. 2022. "Policies to Increase Mitigation of Agricultural Greenhouse Gas Emissions." Issues Brief 22-10, Resources for the Future, Washington, DC. https://media.rff.org/documents/IB_22-10.pdf.

Tribaldos, Theresa, and Teea Kortetmäki. 2022. "Just Transition Principles and Criteria for Food Systems and Beyond." *Environmental Innovation and Societal Transitions* 43: 244–56. https://doi.org/10.1016/j .eist.2022.04.005.

Tubiello, F., K. Karl, A. Flammini, J. Gutschow, G. Obli-Laryea, G. Conchedda, X. Pan, et al. 2022. "Pre- and Post-production Processes Increasingly Dominate Greenhouse Gas Emissions from Agri-food Systems." *Earth System Science Data* 14 (4): 1795–809. https://doi.org/10.5194/essd-14-1795-2022.

UNCCD (United Nations Convention to Combat Desertification). 2022. *The Global Land Outlook.* 2nd ed. Bonn: UNCCD. https://www.unccd.int/sites/default/files/2022-04/UNCCD_GLO2_low-res_2.pdf.

UNEP (United Nations Environment Programme) and Climate and Clean Air Coalition. 2021. *Global Methane Assessment: Benefits and Costs of Mitigating Methane Emissions.* Nairobi: UNEP. https:// wedocs.unep.org/bitstream/handle/20.500.11822/35917/GMA_ES.pdf.

United Nations. 2021. "Climate and Weather-Related Disasters Surge Five-Fold over 50 years, but Early Warnings Save Lives: WMO Report." UN News, September 1. https://news.un.org/en/story /2021/09/1098662.

Verdone, M., and A. Seidl. 2017. "Time, Space, Place, and the Bonn Challenge Global Forest Restoration Target." *Restoration Ecology* 25 (6): 903–11. https://doi.org/10.1111/rec.12512.

Voegele, J. 2023. "Transforming Our Food Systems for Healthy People, Environment, and Economies." *Voices* (blog), January 17. https://blogs.worldbank.org/voices/transforming-our-food-systems-healthy-people-environment-and-economies.

Vranken, Liesbet, Tessa Avermaete, Dimitrios Petalios, and Erik Mathijs. 2014. "Curbing Global Meat Consumption: Emerging Evidence of a Second Nutrition Transition." *Environmental Science and Policy* 39. https://doi.org/10.1016/j.envsci.2014.02.009.

Waldron, A., V. Adams, J. Allan, A. Arnell, J. P. Abrantes, G. Asner, S. Atkinson, et al. 2020. "Protecting 30 Percent of the Planet: Costs, Benefits and Economic Implications." Working paper. https://doi.org/10.13140/RG.2.2.19950.64327.

Wiatros-Motyka, Malgorzata. 2023. *Global Electricity Review 2023*. London: Ember. https://ember-climate.org/insights/research/global-electricity-review-2023/.

Willer, Helga, Jan Trávníček, Claudia Meier, and Bernhard Schlatter, eds. 2021. *The World of Organic Agriculture: Statistics and Emerging Trends 2021*. Bonn: Research Institute of Organic Agriculture FiBL, Frick, and IFOAM—Organics International.

Willett, Walter, Johan Rockström, Brent Loken, Marco Springmann, Tim Lang, Sonja Vermeulen, Tara Garnett, et al. 2019. "Food in the Anthropocene: The EAT–Lancet Commission on Healthy Diets from Sustainable Food Systems." *Lancet* 393 (10170): 447–92. https://doi.org/10.1016/S0140-6736(18)31788-4.

World Bank. 2019. "Zambia: Climate-Smart Agriculture Investment Plan." World Bank, Washington, DC.

World Bank. 2020. *Addressing Food Loss and Waste: A Global Problem with Local Solutions*. Washington, DC: World Bank. http://hdl.handle.net/10986/34521.

World Bank. 2021. "Climate-Smart Agriculture" (web page). Accessed March 30, 2024. https://www.worldbank.org/en/topic/climate-smart-agriculture.

World Bank. 2022. *State and Trends of Carbon Pricing 2022*. Washington, DC: World Bank. http://hdl.handle.net/10986/37455.

World Bank. 2023. "Ending Poverty on a Livable Planet: Report to Governors on World Bank Evolution." Development Committee Report. DC2023-0004, World Bank, Washington, DC. https://www.devcommittee.org/content/dam/sites/devcommittee/doc/documents/2023/Final%20Updated%20Evolution%20Paper%20DC2023-0003.pdf.

World Bank. 2024. "Indicators" (web page). Accessed April 14, 2024. https://data.worldbank.org/indicator.

WRI (World Resources Institute). 2023. "Indicators of Biodiversity and Ecological Services: Greenhouse Gas Fluxes from Forests" (web page). Accessed October 2023. https://research.wri.org/gfr/biodiversity-ecological-services-indicators/greenhouse-gas-fluxes-forests.

WRI (World Resources Institute). 2024. "Navigating the Paris Rulebook: Enhanced Transparency Framework" (web page). Accessed March 30, 2024. https://www.wri.org/paris-rulebook/enhanced-transparency-framework.

Xu, X., P. Sharma, S. Shu, T.-S. Lin, P. Ciais, F. N. Tubiello, P. Smith, N. Campbell, and A. K. Jain. 2021. "Global Greenhouse Gas Emissions from Animal-Based Foods Are Twice Those of Plant-Based Foods." *Nature Food* 2: 724–32. https://doi.org/10.1038/s43016-021-00358-x.

zu Ermgassen, Erasmus K. H. J., Mairon G. Bastos Lima, Helen Bellfield, Adeline Dontenville, Toby Gardner, Javier Godar, Robert Heilmayr, et al. 2022. "Addressing Indirect Sourcing in Zero Deforestation Commodity Supply Chains." *Science Advances* 8 (17). https://doi.org/10.1126/sciadv.abn3132.

ABBREVIATIONS

AEOS	Alberta Emission Offset System
AFOLU	agriculture, forestry, and other land use
AGF GP	Agriculture and Food Global Practice
AI	artificial intelligence
AMB	antimicrobial (resistance)
ASF	animal-source food
AWD	alternate wetting and drying
BAU	business as usual
BII	Biodiversity Intactness Index
BSP	benefit sharing plan
CAP	common agricultural policy
CARB	California Air Resources Board
CBAM	Carbon Border Adjustment Mechanism
CCAFS	Climate Change, Agriculture and Food Security
CCAP	climate change action plan
CCB	climate co-benefit
CCDR	Country Climate and Development Report
CDM	Clean Development Mechanism
CGE	computable general equilibrium
CGIAR	Consultative Group on International Agricultural Research
CH_4	methane
Ci-Dev	Carbon Initiative for Development
CO_2	carbon dioxide
CO_2eq	carbon dioxide equivalent
COP	Conference of the Parties
CPI	Climate Policy Initiative

CRU	carbon removal unit
CSA	climate-smart agriculture
CSRD	Corporate Sustainability Reporting Directive
CTCN	Climate Technology Centre and Network
EEF	enhanced efficiency fertilizer
E/MSY	extinctions per million species-years
EPA	(US) Environmental Protection Agency
ERF	emissions reduction fund
ESD	effort sharing decision
ESG	environmental, social, and governance
ESR	effort sharing regulation
ETF	enhanced transparency framework
ETS	Emissions Trading System
EU	European Union
EUDR	European Union deforestation regulation
FAO	Food and Agriculture Organization
FAOSTAT	Food and Agriculture Organization of the United Nations statistics
FG	farm gate
FOLU	Food and Land Use Coalition
g	gram
GCF	Green Climate Fund
GDP	gross domestic product
GEF	Global Environment Facility
GFANZ	Glasgow Financial Alliance for Net Zero
GHG	greenhouse gas
GHI	Global Hunger Index
Gt	gigaton
$GtCO_2eq$	gigatons of carbon dioxide equivalent
GW	gigawatt
HIC	high-income country
IBRD	International Bank of Reconstruction and Development
ICVCM	Integrity Council for the Voluntary Carbon Market
IDA	International Development Association
IEA	International Energy Agency
IETA	International Emissions Trading Association
IFAD	International Fund for Agricultural Development
IFC	International Finance Corporation
IFPRI	International Food Policy Research Institute
ILO	International Labour Organization
IMPACT	International Model for Policy Analysis of Agricultural Commodities and Trade
INDC	intended nationally determined contribution
IPCC	Intergovernmental Panel on Climate Change
IRENA	International Renewable Energy Agency
IRRI	International Rice Research Institute
ISO	International Organization for Standardization

ITMO	internationally transferred mitigation outcome
kg	kilogram
$kgCO_2eq/kg$	kilogram of carbon dioxide equivalent per kilogram
$kg\ CO_2eq/kg$ protein	kilograms of carbon dioxide equivalent per kilogram of protein
KJWA	Koronivia joint work on agriculture
km^3	cubic kilometer
LIC	low-income country
LMIC	lower-middle-income country
LULUCF	land use, land use change, and forestry
M&E	monitoring and evaluation
MAC	marginal abatement cost
MACC	marginal abatement cost curve
MDB	multilateral development bank
Mha	millions of hectares
MIC	middle-income country
MJ	million joules
MRV	measurement, reporting, and verification
MDB	multilateral development bank
mt	metric ton
$MtCO_2$	megatons of carbon dioxide
$MtCO_2eq$	megatons of carbon dioxide equivalent
MW	megawatt
N	nitrogen
NAMA	Nationally Appropriate Mitigation Action
NDC	nationally determined contribution
ND-GAIN	Notre Dame Global Adaptation Initiative
N_2O	nitrous oxide
OECD	Organisation for Economic Co-operation and Development
P	phosphorus
PPP	pre- and post-production
PPP	public-private partnership
PSIA	poverty and social impact analysis
PV	photovoltaic (technology)
R&D	research and development
RBCF	results-based climate finance
REDD+	reducing emissions from deforestation and forest degradation in developing countries
SB	Senate Bill
SCALE	Scaling Climate Action by Lowering Emissions
SDG	Sustainable Development Goal
SESA	strategic environmental and social assessment
SGiL	Store Grains (Food) in Land (program)
SGiT	Store Grains (Food) in Technology (program)
SME	small and medium enterprises
SSP	Shared Socio-economic Pathway
SRI	system of rice intensification
SRP	Sustainable Rice Platform

t	ton
tCO_2eq	tons of carbon dioxide equivalent
tCO_2eq/km^2	tons of carbon dioxide equivalent per square kilometer
TEC	Technology Executive Committee
TFP	total factor productivity
t/ha/yr	tons per hectare per year
TSVCM	Taskforce on Scaling Voluntary Carbon Markets
UMIC	upper-middle-income country
UNCCD	United Nations Convention to Combat Desertification
UNDP	United Nations Development Programme
UNEP	United Nations Environment Programme
UNFCCC	United Nations Framework Convention on Climate Change
US	United States
VCM	voluntary carbon market
VSS	Voluntary Sustainability Standards
WHO	World Health Organization

All dollar amounts are US dollars unless otherwise indicated.

CHAPTER ONE

A Call to Action

Justification

The top priority for the global agrifood system is ensuring food and nutrition security for everyone. That includes feeding a global population that is expected to grow from 8 billion to 10 billion people by 2050. However, the world will not be able to meet that challenge with today's agrifood system, which is a major contributor to climate change and has harmful consequences for the planet and the societies that depend on it. Thus, there is an urgent need for an agrifood system that emits fewer greenhouse gases (GHGs) and is less damaging to the environment more broadly. Meeting this challenge is made more daunting by the agrifood system's high vulnerability to the worsening climate crisis. The Intergovernmental Panel on Climate Change's (IPCC's) sixth assessment report on climate change impacts states with high confidence that "climate-related extremes have affected the productivity of all agricultural and fishery sectors, with negative consequences for food security and livelihoods" (IPCC 2022a, 717).

The agrifood system contributes significantly more to global heating than previously thought, creating a vicious circle that undermines food and nutrition security. Previous calculations estimated that agriculture, forestry, and other land use (AFOLU) generated about one-fifth of global GHGs (IPCC 2022b). However, recent advances in data collection and analysis have made it possible to more accurately measure emissions from the broader agrifood system, which includes food-related energy emissions and pre- and post-production processes. The newer data show that the global agrifood system is responsible for significantly higher GHG emissions: on average, 16 billion metric tons (or gigatons) of CO_2eq per year, or 30.8 percent of the total (figure 1.1) (Crippa et al. 2021; Tubiello et al. 2022). The vast majority of these agrifood emissions—nearly 80 percent and growing—

FIGURE 1.1 **Greenhouse Gas Emissions from the Agrifood System Are Significantly Higher than Previously Thought**

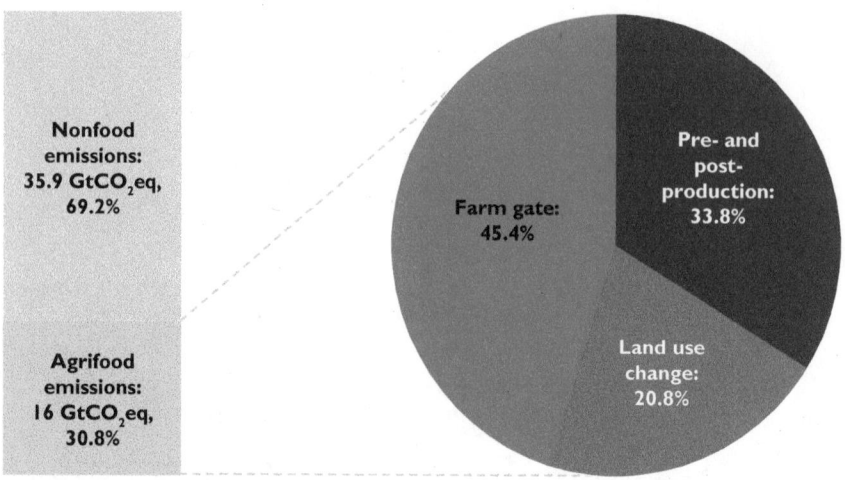

Source: World Bank based on data from FAOSTAT 2023.
Note: Left: Mean annual global greenhouse gas (GHG) emissions from the agrifood system as a share of total GHG emissions, 2018–20. Right: Emissions broken down by the three main subcategories. GtCO$_2$eq = gigatons of carbon dioxide equivalent.

come from developing countries. The COVID-19 pandemic and the Russian Federation invasion of Ukraine have disrupted the production and distribution of staple food crops and fertilizers, exposing the precariousness of the global food system through rising prices and food insecurity. Climate change and its impacts on food production have exacerbated these challenges (IDA 2020). More agrifood activities to feed a growing population increase GHG emissions, which contribute to more global heating, which diminishes agricultural yields—in turn, threatening food security and leading to greater production to cover the shortfalls, whether by converting forests to farms, applying more chemical fertilizers, or increasing animal stocking rates (Bajželj and Richards 2014). This greater production increases GHG emissions even further, resulting in a positive feedback loop, or vicious circle (figure 1.2).

The world cannot achieve the Paris Agreement targets without achieving net zero emissions in the agrifood system, but financing falls far short. The temperature targets enshrined in the Paris Agreement reflect the scientific consensus that warming above 1.5°C from preindustrial levels threatens the most exposed countries, such as low-lying island states, and warming above 2°C would lead to wide-ranging and catastrophic impacts. Recent research finds that even if all fossil fuel emissions are eliminated from every other sector, the emissions from the food system alone would be enough to drive the planet past the 1.5°C threshold, and even put the 2.0°C goal at serious risk (Clark et al. 2020). Therefore, to keep global warming below 1.5°C—as called for in the Paris Agreement—the world would need to reduce GHG emissions from 2010 levels by 45 percent by 2030 and reach net zero emissions by 2050 (IPCC 2022b),[1] including in the agrifood system (IPCC 2018b; UNFCCC 2015). Unfortunately, reducing GHG emissions from the global agrifood system has received scant attention, despite the system's large contribution to global heating. For example, only about half of the Paris Agreement parties originally included agriculture-related GHG targets in their Nationally Determined Contributions (NDCs) (Fransen et al. 2022). Moreover, dedicated climate finance for the agrifood system falls far short of these needs. Overall, climate finance has nearly doubled over the last decade

FIGURE 1.2 **Positive Feedback Loops between Agrifood Activities and the Climate Have Created a Vicious Circle That Precludes Adaptation Alone as a Solution to the Crisis**

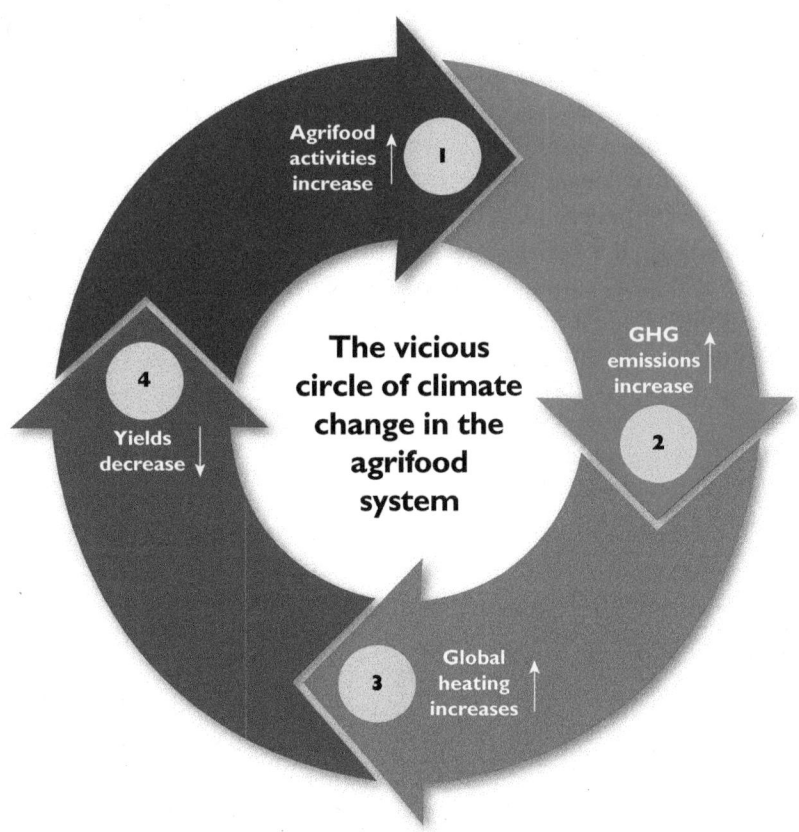

Source: Original figure for this report.
Note: GHG = greenhouse gas.

(Naran et al. 2022), but the agrifood system receives only 4.3 percent of this for adaptation, mitigation, and dual-purpose investments combined, and only 2.4 percent of mitigation finance (Chiriac et al. 2023). This meager support is a consequence of unbalanced financing across sectors and within the agrifood sector.

The agrifood system must balance its climate change efforts with broader developmental objectives. Society relies on the agrifood system to provide jobs, food security, and economic development. The Paris Agreement explicitly states that "the fundamental priority" of the agrifood system is "safeguarding food security and ending hunger" while "foster[ing] climate resilience and low greenhouse gas emissions." The agrifood system must also optimize human health and environmental sustainability (Willett et al. 2019). Conventional agriculture and food production often degrade soils and natural ecosystems and contribute to deforestation, biodiversity loss, ocean acidification, and air and water pollution (IPCC 2022c; WRI 2023). Likewise, common diets, especially in increasingly affluent societies, can undermine nutrition and human development. As a result, the IPCC (2022b, 40) notes that "accelerated and equitable climate action in mitigating, and adapting to, climate change impacts is critical to sustainable development." Thus, the process of transforming the agrifood system to net zero emissions must also contribute to—or at least avoid undermining—myriad other expectations placed on it. Doing so will minimize any trade-offs between mitigating climate change and achieving other development objectives.

The solutions for achieving net zero agrifood system emissions are available and affordable. Over the past three decades, the food system has witnessed remarkable successes. Agricultural producers have dramatically increased their output through enhanced resource-use efficiency and superior technologies. Moreover, conditions are in place to propel the agrifood system into the future. There are new innovations, an engaged private sector, heightened consumer awareness, and advanced digital tools. Moreover, there is no inherent trade-off between climate action and income generation or food security. With the right measures, it is entirely possible to diminish agrifood system emissions while simultaneously bolstering economies, supporting farmers, and feeding the planet. From a pragmatic perspective, the most compelling aspect is that solutions to achieve net zero are already affordable and can improve the trade competitiveness of countries specializing in low-carbon agrifood practices. As evidence shows, the agrifood system has many cost-effective mitigation options, defined as costing less than $100 per ton of GHG emissions (see box 1.1 for an explanation of GHG emissions metrics and units). Estimates have determined that the world can achieve annual reductions of 16.4 gigatons in the agrifood system through cost-effective solutions. This would be more than enough to cover all 16 gigatons of the agrifood system's annual GHG emissions. Furthermore, many of these mitigation options are even cheaper, including a large fraction that generates cost savings or profits. As such, these are no-regret investments.

The World Bank's global leadership in agriculture and climate change makes it well suited to support countries in reaching net zero agrifood emissions. In collaboration with development partners and client countries, the World Bank's Agriculture and Food Global Practice has increased its support for climate-related investments seven times since the Paris Agreement was signed in 2015, to $3 billion in fiscal year 2023. Most of this, or 63 percent, was dedicated to adaptation over the last five years. That progress is built on the World Bank's extensive knowledge and convening work on adaptation (see, for example, MacKinnon, Sobrevila, and Hickey 2008; Padgham 2009; Sutton, Srivastava, and Neumann 2013; Sutton, Srivastava, Neumann, Droogers, et al. 2013; Sutton, Srivastava, Neumann, Iglesias, et al. 2013; Sutton, Srivastava, Neumann, Strzępek, et al. 2013; and World Bank 2015) and the World Bank's mainstreaming of climate resilience into lending projects (Gage and Sutton 2016; World Bank 2021). However, the share of climate investments in the World Bank's agrifood portfolio has plateaued in recent years, settling at just over 50 percent. Moreover, financing for climate change mitigation is only 37 percent of the World Bank's agrifood climate support, leaving ample room to scale up mitigation financing.

Purpose

This report, *Recipe for a Livable Planet: Achieving Net Zero Emissions in the Agrifood System*, provides a recipe for dramatically reducing the global agrifood system's GHG emissions while contributing to the attainment of other key development objectives. It identifies solutions that cost-effectively reduce agrifood emissions while advancing global food security, economic growth, climate resilience, and marginal group inclusion. It describes opportunities for each country income category—high-, middle-, and low-income countries—to tackle their highest concentrations of agrifood system emissions. The logic is that by focusing on the

BOX 1.1 Greenhouse Gas Emissions Metrics and Units

This report employs specific metrics to report greenhouse gas (GHG) emissions quantities clearly and consistently. In this report, metric tons of carbon dioxide (CO_2) equivalent, abbreviated as tCO_2eq, is used as an expression of GHG emissions (IPCC 2018a). CO_2 equivalent accounts for major GHGs and not just CO_2, including nitrous oxide (N_2O), methane (CH_4), and fluorinated gases (F-gases). This metric also accounts for the relative warming potential, as calculated by the Intergovernmental Panel on Climate Change (IPCC) and applied by Food and Agriculture Organization of the United Nations statistics, of each gas compared with CO_2 over a 100-year horizon (IPCC 2022b; FAO 2023) (see table B1.1.1). Adopting these metrics creates a unified measurement standard and a comprehensive understanding of GHGs' overall climate impact.

GHG emissions are quantified in megatons of CO_2 equivalent, denoted as $MtCO_2eq$. This unit provides a standard measure of the mass of emitted gases, where 1 Mt = 1 million metric tons. For larger emissions, this report uses gigatons of CO_2 equivalent, denoted as $GtCO_2eq$ (IPCC 2018a), where 1 Gt = 1,000 Mt = 1 billion metric tons. This report uses both gigatons and megatons as measuring units for GHG emissions, which is consistent with the broader scientific community.

TABLE B1.1.1 Global Warming Potential of Greenhouse Gases

Greenhouse gases	Global warming potential over 100 years
Carbon dioxide (CO_2)	1 times that of CO_2
Methane (CH_4)	28 times that of CO_2
Nitrous oxide (N_2O)	265 times that of CO_2
F-gases	5,195 times that of CO_2 (mean of roughly 20 F-gases)

Source: IPCC 2022c.

biggest emissions sources and the most cost-effective mitigation options, countries will be able to most quickly and cheaply diminish or prevent agrifood GHGs from reaching the atmosphere. This is not to say that these solutions are mutually exclusive; it is simply recognizing that countries have shared, but differentiated, opportunities to combat climate change through the agrifood system. The report also illuminates a path for creating an enabling environment for the agrifood system transformation through six "I"s: investments, incentives, information, innovation, institutions, and inclusion. Collaborative efforts among governments, businesses, and international organizations and frameworks to bolster this environment will give the world its best chance of meeting the Paris Agreement emissions targets.

This flagship report is the first comprehensive global strategic framework for mitigating the agrifood system's contributions to climate change. It is part of a multiyear program of advisory services and analytics on climate change mitigation in the agrifood system led by the World Bank's Agriculture and Food Global Practice's Climate-Smart Agriculture Team. This report marks the first known attempt at developing a comprehensive global strategic road map for climate change mitigation in the agrifood system. The report raises awareness of the agrifood system's role in mitigating climate change and guides decision-makers and development partners in these efforts. It provides a comprehensive analysis of all the main elements of agrifood system mitigation. This includes both the supply and demand sides of emissions at all stages of the agrifood system—including on-farm, land use, and pre- and post-production phases. At the same time, the report does not ignore potential trade-offs. It provides a detailed breakdown of these and other challenges and proposes solutions for managing them.

This report is timely for several reasons. First, there is much more knowledge today about the global agrifood system and its growing climate footprint than there was even a few years ago. Second, it has become clear that virtually all pathways to limiting global warming to 1.5°C by 2050 will require net zero emissions from the agrifood system. Third, now is the time to drastically reorient the agrifood system, as its current form is pushing the planet closer to and beyond its operating limits. Fourth, despite the urgency, the agriculture negotiations under the United Nations Framework Convention on Climate Change (UNFCCC) have stalled,[2] with a particular divide between countries from the global north and south over the approach to mitigation (Puko 2023). Fifth, the World Bank, under the leadership of its new president, has announced a new vision statement and mission that puts climate change mitigation and other global public goods at the center of everything it does, with its new focus on creating a world free from poverty "on a livable planet" (World Bank 2023, 1).

Methodology

This report drew on the knowledge of a large, interdisciplinary team of experts from multiple institutions as well as the latest global research and original analysis. The team includes experts from across practices and sectors within the World Bank and a large team from the Food and Agriculture Organization of the United Nations (FAO). Fortunately, there has been a blossoming of research on different facets of the agrifood climate change challenge over the last few years, which has generated a wealth of new data. Chief among them has been research from organizations such as FAOSTAT that have provided a pioneering time series of emissions data for the entire agrifood system for nearly every country in the world. Academics and international organizations, such as the Consultative Group on International Agricultural Research (CGIAR) and the IPCC, have drilled down on the cost-effectiveness of mitigation measures in different parts of the agrifood system, and an initiative by the Climate Policy Initiative has gathered comprehensive climate finance data by sector, along with other emerging data. This information has been augmented with targeted original research and analysis, including the calculation of climate finance needs and marginal abatement costs and a new examination of climate, emissions, and agrifood system data through the lens of World Bank country income categories (World Bank, n.d.).

Conceptual Framing and Definition of Key Concepts

The global agrifood system, simply put, is the full array of activities through which humankind produces food from agriculture. This system includes seven core *activities*: (1) supplying inputs to agriculture, (2) producing crop and livestock products on farms, (3) processing crop and livestock products into food, and (4) storing, (5) retailing, (6) consuming, and (7) disposing of the food. These systems necessarily develop within broader socioeconomic and environmental systems and generate multiple *outcomes* that are influenced by *drivers* (figure 1.3). The transformation of the agrifood system requires the activation of these drivers through an enabling environment shaped by investments, incentives, information, innovation, institutions, and inclusion in the agrifood, socioeconomic, and environmental systems. These six "I"s need to be used strategically and coordinated across the agrifood system to set it on a low-emissions pathway. There are also feedback loops: for example, increasing GHG emissions from the agrifood system contributes to global heating, which in turn adversely affects agricultural production. Likewise, land, water, and biodiversity degradation from agricultural expansion depletes the resource base upon which agricultural production depends.

The scope of *Recipe for a Livable Planet* is intentionally broad to capture components of the entire agrifood system. This systems approach differs from the approach developed nearly two decades ago by the IPCC (Eggleston et al. 2006), which combined different emissions sources to create national GHG inventories and resulted in sometimes awkward groupings and obscure acronyms such as AFOLU (agriculture, forestry, and other land use) and LULUCF (land use, land use change, and forestry). Not to take anything away from that approach, which helped the world account for economywide emissions trends, but it has not been particularly effective at communicating the problem to a general audience or fostering solutions (Rosenzweig et al. 2020). In comparison, using a broader agrifood systems approach has several advantages. Most importantly, it does not separate the system's complexity into disparate elements but reflects the depth and scale of the challenge, making transformative change more likely. It also helps translate IPCC categories into concepts that are more easily understood by farmers and policy makers (Rosenzweig et al. 2020; Tubiello et al. 2022). Moreover, from an institutional perspective, the World Bank and many of its client country governments are not organized along IPCC emissions categories. Instead, the World Bank's Agriculture and Food Global Practice and many clients take an agrifood systems approach to designing investment projects and engaging in policy dialogue. Fortunately, experts working on FAOSTAT have developed an approach to emissions that bridges the gap. Figure 1.4 shows how this report's agrifood systems approach compares with the IPCC's categories.

This report characterizes GHG emissions and mitigation potential using several lenses but primarily through country income groups. This framework aligns with the World Bank's country income classifications of high-, middle-, and low-income countries. This framework offers several benefits. It is consistent with the World Bank's country-centric approach to development in which individual countries are the World Bank's main clients and shareholders. It also separates countries according to the World Bank's country engagement and financing, which are predicated on country income levels. Likewise, the framework offers a useful typology for analyzing the distinct agrifood system emissions profiles of different country groups without examining every country in the world individually. That said, the report team acknowledges that agrifood mitigation solutions will differ for every country, even among countries of the same income categories. Therefore, the objective of this framework is not to point fingers at specific countries or income groups but to help countries determine where they can focus action now and in the near future. Using country income categories has generated numerous insights into the different agrifood emissions sources and policy and investment priorities. This framework demonstrates that different country categories have different opportunities for combating climate change through the agrifood system, while recognizing that these opportunities could differ wildly from one country to the next.

This report emphasizes climate-smart agriculture (CSA) as an approach to prioritizing solutions. CSA is a concept that was adopted over a decade ago to good effect by the

FIGURE I.3 The Global Agrifood System Is Closely Intertwined with the Global Climate, Environment, Society, and Economy

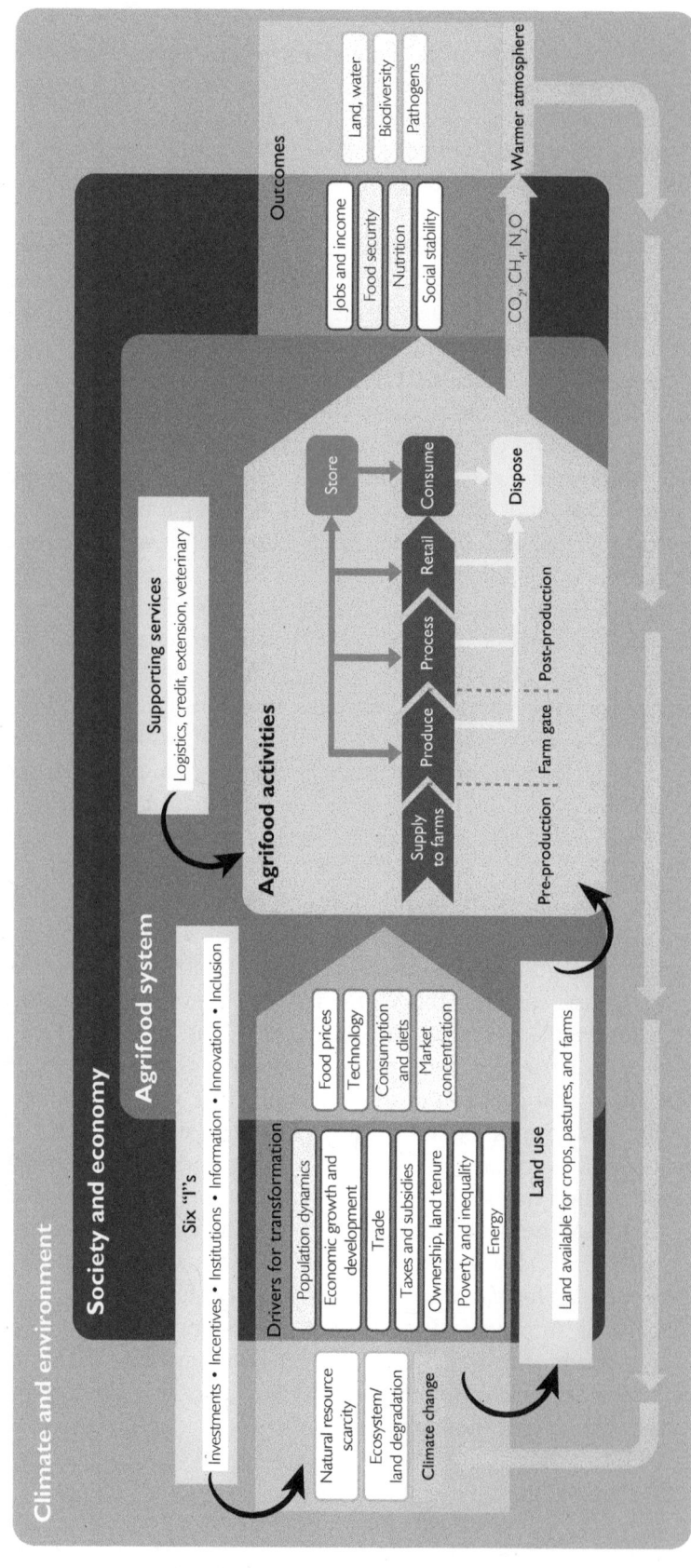

Source: World Bank, adapted from FAO 2022.

Note: CO_2 = carbon dioxide; CH_4 = methane; GHG = greenhouse gas; N_2O = nitrous oxide.

Recipe for a Livable Planet

FIGURE 1.4 Translating the Greenhouse Gas Emissions Inventory Categories of the Intergovernmental Panel on Climate Change into the Food and Agriculture Organization and World Bank's Agrifood Systems Approach

IPCC categories		Food system activity	FAO / World Bank categories	
AFOLU	LULUCF	Net forest conversion	Land use change	Food system
		Peat fires		
		Tropical forest fires		
	Agriculture	Burning (crop residues)	Farm gate	
		Burning (savanna)		
		Crop residues		
		Drained organic soils		
		Drained organic soils		
		Enteric fermentation		
		Manure applied to soils		
		Manure left on pasture		
		Manure management		
		On-farm energy use		
		Rice cultivation		
Energy		Synthetic fertilizers	Pre- and post-production	
		Domestic wastewater		
		Fertilizer manufacturing		
		Household consumption		
		Incineration		
		Industrial wastewater		
		Packaging		
Industry		Processing		
		Transport		
Waste		Retail (energy use)		
		Retail (refrigeration)		
		Solid food waste		

Source: Adapted from Tubiello et al. 2022.
Note: The Food and Agriculture Organization Corporate Statistical Database (FAOSTAT) estimates greenhouse gas (GHG) emissions from 26 sources within agrifood systems. These are gross fluxes of GHG emissions to the atmosphere. Only forest conversion is reported on a net basis, which accounts for both forest conversion emissions and sequestration from reforestation or afforestation.
Note: AFOLU = agriculture, forestry, and other land use; FAO = Food and Agriculture Organization; IPCC = Intergovernmental Panel on Climate Change; LULUCF = land use, land use change, and forestry.

World Bank, FAO, CGIAR, and others (see, for example, CCAFS, n.d.; FAO 2013; and Klytchnikova et al. 2015). CSA's simplicity has made it appealing and widely adopted by governments, farmers' organizations, and other agrifood system actors (Solutions from the Land 2021; World Bank 2019). CSA is an approach that builds on agriculture's unique ability to provide multi-win solutions and guide actions for achieving a sustainable agrifood system transformation. The CSA approach focuses on the following three elements:

(1) **Adaptation,** which builds the resilience of the agrifood system in response to, or in anticipation of, climatic changes, to reduce their harm and even benefit from them where possible;
(2) **Productivity,** which enhances the yield (or output) per unit of input; in other words, "produces more with less" to increase food security and farmer incomes; and
(3) **Mitigation,** which reduces emissions and emissions intensity of food production, minimizes food loss and waste, and supports sequestration.

CSA originally focused on farm-gate activities, but this report broadens the perspective to multi-win solutions across the broader agrifood system wherever possible. The report focuses attention on the biggest emissions sources with the most cost-effective mitigation potential. In doing so, the report touches on all elements of the agrifood system, illustrated by figure 1.4, to varying degrees. However, the reality is that this approach is relatively new, so there is more information on solutions under the traditional AFOLU part of the system. (Chapter 4 explores the need to fill remaining knowledge gaps.) Box 1.2 defines other terms that are common in this report.

A Call to Action

The world must prioritize the agrifood system for dramatic emissions reductions to reach net zero emissions and help heal the planet. Until now, efforts to reduce GHG emissions have focused on other sectors—such as energy, transport, and manufacturing—where scaling up a few key technologies has made an important difference in reducing emissions. However, these low-hanging fruits have mostly been harvested, and the planet is still far from where it needs to be to avoid climate catastrophes. The world has avoided mitigation action in the agrifood system for as long as it could because of the scope and complexity of the task. It is now time to put agriculture and food at the top of the mitigation agenda— both to dramatically reduce its emissions and to sequester excess CO_2 that cannot be cost-effectively eliminated from other sectors—otherwise, the world will not be able to meet the Paris Agreement targets or ensure a livable planet for future generations.

The rest of this report provides the recipe for transforming the world's agrifood system into a net zero emissions model. Chapter 2 describes the problem with the current agrifood system—which, to put it plainly, is that it is no longer conducive to a livable planet—and calculates the price for fixing it. Chapter 3 examines the cost-effective mitigation potential for all countries before delving into the most important sources of agrifood emissions and the relative opportunities for mitigating them in different country contexts. Chapter 4 identifies actions that governments, businesses, and citizens can prioritize to improve the global enabling environment for achieving net zero GHG emissions in the agrifood system. Chapter 5 synthesizes the report's findings and provides a comprehensive global recipe for action, with the most cost-effective pathways for different country types, to achieve net zero emissions in the agrifood system by 2050 and cultivate a more livable planet for all.

BOX 1.2 Definition of Key Terms

This report relies on a variety of technical terms, each with nuanced meanings. These include

- **Net zero emissions:** When the amount of anthropogenic greenhouse gases (GHGs) emitted into the atmosphere is equal to the amount removed anthropogenically (IPCC 2018a).
- **Net negative emissions:** When more GHGs are removed from the atmosphere than are emitted into it from human activities (IPCC 2018a).
- **Decarbonization:** The process by which countries, individuals, or other entities reduce their reliance on fossil carbon, thereby reducing carbon dioxide (CO_2) emissions (IPCC 2018a). Decarbonization is a worthy goal in the transport, industrial, and electricity sectors but is less applicable to the agrifood sector. This is because agrifood systems generate large quantities of other, more potent GHGs besides CO_2, such as methane and nitrous oxide, and because achieving net zero emissions in agrifood systems requires the opposite of decarbonization—specifically, an increase in the amount of carbon stored in soils, plants, and trees.
- **Low-emissions practices:** Agrifood practices with a reduced reliance on GHG-intensive processes or energy sources. Such practices include renewable energy generation, the transition to electric technologies, or fossil fuel use with carbon capture and storage, among many others. Low-carbon practices is a similar term that refers only to practices that reduce CO_2 emissions.
- **Mitigation:** Human interventions to reduce emissions or enhance GHG sinks, thereby alleviating climate change impacts (IPCC 2018a).
- **Adaptation:** Human practices and systems that adjust to the existing or anticipated impacts of climate change to mitigate harm or maximize benefits.
- **Technical mitigation potential:** The maximum amount of GHGs that can be reduced from a particular source using currently available technologies and practices. This does not account for costs.
- **Cost-effective mitigation potential:** The technical mitigation potential that is available and costs no more than $100 per ton of CO_2 equivalent reductions.
- **Cost-saving mitigation potential:** The technical mitigation potential that is available and costs no more than $0 per ton of CO_2 equivalent reductions; that is, mitigation potential that generates cost savings. This is a subset of cost-effective mitigation potential.

Notes

1. The IPCC defines "net zero emissions" as a state where anthropogenic emissions of greenhouse gases to the atmosphere are balanced by anthropogenic removals over a specified period (IPCC 2018a). The global net zero target will be achieved when GHG emissions caused by humans have been reduced as much as feasible, and any residual emissions are balanced by an equivalent amount of permanent removals, that this, the withdrawal of GHGs from the atmosphere as a result of human action. To achieve the temperature goals of the Paris Agreement, all countries are required to set a national GHG emissions reduction target in their nationally determined contributions (NDCs) that is in line with the global net zero target. For more information, see the World Bank Climate Explainer Series: https://www.worldbank.org/en/news/feature/2022/05/23/what-you-need-to-know-about-net-zero.

2. Personal observations by Malte Paul Plewa, William R. Sutton, and Ioannis Vasileiou of the World Bank and communications with participants at UNFCCC 58th Subsidiary Body Meetings held in Bonn, Germany, in June 2023.

References

Bajželj, Bojana, and Keith S. Richards. 2014. "The Positive Feedback Loop between the Impacts of Climate Change and Agricultural Expansion and Relocation." *Land* 2014 (3): 898–916. https://doi.org/10.3390/land3030898.

CCAFS (Consultative Group on International Agricultural Research [CGIAR] Research Program on Climate Change, Agriculture, and Food Security). n.d. "Priorities and Policies for Climate-Smart Agriculture" (web page). Accessed March 30, 2024. https://ccafs.cgiar.org/research/priorities-and-policies-climate-smart-agriculture.

Chiriac, Daniela, Harsha Vishnumolakala, and Paul Rosane. 2023. *Landscape of Climate Finance for Agrifood Systems*. San Francisco, CA: Climate Policy Initiative. https://www.climatepolicyinitiative.org/publication/landscape-of-climate-finance-for-agrifood-systems/.

Clark, Michael A., Nina G. G. Domingo, Kimberly Colgan, Sumil K. Thakrar, David Tilman, John Lynch, Inés L. Azevedo, and Jason D. Hill. 2020. "Global Food System Emissions Could Preclude Achieving the 1.5° and 2°C Climate Change Targets." *Science* 370: 705–08. https://doi.org/10.1126/science.aba7357.

Crippa, M., E. Solazzo, D. Guizzardi, F. Monforti-Ferrario, F. N. Tubiello, and A. Leip. 2021."Food Systems Are Responsible for a Third of Global Anthropogenic GHG Emissions." *Nature Food* 2: 198–209. https://doi.org/10.1038/s43016-021-00225-9.

Eggleston, H. Simon, Leandro Buendia, Kyoko Miwa, Todd Ngara, and Kiyoto Tanabe, eds. 2006. IPCC Guidelines for National Greenhouse Gas Inventories. Vol. 5, *Waste*. Geneva: IPCC. https://www.ipcc-nggip.iges.or.jp/public/2006gl/vol5.html.

FAO (Food and Agriculture Organization of the United Nations). 2013. *Climate-Smart Agriculture Sourcebook*. Rome: FAO. https://www.fao.org/climate-smart-agriculture-sourcebook/en/.

FAO (Food and Agriculture Organization of the United Nations). 2022. *Drivers and Triggers for Transformation*. Future of Food and Agriculture 3. Rome: FAO. https://doi.org/10.4060/cc0959en.

FAO. 2023. "FAOSTAT Domain Emissions Totals. Methodological note, release October 2023." Accessed March 30, 2024, https://fenixservices.fao.org/faostat/static/documents/GT/GT_en.pdf.

FAOSTAT. 2023. "Emissions totals" (data set). Accessed March 30, 2024. https://www.fao.org/faostat/en/#data/Gt.

Fransen, T., C. Henderson, R. O'Connor, N. Alayza, M. Caldwell, S. Chakrabarty, A. Dixit, et al. 2022. *The State of Nationally Determined Contributions: 2022*. Washington, DC: World Resources Institute. https://doi.org/10.46830/wrirpt.22.00043.

Gage, Alessandra, and William R. Sutton. 2016. "China: How Have Farmers Benefited from the World Bank Integrated Modern Agriculture Development Project?" *East Asia and Pacific on the Rise* (blog), July 12. https://blogs.worldbank.org/eastasiapacific/china-how-have-farmers-benefited-from-the-world-bank-integrated-modern-agriculture-development-project.

IDA (International Development Association). 2020. *Responding to the Emerging Food Security Crisis*. Washington, DC: IDA.

IPCC (Intergovernmental Panel on Climate Change). 2018a. "Annex I: Glossary." In *Global Warming of 1.5°C: An IPCC Special Report on the Impacts of Global Warming of 1.5°C above Pre-industrial Levels and Related Global Greenhouse Gas Emission Pathways, in the Context of Strengthening the Global Response to the Threat of Climate Change, Sustainable Development, and Efforts to Eradicate Poverty*, edited by Valérie Masson-Delmotte, P. Zhai, H.-O. Pörtner, D. Roberts, J. Skea, P.R. Shukla, A. Pirani, W. Moufouma-Okia, C. Péan, R. Pidcock, S. Connors, J.B.R. Matthews, Y. Chen, X. Zhou, M.I. Gomis, E. Lonnoy, T. Maycock, M. Tignor, and T. Waterfield, 541–62. Cambridge: Cambridge University Press. https://doi.org/10.1017/9781009157940.008.

IPCC (Intergovernmental Panel on Climate Change). 2018b. "Summary for Policymakers." In *Global Warming of 1.5°C: An IPCC Special Report on the Impacts of Global Warming of 1.5°C above*

Pre-industrial Levels and Related Global Greenhouse Gas Emission Pathways, in the Context of Strengthening the Global Response to the Threat of Climate Change, Sustainable Development, and Efforts to Eradicate Poverty, edited by Valérie Masson-Delmotte, P. Zhai, H.-O. Pörtner, D. Roberts, J. Skea, P.R. Shukla, A. Pirani, W. Moufouma-Okia, C. Péan, R. Pidcock, S. Connors, J.B.R. Matthews, Y. Chen, X. Zhou, M.I. Gomis, E. Lonnoy, T. Maycock, M. Tignor, and T. Waterfield, 3–24. Cambridge: Cambridge University Press. https://doi.org/10.1017/9781009157940.001.

IPCC (Intergovernmental Panel on Climate Change). 2022a. Climate Change 2022: *Impacts, Adaptation and Vulnerability; Contribution of Working Group II to the Sixth Assessment Report of the Intergovernmental Panel on Climate Change.* Cambridge: Cambridge University Press. https://doi .org/10.1017/9781009325844.

IPCC (Intergovernmental Panel on Climate Change). 2022b. "Summary for Policymakers." In *Climate Change 2022: Mitigation of Climate Change. Contribution of Working Group III to the Sixth Assessment Report of the Intergovernmental Panel on Climate Change,* edited by P. R. Shukla, J. Skea, R. Slade, A. Al Khourdajie, R. van Diemen, D. McCollum, M. Pathak, et al., 3–48. Cambridge: Cambridge University Press. https://doi.org/10.1017/9781009157926.001.

IPCC (Intergovernmental Panel on Climate Change). 2022c. *Climate Change and Land: IPCC Special Report on Climate Change, Desertification, Land Degradation, Sustainable Land Management, Food Security, and Greenhouse Gas Fluxes in Terrestrial Ecosystems.* Cambridge: Cambridge University Press. https://doi.org/10.1017/9781009157988.

Klytchnikova, Irina I., Marc Peter Sadler, Robert Townsend, Svetlana Edmeades, Vikas Choudhary, Sarwat Hussain, Holger A. Kray, et al. 2015. *Future of Food: Shaping a Climate-Smart Global Food System.* Washington, DC: World Bank Group. http://documents.worldbank.org/curated/en/645981468189237140 /Future-of-food-shaping-a-climate-smart-global-food-system.

Naran, Baysa, Jake Connolly, Paul Rosane, Dharshan Wignarajah, Githungo Wakaba, and Barbara Buchner. 2022. "Global Landscape of Climate Finance: A Decade of Data 2011–2020." Climate Policy Initiative, Washington, DC. https://www.climatepolicyinitiative.org/wp-content/uploads/2022/10/Global -Landscape-of-Climate-Finance-A-Decade-of-Data.pdf

MacKinnon, Kathy, Claudia Sobrevila, and Valerie Hickey. 2008. *Biodiversity, Climate Change, and Adaptation: Nature-Based Solutions from the World Bank Portfolio.* Washington, DC: World Bank Group. http://documents.worldbank.org/curated/en/149141468320661795/Biodiversity-climate-change -and-adaptation-nature-based-solutions-from-the-World-Bank-portfolio.

Padgham, Jon. 2009. *Agricultural Development under a Changing Climate: Opportunities and Challenges for Adaptation.* Washington, DC: World Bank.

Puko, Timothy. 2023. "Rich Countries Promised Poor Nations Billions for Climate Change. They Aren't Paying." *Washington Post,* October 9, 2023. https://www.washingtonpost.com/climate -environment/2023/10/09/rich-nations-pledged-poor-ones-billions-climate-damages-they-arent-paying/.

Rosenzweig, C., C. Mbow, L. G. Barioni, T. G. Benton, M. Herrero, M. Krishnapillai, E. T. Liwenga, et al. 2020. "Climate Change Responses Benefit from a Global Food System Approach." *Nature Food* 1: 94–97. https://doi.org/10.1038/s43016-020-0031-z.

Solutions from the Land. 2021. *The 21st Century Agriculture Renaissance: Solutions from the Land.* Lutherville, MD: Solutions from the Land. https://www.solutionsfromtheland.org/reports/renaissance-report/.

Sutton, William R., Jitendra P. Srivastava, and James E. Neumann. 2013. *Looking beyond the Horizon: How Climate Change Impacts and Adaptation Responses Will Reshape Agriculture in Eastern Europe and Central Asia.* Directions in Development: Agriculture and Rural Development. Washington, DC: World Bank. http://hdl.handle.net/10986/13119.

Sutton, William R., Jitendra P. Srivastava, James E. Neumann, Peter Droogers, and Brent B. Boehlert. 2013. *Reducing the Vulnerability of Uzbekistan's Agricultural Systems to Climate Change: Impact Assessment and Adaptation Options.* World Bank Study. Washington, DC: World Bank. http://hdl.handle.net /10986/16200.

Sutton, William R., Jitendra P. Srivastava, James E. Neumann, Ana Iglesias, and Brent B. Boehlert. 2013. *Reducing the Vulnerability of Moldova's Agricultural Systems to Climate Change: Impact Assessment and Adaptation Options.* World Bank Study. Washington, DC: World Bank. http://hdl.handle.net/10986/16199.

Sutton, William R., Jitendra P. Srivastava, James E. Neumann, Kenneth M. Strzępek, and Peter Droogers. 2013. *Reducing the Vulnerability of Albania's Agricultural Systems to Climate Change: Impact Assessment and Adaptation Options.* World Bank Study. Washington, DC: World Bank. http://hdl.handle.net /10986/16198.

Tubiello, F., K. Karl, A. Flammini, J. Gutschow, G. Obli-Laryea, G. Conchedda, X. Pan, et al. 2022. "Pre- and Post-production Processes Increasingly Dominate Greenhouse Gas Emissions from Agri-food Systems." *Earth System Science Data* 14 (4): 1795–809. https://doi.org/10.5194/essd-14-1795-2022.

UNFCCC (United Nations Framework Convention on Climate Change) Secretariat. 2021. "Nationally Determined Contributions under the Paris Agreement: Synthesis Report by the Secretariat." Report, UNFCCC, Bonn. https://unfccc.int/documents/306848.

UNFCCC (United Nations Framework Convention on Climate Change). 2015. "The Paris Agreement." UNFCCC, Bonn. https://unfccc.int/process-and-meetings/the-paris-agreement/the-paris-agreement.

Willett, Walter, Johan Rockström, Brent Loken, Marco Springmann, Tim Lang, Sonja Vermeulen, Tara Garnett, et al. 2019. "Food in the Anthropocene: The EAT–Lancet Commission on Healthy Diets from Sustainable Food Systems. Lancet 393 (10170): 447–92. https://doi.org/10.1016/S0140-6736(18)31788-4.

World Bank. 2015. *Future of Food: Shaping a Climate-Smart Global Food System.* Washington, DC: World Bank. https://openknowledge.worldbank.org/handle/10986/22927.

World Bank. 2019. "Climate-Smart Agriculture." Accessed January 2024. https://www.worldbank.org/en /topic/climate-smart-agriculture.

World Bank. 2021. "Climate-Smart Agriculture" (web page). Accessed March 30, 2024. https://www .worldbank.org/en/topic/climate-smart-agriculture.

World Bank. 2023. "Ending Poverty on a Livable Planet: Report to Governors on World Bank Evolution." Development Committee Report DC2023-0004, World Bank, Washington, DC. https://www .devcommittee.org/content/dam/sites/devcommittee/doc/documents/2023/Final%20Updated%20 Evolution%20Paper%20DC2023-0003.pdf.

World Bank. n.d. " Data: How Does the World Bank Classify Countries?" (web page). Accessed March 30, 2024. https://datahelpdesk.worldbank.org/knowledgebase/articles/378834-how-does-the-world-bank -classify-countries.

WRI (World Resources Institute). 2023. "Indicators of Biodiversity and Ecological Services: Greenhouse Gas Fluxes from Forests" (web page). Accessed March 30, 2024. https://research.wri.org/gfr/biodiversity -ecological-services-indicators/greenhouse-gas-fluxes-forests.

CHAPTER TWO

The Agrifood System Has a Big Climate Problem

Introduction

This chapter describes how the current agrifood system is no longer conducive to a livable planet and estimates how much it will cost to fix it. To put it plainly, the world can no longer afford the current agrifood system. It is a major contributor to climate change and has disastrous consequences for the planet and the societies that rely on it. At the same time, people rely on the agrifood system more than ever to provide jobs, food security, and development. It is also a potential source of greenhouse gas (GHG) emissions reductions and sequestration. However, there is a major financing gap between what is currently provided to the agrifood system and what is needed to reach net zero emissions. But the costs of inaction are even higher as climate change, natural resource depletion, and inequitable impacts from the current agrifood system undermine economic development and human and environmental health. Fortunately, there are many cost-effective mitigation actions that the world can take immediately to reduce agrifood system emissions while feeding the planet. This chapter will discuss all of these issues. It first describes the GHG emissions trends from the agrifood system and shows that the agrifood sector's escalating GHG emissions threaten the Paris Agreement's 1.5°C global warming limit, necessitating urgent mitigation measures. Next, it describes the stark financing shortfall for transforming the agrifood system to a low-emissions trajectory. Then it highlights the trade-offs that could emerge from making the agrifood system achieve many disparate goals and looks at the high costs of inaction, such as costly natural disasters and exacerbated food insecurity, and how these consequences are graver than the trade-offs. The chapter concludes by showing the conditions that are in place to start transforming the agrifood system now.

The Global Food System Is a Major, and Underappreciated, Contributor to Climate Change

The world has reduced the probability of warming by 4°C, the most dire projection. In 2012, the scientific community projected that mean global heating would be well over 3°C by the end of the 21st century, with a roughly 20 percent likelihood of exceeding 4°C by 2100 (World Bank 2012) based on national climate pledges and commitments at the time. Since then, GHG emissions projections have fallen. For example, in 2012, the expected emissions increase by 2020 was 17.1 percent; however, the actual increase by 2020 was only 1.3 percent. This was largely the result of high-income countries' increased renewable energy generation and energy and fossil fuel efficiency in industry and transport (Federal Ministry for Economic Affairs and Energy of the Republic of Germany 2020). The most recent synthesis report of Nationally Determined Contributions (NDCs) by the United Nations Framework Convention on Climate Change (UNFCCC) found that countries are bending the arc of GHG emissions predictions downward by increasing their NDC emissions reduction pledges. For example, in 2015, countries pledged to reduce GHG emissions by 31 percent by 2030 from 1990 levels, whereas by 2021 countries had pledged to reduce emissions by 49 percent (UNFCCC Secretariat 2021).

The world would need to reduce net GHG emissions from 52 gigatons annually to zero by 2050 to meet the 1.5°C Paris Agreement target. The temperature targets enshrined in the Paris Agreement reflect the scientific consensus that warming above 1.5°C from preindustrial levels threatens the most exposed countries, such as low-lying island states, and that warming above 2°C would lead to wide-ranging and catastrophic impacts, such as food shortages and more destructive storms, among many others (IPCC 2018). Current projections, with policies in place as of 2020 and no additional action or "business as usual," suggest that global heating would reach 3.2°C by 2100 (figure 2.1) (IPCC 2023). Even if countries follow through and implement all of their NDC commitments—which includes the combined climate pledges of 193 parties under the Paris Agreement—emissions would still increase by 10.6 percent by 2030 compared to 2010 levels. This would put the world on track to warm by about 2.5°C–2.9°C by the end of the century (UNFCCC Secretariat 2021), and by 2.1°C–2.4°C if NDC conditional elements—such as increased financial support, capacity building, and technology transfers, among others— were also implemented. In fact, even if all NDC commitments were implemented, there would still be up to a 23.9 gigatons of carbon dioxide equivalent ($GtCO_2eq$) shortfall in emissions reductions by 2030 (UNFCCC 2023). The Paris Agreement's temperature targets state that for a 67 percent chance of limiting warming to 2°C, the world must reduce global net CO_2 emissions from 2019 levels by 27 percent by 2030 and by 52 percent by 2040. For a 50 percent chance of limiting warming to 1.5°C, the world would need to reduce emissions by 48 percent by 2030 and 80 percent by 2040 (figure 2.1) (IPCC 2023). Put more simply, to meet the 1.5°C target, the world would effectively need to reduce GHG emissions, which averaged 51.9 billion tons per year from 2018 to 2020 to zero annually by 2050 with any unavoidable emissions offset by GHG-capturing activities (IPCC 2022c; World Bank calculations using FAOSTAT [2023] data).

GHG emissions from the agrifood system are significantly higher than previously thought, reaching 16 gigatons per year. Previous approaches to measuring sectoral emissions had used a narrower definition of agricultural-related emissions, restricted to agriculture, forestry, and other land use (AFOLU) combined, which generated around one-fifth of global GHGs (IPCC 2022c). However, recent advances in data collection and analysis have made it possible to accurately measure emissions from the broader agrifood system, which includes farms,

FIGURE 2.1 Limiting Warming to 1.5°C Requires Rapid Reductions in Greenhouse Gas Emissions

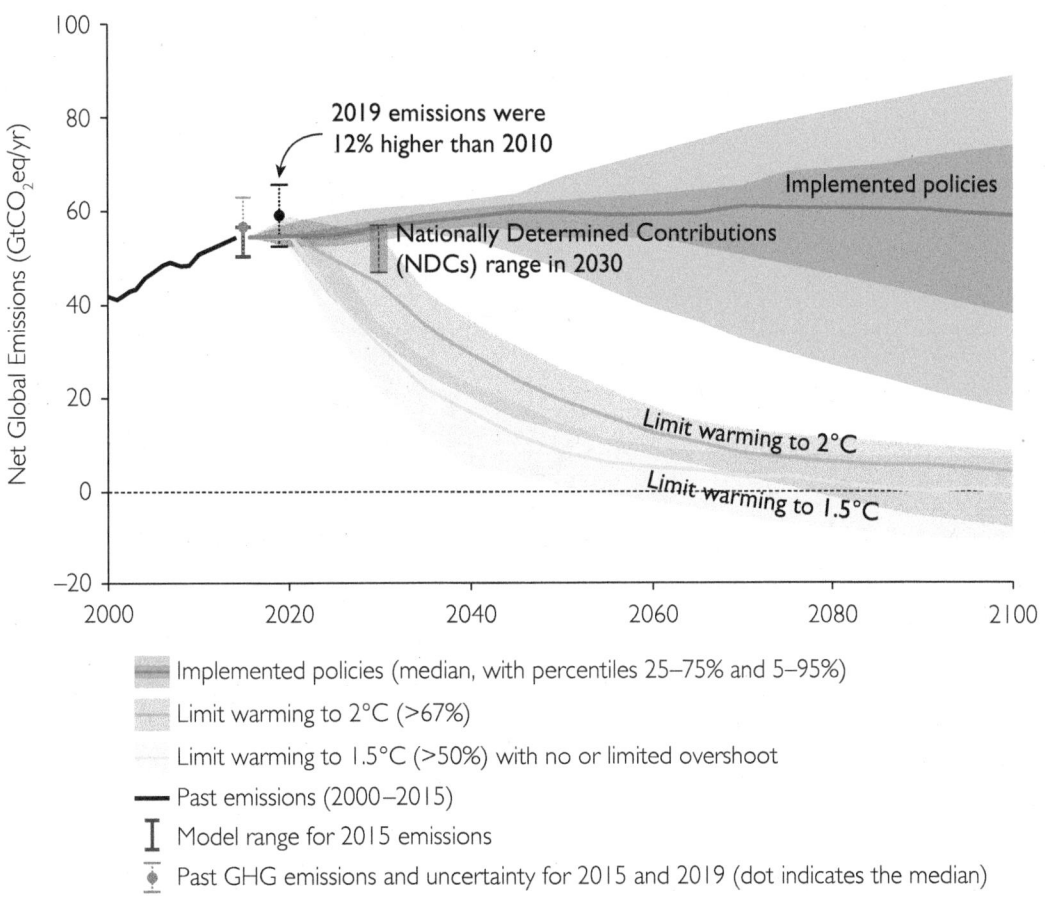

Source: IPCC 2023.

Note: GtCO$_2$eq = gigatons of carbon dioxide equivalent.

food value chains, and land use change linked to agriculture. The broader definition shows that the global agrifood system is responsible for significantly higher GHGs: on average, 16 billion metric tons, or gigatons, of CO$_2$ equivalent per year from 2018 through 2020 out of a global total of 51.9 gigatons per year, or 30.8 percent (figure 2.2 and table 2.1) (Crippa, Solazzo, et al. 2021; Tubiello et al. 2022). To put that into perspective, 16 gigatons is 14 percent more than all the world's heat and electricity emissions over the same period.[1] Moreover, reducing GHG emissions from the global agrifood system has received scant attention, despite its large contribution to global GHG emissions. For example, only about half of the Paris Agreement Parties originally included agriculture-related GHG targets in their NDCs, although the number of agriculture-related targets in the NDCs has more than doubled since the adoption of the agreement (Fransen et al. 2022).

GHG emissions come from a diverse set of sources across agrifood systems. Agrifood system GHG emissions can be broken down into three broad segments of the value chain: farm-gate activities, land use change, and pre- and post-production activities (Tubiello et al. 2022). Figure 2.2 illustrates average GHG emissions in the agrifood system from 2018 through 2020, separated into those three segments of the value chain. Farm-gate emissions refer to all

FIGURE 2.2 Greenhouse Gas Emissions from the Agrifood System Are Significantly Higher Than Previously Thought

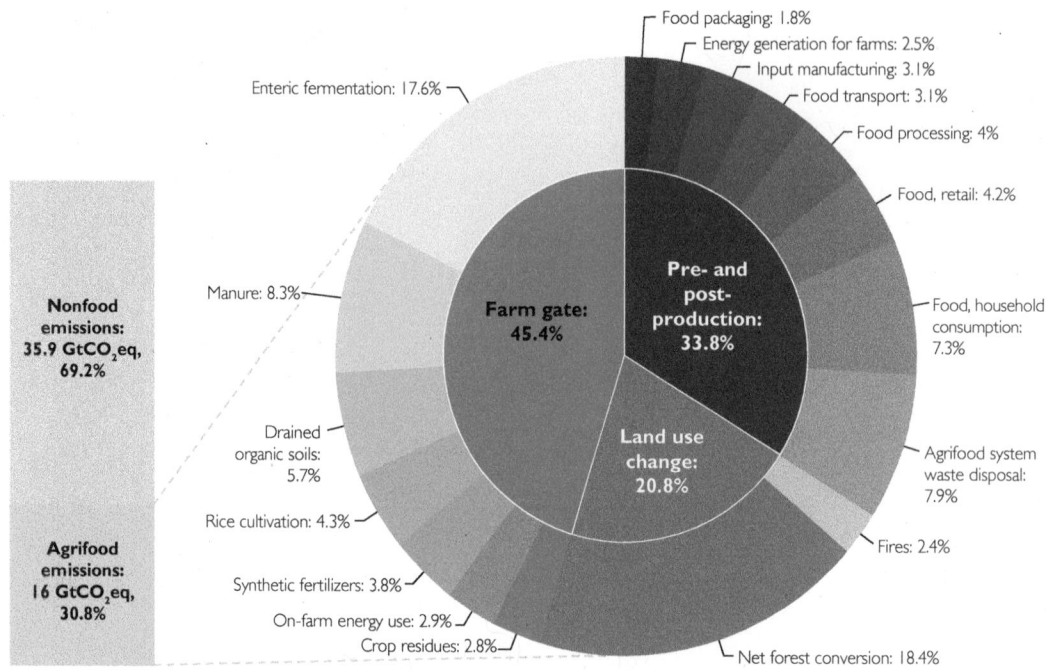

Source: World Bank based on data from FAOSTAT 2023.
Note: Left: Mean annual global greenhouse gas (GHG) emissions from the agrifood system as a share of total GHG emissions, 2018–20. Right: Emissions broken down by the three main subcategories and their individual components. $GtCO_2eq$ = gigatons of carbon dioxide equivalent.

TABLE 2.1 Average Share of Food System Emissions for World Regions, 2018–20

Region	Total GHG emissions, all sectors, including LULUCF, $GtCO_2eq$	Agrifood system GHG emissions, $GtCO_2eq$	Agrifood system share of GHG emissions	Share of global emissions	Agrifood emissions/ number of countries, $GtCO_2eq$	Agrifood emissions per capita, tCO_2eq
World	51.9	16.0	30.8%	100%	0.08	2.1
Region						
East Asia and Pacific	19.8	4.7	23.8%	29.4%	0.12	2.0
Europe and Central Asia	8.1	2.3	28.2%	14.3%	0.04	2.5
Latin America and the Caribbean	4.4	2.8	64.5%	17.7%	0.07	4.4
Middle East and North Africa	4.0	0.6	14.3%	3.6%	0.03	1.2
North America	6.9	1.3	18.9%	8.2%	0.43	3.6
South Asia	4.7	1.8	37.6%	11.0%	0.22	0.9
Sub-Saharan Africa	4.0	2.5	64.0%	15.8%	0.05	2.3

Source: World Bank based on data from FAOSTAT 2023.
Note: Total GHG emissions and agrifood sector emissions vary greatly by region and are dominated by East Asia and Pacific. GHG = greenhouse gas; $GtCO_2eq$ = gigaton carbon dioxide equivalent; LULUCF = land use, land use change, and forestry; tCO_2eq = ton carbon dioxide equivalent.

on-farm emissions from producing food and represent the largest source of agrifood system emissions, at 45.4 percent. Pre- and post-production refers to food system activities outside the agricultural sector that contribute to emissions, including waste disposal, transport, processing, and household food consumption. These activities account for 33.8 percent of total agrifood system emissions. Land use change consists almost entirely of net forest conversion for agriculture, but it also includes fires in organic soils and in humid tropical forests. These land use changes account for 20.8 percent of total agrifood system emissions.

The biggest supply-side contributions to agrifood system emissions come from eight key emissions categories. The supply side of emissions is the emissions sources, or from what or where the GHGs are emitted. The eight largest supply-side emissions categories are shown in figure 2.2 and include the following:

1. Livestock-related emissions represent the largest single subcategory of agrifood system emissions, at 25.9 percent if just enteric fermentation (17.6 percent) and manure left on pasture (8.3 percent) are included.
2. Net forest conversion represents the second largest subcategory, at 18.4 percent.
3. Food system waste accounts for 10.7 percent from waste disposal (7.9 percent) and crop residues (2.8 percent).
4. Household consumption patterns—about 40 percent of which is for electricity for kitchen appliances, about 20 percent, for heat for cooking; and another 20 percent, for heating water and dishwashers (Sims and Flammini 2014)—account for 7.3 percent.
5. Soil-related emissions from fires (2.4 percent) and drainage (5.7 percent) account for another 8.1 percent.
6. Fertilizer production (3.1 percent) and use (3.8 percent) account for 6.9 percent.
7. On-farm energy (2.9 percent) and electricity use (2.5 percent) account for 5.4 percent.
8. Rice production—the only individual crop with sufficiently large emissions to merit a separate subcategory—contributes 4.3 percent of total agrifood system emissions.

These categories represent the supply side of emissions, or the sources from which the GHGs are emitted. It is worth noting that examining agrifood emissions from the demand side would paint a different picture. For example, the global demand for meat leads to much of the production of meat, and related emissions, in developing countries. Chapter 3 explores these issues further and looks at how countries can tackle the demand-side and each of the eight supply-side subcategories, thereby mitigating the lion's share of agrifood system emissions.

The agrifood system's emissions are particularly damaging to the planet because they include powerful methane (CH_4) and nitrous oxide (N_2O) GHGs—not just carbon dioxide (CO_2). As explained in box 1.2, climate change mitigation terminology such as "decarbonization" or "low-carbon" applied to other sectors such as energy and transportation is not entirely appropriate for agriculture and food. That is in part because, while carbon dioxide is the biggest single source of GHG emissions in the agrifood system, at 50.1 percent, methane, at 32.9 percent, and nitrous oxide, at 14.3 percent, account for nearly half of agrifood system emissions (47.2 percent) (figure 2.3) and approximately a quarter of total GHG emissions globally. Moreover, methane and nitrous oxide emissions have accelerated in recent years (NASA 2022). These two GHGs are particularly potent because, on a per-unit basis, they have a much larger global heating effect and greater short-term potency than carbon dioxide does (US EPA 2023). For example, methane's global heating effect is around 80 times greater than that of carbon dioxide per ton emitted over 20 years and around 30 times greater over 100 years. In total, 25 percent of today's warming is driven by

FIGURE 2.3 The Agrifood System Generates Three Major Greenhouse Gases—Carbon Dioxide, Methane, and Nitrous Oxide—Which Come from All Country Income Groups and Parts of the System

Average, 2018–20

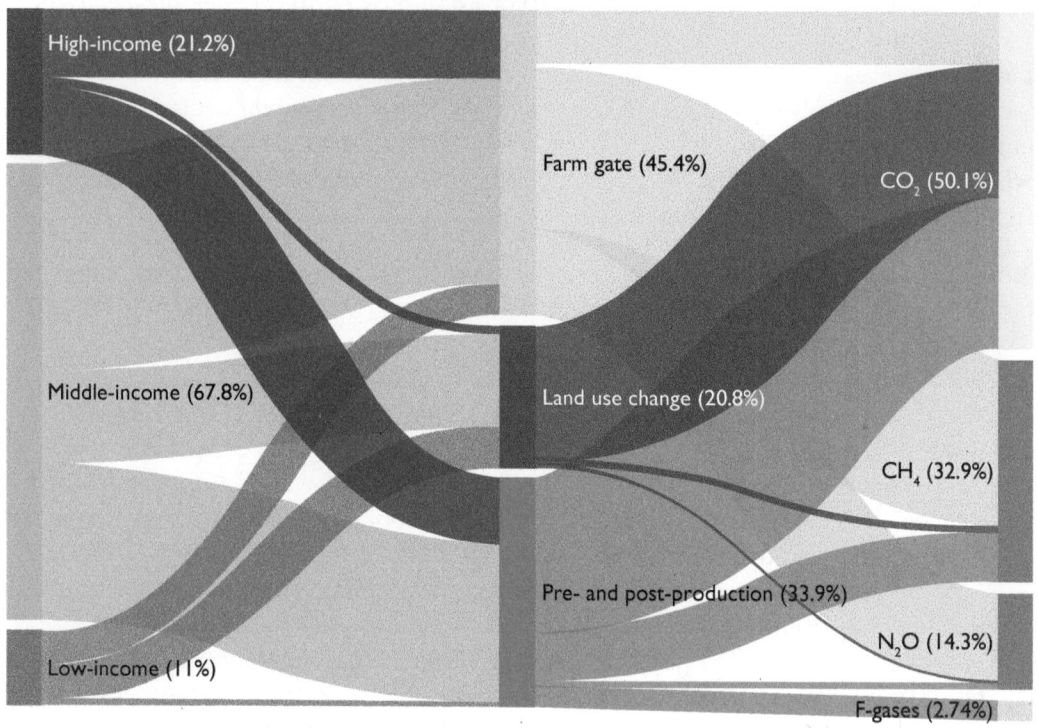

Source: World Bank based on data from World Bank 2024 and FAOSTAT 2023.
Note: Figure is a Sankey diagram of shares of individual greenhouse gas (GHG) emissions by country income group and source category in CO₂ equivalent. In addition to shares of the three major GHGs, the figure includes the share of fluorinated GHGs (F-gases). CH₄ = methane; CO₂ = carbon dioxide; F-gases = fluorinated gases; N₂O = nitrous oxide.

methane from human activities (Department for Business, Energy & Industrial Strategy, and Department for Energy Security & Net Zero, United Kingdom 2022).

The major GHG types are generated in different quantities from the three parts of the agrifood system. Methane and nitrous oxide emissions are disproportionally caused by farm-gate activities, with a smaller but still significant amount of methane stemming from post-production emissions as organic food waste decomposes in landfills. Indeed, the agrifood system is the greatest source of anthropogenic (or human-made) methane emissions, accounting for about 40 percent of economy-wide methane emissions, with livestock manure management and enteric fermentation contributing about 32 percent of such emissions, sanitation and waste about 20 percent, and rice cultivation about 8 percent (UNEP 2021). Among agrifood system emissions, methane represents about one third of the total (figure 2.3, right panel). Agriculture is also the largest source of nitrous oxide emissions (Our World in Data 2023). Notably, carbon dioxide accounts for a smaller portion of farm-gate emissions than the other two gases. That said, carbon dioxide still represents half of agrifood system emissions, and makes up the largest share of pre- and post-production emissions and almost the only type of GHG emitted from land use change (figure 2.3, right panel). The remaining 2.7 percent of agrifood system GHGs are fluorinated gases, or F-gases. These are not discussed in detail in this report because they make up such a small portion of GHGs. However, it is worth noting that these gases generally do not come from low-income countries because those countries have much lower emissions from pre- and post-production activities, which generate the most F-gases.

Middle-income countries are the biggest contributors to agrifood system emissions. Analyzing agrifood system emissions by country income levels—specifically high-, middle-, and low-income countries (HICs, MICs, and LICs) reveals widely diverse emissions profiles, with middle-income countries generating the most agrifood emissions (figure 2.4).

FIGURE 2.4 **Middle-Income Countries Generate Two-Thirds of Agrifood System Emissions**

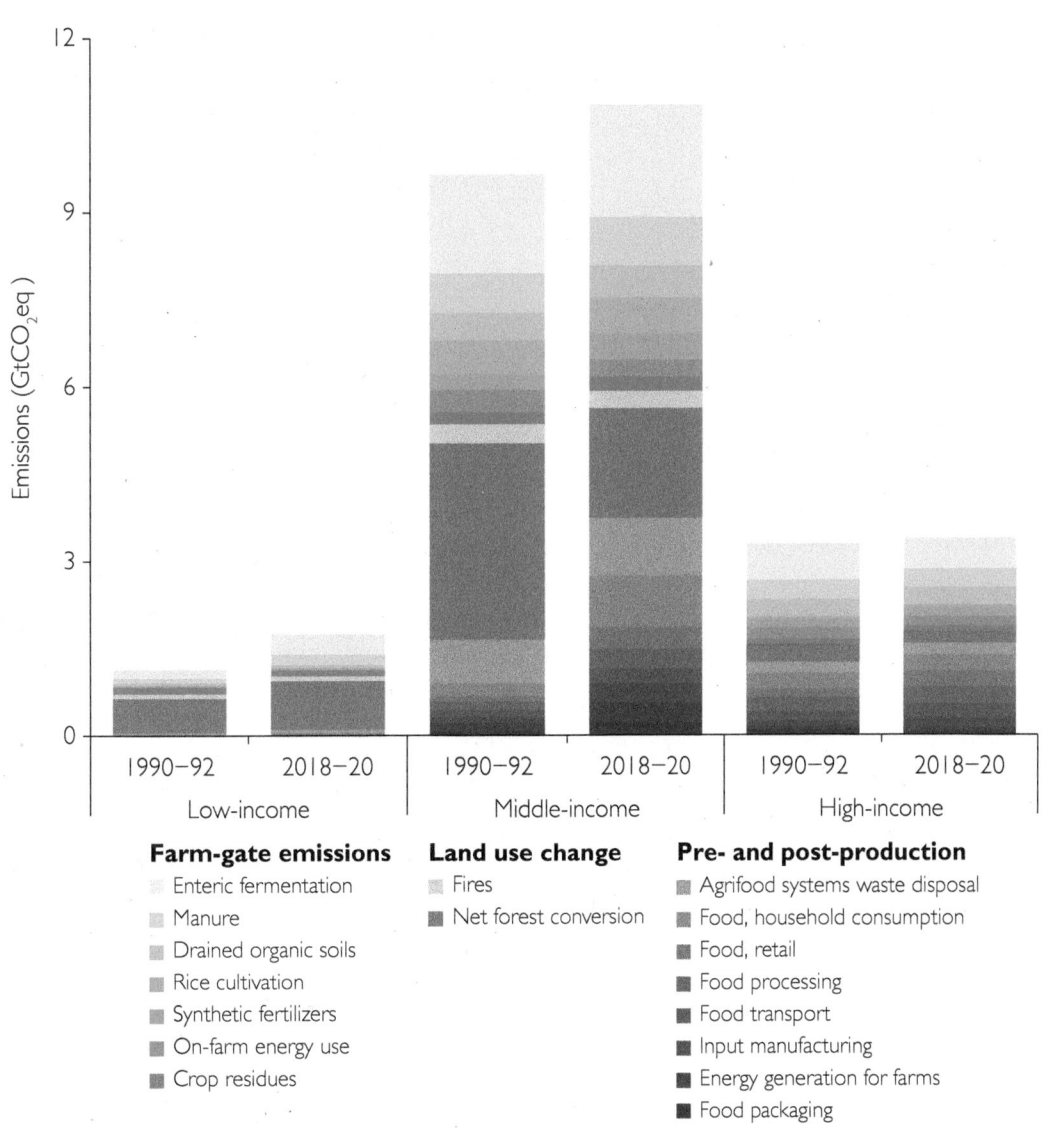

Source: World Bank based on data from World Bank 2024 and FAOSTAT 2023.

Note: Figure shows mean agrifood system emissions for 1990–92 and 2018–20 by source category and country income group. "Manure" consists of manure left on pasture, manure management, and manure applied to soils. "Crop residues" consists of savanna fires, crop residues, and burning—crop residues. "Fires" consists of fires in organic soils and fires in humid tropical forests. "Input manufacturing" consists of fertilizer manufacturing and pesticide manufacturing. "Energy generation for farms" consists of on-farm heat use and on-farm electricity use. $GtCO_2eq$ = gigatons of carbon dioxide equivalent; HICs = high-income countries; LICs = low-income countries; MICs = middle-income countries.

This trend is likely to continue because MICs are undergoing rapid industrialization and consumer income growth. Unfortunately, these countries are largely following the same emissions-heavy development path as HICs, with similar deforestation and land use change patterns (Jones et al. 2023) but with much larger and growing populations. MICs contribute 67.8 percent of global agrifood emissions today compared to 21.2 percent from HICs and 11 percent from LICs (Tubiello et al. 2022). Moreover, MICs accounted for the largest absolute increase in agrifood system emissions between 1990 and 1992 and between 2018 and 2020, with an additional 1.19 $GtCO_2eq$, or 12.3 percent, of emissions entering the atmosphere (figure 2.4). That said, land use change as a contributor to GHG emissions in MICs has decreased from 38.4 percent to 20.2 percent since 1990–92, while pre- and post-production activities as a contributor have grown from 17.1 percent to 34.5 percent over the same time frame (Tubiello et al. 2022). It is important to note that MICs as a country category have the most countries, 108 countries worldwide, compared to 77 HICs and just 28 LICs. In that sense, it should be no surprise that MICs emit the most (FAOSTAT 2023). However, splitting the MIC group into lower-middle-income countries (LMICs) and upper-middle-income countries (UMICs) results in 55 LMICs and 53 UMICs but does not change the result, with agrifood emissions from each MIC subgroup outstripping emissions from either HICs or LICs (figure 2.5). Following this breakdown, UMICs are the world's biggest agrifood system emitters. Newly published research that estimates cumulative GHG emissions from AFOLU going back to 1850 suggests that MICs are also the biggest source of historical agrifood emissions (Jones et al. 2023, with World Bank analysis by country income categories).

The bulk of agrifood emissions is concentrated in a handful of countries. Seven of the top 10 emitter countries are MIC countries, including the top three—China, Brazil, and India (figure 2.6). The United States is the top HIC emitter, and the only HIC among the top five emitters. But even in the top five there is great variation, with China's annual agrifood emissions more than twice those of the United States. The only LIC country in the top 10 is the Democratic Republic of Congo, which comes in sixth, driven almost entirely by converting forests to agriculture (box 3.5). The rest of the top 10 is filled out by four MICs (Indonesia, the Russian Federation, Pakistan, and Argentina) and one HIC (Canada). This is clearly a global problem, with countries in the top 10 encompassing four continents. As a group, the top 10 emitters are responsible for 55 percent of global agrifood emissions, while the top 20 emitters are responsible for 67 percent. Data on agrifood GHG emissions for most countries are provided in appendix A.

HICs are the second biggest source of agrifood system emissions and have the highest per capita emissions. Moreover, some HICs are among the highest historical emitters—for example, the United States has emitted more than any other country on the planet in terms of cumulative emissions (box 2.1). The high per capita emissions are primarily caused by the United States' resource-intensive development model that hinged on fossil fuels for a relatively limited population (Crippa, Guizzardi, et al. 2021). That model brought technological advances and helped the world feed its growing population with a diversity of foods unconstrained by seasons, but it also brought unprecedented pollution, land degradation, obesity and heart disease, and global heating (FAO 2022; FOLU 2019). That said, HICs' share of agrifood emissions has declined as their population growth decelerated, their economies shifted from a reliance on agriculture to manufacturing and services, food production was outsourced to middle- and low-income countries, and investments in food sector productivity and renewable energy have borne fruit (Crippa, Solazzo, et al. 2021). Since 1992, HICs had the lowest increase in agrifood system

FIGURE 2.5 Upper Middle-Income Countries Generate the Highest Agrifood Emissions, Both Today and 30 Years Ago

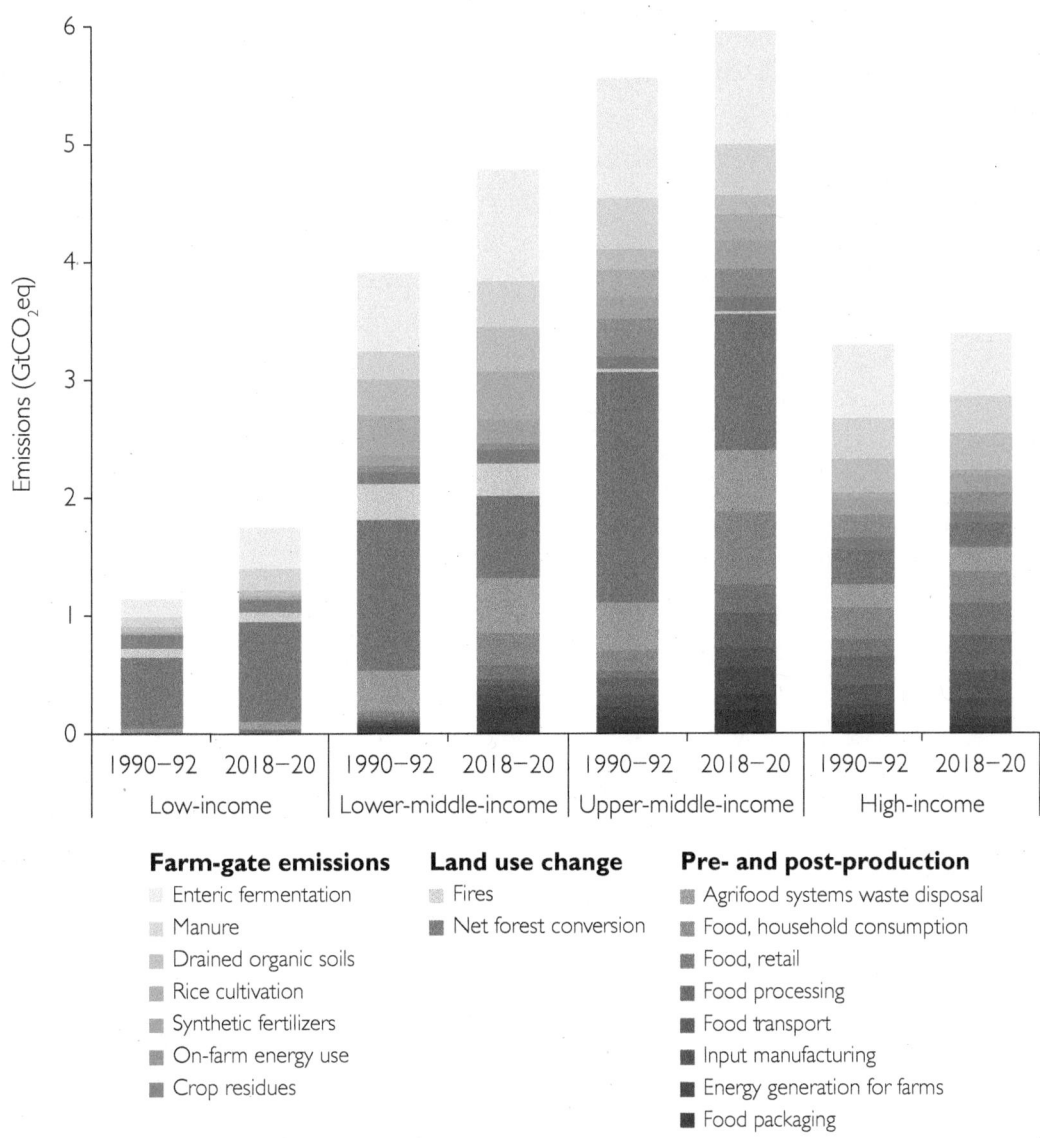

Farm-gate emissions
- Enteric fermentation
- Manure
- Drained organic soils
- Rice cultivation
- Synthetic fertilizers
- On-farm energy use
- Crop residues

Land use change
- Fires
- Net forest conversion

Pre- and post-production
- Agrifood systems waste disposal
- Food, household consumption
- Food, retail
- Food processing
- Food transport
- Input manufacturing
- Energy generation for farms
- Food packaging

Source: World Bank based on data from World Bank 2024 and FAOSTAT 2023.
Note: Figure shows mean agrifood emissions for 1990–92 and 2018–20 by source category and country income group. Categories are grouped to reduce those with small values. "Manure" consists of manure left on pasture, manure management, and manure applied to soils. "Crop residues" consists of savanna fires, crop residues, and burning—crop residues. "Fires" consists of fires in organic soils and fires in humid tropical forests. "Input manufacturing" consists of fertilizer manufacturing and pesticide manufacturing. GtCO$_2$eq = gigatons of carbon dioxide equivalent.

emissions as both a percentage (1.8 percent) and total amount (0.06 GtCO$_2$) (figure 2.7). This is because HIC food systems were already well developed by 1990 and because land use change emissions are barely present in HICs (figure 2.4). Today, HICs contribute only about a third of what MICs contribute to agrifood system emissions (figure 2.4). That said, HICs, including oil-producing developing countries, continue to have the highest per capita emissions (figure 2.7). These per capita agrifood system emissions are driven largely by the heavy consumption of meat and dairy and the increase in food transport, processing,

The Agrifood System Has a Big Climate Problem

FIGURE 2.6 Seven of the Top 10 Agrifood System Emitters Are Middle-Income Countries and One Is a Low-Income Country

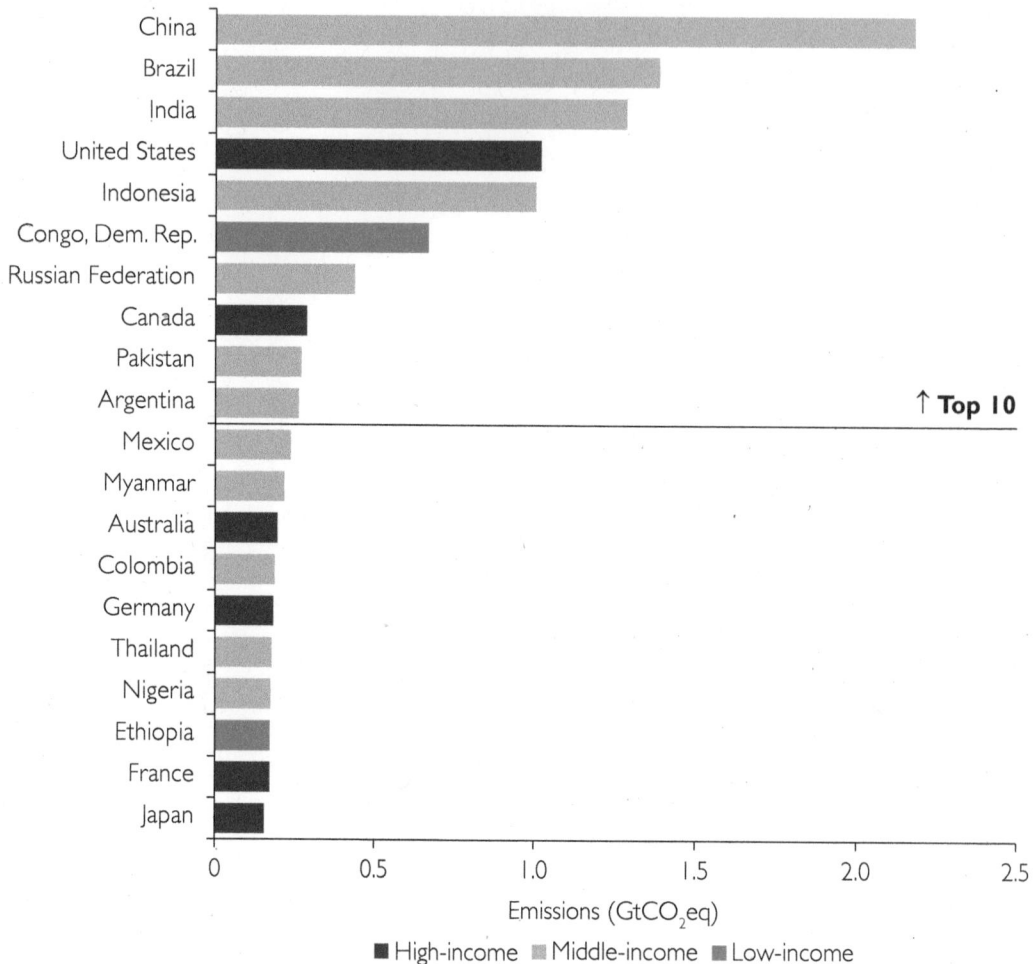

Source: World Bank based on data from World Bank 2024 and FAOSTAT 2023.
Note: Figure shows mean agribusiness emissions for 2018–20. GtCO₂eq = gigatons of carbon dioxide equivalent.

packaging, and waste (FAO 2018). Moreover, almost half of HICs' agrifood system emissions come from pre- and post-production sources (47 percent, 2018–20), which is largely because of the greater use of cold-chain technologies, such as the refrigerated distribution of food along the food chain in HICs (International Institute of Refrigeration 2021).

LICs emit the fewest overall GHG emissions from the agrifood system but have had the fastest rate of increase since the early 1990s. LICs have been a minor source of agrifood emissions because the LIC category comprises fewer countries (28) than MICs (108) and HICs (77) and also because LICs have not seen the rapid fossil fuel–driven industrial development of the other country categories. Even so, total agrifood systems emissions in low-income countries increased from 1.15 GtCO₂eq in 1990–92 to 1.76 GtCO₂eq in 2018–20—a 53.0 percent increase. This is much higher than the 12.3 percent increase in MICs and the 3.0 percent increase in HICs (figure 2.4). Most of these increases are from land use change, such as forest conversion to agricultural land, and on-farm activities, particularly

Agrifood Emissions in Depth: The United States

Historically, the United States is the biggest emitter of greenhouse gases. Today, it is second only to China. Fossil fuel emissions have been the largest source of these emissions, but land use, land use change, and forestry account for 21 percent of the United States' total historical emissions since the 1850s (Jones et al. 2023). Today, the agrifood system represents 18 percent of the US's total GHG emissions. As such, it is among the top five agrifood system emitters along with Brazil, China, India, and Indonesia. Pre- and post-production emissions play a major role, accounting for about half of the United States' total agrifood system emissions, well above the global average of one-third (figure B2.1.1). Retail, food processing, and household consumption alone account for a quarter of the country's agrifood system emissions, and food loss and waste account for 10 percent (FAOSTAT 2023). In fact, more than $160 billion worth of food—or 100 kilograms per person—are wasted annually (USDA, n.d.). The US Department of Agriculture and US

FIGURE B2.1.1 **US Agrifood System Emissions, 1990–92 and 2018–20**

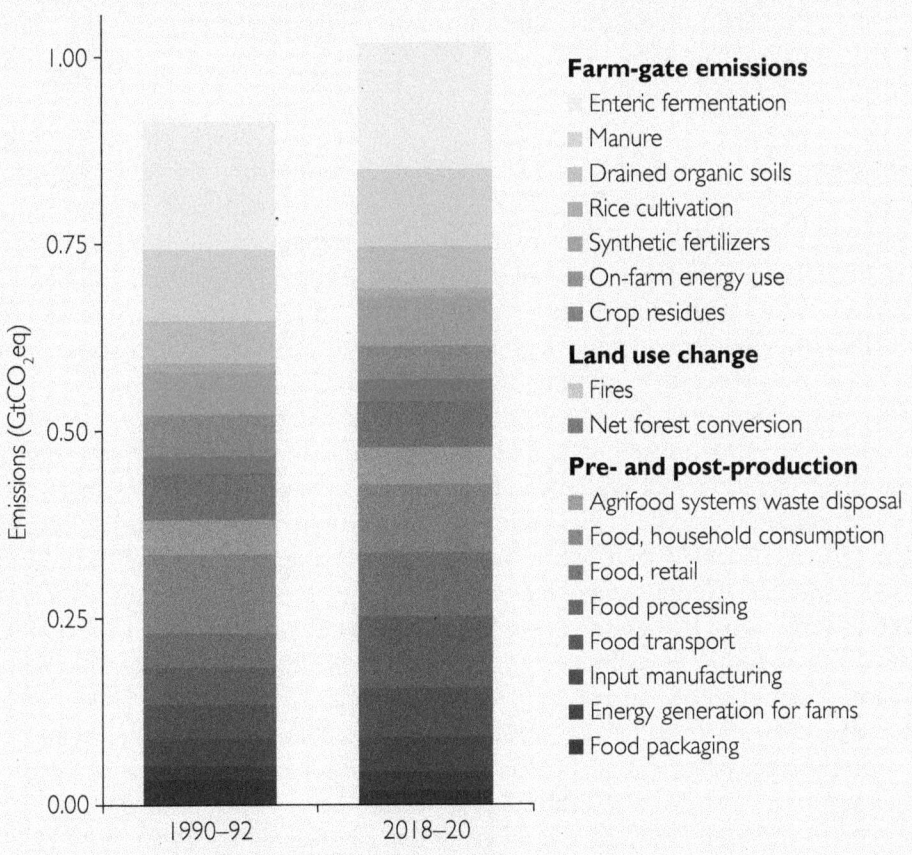

Source: World Bank based on data from World Bank 2024 and FAOSTAT 2023.
Note: Figure shows mean agrifood system emissions for 1990–92 and 2018–20 by source category. Categories are grouped to reduce those with small values. See figure 2.5 note for more detail. GtCO₂eq = gigatons of carbon dioxide equivalent.

(box continued next page)

BOX 2.1 **Agrifood Emissions in Depth: The United States** *(Continued)*

Environmental Protection Agency have set a target to halve this figure by 2030, and enteric fermentation remains the number one source of emissions in the nation's agrifood system (FAOSTAT 2023).

However, there are some encouraging trends in the United States. First, it is among the most productive countries in the world, which leads to a lower demand for land and thus lower emissions from land use and land use change (Blaustein-Rejto 2023). This means that the United States can produce many key food commodities, including maize, beef, and chicken, at a considerably lower carbon footprint than other major producers and exporters of these items. This would well place US industries if any widespread emissions pricing were ever enacted. Second, the United States consumes a lot of meat, but its diet-related emissions declined by 35 percent from 2003 to 2018 and its per capita beef consumption declined by 40 percent. There is a lack of research on the drivers of these dietary changes, but studies show that awareness of climate change and its causes has been steadily rising in the United States over the past decades (Hamilton 2021). Also, the United States has spearheaded the Global Methane Pledge and the associated Food and Agriculture Pathway, which aim to cut methane emissions by 30 percent by 2030 (US Department of State 2022).

livestock production. Very few of LICs' emissions come from pre- and post-production processes, which accounted for only 5.9 percent of their agrifood system emissions in 2018–20 (figure 2.4). Similarly, per capita agrifood system emissions in LICs are growing faster than those from HICs and MICs combined. Per capita agrifood emissions in LICs are already substantially higher than per capita MIC emissions and may soon surpass those from HICs. Agrifood emissions growth in LICs is being propelled by increasing agricultural production and related deforestation (figures 2.4 and 2.7).

Even within country income groups, there are divergent emissions trends. China's emissions are mainly caused by household food consumption emissions, including from cooking, refrigeration, and appliances, followed by emissions from the farm gate. In India, farm-gate emissions are the highest component but with a notable increase in pre- and post-production emissions. By contrast, in Brazil and Indonesia, land use change is the source of agrifood system GHG emissions because these countries continue to convert forested land to agricultural uses. The countries with the most agrifood emissions tend to also be the most populous countries; therefore, countries such as China and India rank high in total emissions but much lower in per capita emissions (map 2.1). Botswana, Guyana, Mongolia, and Suriname—all classified as MICs—make small contributions to global agrifood emissions because of their small populations, but partly for the same reason are among the top per capita emitters (map 2.1; table 2.2; appendix A).

Agrifood emissions vary greatly by geographic region and are driven by big-emitting middle-income countries rather than by per capita emissions. The East Asia and Pacific region accounts for by far the largest regional share of emissions—over 50 percent higher than the next region—because high-emitting, populous countries such as China and Indonesia are located there (figure 2.8). This also means that the region's per capita emissions are low. As East Asia and Pacific economies develop, land use change–related emissions remain low, but pre- and post-production food system emissions are taking on

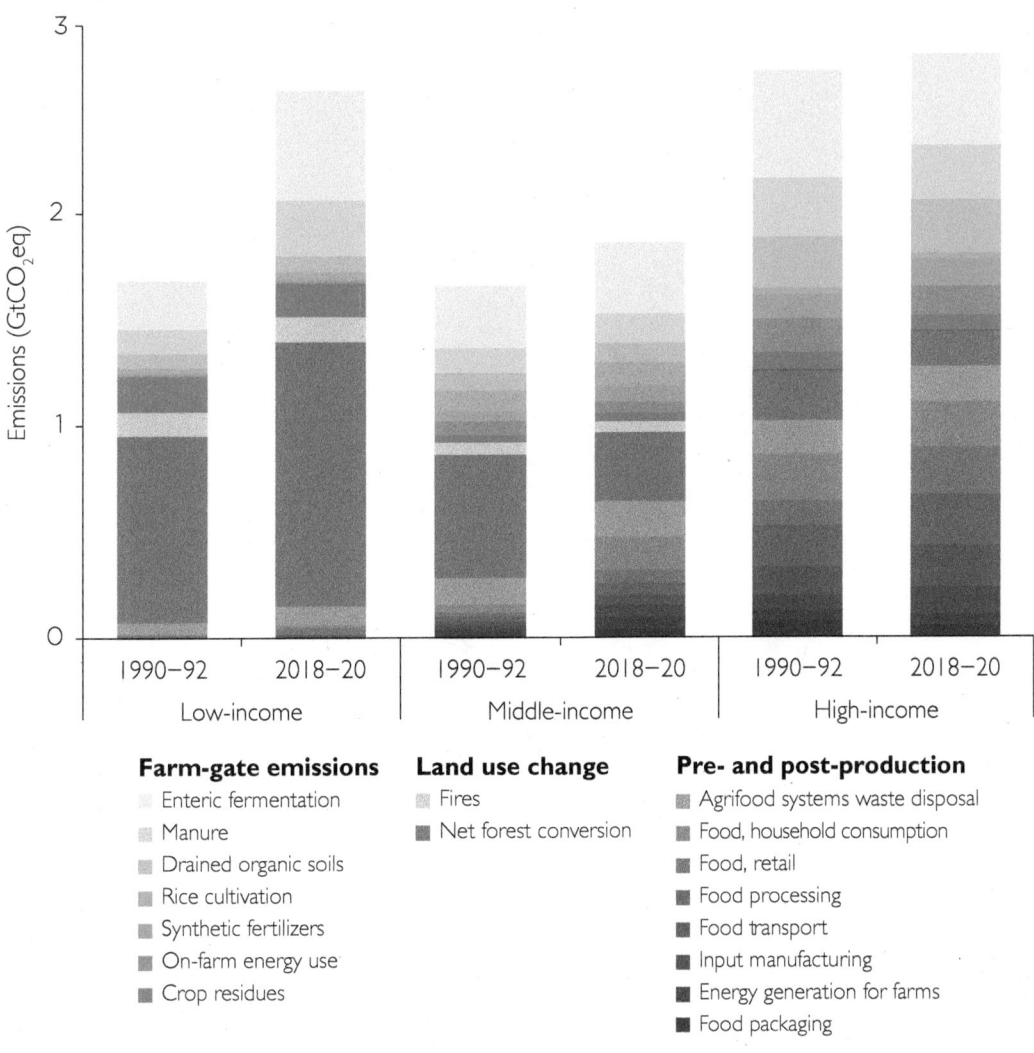

Farm-gate emissions
- Enteric fermentation
- Manure
- Drained organic soils
- Rice cultivation
- Synthetic fertilizers
- On-farm energy use
- Crop residues

Land use change
- Fires
- Net forest conversion

Pre- and post-production
- Agrifood systems waste disposal
- Food, household consumption
- Food, retail
- Food processing
- Food transport
- Input manufacturing
- Energy generation for farms
- Food packaging

Source: World Bank based on data from World Bank 2024 and FAOSTAT 2023.

Note: Figure shows mean per capita agrifood system emissions for 1990–92 and 2018–20 by source category and country income group. Categories are grouped to reduce those with small values. "Manure" consists of manure left on pasture, manure management, and manure applied to soils. "Crop residues" consists of savanna fires, crop residues, and burning—crop residues. "Fires" consists of fires in organic soils and fires in humid tropical forests. "Input manufacturing" consists of fertilizer manufacturing and pesticide manufacturing. "Energy generation for farms" consists of on-farm heat use and on-farm electricity use. GtCO$_2$eq = gigatons of carbon dioxide equivalent.

increasing importance, which is a trend seen in HICs. The Latin America and the Caribbean region accounts for the second largest regional share of agrifood sector emissions, driven by deforestation in countries such Brazil, and the highest per capita emissions among the major regions. This is because the regions with the fewest people tend to have the highest per capita emissions, with Latin America and the Caribbean and North America leading the way. As a result, highly developed but less densely populated North America has per capita emissions several times higher than less developed and highly populated South Asia. Figure 2.8 shows that land use change is the major driver of agrifood emissions in Latin America and the Caribbean and Sub-Saharan Africa. This is due in part to increasing

The Agrifood System Has a Big Climate Problem

MAP 2.1 Countries with the Highest Per Capita Agrifood System Emissions Differ from Those with the Highest Total Agrifood System Emissions

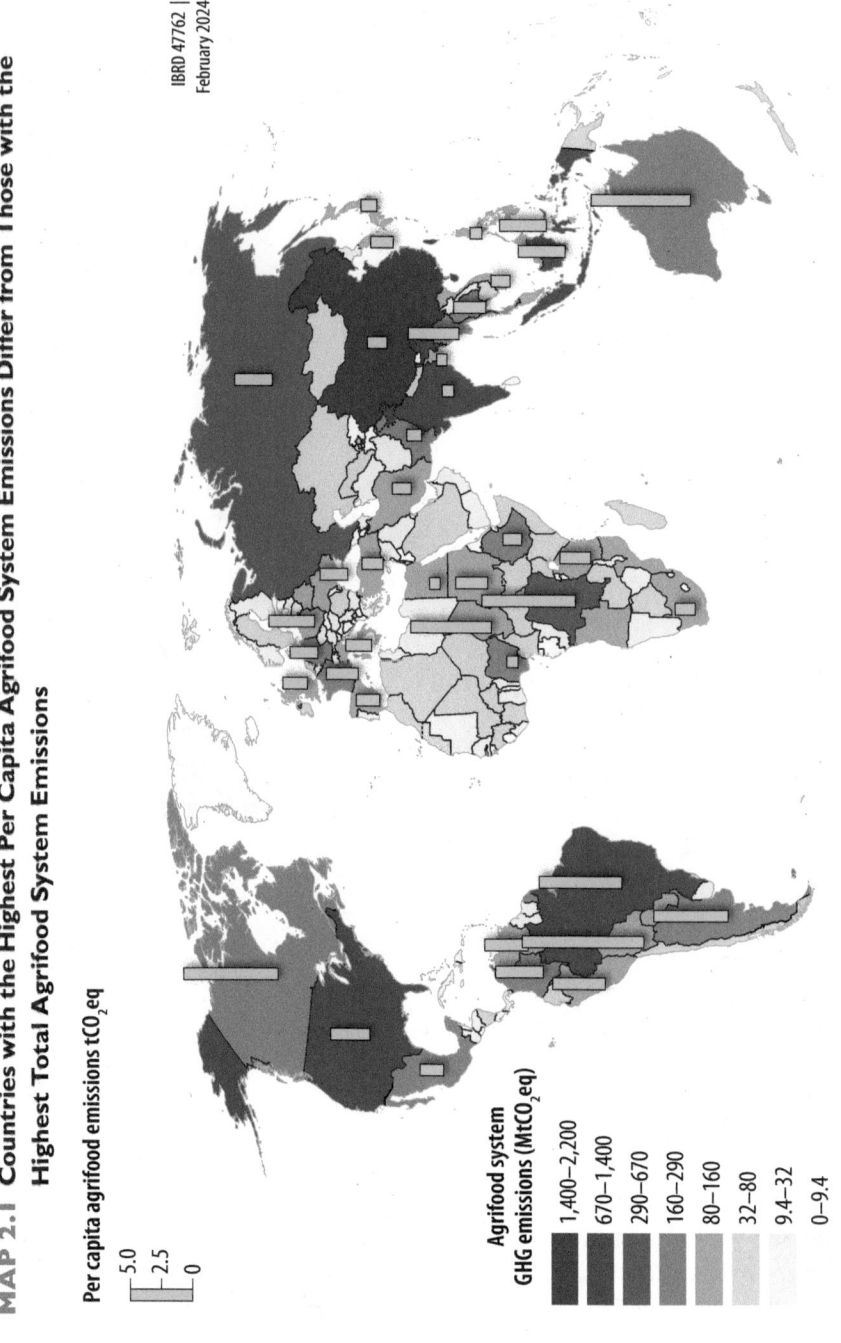

Per capita agrifood emissions tCO$_2$eq

5.0
2.5
0

Agrifood system GHG emissions (MtCO$_2$eq)

1,400–2,200
670–1,400
290–670
160–290
80–160
32–80
9.4–32
0–9.4

IBRD 47762 |
February 2024

Source: World Bank based on data from World Bank 2024 and FAOSTAT 2023.
Note: Map shows for each country total annual agrifood system emissions and, for the top 40 emitters, annual agrifood emissions per capita (green bars). tCO$_2$eq = tons of carbon dioxide equivalent.

Recipe for a Livable Planet

TABLE 2.2 The Top Agrifood System-Emitting Countries and Regions Are Very Different from the Top Per Capita-Emitting Countries and Regions

Total				Per capita			
Rank	Country	Income group	Total MtCO$_2$eq	Rank	Country	Income group	Tons per capita
1	China	Middle	2,176,271	1	Guyana	Middle	20.29
2	Brazil	Middle	1,385,008	2	Botswana	Middle	18.90
3	India	Middle	1,284,493	3	Northern Mariana Islands	Middle	18.62
4	United States	High	1,019,541	4	Mongolia	Middle	17.98
5	Indonesia	Middle	1,003,168	5	Suriname	Middle	17.62

Source: World Bank based on data from World Bank 2024 and FAOSTAT 2023.
Note: MtCO$_2$eq = megatons of carbon dioxide equivalent.

FIGURE 2.8 Regional Agrifood System Emissions Are Driven by Diverse Factors

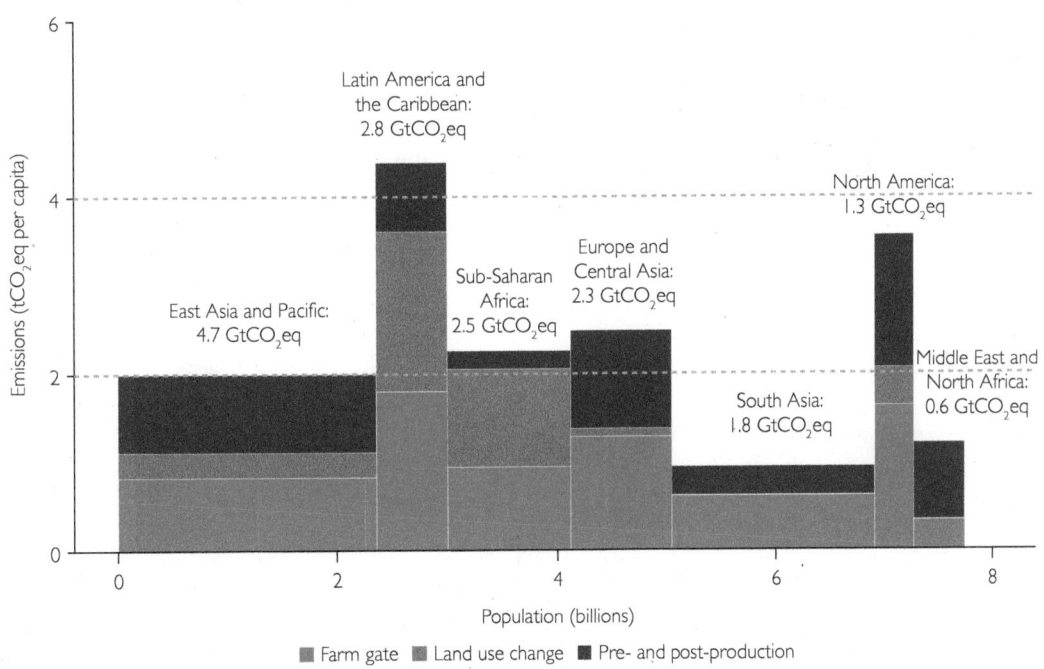

Source: World Bank based on data from World Bank 2024 and FAOSTAT 2023.
Note: Figure shows per capita agrifood system emissions by World Bank region and source category, and populations by region. The area of each bar represents a region's total agrifood system emissions volume (per capita emissions multiplied by the population) in descending order. GtCO$_2$eq = gigatons of carbon dioxide equivalent; tCO$_2$eq = tons of carbon dioxide equivalent.

demand for livestock products from those regions (Foley et al. 2011; Kastner et al. 2012; Weinzettel et al. 2013). Indeed, some might be surprised to learn that Sub-Saharan Africa has the third most agrifood emissions—more than high-income regions such as Europe and Central Asia or North America—and higher per capita emissions than most other developing regions besides Latin America and the Caribbean. This is largely because of

The Agrifood System Has a Big Climate Problem

higher land use change–related emissions. Meanwhile, land use change is the most limited in the richest regions (Europe and Central Asia and North America) because much of the livestock production and associated deforestation have shifted to Asia and Latin America and the Caribbean. That being said, Europe and Central Asia and North America maintain high levels of emissions from pre- and post-production processes. The countries with the highest per capita agrifood emissions tend to be quite small (Figure 2.9), with fewer total emissions (table 2.2; appendix A), so focusing efforts on them may not have much of an impact.

Global agrifood system emissions are predicted to increase even more, pushing the Paris Agreement temperature goals out of reach. Total agrifood system emissions have increased by 14 percent over the past 30 years.[2] Moreover, global food demand will be 35 to 56 percent higher in 2050 than it was in 2010, with the global population projected to reach 10 billion people by then (van Dijk et al. 2021). Another study predicts that the global demand for food calories will rise by almost 70 percent (127×10^{15} kcal) from 2010 through 2050 (Cole et al. 2018). As a result, estimates suggest that global agrifood system emissions will, under a business-as-usual scenario, increase by up to 80 percent by 2050 (Costa et al. 2022). Such an unchecked increase in agrifood system emissions would make it impossible to reach the Paris Agreement's goal of limiting temperature increases to 1.5°C, and may even be unlikely to limit increases to 2°C (Clark et al. 2020; Costa et al. 2022).

FIGURE 2.9 **Agrifood System Emissions Are Growing Fastest in Low- and Middle-Income Countries**

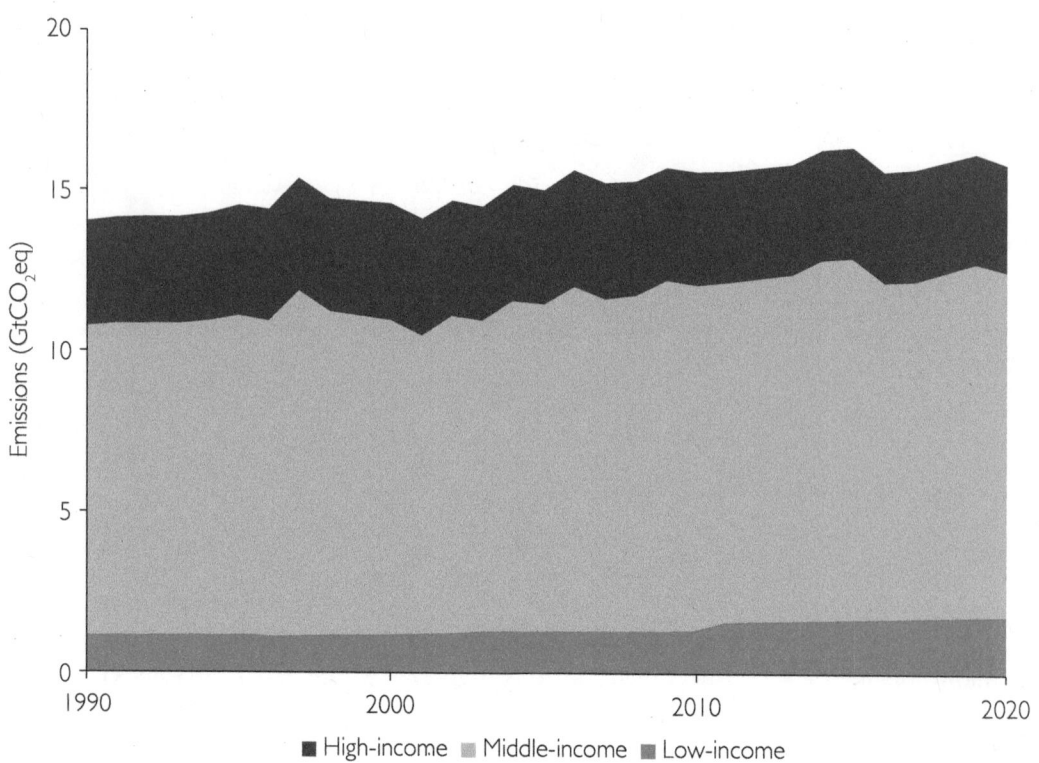

Source: World Bank based on data from World Bank 2024 and FAOSTAT 2023.
Note: GtCO$_2$eq = gigatons of carbon dioxide equivalent.

The world cannot meet the 1.5°C target without dramatic reductions to agrifood system emissions (Clark et al. 2020). Significant reductions in GHG emissions from the global food system will be essential to meeting either the 1.5°C or 2°C Paris Agreement targets. To date, most of the world's efforts to reduce GHG emissions for climate change mitigation have focused on reducing fossil fuel use in the energy, transport, and industrial sectors (Clark et al. 2020). However, reducing emissions from these sectors alone will not be sufficient to achieve the 1.5°C target. As a consequence, even if all nonfood system emissions were halted immediately, business-as-usual emissions from the food system alone would likely exceed the 1.5°C target by the middle of the century and exceed the 2°C limit by the end of the century (figure 2.10) (Clark et al. 2020). To achieve the 1.5°C goal, global GHG emissions—including agrifood emissions—must reach net zero by around 2050, compared to 2010 levels (IPCC 2018). Moreover, global GHG emissions would need to peak in 2025 at the latest to meet the 1.5°C target (UNFCCC 2023). It will also require GHG offset programs because even if all mitigation options are thoroughly applied, they would not entirely eliminate the enteric fermentation of ruminants, emissions from fertilizer production and application, or the energy needs for producing, processing, and transporting foods. Fortunately, the global food system has the potential for offsetting GHG emissions and large-scale GHG mitigation (Clark et al. 2020; Costa et al. 2022). Further, if the technical mitigation potential of these measures is fully realized, agrifood systems could even become a net carbon sink. As discussed later in this chapter and again in chapter 4, this mitigation potential can also be achieved at low costs, with around 40 percent of the technical emission reduction potential costing $100 or less per tCO$_2$eq reduced or removed (Roe et al. 2021).

FIGURE 2.10 Paris Agreement Targets Can Be Reached Only with Significant Reductions in Agrifood System Emissions

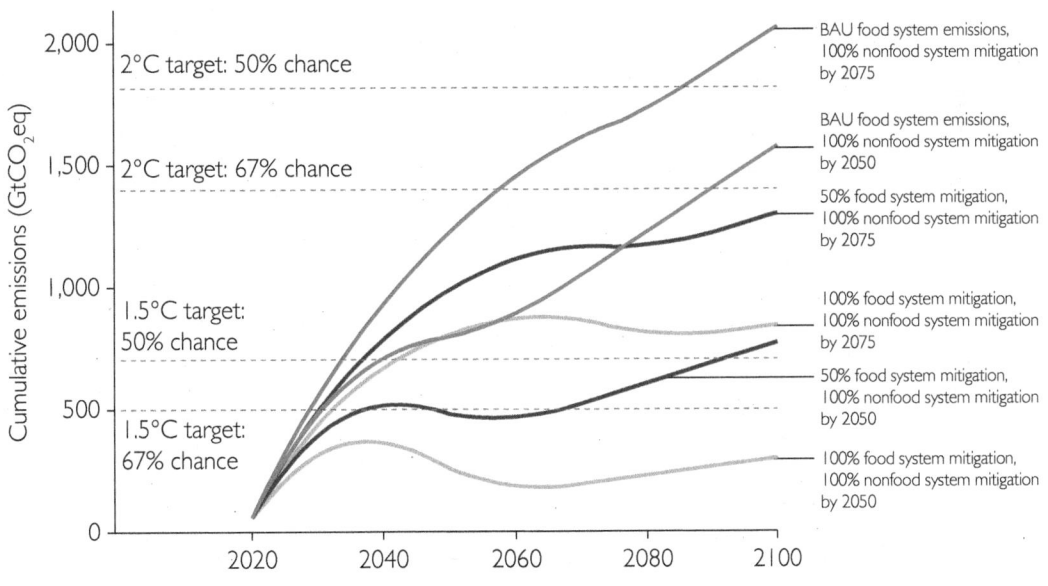

Source: World Bank based on data from Clark et al. 2020.
Note: Figure shows the projected cumulative global emissions pathways and their likelihood of achieving the Paris Agreement targets of 1.5°C or 2°C if all fossil fuel emissions are eliminated by 2050 or 2075 with business as usual, a 50-percent reduction, or a 100-percent reduction in agrifood system emissions by 2050 and 2075. BAU = business as usual; GtCO$_2$eq = gigatons of carbon dioxide equivalent.

The Agrifood System Has a Big Climate Problem

There Is a Major Financing Shortfall for Agrifood System Mitigation

There is a massive gap between the importance of the agrifood system for climate change mitigation and the financing it receives. Overall, climate finance has almost doubled over the last decade (Naran et al. 2022), but climate financing for the agrifood system falls far short of its needs. The Climate Policy Initiative (CPI) provides the most comprehensive analysis yet on climate finance for agrifood systems.[3] The 2023 study covers public, private, and multilateral sources of financing and goes beyond AFOLU to analyze financing for the agrifood system. It found that in 2019–20, agrifood systems received only 4.3 percent of total climate finance at the project level, or an average of $28 billion per year to cover mitigation, adaptation, and dual-benefit investments out of a total of $660.2 billion per year for all sectors (figure 2.11). This is despite one-third of GHG emissions being generated by the agrifood system. Mitigation finance for the agrifood sector was even more anemic, reaching only $14.4 billion in 2019–20, or 2.2 percent of total climate finance and 2.4 percent of total mitigation finance, which was $588.4 billion (figure 2.11).[4] Instead, most climate finance is dedicated to other sectors, such as renewable energy, which receives 51 percent of financing, or low-carbon transportation, which receives 26 percent of financing (Naran et al. 2022).

FIGURE 2.11 Finance for Mitigation in the Agrifood System Is Strikingly Low Relative to Its Importance

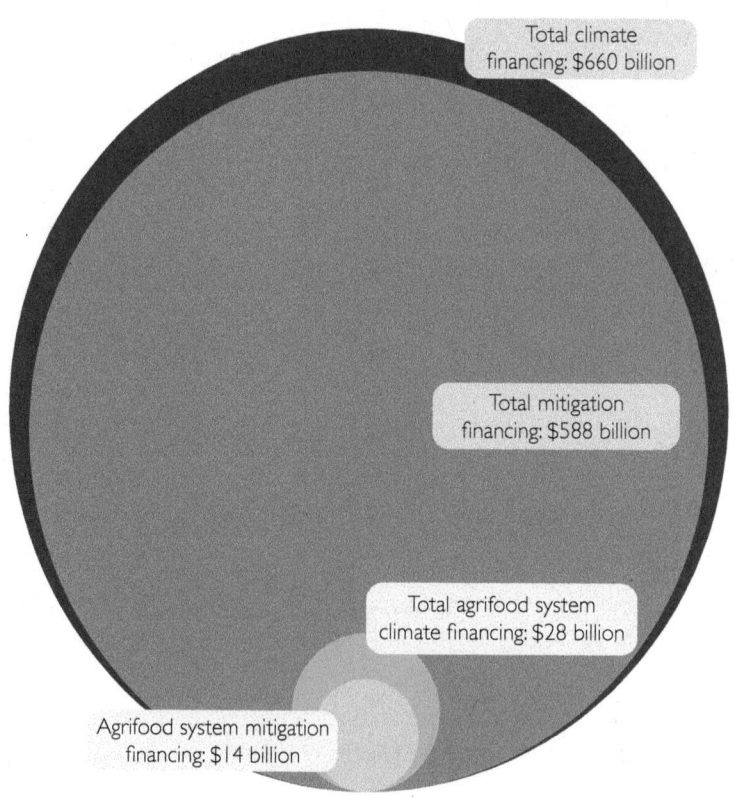

Total climate financing: $660 billion

Total mitigation financing: $588 billion

Total agrifood system climate financing: $28 billion

Agrifood system mitigation financing: $14 billion

Source: World Bank based on data from Naran et al. (2022) and CPI (2023).
Note: Figure shows for 2019/20 global tracked project-level climate finance ($, billions) for adaptation, mitigation, and dual-purpose action economywide and for the agrifood system.

This results from climate finance not flowing to the greatest sources of emissions with the greatest cost-effective mitigation potential, both across sectors and within the agrifood system.

Nearly half of agrifood climate finance goes to MICs, but this is still less than what is warranted by their emissions contribution. MICs receive 48.5 percent of the $28.5 billion in total project-level agrifood climate finance and 51.4 percent of mitigation finance (figure 2.12). This is well below the 67.8 percent of GHG emissions that MICs generate. In general, most climate financing in MICs and HICs is for mitigation, and most climate financing in LICs is for adaptation—53.3 percent of agrifood climate finance in MICs and 61.1 percent in HICs goes to mitigation. LICs, in contrast, receive only 7.7 percent of agrifood climate finance, with 62.3 percent going toward adaptation and 21.3 percent going toward dual-purpose investments, which are resources directed to both mitigation and adaptation, and meeting the criteria for each category. These dual-purpose allocations make sense in LICs given their limited emissions and high vulnerability to climate change. However, less than 3 percent of agrifood climate finance in LICs is for reducing land use change and deforestation-related emissions, despite their high, and growing, contribution to LICs' overall emissions. By contrast, 35 percent of MICs' agrifood finance is for land use change and deforestation. Perhaps more surprisingly, regional or multicountry investments receive 17.9 percent of total agrifood climate finance, a relatively large share.

Climate finance for the agrifood system is distributed unevenly across regions and subsectors. Among subsectors, 83 percent of agrifood climate finance is for agricultural production and forestry, with only 2.8 percent going to policy making and capacity building, and less than 1.0 percent for promoting low-emissions diets or reducing food loss and waste, despite both being key contributors to food system emissions (Chiriac, Vishnumolakala, and Rosane 2023). This disparity is also evident for mitigation finance, where only a fraction of financing goes to the three main agrifood system emissions sources—namely, agricultural production, forestry and land use change, and pre- and

FIGURE 2.12 A Large Share of Agrifood Climate Finance Goes to Middle-Income Countries, but Less than What Is Warranted

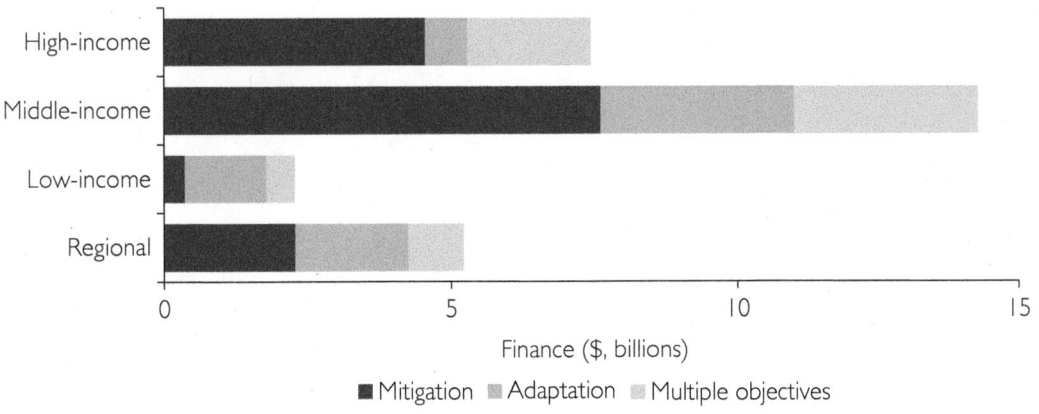

Source: World Bank based on data and analysis by the Climate Policy Initiative.
Note: Figure shows for 2019/20 total tracked agrifood climate finance by country income group and region (multicountry).

The Agrifood System Has a Big Climate Problem

post-production (figure 2.13). This disconnect is particularly striking for agricultural production, which receives only 0.3 percent of mitigation finance despite contributing nearly 14 percent of all global GHG emissions. The largest share of agrifood mitigation finance was devoted to bioenergy, at 42.0 percent, despite questions about this sector's sustainability, as discussed in chapter 3 (Chiriac, Vishnumolakala, and Rosane 2023). Regionally, the East Asia and Pacific region receives a plurality, or 36 percent, of climate finance dedicated to the agrifood sector, followed by Sub-Saharan Africa at 16 percent and North America at 10 percent. Notably, most of the East Asia and Pacific's climate financing originates from East Asia and Pacific countries themselves, particularly China. In contrast, the South Asia region receives only 5 percent of agrifood climate finance and Latin America and the Caribbean just 8 percent (CPI 2023), despite both regions' large contribution to emissions and their vulnerability to climate change.[5]

There are many more opportunities to access concessional climate finance for mitigation than for adaptation, but the agrifood sector is not taking advantage. Nearly 90 percent (89.1 percent) of tracked global concessional climate finance is for mitigation (figure 2.11), leaving only 10 percent for adaptation and dual-purpose climate finance combined.[6] Data, which are available for AFOLU but not the broader agrifood system for the last decade, show that adaptation financing was 34 percent of total AFOLU climate finance in 2019–20, higher than the 7.4 percent average in adaptation financing across sectors (Naran et al. 2022). Meanwhile, mitigation financing in AFOLU increased from $3.6 billion, or 36 percent, in 2013–14 to $10.6 billion, or 52 percent, in 2017–18 (Naran et al. 2022). The remaining $2.2 billion, or 13.5 percent, was for dual-benefit investments. Climate-smart agriculture (CSA) approaches are well adapted to such dual investments

FIGURE 2.13 Agrifood System Mitigation Finance by Subsector Is Not Commensurate with Emissions

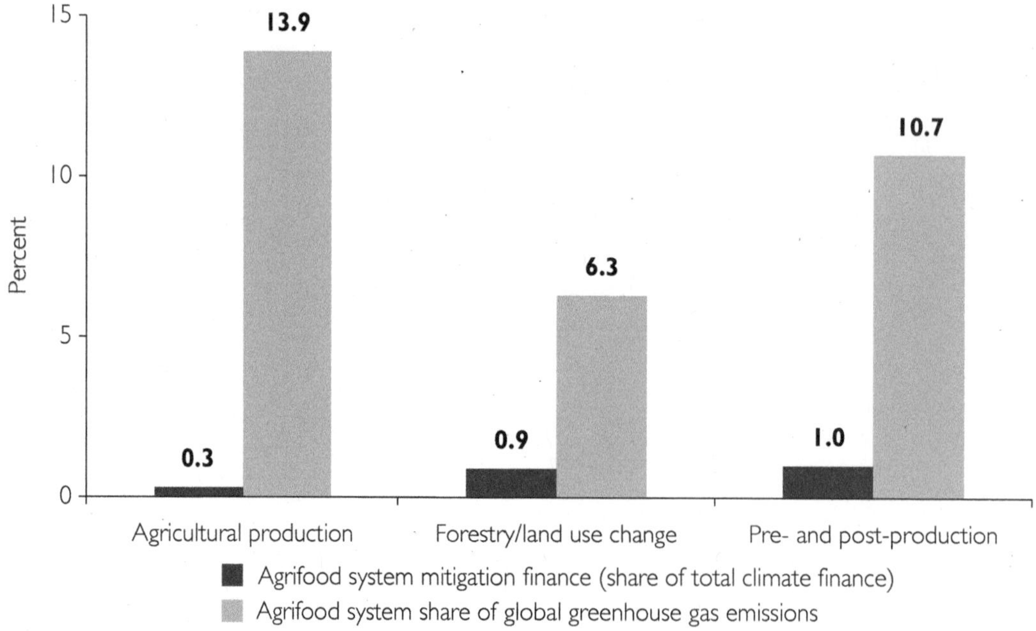

Source: World Bank based on data and analysis from the Climate Policy Initiative.

since the agrifood sector can provide both adaptation and mitigation benefits—as well as productivity and food security benefits. However, total climate finance for AFOLU declined again by $4.2 billion in 2019–20 (Naran et al. 2022). This can be attributed to funding fluctuations, changes in reporting methodologies, and funding changes caused by COVID-19 and the subsequent economic crisis (Naran et al. 2022).

The private sector provides a tiny fraction of finance for reducing emissions in the agrifood system. For AFOLU alone, less than 1 percent of tracked climate finance in 2019–20 was from the private sector, with the rest coming from public sources, such as governments and multilateral and bilateral development finance institutions (Naran et al. 2022). That figure lags far behind private climate financing for other sectors, which averages 49 percent. This is because multiple barriers limit private investments in AFOLU climate action, including low returns (CPI and IFAD 2020; World Bank 2016) long payback periods, high perceived risks and transaction costs, challenges in working with many smallholder farmers, and a lack of adequate measurement, reporting, and verification. Agriculture's high vulnerability to climate change also discourages private investments, creating a vicious circle of low investment, high emissions, and reduced returns. This is reflected in the data, which show that only about $1 out of every $10, or about $2.3 billion, in private venture capital investments in agrifood tech companies in 2019–20 went to companies focused on climate change solutions.[7] Of that, $1.5 billion went to mitigation-focused agrifood tech start-ups, including 1.02 billion for diet-related start-ups focused on producing cultured meats or plant-based proteins.

Blended finance—where public finance reduces the risks behind private investment—is growing in volume and offers opportunities to promote private climate finance. MICs have received the most blended finance, but LICs are also seeing benefits. About half of blended finance transactions across all sectors have been climate oriented (Convergence Blended Finance 2022).

Mitigation finance has been dominant, and renewable energy has accounted for 88 percent of all financing. Thirty-six percent of renewable energy projects were in least developed countries, which have no or very low credit ratings—breaking new ground. Similarly, Sub-Saharan Africa has received the largest proportion, 41 percent, of climate blended finance among all regions between 2019 and 2021, followed by Latin American and the Caribbean with 28 percent. Funds therefore play a key role in bringing scale to these projects. Agriculture-based transactions have accounted for nearly a third of all transactions targeting mitigation and adaptation benefits, and over 60 percent of agriculture transactions have been cross-cutting. The proportion of climate finance transactions targeting smallholders and rural communities increased to 36 percent in 2019–21 from 26 percent in 2016–18 (Convergence Blended Finance 2022).

Annual investments in reducing agrifood emissions will need to increase by 18 times to reduce current food system emissions by half by 2030. As noted, mean annual agrifood system emissions were 16 $GtCO_2eq$ in 2018–20. It is estimated that annual investments in agrifood system mitigation would have to reach an average of $260 billion per year (figure 2.14) to reduce agrifood system GHG emissions to 8 $GtCO_2eq$ by 2030, equivalent to about 15.2 percent of the economywide emissions projected for 2030 (table 2.3). As previously mentioned, the agrifood system received only $14.4 billion in total climate mitigation finance in 2019–20 (Chiriac, Vishnumolakala, and Rosane 2023). This calculation represents a financing gap of $244.6 billion that would require 18 times more funding to bridge it. Other estimates on the financing needs for transforming the

FIGURE 2.14 **Estimated Investment Cost of Agrifood System Mitigation**

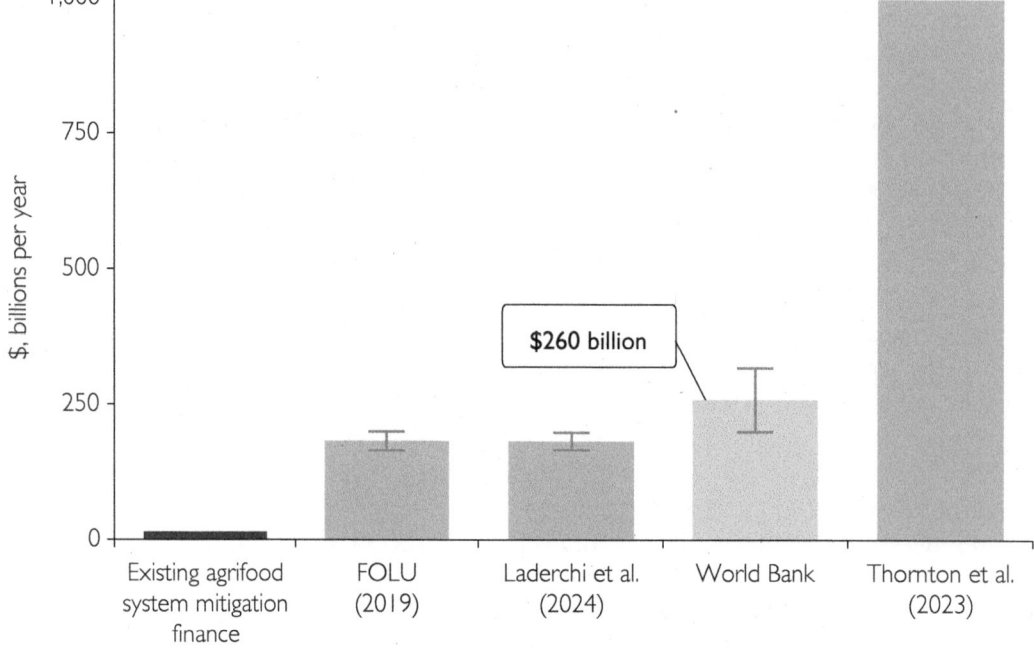

Source: World Bank based on data from FOLU 2019; Laderchi et al. 2024; and Thornton et al. 2023.

agrifood system range from $182 billion (FOLU 2019) to a high of $997 billion annually (FOLU 2019; Thornton et al. 2023). These findings are echoed when restricting our focus to the AFOLU sector, which was responsible for 13–21 percent of global GHG emissions but received only 2.5 percent of total climate finance tracked in 2019–20. In fact, some estimates suggest that a nearly 26-fold increase in annual funding is required to shift the agrifood system to a low-carbon and climate-resilient pathway (Naran et al. 2022).

The benefits from pursuing net zero emissions in the agrifood system far outweigh the investment costs. Table 2.3 shows the World Bank's estimated near-term (by 2030) annual costs (column 2) for implementing six broad actions and an array of measures (column 1) associated with reducing emissions in the agrifood system based on three studies (columns 3–5). Action 1, protecting and restoring nature, represents 37 to 55 percent of our aggregate cost estimate—much more costly than the five other actions. That said, the benefits from implementing agrifood climate change mitigation actions far outweigh the investment costs presented in the table. For example, the gains from scaling up the productive and regenerative agriculture action include freeing up land for reforestation—over 800 million hectares in the FOLU (2019) model—which could remove four additional $GtCO_2eq$ of emissions from the atmosphere annually by 2050, for a value to society of $400 billion a year. More generally, investing in the full set of agrifood system climate change mitigation actions and measures enumerated in table 2.3 would not only reduce net annual GHG emissions by 8 $GtCO_2eq$ (about half the total) but would also generate total annual economic benefits—including reducing hidden costs

TABLE 2.3 Implementing an Array of Agrifood System Climate Change Mitigation Actions Would Cost $260 Billion Per Year by 2030 and Put the World on a Pathway to Net Zero

(1) Agrifood system mitigation actions and specific measures	Annual cost estimates ($, billions)			
	(2) World Bank	(3) FOLU (2019)	(4) Laderchi et al. (2024)	(5) Thornton et al. (2023)[a]
1. Protecting and restoring nature	97–142	45–65	44–64	753
• Avoided conversion of forestland and peatland				
• REDD+ Programme for Forest Conservation				
• Forest restoration				
• Forest management				
2. Productive and regenerative agriculture	35–40	35–40	35–38	181
• Implementation of regenerative farming practices				
• Closing the productivity gap				
• Irrigation efficiency				
• Organic and biofertilizer production				
• Organic and biopesticide production				
• Research and development				
3. Diversifying protein supplies	17–26	15–25	17–25	
• Plant-based meat				
• Plant-based dairy				
• Edible insect protein				
• Research and development				
4. Promoting healthy diets	30–35	30	31	35
• Product reformulation				
• Global nutrition targets				
• Targeted school feeding programs				
• Research and development				
5. Reducing food loss and waste	13–60	30	29	13
• Demand management in developed countries				
• Supply-chain waste				
• Postharvest waste in developing countries				
6. Increasing local loops and linkages	10–15	10	10	15
• Agriculture waste for biogas				
• Vertical farming				
• Greenhouse horticulture				
• Anaerobic digestion				
• Composting				
Total	202–318	165–200	166–198	997
Mean of investment range	260	182.5	182	997

Sources: Column 2: World Bank; Column 3: FOLU 2019; Column 4: Laderchi et al. 2024; Column 5: Thornton et al. 2023.

Note: a. Food system decarbonization actions #2 and #6 overlap with "enable markets" and "public-sector actions incentivize climate-resilient, low emission practices (1.2)" and "transform innovation systems (4.4)" under the Thornton et al. (2023) classification. Laderchi et al. (2024) updates the FOLU 2019 analysis. Thornton et al. (2023) calculates costs for 11 actions and mitigation targets from Steiner et al. (2020).

The Agrifood System Has a Big Climate Problem

from the agrifood system's health, economic, and environmental externalities—of $4.3 trillion by 2030. That is 16 times higher than the estimated annual investment costs of $260 billion and would put the world on a pathway to achieve net zero emissions by 2050. To maximize the impact of these investments, most financing would have to flow to MICs, where the bulk of cost-effective mitigation opportunities are located, as discussed in chapters 3 and 4.

The longer-term investment costs needed to achieve net zero agrifood emissions and limit warming to 1.5°C by 2050 are more uncertain. Comprehensive, long-term estimates of the costs of eliminating net emissions from the agrifood system—in other words, achieving net zero—are not currently available. For the purposes of this report, the World Bank carried out its own alternative analysis using data from Roe et al. (2021), the IPCC (Nabuurs et al. 2022), and other sources. Those estimates show that an annual total investment of $960 billion–$1.2 trillion in available and cost-effective practices and technologies could deliver net zero agrifood emissions through GHG reductions of 16 $GtCO_2eq$ per year, in line with achieving a 1.5°C pathway by 2050. Notably, this investment range represents a high upper limit because the analysis is based on estimated shares of cost-effective mitigation potential under $20 per tCO_2eq and $100 per tCO_2eq in the aforementioned papers, without disclosing their actual marginal abatement costs (MACs). However, based on the global and country-level literature, many on-farm options would cost much less than this and may even achieve cost-saving or negative MACs (McKinsey & Company 2020, 2023).[8] In other words, the investment costs needed to achieve net zero agrifood emissions and meet the 1.5°C target by 2050 is likely to be cheaper than the $960 billion–$1.2 trillion estimate.

There Are Potential Short-Term Social and Economic Trade-Offs in Converting to a Low-Emissions Agrifood System

During its transformation, the agrifood system must balance its climate change efforts with broader developmental objectives. The Paris Agreement's Article 2.1(b) emphasizes "foster[ing] climate resilience and low greenhouse gas emissions development, in a manner that does not threaten food production" and explicitly states that "the fundamental priority" of the agrifood system is "safeguarding food security and ending hunger." The agrifood system must also optimize human health and environmental sustainability (Willett et al. 2019). Today, close to 10 percent of the global population is undernourished (FAO et al. 2022). Further, the monetary valuation of the health benefits from the food system delivering healthier diets is $1.3 trillion (Springmann 2020). The agrifood system is also well positioned to help eradicate poverty and create jobs since 66 percent of the 740 million people living in extreme poverty globally are agricultural workers (Castañeda et al. 2016). As discussed in chapter 4, helping farmers take advantage of new jobs in a future low-emissions agrifood system will be a key priority. Also, agrifood systems can degrade natural ecosystems, and current approaches to food production are increasing pressure on land and water and contributing to deforestation, air pollution, biodiversity loss, impoverished soils, ocean acidification, and water abstraction and pollution. Consequently, the Intergovernmental Panel on Climate Change (IPCC) reports with high confidence that agriculture and related activities "have been the main drivers of land degradation for millennia" (IPCC 2022b, 349). As such, the agrifood system also must deliver environmental benefits. Thus, the agrifood system transformation to low emissions must also contribute to—or at least avoid undermining—the myriad other expectations placed on it.

Poorly designed agrifood system reforms could unintentionally lead to lower agricultural production and higher food prices (Fujimori et al. 2022; Hasegawa et al. 2018). A recent World Bank/IFPRI study (Gautam et al. 2022) shows that removing agriculture subsidies would reduce GHG emissions by 1.5 percent and projected land conversion by 49 percent but could also decrease crop production by 2.6 percent in the developed world and 1 percent in the developing world, increasing the average cost of a basket of healthy food items by 1.8 percent. With increased food prices, real farm incomes per worker would decrease by 4.5 percent globally. Another study showed that developing biofuels—which has dubious climate benefits to begin with (Glauber and Hebebrand 2023)—risks diverting crops from food to industrial use, thereby contributing to further food price inflation (World Bank 2023b). In fact, biofuel demand is expected to increase by a third between 2021 and 2026 (IEA 2021). However, more land for biofuels means less land for food production, resulting in higher food prices, especially in low-income countries (Ahmed et al. 2021), and could potentially put 10 million people at risk of food insecurity (Fujimori et al. 2022). The World Bank/IFPRI simulation also shows that reducing fertilizer or adopting organic farming would reduce emissions by 15 percent but would reduce agricultural production by 5 percent, increase food prices by 13 percent, and raise the cost of healthy diets by 10 percent (European Commission 2020). Other studies were even glummer, projecting that afforestation measures to meet the Paris Agreement's 2°C goal could put 40 million people at risk of food insecurity by 2050 (Fujimori et al. 2022)—and even more to meet the 1.5°C goal (Fujimori et al. 2018). Some fear that the costs of reducing agrifood emissions may be pushed onto marginalized and historically disadvantaged groups (Dalabajan et al. 2022). For example, one study calculates that 60 percent of the people most affected by mitigation policies' food price increases would be in South Asia and Sub-Saharan Africa, areas traditional afflicted by food insecurity (Hasegawa et al. 2018).

Emissions pricing schemes involving the "full-cost pricing" of foods could lead to relative price increases for high-emitting foods in order to reduce emissions. Current food prices do not capture the full cost of food production, including social and environmental externalities. As such, cheaper foods are made possible by overexploiting and exhausting the agrifood system's natural resource inputs, so much so that if only some food system externalities—such as GHG emissions, biodiversity loss, natural resource degradation, and health and social costs—were counted prices, referred to as a Toward Sustainability Scenario, food prices could increase by an additional 30–35 percent relative to the linear historical trend (figure 2.15). Such a price increase could quickly undermine the welfare and livelihoods of poor people (Leippert et al. 2020), but the prices would fall below the historical trend after 2045 in a Toward Sustainability Scenario. Notably, food prices under a business-as-usual scenario, without costing environmental externalities, will remain significantly below both the Toward Sustainability Scenario and historical trends. Other studies echo this, arguing that indiscriminately pricing food-related GHG emissions could potentially increase food prices more than would climate change's impacts on production (Hasegawa et al. 2018). Furthermore, placing carbon prices on energy emissions could increase biofuel demand, posing an additional strain on productive land. In the next section, other studies are presented to argue that climate change's impacts on food prices and hunger, if unchecked, would be even more severe. Full-cost pricing is discussed further in chapter 3, and carbon and emissions pricing are discussed in more detail in chapter 4.

FIGURE 2.15 Food Prices Could Increase with Mitigation Action in the Medium Term Before Declining to Beneath the Historical Trend in the Longer Term

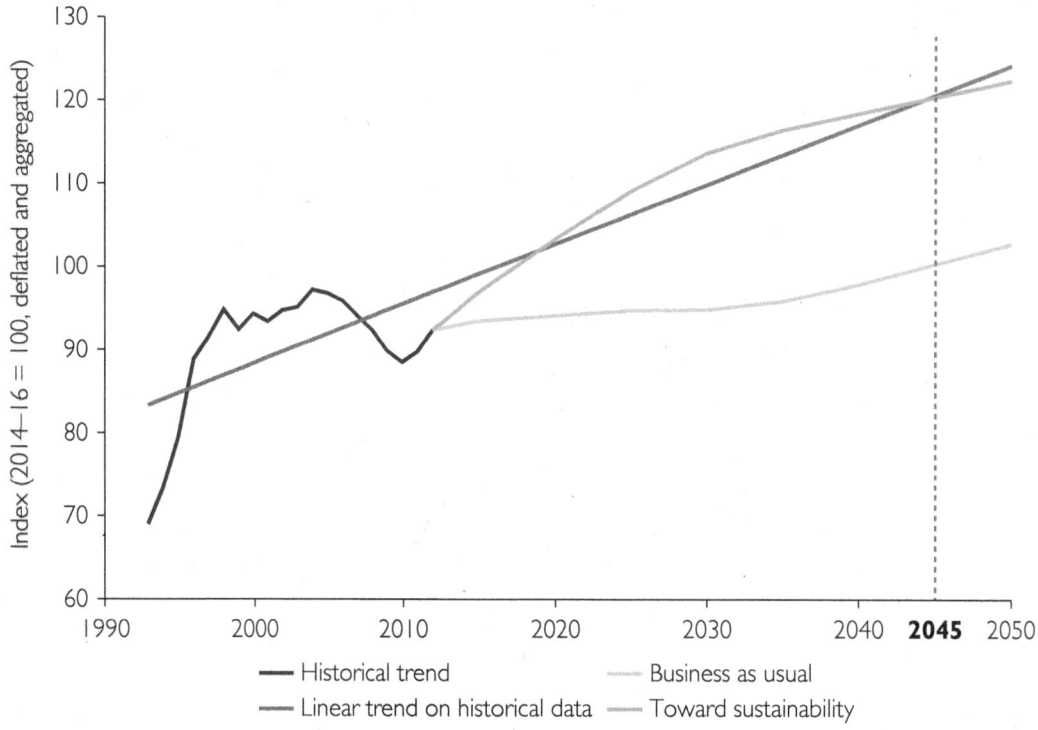

Source: World Bank based on data from FAO 2022.
Note: Figure shows historical trends and projections of food prices under different mitigation scenarios.

Lowering agrifood emissions is likely to have different impacts on jobs in different countries. Reducing agrifood emissions would have the biggest impact in LICs, where the agrifood sector accounts for 64 percent of total employment, compared to 39.1 percent in MICs and 11.1 percent in HICs (European Commission 2020; Guerrero et al. 2022; Nico and Christiaensen 2023). Figure 2.16 shows that 91 percent of agrifood system jobs are on the farm in LICs, 74 percent in MICs, and only 26 percent in HICs, leaving 74 percent of HIC agrifood work off-farm. The figure also shows that mitigation action could affect agrifood jobs in LICs the most, potentially affecting 227 workers for every tCO_2eq reduced, compared to just 161 workers for MICs and just 43 workers for HICs. Moreover, these impacts will be felt differently in different parts of the world. For example, research shows that adopting CSA practices will increase labor requirements in the short run when agricultural mechanization is still limited. A package of conservation agriculture practices[9] is associated with *increased* labor requirements in Sub-Saharan Africa, leading to 55 more workdays per year per hectare in five countries (Montt and Luu 2020) and 45 percent more farm labor time in Malawi and Zimbabwe (Corbeels et al. 2020). Also, the System of Rice Intensification's impact on labor is a function of mechanization, showing reduced labor demand in India (Duvvuru and Motkuri 2013) but increased labor demand in West Africa (Graf and Oya 2021). However, as discussed in chapter 4, mitigation action could accelerate well-established structural transformation trends in which the quality of jobs improves in a country as its share of agrifood system employment declines (Christiaensen, Rutledge, and Taylor 2021).

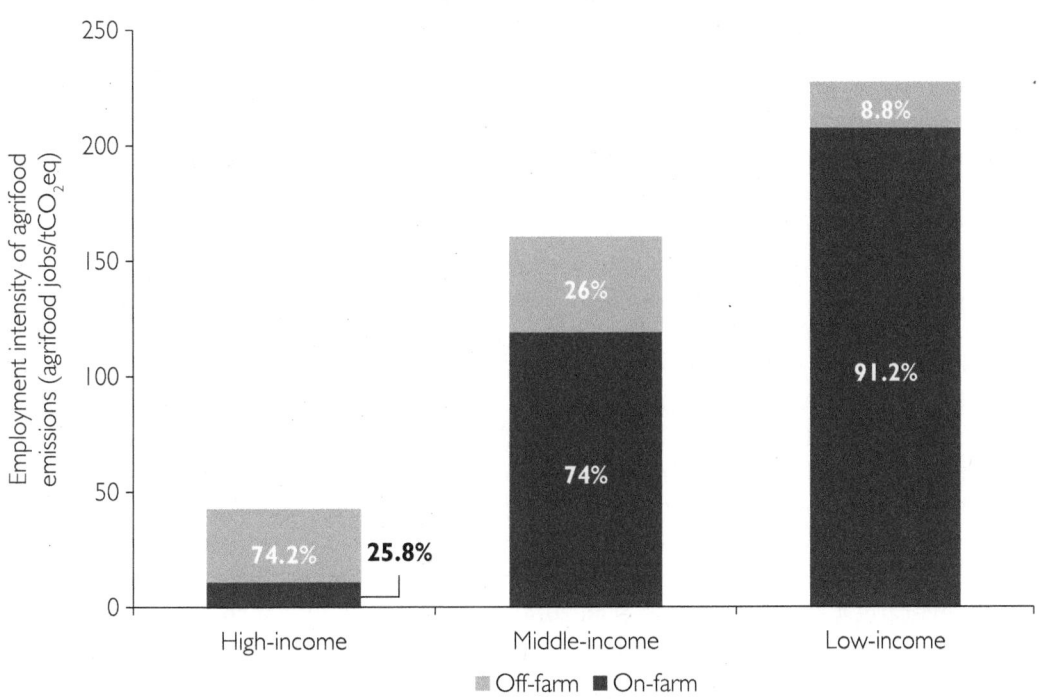

Source: World Bank based on country income data from World Bank 2024; emissions data from FAOSTAT 2023; employment data from ILO 2020.
Note: Figure shows the jobs intensity of agrifood system emissions—that is, how many jobs are associated with every 1 ton of carbon dioxide equivalent (tCO₂eq) produced—and the shares of on- and off-farm employment by country income group. LICs = low-income countries.

Transforming the food system could lead to competition over land, water, and energy resources. The goal of transforming the food system is to produce more food with fewer emissions and less pressure on the land, water, and energy resources (Kumareswaran and Jayasinghe 2022). However, there may be unexpected consequences with inadequately designed mitigation policies related to land, water, or energy. For example, improving agricultural water productivity (crop per drop)[10] generates more food from less land. However, studies show that improved agricultural water productivity through more efficient irrigation can sometimes increase water consumption at the basin level.[11] This is because irrigation can lead to higher evapotranspiration, longer growing seasons, and expanded crop areas (López-Gunn, Mayor, and Dumont 2012). For example, in Andalucia, Spain, modern efficient, pressurized irrigation led to increased water demand. Concomitantly implementing water conservation practices, including water accounting and water allocation policies, and enforcing water-use caps can safeguard against these outcomes (Perez-Blanco et al. 2020). Likewise, deploying land-based mitigation technologies such as biomass production or reforestation could increase competition for land between energy and food production interests, at least in the short term (IPCC 2022b; Vera et al. 2022). For example, in France and Germany, the introduction of biodiesel into the energy matrix led to higher land values (Hill et al. 2006; Matthew 2006; Service 2007). In Brazil, the increased demand for ethanol fuel has pushed up prices for primary agricultural products, thereby increasing the cost for arable land in Paraná and displacing smallholder farmers (Service 2007; Watanabe, Gomes, and Dewes 2007). Overall, biofuel production grew by 44 percent globally between 2011 and 2021, largely due to crop subsidies and other policy mandates (Glauber and Hebebrand 2023). In 2007 in the United States, government-mandated fossil fuel targets increased the opportunity cost of agriculture lands, thereby reducing soybean planted areas by 11 percent and increasing the price of corn, soybeans, and their derivatives in the US domestic market (Hill et al. 2006). However, food production and land-based mitigation do not need to compete. Instead, regenerative carbon farming practices can sequester carbon (Toensmeier 2016) while demand-side changes to consumer diets and less food waste can reduce the land and resources needed for food production (Gerbens-Leenes and Nonhebel 2002; IPCC 2022b; Prudhomme et al. 2020).[12]

The transition to a low-emissions agrifood system is likely to encounter political and cultural obstacles. Almost all food and agriculture policies have redistributive effects or touch on politically sensitive topics such as jobs and food security (OECD 2019a; Wreford, Ignaciuk, and Gruère 2017). As a result, these policies tend to be highly political and bear electoral weight (OECD 2019b). As a result, they often meet the opposition of organized and influential lobby groups and political coalitions (Brunelle, Coat, and Viguié 2017; Swinnen 2018). In Bangladesh and India, rice security is synonymous with food security, and governments provide input subsidies for water, fertilizer, pesticides, and electricity to support rice production. This lowers input costs for farmers but also reduces incentives for farmers to adopt low-carbon practices (Adhya et al. 2014). Attempts to abolish such subsidies have been met with protests and have led to politicians competing for the crucial farmer vote. In 2004, one of the main reasons the sitting party in India's Andhra Pardesh state lost its reelection was its past attempts to remove electricity subsidies (Birner, Gupta, and Sharma 2011). Likewise, policies that promote CSA and other sustainable practices have been criticized by opponents as a technical approach that ignores questions of equality and promotes commercial and political interests (Anderson and Balsera 2019; Clapp, Newell, and Brent 2017). Attempts to influence consumer behavior, for example, toward more sustainable diets are often perceived as culturally intrusive and curtailing individual freedom. For example, in China, people's beliefs and behaviors prevented them from adopting low-emitting rice production practices (Chen and Chen 2022). Moreover, a present bias—the tendency toward short-term gratification—when making decisions can be at odds with sustainable habits (Luoto and Carman 2014). Similarly, loss aversion (the idea that losses cause greater distress than the happiness caused by gains of a similar magnitude) may prevent people from changing their diets. Both present bias and loss aversion may make it difficult to convince people to consume less red meat, for example. At the community level, social norms and identity—the idea that people conform to identities because they create intrinsic utility (Akerlof and Kranton 2000; Gilmore and McAuliffe 2013)—may also reinforce unsustainable eating habits (Serrano Fuentes, Rogers, and Portillo 2019). For example, the national and social identification of Australian, British, and US participants in a study positively predicted their attitudes and intentions toward red-meat-eating habits (Nguyen and Platow 2021).

The Costs of Inaction Are Even Higher Than the Potential Trade-Offs

The world's agrifood system has successfully fed a growing population but has fallen short of promoting optimum health and nutrition goals. In the 1960s and 1970s, many experts forecasted that the developing world would experience widespread hunger and famine as global populations grew. However, investments in agricultural knowledge and innovation, during what is commonly known as the green revolution, led to tripling of agricultural production from 1960 to 2015 (FAO 2017; Fuglie et al. 2020). This outpaced the world's population growth, which had increased by two and half times during the same period (figure 2.17). The production increase was driven mainly by the increased production of calorie-intensive staple foods. The ability to provide sufficient calories to food-insecure populations also improved nutritional indicators for decades. However, starting in 2014, human health outcomes began to decline because the agrifood system's simple focus on increasing calorie availability meant that there was less attention to producing healthier foods (Ambikapathi et al. 2022). Simultaneously, adult and child obesity keeps rising (FAO et al. 2021), and six out of the top 10 risk factors for death and disease in both men and women are diet related (Abbafati et al. 2020). This was likely caused by a low intake of fruits, vegetables, and other healthy foods, combined with the high consumption of processed meats (Afshin et al. 2019). This is complicated by the high cost of healthy diets. By 2020, healthy diets were unaffordable for almost 3.1 billion people, an increase of 119 million from 2019. Partly as a result, 149 million of the world's children under the age of five are stunted, 45 million wasted, and 39 million overweight (FAO et al. 2022). In fact, nearly 30 percent of countries have higher levels of child stunting and are not making progress toward the 2030 Sustainable Development Goal on nutrition (FAO et al. 2021, 2022).

FIGURE 2.17 The World Successfully Overcame Food Production Shortfalls in the 1960s

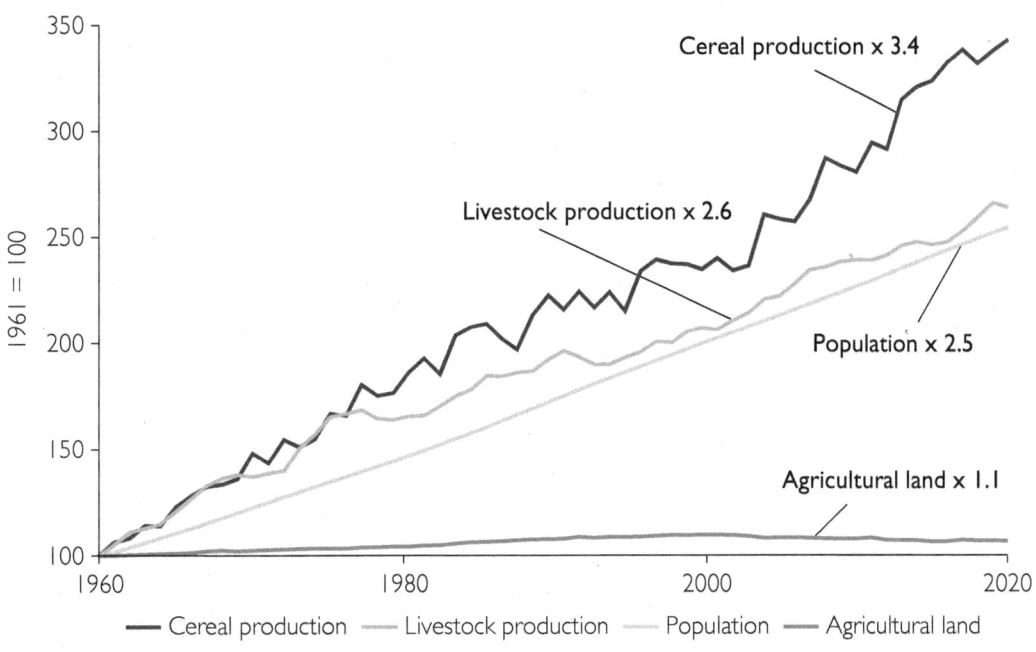

Source: World Bank based on data from FAOSTAT 2023.
Note: Figure shows global trends in food production (cereals and livestock), human population, and agricultural land from 1961 to 2020. All data series are indexed to 100 in 1961. The series label provides the value as of 2020.

The Agrifood System Has a Big Climate Problem

The COVID-19 pandemic and Russia's invasion of Ukraine have exposed the vulnerability of the agrifood system and reinforced inequalities. The global food system's reliance on just-in-time international commodity supply chains, or supply chains that make food and input materials available just when they are needed, makes it susceptible to systemic shocks and high price volatility, as there is no time or redundancy buffer to account for potential supply-chain disruptions (Klimek, Obersteiner, and Thurner 2015; Ringsmuth et al. 2022). The COVID-19 pandemic and its consequences on the entire food value chain highlighted the vulnerability of the food system (Aday and Aday 2020). COVID-19–related restrictions in labor movement constrained food production and processing, and challenges in transporting food and input materials disrupted trade, with freight costs reaching all-time highs (Freightos Data 2023). Russia's invasion of Ukraine adds additional pressure on the food system, as it affects agricultural production in Ukraine, a major grain exporter, and makes shipments fewer, slower, and more expensive. Together, Ukraine and Russia account for 12 percent of all traded calories globally (Glauber and Laborde 2022), meaning that the war-related trade disruptions threaten global food security. In addition, high energy prices related to the war have led to a spike in fertilizer prices, increasing food production costs. Both COVID-19 and the war revealed a strong dependence from several countries and regions on a small number of suppliers for essential items. For example, the Middle East and North Africa import half of their cereals from Russia and Ukraine (FAO 2022; Glauber and Laborde 2022). As a result of these compounding crises, prices for food and input materials increased drastically. For example, FAO's food price index rose by more than 40 percent between 2020 and 2022 (FAO 2023b). This had a direct effect on global food security: between 2019 and 2021, undernourishment rose from 8.0 to 9.8 percent (FAO 2023a) and, since the outbreak of the COVID-19 pandemic, the number of people affected by hunger has increased by 150 million (FAO et al. 2022, 2023). As such, the COVID-19 pandemic has reinforced preexisting inequalities, with the poorest having suffered the worst of this crisis (FAO et al. 2022).

The global agrifood system has often had disproportionately adverse effects on poor communities by uprooting them from their lands and livelihoods or leaving them unable to afford nutritious foods. Industrial agriculture has historically sidelined smallholder farmers who cannot access the resources or afford the technologies to compete, thereby exacerbating rural poverty and increasing landlessness (Clapp, Newell, and Brent 2017). In some countries, the push for industrial agriculture has dispossessed traditional communities of their ancestral lands, detaching them from their primary livelihoods and means of subsistence (Borras et al. 2012). In one example, large tracts of land in Ethiopia's Gambella region were leased to foreign investors, leading to the displacement of local Anuak communities and other traditional groups (Oakland Institute 2011). Second, the global food value chain often prioritizes cash crops for export over subsistence food crops, undermining local food security and depriving communities of essential nutrition (Holt Giménez and Shattuck 2011). Likewise, the food industry produces unhealthy, processed foods more cheaply than nutritious alternatives, making healthy foods unaffordable and scarce in poor communities (Walker, Keane, and Burke 2010). Also, the globalized nature of the agrifood system can lead to food price volatility. For example, FAO estimates that over 122 million more people have faced hunger since 2019 because of supply-chain disruptions caused by COVID-19 and repeated weather shocks and conflicts, including Russia's invasion of Ukraine (FAO et al. 2023).

Nutritious foods are often unaffordable for poor people and other vulnerable groups, particularly in LICs. Lower-income countries and particularly the most underweight people in those countries continue to have the lowest levels of access to healthy foods, such as fruits and vegetables (Springmann et al. 2021). One study observes that keeping nutritious foods affordable is a challenge. The study calculated the "relative caloric price" of 657 foods in 176 countries and found that nutrient-dense foods are expensive relative to staple foods such as rice (Headey and Alderman 2019, figure 1). In Burkina Faso, for example, calories from eggs are around 15 times more expensive than calories from maize, rice, and sorghum. In the United States, on the other hand, egg calories are just 1.9 times more expensive than staple calories. Throughout Sub-Saharan Africa, eggs, fresh milk, and fortified infant cereals are prohibitively expensive for poor people. This problem with affordability, however, is not present in all countries. For example, dairy is inexpensive in India, while fish is relatively inexpensive in Southeast Asia and West and Central Africa.

Today's food system causes trillions of dollars' worth of negative externalities every year, and these are projected to rise under business as usual. Externalities, in this case, refer to indirect costs or benefits that arise from the agrifood system that are not felt by the actor who creates the cost or benefit but by society, or costs that are "externalized" to a third party. The most prominent example of a negative externality from the agrifood system are the GHG emissions that are released, causing climate change. Global food system externalities cause around $20 trillion in costs per year according to one study, or nearly 20 percent of world gross domestic product (GDP). These negative externalities include approximately $7 trillion (between $4 trillion and $11 trillion) in environmental costs, $11 trillion (between $3 trillion and $39 trillion) in costs to human life, and $1 trillion (between $200 billion and $1.7 trillion) in economic costs (Hendriks et al. 2021). Another study estimates that these externality costs total of nearly $12 trillion (FOLU 2019) (table 2.4). These costs are generally not reflected in GDP or other official economic statistics because negative externalities are nonmarket costs not priced by any formal market. Moreover, these costs are expected to rise as the underlying drivers—be they environmental factors, such as

TABLE 2.4 The Agrifood System Generates Costly Externalities: Annual Costs Imposed on Society by the Global Agrifood System in Gross World Product

Externality	Estimated cost ($, trillions)	Gross world product (share)
GHG emissions	1.5	1.7%
Natural capital loss	1.7	1.9%
Obesity-related costs	2.7	3.1%
Undernutrition-related costs	1.8	2.1%
Pollution, pesticides, AMB resistance	2.1	2.4%
Rural welfare losses	0.8	0.9%
Food loss, food waste, fertilizer leakage	1.3	1.5%
Total Costs	11.9	13.6%

Source: World Bank based on data from FOLU 2019.
Note: AMB = antimicrobial (resistance); GHG = greenhouse gas. Gross world product for reference year (2018) was $87.65 trillion.

agrifood system GHG emissions or ecosystem degradation, or socioeconomic factors, such as population growth or geopolitical instability—are all predicted to become more severe (figure 2.18) (FAO 2022). These calculations also do not include large opportunity costs from forgone economic growth (FAO 2022). Table 2.5 shows the risk of negative environmental externalities from agrifood system policies, such as input subsidies or consumer support (Henderson and Lankoski 2021).

Left unabated, climate change will increasingly undercut agricultural production. Climate change has made many agricultural lands uncultivable and has increased the frequency of extreme events since at least the mid 20th century. By one count, climate change has reduced agricultural total factor productivity growth by 21 percent since 1961, undermining seven years' worth of productivity gains (Ortiz-Bobea et al. 2021). Climate change has already caused "regionally different, but mostly negative, impacts on crop yields and the quality and marketability of products" (IPCC 2022a). In the future, climate change is projected to reduce total crop production by 4 percent and total livestock production by 2 percent by 2050 (Guerrero et al. 2022), severely limiting the capacity of the world's

FIGURE 2.18 **Production of Animal Products and Staple Crops Creates the Greatest Environmental Pressures in Agriculture**

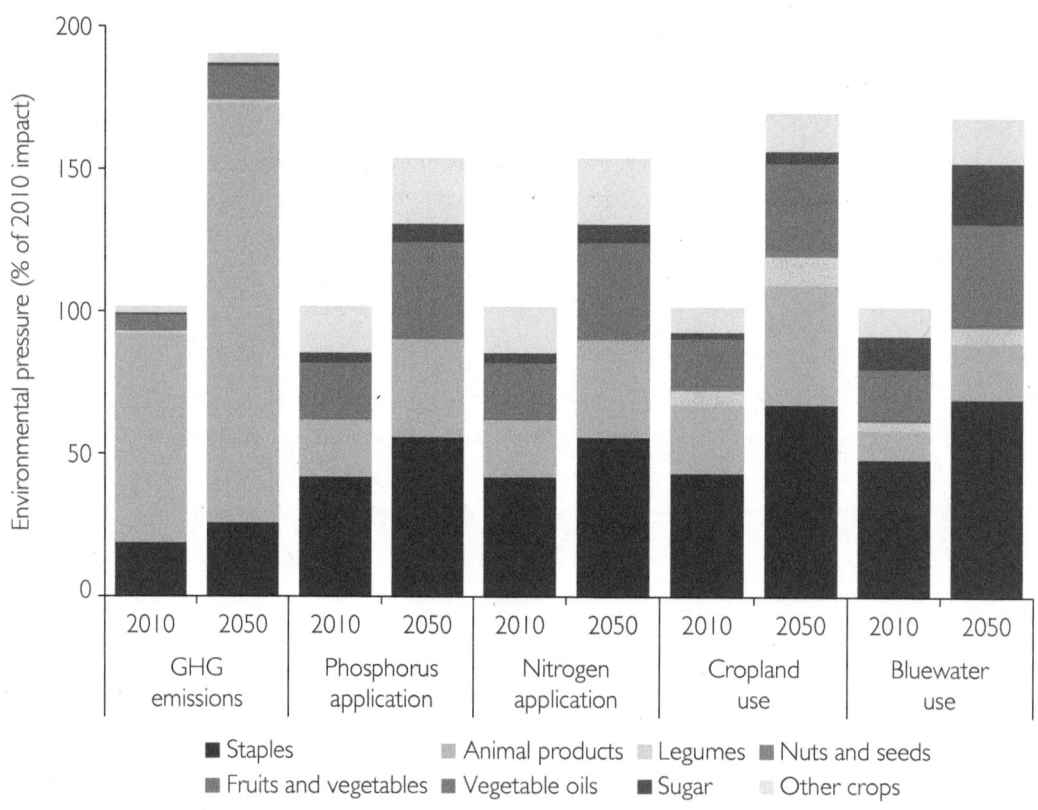

Source: World Bank based on data from Springmann et al. 2018.

Note: Figure shows current (2010) and forecasted (2050) environmental impacts by food group in five key areas: greenhouse gas (GHG) emissions, blue water use, cropland use, nitrogen application, and phosphorus application. These environmental stresses are attributed to the final food product taking into account the usage and implications of primary products. The effects are represented as percentages based on a 2050 baseline projection in the absence of specific mitigation strategies.

TABLE 2.5 **Agrifood System Policies Often Incentivize Maximizing Profits over Protecting the Environment**

Form of support	Risk of negative environmental externalities
Price (dis)incentives	**High:** Influencing prices can distort markets, leading to negative environmental externalities. For example, increasing the price of rice through a tariff or export ban would incentivize rice production, leading to higher methane emissions, displacing other crops, inducing land use change, or bringing marginal land into production. Increasing market prices can be just as disruptive.
Variable input subsides	**High:** These instruments lower the cost of agricultural inputs such as water, energy, pesticides, and fertilizers, leading to their overuse, which causes higher emissions and land degradation.
Output subsidies	**High:** Paying farmers to produce specific commodities encourages excess production, leading to increased emissions—particularly if the commodity is emission intensive, which is the case for rice or beef. It can also induce land use change and input overuse. Likewise, payments based on cattle numbers can also lead to higher emissions by increasing herd sizes.
Technology subsidies	**Moderate:** These could be used to adopt low-emissions technologies, but they are more commonly used to improve productivity, which can reduce environmental impact and emissions intensity. However, without effective management, greater productivity can also lead more intense or expanded production, which creates higher emissions.
Decoupled subsidies	**Low:** Income support that is not linked to production. It is minimally distortive because it does not directly influence production choices.
General support for public goods and services	**Low:** Spending on public goods and services, such as research and development, extension training, and monitoring and surveillance, tend to lower agriculture's emissions footprint. However, some infrastructure public goods may result in higher GHG emissions.
Consumer support	**Low:** This support is usually in-kind or cash consumption subsidies through domestic food aid programs or conditional cash transfers, among others. This support targets vulnerable populations and has a low risk of increasing GHG emissions.

Source: World Bank.
Note: GHG = greenhouse gas.

agricultural areas to produce food (IPCC 2022a). Another study (IFPRI 2022) predicts that climate change will cause substantial and growing reductions in food production globally of 3 percent by 2030 and 5.3 percent by 2050 compared to what it would be without climate change, with even larger reductions in some parts of the world (figure 2.19). For example, the study estimates a 10 percent decline in North America and a 1 percent increase in Southeast Asia by 2030, accelerating to an 18 percent decline in North America and a 2 percent increase in Southeast Asia by 2050. This is happening at the same time that population is expected to increase by up to 2 billion people by midcentury, which is expected to increase the demand for food by at least 60 percent over 2005–07 levels (IFPRI 2022). And, as noted in chapter 1, the positive feedback loop between intensified agrifood activities and higher emissions results in a vicious circle of ever-greater climate impacts.

These production losses would lead to further food price increases and food insecurity (FAO 2018). Real food prices are around 30 percent higher now than they were in the 1990s.[13] This is in part the result of greater food demand from growing populations and, more recently, supply-chain disruptions from global crises such as the COVID-19 pandemic or Russia's invasion of Ukraine. However, it is also the result of climate change–related production losses. These impacts have reduced food availability and increased food

FIGURE 2.19 Climate Change Is Projected to Increasingly Undercut Agricultural Production Globally and in Almost Every Region

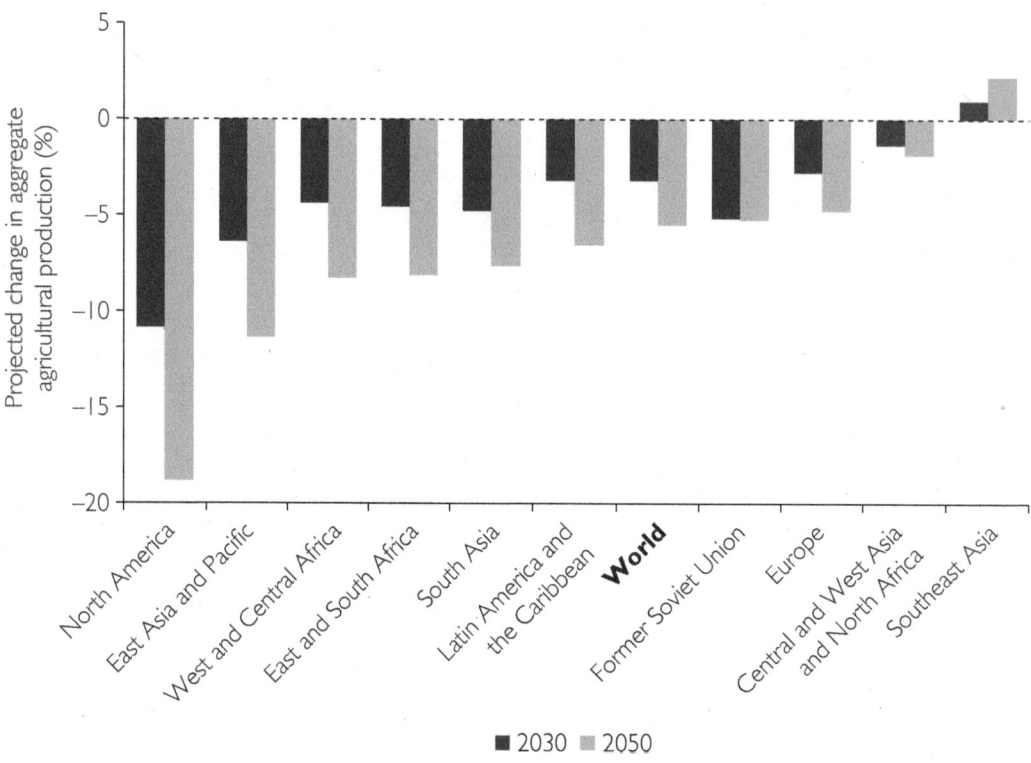

Source: World Bank based on data from IFPRI 2022.
Note: Figure shows projected changes in agricultural production under climate change by geographic region for 2030 and 2050 compared with 2010, in descending order of negative impact (percent change). Countries included in each regional grouping can be found in table 1A of IFPRI 2022.

and commodity prices, thereby threatening the livelihoods, nutrition, and food security of millions (DARA 2012; IPCC 2022a). In fact, unmitigated climate change will cause food prices to increase by up to 3.2 percent per year by 2035 (Kotz et al. 2023). Cereal prices are estimated to increase by up to 29 percent by 2050, and higher prices for feed will increase the costs of animal-sourced products. These price increases are projected to put up to 183 million additional people at risk of hunger (IPCC 2022b). In total, a projected 65 million more people will face hunger as a result of climate change in 2030 and 73 million more in 2050 if no additional measures are taken (figure 2.20). In absolute terms, eastern and southern Africa will be the most affected by this increased hunger, followed by Southeast Asia. In percentage terms, East Asia and Pacific will have the largest increase in hunger, followed by Eastern and Southern Africa (IPCC 2022a). In other words, the poorest communities will suffer the most from these climate change impacts.

Climate change's impacts on the agrifood system will lead to larger economywide impacts. The agrifood system employs 1.2 billion people, representing 36.1 percent of the global workforce (Nico and Christiaensen 2023), and it generates a large share of rural incomes and national GDP (Townsend et al. 2017; World Bank and IFAD 2017). Agriculture's large economic footprint means that climate change's impact on agricultural productivity and employment will have enormous consequences for entire

FIGURE 2.20 Unmitigated Climate Change Could Increase the Number of Hungry People by Tens of Millions, Particularly in Africa and Asia

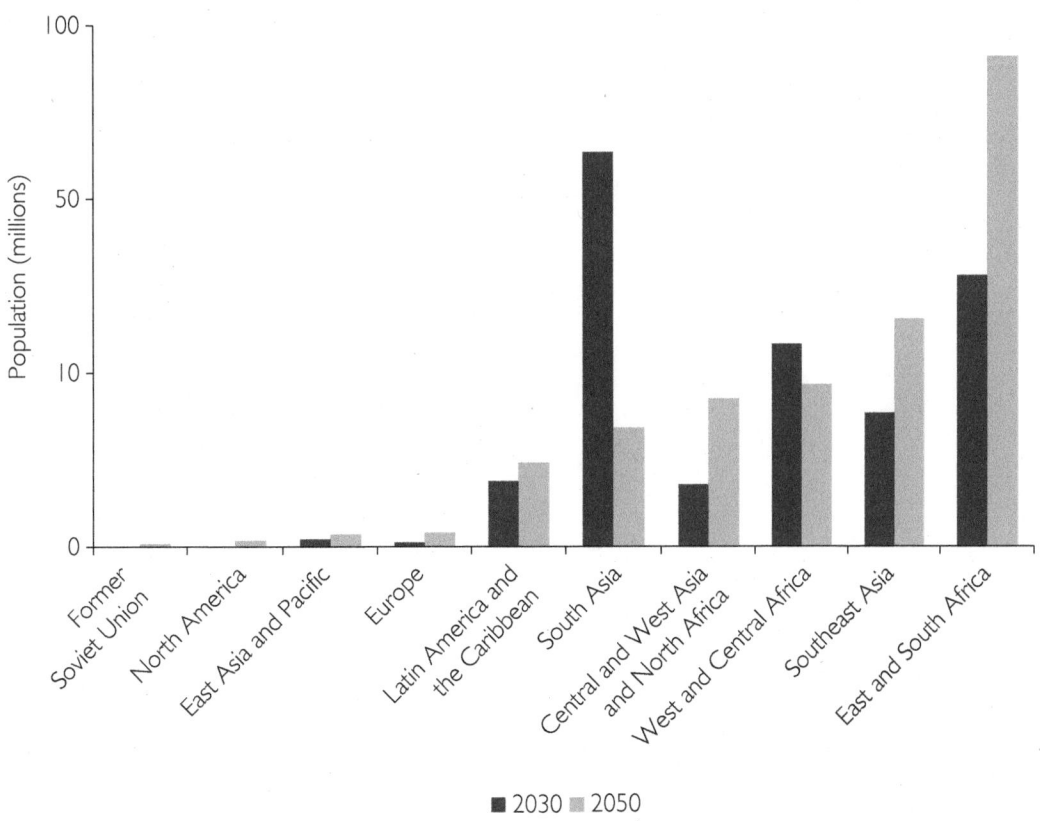

■ 2030 ■ 2050

Source: World Bank based on data from IFPRI 2022.
Note: Figure shows, by region, the projected increase in the number of hungry people in 2030 and 2050 under climate change versus no climate change. Notably, all regions show a projected increase in hunger due to climate change in 2050. However, in South Asia and Central and West Asia and North Africa, this projected increase is smaller in 2050 than in 2030. Countries included in each regional grouping can be found in table 1C of IFPRI 2022.

economies (Christiaensen, Demery, and Kuhl 2011; Hallegatte et al. 2016; Ivanic and Martin 2018), which will imperil food security[14] and create food price volatility (Brenton et al. 2023). Climate change will also cause the geographical distribution of agricultural production potential to change, with increases in mid to high latitudes and decreases in low latitudes (map 2.2) (Huang, von Lampe, and von Tongeren 2011). These impacts are expected to increase net crop imports for poor countries. For example, one study (Barua and Valenzuela 2018) finds that a 1°C increase in temperature lowers the agricultural exports of LMICs by 23 percent and LICs by 39 percent (Barua and Valenzuela 2018). Sub-Saharan Africa is projected to see the largest declines (World Bank 2023a). Taken together, climate change's damage will be greater than the sum of its parts. Another study shows that climate change's combined direct effects on crop yields and water scarcity are significant in all South Asian countries but that climate change's economywide effects are about 26–69 percent greater, on account of its cascading effects on other sectors and other countries through international trade (Taheripour et al. 2018). In Viet Nam, climate shocks to individual sectors are projected to cause annual losses of $27 billion in GDP by 2030 (World Bank 2022a). Another model (World Bank 2022b)

MAP 2.2 Countries with High Climate Vulnerability and High Food Insecurity Also Rely Heavily on Imported Food

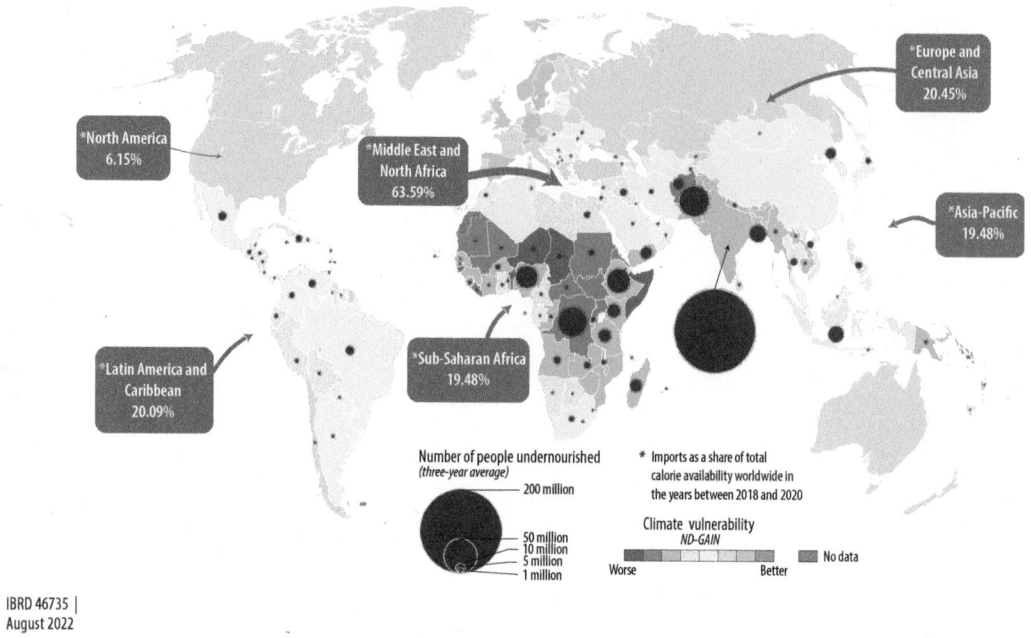

*North America
6.15%

*Europe and Central Asia
20.45%

*Middle East and North Africa
63.59%

*Asia-Pacific
19.48%

*Latin America and Caribbean
20.09%

*Sub-Saharan Africa
19.48%

Number of people undernourished
(three-year average)

200 million
50 million
10 million
5 million
1 million

* Imports as a share of total calorie availability worldwide in the years between 2018 and 2020

Climate vulnerability
ND-GAIN

Worse   Better   No data

IBRD 46735 |
August 2022

Source: Brenton et al. 2023.
Note: Percentages represent net food imports as a share of domestic food supply from 2018 to 2020. ND-GAIN = Notre Dame Global Adaptation Initiative.

estimates total annual losses from climate change in Viet Nam, including indirect losses, to be $44 billion per year.

Efforts to boost food production in response to climate change losses could amplify environmental costs, resulting in a negative feedback loop. Cropland expansion and intensification are the main strategies for boosting agricultural production, but they are also major drivers of biodiversity decline and a significant source of GHG emissions (Zabel et al. 2019). Therefore, boosting production in response to climate change–related losses by expanding croplands and intensifying their production would just accelerate climate change even more in a negative feedback loop. All the while, this would lead to mounting costs and environmental externalities (Dasgupta 2021).

These negative externalities make the current agrifood system unsustainable, as the planet is rapidly reaching and exceeding its planetary boundaries. The externalities are rapidly and irreversibly eroding the very resource base that sustains our livelihoods (Moyer and Sinclair 2020). If left unmitigated, agrifood system externalities could push beyond planetary boundaries (Roson 2017). A planetary boundary is a quantitative limit to how much the planetary system can be disturbed without sending it into a new, unsafe state (Rockström et al. 2009; Steffen et al. 2015). Staying within these boundaries would allow humans to continue to develop and thrive for generations; exceeding them would lead certain natural systems to collapse. Many of these boundaries can be defined in quantitative terms—for example, the global carbon budget to stay within the 1.5°C global heating boundary (Rogelj et al. 2019). Figure 2.21 shows that the planet has already surpassed six operating boundaries, including boundaries that are critical for agrifood systems, such

FIGURE 2.21 Environmental Pressures Are Surpassing Many Planetary Boundaries

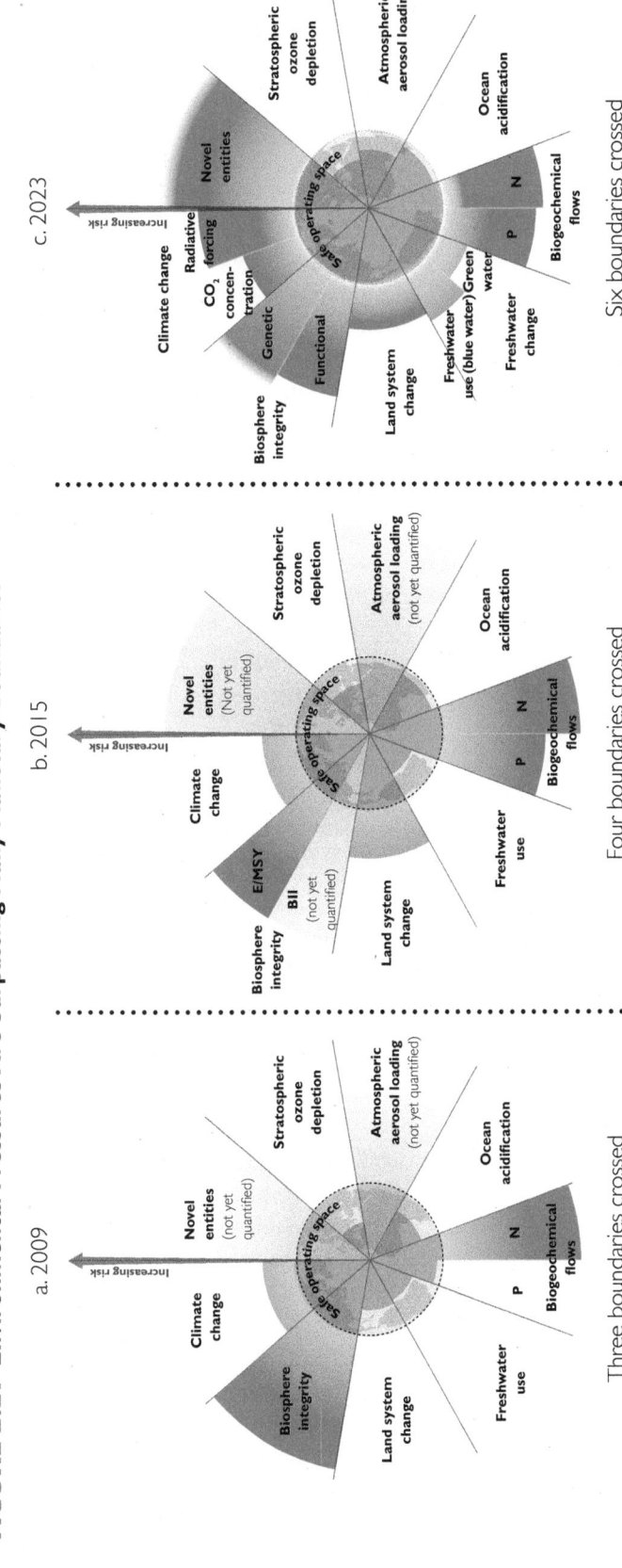

a. 2009

Three boundaries crossed

b. 2015

Four boundaries crossed

c. 2023

Six boundaries crossed

Source: Azote for Stockholm Resilience Centre, Stockholm University. Based on Richardson et al. 2023, Steffen et al. 2015, and Rockström et al. 2009.

Note: BII = Biodiversity Intactness Index; CO_2 = carbon dioxide; E/MSY = extinctions per million species-years; N = nitrogen; P = phosphorus.

The Agrifood System Has a Big Climate Problem

as climate change, land system change, freshwater, biogeochemical flows, and biosphere integrity (Stockholm Resilience Centre 2023). Each of the figure's segments represents an environmental pressure that, if it gets high enough, takes the planetary system into an unsafe state. In many cases, food production systems are applying this pressure, at least in part (Wang-Erlandsson et al. 2022). Moreover, environmental pressures from food production are highly concentrated, with 92.5 percent of all pressure being exerted on 10 percent of the planet's land area and more than half concentrated in just five countries: Brazil, China, India, Pakistan, and the United States.[15] Avoiding or delaying action to prevent these externality pressures will lead to runaway costs and potentially irreversible damage to earth systems. For example, economic costs from GHG emissions are estimated to be hundreds of billions of dollars with every year of delayed mitigation action (Sanderson and O'Neill 2020). Moreover, restoring critical ecosystems after their boundaries have been exceeded is costlier than protecting them in the first place. This is certainly true for the ecosystem's lost environmental services.

The Conditions Are in Place to Start the Agrifood System's Transformation to Net Zero

The food system transformation can build on productivity growth and other food system successes from the past three decades. Agriculture producers have increased agricultural output since 1990 through improved resource-use efficiency, or productivity, and better technology and practices. Many of these efforts focused on boosting the total factor productivity (TFP) of agriculture, which reduces the need for converting forested land to agriculture or depleting natural resource inputs, thereby reducing biodiversity loss, GHG emissions, and water contamination (figure 2.22). Empirical estimates show that improvements in TFP between 2001 and 2015 accounted for two-thirds of global agricultural growth and close to 60 percent of agricultural growth in developing economies (Fuglie et al. 2020). In high-income countries, improved TFP has slowed the expansion of agricultural lands and converted agricultural land into vegetated areas. Food producers have also introduced better technologies and practices, such as mechanization, improved seed varieties, improved irrigation techniques, more sustainable livestock feeding practices, and the introduction of genetic management techniques. Global agricultural TFP grew at a very healthy 1.86 percent annually from 1991 to 2010, driven largely by increases in China and countries in Latin America and the Caribbean, South Asia, and Southeast Asia (Steensland 2022).

However, global TFP growth has slowed dramatically while agricultural land expansion has grown over the past decade. Global TFP growth has been only 1.12 percent annually since 2010, which is below the estimated 1.73 percent required to satisfy the increased food demand from a growing population by 2050. This coincides with agricultural land expansion over the past three decades from a low in the 1990s (figure 2.23). Both trends contribute to higher agriculture-related GHG emissions. Additional trends become apparent when looking at country income groups. Most notably, TFP growth in LICs—where it is most needed to boost low yields—lags far behind that of MICs and HICs and dropped from 1.4 percent in 1991–2000 to only 0.1 percent in 2011–20. Instead, LICs, and MICs to a lesser extent, have relied on converting land to agriculture to boost production. In contrast, agricultural land expansion has been reversed in HICs. LICs have also turned to the greater use of inputs, such as fertilizer, rather than TFP growth

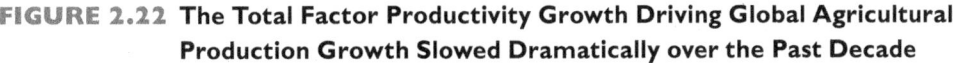

FIGURE 2.22 The Total Factor Productivity Growth Driving Global Agricultural Production Growth Slowed Dramatically over the Past Decade

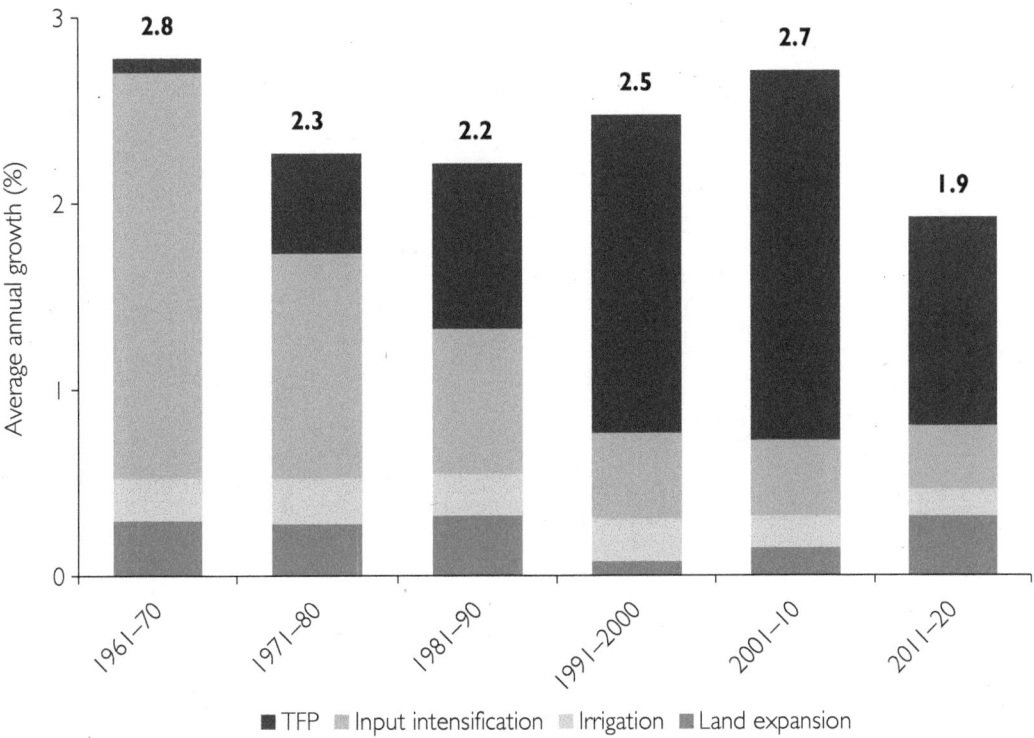

Source: World Bank based on data from the Economic Research Service of the US Department of Agriculture.
Note: Figure shows the global sources of agricultural output growth by decade for 1961–2020. The total percentage growth of output per decade appears above each bar. TFP = total factor productivity.

to increase agricultural output. That said, the rapid introduction of new technologies can boost productivity growth, and—as discussed in chapter 4—policy makers can provide incentives and a friendly policy environment to public research institutions and the private sector to accelerate innovation, as they have in the past, to enhance productivity.

Recent crises have highlighted opportunities for "building back better" with more-resilient supply chains and lower-emission food systems (CGIAR Research Program on Agriculture for Nutrition and Health 2023). As discussed, COVID-19 and Russia's invasion of Ukraine exposed vulnerabilities in the agrifood system, creating an opportunity to make the system more resilient. A resilient food system provides sufficient, accessible, adequate, and nutritious food to all despite being exposed to various shocks (Ebata, Nisbett, and Gillespie 2020). Such a system is built with redundancy, replicating system components to increase tolerance against faults; modularity, lessening faults to one part of a system by spreading them across the entire system; and diversity by increasing the number of categories and reducing their disparity within a system (Ringsmuth et al. 2022). Resilience is also enhanced by reducing long-distance just-in-time deliveries of basic commodities (Ringsmuth et al. 2022) and the dependence on single suppliers for critical commodities. Measures to increase food system resilience can also reduce GHG emissions. Shorter supply chains and more locally sourced basic goods can reduce transportation-related emissions.

FIGURE 2.23 Total Factor Productivity Growth in Agriculture Has Slowed the Most in Low-Income Countries, Where Land Expansion and Input Intensification Instead Drive Agricultural Output Growth

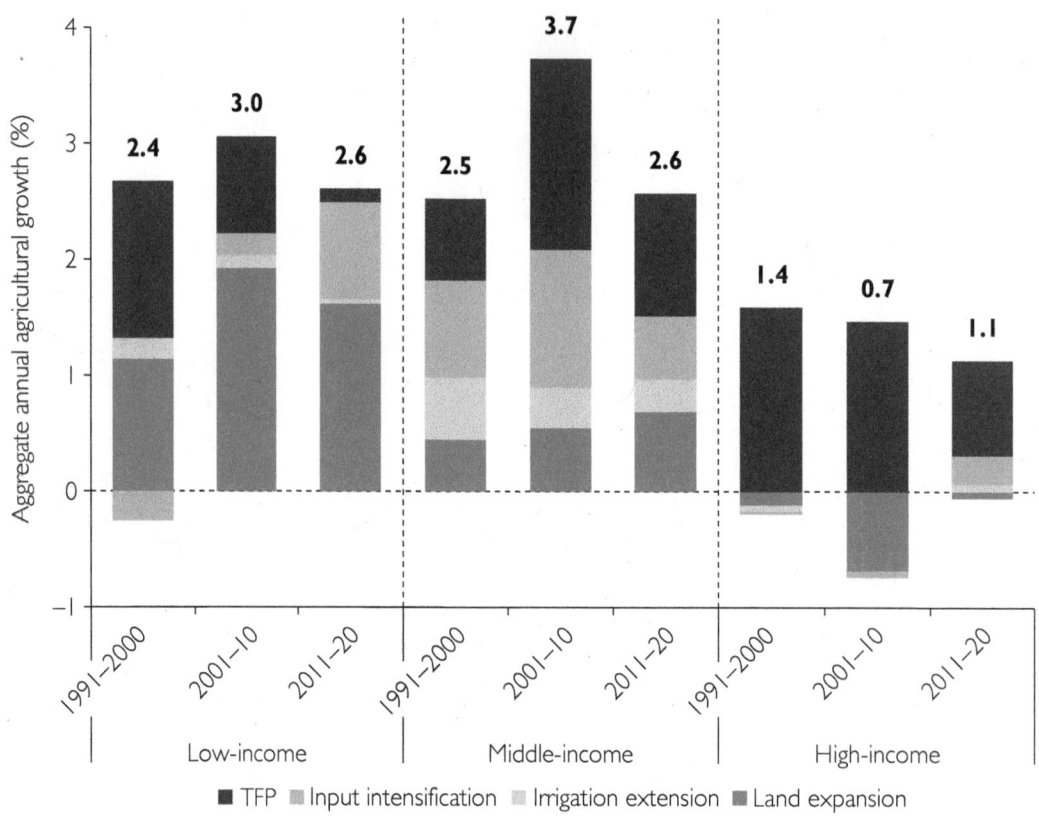

Source: World Bank based on data from the Economic Research Service of the US Department of Agriculture, and the World Bank 2024.
Note: Figure shows sources of agricultural output growth by country income category and decade for 1991–2020. Total output growth appears above each bar. TFP = total factor productivity.

For example, producing input materials, such as fertilizers, closer to where they are applied and using renewable energy instead of fossil fuels can help countries withstand international supply-chain problems and reduce the reliance on imported fossil feedstocks. The same applies to on-farm energy supplies: generated locally produced renewable energy instead of imported fossil fuels reduces both the local system's vulnerability and its emissions. Moreover, as discussed in chapter 3, increased food system circularity can help mitigate climate change while increasing resilience to shocks. For example, using food production and consumption by-products to enrich soils and feed animals creates resource security and efficiency while reducing emissions (de Boer and van Ittersum 2018). However, such approaches should not come at the cost of increased protectionism in the international food trade, which disproportionately affects LICs and poor consumers (Pangestu and van Trotsenburg 2022).

Early mitigation action will lead to short-, medium-, and long-term dividends, while delaying these actions will be particularly costly. If climate mitigation action is delayed and temperature targets are exceeded, it will require large-scale carbon dioxide removal in the second half of this century. Removing methane and nitrous oxide from the atmosphere is even more technically challenging (Bond 2023). For example, avoiding land conversion to agriculture is much more cost-effective, in both economic and noneconomic costs, than converting those lands back to forest (Hasegawa et al. 2021). The world would need an unrealistic 1.2 billion hectares—equivalent to the world's total cropland area—to remove the amount of biological carbon needed to meet national climate pledges (Dooley 2022). Early action to prevent emissions will likely entail both short- and medium-term costs and benefits. For example, to achieve the goals of the Paris Agreement, the IPCC projects that land use for energy crops may need to expand by more than 20 million hectares per year, which could lead to an increase in food prices from increased competition for land (IPCC 2022b). At the same time, early mitigation action could also lead to some short-term economic gains, amounting to up to $4.3 trillion annually by 2030 (FOLU 2019). Transforming the food system more generally creates business opportunities from delivering healthier food, reducing food waste, and monetizing environmental services that will have an estimated worth of $4.5 trillion by 2030 (FOLU 2019). Over the long term (2080–2100), the benefits are much clearer. Early mitigation action lowers long-term food prices by 4.2 percent, hunger risk for 4.8 million people, and water demand for irrigation by 7.2 cubic kilometers per year (Hasegawa et al. 2021). Not to mention that early action will limit global heating and prevent the direst, and most costly, consequences of climate change.

There is no inherent trade-off between agrifood sector mitigation and food security and other development objectives because climate action can deliver multiple wins. Evidence shows that it is possible to reduce GHG emissions and increase food production, while preserving biodiversity, through better and more efficient land, water, and resource allocation and management. New research by the World Bank and its partners (Damania et al. 2023)

FIGURE 2.24 **More Efficient Land Use Will Allow the World to Sequester Significantly More Carbon Dioxide While Still Feeding More People**

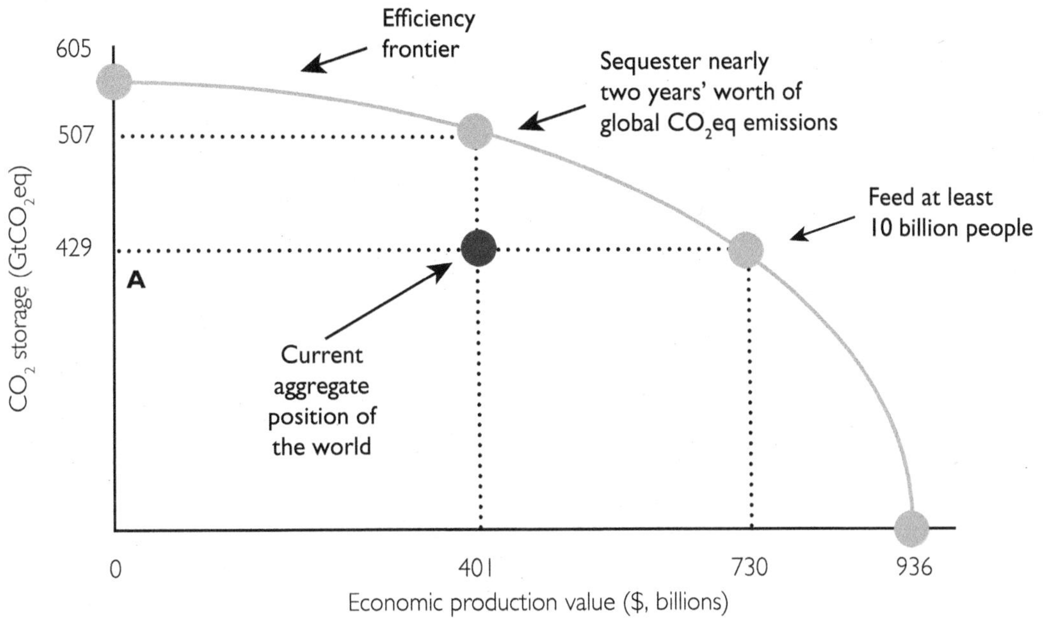

Source: Damania et al. 2023.
Note: CO_2 = carbon dioxide; CO_2eq = carbon dioxide equivalent; $GtCO_2$eq = gigatons of carbon dioxide equivalent.

The Agrifood System Has a Big Climate Problem

assesses how countries can sustainably use their natural capital—particularly land—in more efficient ways, or build "sustainable resource efficiency frontiers." It finds there are natural capital management efficiency gaps in nearly every country in the world, where land and resources are not optimally allocated for their best use. Closing these gaps to achieve maximum efficiency—in what economists refer to as Pareto efficiency[16]—could contribute to global development and sequester an additional 78.1 billion metric tons of CO_2eq with no adverse impacts on crop and livestock production or biodiversity loss in the 147 countries for which data were available (figure 2.24). In addition, better production strategies and smarter spatial planning can improve crop yields and reduce agriculture's land footprint while limiting its GHG footprint and increasing global calorie production by more than 150 percent (Damania et al. 2023). This translates to an 82 percent increase in net value from crop, livestock, and timber production globally. Figure 2.25 reveals that economic efficiency scores are significantly higher in HICs than in MICs, which are in turn higher than in LICs. That implies that LICs and MICs have ample opportunity to boost agricultural yields and rural incomes—without compromising carbon sequestration or biodiversity—simply

FIGURE 2.25 Low- and Middle-Income Countries Have Opportunities to Improve Rural Incomes without Sacrificing Natural Capital

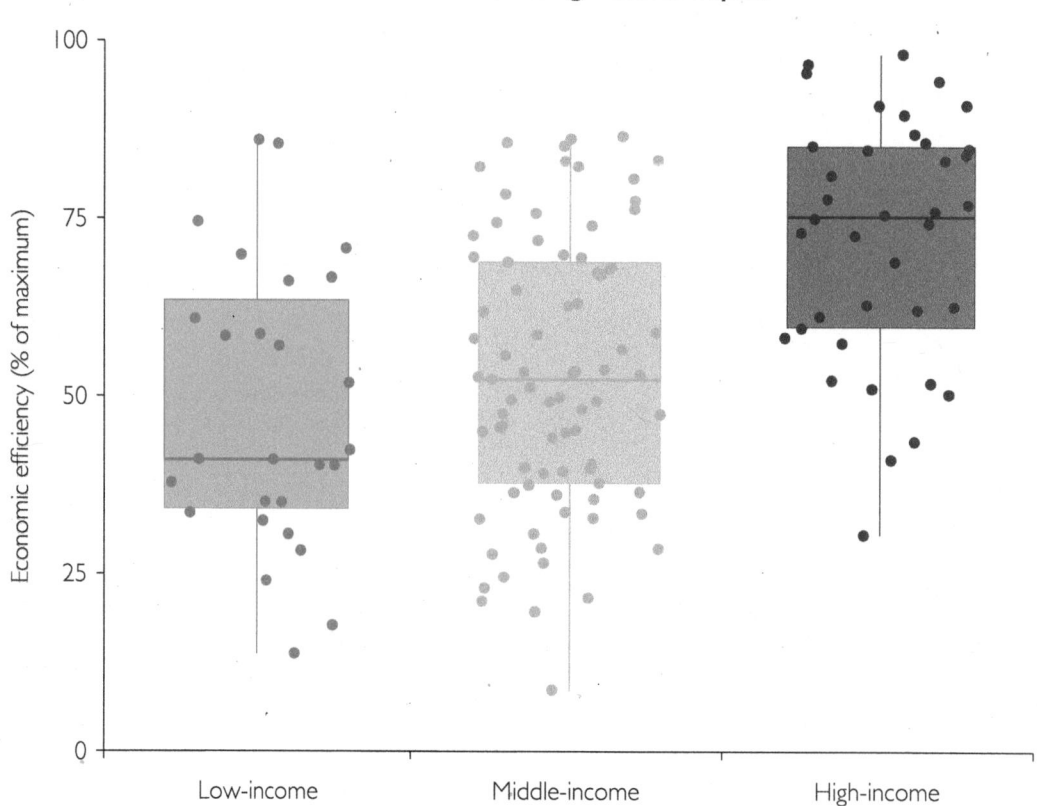

Source: World Bank based on data from Damania et al. 2023 and World Bank 2024.
Note: The figure depicts a box and whisker plot illustrating the percentage of maximum possible monetary returns within the Pareto space achieved by the current landscape. In Pareto analysis, results reflect what is accomplished in each dimension relative to the maximum feasible scenario without compromising other dimensions. Each country point is plotted within its respective income group, with box size representing the interquartile range. A solid horizontal line denotes the median percentage of economic efficiency within each income group, while the length of the vertical bar, or "whisker", indicates the range between minimum and maximum data values (Damania et al. 2023).

Recipe for a Livable Planet

by bridging the economic efficiency gap with HICs. Likewise, even HICs have room for improvement, with a median economic efficiency score of only 76 percent. Therefore, the agrifood system transformation will create many more employment opportunities and raise incomes in the future despite some short-term income losses.

Notes

1. World Bank calculations using IEA and FAOSTAT data covering 2018–20.

2. World Bank analysis using FAOSTAT data (2023).

3. Chiriac, Vishnumolakala, and Rosane 2023 and new analysis carried out by CPI in 2023 for the World Bank for the purposes of this report.

4. Naran et al. 2022; and CPI analysis for this report.

5. Based on the ND-GAIN Index.

6. Naran et al. 2022 and new analysis carried out by the Climate Policy Initiative (CPI) in 2023 for the World Bank for the purposes of this report.

7. Chiriac, Vishnumolakala, and Rosane 2023, and new analysis carried out by CPI in 2023 for this report using data from AgFunder.

8. Examples from McKinsey and Co. 2023 include advanced feed additives ($99/tCO$_2$e), nitrogen inhibitors on pastures ($34/tCO$_2$e), incorporation of cover crops ($10/tCO$_2$e), and even net cost-saving technologies like increased concentrate to-forage ratio (–$306/tCO$_2$e), biologicals (–$177/tCO$_2$e), and direct seeding of rice (–$159/tCO$_2$e). Examples from McKinsey and Co. 2020 include anerobic manure digestion ($92/tCO$_2$e), improved fertilization ($3/tCO$_2$e), and even net cost-saving technologies like zero emissions on-farm machinery (–$229/tCO$_2$e), low or no tillage (–$41/tCO$_2$e), and improved rice paddy water management (–$12/tCO$_2$e).

9. The packages of strategies under conservation agriculture differed across studies and usually included some combination of crop rotation, intercropping, residue retention, use of inorganic fertilizer, and minimum tillage

10. Agricultural water productivity is the measure of output (biomass, crop yield, or revenue) divided by some measure of water consumed in production (for example, kilograms of output per cubic meter of water consumed).

11. This counterintuitive effect of higher productivity leading to higher water consumptions is explained by the rebound effect and Jevons paradox (which states that, in the long term, an increase in efficiency in resource use will generate an increase in resource consumption rather than a decrease). Farmers, as economic agents, increase the area irrigated (or intensify under the same irrigation area) if new technologies allow them to use less water or increase the number of croppings in a year, unless there are water conservation policies that prevent this behavior.

12. For a more in-depth analysis of competing land uses, see Damania et al. 2023.

13. As measured by the real FAO Food Price Index, a measure of the monthly change in international prices of a basket of food commodities. It consists of the average of five commodity group price indices weighted by the average export shares of each of the groups over the 2014 –16 period. See FAO 2023b.

14. Some estimates suggest that at the regional level, declining rice yields in LAC, MENA, Oceania, and SSA will be offset by rising yields in Europe. For maize, declining yields in Europe and NA are accompanied by increases in Oceania, MENA, and Asia (Glauber and Laborde 2022).

15. Halpern et al. (2022) defined disturbance to land and biodiversity as the proportion of native plants and animals displaced by agricultural activities within a region, and this pressure is reported in units of square kilometer equivalents (km$_2$eq), which incorporate both the occupancy area and a measure of disruption.

16. Pareto efficiency implies that it is not possible to increase one output without decreasing another output (Damania et al. 2023, 25).

References

Abbafati, C., et al. 2020 "Global Burden of 369 Diseases and Injuries in 204 Countries and Territories, 1990–2019: A Systematic Analysis for the Global Burden of Disease Study 2019." *Lancet* 396, (10258): 1204–22. https://doi.org/10.1016/S0140-6736(20)30925-9.

Aday, S., and M. S. Aday. 2020. "Impact of COVID-19 on the Food Supply Chain." *Food Quality and Safety* 4 (4): 167–80. https://doi.org/10.1093/fqsafe/fyaa024.

Adhya, Tapan K., Bruce Lindquist, Tim Searchinger, Reiner Wassmann, and Xiaoyuan Yan. 2014. "Wetting and Drying: Reducing Greenhouse Gas Emissions and Saving Water from Rice Production." Working paper (Installment 8 of "Creating a Sustainable Food Future), World Resource Institute. https://files.wri.org/d8/s3fs-public/wfetting-drying-reducing-greenhouse-gas-emissions-saving-water-rice-production.pdf.

Afshin, Ashkan, et al. 2019. "Health Effects of Dietary Risks in 195 Countries, 1990–2017: A Systematic Analysis for the Global Burden of Disease Study 2017." *Lancet* 393 (10184): 1958–72. https://doi.org/10.1016/S0140-6736(19)30041-8.

Ahmed, S., T. Warne, E. Smith, H. Goemann, G. Linse, M. Greenwood, J. Kedziora, et al. 2021. "Systematic Review on Effects of Bioenergy from Edible versus Inedible Feedstocks on Food Security." *NPJ Science of Food* 5: 9. https://doi.org/10.1038/s41538-021-00091-6.

Akerlof, George A., and Rachel E. Kranton. 2000. "Economics and Identity." *Quarterly Journal of Economics* 115 (3): 715–53. https://doi.org/10.1162/003355300554881.

Ambikapathi, R., K. R. Schneider, B. Davis, M. Herrero, P. Winters, and J. C. Fanzo. 2022. "Global Food Systems Transitions Have Enabled Affordable Diets but Had Less Favourable Outcomes for Nutrition, Environmental Health, Inclusion and Equity." *Nature Food* 3: 764–79. https://doi.org/10.1038/s43016-022-00588-7.

Anderson, T., and M. R. Balsera. 2019. *Principles for a Just Transition in Agriculture*. Johannesburg: ActionAid International. https://actionaid.org/publications/2019/principles-just-transition-agriculture.

Barua, S., and E. Valenzuela. 2018. "Climate Change Impacts on Global Agricultural Trade Patterns: Evidence from the Past 50 Years." In *Proceedings of the Sixth International Conference on Sustainable Development 2018, Columbia University*. Columbia University, New York.

Birner, Regina, Surupa Gupta, and Neeru Sharma. 2011. *The Political Economy of Agricultural Policy Reform in India: Fertilizers and Electricity for Irrigation*. Research Monograph 174. Washington, DC: International Food Policy Research Institute. https://citeseerx.ist.psu.edu/document?repid=rep1&type=pdf&doi=a58f7b99ac34a61b52e8edd79bfb3a1c6915271a.

Blaustein-Rejto, Dan. 2023. "How to Cut Emissions through Agricultural Trade" (article). Accessed April 3, 2024. https://thebreakthrough.org/issues/food-agriculture-environment/how-to-cut-emissions-through-agricultural-trade.

Bond, Camille. 2023. "Why Capturing Methane Is So Difficult." *Scientific American*, January 17. https://www.scientificamerican.com/article/why-capturing-methane-is-so-difficult/#:~:text=But%20methane%20is%20200%20times,unfeasibly%20large%20amount%20of%20energy.

Borras, Saturnino, Cristobal Kay, Sergio Gómez, and John Wilkinson. 2012. "Land Grabbing and Global Capitalist Accumulation: Key Features in Latin America." *Canadian Journal of Development Studies/Revue canadienne d'études du développement* 33 (4): 402–16. https://doi.org/10.1080/02255189.2012.745394.

Brenton, P., V. Chemutai, M. Maliszewska, and I. Sikora. 2023. *Trade and the Climate Emergency: Policy Priorities for Developing Countries*. Washington, DC: World Bank.

Brunelle, Thierry, Mathilde Coat, and Vincent Viguié. 2017. "Demand-Side Mitigation Options of the Agricultural Sector: Potential, Barriers and Ways Forward." *OCL [Oilseeds & fats Crops and Lipids]* 24 (1): D104. doi: 10.1051/ocl/2016051.

Castañeda, Andes, Dung Doan, David Newhouse, Minh Cong Nguyen, Hiroki Uematsu, and Joao Pedro Azevedo. 2016. "Who Are the Poor in the Developing World?" Policy Research Working Paper 7844, World Bank, Washington, DC. http://hdl.handle.net/10986/25161.

CGIAR Research Program on Agriculture for Nutrition and Health. 2023. "CGIAR COVID Hub Focus: Addressing Food Systems' Fragilities and Building Back Better" (web page). Accessed November

25, 2023. https://a4nh.cgiar.org/covidhub/covid-hub-focus-addressing-food-systems-fragility-and -building-back-better/.

Chen, Zhong-Du, and Fu Chen. 2022. "Socio-economic Factors Influencing the Adoption of Low Carbon Technologies under Rice Production Systems in China." *Carbon Balance and Management* 17 (1): 19. doi:10.1186/s13021-022-00218-6.

Chiriac, Daniela, Harsha Vishnumolakala, and Paul Rosane. 2023. "Landscape of Climate Finance for Agrifood Systems. Climate Policy Initiative." https://www.climatepolicyinitiative.org/publication /landscape-of-climate-finance-for-agrifood-systems/.

Christiaensen, Luc, Lionel Demery, and Jesper Kuhl. 2011. "The (Evolving) Role of Agriculture in Poverty Reduction—An Empirical Perspective." *Journal of Development Economics* 96 (2): 239–54. https://doi .org/10.1016/j.jdeveco.2010.10.006.

Christiaensen, L., Z. Rutledge, and J. E. Taylor. 2021. "Viewpoint: The Future of Work in Agri-food." *Food Policy* 99: 101963.https://doi.org/10.1016/j.foodpol.2020.101963.

Clapp, J., P. Newell, and Z. Brent. 2017. "The Global Political Economy of Climate Change, Agriculture, and Food Systems." *Journal of Peasant Studies* 45 (1): 60–66. https://doi.org/10.1080/03066150.2017.1381602.

Clark, Michael A., Nina G. G. Domingo, Kimberly Colgan, Sumil K. Thakrar, David Tilman, John Lynch, Inés L. Azevedo, and Jason D. Hill. 2020. "Global Food System Emissions Could Preclude Achieving the 1.5° and 2°C Climate Change Targets." *Science* 370: 705–8. https://doi.org/10.1126/science.aba7357.

Cole, Martin Barry, Mary Ann Augustin, Michael John Robertson, and John Michael Manners. 2018. "The Science of Food Security." *NPJ Science of Food* 2: 14. https://doi.org/10.1038/s41538-018-0021-.

Convergence Blended Finance. 2022. "State of Blended Finance: Climate Edition 2022." https://www .convergence.finance/resource/state-of-blended-finance-2022.

Corbeels, M., K. Naudin, A. M. Whitbread, R. Kühne, and P. Letourmy. 2020. "Limits of Conservation Agriculture to Overcome Low Crop Yields in Sub-Saharan Africa." *Nature Food* 1 (7): 447–54. https:// doi.org/10.1038/s43016-020-0114-x.

Costa Jr., C., E. Wollenberg, M. Benitez, R. Newman, N. Gardner, and F. Bellone. 2022. "Roadmap for Achieving Net-Zero Emissions in Global Food Systems by 2050." *Scientific Reports* 12 (1): 15064. https:// doi.org/10.1038/s41598-022-18601-1.

CPI (Climate Policy Institute). 2023. "Global Landscape of Climate Finance 2023." CPI, San Francisco, CA. https://www.climatepolicyinitiative.org/publication/global-landscape-of-climate-finance-2023/.

CPI (Climate Policy Initiative) and IFAD. 2020. "Examining the Climate Finance Gap for Small-Scale Agriculture." https://www.ifad.org/en/web/knowledge/-/publication/examining-the-climate-finance -gap-for-small-scale-agriculture.

Crippa, M., D. Guizzardi, E. Solazzo, M. Muntean, E. Schaaf, F. Monforti-Ferrario, M. Banja, et al. 2021. *GHG Emissions of All World Countries—2021 Report*. EUR 30831 EN. Luxembourg: Publications Office of the European Union. https://edgar.jrc.ec.europa.eu/report_2021.

Crippa, M., E. Solazzo, D. Guizzardi, F. Monforti-Ferrario, F. N. Tubiello, and A. Leip. 2021. "Food Systems Are Responsible for a Third of Global Anthropogenic GHG Emissions." *Nature Food* 2: 198–209. https:// doi.org/10.1038/s43016-021-00225-9.

Dalabajan, Dante, Ruth Mayne, Blandina Bobson, Hadeel Qazzaz, Henry Ushie, Jacobo Ocharan, Jason Farr, et al. 2022. *Towards a Just Energy Transition: Implications for Communities in Lower- and Middle-Income Countries*. Oxford, UK: Oxfam International. https://doi.org/10.21201/2022.9936.

Damania, Richard, Stephen Polasky, Mary Ruckelshaus, Jason Russ, Markus Amann, Rebecca Chaplin-Kramer, James Gerber, et al. 2023. *Nature's Frontiers: Achieving Sustainability, Efficiency, and Prosperity with Natural Capital*. Environment and Sustainable Development series. Washington, DC: World Bank. https://doi.org/10.1596/978-1-4648-1923-0.

DARA. 2012. *Methodological Documentation for the Climate Vulnerability Monitor*. 2nd ed. Madrid: DARA. https://daraint.org/wp-content/uploads/2012/09/CVM2_Methodology.pdf.

Dasgupta, P. 2021. *The Economics of Biodiversity: The Dasgupta Review*. London: HM Treasury. https://assets .publishing.service.gov.uk/government/uploads/system/uploads/attachment_data/file/962785/The _Economics_of_Biodiversity_The_Dasgupta_Review_Full_Report.pdf.

de Boer, I. J. M., and M. K. van Ittersum. 2018. *Circularity in Agricultural Production*. Wageningen, The Netherlands: Wageningen University and Research. https://library.wur.nl/WebQuery/wurpubs/547719.

Department for Business, Energy and Industrial Strategy, and Department for Energy Security and Net Zero, United Kingdom. 2022. "United Kingdom Methane Memorandum" (notice). Accessed April 3, 2024. https://www.gov.uk/government/publications/united-kingdom-methane-memorandum/united -kingdom-methane-memorandum.

Dooley, K., H. Keith, A. Larson, G. Catacora-Vargas, W. Carton, K. L. Christiansen, O. Enokenwa Baa, A. Frechette, S. Hugh, N. Ivetic, L. C. Lim, J. F. Lund, M. Luqman, B. Mackey, I. Monterroso, H. Ojha, I. Perfecto, K. Riamit, Y. Robiou du Pont, and V. Young. 2022. *The Land Gap Report 2022*. Accessed April 1, 2024. https://www.landgap.org/.

Duvvuru, Narasimha Reddy, and Venkatanarayana Motkuri. 2013. "Declining Labour Use in Agriculture: A Case of Rice Cultivation in Andhra Pradesh." MPRA Paper 49204, University Library of Munich. https://doi.org/10.13140/RG.2.2.16594.04809.

Ebata, Ayako, Nick Nisbett, and Stuart Gillespie. 2020. "Food Systems and Building Back Better." Positioning paper, Institute of Development Studies, Brighton, UK. https://opendocs.ids.ac.uk/opendocs/handle /20.500.12413/15677.

European Commission. 2020. "Factsheet: How the Future CAP Will Contribute to the EU Green Deal" (web page). Accessed April 3, 2024. https://ec.europa.eu/commission/presscorner/detail/en/fs_20_910.

FAO (Food and Agriculture Organization of the United Nations), IFAD (International Fund for Agricultural Development), UNICEF (United Nations Children's Fund), WFP (World Food Programme), and WHO (World Health Organization). 2021. *The State of Food Security and Nutrition in the World 2021: Transforming Food Systems for Food Security, Improved Nutrition and Affordable Healthy Diets for All*. Rome: FAO. https://doi.org/10.4060/cb4474en.

FAO (Food and Agriculture Organization of the United Nations), IFAD (International Fund for Agricultural Development), UNICEF (United Nations Children's Fund), WFP (World Food Programme), and WHO (World Health Organization). 2022. *The State of Food Security and Nutrition in the World 2022: Repurposing Food and Agricultural Policies to Make Healthy Diets More Affordable*. Rome: FAO. https:// doi.org/10.4060/cc0639en.

FAO (Food and Agriculture Organization of the United Nations), IFAD (International Fund for Agricultural Development), UNICEF (United Nations Children's Fund), WFP (World Food Programme), and WHO (World Health Organization). 2023. *The State of Food Security and Nutrition in the World 2023: Urbanization, Agrifood Systems Transformation and Healthy Diets across the Rural-Urban Continuum*. Rome: FAO. https://doi.org/10.4060/cc3017en.

FAO (Food and Agriculture Organization of the United Nations). 2017. *The Future of Food and Agriculture: Trends and Challenges*. Rome. https://www.fao.org/3/i6583e/i6583e.pdf.

FAO (Food and Agriculture Organization of the United Nations). 2018. *The Future of Food and Agriculture: Alternative Pathways to 2050*. Rome: FAO. https://www.fao.org/global-perspectives-studies/resources /detail/en/c/1157074/.

FAO (Food and Agriculture Organization of the United Nations). 2022. *Drivers and Triggers for Transformation*. Future of Food and Agriculture 3. Rome: FAO. https://doi.org/10.4060/cc0959en.

FAO (Food and Agriculture Organization of the United Nations). 2023a. "Sustainable Development Goals 2.1.1: Prevalence of Undernourishment." Accessed April 3, 2024. https://www.fao.org/sustainable -development-goals/indicators/211/en/.

FAO (Food and Agriculture Organization of the United Nations). 2023b. "World Food Situation: FAO Food Price Index" (web page). Accessed April 3, 2024. https://www.fao.org/worldfoodsituation /foodpricesindex/en/.

FAOSTAT. 2023. (web page). Accessed April 3, 2024. https://www.fao.org/faostat/en/#data.

Federal Ministry for Economic Affairs and Energy (BMWK), Germany. 2020. *Renewable Energy Sources in Figures: National and International Development, 2020*. Berlin: Federal Ministry for Economic Affairs and Energy. https://www.bmwk.de/Redaktion/EN/Publikationen/Energie/renewable-energy-sources-in -figures-2020.pdf?__blob=publicationFile&v=1.

Foley, J., N. Ramankutty, K. Brauman, et al. 2011. "Solutions for a Cultivated Planet." *Nature* 478: 337–42. https://doi.org/10.1038/nature10452.

FOLU (Food and Land Use Coalition). 2019. *Growing Better: Ten Critical Transitions to Transform Food and Land Use; The Global Consultation Report of the Food and Land Use Coalition*. https://www.foodandlandusecoalition.org/wp-content/uploads/2019/09/FOLU-GrowingBetter-GlobalReport.pdf.

Fransen, T., C. Henderson, R. O'Connor, N. Alayza, M. Caldwell, S. Chakrabarty, A. Dixit, et al. 2022. *The State of Nationally Determined Contributions: 2022*. Washington, DC: World Resources Institute. doi:10.46830/wrirpt.22.00043.

Freightos Data. 2023. "Freightos Baltic Index (GBX): Global Container Pricing Index" (web page). Accessed April 3, 2024. https://fbx.freightos.com/.

Fuglie, Keith, Madhur Gautam, Aparajita Goyal, and William F. Maloney. 2020. *Harvesting Prosperity: Technology and Productivity Growth in Agriculture*. Washington, DC: World Bank. https://doi.org/10.1596/978-1-4648-1393-1.

Fujimori, S., T. Hasegawa, J. Rogelj, X. Su, P. Havlik, V. Krey, K. Takahashi, and K. Riahi. 2018. "Inclusive Climate Change Mitigation and Food Security Policy under 1.5°C Climate Goal." *Environmental Research Letters* 13 (7): 074033.

Fujimori, S., W. Wu, J. Doelman, S. Frank, J. Hristov, P. Kyle, R. Sands, et al. 2022. "Land-Based Climate Change Mitigation Measures Can Affect Agricultural Markets and Food Security." *Nature Food* 3: 110–21. https://doi.org/10.1038/s43016-022-00464-4.

Gautam, M., D. Laborde, A. Mamun, W. Martin, V. Pineiro, and R. Vos. 2022. *Repurposing Agricultural Policies and Support: Options to Transform Agriculture and Food Systems to Better Serve the Health of People, Economies, and the Planet*. Washington, DC: World Bank. http://hdl.handle.net/10986/36875.

Gerbens-Leenes, P. W., and S. Nonhebel. 2002. "Consumption Patterns and Their Effects on Land Required for Food." *Ecological Economics* 42 (1–2): 185–99.

Gilmore, B., and E. McAuliffe. 2013. "Effectiveness of Community Health Workers Delivering Preventive Interventions for Maternal and Child Health in Low- and Middle-Income Countries: A Systematic Review." *BMC Public Health* 13: 847. https://doi.org/10.1186/1471-2458-13-847.

Glauber, Joseph, and Charlotte Hebebrand. 2023. "Food versus Fuel v2.0: Biofuel Policies and the Current Food Crisis." *IFPRI Blog*, April 11. https://www.ifpri.org/blog/food-versus-fuel-v20-biofuel-policies-and-current-food-crisis.

Glauber, Joseph, and David Laborde. 2022. *How Will Russia's Invasion of Ukraine Affect Global Food Security?* Washington, DC: International Food Policy Research Institute. https://www.ifpri.org/blog/how-will-russias-invasion-ukraine-affect-global-food-security.

Graf, Sarah Lena, and Carlos Oya. 2021. "Is the System of Rice Intensification (SRI) Pro Poor? Labour, Class and Technological Change in West Africa." *Agricultural Systems* 193: 103229. https://doi.org/10.1016/j.agsy.2021.103229.

Guerrero, Santiago, Ben Henderson, Hugo Valin, Charlotte Janssens, Petr Havlik, and Amanda Palazzo. 2022. "The Impacts of Agricultural Trade and Support Policy Reform on Climate Change Adaptation and Environmental Performance: A Model-Based Analysis." OECD Food, Agriculture and Fisheries Papers 180, Organisation for Economic Co-operation and Development Publishing, Paris. https://doi.org/10.1787/520dd70d-en.

Hallegatte, Stephane, Mook Bangalore, Laura Bonzanigo, Marianne Fay, Tamaro Kane, Ulf Narloch, Julie Rozenberg, David Treguer, and Adrien Vogt-Schilb. 2016. *Shock Waves: Managing the Impacts of Climate Change on Poverty*. Washington, DC: World Bank. https://documents1.worldbank.org/curated/en/260011486755946625/pdf/Shock-waves-managing-the-impacts-of-climate-change-on-poverty.pdf.

Halpern, Benjamin S., Melanie Frazier, Juliette Verstaen, Paul-Eric Rayner., Gage Clawson, Julia L. Blanchard, Richard S. Cottrell, et al. 2022. "The Environmental Footprint of Global Food Production." *Nature Sustainability* 5: 1027–39. https://doi.org/10.1038/s41893-022-00965-x.

Hamilton, Lawrence C. 2021. "The Slow Dawn of Climate-Change Awareness, and Its Challenge for a Sustainable Planet." *Carsey Perspectives,* Carsey School of Public Policy, University of New Hampshire, April 22. https://carsey.unh.edu/publication/slow-dawn-climate-change-awareness.

Hasegawa, Tomoko, Shinichiro Fujimori, Stefan Frank, Florian Humpenöder, Christoph Bertram, Jacques Després, Laurent Drouet, et al. 2021. "Land-Based Implications of Early Climate Actions without Global Net-Negative Emissions." *Nature Sustainability* 4: 1052–59. https://doi.org/10.1038/s41893-021-00772-w.

Hasegawa, Tomoko, Shinichiro Fujimori, Petr Havlík, Hugo Valin, Benjamin Leon Bodirsky, Jonathan C. Doelman, Thomas Fellmann, et al. 2018. "Risk of Increased Food Insecurity under Stringent Global Climate Change Mitigation Policy." *Nature Climate Change* 8: 699–703. https://doi.org/10.1038/s41558-018-0230-x.

Headey, Derek D., and Harold H. Alderman. 2019. "The Relative Caloric Prices of Healthy and Unhealthy Foods Differ Systematically across Income Levels and Continents." *Journal of Nutrition* 149 (11): 2020–33. https://doi.org/10.1093/jn/nxz158.

Henderson, B., and J. Lankoski. 2021. "Assessing the Environmental Impacts of Agricultural Policies." *Applied Economic Perspectives and Policy* 43: 1487–502. https://doi.org/10.1002/aepp.13081.

Hendriks, S., A. D. G. Ruiz, M. H. Acosta, H. Baumers, P. Galgani, D. Mason-D'Croz, C. Godde, et al. 2021. "The True Cost and True Price of Food." Paper prepared for the UN Food Systems Summit 2021, New York, September 23. https://sc-fss2021.org/wp-content/uploads/2021/06/UNFSS_true_cost_of_food.pdf.

Hill, J., E. Nelson, D. Tilman, S. Polasky, and D. Tiffany. 2006. "Environmental, Economic, and Energetic Costs and Benefits of Biodiesel and Ethanol Biofuels." *Proceedings of the National Academy of Sciences of the United States of America* 103 (30): 11206–10. https://doi.org/10.1073/pnas.0604600103.

Holt Giménez, Eric, and Annie Shattuck. 2011. "Food Crises, Food Regimes and Food Movements: Rumblings of Reform or Tides of Transformation?" *Journal of Peasant Studies* 38 (1): 109–44. https://doi.org/10.1080/03066150.2010.538578.

Huang, Hsin, Martin von Lampe, and Frank van Tongeren. 2011. "Climate Change and Trade in Agriculture." *Food Policy* 36 (S1): S9–S13. https//:doi.org/10.1016/j.foodpol.2010.10.008.

IEA (International Energy Agency). 2021. *Renewables 2021: Analysis and Forecasts to 2026.* Paris: IEA. https://www.iea.org/reports/renewables-2021.

IFPRI (International Food Policy Research Institute). 2022. *2022 Global Food Policy Report: Climate Change and Food Systems.* Washington, DC: International Food Policy Research Institute. https://doi.org/10.2499/9780896294257.

ILO (International Labour Organization). 2020. "ILO modelled estimates database (ILOSTAT)" (database). Accessed April 3, 2024. https://ilostat.ilo.org/data/.

International Institute of Refrigeration. 2021. "The Carbon Footprint of the Cold Chain." 7th Informatory Note on Refrigeration and Food, International Institute of Refrigeration, Paris. https://iifiir.org/en/fridoc/the-carbon-footprint-of-the-cold-chain-7-lt-sup-gt-th-lt-sup-gt-informatory-143457.

IPCC (Intergovernmental Panel on Climate Change). 2018. "Summary for Policymakers." In *Global Warming of 1.5°C: An IPCC Special Report on the Impacts of Global Warming of 1.5°C above Pre-industrial Levels and Related Global Greenhouse Gas Emission Pathways, in the Context of Strengthening the Global Response to the Threat of Climate Change, Sustainable Development, and Efforts to Eradicate Poverty*, 3–24. Cambridge: Cambridge University Press. https://doi.org/10.1017/9781009157940.001.

IPCC (Intergovernmental Panel on Climate Change). 2022a. *Climate Change 2022: Impacts, Adaptation and Vulnerability; Contribution of Working Group II to the Sixth Assessment Report of the Intergovernmental Panel on Climate Change* Cambridge: Cambridge University Press. https://doi.org/10.1017/9781009325844.

IPCC (Intergovernmental Panel on Climate Change). 2022b. *Climate Change and Land: An IPCC Special Report on Climate Change, Desertification, Land Degradation, Sustainable Land Management, Food Security, and Greenhouse Gas Fluxes in Terrestrial Ecosystems.* Cambridge: Cambridge University Press. https://doi.org/10.1017/9781009157988.

IPCC (Intergovernmental Panel on Climate Change). 2022c. "Summary for Policymakers." In *Climate Change 2022: Mitigation of Climate Change. Contribution of Working Group III to the Sixth Assessment Report of the Intergovernmental Panel on Climate Change*, edited by P. R. Shukla, J. Skea, R. Slade,

A. Al Khourdajie, R. van Diemen, D. McCollum, M. Pathak, et al., 6–51. Cambridge: Cambridge University Press. https://doi.org/10.1017/9781009157926.001.

IPCC (Intergovernmental Panel on Climate Change). 2023. *Climate Change 2023: Synthesis Report; Contribution of Working Groups I, II and III to the Sixth Assessment Report of the Intergovernmental Panel on Climate Change,* edited by H. Lee and J. Romero. Geneva: IPCC. https://doi.org/10.59327/IPCC/AR6-9789291691647.

Ivanic, Maros, and Will Martin. 2018. "Sectoral Productivity Growth and Poverty Reduction: National and Global Impacts." *World Development* 109: 429–39. https://doi.org/10.1016/j.worlddev.2017.07.004.

Jones, M. W., G. P. Peters, T. Gasser, R. M. Andrew, C. Schwingshackl, J. Gütschow, R. A. Houghton, P. Friedlingstein, J. Pongratz, and C. Le Quéré. 2023. "National Contributions to Climate Change Due to Historical Emissions of Carbon Dioxide, Methane, and Nitrous Oxide since 1850." *Scientific Data* 10: 155. https://doi.org/10.1038/s41597-023-02041-1.

Kastner, Thomas, Maria Jose Ibarro-la Rivas, Wolfgang Koch, and Sanderine Nonhebel. 2012. "Global Changes in Diets and the Consequences for Land Requirements for Food." *Proceedings of the National Academy of Sciences (PNAS)* 109 (18): 6868–72. https://doi.org/10.1073/pnas.1117054109.

Klimek, Peter, Michael Obersteiner, and Stefan Thurner. 2015. "Systemic Trade Risk of Critical Resources." *Science Advances* 1 (10). https://www.science.org/doi/epdf/10.1126/sciadv.1500522.

Kotz, Maximilian, Friderike Kuik, Eliz Lis, and Christiane Nickel. 2023. "The Impact of Global Warming on Inflation: Averages, Seasonality and Extremes." ECB Working Paper 2821, European Central Bank, Frankfurt am Main. https://doi.org/10.2866/46035.

Kumareswaran, K., and G. Y. Jayasinghe. 2022. "Systematic Review on Ensuring the Global Food Security and COVID-19 Pandemic Resilient Food Systems: Towards Accomplishing Sustainable Development Goals Targets." *Discover Sustainability* 3 (1): 29. https://doi.org/10.1007/s43621-022-00096-5. Epub 2022 Aug 31.

Laderchi, C. R., H. Lotze-Campen, F. DeClerck, B. L. Bodirsky, Q. Collignon, M. S. Crawford, S. Dietz, et al. 2024. *The Economics of the Food System Transformation.* Global Policy Report. Oslo, Norway: Food System Economics Commission.

Leippert, F., M. Darmaun, M. Bernoux, and M. Mpheshea. 2020. *The Potential of Agroecology to Build Climate-Resilient Livelihoods and Food Systems.* Rome: FAO and Biovision. https://doi.org/10.4060/cb0438en.

López-Gunn, E., B. Mayor, and A. Dumont. 2012. "Implications of the Modernization of Irrigation Systems." In *Water, Agriculture and the Environment in Spain: Can We Square the Circle?,* edited by L. De Stefano and M. R. Llamas, 241–55. Leiden, the Netherlands: CRC Press/Balkema. https://www.fundacionbotin.org/89dguuytdfr276ed_uploads/Observatorio%20Tendencias/PUBLICACIONES/LIBROS%20SEM%20INTERN/water-agriculture-environment/capitulo19-wagriculture.pdf.

Luoto, Jill, and Katherine Grace Carman. 2014. "Behavioral Economics Guidelines with Applications for Health Interventions." Technical Note IDB-TN-66, Social Protection and Health Division, Inter-American Development Bank, Washington, DC. https://publications.iadb.org/en/behavioral-economics-guidelines-applications-health-interventions.

Matthew, L. 2006. "Corn Farmers Smile as Ethanol Prices Rise, but Experts on Food Supplies Worry." *New York Times,* January 16. https://www.nytimes.com/2006/01/16/us/corn-farmers-smile-as-ethanol-prices-rise-but-experts-on-food-supplies.html.

McKinsey & Company. 2020. *Agriculture and Climate Change: Reducing Emissions through Improved Farming Practices.* New York: McKinsey & Company. https://www.mckinsey.com/industries/agriculture/our-insights/reducing-agriculture-emissions-through-improved-farming-practices.

McKinsey & Company. 2023. *The Agricultural Transition: Building a Sustainable Future.* New York: McKinsey & Company. https://www.mckinsey.com/industries/agriculture/our-insights/the-agricultural-transition-building-a-sustainable-future.

Montt, Guillermo, and Trang Luu. 2020. "Does Conservation Agriculture Change Labour Requirements? Evidence of Sustainable Intensification in Sub-Saharan Africa." *Journal of Agricultural Economics* 71 (2): 556–80. https://doi.org/10.1111/1477-9552.12353.

Moyer, J. M., and A. J. Sinclair. 2020. "Learning for Sustainability: Considering Pathways to Transformation." *Adult Education Quarterly* 70 (4): 340–59. https://doi.org/10.1177/0741713620912219.

Nabuurs, G.-J., R. Mrabet, A. Abu Hatab, M. Bustamante, H. Clark, P. Havlík, J. House, et al. 2022. "Agriculture, Forestry and Other Land Uses (AFOLU)." In *Climate Change 2022: Mitigation of Climate Change; Contribution of Working Group III to the Sixth Assessment Report of the Intergovernmental Panel on Climate Change,* edited by P. R. Shukla, J. Skea, R. Slade, A. Al Khourdajie, R. van Diemen, D. McCollum, M. Pathak, et al., chap. 7. Cambridge, UK: Cambridge University Press. https://doi.org/10.1017/9781009157926.009.

Naran, Baysa, Jake Connolly, Paul Rosane, Dharshan Wignarajah, and Githungo Wakaba. 2022. *Global Landscape of Climate Finance: A Decade of Data; 2011–2020.* Washington, DC: Climate Policy Initiative. https://www.climatepolicyinitiative.org/wp-content/uploads/2022/10/Global-Landscape-of-Climate-Finance-A-Decade-of-Data.pdf.

NASA (National Aeronautics and Space Administration). 2022. "Vital Signs: Methane" (web page). Accessed April 3, 2024. https://climate.nasa.gov/vital-signs/methane/.

Nguyen, Angela, and Michael J. Platow. 2021. "'I'll Eat Meat Because That's What We Do': The Role of National Norms and National Social Identification on Meat Eating." *Appetite* 164: 105287. https://doi.org/10.1016/j.appet.2021.105287.

Nico, Gianluigi, and Luc Christiaensen. 2023. "Jobs, Food and Greening: Exploring Implications of the Green Transition for Jobs in the Agri-food System." World Bank Jobs Working Paper 75, World Bank, Washington, DC. http://hdl.handle.net/10986/39819.

Oakland Institute. 2011. "Understanding Land Investment Deals in Africa, Country Report: Ethiopia. 2011." Accessed April 3, 2004. https://www.oaklandinstitute.org/sites/oaklandinstitute.org/files/OI_Ethiopa_Land_Investment_report.pdf.

OECD (Organisation for Economic Co-operation and Development). 2019a. *Enhancing Climate Change Mitigation through Agriculture.* Paris: OECD Publishing. https://doi.org/10.1787/e9a79226-en.

OECD (Organisation for Economic Co-operation and Development). 2019b. "Policy Coherence in Food and Agriculture." In *Innovation, Productivity and Sustainability in Food and Agriculture: Main Findings from Country Reviews and Policy Lessons.* Paris: OECD Publishing. https://www.oecd-ilibrary.org/sites/f13335a7-en/index.html?itemId=/content/component/f13335a7-en.

Ortiz-Bobea, A., T. R. Ault, C. M. Carrillo, R. G. Chambers, and D. B. Lobell. 2021. "Anthropogenic Climate Change Has Slowed Global Agricultural Productivity Growth." *Nature Climate Change* 11: 306–12. https://doi.org/10.1038/s41558-021-01000-1.

Our World in Data. 2023. "Nitrous Oxide Emissions by Sector." Accessed April 1, 2024. https://ourworldindata.org/grapher/nitrous-oxide-emissions-by-sector.

Pangestu, Mari Elka, and Axel van Trotsenburg. 2022. "Trade Restrictions Are Inflaming the Worst Food Crisis in a Decade." *Voices* (blog), July 6. https://blogs.worldbank.org/voices/trade-restrictions-are-inflaming-worst-food-crisis-decade.

Pérez-Blanco, C. Dionisio, Arthur Hrast-Essenfelder, and Chris Perry. 2020. "Irrigation Technology and Water Conservation: A Review of the Theory and Evidence." *Review of Environmental Economics and Policy* 14 (2) https://www.journals.uchicago.edu/doi/full/10.1093/reep/reaa004.

Prudhomme, Rémi, Adriana De Palma, Patrice Dumas, Ricardo Gonzalez, Paul Leadley, Harold Levrel, Andy Purvis, and Thierry Brunelle. 2020. "Combining Mitigation Strategies to Increase Co-Benefits for Biodiversity and Food Security." *Environmental Research Letters* 15 (11): 114005. https://doi.org/10.1088/1748-9326/abb10a.

Richardson, R., M. P. Prescott, and B. Ellison. 2020. "Impact of Plate Shape and Size on Individual Food Waste in a University Dining Hall." *Resources, Conservation and Recycling* 168: 105293. https://doi.org/10.1016/j.resconrec.2020.105293.

Richardson, J., W. Steffen, W. Lucht, J. Bendtsen, S.E. Cornell, et al. 2023. "Earth Beyond Six of Nine Planetary Boundaries." *Science Advances,* 9, 37. https://www.science.org/doi/10.1126/sciadv.adh2458.

Ringsmuth, Andrew K., Ilona M. Otto, Bart van den Hurk, Glada Lahn, Christopher P. O. Reyer, Timothy R. Carter, Piotr Magnuszewski, et al. 2022. "Lessons from COVID-19 for Managing Transboundary Climate Risks and Building Resilience." *Climate Risk Management* 35: 100395. https://doi.org/10.1016/j.crm.2022.100395.

Rockström, Johan, Will Steffen, Kevin Noone, Åsa Persson, F. Stuart Chapin III, Eric Lambin, Timoth M. Lenton, et al. 2009. "Planetary Boundaries: Exploring the Safe Operating Space for Humanity." *Ecology and Society* 14 (2): 32. http://www.ecologyandsociety.org/vol14/iss2/art32/.

Roe, S., C. Streck, R. Beach, J. Busch, M. Chapman, V. Daioglou, A. Deppermann, et al. 2021. "Land-Based Measures to Mitigate Climate Change: Potential and Feasibility by Country." *Global Change Biology* 27 (23): 6025–58. https://doi.org/10.1111/gcb.15873.

Rogelj, J., P. M. Forster, E. Kriegler, et al. 2019. "Estimating and Tracking the Remaining Carbon Budget for Stringent Climate Targets." *Nature* 571 (7765): 335–42. https://doi.org/10.1038/s41586-019-1368-z.

Roson, Roberto. 2017. "Simulating the Macroeconomic Impact of Future Water Scarcity." Discussion Paper, World Bank, Washington, DC. https://doi.org/10.1596/26027.

Sanderson, Brian M., and Brian C. O'Neill. 2020. "Assessing the Costs of Historical Inaction on Climate Change." *Scientific Reports* 10: 9173. https://doi.org/10.1038/s41598-020-66275-4.

Serrano Fuentes, N., A. Rogers, and M. C. Portillo. 2019. "Social Network Influences and the Adoption of Obesity-Related Behaviors in Adults: A Critical Interpretative Synthesis Review." *BMC Public Health* 19: 1178. https://doi.org/10.1186/s12889-019-7467-9.

Service, Robert F. 2007. "Biofuel Researchers Prepare to Reap a New Harvest." *Science* 315: 1488–91. https://doi.org/10.1126/science.315.5818.1488.

Sims, R. E. H., and A. Flammini. 2014. "Energy-Smart Food—Technologies, Practices, and Policies." In *Sustainable Energy Solutions in Agriculture*, edited by J. Bundschuh and G. Chen. Cited in F. N. Tubiello, A. Flammini, K. Karl, G. Obli-Laryea, S. Y. Qiu, H. Heiðarsdóttir, X. Pan, and G. Conchedda. 2021. "Methods for Estimating Greenhouse Gas Emissions from Food Systems. Part III: Energy Use in Fertilizer Manufacturing, Food Processing, Packaging, Retail, and Household Consumption." FAO Statistics Working Paper 29, Rome, Food and Agriculture Organization of the United Nations. https://doi.org/10.4060/cb7473en.

Springmann, M. 2020. "Valuation of the Health and Climate-Change Benefits of Healthy Diets." Background paper for *The State of Food Security and Nutrition in the World 2020*. FAO Agricultural Development Economics Working Paper 20-03. FAO, Rome. https://doi.org/10.4060/cb1699en.

Springmann, Marco, Michael Clark, Daniel Mason-D'Croz, Keith Weibe, Benjamin Leon Bodirsky, Luis Lassaletta, Wim de Vries, et al. 2018. "Options for Keeping the Food System within Environmental Limits." *Nature* 562: 519–25. https://doi.org/10.1038/s41586-018-0594-0.

Springmann, M., D. Mozaffarian, C. Rosenzweig, and R. Micha. 2021. "What We Eat Matters: Health and Environmental Impacts of Diets Worldwide." Chap. 2 in *Global Nutrition Report 2021: The State of Global Nutrition*. Bristol, UK: Development Initiatives, 15. https://globalnutritionreport.org/reports/2021-global-nutrition-report/health-and-environmental-impacts-of-diets-worldwide/.

Steensland, Aaron. 2022. *2022 Global Agricultural Productivity Report: Troublesome Trends and System Shocks*, edited by T. Thompson and J. Agnew. Blacksburg, VA: Virginia Tech College of Agriculture and Life Sciences. https://globalagriculturalproductivity.org/wp-content/uploads/2022/11/2022-GAP_Report_final_110922.pdf.

Steffen, Will, Katherine Richardson, Johan Rockström, Sarah E. Cornell, Ingo Fetzer, Elena M. Bennett, Reinette Biggs, et al. 2015. "Planetary Boundaries: Guiding Human Development on a Changing Planet." *Science* 347 (6223): 1259855. https://doi.org/10.1126/science.1259855.

Steiner, A., G. Aguilar, K. Bomba, J. P. Bonilla, A. Campbell, R. Echeverria, R. Gandhi et al. 2020. "Actions to transform food systems under climate change." Wageningen, The Netherlands: CGIAR Research Program on Climate Change, Agriculture and Food Security (CCAFS).

Stockholm Resilience Centre. 2023. "Planetary Boundaries" (web page). Accessed April 3, 2024. https://www.stockholmresilience.org/research/planetary-boundaries.html.

Swinnen, J. 2018. "The Political Economy of Agricultural and Food Policies." In *The Routledge Handbook of Agricultural Economics*, edited by G. Cramer, K. Paudel, and A. Schmitz, 381–98. Abingdon, UK: Routledge.

Taheripour, F., T. W. Hertel, B. N. Gopalakrishnan, S. Sahin, A. Markandya, and B. K. Mitra. 2018. "Climate Change and Water Scarcity: Growing Risks for Agricultural-Based Economies in South Asia." In *Routledge Handbook of Sustainable Development in Asia*, edited by S. Hsu, 104–32. London and New York: Routledge, Taylor and Francis Group.

Thornton, Philip, Yuling Chang, Ana Maria Loboguerrero, and Bruce Campbell. 2023. "Perspective: What Might It Cost to Reconfigure Food Systems?" *Global Food Security* 36:100669. https://doi.org/10.1016/j.gfs.2022.100669.

Toensmeier, Eric. 2016. *The Carbon Farming Solution: A Global Toolkit of Perennial Crops and Regenerative Agriculture Practices for Climate Change Mitigation and Food Security*. White River Junction, VT: Chelsea Green Publishing.

Townsend, Robert, Rui Manuel Benfica, Ashesh Prasann, Maria Lee, and Parmesh Shah. 2017. *Future of Food: Shaping the Food System to Deliver Jobs*. Washington, DC: World Bank Group. http://documents.worldbank.org/curated/en/406511492528621198/Future-of-food-shaping-the-food-system-to-deliver-jobs.

Tubiello, F., K. Karl, A. Flammini, J. Gutschow, G. Obli-Laryea, G. Conchedda, X. Pan, et al. 2022. "Pre- and Post-production Processes Increasingly Dominate Greenhouse Gas Emissions from Agri-food Systems." *Earth System Science Data* 14 (4): 1795–809. https://doi.org/10.5194/essd-14-1795-2022.

UNEP (United Nations Environment Programme). 2021. *Global Methane Assessment: Benefits and Costs of Mitigating Methane Emissions*. Nairobi: UNEP. https://www.unep.org/resources/report/global-methane-assessment-benefits-and-costs-mitigating-methane-emissions.

UNFCCC (United Nations Framework Convention on Climate Change) Secretariat. 2021. "Nationally Determined Contributions under the Paris Agreement: Synthesis Report by the Secretariat." Report, UNFCCC, Bonn. https://unfccc.int/documents/306848.

UNFCCC (United Nations Framework Convention on Climate Change). 2023. "Technical Dialogue of the First Global Stocktake: Synthesis Report by the Co-Facilitators on the Technical Dialogue." Advance version. unfccc.int/sites/default/files/resource/sb2023_09_adv.pdf.

USDA (US Department of Agriculture). n.d. "Food Waste FAQs" (web page). Accessed April 3, 2024. https://www.usda.gov/foodwaste/faqs.

US Department of State. 2022. "Global Methane Pledge: From Moment to Momentum. Factsheet" (web page). Accessed April 3, 2024. https://www.state.gov/global-methane-pledge-from-moment-to-momentum/#:~:text=New%20GMP%20Food%20and%20Agriculture,of%20agriculture%20in%20the%20future.

US EPA (United States Environmental Protection Agency). 2023. "Understanding Global Warming Potentials" (web page). Updated April 18, 2023. https://www.epa.gov/ghgemissions/understanding-global-warming-potentials.

van Dijk, Michiel, Tom Morley, Marie Luise Rau, and Yashar Saghai. 2021. "A Meta-analysis of Projected Global Food Demand and Population at Risk of Hunger for the Period 2010–2050." *Nature Food* 2: 494–501. https://doi.org/10.1038/s43016-021-00322-9.

Vera, Ivan, Birka Wicke, Patrick Lamers, Annette Cowie, Anna Repo, Bas Heukels, Colleen Zumpf, et al. 2022. "Land Use for Bioenergy: Synergies and Trade-Offs between Sustainable Development Goals." *Renewable and Sustainable Energy Reviews* 161: 112409. https://doi.org/10.1016/j.rser.2022.112409.

Walker, Renee E., Christopher R. Keane, and Jessica G. Burke. 2010. "Disparities and Access to Healthy Food in the United States: A Review of Food Deserts Literature." *Health and Place* 16 (5): 876–84. https://doi.org/10.1016/j.healthplace.2010.04.013.

Wang-Erlandsson, L., Arne Tobian, Ruud J. van der Ent, Ingo Fetzer, Sofie te Wierik, Miina Porkka, Arie Staal, et al. 2022. "A Planetary Boundary for Green Water." *Nature Reviews: Earth and Environment* 3: 380–92. https://doi.org/10.1038/s43017-022-00287-8.

Watanabe, M., J. Gomes, and H. Dewes. 2007. "Sugarcane-Induced Changes in the Land Use in the Parana State, Brazil." In *VI International Pensa Conference*, 1–3. Ribeirão Preto, Brazil: Universidade de São Paulo.

Weinzettel, Jan, Edgar G. Hertwich, Glen P. Peters, Kjartan Steen-Olsen, and Alessandro Galli. 2013. "Affluence Drives the Global Displacement of Land Use." *Global Environmental Change* 23 (2): 433–38. https://doi.org/10.1016/j.gloenvcha.2012.12.010.

Willett, Walter, Johan Rockström, Brent Loken, Marco Springmann, Tim Lang, Sonja Vermeulen, Tara Garnett, et al. 2019. "Food in the Anthropocene: The EAT–Lancet Commission on Healthy Diets from Sustainable Food Systems. *Lancet* 393 (10170): 447–92. https://doi.org/10.1016/S0140-6736(18)31788-4.

World Bank. 2012. *Turn Down the Heat: Why a 4°C Warmer World Must Be Avoided*. Report for the World Bank by the Potsdam Institute for Climate Impact Research and Climate Analytics. Washington, DC: World Bank. http://hdl.handle.net/10986/11860.

World Bank. 2016. "Making Climate Finance Work in Agriculture." World Bank (blog). Accessed April 2, 2014. https://www.worldbank.org/en/topic/agriculture/publication/making-climate-finance-work-in-agriculture.

World Bank. 2022a. *Accelerating Clean, Green, and Climate-Resilient Growth in Vietnam: A Country Environmental Analysis*. Washington, DC: World Bank. https://doi.org/10.1596/10986/37704.

World Bank. 2022b. "Spearheading Vietnam's Green Agricultural Transformation: Moving to Low-Carbon Rice." World Bank, Washington, DC. https://documents.worldbank.org/en/publication/documents-reports/documentdetail/099735109222222315/p17448205335130730bb7e0a6e231e1f667.

World Bank. 2023a. *The Development, Climate, and Nature Crisis: Solutions to End Poverty on a Livable Planet; Insights from World Bank Country Climate and Development Reports Covering 42 Economies*. Washington, DC: World Bank. http://hdl.handle.net/10986/40652.

World Bank. 2023b. "Food Security Update LXXXIII." April 20. World Bank, Washington, DC. https://thedocs.worldbank.org/en/doc/40ebbf38f5a6b68bfc11e5273e1405d4-0090012022/related/Food-Security-Update-LXXXIII-April-20-2023.pdf.

World Bank. 2024. "Indicators" (web page). Accessed April 14, 2024. https://data.worldbank.org/indicator.

World Bank and IFAD (International Fund for Agriculture Development). 2017. "Rural Youth Employment." Paper prepared as input document for the G20 Development Working Group. World Bank, Washington, DC, and IFAD, Rome. https://www.researchgate.net/publication/322578396_Rural_Youth_Employment.

Wreford, A., A. Ignaciuk, and G. Gruère. 2017. "Overcoming Barriers to the Adoption of Climate-Friendly Practices in Agriculture." OECD Food, Agriculture and Fisheries Paper 101, OECD Publishing, Paris. https://doi.org/10.1787/97767de8-en.

Zabel, Florian, Ruth Delzeit, Julia M. Schneider, Ralf Seppelt, Wolfram Mauser, and Tomáš Václavik. 2019. "Global Impacts of Future Cropland Expansion and Intensification on Agricultural Markets and Biodiversity." *Nature Communications* 10: 2844. https://doi.org/10.1038/s41467-019-10775-z.

CHAPTER THREE

Every Country Can Harness Priority Opportunities to Achieve Net Zero Agrifood Emissions While Advancing Development

All countries should take comprehensive action to reduce emissions in their agrifood sectors, but different countries have different challenges and pathways for doing so. This chapter analyzes some of these challenges and pathways, specifically looking at the largest sources of agrifood system emissions and the technical and cost-effective mitigation potential for addressing them. To aid this analysis, the study team clustered countries into three categories: high-income, middle-income, and low-income countries (HICs, MICs, and LICs, respectively), which, as shown in chapter 2, generally correspond to historically high emitters, current high emitters, and low emitters, respectively. Arranging the chapter into these three country groups offers insights into where the greatest opportunities lie for each group to prioritize its contributions to net zero emissions in the agrifood system. That said, these opportunities and solutions are not mutually exclusive for the country categories, and solutions can be applied by multiple country types concurrently. For example, the fact that livestock emissions are highest in MICs and that targeting this sector offers those countries considerable opportunities to reduce total agrifood emissions does not mean that HICs should not also tackle this important climate challenge. The point is that individual countries vary in where they have the greatest relative opportunities to contribute to net zero agrifood emissions and have unique pathways that are specific to their context and are aligned with their national development objectives. In practice, countries should implement mitigation actions where they are the cheapest and they deliver the greatest climate and development co-benefits.

This chapter begins by looking at the global cost-effective mitigation that is available for all countries. It then takes a close look at where different country income groups hold the greatest opportunities for contributing to net zero agrifood emissions, starting with HICs. HICs can (1) fuel the transition toward more efficient and renewable energy to power agrifood system activities, (2) provide financial and technical solutions to help MICs and LICs mitigate agrifood system emissions, and (3) lead the way in full-cost pricing of foods and in promoting low-emissions diets. The chapter then looks at where MICs hold the greatest opportunities for contributing to net zero agrifood emissions. MICs, as a group, are the world's biggest agrifood emitters and have many available options to reduce on-farm emissions from (1) livestock production; (2) rice production; (3) soil degradation; and (4) pre- and post-production emissions from fertilizer production and use, food loss and waste, wastewater, and household food consumption. The chapter concludes by examining where LICs hold the greatest opportunities for contributing to net zero agrifood emissions. It shows the following: (1) LICs contribute the least to emissions but in many ways suffer the most from climate change. (2) LICs are the fastest-growing source of land use change–related emissions because of their natural forests and have an opportunity to profit from this by accessing carbon credits. (3) LICs have opportunities to forge a low-emissions development path through greater agrifood system productivity and efficiency and by supplying new food retail markets. (4) LICs can use these opportunities to make economic and rural development gains through climate-smart practices.

There Are Cost-Effective Mitigation Opportunities for All Countries, but These Opportunities Depend on Each Country's Relative Circumstances

There are many established mitigation options that are also cost-effective

Many established mitigation practices can be applied in all countries to all phases of the agrifood system to reduce emissions. Table 3.1 provides an overview of these measures within on-farm, land use, and pre- and post-production activities. It shows both the technical and the cost-effective mitigation potential of each measure. Technical mitigation potential is the amount of emissions reduction that is possible with available technology, regardless of cost. Cost-effective mitigation potential is the mitigation potential that is available and costs no more than $100 per ton of carbon dioxide equivalent (tCO_2eq) reductions, thus representing a realistic target for policy. Cost-effective mitigation options can have a negative cost as well, thereby generating savings. This can result from, for example, enhanced nutrient-use efficiency, which reduces the money spent on fertilizer, or improved soil health, which can increase yields, resulting in higher profits. Similarly, to reduce deforestation, effective practices include silvo-pastoral systems, agroforestry systems, crop diversification, increased crop productivity, and forest fire management and preparedness. On-farm practices to reduce rice paddy emissions include direct seeding, midseason drainage, residue management, improved fertilization, alternate wetting and drying (AWD), and integrated rice and fish farming.

Many of these established practices create adaptation and resilience co-benefits and are already at scale (Pretty, Toulmin, and Williams 2011; Tilman et al. 2011). For example, India and Mexico are applying precision nutrient management and other practices to improve the nutrient-use efficiency of crops, thereby optimizing fertilizer application without affecting yields or national food security targets (Sapkota et al. 2019; Sapkota et al. 2020; World Bank 2018). Likewise, the World Bank has implemented several climate-smart agriculture (CSA) projects at scale through its Climate Change Action Plan (2021–25). For example, in Bangladesh, the Livestock and Dairy Development Project (World Bank 2023e) boosts the resilience and production efficiency of livestock farms while reducing emissions intensity, through improved feeding strategies, animal health, breeding, manure and waste management, and low-emission technologies for downstream activities such as milk chilling and transport. In Pakistan, the SMART Punjab Program (World Bank 2022b) subsidizes the use of improved seeds and phosphatic and potash fertilizers, enabling farmers to switch from urea, which is produced by energy- and emission-intensive methods, to more efficient alternatives that increase productivity and profitability. In Colombia, the Mainstreaming Sustainable Cattle Ranching Project (World Bank 2019c) helped farmers plant 3.1 million trees and adopt silvo-pastoral techniques, leading to increased carbon sequestration and greater availability and diversity of food sources. In China, the World Bank invested $755 million in CSA to support resilient and lower-emissions agriculture practices, greater water-use efficiency, and more rice and maize production. The emerging results from the World Bank's CSA portfolio show that mitigation and food production can be delivered simultaneously at scale. Table 3.1 reinforces this, showing that most mitigation measures in the agrifood system also generate adaptation and resilience co-benefits. Table B.1 in appendix B expands on this, showing the specific and various co-benefits that different agrifood system mitigation practices generate.

The agrifood system is a prime source of cost-effective mitigation solutions under $100 per tCO_2eq, including cost-saving solutions under $0 per tCO_2eq. Existing agrifood system mitigation practices and technologies have the potential to achieve large emission reductions at low costs, defined in this report as having a marginal abatement cost (MAC) at or below $100 per tCO_2eq. This report calls these practices cost-effective. This is also the selected threshold for economic mitigation potential in the Intergovernmental Panel on Climate Change (IPCC) Sixth Assessment Report (AR6) chapter on agriculture, forestry, and other land use (AFOLU) (IPCC 2022c) and is the high estimate for the World Bank's shadow price of carbon in 2030 (World Bank 2017). It is also policy relevant, given that it falls within the 2030 carbon price corridor based on the recommendations of the High-Level Commission on Carbon Prices adjusted for inflation (Roe et al. 2021; World Bank 2023f). Roe et al. (2021) calculate that cost-effective mitigation practices in AFOLU, a subset of the agrifood system that excludes upstream and downstream activities, can reduce emissions by up to approximately 14 gigatons carbon dioxide equivalent ($GtCO_2eq$) on average per year, about 40 percent of AFOLU's available technical potential and in line with achieving a 1.5°C pathway by 2050. Fifty percent of this mitigation, or *abatement*, potential is from protecting forests and other ecosystems, 35 percent is from improving on-farm production practices, and 15 percent is from demand-side measures such as shifting to low-emission diets (Roe et al. 2021). Further, a recent global study (McKinsey & Company 2023) shows that 13 of the top 28 on-farm mitigation options—including increased concentrate-to-forage ratios, direct rice seeding, and reduced fertilizer overapplication—lead to cost savings,[1] underscoring the no-regret nature of many mitigation practices. Three of these options come at zero cost, and five options cost less than $35 per ton of carbon dioxide equivalent (tCO_2eq).[2] Another study (Frank et al. 2019) shows that at a carbon price of $100

TABLE 3.1 Many Agrifood Mitigation Options Are Cost-Effective and Provide Adaptation Co-benefits

Emissions category	Established mitigation measures	Technical mitigation potential (MtCO$_2$eq/ year)[a]	Cost-effective mitigation potential (MtCO$_2$eq/ year)[b]	Adaptation and resilience co-benefits (CSA)
LULUCF	Reduced deforestation	6,008	3,563	Yes
	Improved forest management	1,834	903	Yes
	Afforestation and reforestation	8,471	1,208	Yes
	Reduced mangrove conversion and mangrove restoration	92	70	Yes
	Reduced peatland degradation and conversion	433	205	Yes
	Peatland restoration	1,310	593	Yes
	Grassland and savanna fire management	104	31	Yes
	All LULUCF measures	**18,252**	**6,573**	**n.a.**
On-farm	Enteric fermentation: productivity enhancement[c]	179	98	Yes
	Manure management	118	91	Yes
	Improved rice cultivation	243	171	Yes
	Agroforestry	5,605	1,121	Yes
	Bioenergy with carbon capture and storage	2,390	499	No
	Nutrient management	255	222	Yes
	Biochar from crop residues	2,364	1,815	Yes
	Increased soil organic carbon in croplands	1,024	922	Yes
	Increased soil organic carbon in grasslands	1,487	892	Yes
	Enteric fermentation: feed additives[d]	>380	380	No
	Enteric fermentation: improved feed digestibility (Thornton and Herrero 2010)	680	120[e]	No
	Electrified farm machinery (McKinsey & Company 2023)	>167	167	Yes
	On-farm renewable energy/energy efficiency (IEA et al. 2022)	>330	330	Yes
	All on-farm measures	**15,222**	**6,830**	**n.a.**
Pre- and post-production	Dietary change[f]	2,277	1,433	Yes
	Reduced food waste	865	452	Yes
	Clean cookstoves	352	105	Yes
	Low GHG fertilizer production (Gao and Cabrera Serrenho 2023; IEA 2021a; Royal Society 2020)	480	300[g]	No
	Green cold chain (Becken et al. 2011; Cerutti et al. 2023)	900	400[h]	Yes
	Alternative proteins[i]	6,100	300[j]	Yes
	All pre- and post-production measures	**10,974**	**2,990**	**n.a.**

Source: World Bank based on data from Roe et al. 2021 (unless indicated otherwise).
Note: CSA = climate-smart agriculture; GHG = greenhouse gas; LULUCF = land use, land use change, and forestry; MtCO$_2$eq = megatons of carbon dioxide equivalent; n.a. = not applicable.
a. Annual technical mitigation potential.
b. Annual mitigation potential achievable at <$100 per tCO$_2$eq (tons of carbon dioxide equivalent).
c. Enteric fermentation refers to avoided methane emissions from ruminant livestock enteric fermentation through improved feed conversion (amount of feed fed by the amount of livestock weight gain), antibiotics, bovine somatotropin, propionate precursors, antimethanogens, and intensive grazing. All are aimed at increasing productivity.
d. World Bank calculation based on Ungerfeld (2022).
e. Range, 120–150.
f. Dietary change refers to emissions reductions from diverted agricultural production from the adoption of sustainable healthy diets.
g. Range, 300–450.
h. Range, 400–600.
i. World Bank analysis based on BCG (2022) and Xu et al. (2021).
j. Range, 300–1,900.

per tCO$_2$eq, the agriculture sector alone could reduce non-CO$_2$ emissions by 31–35 percent relative to baseline emissions.[3] Other estimates suggest that new agricultural practices, even at a much lower price of $5 per tCO$_2$eq, can still mitigate 5–7 percent of baseline non-CO$_2$ emissions (Beach et al. 2015).

Measures to reduce methane emissions are also readily available and, in some cases, very cost-effective. As discussed in chapter 2, agriculture generates large methane emissions from livestock and nitrous oxide emissions from fertilizers, both of which are much higher than CO$_2$ in global heating potential.[4] Fortunately, many methane-reducing measures are also cost-effective. For example, 40 percent of current methane emissions could be avoided at no net cost when co-benefits are accounted for (IEA 2023b). In fact, available methane mitigation measures for energy use, agriculture, and waste management could reduce methane emissions by up to 45 percent by 2030 (UNEP and Climate and Clean Air Coalition 2021). For example, methane emissions from energy consumption can be cut effectively at very low cost by adopting well-established operational standards, implementing firm policy action, and deploying technologies to detect and repair methane leaks and control methane emissions (IEA 2022b). For emissions from agriculture, the lowest-cost methane mitigation options are from adopting technologies for rice cultivation, such as systems of rice intensification, which include alternate wetting and drying, and methane waste recovery for power generation (UNEP and Climate and Clean Air Coalition 2021).

Fifteen large, mostly middle-income, countries account for 62 percent of the world's cost-effective mitigation potential. The 15 countries include 11 MICs: Argentina, Bolivia, Brazil, China, Colombia, India, Indonesia, Mexico, Myanmar, Peru, and the Russian Federation; 3 HICs: Australia, Canada, and the United States; and 1 LIC: the Democratic Republic of Congo (figure 3.1). Likewise, cost-effective mitigation potential is highest for MICs as a

FIGURE 3.1 Sixty-Two Percent of the Global Cost-Effective Potential to Reduce Emissions from Demand-Side Measures and from Agriculture, Forestry, and Other Land Use Is Concentrated in 15 Countries

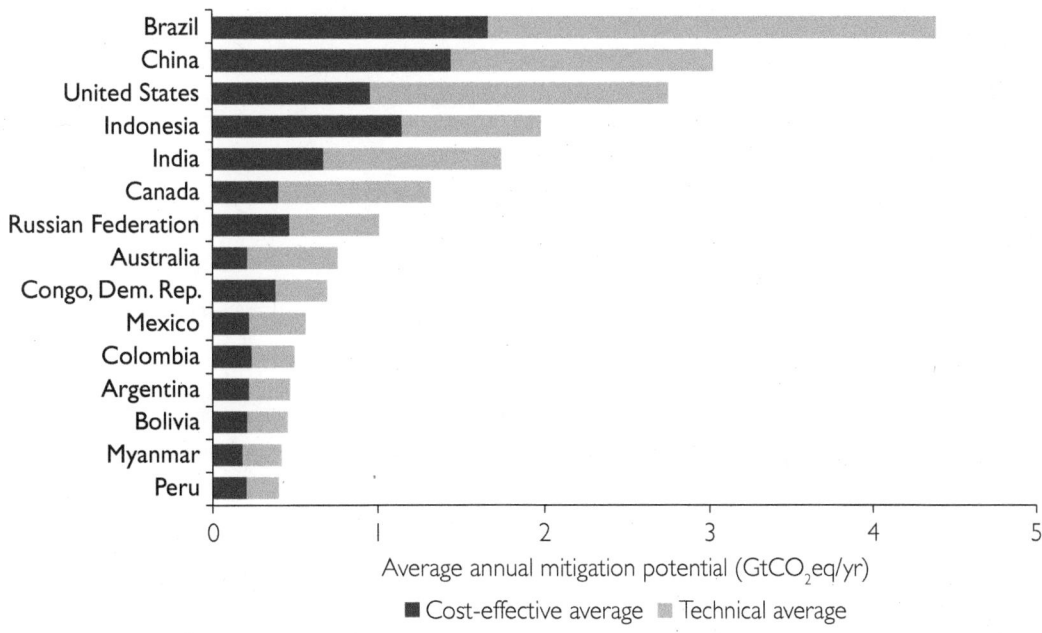

Average annual mitigation potential (GtCO$_2$eq/yr)

■ Cost-effective average ■ Technical average

Source: World Bank based on data from Roe et al. 2021.
Note: Figure shows the technical versus cost-effective average annual mitigation potential for 2020–50. GtCO$_2$eq/yr = gigatons of carbon dioxide equivalent per year.

country income group, underscoring their critical role in reducing emissions in the agrifood system and achieving the 1.5°C target (figure 3.2). Among regions, cost-effective mitigation potential is highest in East Asia and Pacific, reflecting China and Indonesia's large carbon footprints. However, it is noteworthy that cost-effective mitigation potential as a share of total mitigation potential is highest in LICs and Sub-Saharan African countries, underscoring the opportunity for those countries to largely avoid high-emissions agricultural production practices altogether (figure 3.3). Small states endowed with forests and wetlands—such as Brunei Darussalam, Maldives, Malta, Mauritius, and Trinidad and Tobago—rank in the top 15 globally when cost-effective mitigation potential is considered on a per hectare basis,

FIGURE 3.2 Cost-Effective Mitigation Potential Is the Low-Hanging Fruit for Different Regions and Country Income Groups

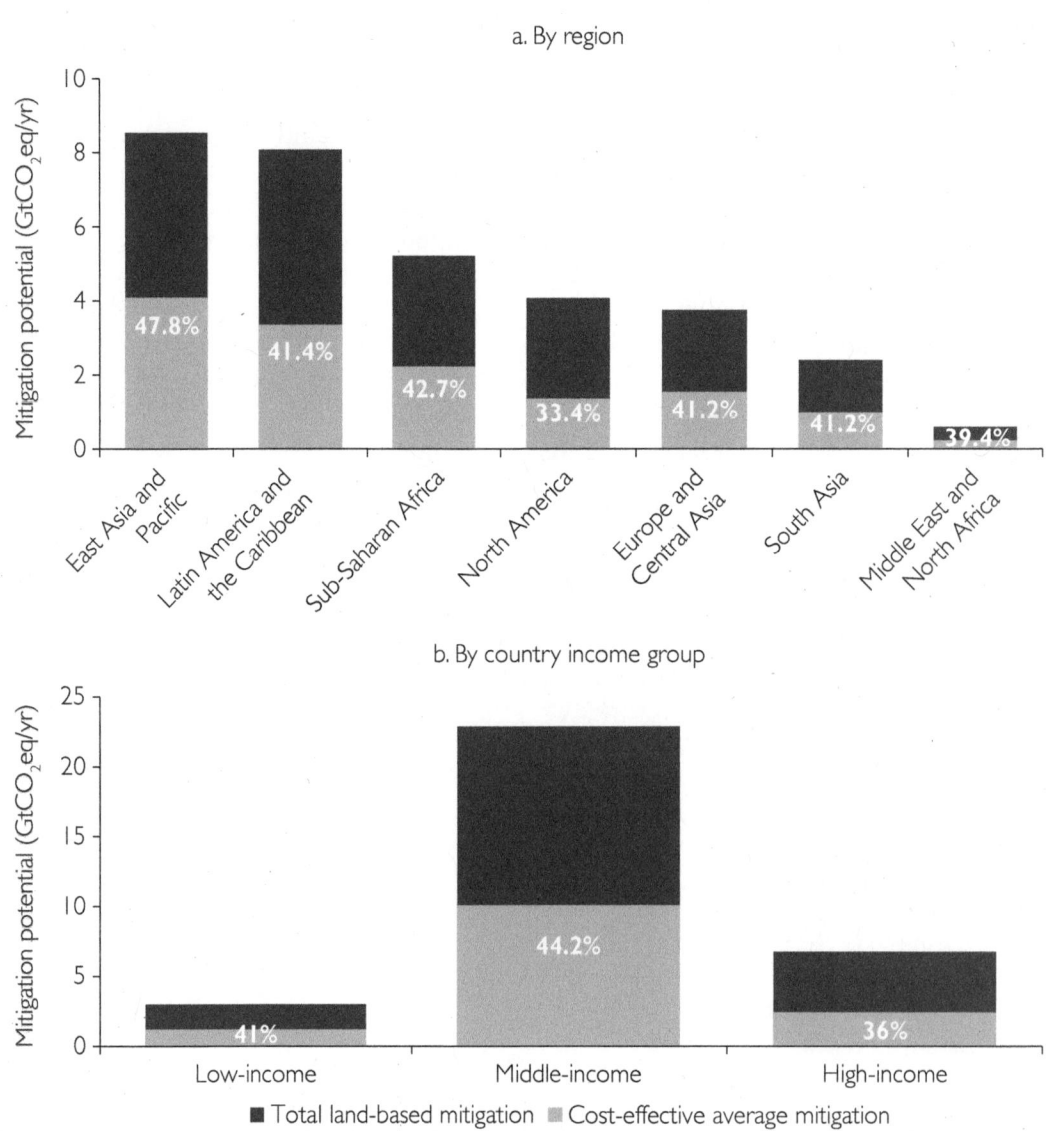

Source: World Bank based on data from Roe et al. 2021 and World Bank 2023d.
Note: Figure shows for 2020–50 the average annual volume and percentage share of cost-effective agriculture, forestry, and other land use and demand-side mitigation potential by region and country income group. GtCO$_2$eq/year = gigatons of carbon dioxide equivalent per year.

Recipe for a Livable Planet

FIGURE 3.3 Countries Have Different Pathways to Fulfilling Their Cost-Effective Mitigation Potential

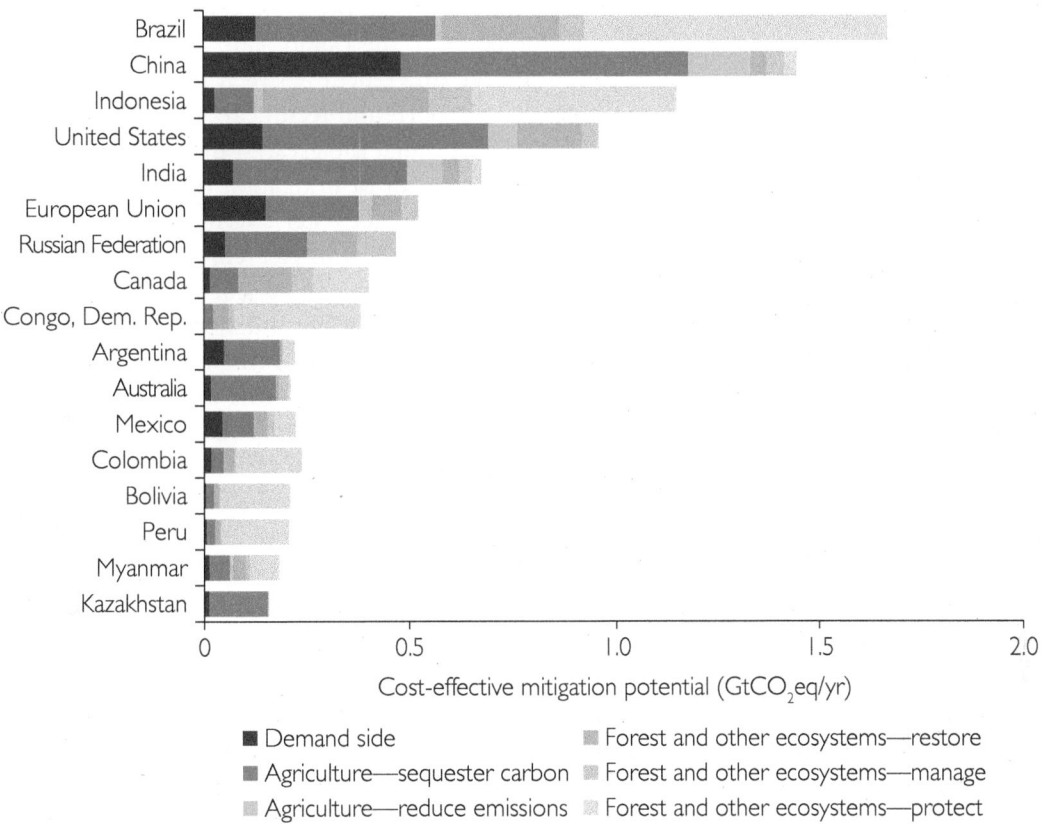

Source: World Bank based on data from Roe et al. 2021.

Note: Figure shows for the top 16 countries and the European Union the total cost-effective mitigation potential by mitigation category and measure. Much of the cost-effective mitigation potential is from sustainable land use, on-farm carbon sequestration, and demand-side measures. GtCO₂eq/yr = gigatons per carbon dioxide equivalent per year.

with Rwanda being the only LIC on this list.[5] Notably, no country from the Middle East or North Africa ranks in the top 15 in mitigation potential (figure 3.1). In fact, the Middle East and North Africa have the lowest total and cost-effective mitigation potentials among all regions (figure 3.2). Among country categories, 71.5 percent of cost-effective AFOLU mitigation opportunities are in MICs, 20.6 percent are in HICs, and 8 percent are in LICs. IPCC estimates that 30–50 percent of the cost-effective mitigation potential is achievable at costs below $20 per tCO₂eq, showing that several options are within reach in low- and middle-income settings (Nabuurs et al. 2022).

A country's pathway to cost-effective emissions reductions is shaped by its natural endowments and other factors. For example, Brazil is a large, heavily forested, meat-producing and -consuming MIC that has the highest cost-effective mitigation potential in Latin America and the Caribbean. This is because there are many cost-effective measures the country can take to reduce food system emissions, from protecting and restoring forests to shifting to healthy and sustainable diets and sequestering carbon in agriculture (figure 3.3) (Roe et al. 2021). In contrast, the pathway to cost-effective decarbonization is much narrower for the Democratic Republic of Congo. This is because that country has a significantly lower income per capita and less meat production and consumption. As a result, the only real pathway to cost-effective decarbonization is to protect forests and other ecosystems in the similarly large and heavily forested nation. That said, the feasibility of long-term mitigation actions, like forest protection, in the Democratic Republic of Congo is much less than it is for Brazil because of large differences between the two countries' national financial resources; external financial support; and technical, jurisdictional, and institutional capacities. Meanwhile, for China and India, the greatest mitigation potential is from carbon sequestration in agriculture (48 percent of mitigation potential in China and 63 percent in India). This includes measures to reduce enteric fermentation, increase synthetic fertilizer efficiency, and manage water resources in rice cultivation. However, China has more mitigation potential (34 percent) through demand-side measures, such as shifting toward low-emissions diets and reducing food waste. For Indonesia—another large Asian MIC—the pathway is different from those for India and China but similar to that for Brazil, with protection of forests and other ecosystems accounting for about half of its cost-effective mitigation potential. Among HIC countries, the United States has the greatest cost-effective mitigation potential, and carbon sequestration in agriculture constitutes a major part of its emissions reduction pathway, followed by demand-side measures such as shifting from livestock to plant- and lab-based proteins (Costa et al. 2022). Figure 3.3 also shows that the European Union's (EU's) cost-effective mitigation potential is significantly less than that of the United States despite their having similar decarbonization pathways, with carbon sequestration in agriculture and demand-side measures accounting for large shares of cost-effective mitigation potential in both regions.

A country's context also determines its opportunities for cost-saving agrifood mitigation, with negative abatement costs, that can increase farm profitability. Cost-saving mitigation options, or negative MACs, account for more than 35 percent of technical mitigation potential in China's agriculture sector, 80 percent in India's, and 75 percent in Bangladesh's (figures 3.4–3.6). Rice and crop producers in all three countries have multiple cost-saving mitigation options—such as fertilizer management, conservation and zero tillage, and rice water management—given the prevalence of rice cultivation and other crop production. In contrast, only China has cost-saving mitigation options in livestock production, including animal feed additive use, manure management, and improved breeding (figure 3.4). According to studies covering the entire AFOLU sector in Mexico (Sapkota et al. 2020), Nigeria (Cervigni, Dvorak, and Rogers 2013), South Africa (South Africa Department of Environmental Affairs 2014), and Viet Nam (Escobar Carbonari et al. 2019), forest management and agroforestry are cost-saving mitigation options, reflecting the value of these options in carbon sequestration (appendix B, table B.1). In Viet Nam, there are also multiple cost-saving mitigation options for land use changes, namely, replacing rice areas with shrimp farming and planting trees, such as rubber or acacia trees, on bare land. Meanwhile, other studies show that Kenya's dairy production (Khatri-Chhetri, Wilkes, and Odhong 2020) and Latvia's crop production (Popluga et al. 2017) have cost-saving mitigation options similar to the livestock and crop production options in other countries. Livestock mitigation options, such as supplementing fodder and providing concentrated feed to large ruminants, also have negative MACs when spillover benefits are factored in (Sapkota et al. 2019).

Country-specific MAC information can guide policies and strategic investments in food system decarbonization. A key challenge for policy makers is the lack of accurate, relevant,

FIGURE 3.4 In China, the Marginal Abatement Cost Curve Indicates That the Most Cost-Effective Mitigation Options for Livestock and Crop Production Include Better Livestock Feeding and Breeding, Fertilizer Management, and Water Management in Rice Paddies

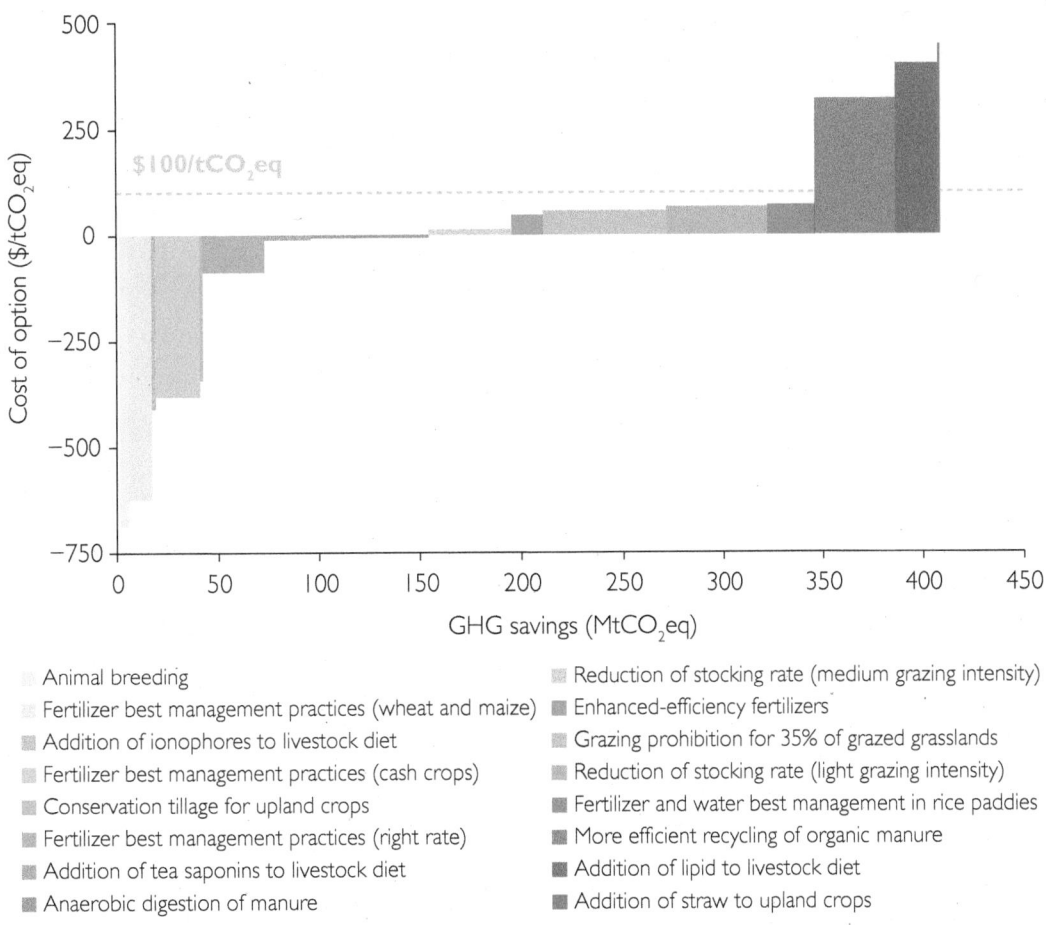

Animal breeding

Fertilizer best management practices (wheat and maize)

Addition of ionophores to livestock diet

Fertilizer best management practices (cash crops)

Conservation tillage for upland crops

Fertilizer best management practices (right rate)

Addition of tea saponins to livestock diet

Anaerobic digestion of manure

Reduction of stocking rate (medium grazing intensity)

Enhanced-efficiency fertilizers

Grazing prohibition for 35% of grazed grasslands

Reduction of stocking rate (light grazing intensity)

Fertilizer and water best management in rice paddies

More efficient recycling of organic manure

Addition of lipid to livestock diet

Addition of straw to upland crops

Source: World Bank based on data from Nayak et al. 2015.

Note: Figure shows the cost of mitigation options associated with livestock and crop production (represented in shades of green and red, respectively) in relation to the savings in greenhouse gases (GHGs). When arranged from least to most costly along the x-axis these mitigation options, represented as scaled bars, form a "curve" referred to as marginal abatement cost curve. The area of each bar represents the total cost of the respective mitigation option (that is, the volume, expressed in $MtCO_2eq$ on the x-axis, multiplied by the unit cost, expressed in $/tCO_2eq$ on the y-axis). Several mitigation options toward the left of the graph have negative marginal abatement costs—that is, their implementation saves money. Two mitigation options, the least cost-effective, are not represented in the figure to enable visualization: (1) addition of probiotics to livestock diet, $7,080/tCO_2eq$ (tons of carbon dioxide equivalent) and (2) addition of biochar to soil, $5,478/tCO_2eq$. Exchange rate: $1 = ¥ 4.94; $MtCO_2eq$ = megatons of carbon dioxide equivalent; tCO_2eq = tons of carbon dioxide equivalent; ¥ = yuan.

and globally comparable MAC information for cost-effective mitigation actions and defining realistic and actionable targets for Nationally Determined Contributions (NDCs) and agriculture and food sector commitments. There are three main reasons for this challenge. First, country-level assessments of food system MACs have limited geographical coverage, especially for the Middle East and North Africa, Europe and Central Asia, and some countries with the greatest mitigation potential, such as the Arab Republic of Egypt and Russia. Second, existing MAC estimates focus on mitigation options in AFOLU, the agriculture sector, or subsectors (crops or livestock) but do not cover food transport and

FIGURE 3.5 In India, the Marginal Abatement Cost Curve Indicates That 80 Percent of the Technical Mitigation Potential for Agriculture Could Be Achieved by Adopting Cost-Saving Measures Alone

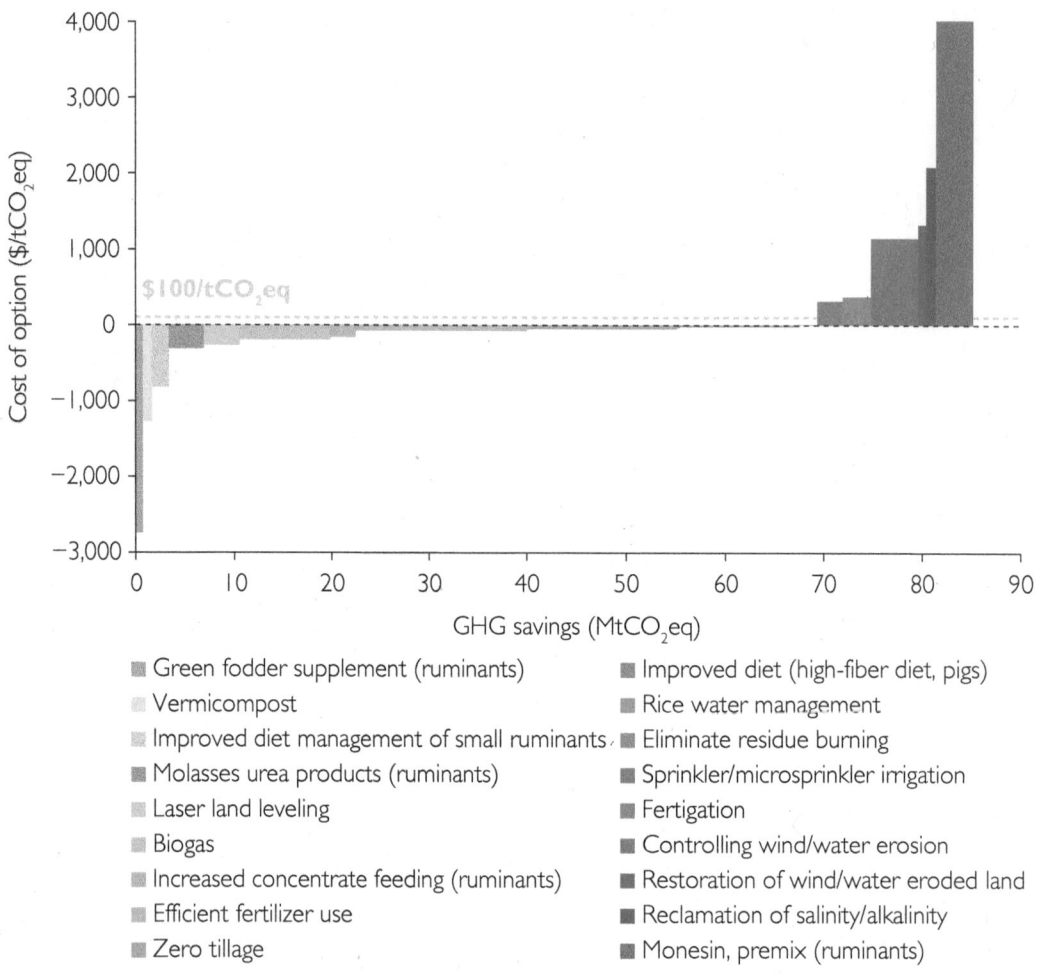

- Green fodder supplement (ruminants)
- Vermicompost
- Improved diet management of small ruminants
- Molasses urea products (ruminants)
- Laser land leveling
- Biogas
- Increased concentrate feeding (ruminants)
- Efficient fertilizer use
- Zero tillage
- Improved diet (high-fiber diet, pigs)
- Rice water management
- Eliminate residue burning
- Sprinkler/microsprinkler irrigation
- Fertigation
- Controlling wind/water erosion
- Restoration of wind/water eroded land
- Reclamation of salinity/alkalinity
- Monesin, premix (ruminants)

Source: World Bank based on data from Sapkota et al. 2019.

Note: Figure shows the cost of mitigation options associated with livestock and crop production (represented in shades of green and red, respectively) in relation to the savings in greenhouse gases (GHGs). Three mitigation options—efficient fertilizer use, zero tillage, and rice water management—could deliver more than 50 percent of the total technical abatement potential. One mitigation option, the least cost-effective, is not represented in the figure to enable visualization: reclamation of waterlogged soil, $5,014/tCO$_2$eq (tons of carbon dioxide equivalent). Exchange rate: $1 = Rs 82.67; MtCO$_2$eq = megatons of carbon dioxide equivalent.

processing, food loss and waste, dietary changes, or other upstream and downstream parts of the agrifood system with implications for GHG emissions. Third, there is limited (1) analysis of public investments in food system mitigation, (2) knowledge of public and private costs of adopting mitigation practices, and (3) understanding of mitigation actions' yields, income gains, and gross and net costs. To address these gaps, the World Bank is developing a MAC database with country-specific estimates for its food system investments. This database will span major food production systems and abatement options with policy-relevant and country-specific detail, while specifying its scope and limitations.[6] The database will be an important tool for upstream sector planning and for determining future investments in food system decarbonization that are in line with the 1.5°C goal.

FIGURE 3.6 **In Bangladesh, the Marginal Abatement Cost Curve Indicates That 75 Percent of the Technical Mitigation Potential for Agriculture Could Be Achieved by Adopting Cost-Saving Measures Alone**

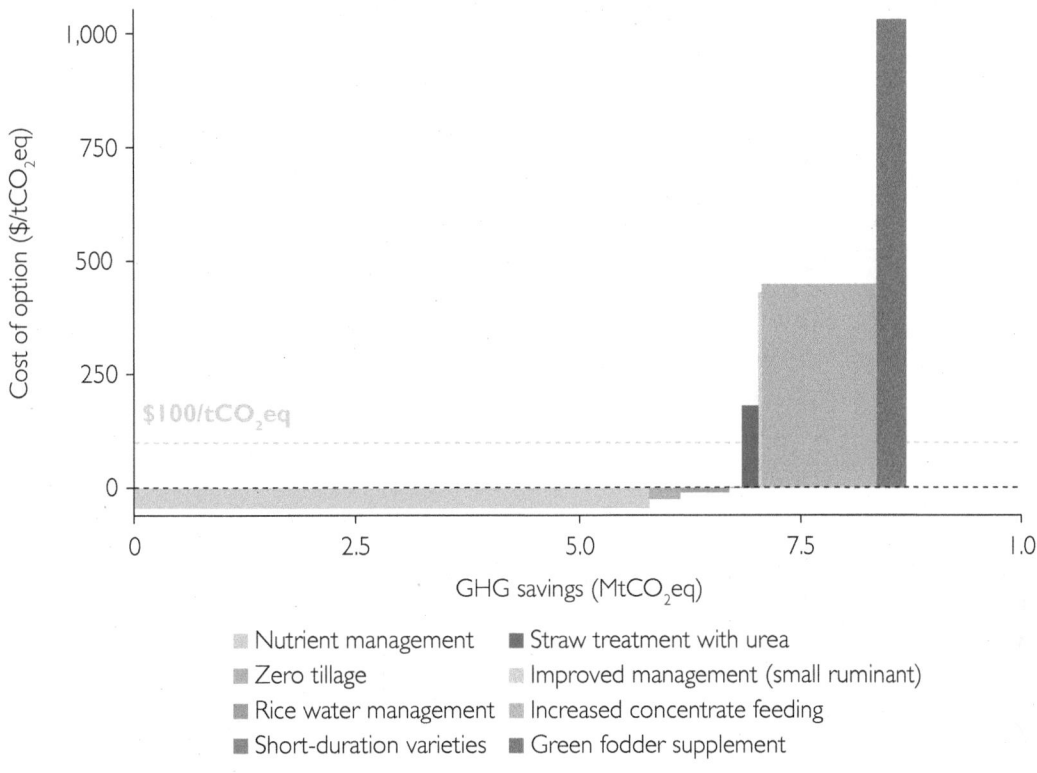

Source: World Bank based on data from Sapkota et al. 2021.

Note: Figure shows the mitigation options associated with livestock and crop production (represented in shades of green and red, respectively) in relation to the savings in greenhouse gases (GHGs). Three mitigation options—nutrient management, zero tillage, and rice water management—are cost-saving. One mitigation option, the least cost-effective, is not represented in the figure to enable visualization: vermicompost, $5,623.7/tCO$_2$eq (tons of carbon dioxide equivalent). Exchange rate: $1 = Tk 106.5; MtCO$_2$eq = million tons of carbon dioxide equivalent; Tk = taka.

The adoption of cost-effective mitigation solutions can be hindered by inertia in the agrifood system. There are several factors that contribute to this inertia. First are cost factors. The need to build infrastructure or make long-lived investments, for example in plantations or irrigation systems, can be costly initially. Second are policy factors. Companies often cite the lack of a robust policy framework as a barrier to following through on their low-emissions or net zero commitments. Likewise, changing trade policies or government support programs can be a time-consuming political process. Third are capacity factors. Applying low-emissions practices and new technologies requires reskilling workers, and the reallocation of land to cropping, forestry, or conservation requires experienced long term-land use planning. Fourth are engagement factors. Transitioning the agrifood system requires engagement from many stakeholders, including governments, businesses, and citizens, many of whom may not prioritize changing their behaviors for planetary concerns. That said, chapter 4 shows that there are many effective and innovative solutions to address these factors of inertia and improve the enabling environment for reduced agrifood system emissions.

High-Income Countries' Greatest Opportunities for Reducing Agrifood System Emissions Are from Curbing Energy Emissions, Aiding Developing Nations in Their Shift to Low-Emission Pathways, and Promoting Low-Emission Foods

This section shows that HICs are major contributors to both historical and current agrifood system emissions and can aid developing countries in transforming to low-emission pathways. As described in chapter 2, HICs contribute fewer source emissions than MICs. However, the consumer demand for high-emitting food products, particularly meat, in HICs drives 60 percent of emissions across all sources. This makes dietary changes in HICs a major opportunity area for reducing global agrifood system emissions. The pie chart in figure 3.7 also shows that pre- and post-production emissions make up a larger part of HICs' emissions profile than they do in LICs. But when the 108 MICs are divided into upper- and lower-middle-income countries (UMICs and LMICs, respectively, each of about the same number of countries), HICs contribute more to pre- and post-production emissions than either UMICs or LMICs. Moreover, HICs were the first countries to embark on a fossil fuel–based development model, which several MICs later followed. HICs are also the best positioned to offer financial and technical support to MICs and LICs in their transition to a low-emitting agrifood system. Therefore, this section on HICs will (1) examine how energy

FIGURE 3.7 High-Income Countries Are Major Contributors to Annual Agrifood System Emissions

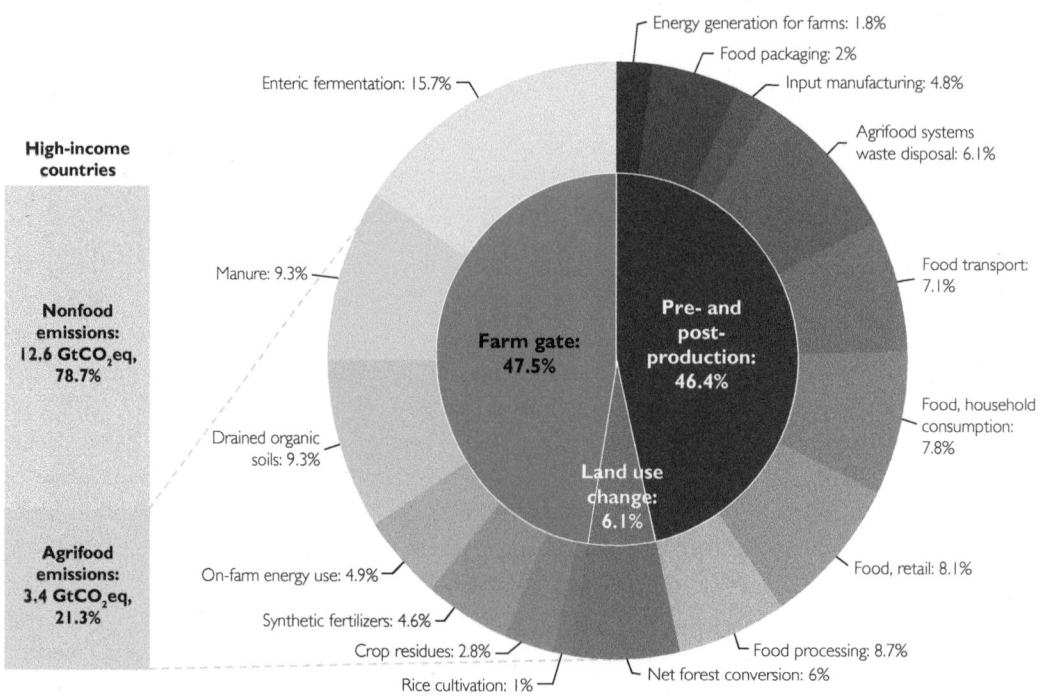

Source: World Bank based on data from FAOSTAT 2023c and World Bank 2023d.
Note: Left: Agrifood system emissions as share of total global greenhouse gas emissions (data account for methane, nitrous oxide, and carbon dioxide emissions), 2018–20 annual average. Right: Emissions categorized by three main subcategories and their individual components. GtCO$_2$eq = gigatons of carbon dioxide equivalent.

efficiency and renewable energy can bring down emissions, (2) analyze HICs' comparative capacity to offer financial and technical mitigation solutions to MICs and LICs, and (3) discuss how consumer demand for animal-source foods (ASFs) drives emissions and how HICs can contribute to widespread dietary changes that can drastically reduce global emissions.

The high economic costs of climate-related events in HICs underscore their motivation to slash global agrifood system emissions. Fourteen of the 20 costliest climate-related extreme events since 1990 took place in high-income countries, including 12 in the United States. Seven of the 10 economies with the largest economic disaster–related losses since 1990 are categorized as high income—namely, from highest to lowest losses, the United States, Japan, Germany, Puerto Rico (US), Australia, France, and Italy (Guha-Sapir, Hoyois, and Below 2015). Since 1998, high-income countries reported $2 trillion in losses from climate-related disasters such as floods, droughts, heat waves, and forest fires (Guha-Sapir, Hoyois, and Below 2015; IPCC 2022c). These high costs are driven up by the increased intensity and frequency of extreme events (Hoeppe 2016), population density, and economic development in exposed areas (Botzen, Deschenes, and Sanders 2019). Moreover, real disaster-related economic losses are even higher because of the omission of indirect losses and the underreporting of small-scale and slow-onset events, such as sea level rise, which are predicted to increasingly cause human and economic losses (Eckstein, Kuenzel, and Schaefer 2021). Research shows that agriculture absorbs around a quarter of all disaster-related losses in all countries (FAO 2015). But the Food and Agriculture Organization of the United Nations (FAO) also found that upper-middle-income and high-income countries experienced the greatest disaster-related agricultural losses, costing more than $170 billion between 2008 and 2018. Moreover, actual losses are suspected to be much higher, given limited data and measurement methodologies (FAO 2021a). That said, high-income countries face a lower burden than middle- and low-income countries (United Nations Office for Disaster Risk Reduction 2022) in the percentage of total gross domestic product (GDP) lost, and no high-income country is among the most affected in terms of disaster-related fatalities.

The Global Agrifood System's Energy Demands Are Highest in HICs and on the Rise Globally, but Alternative Low-Emission Energy Sources Provide a Counterbalance

The global agrifood system is becoming more energy intensive. Energy is consumed at three main stages of the agrifood system: (1) preharvest, during manufacture of fertilizers and pesticides; (2) primary production, to operate farm machinery and buildings; and (3) postharvest, for the heating and cooling needs of food processing, packaging, transport, and retail, plus final cooking. Energy and fuel consumption is directly proportional to the length and complexity of food chains, use of refrigerated transport, and the stringency of local food safety regulations (OECD 2017). Today, most of these energy needs are met by fossil fuel–based energy. As shown in chapter 2, on-farm energy and electricity use accounts for 5.8 percent of all agrifood system emissions, though the agrifood system's total energy use is much higher when energy needs in all aspects of the agrifood value chain are included. Indeed, one-third of the world's total global energy consumption is related to agrifood systems (FAO 2011), and energy use accounts for a third of all agrifood system emissions (Crippa et al. 2021). The doubling of energy-intensive pre- and post-production emissions, especially in HICs (Tubiello et al. 2022), led to a 17 percent increase of agrifood systems emissions between 1990 and 2015 (Crippa et al. 2021). The agrifood system's 15 percent increase in energy use since 1990 was caused largely by increased mechanization and fertilizer and pesticide use in MICs (fertilizer production and use is discussed in the MIC section of this chapter) (Abdelaziz, Saidur, and Mekhilef 2011). In 2019, agriculture emissions from energy use reached 1,029 megatons carbon dioxide equivalent (MtCO$_2$eq) per year, a 7 percent increase since 1990, roughly half of which resulted from fossil fuel combustion to generate electricity. In fact, on-farm emissions from electricity had a mean annual growth rate of more than 6 percent, a threefold increase, making electricity the largest source of energy use in agriculture since 2005, exceeding coal, fuel oil, natural gas, and motor gasoline (Flammini et al. 2022). Greater energy needs translate into higher food prices (World Bank Group 2022).

Most food processing-to-consumption emissions come from energy use in HICs. Forty-six percent of agrifood system emissions in HICs come from pre- and post-production processes. For comparison, 35 percent of agrifood system emissions in MICs and only 6 percent in LICs come from these processes. The biggest difference between HICs and MICs is that the processing, packaging, transport, and retail stages emit a much larger share of emissions in HICs than in MICs: these stages account for a quarter of all agrifood system emissions in HICs, but only 11 percent in MICs and less than 2 percent in LICs. Overall, these post-production phases account for 13.1 percent of total agrifood system emissions (figure 2.2) and 18 percent of AFOLU emissions (Poore and Nemecek 2018). This includes food processing, which contributes 4 percent to the agrifood system's total footprint. The most energy-intensive food processing comes from cheese production, sugar production, vegetable oil refining, and other fruit and vegetable processing. A study (Brueske et al. 2012) shows that 46 percent of the electricity used in the US's food and beverage processing sector is consumed by pumps, fans, mixers, and other machines. A total of 27 percent is consumed by cooling and refrigeration systems, 19 percent is consumed by the everyday operating needs of processing facilities, and the rest is consumed by heating needs. Likewise, another study shows that 10 percent of all energy consumed worldwide is used to produce food that is lost or wasted, which is discussed in greater detail in the MIC section of this chapter (FAO 2017b).

Renewable energy mitigation options are already cost-effective, and costs continue to decline. Renewable energy is a cost-effective mitigation strategy, with abatement costs of only $20–$50 per ton of carbon dioxide (Elshurafa et al. 2021). Table 3.1 shows that improved energy efficiency measures—including electrified farm machinery, on-farm renewable energy, and green cold chains—have a technical mitigation potential of at least 1.4 GtCO$_2$eq per year, with about 0.9 gigatons obtainable cost-effectively. Moreover, these low costs have continued to decline. For example, the cost for solar installations declined by 82 percent between 2010 and 2021, and the cost for onshore wind installations declined by 35 percent over the same period (IRENA 2023).

Renewable energy can reduce the agrifood system's dependence on fossil fuel energy and prevent greenhouse gas emissions (Karwacka et al. 2020). In 2022 alone, renewable-generated electricity avoided 600 million tons of CO$_2$ (IEA 2022d) that would have been emitted had that electricity come from fossil fuels (Wiatros-Motyka 2023). As an example, estimates (Elshurafa et al. 2021) suggest that deploying renewable energy in Saudi Arabia's power sector would reduce carbon emissions by 25–41 percent by 2040, which is equivalent to 66–114 million tons of emissions. Likewise, Europe's greenhouse gas emissions would have been 7 percent higher by 2012 if the EU had not started adopting renewable energy sources in 2005 (European Environment Agency 2015). The adoption of renewable energy in the agrifood system can drastically cut the sector's emissions. For instance, replacing one-quarter of India's 8.8 million diesel irrigation pumps with solar ones would reduce emissions by 11.5 million tons per year. This is more than twice the 5 million tons in global emissions that electric vehicles and solar panels prevented in 2020.[7] That said, measures should be put in place to ensure that powering irrigation with affordable and accessible clean energy does not lead to unsustainable water use (Rodella, Zaveri, and Bertone 2023).

Deploying renewables leads to other positive outcomes, such as increased employment and reduced pollution. For example, expanding renewable energy generation has created job opportunities (IRENA and ILO 2022) and spurred innovation in the energy sector (GGI Insights 2023). As of 2021, the renewable energy sector employed 12.7 million individuals, compared to 65 million employed in the general energy sector in 2019 (IEA 2022c). Moreover, this number is expected to climb, reaching 38.2 million employed by 2030 (IRENA and ILO 2022). For example, in Kenya, 50,000 people were directly employed in decentralized renewable energy in 2021, outnumbering people employed by the utility-scale power sector by a ratio of more than three to one (IRENA and ILO 2022). Renewable energy is also cleaner than fossil fuel energy, contributing fewer air pollutants (Galimova, Ram, and Breyer 2022). Indeed, annual deaths attributed to energy sector–related air pollution would fall by approximately 97 percent if that energy came from renewable energy sources; that is equivalent to preventing 150,000 pollution-related deaths by 2050 (Galimova, Ram, and Breyer 2022). Renewables also increase energy efficiency throughout the agrifood value chain, reduce the cost of inputs, waste less, and boost profits (Conti, Zanello, and Hall 2021; FAO and IRENA 2021; Gokarn and Kuthambalayan 2017).

Renewable energy has bolstered both pre- and post-production activities within the agrifood system. In the pre-production phase, it offers a sustainable solution to powering fertilizer production. Traditional nitrogen fertilizer production, including ammonia production, relies heavily on energy-intensive, high-emission fossil fuels, but renewable energy can replace the need for them. In the post-production phase, renewable energy fortifies key areas like cold storage, transportation, and distribution, optimizing food product quality and safety while curbing emissions. For instance, solar-powered refrigeration units can substantially decrease food waste and bolster food security in remote, off-grid areas (FAO and IRENA 2021). Additionally, solar dryers tailored for marine products (Sethi et al. 2021) and biomass-based dryers designed for rice paddies (Yahya, Fahmi, and Hasibuan 2022) have demonstrated superior performance over conventional drying methods. It is noteworthy that in developing countries, cooking, an essential post-production activity, consumes more energy than on-farm operations. As of 2019, 35 percent of the populations in such countries still relied on wood fuel (FAO and IRENA 2021), a practice that carries environmental burdens and health risks (IRENA 2022). In fact, wood-fuel cooking has been linked to approximately 3.2 million premature deaths every year (WHO 2022a), with women and children disproportionately affected (FAO and IRENA 2021). Clean cooking, which is healthier, uses lower-emitting stoves, and is discussed in greater detail in the MIC section of this chapter, can fuel stoves with sustainable biomass, biogas (IRENA 2022), solar power (IEA 2023a), or other renewable-based electricity.

The adoption of solar technologies has unlocked new avenues for sustainability and energy efficiency in agriculture. Solar-powered irrigation has been gaining traction since the 1970s (Hartung and Pluschke 2018), by improved efficiency and innovative financing models (FAO and IRENA 2021). As of December 2020, India has been at the forefront of its adoption, deploying over 272,000 solar-powered irrigation systems (Ministry of New and Renewable Energy, Government of India 2021), while Bangladesh, with just over 1,500 systems, aims for 10,000 by 2027. Farmers in India and East Africa have seen tangible benefits from installing solar-powered water pumps with approximately half of Indian users reporting a 50 percent income boost compared to rain-fed irrigation (Suman 2018), and Rwandan farmers achieved one-third-higher yields, even cultivating crops during dry seasons for the first time (Energy 4 Impact 2021). This shift toward solar irrigation could reduce the energy demands and mitigate the environmental consequences of the projected doubling of irrigated areas in Sub-Saharan Africa by 2050 (FAO 2020), especially if solar power is used to replace diesel or grid-connected pumps. Similarly, agrifood system actors in countries such as Kenya (SunCulture 2023), Nigeria (Cold Hubs, n.d.), and Rwanda (Puri, Rincon, and Maltsoglou 2021) are already deploying low-cost solar panels and batteries to power primary production. Likewise, decentralized solar-powered mini-grids can make these energy sources and electricity accessible to farmers in remote areas (Amjith and Bavanish 2022; FAO and IRENA 2021). Agrivoltaics, which places solar panels among crops or livestock, has been shown to maintain yields while boosting land and water productivity (AL-agele et al. 2021; Gonocruz et al. 2021; Trommsdorff et al. 2021). In some HICs, including France and Israel, agrivoltaics has increased land use efficiency by 60–70 percent and reduced water needs by 14 to 29 percent (Dupraz et al. 2011). To date, 14 gigawatts (GW) of agrivoltaics has been installed globally (Agrivoltaics, n.d.).

There are additional innovative practices that have been shown to reduce the agrifood system's energy needs. One such practice is the use of tidal energy, renewable energy powered by the natural ocean currents, to power desalination systems. Such an application would reduce energy costs by 31 to 42 percent compared to those of conventional systems (Ling et al. 2018). On-farm batteries, thermal storage, and other energy storage systems can stabilize the supply of renewable electricity by storing excess energy when energy generation is high and stabilize the energy grid when generation is low (Clairand et al. 2020; Koçak, Fernandez, and Paksoy 2020). Another option is using geothermal energy, heat energy that can be harvested from the earth. It is an abundant renewable energy source that can heat buildings and greenhouses, thereby reducing both energy consumption and costs while maintaining productivity (Bundschuh et al. 2017).

The adoption of renewable energy sources is growing, particularly in major economies. According to the International Renewable Energy Agency (IRENA), renewables accounted for 83 percent of all new electricity capacity and 30 percent of global electricity generation in 2022 (IEA 2022d). Concurrently, the market share of fossil fuel energy has declined since 2015 as renewables such as wind and solar have increased (figure 3.8). In 2022, wind and solar provided 12 percent of the world's electricity, a new high, jointly making up more than 50 percent of total installed renewables capacity. Renewables other than wind and solar, such as hydropower, marine energy, geothermal, and bioenergy, are also becoming more prevalent, albeit to a lesser extent (figure 3.8). Projections by the International Energy Agency (IEA) indicate that within the next three years, renewables are expected to become the primary energy source for electricity generation globally, overtaking coal (IEA 2022d). National efforts have also contributed to the growth of renewables. For example, China's 14th Five-Year Plan for Renewable Energy, published in 2022, sets ambitious targets for renewable energy use. Similarly, in April 2023, India set a target of 500 GW of non-fossil fuel power capacity by 2030. The EU, for its part, has accelerated its solar photovoltaics and wind deployment in response to the recent energy crisis that arose from Russia's

FIGURE 3.8 Wind and Solar Energy Are Reducing Dependence on Fossil Fuels

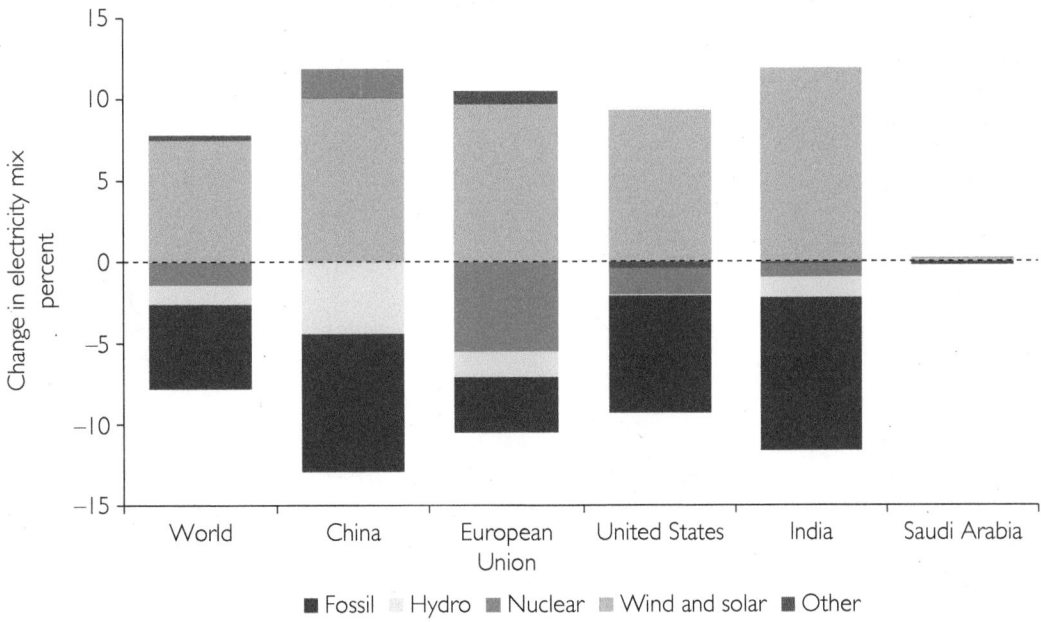

Source: World Bank based on data from Wiatros-Motyka 2023.
Note: Figure shows the change in the electricity mix for the world and selected countries between 2015 and 2022. The European Union had an exceptional year in 2022 with record low nuclear and hydro generation.

invasion of Ukraine. These deployments added 50 GW in renewable energy capacity in 2022, a 45 percent increase since 2021. To spur further growth, the EU enacted new policies and targets in its REPowerEU Plan and Green Deal Industrial Plan (IEA 2022d).

Renewable technologies have penetrated some countries more than others. Among all countries, China generates the most electricity from renewables into its energy systems, surpassing the United States and the EU combined (IRENA 2023), reaching 1,161 GW in 2022 (figure 3.9). China is also expanding its renewable electricity generation capacity annually, reaching 160 GW of expanded capacity in 2022, which equals half of the world's expanded generation capacity for that year (IEA, n.d.-a). Germany and the United States, along with other HICs, also invest heavily in renewable energy infrastructure, with Germany's capacity amounting to 148 GW in 2022 and the United States reaching 352 GW in the same year (IRENA 2023). Other major MICs besides China are expanding their renewable installations. For example, Brazil had 175 GW of renewable energy generation capacity in 2022 and India had 163 GW (IRENA 2023). Among low-income countries, Ethiopia has the greatest renewable energy capacity, amounting to almost 6 GW in 2022 (IRENA 2023).

Governments can incentivize the further expansion of energy efficiency in pre- and postharvest operations. The world is offtrack to meet the Sustainable Development Goal (SDG) 7.3 target of doubling the global energy efficiency rate by 2030.[8] Part of the reason is that the food industry has the slowest progress in energy efficiency among economic sectors (IEA 2022a) because the growing emissions intensity from pre- and post-production operations offsets energy efficiency gains in other parts of the agrifood sector (Tubiello et al. 2022). There are several policy actions that can improve agrifood system energy efficiency. For example, governments could repurpose the $1 trillion worth of fossil fuel subsidies (IEA, n.d-b.) toward building energy efficiency. Other proven policies include regulating

FIGURE 3.9 China Leads Global Growth in Renewable Electricity Generation

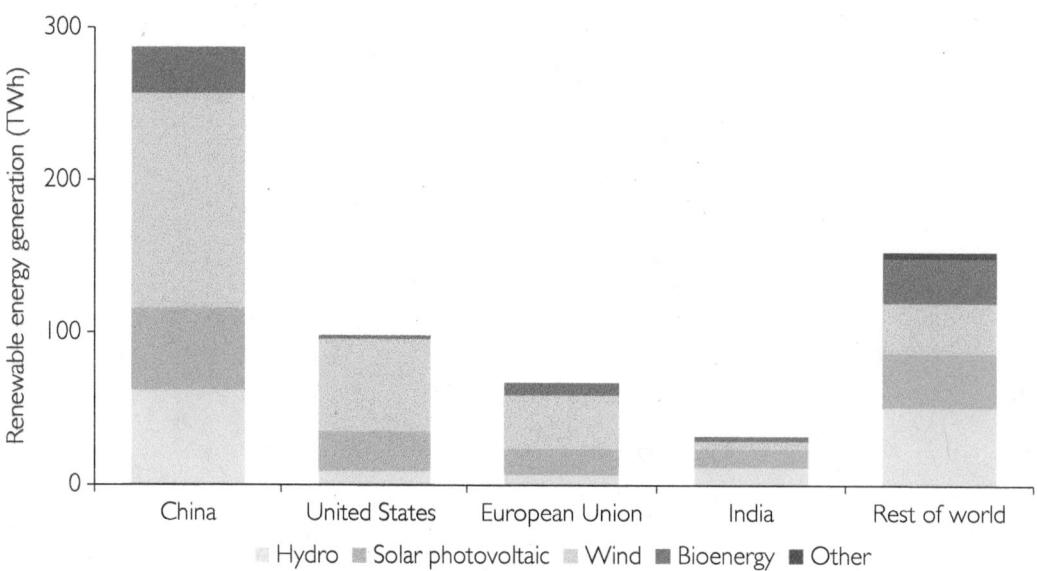

Source: World Bank based on data from IEA 2022d.
Note: Figure shows the increase in renewable electricity generation by technology and country and region for 2020–21. TWh = terawatt-hours.

minimum energy performance standards for appliances; fuel economy standards for heavy-duty vehicles; voluntary schemes, such as International Organization for Standardization (ISO) certification, for energy savings; and research and development (R&D) investments for more energy-efficient appliances, vehicles, and machinery (UNECE 2015). Policy incentives for installing and maintaining energy management systems, such as insulation and dehumidification systems (Licina and Sekhar 2012; Martzopoulou, Firfiris, and Kotsopoulos 2020; Metzger 2017), can save 5–30 percent of the energy used in food processing (Aziz, Sumiyoshi, and Akashi 2017; Jo et al. 2017). Other incentives, for example, to reduce transport distances between production and processing sites and to develop horizontal bunker silos, could reduce the energy intensity of food transport and storage (Niesseron et al. 2020; Wieben 2019). Notably, NDCs include several policy actions and incentives that target energy efficiencies in the food system. An analysis of 163 NDCs found that 45 refer to specific measures to reduce GHG emissions from agrifood systems, with the majority of them referring to utilizing biomass waste for energy generation.

HICs Are Positioned to Transfer Financial and Technical Support to LICs and MICs

High-income countries are uniquely positioned to assist low- and middle-income countries in reducing agrifood system emissions. One of the primary ways they can help is by providing financial support. This could be in the form of grants, concessional loans, or climate finance. Moreover, many high-income countries are at the forefront of technological advancements. Thus, they can leverage their expertise to transfer advanced technologies to low- and middle-income nations, empowering them to adopt low-emission agrifood system practices. However, merely transferring technology is not enough. Comprehensive capacity-building initiatives are also needed to ensure that low- and middle-income countries can effectively utilize these technologies. Chapter 4 reviews international climate frameworks that govern such financial and capacity transfers from HICs to developing countries. That being said, middle-income countries must also recognize their own contributions to GHG emissions, especially from agricultural activities. Potential areas for HICs to support MICs and LICs in mitigating agrifood system emissions include the following:

1. **Financial assistance:** Allocate funds for climate projects, focusing on mitigation, adaptation, renewable energy, technology transfer, and capacity building.
2. **Technology transfer:** Share cutting-edge technologies and expertise, particularly in areas such as renewable energy, agriculture, and waste management.
3. **Capacity building:** Offer tailored programs to help middle-income countries develop the necessary infrastructure and skill sets.
4. **Knowledge sharing and best practices:** Create platforms for exchanging experiences and insights to help middle-income countries refine their climate strategies.
5. **Policy support and advocacy:** Champion global climate action and support middle-income nations in international arenas, promoting sustainable policies and facilitating access to global resources.
6. **Collaborative projects:** Initiate joint ventures that address shared climate challenges, fostering mutual growth and knowledge exchange.
7. **Trade and investment:** Encourage sustainable trading practices and invest in green initiatives in middle-income countries.
8. **Climate diplomacy:** Use diplomatic channels to amplify the concerns and needs of low- and middle-income countries during global climate discussions.
9. **Debt relief and green debt swaps:** Consider financial mechanisms such as debt relief, allowing resources to be redirected toward eco-friendly initiatives.
10. **Support for vulnerable communities:** Focus on aiding those disproportionately affected by climate change, ensuring that they have access to resilient infrastructure and support systems.

HICs Can Decrease Consumer Demand for Emissions-Intensive Foods by Fully Pricing Animal-Source Foods through Repurposed Subsidies and Promoting Sustainable Food Options

As global populations become wealthier, they consume more emissions-intensive foods, such as meat and dairy. As discussed in chapter 2, the food system transitioned a half-century ago to meet food shortages by increasing the availability and affordability of calories through increased staple crop production (FAO 2022c). However, the agrifood system transitioned again over the last couple of decades to meet a greater demand for resource-intensive foods (figure 3.10) (Clark et al. 2020; Miller et al. 2022). Cattle meat production grew from 53 to 68 million tons from 1990 to 2020, a 30 percent increase, and added close to 0.25 $GtCO_2eq$ to the atmosphere. By comparison, the tripling of poultry meat production during that period, from 35 to 120 million tons, added only 0.04 $GtCO_2eq$ (FAOSTAT 2023a, 2023b). This transition was spurred by income growth and urbanization, which are linked to higher demand for animal-source foods (Popkin and Gordon-Larsen 2004). For example, an assessment (Vranken et al. 2014) of dietary transitions in 120 countries showed that meat consumption grows as per capita GDP grows. HICs have the highest per capita incomes, so demand for and consumption of animal-source foods are greatest there. For example, in North America, the average citizen consumes 36 kilograms

FIGURE 3.10 Animal-Source Food Intake and Meat Consumption Are Unevenly Distributed across Global Regions, with Richer Countries Consuming More Than Poorer Ones

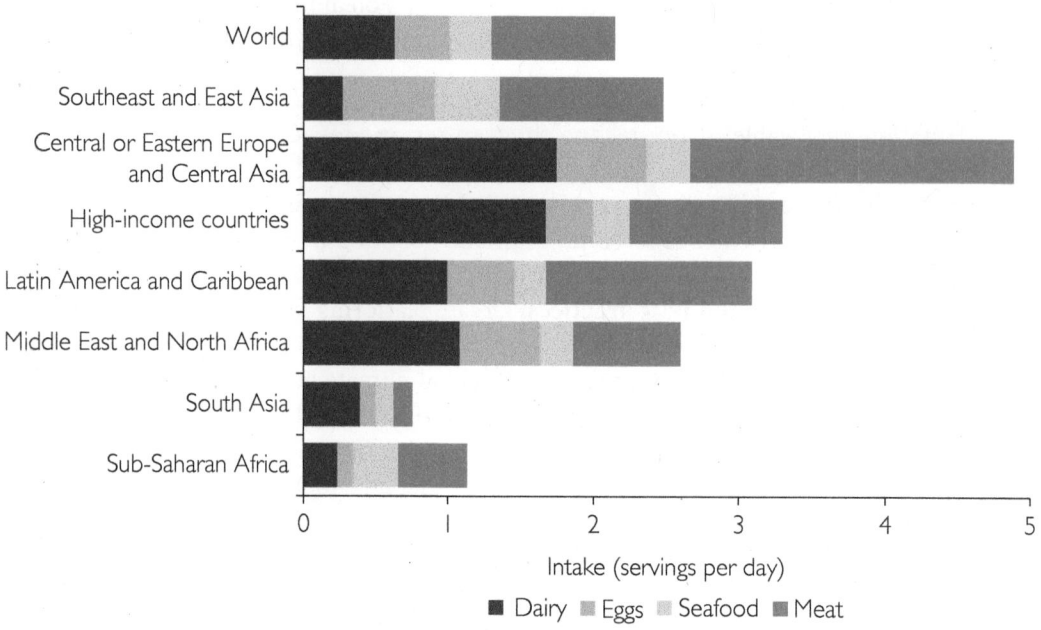

Source: World Bank based on data from Miller et al. 2022.
Note: Figure shows servings per day per person of animal-source foods in 2018. The following standardized serving sizes were used for this analysis: meat: unprocessed red meat (100 grams) and processed meat (50 grams); seafood (100 grams); eggs (55 grams); dairy: cheese (42 grams), yogurt (245 grams), milk (245 grams).

(kg) of bovine meat per year, whereas in Africa, the average citizen consumes only 6 kg per capita per year (FAOSTAT 2023d). The global average is 9 kg of bovine meat per capita per year. This trend of increased meat consumption is also occurring in MICs and LICs as their populations graduate out of poverty (Clark and Tilman 2017; Clark et al. 2020). For example, meat consumption is expected to increase by about 37 percent in LICs this decade, the most of any country income group (OECD and FAO 2021). Diets in these lower-income countries are projected to contain fewer animal-source foods than current diets in high-income countries, but emissions are estimated to be higher since most of that production will occur in less efficient production systems (Herrero et al. 2013; Poore and Nemecek 2018; Springmann et al. 2018). If trends in eating animal-source foods continue, the world would need to close a 50 percent gap between the animal-source food calories available in 2013 and the expected demand for them in 2050, which would, in turn, contribute to even more animal-source food production and related emissions (FAO 2017b).

Diet-related emissions are highest in HICs, though most of these emissions are attributed to MICs. As shown in chapter 2, livestock-related emissions represent over 25 percent of agrifood system emissions, the single largest source. However, what is not shown in those emissions figures is how demand drives those emissions. The demand for animal-source diets accounts for almost 60 percent of total agrifood emissions across all emissions categories, including on-farm activities, land use changes, and pre- and post-production processes (Xu et al. 2021). Therefore, there is greater mitigation potential from shifting diets away from animal-source food than from changing production methods. FAO estimates that the mitigation potential from modifying livestock production practices, such as improving pasture management or improving animal diets, would be from 1.1 to 1.8 $GtCO_2$eq per year (Gerber et al. 2013). By contrast, the mitigation potential from humans changing their own diets, for example, through the reduced consumption of meat and other carbon-intensive food commodities, would be from 0.7 to 8 $GtCO_2$eq per year, a much higher ceiling (IPCC 2019). Moreover, dietary changes in HICs would have a greater impact on emissions than dietary changes in MICs. For example, adopting nationally recommended diets in MICs would reduce livestock-related GHG emissions by only 4.4 percent but would reduce emissions by 13–17 percent in HICs (Behrens et al. 2017). Part of the reason for this is that reducing meat consumption in HICs would reduce livestock production in both HICs and MICs because of trade.

Consumption of animal-source foods has damaged the planet. As discussed in chapter 2 and the examination of MICs in the next section, livestock-related emissions are the single largest source of agrifood system emissions and the largest source of methane emissions. The production of animal-source foods is also damaging to the planet for several other reasons. First, it drives land use change, as many farmers expand croplands to produce cattle feed and other livestock inputs. Second, it depletes land, water, and energy resources to maintain those feed croplands and manage livestock populations. Third, meat production is a very inefficient process for converting inputs from feed to food (Herrero et al. 2013). As a result, per capita diet-related environmental impacts in high-income and upper-middle-income countries are greater than in poorer countries (Clark et al. 2020). Similarly, the agrifood system's transition to animal-source foods has depleted lands and contributed to higher greenhouse gas emissions (Bodirsky et al. 2020; Springmann et al. 2018). Therefore, a shift in diets away from animal-source foods, especially beef (figure 3.11), can help promote greater biodiversity and reduce environmental pressures (Clark and Tilman 2017; Foley et al. 2011; Springmann et al. 2018). Moving from current diets to a diet that excludes animal products could reduce land use by 76 percent, GHG emissions by 49 percent, acidification by 50 percent, eutrophication by 49 percent, and freshwater withdrawals by 19 percent (Poore and Nemecek 2018).

Food systems are also failing to provide healthy diets, with current diets leading to significant health burdens (FAO et al. 2021). These health burdens are more pronounced in HICs than in low- and lower-middle-income countries. A healthy diet with no more than 43 grams of red meat and at least five portions of fruit and vegetables per day could avoid 5 million deaths a year from strokes, cancer, heart disease, and type II diabetes. In poor regions, people would mostly benefit from consuming more fruits and vegetables, and in richer regions they would benefit from consuming less red meat (Springmann et al. 2016). In some high-income countries, a dietary shift is already underway. Research in France has shown that people are self-selecting nutritious and relatively low-carbon diets and that these changes, if widespread, could reduce emissions by 30 percent without compromising the foods' affordability or nutritional value compared to those of the average French diet (Perignon et al. 2017). Despite these health risks, animal-source foods make a critical contribution to diets by providing protein and micronutrients such as zinc, iron, vitamin B_{12}, vitamins A and D, and essential amino acids (Beal et al. 2023). However, consumers can access these nutrients from foods other than animal-source foods, thereby avoiding the health risks of ASF and lowering the climate impact of their diets. Access to alternative healthy diets is highest in HICs but is increasing in MICs and LICs (Good Food Institute 2022).

FIGURE 3.11 Beef Is the Most Emissions-Intensive Food

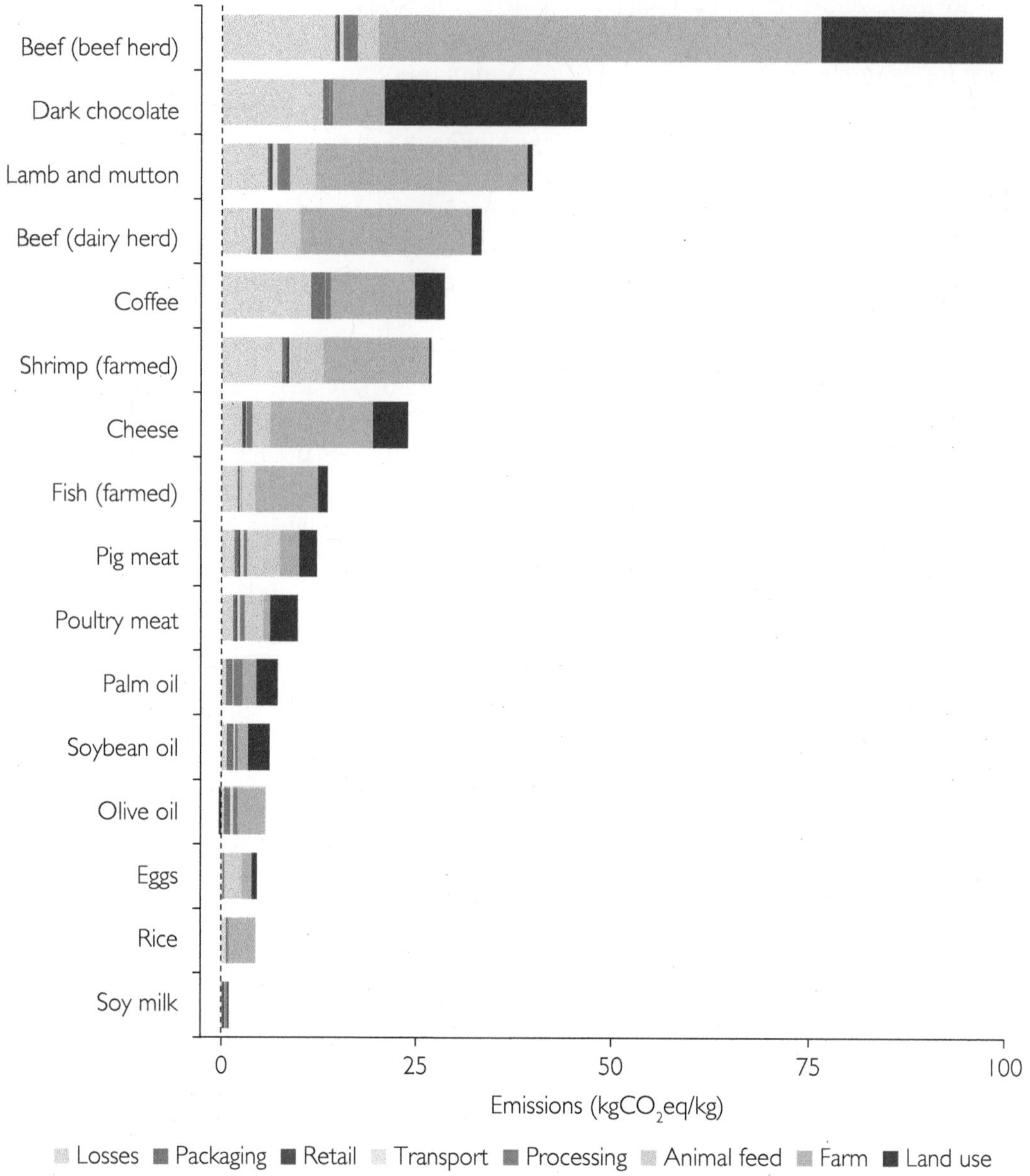

Sources: World Bank based on data from Ritchie, Rosado, and Roser 2022; Poore and Nemecek 2018.
Note: Figure shows greenhouse gas emissions across the supply chain for different foods broken down by sources of emissions. kgCO$_2$eq/kg = kilograms of carbon dioxide equivalent per kilogram.

Changing the source of animal protein in diets from red meat to other sources is a highly cost-effective option for drastically reducing agrifood emissions (Foley et al. 2011). Table 3.1 shows that the technical mitigation potential of changing diets is nearly 2.3 GtCO$_2$eq per year, including 1.4 GtCO$_2$eq per year from cost-effective options. In contrast, the technical and cost-effective mitigation potential from on-farm emissions reductions—from productivity enhancements, improved manure management, feed additives, and improved feed digestibility—have the combined technical potential to mitigate about 1 GtCO$_2$eq per year and cost-effective potential to mitigate less than 0.7 GtCO$_2$eq. Consumer changes

Recipe for a Livable Planet

FIGURE 3.12 **Changes in Diets Can Significantly Reduce Food's Carbon Footprint**

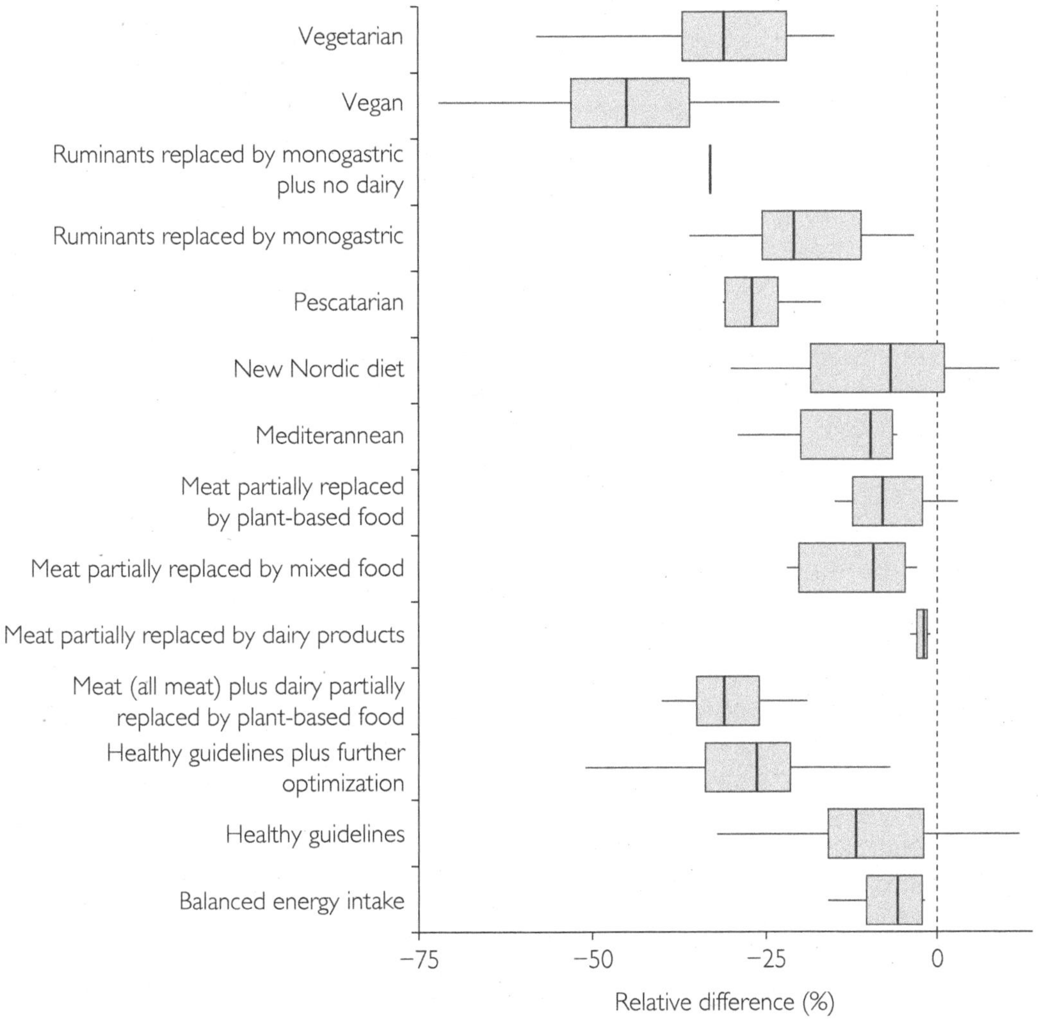

Source: World Bank based on data from Aleksandrowicz et al. 2016.

Note: Figure shows the relative differences in greenhouse gas emissions (in kilotons of carbon dioxide equivalent per capita per year) between common diets and more sustainable diets. Whisker plots show the median percentage difference (vertical line) and the range between the 25th and 75th percentiles (box) of the relative difference in emission reductions.

to healthy, low-emissions diets would reduce food-related emissions by an estimated 30 percent, relative to current dietary trends (FAO et al. 2020). Changing current diets to 14 common alternative diets—including vegan, vegetarian, pescatarian, monogastric meat, Mediterranean, new Nordic, and others (Aleksandrowicz et al. 2016)—would reduce diet-related emissions by up to 70–80 percent and reduce land and water use by 50 percent (see figure 3.12). Another study shows that the median emissions reduction from shifting to ovolactovegetarian diets—which do not include fish, fowl, or red meat but do include animal by-products such as eggs, milk, and honey—is estimated at 35 percent, while vegan diets could cut emissions by 49 percent (Fresán and Sabaté 2019). Emerging protein alternatives, which are discussed in more detail in chapter 4, have the technical potential to reduce emissions by 6.1 $GtCO_2eq$ per year, but as of yet only 0.3 $GtCO_2eq$ per year can be achieved cost-effectively.

People's beliefs and biases can prevent their adoption of low-emission diets. Individual decision-making biases can also influence the transition to low-emissions food systems. For example, a present bias—the tendency toward short-term gratification—when making decisions can be at odds with sustainable habits (Luoto and Carman 2014). Similarly, a loss aversion bias—the idea that the distress caused by losses is greater than the happiness caused by gains of a similar magnitude—may prevent people from changing their diets. For example, a study on selling cold cuts in grocery stores shows that meats described as "90% fat-free" tend to sell better than meats that have "10% fat" (Pink 2012). At the community level, social norms and identity—the idea that people conform to identities because they create intrinsic utility (Akerlof and Kranton 2000)—may also reinforce unsustainable eating habits such as widespread meat consumption in Australia, Great Britain, or the United States (Nguyen and Platow 2021). Similarly, social ties have been linked to long-term eating patterns and obesity (Serrano Fuentes, Rogers, and Portillo 2019). Other studies describe a "licensing effect"—that is, people do not feel as motivated to reduce emissions if they think emissions are harmless. For example, people who do not believe that climate change is caused by human behavior are less likely to modify their dietary behaviors (Bernard, Tzamourani, and Weber 2022).

Poverty can also prevent dietary changes. Decision-making among poor populations, including those in rich countries, involves monetary and welfare trade-offs that are not present for more affluent populations (Mani et al. 2013; Spears 2011). Material scarcity forces people to focus on immediate needs over longer-term goals (Mani et al. 2013). In these situations, environmental or sustainability decisions take second place to more urgent needs, such as hunger and affordability. Taking that into account, as seen in chapter 2, food system transformation could raise food prices, at least temporarily. Similarly, healthy diets are around five times more expensive than basic staple diets, on average. At least 3 billion people worldwide cannot afford healthy diets. Yet the prevalence of unhealthy diets leads to public health costs that are projected to reach $1.3 trillion per year by 2030 (FAO et al. 2020).

Full-cost pricing of animal-source food to reflect its true planetary costs would make low-emission food options more competitive. Meat and dairy producers still receive large subsidies in many HICs and MICs. Globally, one-third of agricultural support was directed toward meat and milk products in 2016, with the top five subsidized economies being China, the EU, India, Russia, and the US (Springmann and Freund 2022). These subsidies, combined with the free or cheap use of water and nutrient resources and the costless nature of their externalities, reduce animal-source foods' market prices and contribute to their large share in diets (Instituto Escolhas 2020; Vallone and Lambin 2023). Indeed, studies have shown that if prices were to reflect the true health, climate, and environmental costs of meat, meat prices would be 20–60 percent higher, depending on the type of meat (Funke et al. 2022). That said, the prices of meat and dairy products are highly elastic compared to those of other food products (Andreyeva, Long, and Brownell 2010), meaning that the repurposing of red-meat subsidies toward low-emission foods, such as poultry or fruits and vegetables, could lead to large changes in consumption patterns and large emissions reductions while also improving many health indicators, especially cardiovascular health (Pearson-Stuttard et al. 2017). Notably, fossil fuels are similarly underpriced, resulting in emissions of GHGs and harmful local air pollutants. For example, 80 percent of global coal consumption was priced at less than half of its efficient level in 2022 (Black et al. 2023).

There are policy measures that can expand low-emission dietary options and tackle the behavioral factors that influence food consumption patterns (Steg and Vlek 2009). In recent

Recipe for a Livable Planet

years, several governments have adopted policies to counteract harmful dietary behaviors (GLOPAN 2017; Gonzalez Fischer and Garnett 2016; Vermeir et al. 2020; Wellesley, Happer, and Froggatt 2015). These policies include the following: (1) financial measures, (2) choice architecture strategies, (3) food labeling, and (4) education and communication campaigns. Each of these is analyzed separately. In general, stand-alone and less intrusive interventions, such as labeling and choice architecture, are more widespread but also less visible and less influential on consumer behaviors (Annunziata, Mariani, and Vecchio 2019; Grunert, Hieke, and Wills 2014; Vermeir and Verbeke 2006). For example, emissions labeling in Scandinavia led to 9 percent less demand for meat dishes at cafeterias (Slapø and Karevold 2019). Further, the impacts of these interventions on consumer choices are context specific (Grunert 2011; Song, Semakula, and Fullana-i-Palmer 2019) and range from small to moderate, because for consumers, sustainability is often a trade-off against other criteria such as the food's price, taste, brand, quantity, expiration date, and healthiness (Grunert, Hieke, and Wills 2014; Song, Semakula, and Fullana-i-Palmer 2019). By contrast, more intrusive instruments, such as taxes or the banning of food products with large environmental footprints, are more effective (Ammann et al. 2023). Comprehensive approaches that combine various policy tools have been the most effective (Ammann et al. 2023; Clark et al. 2020; Garnett et al. 2015). All that being said, trust in the government is positively associated with people's support for environmental policy (Fairbrother 2013; Konisky, Milyo, and Richardson 2008; Zannakis, Wallin, and Johansson 2015) and their willingness to sacrifice for the environment (Harring 2013; Jones, Clark, and Malesios 2015; Koerth et al. 2013; Smith and Mayer 2018). Therefore, there must be trust among the stakeholders for these interventions to work (Ammann et al. 2023; Wolff, Schönherr, and Heyen 2017). Likewise, modeling in high-income countries shows that these policies can have unintended consequences and disproportionately affect poor and income-constrained households (Springmann et al. 2017). Figure 3.13 shows the following factors that influence dietary behaviors and identities.

FIGURE 3.13 Diets Are Influenced by Many Factors

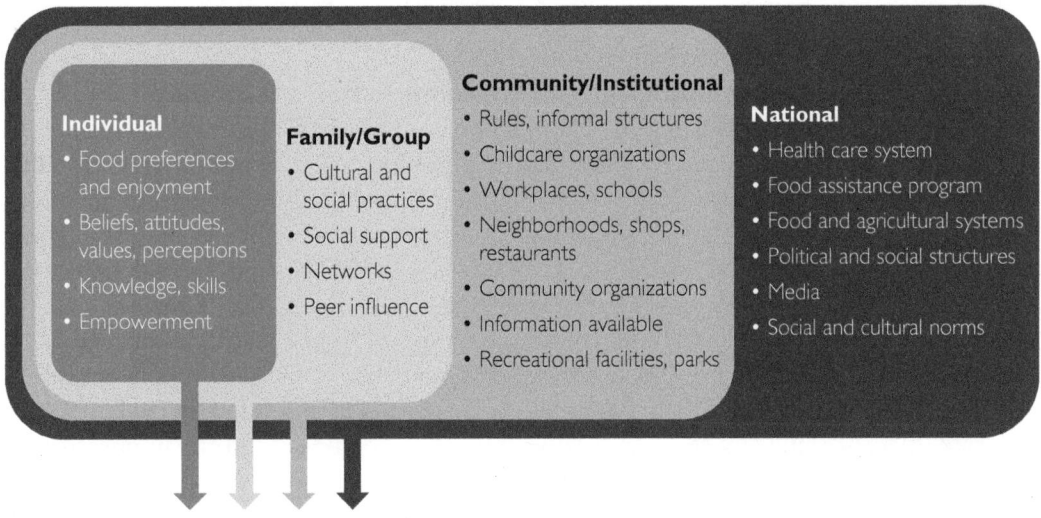

Food and nutrition education works at all levels.

Source: Adapted from GLOPAN 2017.
Note: Figure shows the entry points to changes in diet at the individual, family, community, and national levels.

- **Financial measures** can restrict, discourage, or incentivize choices, thereby leading to more sustainable diets (Park et al. 2023). For example, introducing a food-waste levy or providing tax incentives for food donations can reduce food waste (WHO 2016). Similarly, taxing sugar-sweetened beverages can combat obesity and noncommunicable diseases (Carriedo et al. 2021; Teng et al. 2019; World Bank 2020b). However, taxing these products would affect primarily the poor, unless accompanied by affordable alternatives (Mancino et al. 2018; Springmann et al. 2017; Thow et al. 2018), and would likely face consumer resistance (Latka et al. 2021). Overall, studies show that a 20 percent food price increase would decrease that food's carbon footprint by up to 19 percent, though evidence on emissions impacts from financial incentives is still sparse (Ammann et al. 2023). Other financial measures, such as cash transfer programs, can also influence consumer behavior (Abila and Kantola 2019; Hong Kong Waste Reduction Website, n.d.).
- **Choice architecture strategies** can influence and guide consumers on dietary choices (Kallbekken and Sælen 2013). An example of choice architecture—presenting choices in different ways to influence decision-making—is when the government mandates restaurants and supermarkets (or at least state-controlled entities [Park et al. 2023]) to reduce portion sizes (Richardson, Prescott, and Ellison 2021), display food in a specific order that makes green foods the default option (Bacon and Krpan 2018), or normalize plant-based foods by displaying them side by side with more traditional choices (Bacon and Krpan 2018).
- **Food labeling** on the food's origin, carbon footprint, nutrient composition, or production conditions for workers or animals (Apostolidis and McLeay 2019; Koistinen et al. 2013; Tobi et al. 2019; Van Loo et al. 2014) can also influence consumer choices. Food labeling, which is highly regulated in most wealthy countries, can provide consumers with important information on the social and environmental impacts of food products (Abrahamse 2020; Shangguan et al. 2019; Tzilivakis et al. 2012). A recent literature review shows that higher income and education are positively correlated with GHG footprint labels and that environmentally conscious individuals are willing to pay more for GHG footprint–labeled foods. However, it also highlights that the effectiveness of emissions labels is limited because of inaccurate systems for measuring the GHG footprints of foods (Rondoni and Grasso 2021).
- **Education and communication** measures informed by behavioral science (Behavioural Insights Team 2018) that provide information in a timely (Whitehair, Shanklin, and Brannon 2013) and attractive (Bartiaux and Salmón 2012; Hanss and Böhm 2013; Ludden and de Ruijter 2016) manner and target specific group identities (De Boer, Schösler, and Aiking 2014) have shown positive results (Farmer et al. 2017). These measures (Garnett et al. 2015) are most effective when they go beyond knowledge sharing, which by itself does not lead to lasting behavioral change (Graziose and Ang 2019; Martins et al. 2020), and are accompanied by choice architecture and other policy tools that make healthy, low-emissions food choices more common, appealing, affordable, and effortless (Abrahamse 2020; Leonard 2008; Ruel and Fanzo 2022). That said, there are still challenges in getting consumers to understand the implications of their food choices (Grunert 2011) and in overcoming more traditional influences in food shopping, such as price, taste, or brand (Grunert, Hieke, and Wills 2014; Song, Semakula, and Fullana-i-Palmer 2019).

Recipe for a Livable Planet

- **Research and innovation** in alternative proteins by governments to incentivize private sector solutions and create an enabling environment that would get these solutions to market (see more on R&D in chapter 4).

Consumer-driven efforts to promote low-emission diets are also important. Formal consumer organizations have a wide range of functions in the agrifood system, including monitoring consumer rights, denouncing noncompliance with regulations, demanding accountability from industries and the government, and influencing policy and industry practices. Individuals can be responsible consumers or issue voters (Isenhour 2012; Vermeir and Verbeke 2006) but can also be more active agents of change. Social media influencers, in particular, can shape consumer attitudes and purchasing decisions (Simeone and Scarpato 2020), though their messages compete with other information available to consumers. Consumer activism and advocacy, ranging from boycotts to petitions, have also been effective but require continuous resources and effective, coordinated alliances (Delacote 2009). Consumer actions are most effective when they have buy-in from producers and show alternative pathways. For example, consumer activism in Germany achieved dramatic reductions in food waste over two years (Gollnhofer, Weijo, and Schouten 2019). Likewise, in the Netherlands, consumer movements for more organic foods were successful because the movement's objectives shared the core cultural-historical values of the wider population, described in a research paper (Schösler, Boer, and Boersema 2013) as embracing a natural lifestyle, moving away from materialistic behaviors, and connecting with nature. See box 3.1 for an example how another country's culture affects its agrifood emissions.

BOX 3.1 Agrifood Emissions In-Depth: India

India's large population makes it one of the world's largest agrifood greenhouse gas (GHG) emitters, but its vegetarian diets mitigate this. India has roughly four times the population of the United States but emits only 30 percent more GHG. This is because cumulatively India's massive population emits more than less populated countries, but each individual emits much less than the global average per person. One reason is India's low-carbon diets (Kim et al. 2020), with India having a larger share of vegetarians than any other country worldwide (Buchholz 2022). However, another reason is India's pervasive poverty and malnutrition levels, meaning that large shares of the population cannot afford to consume much. This creates a perverse scenario; for most of the planet, a shift to healthy diets would reduce GHG emissions, but in India, such a shift would slightly increase emissions (Aleksandrowicz et al. 2019). Sixty percent of India's agrifood system emissions come from the farm gate, with enteric fermentation making up the largest share (figure B3.1.1). Again, this is ironic because most of the country is vegetarian; however, India's livestock sector is highly inefficient, with its emission intensity per unit of both milk and beef among the highest worldwide (FAOSTAT 2023b). In contrast, the emission intensity of India's rice production is among the lowest in the world, generating less than 1 kilogram of carbon dioxide equivalent per kilogram of rice produced. However, emissions from this subsector are nevertheless considerable (4 percent), since India is the second-largest rice producer globally, after China. That said, India's Nationally Determined Contribution to the Paris Agreement and National Mission for Sustainable Agriculture set ambitious targets to reduce agrifood system emissions (Ministry of Agriculture and Farmers Welfare, Government of India 2018).

(box continued next page)

FIGURE B3.1.1 India's Agrifood System Emissions, 1990–92 and 2018–20

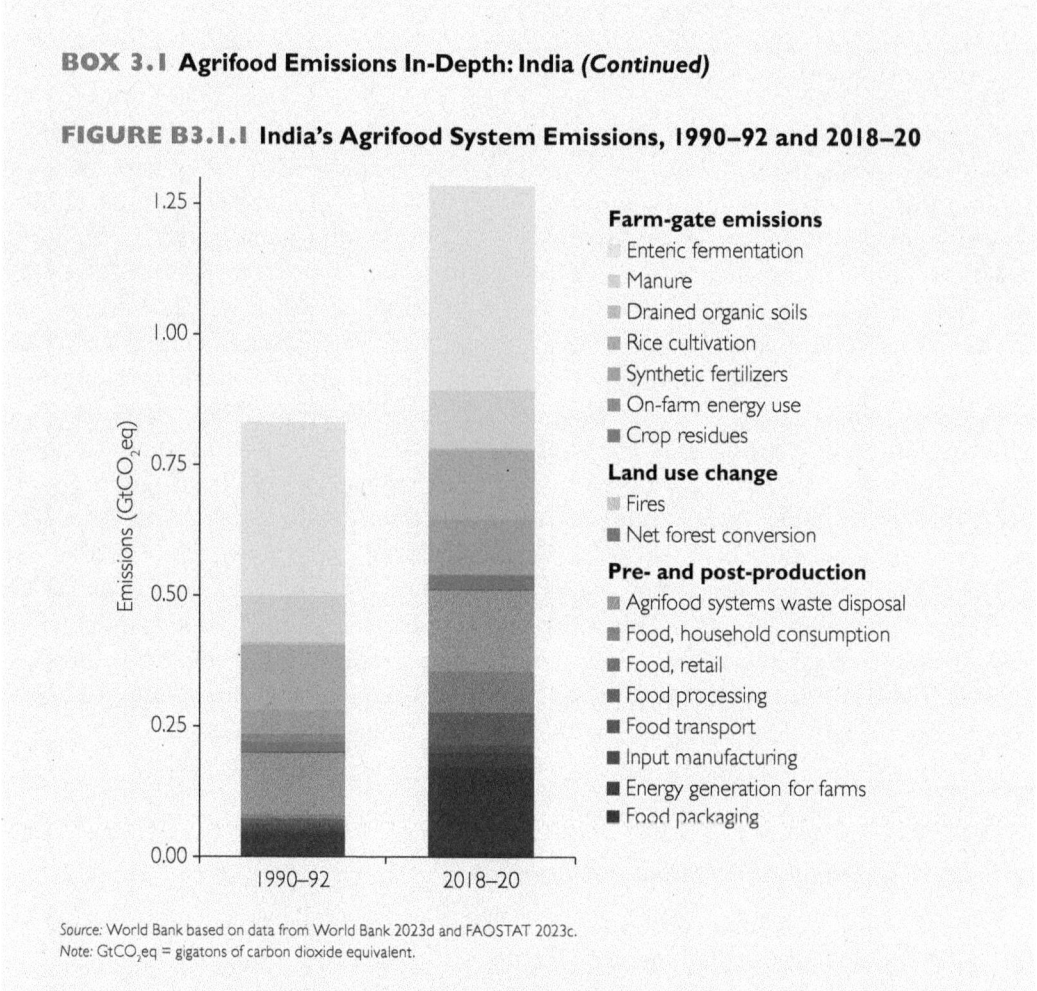

Source: World Bank based on data from World Bank 2023d and FAOSTAT 2023c.
Note: GtCO$_2$eq = gigatons of carbon dioxide equivalent.

Middle-Income Countries Have the Opportunity to Curb up to Two-Thirds of Global Agrifood Emissions through Sustainable Land Use, Low-Emissions Farming Practices, and Cleaner Pre- and Post-production Processes

Middle-income countries dominate global GHG emissions, both from all sources and from only the agrifood system. About half of all countries, or 108 of 213 countries, are classified as MICs by the World Bank. By this count, it would make sense that MICs have the largest cumulative emissions. However, as shown in chapter 2, even when MICs are split into LMICs and UMICs, those two smaller groups still emit more than the larger group of HICs and much more than the smaller group of LICs. In 2019, MICs accounted for almost 70 percent of emissions from all sources and for 47 percent of emissions from the agrifood system. MICs have contributed the most agrifood system emissions historically as well, also as described in chapter 2. Cumulatively, MICs emit the most from the individual emissions categories listed in figure 3.14, which shows supply-side emissions, meaning where the GHGs were emitted from, not necessarily the sources of demand for those emissions. As a result,

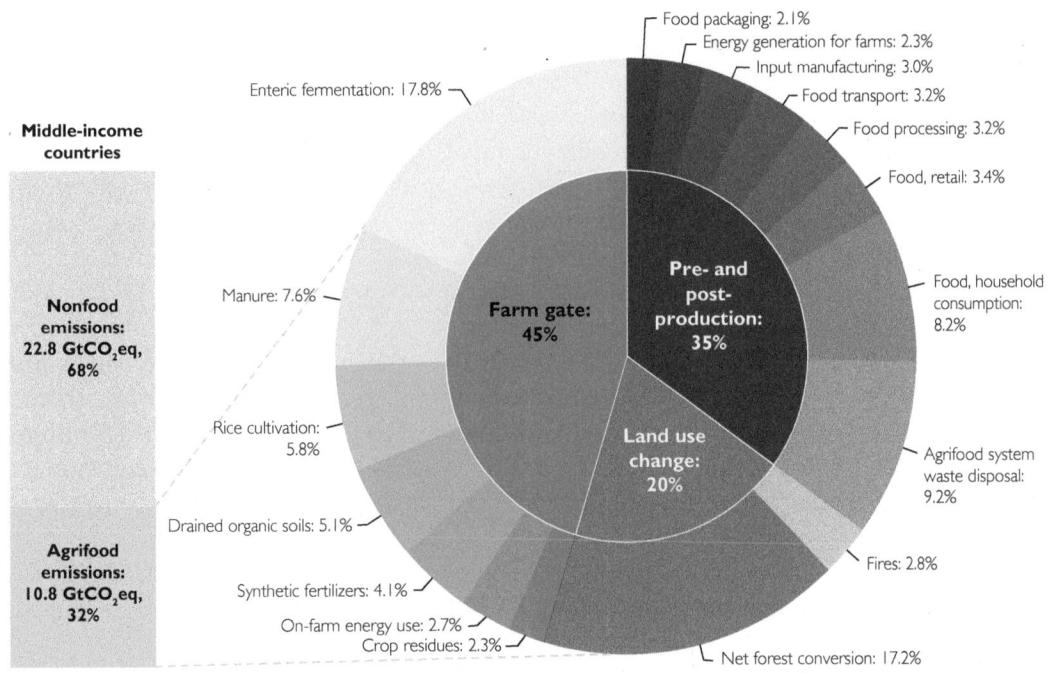

FIGURE 3.14 Middle-Income Countries Are the Largest Source of Agrifood System Emissions, with High Levels across All Emission Categories

Middle-income countries

Nonfood emissions: 22.8 GtCO$_2$eq, 68%

Agrifood emissions: 10.8 GtCO$_2$eq, 32%

Enteric fermentation: 17.8%
Manure: 7.6%
Rice cultivation: 5.8%
Drained organic soils: 5.1%
Synthetic fertilizers: 4.1%
On-farm energy use: 2.7%
Crop residues: 2.3%

Farm gate: 45%

Land use change: 20%

Pre- and post-production: 35%

Food packaging: 2.1%
Energy generation for farms: 2.3%
Input manufacturing: 3.0%
Food transport: 3.2%
Food processing: 3.2%
Food, retail: 3.4%
Food, household consumption: 8.2%
Agrifood system waste disposal: 9.2%
Fires: 2.8%
Net forest conversion: 17.2%

Source: World Bank based on data from FAOSTAT 2023c and World Bank 2023d.

Note: Left: Agrifood system emissions as share of total global greenhouse gas emissions (data account for methane, nitrous oxide, and carbon dioxide emissions), 2018–20 annual average. Right: Emissions categorized by three main subcategories and their individual components. GtCO$_2$eq = gigatons of carbon dioxide equivalent.

MICs have the greatest potential for reducing supply-side emissions. In aggregate, MICs' largest shares of agrifood emissions come from the farm gate and pre- and post-production processes. Combined, these two MIC subcategories account for 80 percent of global agrifood system emissions. Within the farm gate, the biggest emissions sources in MICs are livestock production, rice production, and practices that reduce soil carbon; within pre- and post-production, the biggest emissions sources are fertilizer production and use, food and water waste and loss, and household food consumption. While land use emissions are only one-fifth of MICs' overall emissions, in absolute terms MICs account for the largest share of deforestation and land use–related emissions globally, especially in large MICs such as Brazil and Indonesia. At the same time, the risk of forest conversion due to agricultural activities in LICs is escalating. Stubbornly high rates of deforestation also remain a major issue in MICs, and reducing them is a priority in those countries. This section focuses on opportunities arising from sustainable land use, low-emissions on-farm practices, and cleaner pre- and post-production.

A shift to more sustainable land use in MICs could reduce a third of global agrifood emissions cost-effectively

Commodity production in MICs drives deforestation. Cropland expansion and deforestation leave a massive carbon footprint in middle-income economies. Once lost, the carbon in forests is very difficult to recover, as are the forest's biodiversity and other important ecological functions. Deforestation contributes 11 percent of total CO$_2$ emissions, with 90 percent of that caused by expanding croplands (52 percent) and livestock pastures (38 percent). Globally, about a quarter to a third of permanent forest loss is linked to the production of seven commodities—which in descending order are cattle, palm oil, soy, cocoa, rubber, coffee, and plantation wood fiber—with the remaining three-quarters shared among wildfire, forestry, and shifting agriculture (figure 3.15). Since 2001, a few middle-income economies with large forest cover have caused over 80 percent of commodity-driven deforestation emissions, with Brazil contributing 31 percent and Indonesia 36 percent, followed by Malaysia (7 percent), Bolivia (4 percent), and Viet Nam (3 percent) (figure 3.16). Indonesia lost 11 percent of its forests because of oil palm expansion. This is equal to 10 million hectares of forest and one-third of Indonesia's old-growth forests. In Brazil, the expansion of soy plantations has contributed to the country's deforestation. Brazil's total deforestation and conversion of native vegetation escalated from 1.6 million hectares in 2018 to 1.84 million in 2019 and 1.83 million in 2020. Soy cultivation was the second biggest cause of this forest loss, behind only pasture expansion for cattle farming. The overall area dedicated to soy cultivation also continues its upward trend, expanding from 34.8 million hectares in 2018 to 37.2 million hectares by 2020 (Reis and Prada Moro 2022). As mentioned elsewhere in this report, 70 percent of that soy is exported to China, where it is converted to soy meal to feed China's livestock.

Reducing forest conversion holds a lot of cost-effective mitigation potential globally. The largest share of the economic potential from AFOLU mitigation options comes from the

FIGURE 3.15 Emissions from Converting Forests to Agriculture Have Increased since 2001 and Account for More Than Half of the Permanent Loss of Forests Globally

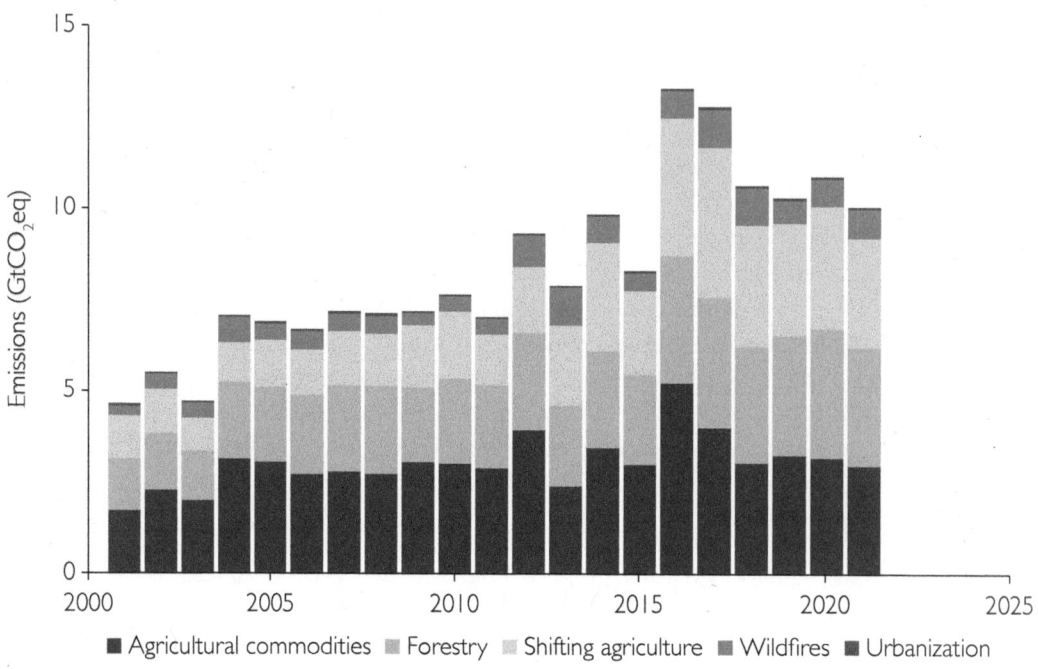

Source: World Bank based on data from Harris et al. 2021.
Note: Figure shows the annual global greenhouse gas emissions from forest loss by driver for 2001–21. Emissions—carbon dioxide, nitrous oxide, and methane—from the gross forest loss globally are disaggregated by drivers (forest gain from forestry plantations, for example, is not accounted for). Forest clearing for agricultural commodities such as oil palm or cattle and shifting cultivation make up more than half of deforestation emissions. Forestry contributes to emissions through unsustainable practices, such as the impacts of extractive logging. $GtCO_2eq$ = gigatons of carbon dioxide equivalent.

FIGURE 3.16 A Few Middle-Income Countries Are Driving the Growth in Global Emissions from Commodity-Linked Deforestation

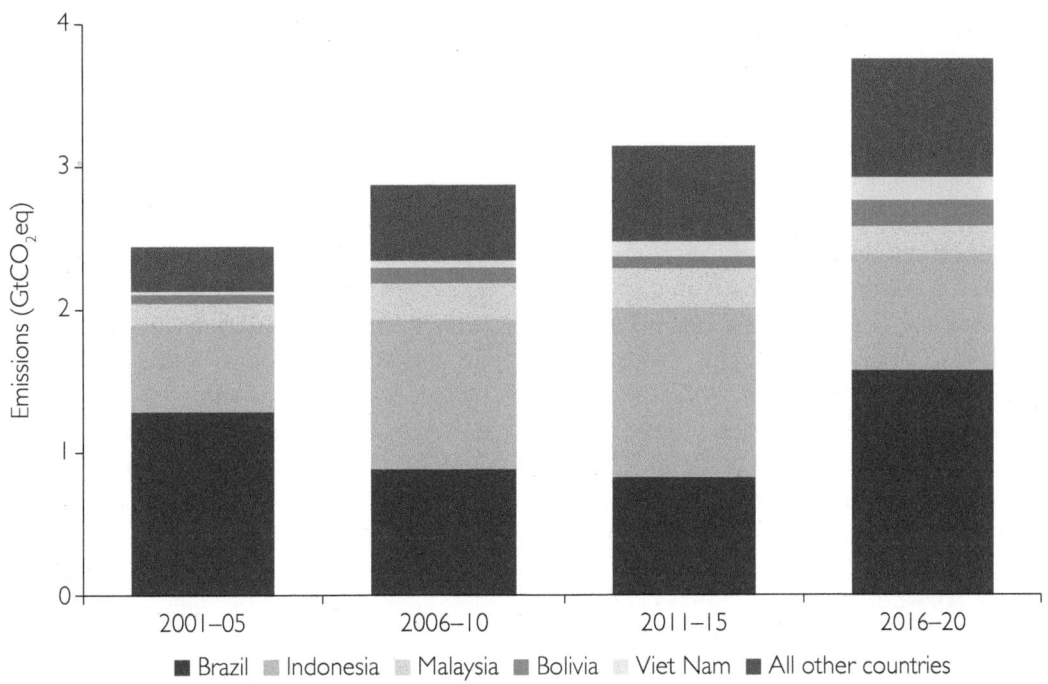

Source: World Bank based on data from Harris et al. 2021.
Note: Figure shows top country emitters of average annual global greenhouse gas emissions from commodity-driven deforestation for 2001–20.

conservation, improved management, and restoration of forests and other ecosystems—such as peatlands, grasslands, savannas, and coastal wetlands, among others—with reduced deforestation in tropical regions having the highest total contribution to agrifood sector mitigation.[9] Using cost-effective mitigation measures in land use, land use change, and forestry (LULUCF) could avoid 6.5 gigatons of emissions per year, which is 40 percent of all cost-effective mitigation potential shown in table 3.1. Higher-cost measures, such as afforestation and reforestation, could avoid even more emissions, or about 7.3 $GtCO_2eq$ per year excluding cost-effective options, though these measures could also raise commodity prices (Roe et al. 2021). The deforestation-reducing measures that cost less than $100 per tCO_2eq represent 54 percent of all emission reduction potential from low-cost land-based mitigation options. By some estimates, the cost of protecting 30 percent of the world's forests and mangroves would require an annual investment of just $140 billion (Waldron et al. 2020), which is less than one-quarter of global agricultural support. A growing number of commodity producers in these countries have introduced sectoral programs to reduce their deforestation footprint, but results are limited. There is also still a lack of transparency about where many commodities come from and whether they contribute to deforestation (zu Ermgassen et al. 2022). See table 3.1 for more details on the technical and cost-effective mitigation potentials from land use and forestry-related mitigation measures.

Governments and businesses both have roles to play in reducing deforestation. Many companies have adopted measures to ensure sustainability in their supply chains, such as codes of conduct, due diligence, certification schemes, and traceability instruments

(Lambin et al. 2018; FAO 2022). The market share of companies with some form of deforestation-free commitments varies across products, ranging from about 12 percent of companies for soy, livestock, and paper pulp to 65 percent of companies for palm oil (Garrett et al. 2019). These gaps show that much more can be done. Tools such as the OECD-FAO Guidance for Responsible Agricultural Supply Chains (a global standard) help companies rid their supply chains of deforestation, but so far these tools are underutilized. Governments can also dictate levels of deforestation. For example, in Brazil, the deforestation rate declined by more than 80 percent between 2004 and 2014. This has been attributed to a combination of government policies, such as stronger law enforcement; supply-chain interventions, including private commitments on soy and cattle production; and changes in market conditions (Hanusch and Strand 2023). However, those trends worsened when the government de-emphasized deforestation after 2019, with deforestation reaching a 15-year high in 2021 (Roy 2022). The deforestation rate improved again almost immediately after new leadership took over in 2023 because of resumed antilogging raids (Araujo 2023). Governments can also take more direct legal action against deforestation—for example, Viet Nam's moratoria on logging (GIZ Programme on Conservation, Sustainable Use of Forest Biodiversity and Ecosystem Services in Viet Nam 2022) or Indonesia's moratoria on new palm oil plantations (Yusuf, Roos, and Horridge 2018). Public-private approaches are increasingly used as a model to reduce deforestation connected to agricultural commodity production—for instance, the zero-deforestation commitments for key commodities in Colombia and West Africa. Yet, while showing promising results for some value chains, a siloed approach by individual companies has hampered deeper transformation of production systems. A more effective stakeholder engagement and stronger public regulatory measures are needed to have a measurable effect across larger areas and on a region's deforestation rate. International institutions can provide financing and technical support for deforestation initiatives but also can support efforts to decouple agricultural production from deforestation through binding national or commodity-specific social and environmental standards, assurance systems, and branding strategies to make products that do not cause deforestation more appealing to international markets (DeValue et al. 2022).

More than a quarter of MICs' agrifood system emissions are in the livestock sector

Most livestock-related GHG emissions are taking place in the rapidly growing economies of MICs. MICs are responsible for nearly three-quarters (72.4 percent) of GHG direct emissions from livestock, compared to 6.1 percent for LICs and 21.5 percent for HICs (figure 3.17, left panel). Large ruminants (cattle) account for 70 percent of global livestock emissions (figure 3.17, right panel). Figure 3.14 shows that enteric fermentation and manure left on pasture combined cause a quarter of total GHG emissions from MICs' agrifood sector, and this does not include feed production, which is attributed to the land use change category. Moreover, MIC livestock emissions are on the rise. Between 2010 and 2019, MIC livestock emissions grew by 6 percent, compared to a decrease of 2 percent for HICs, and LICs' emissions increased by an astounding 64 percent, although from a much lower level of total emissions. The surge of emissions in MICs is driven by population growth, economic growth, and urbanization, with more affluent urban consumers eating more animal-source foods (Delgado et al. 1999).

Livestock technical mitigation potential is high in MICs because of their high emissions intensity and the greater opportunity in MICs to alter production practices than in HICs

FIGURE 3.17 Nearly 80 Percent of Global Livestock Emissions Are from Enteric Fermentation and Feed Production, and Middle-Income Countries Contribute Nearly Three-Quarters of Those Emissions to the Global Total

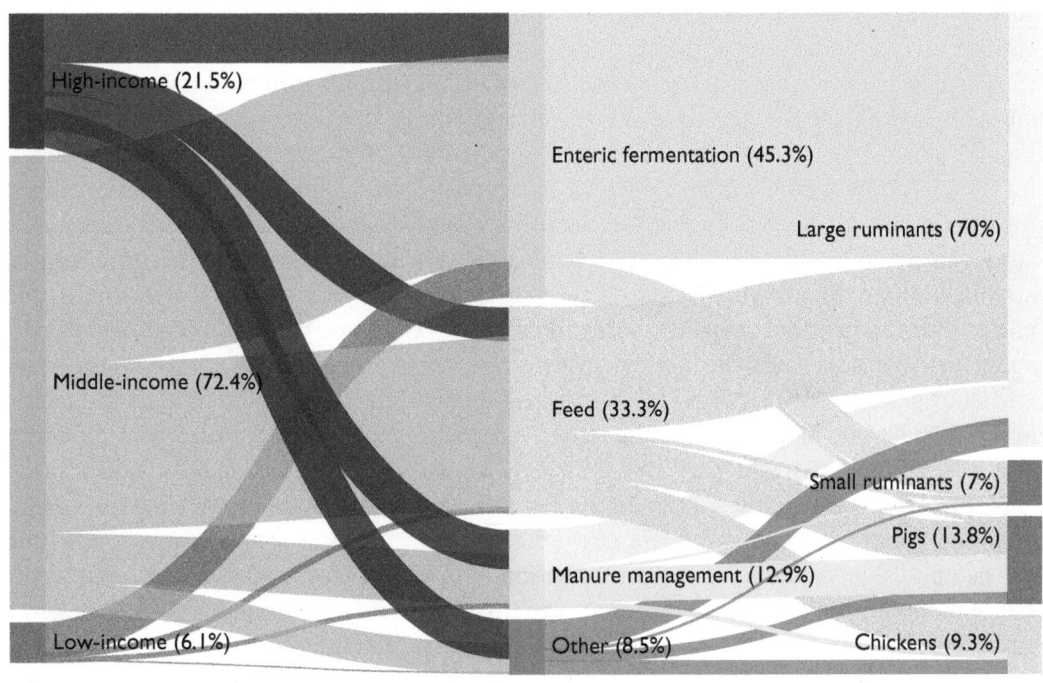

Source: FAO 2023a.

Note: Figure is a Sankey diagram of livestock emissions in high-, middle-, and low-income countries in 2015 (left) and their distribution relative to emission sources (center) and animal species (right).

MAP 3.1 Virtually Every Country Contributes to Livestock Emissions, but the Spatial Distribution Is Uneven

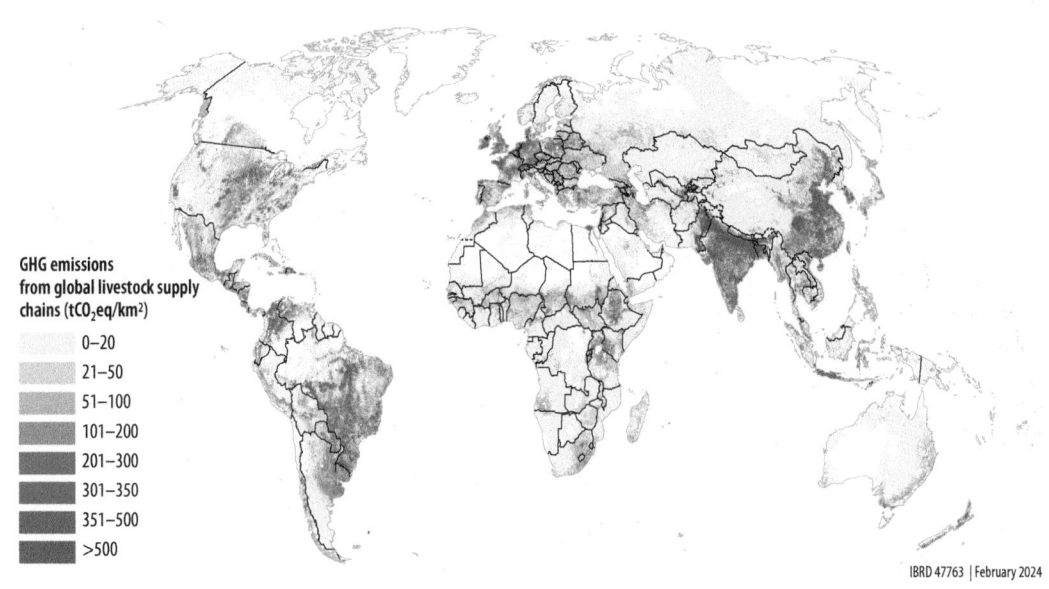

Source: FAOSTAT 2023b.

Note: GHG = greenhouse gas; tCO$_2$eq/km^2 = tons of carbon dioxide equivalent per square kilometer.

and LICs. Every country in the world generates livestock emissions, but map 3.1 shows that some generate much more than others. Most livestock production takes place in MICs (FAO 2019a). Its efficiency in MICs is limited because of weak policy frameworks in those countries, especially environmental regulations, and because of the high prices for inputs, such as energy and fertilizers (Steinfeld et al. 2010). As a result, the intensity of GHG emissions from livestock in MICs is 121 kg of CO_2eq per kg of proteins, compared to only 79 kg of CO_2eq per kg of proteins in HICs (FAOSTAT 2023b), with ruminants, both large and small, generating far more emissions per kilogram of protein than pigs or chickens (figure 3.18). This means there is greater opportunity to reduce this intensity through improved productivity in MICs than in HICs. Meanwhile, the livestock emissions intensity for LICs is even higher, at 232 kg of CO_2eq per kg of proteins. However, producers in those countries struggle with harsher climatic conditions and less access to finances, information, and technology than their peers in MICs. Livestock value chains are also better structured and markets are more diversified and segmented in MICs. These conditions do not generally apply to MIC smallholders, but, on a general level, conditions are more conducive to efficiency gains in MICs than in LICs. Meanwhile, protecting land from pasture expansion or feed production has great cost-effective mitigation potential relative to on-farm measures and new technologies, which are not yet widely available (see figure 3.3).

There are many supply-side solutions for reducing livestock production–related GHG emissions, but they tend to be less cost-effective than demand-side solutions. Targeting the demand side, or reducing the consumption of livestock products, was discussed in the HIC section of this chapter and would make the biggest dent in reducing livestock-related emissions. It would also be more affordable, with the cost-effective mitigation potential from changing diets double that of the four supply-side livestock mitigation options from table 3.1 combined. That said, targeting the supply side, or reducing emissions per unit of production, would also reduce emissions significantly if all technical mitigation solutions

FIGURE 3.18 **Livestock Production in Low- and Middle-Income Countries Is Inefficient, Especially for Ruminants**

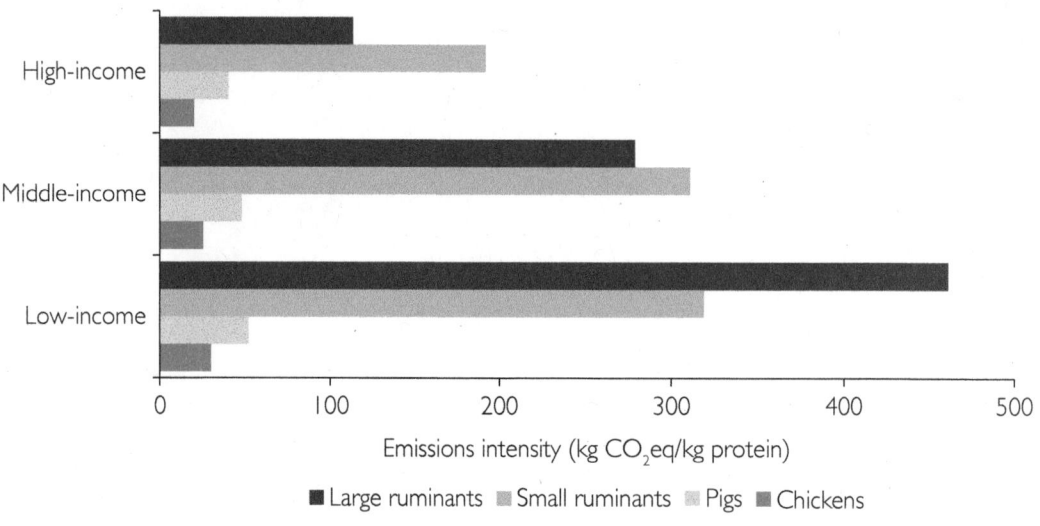

Source: FAOSTAT 2023b.
Note: Figure shows the average emissions intensity by animal type and country income group in 2015. Large ruminants are cattle, and small ruminants are goats, sheep, and other species. kg CO_2eq/kg protein = kilograms of carbon dioxide equivalent per kilogram of protein.

Recipe for a Livable Planet

were adopted. However, these solutions are interdependent, so a simple aggregation of their mitigation potential would be misleading. For example, improved production efficiency will likely be associated with smaller herd sizes and therefore a reduced grassland area with reduced sequestration potential. Moreover, rebound effects, for instance, expanding production to take advantage of efficiency gains, can reduce or even reverse emission intensity improvements, especially where the demand for animal products is elastic or changes drastically as the price changes (Hawkins et al. 2021; Valin et al. 2013). The following supply-side options all present opportunities to reduce livestock emissions:

- **Reducing animal-source food loss and waste.** This will be discussed for the broader agrifood system later, but food losses and waste for ASFs are generally less than food losses for non-ASFs, though still significant. These ASF losses are caused by inadequate slaughtering and cooling facilities and inappropriate handling and sanitation. FAOSTAT data suggest that food losses in most primary production chains (excluding slaughter and harvest losses) for all animal products are around 3 percent globally, with losses in high-income countries generally less than 1 percent. A global reduction of losses from 3 percent to 1 percent would save 167 $MtCO_2$eq per year. Meanwhile, ASF waste at the consumption stage is generally higher in high-income countries. For example, food waste for ASFs in Northern America and Europe was estimated at 15–35 percent. A global halving of food waste by 2050, from 12 percent to 6 percent, would reduce livestock emission by 502 $MtCO_2$eq. A further consideration is the recycling of ASF waste as swill to feed livestock (Uwizeye et al. 2019).

- **Increasing livestock productivity.** Livestock emissions can be cut by up to 30 percent if best practices on improving productivity and resource use efficiency are followed (Gerber et al. 2013). One way to improve livestock productivity is by improving animal health and preventing illnesses, which will lower emissions per unit of output (Özkan et al. 2022). One study (McKinsey & Company 2020) estimates the GHG mitigation potential from animal health interventions to be 411 $MtCO_2$eq and the economic benefits to be $5 per tCO_2eq mitigated. The potential for improvements in productivity through animal health interventions is generally greater in LICs and LMICs, as are most productivity interventions, because such countries lack resources and capacity. Broader productivity improvements are discussed in the LIC section of this chapter.

- **Limiting pasture expansion.** Preventing pasture expansion into forests and sustainably sourcing feed would prevent the biggest land use changes associated with livestock. There are several methods for achieving this. First is intensification of livestock production on pastures, reducing the land used per head of livestock (Bogaerts et al. 2017). Second is enactment of policies that ensure that imported products do not contribute to large-scale deforestation. Evidence suggests that deforestation is often displaced to other countries if national forest protection measures are scaled up (Pendrill et al. 2019). For example, China promotes widespread reforestation within its borders but imports soybeans from Brazil, which contributes to the Amazon's deforestation (see box 3.2). Third is application of rotational grazing and reduction of grazing intensity. Grazing can have a positive impact on vegetation productivity, but overgrazing degrades soils and leads to loss of soil organic carbon (Godde et al. 2020).

- **Adopting technical solutions.** There are several relatively modern innovations that would help reduce livestock-related GHG emissions (McKinsey & Company 2020). For example, breeding cattle for low enteric fermentation would reduce emissions by 506 $MtCO_2$eq by 2050. Changing animal diets could also reduce emissions, with optimized,

BOX 3.2 Agrifood Emissions In-Depth: Brazil

Brazil's beef and soybean production makes it the world's second-largest emitter of agrifood system greenhouse gases (Roe et al. 2021). Eighty-six percent of Brazil's overall greenhouse gas (GHG) emissions are linked to its food system (figure B3.2.1). Specifically, Brazil is the largest historic emitter of land use, land use change, and forestry-related greenhouse gas emissions (Jones et al. 2023). The major cause of these emissions is the destruction of Brazil's vast tropical forests to make way for agricultural land for beef and soybean production (Mota dos Santos et al. 2021). Both of these commodities supply the world's demand for meat. Beef is consumed directly, often domestically, with Brazil having one of the highest diet-related per capita emission levels in the world, more than 4 tons of CO_2eq per year, or twice that of the United States (Kim et al. 2020). Unfortunately, Brazil's meat industry is highly emissions intensive because of the widespread deforestation (Reis et al. 2023). As a result, producing 1 kilogram of bovine meat in Brazil emits roughly 17 times more greenhouse gases than doing the same in Denmark. Similarly, Brazil's soy production, which is the largest in the world, is also meant to satisfy global demand, primarily in China. Brazil's large swaths of Amazon rainforest are attractive to soy producers because the land is rich with nutrients and water and the climate is ideal for producing multiple soybean harvests per year. Nearly 70 percent of this soy is shipped off

FIGURE B3.2.1 Brazil's Agrifood System Emissions, 1990–92 and 2018–20

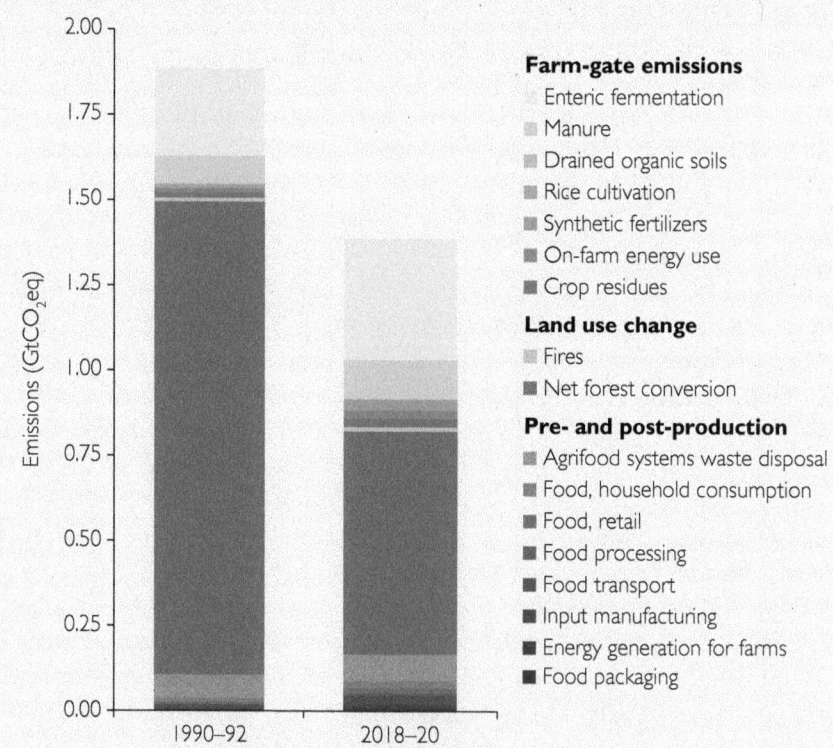

Source: World Bank based on data from World Bank 2023d and FAOSTAT 2023c.
Note: GtCO₂eq = gigatons of carbon dioxide equivalent.

(box continued next page)

BOX 3.2 **Agrifood Emissions In-Depth: Brazil** *(Continued)*

to China, where it is crushed into soybean meal and fed to livestock (International Trade Centre, n.d.).

Brazil has a few crucial opportunities to reduce its deforestation and its agrifood system emissions more generally. First, Brazil established ambitious low-carbon agriculture plans (ABC Plans) for 2010–20 and 2020–30. More than $3.5 billion has been channeled toward agricultural mitigation through these plans (Federative Republic of Brazil 2022). Second, Brazil has the potential to sequester vast amounts of carbon at relatively low costs. Brazil's agrifood system can cost-effectively (less than $100 per ton of carbon dioxide equivalent) mitigate 1,664 $MtCO_2eq$ per year, mostly through avoiding deforestation (Roe et al. 2021). This equals 3 percent of the world's greenhouse gas emissions and exceeds Brazil overall annual GHG emissions when negative emissions are factored in. Third, protecting Brazil's forests generates more value from ecosystem services ($300 billion annually) than it does from economic gains ($100 billion annually) (Hanusch and Strand 2023).

higher-fat diets saving 370 $MtCO_2eq$ by 2050 and feed additives saving 299 $MtCO_2eq$ by 2050. Expanding anaerobic manure digestion has the potential to save another 260 $MtCO_2eq$ by 2050. Likewise, applying nitrification inhibitors to pasture could further bring down emissions by 123 $MtCO_2eq$ by 2050. Using manure to generate biogas can offset energy costs, and biogas digesters, which convert methane and carbon dioxide into energy, can capture up to 80 percent of the methane from manure that would otherwise be emitted into the atmosphere. Several studies describe a more comprehensive range of technical solutions for livestock mitigation (Gerber et al. 2013).

There are multiple avenues for mitigating emissions, particularly methane, in rice production in Asian MICs

Rice production is a significant source of global methane emissions, particularly in Asian MICs. Rice supplies around 20 percent of the world's calories (Fukagawa and Ziska 2019). The warm, water-logged soil of flooded rice paddies provides ideal conditions for bacterial processes that produce methane, most of which is released into the atmosphere (Schimel 2000). As a result, paddy rice production is responsible, on average, for 16 percent of agricultural methane emissions, or 4.3 percent of global agrifood emissions (figure 2.2), which corresponds to 1.5 percent of total anthropogenic GHG emissions (Searchinger et al. 2021). The high methane content of rice emissions means that rice's yield-scaled global heating potential is about four times higher than that of wheat or maize (Linquist et al. 2012). Rice also emits carbon dioxide and nitrous oxide, whose quantities depend on several factors, such as crop residues management, fertilizer management, rice varieties, and soil types. Nitrous oxide emissions from rice cultivation are also likely higher than originally thought. A report by the US Environmental Protection Agency (EPA) finds that nitrous oxide accounts for 35 percent of non-CO_2 emissions in rice production, while methane accounts for 65 percent (US EPA 2013). Notably, virtually all rice-related GHG emissions originate in middle-income countries, and the vast majority originate in Asian countries (figure 3.19).

FIGURE 3.19 Most Rice Emissions Are from Larger Countries with the Most Rice Production—That Is, Asian Middle-Income Countries Such as China, India, and Indonesia—but Emissions Intensity Varies Widely Among Them

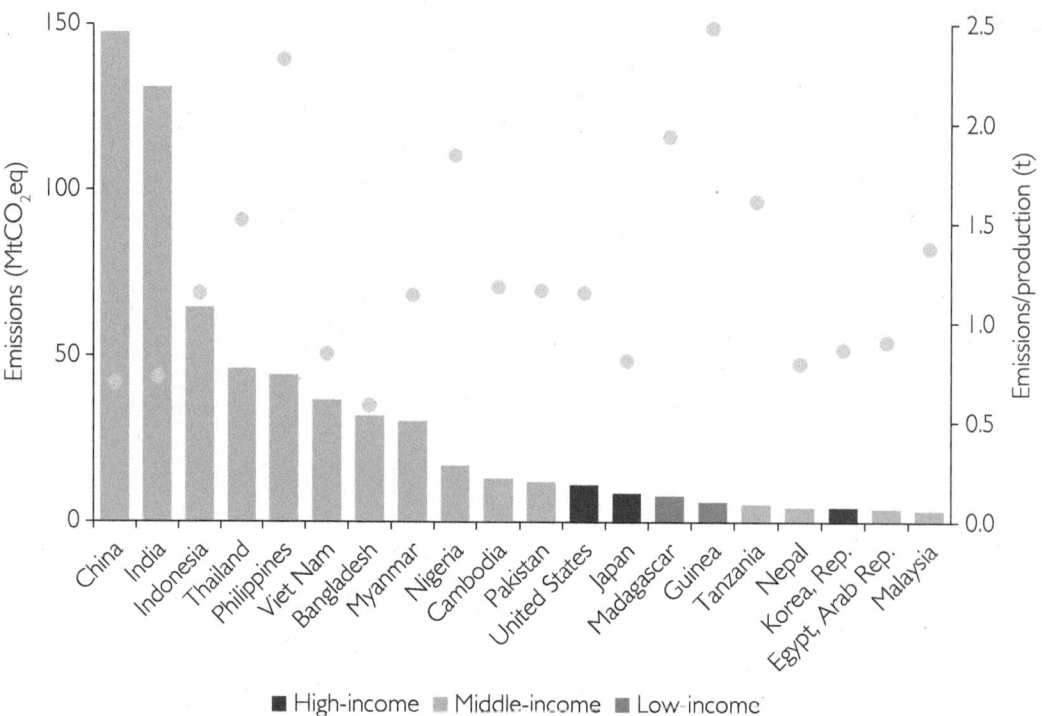

Source: World Bank based on data from World Bank 2023d, FAOSTAT 2023b, and FAOSTAT 2023c.
Note: Figure shows the average annual emissions from rice cultivation for the top 20 countries for 2018–20. Normalized emissions by national production are indicated by yellow dots. Larger density values indicate a greater scope to reduce emission intensity. HICs = high-income countries; LICs = low-income countries; MICs = middle-income countries; MtCO$_2$eq = megatons of carbon dioxide equivalent; t = tons.

Intermittent water application methods reduce net GHG emissions from rice. These methods consistently draw down the water levels in rice fields, thereby limiting the time that rice fields are flooded. The methods include single drainage, midseason drainage, and AWD practices. Each of these methods reduces methane and carbon dioxide emissions but can also increase nitrous oxide emissions, depending on soil type, management practices, and climate conditions (Lagomarsino et al. 2016; Ma et al. 2013). That said, the reduction in methane emissions generally outweighs the increase in nitrous oxide emissions; therefore, the global heating potential of AWD and other intermittent water applications is generally less than that of continuous flooding (Chidthaisong et al. 2018; Islam et al. 2018; Linquist et al. 2015; Setyanto et al. 2018). GHG reductions from AWD range from 15 to 45 percent less than emissions from continuous flooding, with some studies estimating that 90 percent less GHG is emitted (Adhya et al. 2014; Cai et al. 2003; Searchinger et al. 2021; Wang et al. 2018). Total annual rice methane emissions are about 624 million tons of CO$_2$eq (FAOSTAT 2023c); therefore, reductions would approximately be in the range of 100–300 million tons CO$_2$eq per year (IRRI 2013; McKinsey & Company 2020; Nelson 2009). Direct seeding of rice instead of transplanting rice seedlings from a nursery also reduces the time a field needs to be flooded by a month, limiting the activity of methane-producing microorganisms and cutting emissions by approximately 45 percent per hectare (Chakraborty et al. 2020).

Aerobic rice production holds the greatest potential for reducing rice-related GHG emissions, though improved rice cultivation has limited cost-effective mitigation potential.

Aerobic rice refers to varieties grown in nonflooded fields, or aerobic soils. This practice enables a greater decrease in emissions than intermittent water application practices and, in some cases, nearly eliminates methane emissions. As a result, creating aerobic conditions is the most effective and feasible option to reduce emissions from rice systems (Roe et al. 2021; Searchinger and Adhya 2015). The drawback of aerobic rice is that it tends to produce low yields. However, in recent years, new, higher-yielding aerobic rice varieties have been developed, and farmers increasingly use them as a cash crop (McKinsey & Company 2020). Table 3.1 shows that the technical mitigation potential from improved rice cultivation is less than 0.25 $GtCO_2$eq per year and its cost-effective mitigation is 0.17 $GtCO_2$eq per year—a mere 1.5 percent of MICs' overall agrifood system cost-effective mitigation potential. However, this is still higher than the 20.6 million tons of CO_2eq per year in total quantified greenhouse gas reductions from improved rice cultivation promised in the new and updated NDCs (Trang et al. 2022).

Most rice producers still rely on continuous-flooding methods to grow rice (Sriphirom et al. 2020). Some studies optimistically estimate that up to 40 percent of rice producers in China already use AWD methods (Arnaoudov, Sibayan, and Caguioa 2015; Li and Barker 2004; Sander et al. 2017) but most evidence suggests that other major rice-producing regions, such as South Asia and southeast Asia, still grow rice under continuous-flooding conditions. Farmers have several reasons for not adopting new emissions-saving practices. They often lack economic incentives to save water; for example, many farmers pay flat rates to irrigation agencies, and the payments are not tied to water use volumes (Pandey et al. 2020). Likewise, many rice farmers live in wet or humid regions with monsoon seasons, thereby limiting their ability to dry their rice fields. In many poor regions, irrigation schemes are unreliable for delivering timely water supplies or draining water, and rice fields are often grown on uneven land, making it difficult for farmers to control water flow (McKinsey & Company 2020).

Governments must apply policy and financing incentives and share technical knowledge with rice farmers to accelerate their adoption of low-emission practices. Some of these incentives are (1) limiting subsidies for water use and irrigation to incentivize farmers to save water and limit continuous flooding (Searchinger et al. 2021); (2) de-risking innovation, for example, by offering premium irrigation services to those who employ AWD or other conservation methods (Searchinger and Adhya 2015); and (3) facilitating better access to markets and climate finance (Pangestu and van Trotsenburg 2022). Yet most rice-producing countries still lack the expertise and resources to implement rice-specific measurement, reporting, and verification (MRV) systems to access climate finance. Governments should bring these incentives together in a comprehensive policy package that also applies incentives to other parts of the value change besides the farm gate (Searchinger and Adhya 2015). For instance, the system of rice intensification (SRI) is a broad set of practices to increase rice yields while using fewer resources and reducing environmental impacts. Such comprehensive packages are gaining traction. Twenty-four countries mentioned rice-related mitigation actions in their NDCs, and eight of them focused on a comprehensive rice management package that incorporates water management into broader approaches to sustainable agriculture, rather than focusing on individual stand-alone rice emissions mitigation practices (Roe et al. 2021). Similarly, Ghana and Switzerland agreed to the first-ever internationally transferred mitigation outcomes (ITMOs), with additional ITMOs planned for other countries (Manuell 2022). The ITMO allows countries to trade or purchase carbon credits for rice emissions reductions (United Nations 2022a).

Soils could sequester about 1 billion tons of solid carbon per year cost-effectively

Soils are the largest terrestrial carbon sink. Terrestrial ecosystems—such as forests, grasslands, deserts, and others—absorb around 30 percent of total anthropogenic CO_2 emissions (Terrer, Phillips, and Hungate 2021). The top meter of soil stores approximately 2,500 billion tons of carbon, both soil organic carbon (such as decaying plants and microbes) and soil inorganic carbon (which encompasses mineral forms of carbon). This is almost three times the carbon found in the atmosphere (Lal et al. 2021) and 80 percent of all terrestrial carbon (Ontl and Schulte 2012). This easily makes soils the biggest terrestrial carbon sink.

Middle-income countries have the greatest soil organic carbon sequestration potential. Twelve of the 15 countries with the highest organic carbon sequestration potential in the top 30 centimeters of soil are middle-income countries. These 12 countries account for almost half of the world's soil organic carbon sequestration potential, with China, Brazil, and India accounting for around a quarter (FAO 2022d). Furthermore, black soils, which are particularly carbon rich and productive, are found almost exclusively in MICs, with Russia, China, and Kazakhstan having two-thirds of the world's black soils (map 3.2) (FAO 2022a). MICs apply more fertilizer to croplands than low- or high-income countries and produce nearly all the world's rice (FAOSTAT 2023e). The high reliance of these countries on fertilizers and rice means they have ample opportunities for reducing methane and nitrous oxide emissions from soils.

Unsustainable land management practices, which include conventional agriculture, have released large amounts of soil carbon into the atmosphere. Deforestation and destructive farming practices, including intensive and repetitive tillage, break up soil aggregates, cause soil water evaporation, and increase the soil's organic carbon decomposition, thereby releasing CO_2 into the atmosphere (Lal 2011). As a result, soil organic carbon stocks in

MAP 3.2 Sustainable Soil Management Practices Have the Potential to Restore the World's Soil Organic Carbon

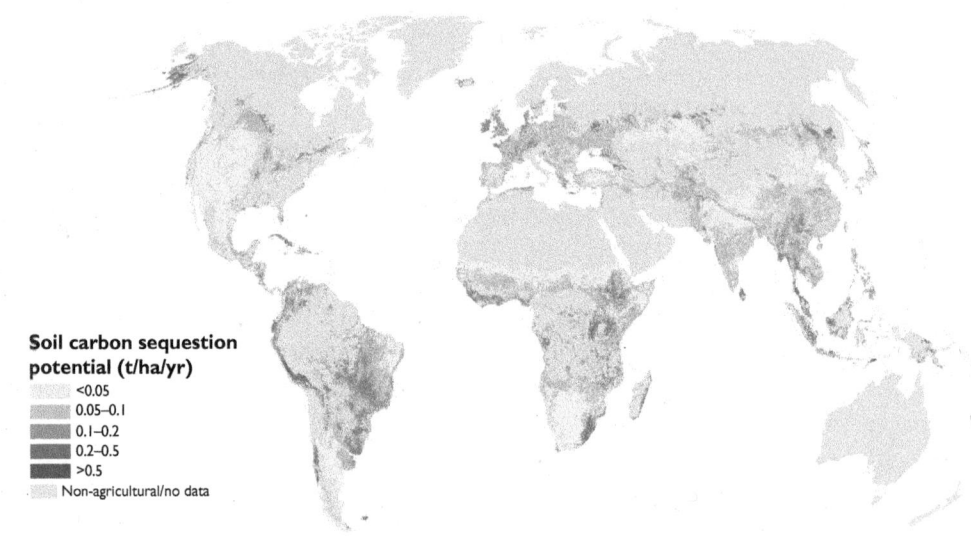

Soil carbon sequestion
potential (t/ha/yr)
<0.05
0.05–0.1
0.1–0.2
0.2–0.5
>0.5
Non-agricultural/no data

Source: FAO 2022d.
Note: Map shows the average annual soil organic carbon sequestration potential. The estimates of sequestration potential are based on 20 years of implementation of sustainable soil management practices that generated a 10 percent increase in carbon inputs. t/ha/yr = tons per hectare per year.

Recipe for a Livable Planet

croplands and grazed grasslands are 25 to 75 percent lower than they are in undisturbed soil ecosystems (IPCC 2000). Today, 52 percent of the world's agricultural soils are considered carbon depleted (UNCCD 2022), most of them found in China, then the United States, Australia, and Brazil (Sanderman, Hengl, and Fiske 2017). Historically, anthropogenic land use changes have led to 135 billion tons of soil organic carbon being lost (Lal 2018). Soil with little organic matter retains less water and requires more frequent irrigation. An assessment of the global impact of 21st-century land use change on soil erosion estimates a total yearly erosion loss of 35.9 billion tons of soil (Borrelli et al. 2017). The same study predicts that current cropland expansion will increase the erosion rate, with the greatest increases in Sub-Saharan Africa, South America, and Southeast Asia. Climate change is also having an impact, especially in areas with increased precipitation, since increased soil moisture variability negatively affects soils' ability to sequester carbon (Green et al. 2019). By contrast, regenerative organic farming practices that reduce or eliminate tillage and preserve organic matter can revive the water cycle and build drought-resilient soils.

The methane and nitrous oxide released from the soil during traditional agriculture practices contribute to global emissions. Nitrous oxide released from agricultural lands—particularly soils, mainly because of the overuse of fertilizer—accounts for approximately two-thirds of total anthropogenic nitrous oxide emissions (Fowler et al. 2015). Soil methane emissions stem primarily from wetlands and rice paddies (Singh et al. 2022). Soil methane emissions from rice cultivation are responsible for 12 percent of global methane emissions and 1.5 percent of total global GHG emissions (IPCC 2014). Forest soils absorb methane through a process called methanotrophy (Tate 2015), but the capacity of forest soils to sequester methane has decreased by 77 percent over the past three decades because of climate change–related hydrological fluxes from water runoff, drainage, infiltration, and evaporation (Ni and Groffman 2018).

Restoration and sustainable management of soils can recarbonize landscapes and reduce GHG emissions. Soils have the technical potential to sequester 2–5 billion tons of carbon per year (Bossio et al. 2020; Fuss et al. 2018). Five billion tons is equivalent to a quarter of the world's annual mitigation potential from natural climate solutions, such as afforestation, reforestation, peatland protection, grassland management, and others (Bossio et al. 2020). Soils are thus an important instrument for reducing GHG emissions. Forty percent of this mitigation potential can be realized by protecting existing stocks of soil organic carbon, and 60 percent can be achieved by restoring, or recarbonizing, depleted soils (Bossio et al. 2020). Practices to enhance soils' carbon content entail, for example, preventing erosion, reducing soil disturbances, optimizing inputs such as water and fertilizer, and raising carbon levels through agroforestry and other practices (Sykes et al. 2019) (figure 3.20). These measures must be adapted to local soil conditions to yield optimal results (Bossio et al. 2020). Sustainable soil management and restoration should take nitrous oxide and methane dynamics into account because if they do not, they can increase non-CO_2 emissions (FAO and ITPS 2021; Hassan et al. 2022). Measures to reduce soil methane emissions include sustainable rice production practices, such as alternate wetting and drying, use of improved rice varieties, and ecosystem restoration. For nitrous oxide, the more efficient use of fertilizer and manure can reduce its soil emissions; fertilizer-related emissions are discussed later in this section.

Sustainable soil management is a low-cost mitigation option that could sequester about 3.8 billion tons of CO_2eq per year, or 1 billion tons of solid carbon. Soil management is one of the most cost-effective options for reducing GHG emissions (Sperow 2020) and

FIGURE 3.20 Many Measures Can Be Used to Increase Soil Carbon Sequestration

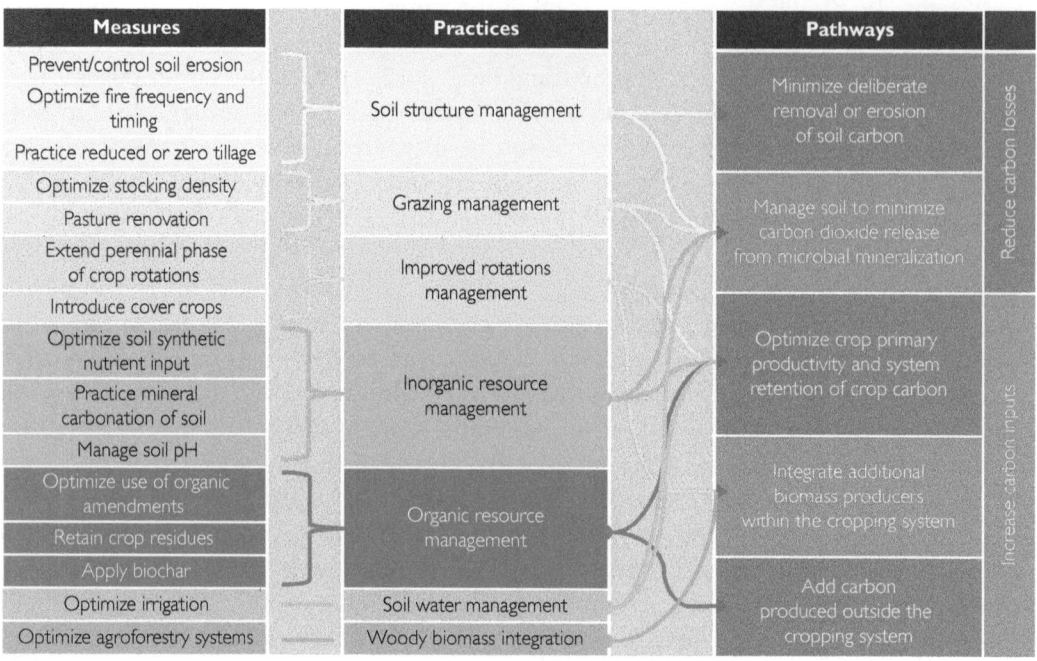

Source: Sykes et al. 2019.

includes measures such as biochar carbon removal, better nutrient application, and grass- and cropland management. According to the IPCC, around half of the soil organic carbon sequestration potential would cost less than $100 per ton of CO_2eq (IPCC 2022c), and about a quarter would cost less than $10 per ton of CO_2eq (Bossio et al. 2020). Among the four soil sequestration practices listed in table 3.1, about three-quarters of their technical potential can be achieved cost-effectively. In fact, several soil management practices to mitigate greenhouse gas emissions, such as using no-till practices and enhancing the efficiency of nitrogen use, can be implemented at negative costs because they reduce the need for labor and fertilizer (McKinsey & Company 2020). Table 3.1 shows that sustainable soil management has the potential to sequester 3.8 $GtCO_2$eq annually for less than $10 per tCO_2eq, equal to just over 1 billion tons of solid carbon, with three-quarters of that potential in MICs. Sustainable soil management can also be implemented on existing agricultural lands, avoiding competition for sparse land (FAO and ITPS 2021).

Sustainable soil management provides co-benefits besides reduced GHG emissions (figure 3.21). It enhances agricultural resilience by improving the soils' water retention capacity, protecting soil biodiversity, and reducing erosion (Amelung et al. 2020). Soil erosion alone leads to annual crop losses of 0.3 percent, equivalent to the production capacity of 4.5 million hectares of cropland per year until 2050 (FAO and ITPS 2021), and annual economic losses of $8 billion, with MICs including Brazil, China, and India being the most affected (Sartori et al. 2019). Sustainable soil management practices also contribute to the soil's overall health, fertility, and ultimately food quality and productivity, thereby increasing incomes and food security (Sykes et al. 2019). For example, water-logged soils cause annual wheat yield losses of 20–50 percent globally (Manik et al. 2019). A study in the United States found that a 1 percent increase of soil organic matter from sustainable soil

FIGURE 3.21 Sustainable Soil Management Generates Multiple Benefits in Addition to Increased Carbon Sequestration

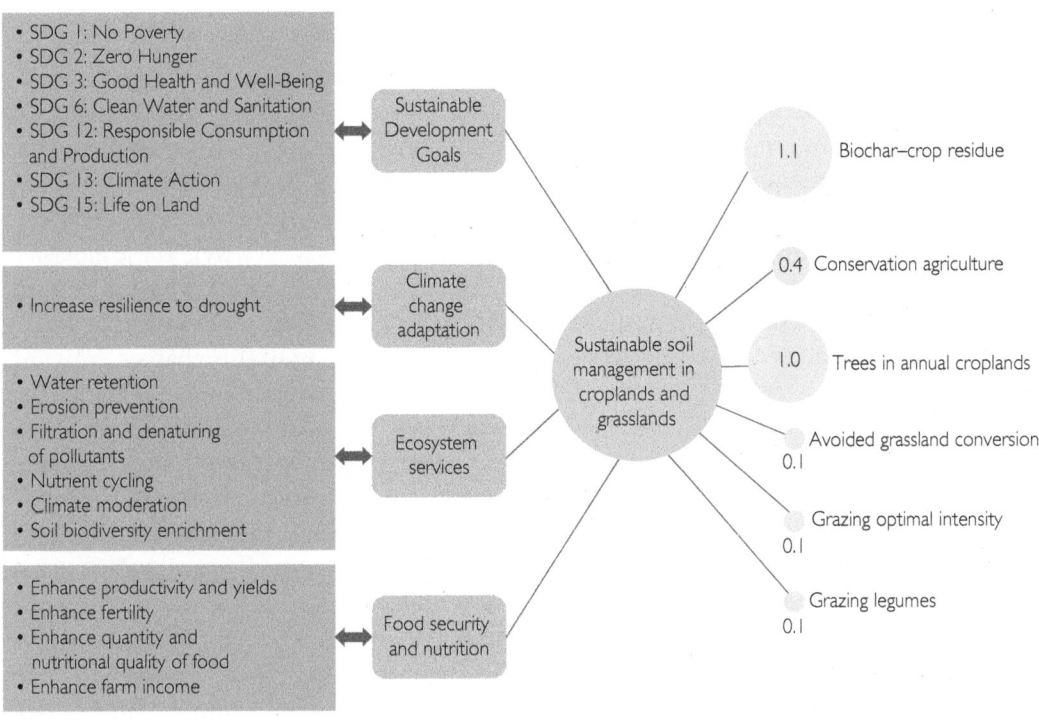

Source: World Bank based on Bossio et al. 2020.
Note: GtCO$_2$eq/yr = gigatons of carbon dioxide per year; SDG = Sustainable Development Goal.

management reduced agricultural insurance payouts after a severe drought by 36 percent and increased yields by 2.2 tons per hectare (Kane et al. 2021).

The measurement, reporting, and verification of soil GHG fluxes can improve soil management and payments to farmers for ecosystem services. MRV of soil carbon sequestration can be expensive and labor-intensive, reducing the economic viability of ecosystem service schemes (Frelih-Larsen et al. 2020). Exact measurements of soil organic carbon, methane, and nitrous oxide fluxes are needed to accurately quantify emission balances for ecosystem service payments. However, such measurements often require field sampling and laboratory analyses, which are complex, time-consuming, and labor-intensive and therefore expensive. In other words, there is a trade-off between a measurement's accuracy and its costs (World Bank 2021b). Therefore, making accurate soil carbon, methane, or nitrous oxide MRV more cost-effective would help farmers access climate finance for their sustainable soil management practices. Emerging remote-sensing technologies using satellite data can accurately measure soil emissions without the need for physical soil sampling, which can help farmers track their soil carbon sequestration at lower costs. The rapid improvement of satellite technologies, such as the European Space Agency's Sentinel-5P satellite platform, has drastically increased emission data availability and quality, especially for methane emissions. This technology can also close knowledge gaps on methane emissions from rice production and quantify the effectiveness of local soil management practices (Nelson et al. 2022). That said, use of these remote-sensing technologies remains costly and problematic for monitoring small areas.

Pre- and post-production processes are a significant and growing source of agrifood system emissions in MICs

High- and middle-income countries are responsible for almost all pre- and post-production emissions. Globally, pre- and post-production emissions account for a third of all agrifood system–related emissions. In high-income countries, pre- and post-production emissions make up 46 percent of the agrifood system emissions; for MICs, this value is 35 percent; and for LICs, it is only 6 percent (figures 3.7, 3.14, and 3.24, respectively). These emissions entail waste disposal; household consumption; on-farm heat and electricity usage; input manufacturing, for example, of pesticides and fertilizers; and food processing, packaging, transport, and retail (FAO 2023b). As evident in the HIC section of this chapter, emissions from the last four categories, the so-called processing-to-consumption phase, are greatest in HICs in comparison with UMICs, LMICs, and LICs, representing a quarter of all HIC agrifood system emissions. The lower-emissions categories are discussed in the HIC energy section of this chapter because most of those emissions come from electricity use during that phase. When those categories are removed, MICs then have the largest share of pre- and post-production emissions. The post-production phase of waste disposal and household consumption emissions makes up the largest share of these emissions in MICs: 17.4 percent, or nearly 1.9 $GtCO_2eq$ emissions, compared to 0.47 $GtCO_2eq$ for HICs. Even when household food consumption emissions in MICs are broken up between upper- and lower-middle-income countries, LMICs have the highest emissions in this category. Similarly, the pre-production phase of input manufacturing, which includes fertilizer production, emits the most GHGs in MICs. Thus, this section first looks at fertilizer production and use before turning to food loss and waste and household food consumption.

Fertilizer production and use

Middle-income countries produce and consume the most fertilizer. Mineral fertilizers have revolutionized agriculture and play a vital role in reducing global hunger. Since the 1960s, nitrogen fertilizer use has increased by 800 percent and was a major driver of the world's efforts to increase calorie availability (IPCC 2022b). It is estimated that half of the global population is fed with crops that are grown with synthetic fertilizers (Erisman et al. 2008; Stewart et al. 2005). A total of 80 percent of the world's fertilizer is consumed in middle-income countries, with Brazil, China, India, and Indonesia among the top five fertilizer consumers worldwide (International Fertilizer Association 2022). Moreover, fertilizer application in these countries is often wastefully high: on average, MICs apply 168 kg of fertilizer per hectare, compared to 141 kg in high-income countries and 12 kg in low-income countries (FAOSTAT 2023f). As a result, nitrogen use efficiency in MICs is just 42 percent,[10] with that in China and India considerably lower (Lassaletta et al. 2014). MICs are also some of the world's largest fertilizer producers, with China, India, and Russia producing more than a third of the world's nitrogen fertilizer (FAO 2023b).

Fertilizer production and use damage the environment and are major sources of GHG emissions. Chapter 2 shows that fertilizer production (2.6 percent) and use (3.8 percent) account for 6.4 percent of total agrifood emissions and are the biggest sources of agrifood emissions in the pre-production phase. Nitrogen fertilizer production and use are greenhouse gas–intensive, since production typically uses natural gas and coal as feedstock (IEA 2021a).

Meanwhile, fertilizer use generates nitrous oxide and CO_2 emissions. The manufacturing of ammonia alone emits around 420 million tCO_2eq per year, equivalent to around 1 percent of global GHG emissions (Liu, Elgowainy, and Wang 2020). Moreover, ammonia demand is predicted to increase by 25–40 percent by 2050 (IEA 2021a). Virtually all ammonia produced today is derived from coal and natural gas. Nitric acid manufacturing, another chemical process in nitrogen fertilizer production, generates nitrous oxide emissions of around 85 million tCO_2eq per year (Eggleston et al. 2006; Gao and Cabrera Serrenho 2023). Around half of all fertilizer-related emissions are caused by direct and indirect nitrous oxide emissions from fields (Gao and Cabrera Serrenho 2023). Additionally, the application of urea releases CO_2 into the atmosphere. Fertilizers damage the planet in other ways, too. Less than half of the 109 million metric tons of synthetic nitrogen fertilizer used each year is absorbed by crops, with the rest either leached into groundwater, thus creating marine dead zones, or lost as potent nitrous oxide greenhouse gas emissions (Peoples et al. 2019). The excessive use of inorganic fertilizers, herbicides, and pesticides acidifies soils, undermines plant nutrition, and disrupts soil microbiology, especially fungal networks, which are key to a plant's nutrition and defense from disease (AL-Ani et al. 2019; Huber 2010; Johal and Huber 2009; Levesque and Rahe 1992).

Emissions from fertilizer production and use can be drastically reduced cost-effectively. Recent research shows that a combination of interventions could reduce emissions from nitrogen fertilizer production and use by up to 84 percent (Gao and Cabrera Serrenho 2023). A global shift to green ammonia production that uses renewables to power the process would reduce 75 percent of fertilizer production-related emissions (Gao and Cabrera Serrenho 2023). Carbon capture and storage technologies can provide further emissions reductions (IEA 2021a). Installing catalyst technology in nitric acid facilities could almost completely eliminate nitrous oxide emissions from nitric acid production (Menegat, Ledo, and Tirado 2022). Similarly, nitrification and urea inhibitors can reduce nitrous oxide emissions from fertilizer use (Kim, Saggar, and Roudier 2012). A switch from urea to ammonium nitrate fertilizer would further reduce emissions from fertilizer use (Gao and Cabrera Serrenho 2023; IEA 2021a). Overall, low-emissions fertilizer production has the technical potential to reduce emissions by 0.48 $GtCO_2eq$ annually, and between 63 percent and 100 percent of this could be achieved cost-effectively. Meanwhile, reducing fertilizer demand offers the greatest mitigation opportunity for reducing emissions from fertilizer use, because high demand is often linked to low nutrient-use efficiency. Increasing nitrogen use efficiency from its current level of 42 percent to 67 percent could halve nitrogen demand (Gao and Cabrera Serrenho 2023). Integrated soil fertility management, diversified crop production, soil fertility mapping, and use of slow-release and smart fertilizers can help minimize soil nutrient losses and further reduce fertilizer demand. Reducing fertilizer use would also provide economic and environmental co-benefits (Cui et al. 2018). For example, reducing fertilizer application lowers the overall cost of food production, when coupled with enhanced nutrient management practices, and reduces waterbody pollution.

Food loss and waste

Food loss and waste cause unnecessary emissions across the entire food chain. According to FAO, *food loss* refers to the decrease in edible food at the production, postharvest, and processing stages of the food chain, mostly in developing countries. *Food waste* refers to the discard of edible foods at the retail and consumer levels, mostly in developed countries (FAO 2023d). The amount of food lost or wasted is around 30 percent of the world's food supply (World Bank 2020a). The amount of all food loss is estimated at 14 percent globally (UNEP 2021), with large regional variations (FAO 2019b). Currently, 28 percent of the world's agriculture area is used to produce food that is wasted (World Bank 2020a). This is land that could otherwise be storing carbon and food that would no longer require emissions-intensive processing, transportation, or disposal. Reduction of waste, especially of rice and meats, would avoid methane emissions from producing unused food. In fact, reducing food waste reduces methane at a negative cost, since farms generate higher incomes when they reduce postharvest losses (UNEP and Climate and Clean Air Coalition 2021). Estimates indicate that feasible measures to limit postharvest food waste could reduce emissions by about 1.05 billion tons of CO_2eq per year by 2030 (Thornton et al. 2023). Chapter 2 also shows that crop residues generate 1.2 percent of all agrifood system waste. At the household level, food waste emissions shares are similar in richer and poorer countries but are cumulatively the highest in lower-middle-income countries (figure 3.22).

Food waste disposal is a major source of agrifood emissions, especially methane. Solid food waste is disposed through incineration, composting, or circular practices (discussed next), such as biogas production (Karl and Tubiello 2021). However, in most countries the majority of solid food waste ends up in landfills and open dumps, where the anaerobic decomposition of organic material releases methane gas (CH_4) (Thi, Kumar, and Lin 2015). Much of the food that is produced but not eaten ends up in landfills and generates 3.3 billion tons of CO_2 eq a year, equal to about 7.9 percent of agrifood system GHGs (as shown in chapter 2). This food waste also generates local air pollutants. Reducing waste disposal emissions should be a priority for both HICs and MICs.

There are many cost-effective measures to reduce food waste (Willett et al. 2019; Yontar 2023). One important method is to match food supply to demand. Producers often overproduce and retailers often overstock to account for uncertain demand, and consumers often overbuy to account for uncertain needs. Matching supply to demand would prevent food waste from ever reaching landfills or water systems (Chauhan et al. 2021). Emerging digital solutions—including big data, blockchain technology, and cloud computing, among others—could help match supply to demand and manage the timely transfer, and guarantee the safety, of foods across the supply chain, thus reducing waste and securing a better food shelf life for the consumer (Annosi et al. 2021). Improved access to roads and railways is a particularly effective way for low-income countries to prevent foods from spoiling during

FIGURE 3.22 Lower-Middle-Income Countries Generate the Most Food Waste

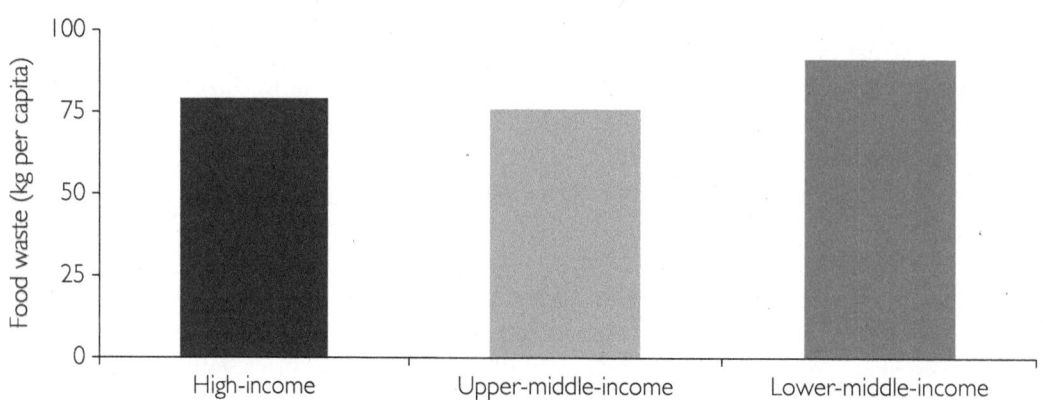

Source: UNEP 2021.
Note: There are insufficient data for low-income countries. kg = kilogram.

Recipe for a Livable Planet

road blockages or delays. Other opportunities to avoid food loss during transportation include cold handling and storage, timely and efficient trade logistics, good physical infrastructure, and adequate processing and packaging to preserve foods (FAO 2019b). However, many lower-income countries lack the resources for these solutions. Overall, table 3.1 shows that measures to reduce food waste have the technical potential to mitigate nearly 0.9 $GtCO_2eq$ per year, with half of that being achievable by cost-effective measures.

Citizens also have a role to play in reducing food waste at all phases of food consumption. These phases involve the purchasing, storage, handling, and disposal of foods. At the purchasing phase, consumers can shop for appropriate amounts of food, buy low-emitting and nonperishable foods, or prioritize food with near expiration dates. In the storage phase, consumers can keep food refrigerated or freeze it for later use. In the handling phase, citizens can prepare the right amount of food to reduce leftovers and cook closer to the food's expiration date. In the disposal phase, citizens can eat leftovers, compost waste, or donate unused food. Overall, 17 percent of food is wasted in retail and by consumers, particularly in households (UNEP 2021).

Applying on-farm circular practices reduces food loss and waste[11] and avoids GHG emissions (FAO 2018). Circular agriculture uses no more acreage or resources than strictly necessary and sees waste as a raw material to produce new food products, including crops, food, feed, and energy, among others. A Netherlands study (van Bodegom, van Middelaar, and Metz 2019) concludes that circular agriculture creates jobs, lowers CO_2 emissions, reduces natural resource exploitation, and improves living conditions because of less pollution and fewer malodorous smells. Moreover, bioenergy technologies can convert agrifood waste to energy. Residues with high lignocellulosic content, such as pellets and briquettes, are suitable for biogas production, which can be used for cooking, heating, or electricity. For example, a study in Egypt found that livestock residues, sunflower heads, and sugar beet haulms could be reused to generate around 30 megawatts of electricity, enough to supplement the energy needs of three governorates (FAO 2017b). In Azerbaijan, FAO estimates that at any given time there were 45,000 tons of hazelnut husks and 40,000 tons of pruning residues, which can be made into pellets or charcoal briquettes for energy (FAO 2022b). These pellets could meet the cooking and heating energy needs of more than 10,000 households, and charcoal briquettes could meet the needs of around 13,000 households. This would avoid approximately 32,400 tons of CO_2eq per year for pellets and 42,356 tons of CO_2eq per year for charcoal briquettes compared to using natural gas. The total investment to carry this out was $1.2 million for pellet production and $1.9 million for briquette production. A groundbreaking World Bank study (Verner et al. 2021) shows how insects can be farmed to consume crop residues, thereby reducing farm waste and providing a valuable source of protein for animal feed. The study calculates that insect farming in Africa using agricultural waste as feed could annually generate crude protein worth up to $2.6 billion and biofertilizers worth up to $19.4 billion. That is enough protein meal to meet up to 14 percent of the crude protein needed to rear all the pigs, goats, fish, and poultry in Africa.

Wastewater

Agrifood system wastewater and wastewater treatment processes release greenhouse gases. The world's water and wastewater utilities account for 3–7 percent of all emissions (UNESCO 2020). Untreated or poorly treated wastewater releases large amounts of methane and nitrous oxide into the atmosphere, and more than 80 percent of all wastewater released into the environment is not treated (WWAP 2017). That said, wastewater treatment in itself is an energy-intensive process that can release GHGs but, as will be discussed, provides important benefits as well. Runoff from agricultural fields into waterbodies can also increase greenhouse gas emissions, as river denitrification converts nitrogen to nitrous oxide (Winnick 2021). Similarly, wastewater from palm oil production—so-called palm oil mill effluent—is a source of methane emissions (Mahmod et al. 2020). Wastewater emissions of nitrous oxide make up only 3 percent of total anthropogenic nitrous oxide emissions, but they can account for 26 percent of the global "water chain" GHG footprint (Kampschreur et al. 2009). Notably, these are rough estimates, since information on wastewater generation and treatment is not systematically monitored or not reported on in many countries, particularly in rural areas (Mateo-Sagasta, Raschid-Sally, and Thebo 2015). Thus, it is difficult to determine the exact contribution of wastewater-related emissions in the agrifood sector.

Wastewater from agrifood systems causes negative environmental externalities. Currently, global industries discharge about 2,250 cubic kilometers (km^3) of effluent into the environment per year, of which agriculture discharges 1,260 km^3 per year as drainage (FAO 2021b). Examples of agricultural wastewater include manure water, milking center wash water, barnyard and feedlot runoff, egg-washing and -processing water, slaughterhouse wastewaters, horse-washing waters, and composting runoff. Cropland runoff can contribute sedimentation and release concentrated streams of fertilizers and pesticides into surface waters. If inadequately treated, these waste streams can have serious ecological ramifications (Liu 2008; WWAP 2017). For instance, nitrate- and phosphorous-laden agricultural wastewater released into freshwater bodies causes eutrophication and oxygen depletion in those waters. Increased phosphorus loading from agriculture is one of several factors that have led to algal blooms in Lake Erie and Lake Winnipeg (Michalak et al. 2013; Schindler, Hecky, and McCullough 2012). The northern Gulf of Mexico is the second-largest zone of coastal hypoxia (Rabalais, Turner, and Wiseman 2002), known as a "dead zone," which is caused largely by nitrate flux draining from agricultural land in the Mississippi River basin (McIsaac et al. 2001). Planetary limits for nitrogen and phosphorous flows are already beyond safe levels, threatening the functioning of earth systems such as biomes, basins, sources, and sinks (Steffen et al. 2015).

Some agrifood wastewater management practices can mitigate emissions. These practices include minimizing runoff, enhancing nutrient management, and improving wastewater treatment. Projects that introduced GHG reduction technologies at water utility companies decreased GHG emissions from water and wastewater systems by 23 percent in Mexico, 32 percent in Thailand, and 34 percent in Peru.[12] Moreover, treating and reusing wastewater can abate GHG emissions. Reusing treated wastewater for irrigation reduces the need for energy-intensive surface and groundwater pumping and alleviates irrigation pressures on scarce freshwater resources. In Jordan, approximately 90 percent of treated wastewater was reused in agricultural activities in 2019 (UN-Habitat and WHO 2021). If this could be applied to the approximately 330 km^3 per year of the world's municipal wastewater, it would theoretically generate enough treated water to irrigate and fertilize millions of hectares of crops and produce enough biogas to supply energy to millions of households. However, very little wastewater is treated, and even less is reused after treatment (Mateo-Sagasta, Raschid-Sally, and Thebo 2015). According to Water Reuse Europe (2018), only 2 percent of treated wastewater is reused in Europe, although this is expected to grow, with the greatest growth potential in Portugal and Spain (WWAP 2017). The cost of water treatment is determined

Recipe for a Livable Planet

by the daily volume of wastewater streams and the relative concentrations of contaminants (Liu 2014). Constructed wetlands are a cost-effective and low-maintenance treatment option that uses microbial and plant activity to break down waste and is applicable to various wastewater types (Rozema et al. 2016). For instance, studies suggest that constructed wetlands reduce nitrogen and phosphorous concentrations from cropland-dominated watersheds by 14–45 percent, depending on design and climatic characteristics (Messer et al. 2021). The application of biochar—charcoal produced from plant matter and stored in the soil that would otherwise decompose and emit carbon dioxide into the atmosphere—is another low-cost treatment method for removing toxic contaminants, such as pesticides, from wastewater (Cao et al. 2009; Chun et al. 2004; Qambrani et al. 2017; Zheng et al. 2010).

Wastewater treatment can also transform waste into a resource. This is especially the case when treated wastewater is used to produce bioenergy, biochemicals, and other valuable products while reducing pollution and emissions. Biological processes involved in this treatment include fermentation, microbial fuel cell generation, biological hydrogen production, and methanogenic anaerobic digestion (Angenent et al. 2004). One example of this type of circular economy is from Jordan's As-Samra Wastewater Treatment Plant. The plant treats between 267,000 and 840,000 cubic meters of wastewater per day by mixing it with rainwater. Over 80 percent of this treated water is used for agriculture, particularly irrigation, and serves 2.2 million people (World Bank 2018). The plant also produces nearly 13 megawatts of energy from biogas and hydropower, meeting 80 percent of the plant's own energy needs, making it one of the most modern and energy-efficient treatment plants in the Middle East (Millennium Challenge Corporation 2022). More generally, the water treatment process produces biogas, which can be recovered and used to power the treatment plant itself, rendering it energy neutral and avoiding fossil energy-related emissions. Advanced wastewater treatment systems can also recover nutrients from the wastewater that can be transformed into fertilizers, diminishing the reliance on high-emitting synthetic fertilizers (WWAP 2017).

Household food consumption

Household food consumption is the largest emissions category within pre- and post-production processes. These processes make up 7.3 percent of all agrifood emissions, including 8.2 percent of MIC emissions, 7.8 percent of HIC emissions, and a fraction of a percent of LIC emissions. Most of the emissions in this category come from running of household kitchen appliances. Cooking is another source of household food consumption emissions. Globally, natural gas dominates as the chief cooking fuel, accounting for 51 percent in 2019. Meanwhile, electricity's share has surged since 2010, powering 10 percent of all cooking in 2019. Biomass and charcoal constitute most of the rest, averaging 35 percent of all cooking fuels (WHO 2022b). However, in Africa, the use of biomass and charcoal for cooking hovers around 75 percent (IEA et al. 2022). This is common in many remote and rural communities that maintain off-grid cooking in the absence of municipal gas or electricity connections. Household food consumption emissions in MICs have seen the sharpest rise, with a 167 percent increase from 2000 to 2020 (figure 3.23).[13] This rise was driven by households shifting from traditional wood fuels to fossil fuels, particularly liquified petroleum gas and electricity, for food preparation and consumption. The same dynamic is expected in LICs as those countries move away from wood fire cooking. For example, southeast Asia witnessed a substantial decline in traditional fuel use, with its share plunging from 58 percent in 2011 to 36 percent in 2019 (WHO 2022b). Generally, this is good for people, because it reduces health risks, and for the climate, because 34 percent of wood fuel is harvested unsustainably (US EPA 2023), contributing to deforestation. However, this does not necessarily reduce net emissions, since switching from wood fuel– to fossil fuel–based cooking just means that many of the cooking-related emissions move from land use change categories (basically, deforestation to supply wood stoves) to household consumption categories. That said, as households become wealthier they not only convert wood stoves to gas stoves, but also start using appliances—such as refrigerators, freezers, or microwaves—that also increase these households' carbon footprint (figure 3.23). See box 3.3 on China's growth in household food consumption emissions.

Clean cooking reduces emissions and bolsters health and food security in developing countries, but acquiring clean cookstoves is not yet cost-effective. *Clean cooking* refers to adopting modern, energy-efficient stoves that use clean energy to operate. Greenhouse gas emissions from cooking with nonrenewable fuels are estimated to equal a gigaton (1 billion tons) of carbon dioxide annually (US EPA 2023). This volume represents about 2 percent of all global CO_2 emissions, mirroring the emissions from global aviation or shipping (US EPA 2023). A typical cookstove releases between 2 and 6 tons of CO_2 each year. However, improved stoves can curtail these emissions by 50–80 percent, rendering many clean-cookstove initiatives eligible for carbon credits (US EPA 2023). Compounded by population growth and sluggish economic progression, the number of individuals in Sub-Saharan Africa lacking clean cooking access swelled from 777 million in 2010 to 964 million in 2020 (IEA et al. 2022). Clean cooking also diminishes indoor air pollution and exposure to harmful air contaminants, safeguarding women and children in particular. High- and middle-income countries spearhead global progress in applying clean-cooking solutions, but low-income countries trail. In 2020, a mere 15 percent of the populace in low-income countries had access to clean cooking, compared to 84 percent in upper-middle-income countries and 59 percent in lower-middle-income countries (World Bank 2023a). Overall, SDG7's goal of achieving universal clean-cooking access by 2030 remains elusive, particularly in Sub-Saharan Africa, where there is inadequate access to clean fuels and modern stoves (IEA et al. 2022). Part of the reason for this is that less than 30 percent of the technical mitigation potential from converting to clean cookstoves can be achieved cost-effectively (table 3.1).

FIGURE 3.23 Per Capita Energy Use Arising from Household Food Consumption Grew Rapidly in Middle-Income Countries from 2000 to 2020

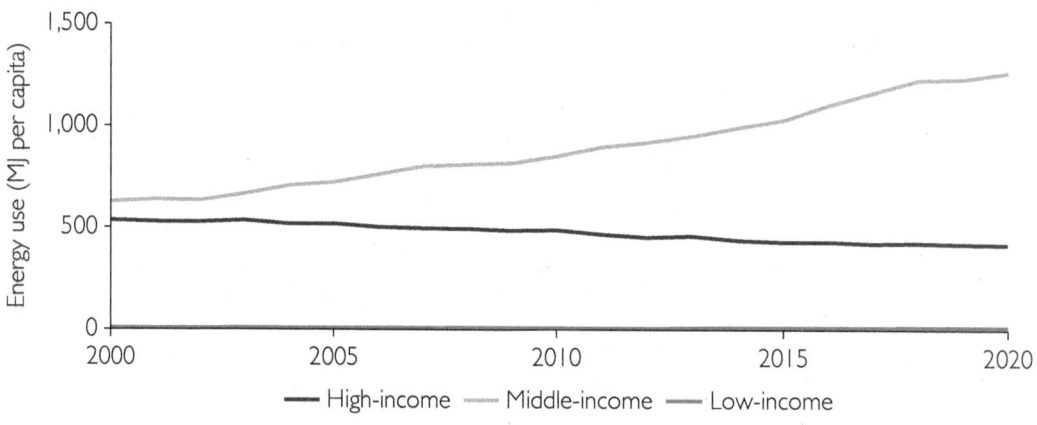

Source: World Bank based on data from FAOSTAT n.d.
Note: Energy sources for household food consumption include electricity, coal, natural gas, and petroleum products. MJ = million joules.

BOX 3.3 Agrifood Emissions In-Depth: China

China's household food consumption helps make it the world leader in both total emissions and agrifood system emissions. China's agrifood system emits 2.2 gigatons of carbon dioxide equivalent ($GtCO_2eq$) per year (figure B3.3.1), almost three times the emissions from all airplane flights in a given year combined. Two-thirds of these emissions are caused by pre- and post-production processes, with household food consumption making up 32 percent of all agrifood system emissions, food processing making up 13 percent, and food waste making up 12 percent (FAOSTAT 2023c). These high emissions are a function of China's enormous population and its rapid development and poverty reduction over the last several decades. As a result, China's large population is emitting more greenhouse gas (GHG) than ever before.

FIGURE B3.3.1 China's Agrifood System Emissions, 1990–92 and 2018–20

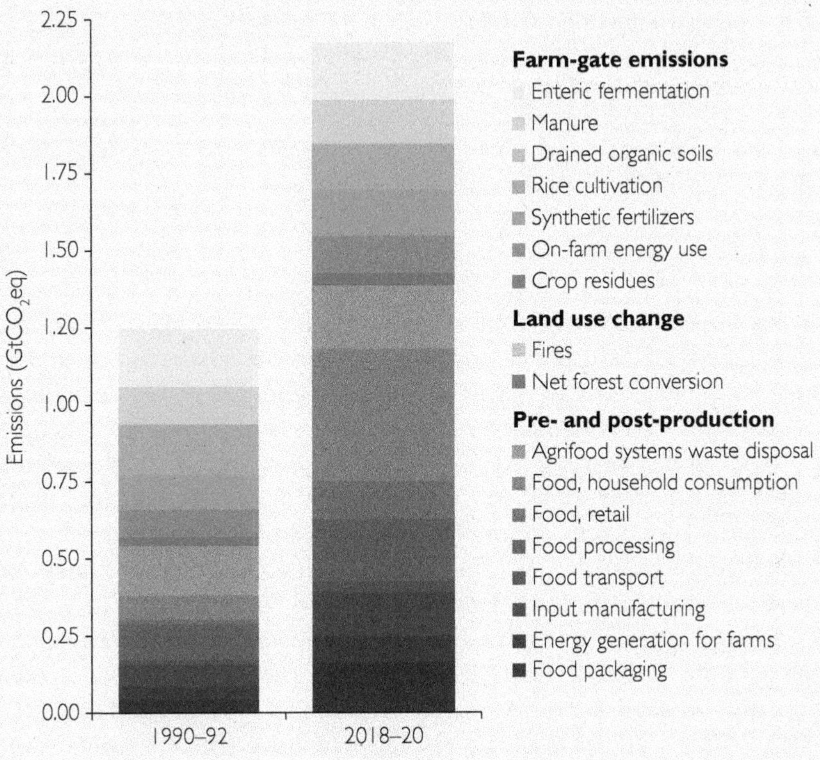

Emissions ($GtCO_2eq$)
2.25
2.00
1.75
1.50
1.20
1.00
0.75
0.50
0.25
0.00
1990–92
2018–20
Farm-gate emissions
Enteric fermentation
Manure
Drained organic soils
Rice cultivation
Synthetic fertilizers
On-farm energy use
Crop residues
Land use change
Fires
Net forest conversion
Pre- and post-production
Agrifood systems waste disposal
Food, household consumption
Food, retail
Food processing
Food transport
Input manufacturing
Energy generation for farms
Food packaging

Source: World Bank based on data from World Bank 2023d and FAOSTAT 2023c.

China emits almost nothing from its land use, land use change, and forestry (LULUCF) sector because of policy and trade. China's massive reforestation and afforestation efforts are a big reason for the limited LULUCF emissions. Between 2000 and 2017, China accounted for 25 percent of the world's increase in forest cover (Chen et al. 2019). Today, China's forests absorb around 5 percent of its GHG emissions. Much of this can be

(box continued next page)

BOX 3.3 **Agrifood Emissions In-Depth: China** *(Continued)*

attributed to China's Great Green Wall project, which started in 1978 and aims to increase the region's forest cover by 15 percent (Wolosin 2017). However, this project was never meant to reduce emissions but to safeguard food security by protecting the country's food production in the agricultural regions close to the Gobi Desert. This region was experiencing desertification and frequent flash floods, making it less and less productive. The reforestation efforts were a way of recuperating these lands before they were lost for good. Nevertheless, the GHG mitigation effects were large and cost-effective, with an estimated cost of around $25 per ton of CO_2eq removed (Wolosin 2017). However, another reason for China's limited LULUCF emissions is that land-consuming commodity production has shifted to countries that can meet the demand and produce commodities more efficiently. As a result, Brazil sends 70 percent of its soybean production, a leading cause of emissions from deforestation in Brazil, to China to feed livestock. That said, Chinese commodity importers are taking some steps to reduce their footprint on Brazil's forests by setting deforestation-free standards and terms with producers (Reuters 2023). Domestically, China has also been proactive in climate change mitigation efforts, setting ambitious targets in its 2022 Implementation Plan for Emission Reduction and Carbon Sequestration in Agriculture and Rural Areas and its 14th five-year development plan. It is also the world leader in renewable energy investments and in pursuing alternative protein sources from plants and lab-grown meat (Rouzi 2022).

The transition to clean cooking requires addressing both the supply of clean cooking fuels and the demand for them, which is closely related to consumer behavior. Sociodemographic determinants such as education, gender, culture, and habits are equally important (Galimberti 2021). Many Sub-Saharan African countries lack the infrastructure for rapid deployment of electricity or natural gas for cooking, necessitating a phased transition to clean cooking. In urban areas where infrastructure exists, introducing electricity and nonbiomass alternatives becomes more feasible, with efforts then centered on promoting behavioral change. In rural settings, the transition might first involve adopting modern solid and gaseous biofuels. On the supply side, this can be achieved by leveraging unused, sustainably sourced agricultural residues and introducing efficient charcoal production technologies. Unlike earlier generations of biofuels (such as corn-based ethanol) that create competition for land and other inputs, modern fuel sources avoid these trade-offs by recycling organic material that would otherwise go to waste. This approach would alleviate pressures on forests and offer additional income opportunities for farmers. Concurrently, increasing demand for modern biofuels could involve introducing clean-cooking stoves and spearheading dedicated behavioral change initiatives.

Many countries, especially HICs, have taken proactive steps to reduce cooking-related emissions. These steps include banning gas-based cooking and gas-powered cooking appliances. For instance, New York enacted regulations in 2023 to phase out natural gas appliances in new residential buildings, encouraging the use of electric alternatives (Stack 2023). California enacted a similar ban in 2021 for both residential and commercial buildings before it was overturned in 2023 on the grounds that it violated the US's 1975 Energy Policy and Conservation Act (Medora 2023). In the United Kingdom, the government is promoting heat pumps and electric stoves to eliminate gas for cooking in new homes by 2025 (Taylor 2019; Vishnubhotla 2024). Similarly, since 2018, the Netherlands has banned newly built homes from connecting to the gas network (Pont Omgeving 2018). Other cities, such as Seattle, are exploring similar measures to limit gas use in both residential and commercial kitchens (Iaconangelo 2023; Ryan 2021). These steps toward clean cooking have helped HICs curb their per capita household food consumption emissions. That said, there is additional work that needs to be done, especially in MICs and LICs. For example, cooking traditions are engrained in societies, so transitioning to clean cooking requires addressing many sociodemographic determinants, such as gender, culture, habits, and education (Galimberti 2021). Also, as mentioned, many communities, especially in rural areas, remain off-grid, and a clean-energy infrastructure must be put in place to allow access to clean cooking.

Low-Income Countries Can Bypass a High-Emissions Development Path, Seizing Climate-Smart Opportunities for Greener, More Competitive Economies

Low-income countries'[14] contribution to global greenhouse gas emissions is small compared to that of richer countries, but most of their emissions come from the agrifood system. They contribute 4.2 percent to global greenhouse gas emissions and 5.8 percent to global agrifood system emissions (Climate Watch 2023). Indeed, over 82 percent of LIC emissions come from the agrifood system, well above the global average of 31 percent (Crippa et al. 2021; figure 3.24). Half of LICs' agrifood emissions come from LULUCF. This is because of the prominence of the agriculture sector in these countries: agriculture contributes more than a quarter of the GDP for LICs. Overall, agrifood systems in low-income countries emit 1.8 billion tons of CO_2eq per year (figure 3.25), which is less than 10 percent of total global food system emissions. Notably, more than 40 percent of food system emissions in LICs come from just two countries: Ethiopia, because of large livestock populations, and the Democratic Republic of Congo, because of high deforestation rates. Moreover, agrifood systems in low-income countries are more GHG intensive. This reflects the lower productivity and efficiency of LIC food systems compared to those of middle- and high-income countries (Laborde et al. 2021). Put simply, cropping in LICs requires more land for the same amount of output. Similarly, livestock production in LICs entails suboptimal feeding or pasture management, resulting in more emissions, notably methane, per unit of dairy or meat (see figure 3.18). As a result, GHG emissions per hectare of arable land or per animal in LICs are below the global average but higher per unit of yield.

LICs contribute the least to climate change but suffer the most

Climate change disproportionately affects agrifood systems in low-income countries. These countries are highly dependent on primary industries, such as agriculture and fisheries, and have little adaptive capacity (IPCC 2022a). The agriculture sector in low-income countries contributes more than a quarter to their GDPs but only 4.4 percent to GDP globally (World Bank 2023d). Moreover, 59 percent of the workforce in LICs is employed in (often unpaid) agriculture (Rud and Trapeznikova 2021), compared to 26 percent globally and only 3 percent in high-income countries (ILO 2020). The high economic importance of the agrifood sector in low-income countries makes any negative climatic impacts disproportionally felt, especially by subsistence farmers, who rely on natural resources and rain-fed systems (Williams et al. 2018). Indeed, the agricultural sector sustains 82 percent of all drought

FIGURE 3.24 Low-Income Countries Contribute the Least to Global Agrifood System Emissions, Although Most of These Emissions Are from Deforestation

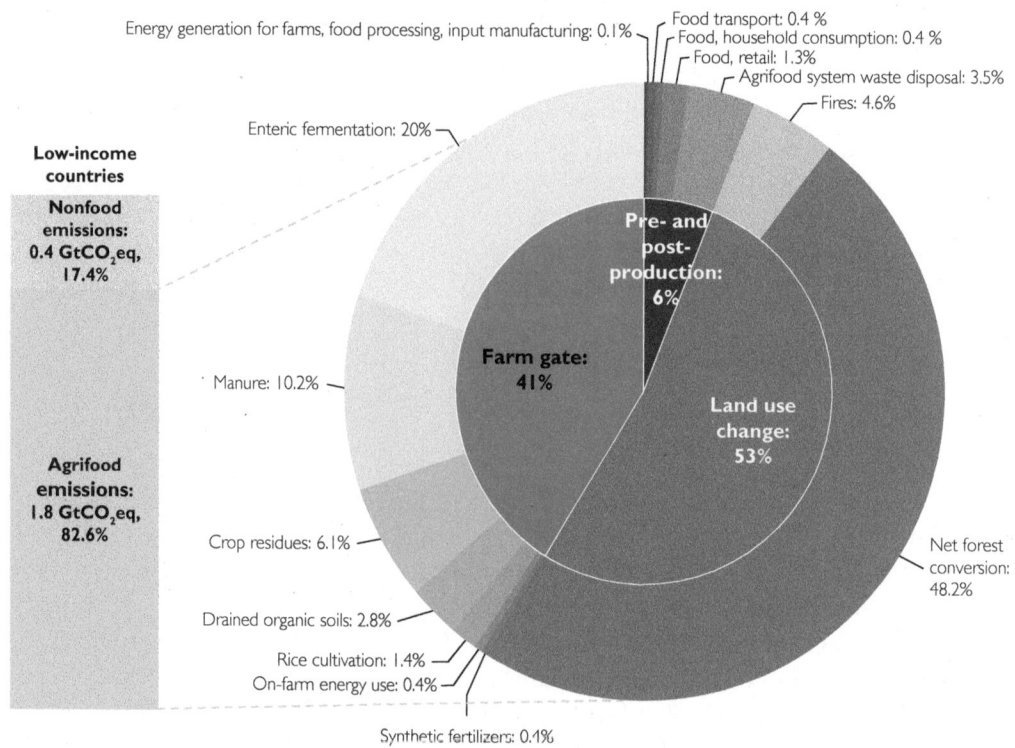

Source: World Bank based on data from FAOSTAT 2023c and World Bank 2023d.

Note: Left: Agrifood system emissions as share of total global greenhouse gas emissions (data account for methane, nitrous oxide, and carbon dioxide emissions), 2018–20 annual average. Right: Emissions categorized by three main subcategories and their individual components. GtCO$_2$eq = gigatons of carbon dioxide equivalent.

impacts in LICs, compared to 18 percent for all other sectors combined. Between 2008 and 2018, low-income countries experienced disaster-related agricultural losses of $14.7 billion (FAO 2021a), and between 1998 and 2017, LICs experienced disaster-related economic losses equal to 1.8 percent of their GDP. The Sahel region accounts for more than half of these losses, mostly from floods and droughts. Climate change has also slowed agricultural productivity in tropical regions, which are overrepresented by LICs (Ortiz-Bobea et al. 2021). Between 2008 and 2018, LICs suffered disaster-related losses of around $3.5 million per day (FAO 2021a). These economic impacts, though severe, are still lower than global averages, which increased sevenfold from the 1970s to the 2010s, going from $49 million to $383 million per day (United Nations 2021). However, the human toll in developing countries is much costlier than in developed countries, with a staggering 91 percent of disaster-related deaths occurring in poorer countries (United Nations 2021). Impacts from extreme weather events in LICs are expected to grow going forward (O'Neill, van Aalst, and Ibrahim 2022). For the poorest populations, climate change and natural disasters are predicted to increase extreme poverty by 35 million to 122 million people by 2030 (Hallegatte et al. 2016). For a specific example of climate change's disastrous consequences in poor countries, see box 3.4 on drought impacts in the Horn of Africa.

Climate change negatively affects food security, especially in low-income countries. The number of people affected by hunger is on the rise, with global undernourishment having risen from 8 percent to almost 10 percent between 2019 and 2022 (FAO et al. 2022). Climate change drives this food insecurity, especially in LICs. Between 2008 and 2018, disasters caused crop and livestock losses in low- and lower-middle-income countries that could have fed 7 million adults (FAO 2021a). Climate change will likely cause cereal prices to increase by 29 percent by 2050 (IPCC 2022a), which is especially problematic for poor people, given their significant food price sensitivity (Colen et al. 2018). In LICs, poor populations would see health benefits from increasing their consumption of fruits, vegetables, and ASF and decreasing their consumption of some oils, starches, and highly processed foods (Beal et al. 2023; Herrero et al. 2023). This is particularly true for certain life stages, such as early childhood and adolescence, as well as during pregnancy and lactation periods. However, as mentioned in the HIC section of this chapter, healthy diets are often prohibitively expensive for the poor. More broadly, food price increases and yield declines from climate change will result in greater hunger in Sub-Saharan Africa and the poorer parts of South Asia and Southeast Asia (see chapter 2). This will only exacerbate an already existing trend that saw health indicators plummet 31 percent between 2000 and 2014 and health conditions further undermined by the COVID-19 (coronavirus) pandemic and Russia's invasion of Ukraine. As a result, the share of people who lack regular access to sufficient calories is increasing, with as many as 828 million people undernourished in 2021.[15]

Most of the climate finance in low-income countries has been for adaptation and fails to help small-scale farmers reduce agricultural emissions. Between 2016 and 2020, low-income countries received around $30 billion of climate finance from developed countries, accounting for 8 percent of total climate finance contributions. Around half of this has been for adaptation and 40 percent for mitigation, with the remaining 10 percent having mitigation and adaptation dual benefits (OECD 2022). Adaptation finance is important for LICs, given the severe impacts already being felt in these countries (see box 3.4 on the Horn of Africa). FAO estimates that developing countries require $105 billion annually for adaptation in the

BOX 3.4 Climate Change Impacts in the Horn of Africa in 2022

Climate change impacts combined with poverty and conflict have led to disastrous consequences in the Horn of Africa. In December 2022, the Horn of Africa faced its third catastrophic drought in the region since 2010 and its fifth consecutive failed farming season. The region is heavily dependent on agriculture: in Somalia, four out of five people are employed in the agriculture sector. In Ethiopia and Kenya, the agriculture sector is also by far the largest employer (ILO 2020). Agriculture contributes over 60 percent to Somalia's gross national product, the highest value for any country in the world (World Bank 2023b). Water-dependent livestock herding is a major source of income in the region, and around 9 million livestock are estimated to have died because of the drought (UNOCHA 2022). Extreme climatic events, such as these droughts, are devastating local economies and livelihoods. In total, 36 million people in parts of Ethiopia, Kenya, and Somalia are affected by severe drought, which caused food prices to spike, leaving 22 million people in acute food insecurity (United Nations 2022b). Combined with poverty and conflict, this contributed to the internal displacement of 1.3 million people in these countries. Development donors recognize the severity of the problem. The World Bank, for example, is providing $385 million to improve climate resilience in the region by enhancing the use of untapped groundwater resources.

agrifood sector (FAO 2017b). This is more than the total climate finance provided annually, as donor countries continue to fall short in providing the $100 billion annually for developing countries promised at the UN Climate Change Conference in 2009 (COP15) (OECD 2022). However, the growing emissions in LICs also call for greater finance for mitigation actions. As described, just 2.5 percent of the world's climate finance goes to the agriculture, forestry, and other land use sector (Naran et al. 2022), and an even smaller portion goes to small-scale agriculture, both of which are predominant in low-income countries (Lowder, Sánchez, and Bertini 2021). More than 80 percent of farms in LICs are smaller than 1 hectare, and virtually all farms in LICs are smaller than 10 hectares (Lowder, Sánchez, and Bertini 2021). Yet small-scale agriculture, which produces around a third of the global food supply, receives less than 2 percent of climate finance (Chiriac and Naran 2020).

Preserving and restoring forests is a cost-effective way to promote development and limit LICs' growth in emissions

Forest conversion contributes over 90 percent of land use emissions in LICs and about half of all agrifood system emissions in LICs, compared to 17 percent of agrifood system emissions in MICs and 6 percent in HICs. Moreover, LICs also have greater potential for deforestation, on average, than countries from other income groups. For example, except for Brazil, Sub-Saharan Africa, which contains 23 of the world's 28 LICs, has the largest block of primary forest in the world. However, it is shrinking. In 1990, 31.3 percent of Sub-Saharan Africa was forest area, but in 2020 the forest area was already down to 26.3 percent.

The rate of commodity-driven forest loss is highest in some LICs and is set to accelerate. In Congo basin countries, there has been a 40 percent increase in land allocated for oil palm from 1990 to 2017 (Ordway et al. 2019). In southwest Cameroon, palm oil expansion caused 67 percent of the country's forest loss between 2000 and 2015 (Ordway et al. 2019). To take advantage of global palm oil demand and the domestic economic potential, several African LICs have set ambitious production targets for oil palm, which almost assuredly locks them into future deforestation and related emissions. In Côte d'Ivoire, the world's largest producer of cocoa, the production of this tree crop has led to the loss of 80 percent of the country's forest since the 1960s (World Bank 2023c). Moreover, shifting cultivation to forested areas is a common land use practice in MICs and LICs. This practice is generally driven by local food demand rather than international commodity demand, but it is also a major, and growing, contributor to forest conversion emissions (figure 3.25).

Forest restoration can achieve climate objectives and drive development. Once lost, the carbon in forests is very difficult to recover, as are the forest's biodiversity and other important ecological functions; therefore, avoiding deforestation is the best option. That said, the planet has 2.2 billion hectares of degraded land that is unused but available for restoration. Forest restoration of degraded land, or returning lands to their natural forested state, including by afforestation—planting new forests—could cost-effectively take 0.9–1.5 $GtCO_2eq$, or close to 3 percent of total global GHG emissions, per year out of the atmosphere by 2050. This would boost the capacity for forests to sequester carbon and avoid projected global biodiversity losses (FAO 2022c). The financial benefits of restoration would also be considerable. By one estimate, the restoration of 350 million hectares of deforested and degraded land by 2030 could deliver a net benefit of up to $9 trillion, or $7 to $30 for every dollar invested (Verdone and Seidl 2017) through ecosystem services.

Agroforestry in MICs and LICs (FAO 2023c) delivers multiple biophysical and socioeconomic co-benefits. Agroforestry is the practice of integrating trees in croplands.

FIGURE 3.25 Low-Income Countries Contribute Nearly Half of the Global Emissions from Shifting Agriculture

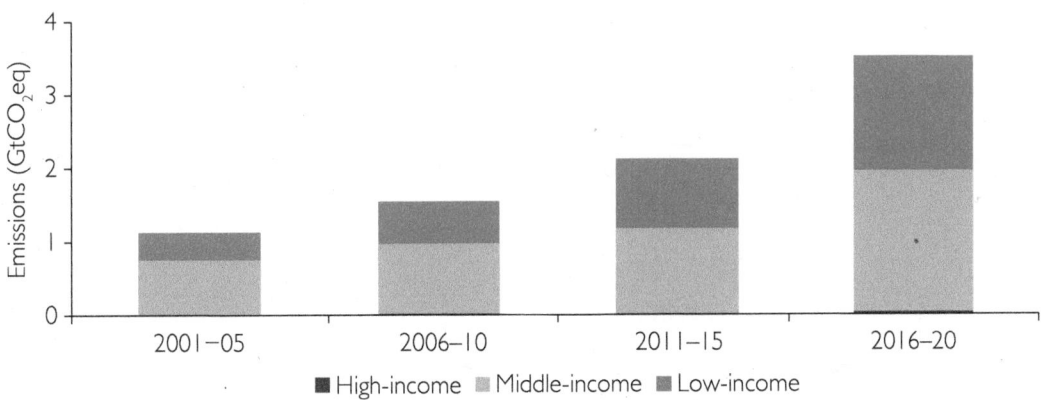

Source: World Bank based on data from Harris et al. 2021.
Note: Figure shows the share of global emissions linked to shifting cultivation by country income group for 2001–20. GtCO₂eq = gigatons of carbon dioxide equivalent.

Trees in agricultural landscapes comprise 75 percent of stored carbon on agricultural lands and can sequester an additional 12–228 tons of carbon per hectare, or an average of 95 tons per hectare (Zomer et al. 2016). In one scenario, increasing tree cover on agricultural lands by 10 percent would sequester more than 18 gigatons of carbon globally, with South America having the most potential, followed by Southeast Asia, West and Central Africa, and North America (figure 3.26) (Zomer et al. 2022). In fact, 1.5 billion of the 2.2 billion hectares of degraded land that is capable of forest restoration may be best suited for mosaic restoration through agroforestry systems that combine trees with agriculture (FAO 2022e). This is because agroforestry produces benefits beyond carbon storage, such as better land productivity, livelihood opportunities, diversified diets, and greater ecosystem resilience and services, although forest restoration is better for biodiversity (FAO 2023c). As such, agroforestry could increase the productivity and ecosystem services of a further 1 billion hectares of croplands. To date, however, agroforestry has been used mainly for subsistence farming by smallholders. This is because small-scale agroforestry systems cost very little, but scaling up agroforestry requires high start-up costs, long-term investments, consistent risk management, and context-specific knowledge (FAO 2022e; Ollinaho and Kröger 2021).

Silvo-pastoral systems improve livestock productivity while mitigating climate change. Similar to agroforestry, silvo-pastoralism—trees on grazed pastures and rangelands—is equally effective at capturing carbon in soils and trees (Mottet et al. 2017). Recent studies show that silvo-pastoral systems can produce more meat and milk of better quality, restore degraded lands, and reduce GHG emissions per head of cattle (Chará et al. 2019). Latin American countries have experimented with silvo-pastoral systems and found that they sequestered 5–148.4 metric tons of aboveground carbon per hectare per year, considerably more than the standard grassland pastures. Even in dry or mountainous areas that cannot sustain forests naturally, the restoration of rangelands into grasslands, savannas, or silvo-pastoral systems (Curtis et al. 2018) could curb the economic losses from land degradation, which are estimated to be $6.3 trillion to $10.6 trillion per year (Stewart 2015). Rangelands have relatively low carbon sequestration rates on a per-hectare basis but could sequester 2–4 percent of the world's annual anthropogenic greenhouse gas emissions if silvo-pastoral

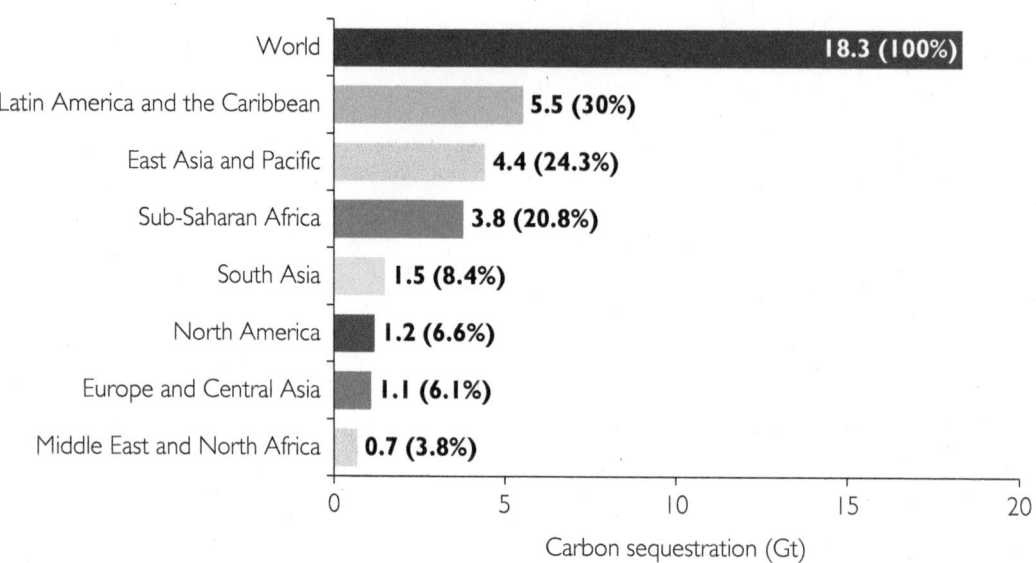

FIGURE 3.26 Increasing Tree Cover on Agricultural Lands Would Increase Carbon Uptake Significantly

Source: World Bank based on data from Zomer et al. 2022.
Note: Figure shows estimated carbon sequestration in biomass both above and below ground arising from increasing tree cover on all agricultural land by 10 percent, globally and regionally. Percentages in parenthesis indicate the regional share of the global carbon sequestration potential. Gt = gigatons.

or sustainable grazing practices were applied, because of the vast areas rangelands cover (FAO 2017a).

Emerging economies are beginning to monetize their forest cover and agrifood emissions reductions through carbon credits and emissions trading. A global study of all country types shows that LICs can earn the most potential income from carbon sequestration. However, this value is still rather low, at $4 per ton compared to $56 per ton in the EU's emissions trading system.[16] Emissions trading and carbon credits incentivize developing countries to meet their NDC targets. The main mechanisms for LICs to access carbon credits are as follows: (1) results-based climate finance (RBCF), (2) voluntary carbon markets (VCMs), and (3) domestic and international compliance carbon markets. RBCFs are financing instruments from international donors that provide funds to participating countries once their RBCF project's climate results are achieved and verified. The World Bank and other donors are increasingly using this tool to help LICs access carbon credits. In VCMs, state and nonstate actors reduce their GHG emissions, which is verified by an independent crediting standard, in return for carbon credits, which high-emitting countries or businesses can buy to offset their own emissions. In 2019, 86 percent of voluntary carbon offsets from reduced deforestation activities originated from just eight countries, including Ethiopia, Guatemala, Indonesia, Kenya, Peru, and Zimbabwe (Ecosystem Marketplace Insights Team 2023). The issuance of carbon credits for protecting forests and reducing land use change–related emissions has increased in recent years and amounted to a third of all carbon credit issuances in 2021 (World Bank 2022a). However, most of these VCMs are active in middle-income countries, not LICs (OECD 2021). International and domestic compliance markets tax emissions or provide carbon credits for complying with emissions limits. Several countries allow companies to use credits to reduce or avoid carbon tax liabilities. For example, under Colombia's carbon tax, taxable entities implementing emissions-saving projects can use credits to fully or partially reduce their carbon tax liabilities. International compliance markets under the Paris Agreement, specifically under Article 6, allow parties to the agreement to trade authorized emission reductions, or "mitigation outcomes." Chapter 4 discusses RBCFs, VCMs, and compliance markets in more detail. Box 3.5 highlights the Democratic Republic of Congo, the only LIC among top GHG-emitting countries.

BOX 3.5 Agrifood Emissions In-Depth: The Democratic Republic of Congo

The Democratic Republic of Congo is the only low-income country among the top 15 greenhouse gas (GHG)–emitting countries in the world. It ranks as the 12th-highest GHG-emitting country globally, with annual emissions of 668 metric tons of carbon dioxide equivalent (MtCO$_2$eq) per year (FAOSTAT 2023c). More than 95 percent of the Democratic Republic of Congo's GHG emissions stem from deforestation (figure B3.5.1). Both commercial and subsistence-level agriculture, including firewood harvesting, drives this deforestation. The agriculture sector employs 70 percent of the country's population (IMF 2022) and accounts for 20 percent of the country's GDP (World Bank 2023b). The Democratic Republic of Congo is home to the world's second-largest rainforest and has the

FIGURE B3.5.1 Democratic Republic of Congo's Agrifood System Emissions, 1990–92 and 2018–20

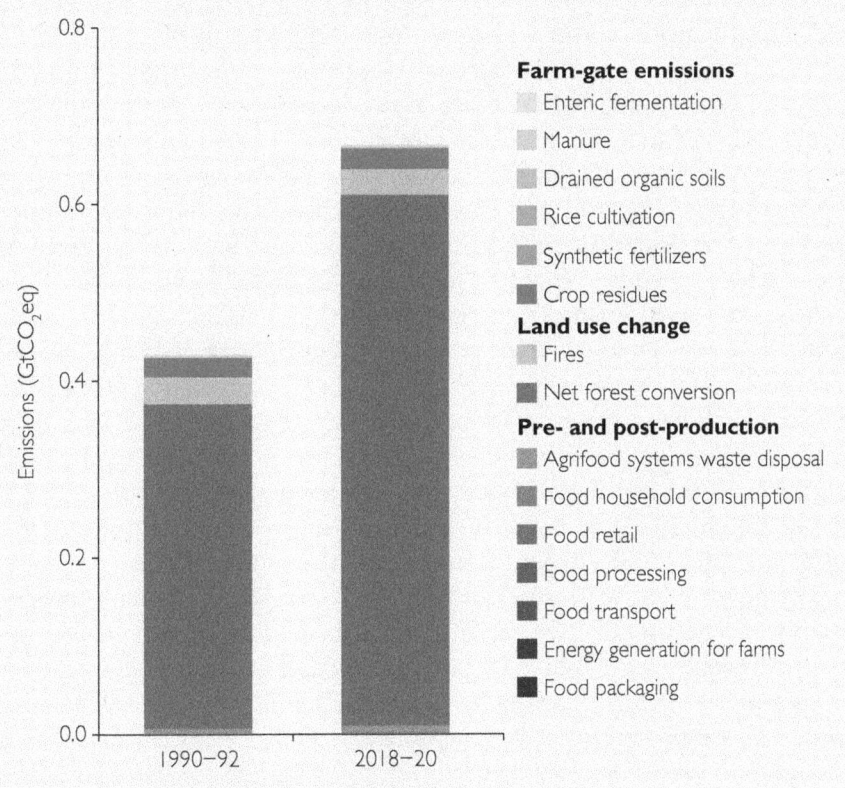

Source: World Bank based on data from World Bank 2023d and FAOSTAT 2023c.
Note: GtCO$_2$eq = gigatons of carbon dioxide equivalent.

(box continued next page)

potential to become a net carbon sink if deforestation is halted and forests are adequately managed. As a consequence, forest protection measures and carbon sequestration in that country's forests are among the most cost-effective mitigation options in the world (Roe et al. 2021). However, the Democratic Republic of Congo's populations are among the fastest growing in the world, so economic pressures on the country's rainforest are increasing (World Bank 2023c). As such, creating alternative sources of income and delinking agriculture and deforestation are key to protecting the country's forests, as is helping the country to access carbon markets and external technical and resource support to protect the forests. One mechanism is the Central African Forest Initiative, which is funded by EU countries to reduce deforestation and forest degradation and through the development of national investment frameworks.

LICs can avoid GHG lock-in by improving agrifood system efficiency and by marketing sustainable products

LICs are rapidly increasing food systems emissions, but their agrifood systems are not yet locked into a high-emissions trajectory. This GHG lock-in occurs when a country's investments or policies support infrastructure, institutions, or behaviors that hinder the transition to lower-emissions alternatives even when they are technically feasible and economically viable. Currently, 53 percent of agrifood system emissions in HICs come from the energy-intensive postharvest stages, whereas the emissions from these stages are negligible in LICs. That said, this is starting to change. As countries industrialize and move up the income ladder, energy-consuming technology, such as refrigeration or food-processing machinery, tends to enter the food value chain and increase energy demand. As a result, agriculture emissions from energy use have increased by 15 percent globally since 1990 and by 50 percent in low-income economies, though starting from a low baseline of energy use. This reflects the salient global trend since 1990 of slowing farm-gate emissions in high-income countries being offset by increasing farm-gate emissions in MICs and LICs (figure 3.27, panel a) (Flammini et al. 2022). Many of these MICs are now among the top 10 highest-emitting countries globally in on-farm energy use (figure 3.27, panel b), an indication of the improving access to fuels, machinery, and electricity in these countries. LICs thus have an opportunity to benefit from renewable sources of energy that have become cost competitive in recent years and can help drive increases in agricultural productivity and low-emissions post-production activities, such as solar-powered cold chains.

LICs can still avoid being locked into a high-emissions development path for their agrifood systems. Lock-in has already largely occurred in HICs and MICs where infrastructure and other long-lived assets are costly to decommission and where persistent barriers along the entire agrifood value chain prevent them from shifting to low-emissions development pathways (Seto et al. 2016). By contrast, these barriers are less entrenched in LICs than they are in MICs and HICs. The emissions-intensive agriculture sector development that has increased yields in MICs and HICs has mostly not yet reached LICs. Conversely, the limited

FIGURE 3.27 On-Farm Energy Emissions Have Remained Constant in High-Income Countries, but Have Increased in Middle-Income Countries and Remain Marginal in Low-Income Countries

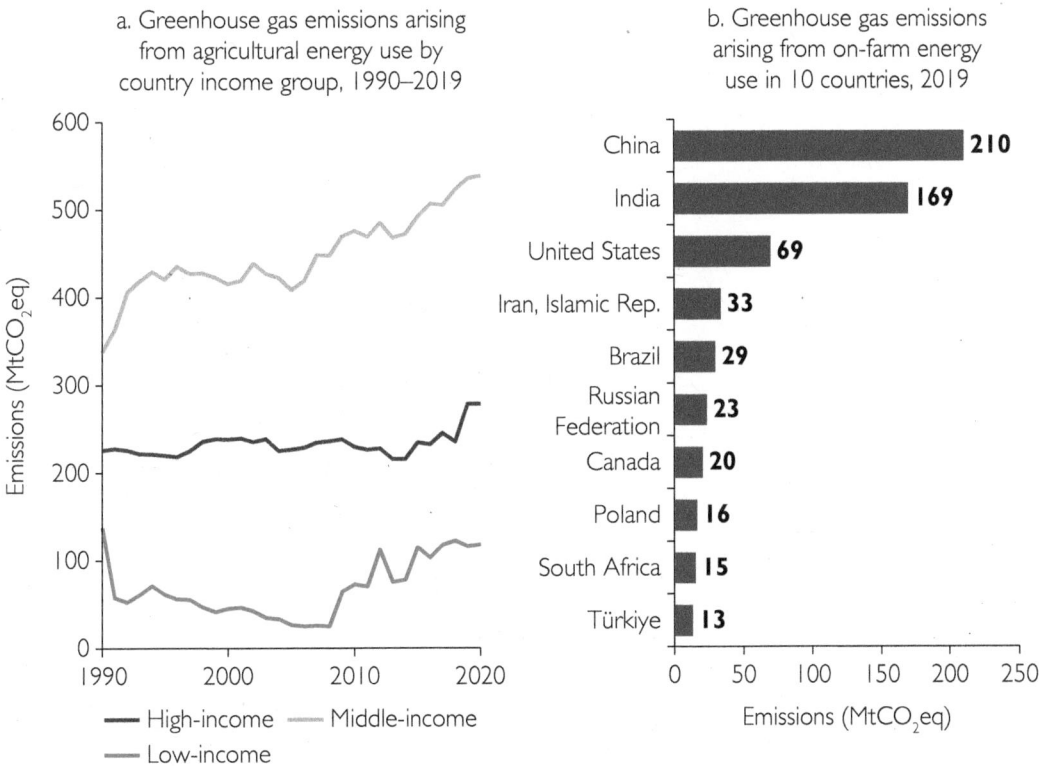

a. Greenhouse gas emissions arising from agricultural energy use by country income group, 1990–2019

b. Greenhouse gas emissions arising from on-farm energy use in 10 countries, 2019

Sources: World Bank based on data from FAOSTAT 2023c; IEA and UNSD 2021; World Bank 2023d.
Note: MtCO₂eq = megatons of carbon dioxide equivalent.

energy use per hectare in LICs is one of the causes for low emissions but also stubbornly low productivity in those countries. Figure 3.28 shows that LICs have avoided the rapid increase in emissions that was experienced in HICs and is now happening in MICs. Instead, LICs still lag far behind and thus have opportunities to forge an alternative development pathway from those of HICs and MICs, one that is less damaging to the planet. The challenges for LICs are acquiring the resources to invest in long-term low-emission solutions and innovative technologies and resisting pressure from foreign investors to outsource GHG-emitting production processes to other LICs (Conti, Zanello, and Hall 2021; Tong et al. 2019). Avoiding GHG lock-in would also require assessing the lock-in risks of policies and investments and then developing sector- and context-specific policies and regulations based on those assessments. As discussed in the HIC section of this chapter, HICs have an important role in financing the low-emissions pathway in LICs and transferring technical assistance in low-emission practices and innovative technologies. Likewise, avoiding lock-in would also require avoiding high-carbon consumer behavior, such as wasting food or excessive meat consumption. There are several cost-effective steps that LICs can pursue immediately to avoid GHG lock-in. They include (1) improving productivity, (2) accessing carbon markets, and (3) gearing agricultural production toward sustainable food markets. Each of these is discussed further.

FIGURE 3.28 **Low-Income Countries Are Not Yet Locked into an Energy-Intensive Agrifood System Model, Lagging Far Behind Middle- and High-Income Countries in On-Farm Energy Use**

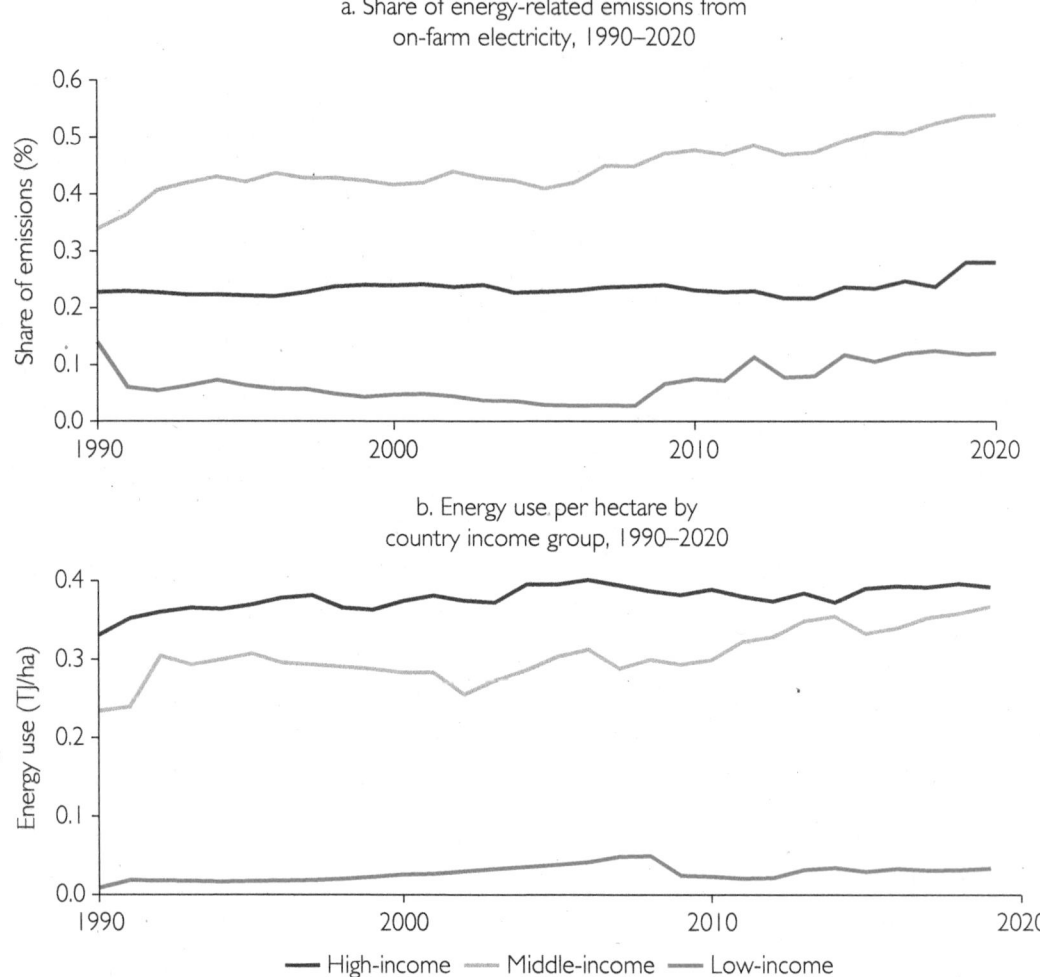

a. Share of energy-related emissions from
on-farm electricity, 1990–2020

b. Energy use per hectare by
country income group, 1990–2020

High-income — Middle-income — Low-income

Source: World Bank based on data from FAOSTAT 2023c.
Note: TJ/ha = terajoules per hectare.

There is significant scope for LICs to improve their food system efficiency and productivity. As discussed in this chapter, the world's use of natural resources, especially in developing countries, is inefficient (for example, see figure 3.18 on LICs' livestock emissions intensity) (Damania et al. 2023). More efficient land use means less land is required to grow food, and therefore emissions from land clearing are lower. Most low- and middle-income countries are achieving less than half of their potential agricultural output, whereas high-income countries are achieving 70 percent of their potential output (see chapter 2). More efficient use of land could sequester an additional total of 85.6 billion metric tons of CO_2eq with no adverse economic impacts (Damania et al. 2023). In fact, more efficient land use has positive economic impacts. Agriculture value added in LICs is only $210 per hectare, whereas in middle-income countries, it is five times that at $1,100 per hectare (World Bank 2023d). Yet countries that have graduated from low income in the 1990s to middle income in this century have also had major increases in value-added per hectare. For example, between 1990 and 2021, Viet Nam improved its value added per hectare by 65 percent and China improved it by 217 percent. Total factor productivity (TFP) is a comprehensive indicator of agriculture productivity and efficiency that measures agriculture outputs per unit of inputs. TFP growth rates have increased for all country income groups except LICs, which have experienced a contraction. From 2011 to 2020, TFP increased by 1.58 percent in lower MICs, 1.60 percent in upper MICs, and 0.76 percent in HICs but declined by 0.04 percent in LICs (Steensland 2022). Overall, climate change and a reduction in research and development investments have contributed to the reduced TFP growth over the last decade, particularly in LICs (Alston, Pardey, and Rao 2022; Ortiz-Bobea et al. 2021). Climate change has caused a TFP decline of up to 34 percent in the Africa and Latin America and Caribbean regions (Ortiz-Bobea et al. 2021). Moreover, climate change–induced heat stress is expected to reduce labor productivity even more (Kjellstrom et al. 2019).

Likewise, agricultural productivity in LICs can improve significantly (Damania et al. 2023; Dooley et al. 2022). Increasing productivity reduces the need to expand agricultural production into carbon-rich forests. Producing food on less land can spare important natural systems from land conversion. This retains critical environmental functions and preserves natural carbon sinks—an important knock-on effect. For example, in Central America, shifting from slash-and-burn agriculture to agroforestry led to more efficient land use, higher crop yields, and lower operating costs, thereby reducing the need to convert land. In the Syrian Arab Republic, participatory land management by local communities reduced herders' vulnerability to climate change and restored the long-term productivity of rangelands. In Kenya, livestock farmers implemented a grazing plan for 6,000 cattle and 3,000 sheep and goats to boost productivity during the dry season. Improving the reliability of water access for farmers in the Chiquitania region of Santa Cruz, Bolivia, and the Huang-Huai-Hai Plain of China increased the efficiency of irrigation systems, thereby improving productivity (FAO 2013). That said, such measures require adequate finance. In Ethiopia, for example, finance allowed farmers to store sesame, commercialize sorghum, and provide short-term capital loans for barley, all of which have increased agriculture productivity. Similarly, in Mali, different financing instruments boosted productivity in several value chains through project finance, credit for users, debt instruments, short-term working capital, and blended finance. In Senegal, risk transfer instruments, such as guarantees to cover initial losses from expanding solar-powered irrigation pumps, increased groundnut and vegetable production (Agyekumhene et al. 2022). Removing distortive policies and investing in innovative practices could also boost TFP in LICs.

LICs could orient their agrifood systems to deliver healthy, organic, or circular food system products to emerging retail markets; however, the emissions impacts from doing so are not yet clear. Global markets for certified organic products have grown rapidly, by 102 percent between 2009 and 2019 (Willer et al. 2021). Eighty-eight percent of these sales are concentrated in Europe and North America, but developing countries have been able to supply some of these foods (Willer et al. 2021). Recent studies of Asia, Africa, and Latin America indicate that organic farmers generally earn higher incomes than their conventional counterparts because of expanding organic markets and price premiums for organic products (UNCTAD and UNEP 2008). Moreover, the production methods for these foods tend to require fewer inputs, such as synthetic fertilizers or pesticides, and contribute to soil carbon sequestration, so they are less environmentally damaging and more sustainable. Still, only 1.5 percent of all agricultural land in 2019 was geared toward producing organic foods (Willer et al. 2021), meaning that there are opportunities for LICs to help fill this market demand. However, sometimes these new products lead to unintended emissions increases. For example, studies show that organic food production in the United Kingdom generated smaller yields than traditional agriculture, which led traditional agriculture to expand to meet supply shortfalls, thereby contributing to a net increase in emissions (Smith et al. 2019). That said, it is not always the case that organic yields are lower in low- and middle-income countries. A study of smallholder adoption of organic practices in Cambodia, China, the Lao People's Democratic Republic, Sri Lanka, and Thailand found that organic farms obtained higher yields than comparable conventional farms while sequestering soil carbon (Setboonarng and Markandya 2015).

Climate-smart agriculture provides LICs an avenue to low-emission rural development

LICs should take advantage of climate-smart agriculture to achieve three gains. Climate-smart agriculture is an integrated approach to managing agricultural production that achieves the triple win of (1) economic gains, (2) climate resilience, and (3) lower GHG emissions (World Bank 2021a). There are 1,700 combinations of production systems and technology that could be classified as CSA, with two-thirds pertaining to cropping systems for maize, wheat, rice, and cash crops. Only 18 percent of CSA technologies are for livestock systems and just 2 percent are for aquaculture systems (Sova et al. 2018).

Adopting CSA practices reduces emissions and contributes to economic development. The expansion of conservation agriculture, commercial horticulture, and agroforestry and the reduction of postharvest losses in Zambia, for instance, have an economic rate of return of 27–34 percent, which gets a boost from carbon payments for emission reductions (World Bank 2019d). Similarly, in Mali, four climate-smart measures have high rates of return on investment: using agroforestry to produce nontimber forest products (53 percent rate of return), building infrastructure to harness floodwater for agriculture (46 percent), integrating crop and livestock management practices (88 percent), and providing accurate geospatial information for farmers (126 percent). These measures also produce mitigation benefits. For example, the mitigation benefits from every $5 per ton in economic benefits were 6 percent for nontimber forest products, 5 percent for flood recession agriculture, 4 percent for crop-livestock integration, and 7 percent for providing geospatial data (World Bank 2019b). In Bangladesh, a portfolio of investments—in improved crop varieties research; small, women-led livestock enterprises; crop diversification; and climate-smart intensification of rice—had economic rates of return of over 30 percent, while reducing emissions by 9 percent (World Bank 2019a). These successful examples of CSA practices highlight the potential of these measures to boost economic development in low- and middle-income countries, especially among the poorest communities, which often make a living from agriculture.

Agrifood system actors can make low-carbon energy sources, such as solar power and bioenergy, sustainable and able to contribute to rural electrification in LICs (Christiaensen, Rutledge, and Taylor 2021). Large-scale food producers often provide the most consistent demand for photovoltaic-powered mini- and micro-energy grids in rural areas. These producers act as reliable paying customers with consistent energy needs, from irrigation or processing activities, that provide a predictable revenue source for grid developers and operators. This makes the micro-grids more economically viable and sustainable (Vourdoubas and Dubois 2016). Rural businesses and communities can also connect to the micro-grid, making renewable energy access available in rural areas and allowing nearby business and communities to connect to the micro-grid through energy kiosks and other access points (Dubois et al. 2017). Likewise, farms and other food producers and processors can create bioenergy from their waste materials, such as lignocellulosic biomass like wood, straw, and bagasse. Biogas systems can generate electricity, resulting in decreased electricity costs for farmers and food producers and making their operations more financially viable (Rincón et al. 2019). Biogas electricity surpluses can be exported to nearby grids, benefiting local rural communities. The technical energy generation potential of agriculture and forestry residues and other organic waste ranges between 50 and 150 exajoules. Bioenergy also reduces a community's dependency on fossil fuels (Chel and Kaushik 2011). However, the cost-effectiveness of the bioenergy generated from agriculture residues depends on several local factors, including the logistics of residue mobilization, homogeneity of residues, and the local availability of alternatives (Röder and Welfle 2018). Other factors affecting the profitability of bioenergy are irregular consumption patterns and unaffordability in rural settings. As with photovoltaic micro-grids, this challenge can be met by establishing large food producers in rural areas as consistent bioenergy consumers for private energy producers. These rural renewable energy sources can create jobs, stimulate local economic development, and build more resilient and low-carbon food systems (Vourdoubas and Dubois 2016).

Notes

1. The top four net cost-saving mitigation options are increasing the concentrate-to-forage ratio (–$306/tCO$_2$eq), biologicals (–$177/tCO$_2$eq), direct seeding of rice (–$159/tCO$_2$eq), and reducing overapplication of fertilizer (–$146/tCO$_2$eq).

2. The zero- and low-cost mitigation options include biochar as a fertilizer ($0/tCO$_2$eq), improved animal health and disease treatments ($0/tCO$_2$eq), GHG-focused breeding and genetic selection ($0/tCO2eq), feed grain processing for digestibility ($1/tCO$_2$eq), and conversion to hybrid and electric fishing vessels ($5/tCO$_2$eq).

3. The baseline scenario is based on the Shared Socio-economic Pathway 2 (SSP2) from the Fifth Assessment Report of the IPCC, which represents a business-as-usual scenario with continuation of current trends and medium levels of challenges for mitigation and adaptation. In this scenario, world population is projected to increase to about 9.2 billion until 2050, and GDP per capita is expected to more than double globally to about $25,000 (2005 dollars) per capita.

4. According to the EPA, methane is estimated to have a global warming potential of 27–30 times that of carbon dioxide over 100 years. Methane emitted today lasts about a decade, on average, which is much less time than carbon dioxide. But methane also absorbs much more energy than carbon dioxide. The net effect of the shorter lifetime and higher energy absorption is reflected in the global warming potential. Nitrous oxide is a powerful greenhouse gas, with an estimated atmospheric lifetime of 114 years. It has a global warming potential 273 times that of carbon dioxide for a 100-year time scale. Other non-carbon-dioxide emissions are from chlorofluorocarbons, hydrofluorocarbons, hydrochlorofluorocarbons, perfluorocarbons, and sulfur hexafluoride.

5. The top 15 countries by density of mitigation potential (per hectare of land), ranked from first to last, are Maldives (MIC), Brunei Darussalam (HIC), Bangladesh (MIC), Indonesia (MIC), Viet Nam (MIC), Trinidad and Tobago (HIC), Malaysia (MIC), Malta (HIC), Rwanda (LIC), Republic of Korea (HIC), the Netherlands (HIC), Cambodia (MIC), Mauritius (MIC), the Philippines (MIC), and El Salvador (MIC).

6. MACs may not be accurate when interventions interact among one another, an intervention takes a long time to implement, technological progress is expected to reduce costs as we invest, or transaction costs for implementing interventions are high.

7. See calculations for this example at The James E. Rogers Energy Access Project at Duke (available at https://energyaccess.duke.edu/low-carbon-ag-tech-mitigation-potentials-by-market-assumptions -data/).

8. Between 2010 and 2019, energy efficiency increased by 1.9 percent, far lower than 3.2 percent, the rate needed to achieve the SDG 7.3 target.

9. IPCC Sixth Assessment Report Working Group III report on mitigation (Riahi et al. 2022).

10. Authors' calculations based on data from Lassaletta et al. 2014 and FAOSTAT 2023.

11. Food loss, as reported by FAO 2019b, occurs from postharvest up to—but not including—the retail level. Food waste, as reported by UNEP 2021, occurs at the retail, food service, and consumer levels.

12. IWA (International Water Association), "Climate Smart Case Stories," Climate Smart Utilities (accessed April 15, 2024), https://climatesmartwater.org/case-studies/.

13. Analysis was carried out for Annex I and non-Annex I countries.

14. Low-income economies are defined as those with a gross national income per capita of $1,085 or less in 2021. See World Bank, n.d.

15. Global, Regional, and National Trends—Global Hunger Index (GHI)—is a database that comprehensively measures and tracks hunger at the global, regional, and country levels https://www .globalhungerindex.org/.

16. Information on the price in the voluntary markets is from Ecosystem Marketplace Insights Team 2023. EU Emissions Trading System mid-year values are from Carbon Credits, n.d.

References

Abdelaziz, E. A., R. Saidur, and S. Mekhilef. 2011. "A Review on Energy Saving Strategies in Industrial Sector." *Renewable and Sustainable Energy Reviews* 15 (1): 150–68. https://doi.org/10.1016/j.rser .2010.09.003.

Abila, Beatrice, and Jussi Kantola. 2019. "The Perceived Role of Financial Incentives in Promoting Waste Recycling—Empirical Evidence from Finland." *Recycling* 4 (1): 4. https://doi.org/10.3390 /recycling4010004.

Abrahamse, W. 2020. "How to Effectively Encourage Sustainable Food Choices: A Mini-review of Available Evidence." *Frontiers in Psychology* 9. https://doi.org/10.3389/fpsyg.2020.589674.

Adhya, Tapan K., Bruce Lindquist, Tim Searchinger, Reiner Wassmann, and Xiaoyuan Yan. 2014. "Wetting and Drying: Reducing Greenhouse Gas Emissions and Saving Water from Rice Production." Working Paper (Installment 8 of "Creating a Sustainable Food Future"), World Resources Institute, Washington, DC. https://files.wri.org/d8/s3fs-public/wetting-drying-reducing-greenhouse-gas-emissions-saving -water-rice-production.pdf.

Agrivoltaics. n.d. "Agrivoltaics: Opportunities for Agriculture and Energy Transition" (web page). Accessed April 14, 2024. https://agri-pv.org/en/.

Agyekumhene, C., M. Derenoncourt, C. Costa Jr, P. Tetteh-Addo, W. Wathuta, R. Newman, and G. Grosjean. 2022. *Impact Investment in Agriculture in Africa: A Case Study of Ethiopia, Sudan, Mali, and Senegal.* Montpellier, France: Consultative Group on International Agricultural Research Initiative on Climate Resilience.

Akerlof, George A., and Rachel E. Kranton. 2000. "Economics and Identity." *Quarterly Journal of Economics* 115 (3): 715–53. https://doi.org/10.1162/003355300554881.

AL-agele, Hadi A., Kyle Proctor, Ganti Murthy, and Chad Higgins. 2021. "A Case Study of Tomato (Solanum lycopersicon var. Legend) Production and Water Productivity in Agrivoltaic Systems." *Sustainability* 13 (5): 2850. https://doi.org/10.3390/su13052850.

AL-Ani, M. A., R. M. Hmoshi, I. A. Kanaan, and A. A. Thanoon. 2019. "Effect of Pesticides on Soil Microorganisms." *Journal of Physics: Conference Series* 1294 (7): 072007. https://doi.org/10.1088/1742 -6596/1294/7/072007.

Aleksandrowicz, L., R. Green, E. J. M. Joy, F. Harris, J. Hillier, S. H. Vetter, P. Smith, B. Kulkarni, A. D. Dangour, and A. Haines. 2019. "Environmental Impacts of Dietary Shifts in India: A Modeling Study Using Nationally-Representative Data." *Environment International* 126: 207–15. https://doi .org/10.1016/j.envint.2019.02.004.

Aleksandrowicz, L., R. Green, E. J. M. Joy, P. Smith, and A. Haines. 2016. "The Impacts of Dietary Change on Greenhouse Gas Emissions, Land Use, Water Use, and Health: A Systematic Review. " *PLoS ONE* 11 (11): e0165797. https://doi.org/10.1371/journal.pone.0165797.

Alston, J. M., P. Pardey, and X. Rao. 2022. "Payoffs to a Half Century of CGIAR Research." *American Journal of Agricultural Economics* 104: 502–29. https://doi.org/10.1111/ajae.12255.

Amelung, W., D. Bossio, W. de Vries, I. Kögel-Knabner, J. Lehmann, R. Amundson, R. Bol, et al. 2020. "Towards a Global-Scale Soil Climate Mitigation Strategy." *Nature Communications* 11: 5427. https://doi.org/10.1038/s41467-020-18887-7.

Amjith, L. R., and B. Bavanish. 2022. "A Review on Biomass and Wind as Renewable Energy for Sustainable Environment." *Chemosphere* 293. https://doi.org/10.1016/j.chemosphere.2022.133579.

Ammann, J., A. Arbenz, G. Mack, T. Nemecek, and N. El Benni. 2023. "A Review on Policy Instruments for Sustainable Food Consumption." *Sustainable Production and Consumption* 36: 338–53. https://doi .org/10.1016/j.spc.2023.01.012.

Andreyeva, T., M. W. Long, and K. D. Brownell. 2010. "The Impact of Food Prices on Consumption: A Systematic Review of Research on the Price Elasticity of Demand for Food." *American Journal of Public Health* 100 (2): 216–22. https://doi.org/10.2105/AJPH.2008.151415.

Angenent, L. T., K. Karim, M. H. Al-Dahhan, and B. A. Wrenn. 2004. "Production of Bioenergy and Biochemicals from Industrial and Agricultural Wastewater." *Trends in Biotechnology* 22 (9): 477–85. https://doi.org/10.1016/j.tibtech.2004.07.001.

Annosi, M. C., F. Brunetta, F. Bimbo, and M. Kostoula. 2021. "Digitalization within Food Supply Chains to Prevent Food Waste: Drivers, Barriers, and Collaboration Practices." *Industrial Marketing Management* 93: 208–20. https://doi.org/10.1016/j.indmarman.2021.01.005.

Annunziata, A., A. Mariani, and R. Vecchio. 2019. "Effectiveness of Sustainability Labels in Guiding Food Choices: Analysis of Visibility and Understanding among Young Adults." *Sustainable Production and Consumption* 17: 108–15. https://doi.org/10.1016/j.spc.2018.09.005.

Apostolidis, Chrysostomos, and Fraser McLeay. 2019. "To Meat or Not to Meat? Comparing Empowered Meat Consumers' and Anti-Consumers' Preferences for Sustainability Labels." *Food Quality and Preference* 77: 109–22. https://www.sciencedirect.com/science/article/abs/pii/S0950329318309005.

Araujo, Gabriel. 2023. "Deforestation in Brazil's Amazon Falls in First Month under Lula." Reuters, February 10, 2023. https://www.reuters.com/world/americas/deforestation-brazils-amazon-falls-first-month -under-lula-2023-02-10/.

Arnaoudov, Vladislav, Evangeline B. Sibayan, and Raymond C. Caguioa. 2015. "Adaptation and Mitigation Initiatives in Philippine Rice Cultivation." UNDP, November 5, 2015. https://www.undp.org/sites/g/files /zskgke326/files/publications/AMIA%20Philippines%20Final.pdf.

Aziz, A. A., D. Sumiyoshi, and Y. Akashi. 2017. "Low-Cost Humidity Controlled Air-Conditioning System for Building Energy Savings in Tropical Climate." *Journal of Building Engineering* 11: 9–16. https://doi .org/10.1016/j.jobe.2017.03.005.

Bacon, L., and D. Krpan. 2018. "(Not) Eating for the Environment: The Impact of Restaurant Menu Design on Vegetarian Food Choice." *Appetite* 125: 190–200. https://doi.org/10.1016/j.appet.2018.02.006.

Bartiaux, F., and L. R. Salmón. 2012. "Are There Domino Effects between Consumers' Ordinary and 'Green' Practices? An Analysis of Quantitative Data from a Sensitization Campaign on Personal Carbon Footprint." *International Review of Sociology* 22 (3): 471–91. https://doi.org/10.1080/03906701.2012.725473.

BCG (Boston Consulting Group). 2022. "The Untapped Climate Opportunity in Alternative Proteins." Accessed April 10, 2024. https://web-assets.bcg.com/6f/f1/087a0cc74221ac3fe6332a2ac765/the -untapped-climate-opportunity-in-alternative-proteins-july-2022.pdf.

Beach, Robert H., Jared Creason, Sara Bushey Ohrel, Shaun Ragnauth, Stephen Ogle, Changsheng Li, Pete Ingraham, and William Salas. 2015. "Global Mitigation Potential and Costs of Reducing Agricultural

Non-CO$_2$ Greenhouse Gas Emissions through 2030." *Journal of Integrative Environmental Sciences* 12 (S1): 87–105. https://doi.org/10.1080/1943815X.2015.1110183.

Beal, Ty, Christopher D. Gardner, Mario Herrero, Lora L. Iannotti, Lutz Merbold, Stella Nordhagen, and Anne Mottet. 2023. "Friend or Foe? The Role of Animal-Source Foods in Healthy and Environmentally Sustainable Diets." *Journal of Nutrition* 153 (2): 409–25. https://doi.org/10.1093/jn/nxac054.

Becken, K., et al. 2011. "Avoiding Fluorinated Greenhouse Gases: Prospects for Phasing Out." German Federal Environment Agency, Dessau-Rosslau. Accessed April 12, 2024. https://www.umweltbundesamt.de/sites/default/files/medien/publikation/long/3977.pdf.

Behavioural Insights Team. 2018. *Applying Behavioral Insights to Increase Food Waste in Wigan: Final Report.* London: Behavioural Insights Team. https://www.bi.team/wp-content/uploads/2020/12/Applying-behavioural-insights-to-improve-food-recycling-in-Wigan-Final-Report-1.pdf.

Behrens, Paul, Jessica C. Kiefte-de Jong, Thijs Bosker, João F. D. Rodrigues, Arjan de Koning, and Arnold Tukker. 2017. "Evaluating the Environmental Impacts of Dietary Recommendations." *Proceedings of the National Academy of Sciences* 114 (51): 13412–17. https://doi.org/10.1073/pnas.1711889114.

Bernard, René, Panagiota Tzamourani, and Michael Weber. 2022. "Climate Change and Individual Behavior." Chicago Booth Research Paper 22-13, University of Chicago, Chicago. https://doi.org/10.2139/ssrn.4112620.

Black, Simon, Antung A. Liu, Ian W.H. Parry, and Nate Vernon. 2023. "IMF Fossil Fuel Subsidies Data: 2023 Update." IMF Working Paper 2023/169, August 24, 2023. https://www.imf.org/en/Publications/WP/Issues/2023/08/22/IMF-Fossil-Fuel-Subsidies-Data-2023-Update-537281.

Bodirsky, Benjamin Leon, Jan Philipp Dietrich, Eleonora Martinelli, Antonia Stenstad, Prajal Pradhan, Sabine Gabrysch, Abhijeet Mishra, et al. 2020. "The Ongoing Nutrition Transition Thwarts Long-Term Targets for Food Security, Public Health and Environmental Protection." *Scientific Reports* 10 (2020): 19778. https://doi.org/10.1038/s41598-020-75213-3.

Bogaerts, Meghan, Lora Cirhigiri, Ian Robinson, Mikaela Rodkin, Reem Hajjar, Ciniro Costa Jr., and Peter Newton. 2017. "Climate Change Mitigation through Intensified Pasture Management: Estimating Greenhouse Gas Emissions on Cattle Farms in the Brazilian Amazon." *Journal of Cleaner Production* 162: 1539–50. https://doi.org/10.1016/j.jclepro.2017.06.130.

Borrelli, Pasquale, David A. Robinson, Larissa R. Fleischer, Emanuele Lugato, Cristiano Ballabio, Christine Alewell, Katrin Meusburger, et al. 2017. "An Assessment of the Global Impact of 21st Century Land Use Change on Soil Erosion." *Nature Communications* 8: 2013. https://doi.org/10.1038/s41467-017-02142-7.

Bossio, D. A., S. C. Cook-Patton, P. W. Ellis, J. Fargione, J. Sanderman, P. Smith, S. Wood, et al. 2020. "The Role of Soil Carbon in Natural Climate Solutions." *Nature Sustainability* 3: 391–98. https://doi.org/10.1038/s41893-020-0491-z.

Botzen, Wouter J., Olivier Deschenes, and Maarten Sanders. 2019. "The Economic Impacts of Natural Disasters: A Review of Models and Empirical Studies." *Review of Environmental Economics and Policy* 13 (2): 167–88. https://doi.org/10.1093/reep/rez004.

Brueske, S., R. Sabouni, C. Zach, and H. Andres. 2012. *U.S. Manufacturing Energy Use and Greenhouse Gas Emissions Analysis.* ORNL/TM-2012/504. Washington, DC: US Department of Energy. https://www.energy.gov/sites/default/files/2013/11/f4/energy_use_and_loss_and_emissions.pdf.

Buchholz, Katharina. 2022. "Agriculture, Food and Beverage: Here's How Attitudes to Vegetarianism Are Changing around the World" (article). World Economic Forum, November 8, 2022. https://www.weforum.org/agenda/2022/11/vegetarianism-rise-fall-world-chart/.

Bundschuh, J., G. Chen, D. Chandrasekharam, and J. Piechocki. 2017. *Geothermal, Wind and Solar Energy Applications in Agriculture and Aquaculture.* London: Taylor and Francis. https://doi.org/10.1201/9781315158969.

Cai, Z., H. Tsuruta, M. Gao, H. Xu, and C. Wei. 2003. "Options for Mitigating Methane Emission from a Permanently Flooded Rice Field." *Global Change Biology* 9: 37–45. https://doi.org/10.1046/j.1365-2486.2003.00562.x.

Cao, Xinde, Lena Ma, Bin Gao, and Willie Harris. 2009. "Dairy-Manure Derived Biochar Effectively Sorbs Lead and Atrazine." *Environmental Science and Technology* 43 (9): 3285–91. https://doi.org/10.1021/es803092k.

Carbon Credits. n.d. "Live Carbon Prices Today" (data portal). Accessed April 14, 2024. https://carboncredits.com/carbon-prices-today/.

Carriedo, Angela, Adam D. Koon, Luis Manuel Encarnación, Kelley Lee, Richard Smith, and Helen Walls. 2021. "The Political Economy of Sugar-Sweetened Beverage Taxation in Latin America: Lessons from Mexico, Chile, and Colombia." *Globalization and Health* 17 (1): 5. https://doi.org/10.1186/s12992-020-00656-2.

Cerutti, N., W. F. Lamb, M. Crippa, A. Leip, E. Solazzo, F. N. Tubiello, and J. C. Minx. 2023. "Food System Emissions: A Review of Trends, Drivers, and Policy Approaches, 1990–2018." *Environmental Research Letters* 18 (7): 074030. https://doi.org/10.1088/1748-9326/acddfd.

Cervigni, Raffaello, Irina Dvorak, and John Allen Rogers. 2013. *Assessing Low-Carbon Development in Nigeria: An Analysis of Four Sectors.* Washington, DC: World Bank Group. https://doi.org/10.1596/978-0-8213-9973-6.

Chakraborty, Debashis, Justin Ahmed, Elaine Almeida, Daniel Aminetzah, Nicolas Denis, Kimberly Henderson, Joshua Katz, et al. 2020. "A Global Analysis of Alternative Tillage and Crop Establishment Practices." In *McKinsey & Company, Agriculture and Climate Change*, 20. New York: McKinsey & Company. https://www.mckinsey.com/~/media/mckinsey/industries/agriculture/our%20insights/reducing%20agriculture%20emissions%20through%20improved%20farming%20practices/agriculture-and-climate-change.pdf.

Chará, J., E. Reyes, P. Peri, J. Otte, E. Arce, and F. Schneider. 2019. "Silvopastoral Systems and Their Contribution to Improved Resource Use and Sustainable Development Goals (SDG): Evidence from Latin America." Food and Agriculture Organization of the United Nations, Centre for Research on Sustainable Agriculture, and Agri Bechmark, Cali, Colombia. https://www.fao.org/publications/card/en/c/CA2792EN/.

Chauhan, Chetna, Amandeep Dhir, Manzoor Ul Akram, and Jari Salo. 2021. "Food Loss and Waste in Food Supply Chains: A Systematic Literature Review and Framework Development Approach." *Journal of Cleaner Production* 295: 126438. https://doi.org/10.1016/j.jclepro.2021.126438.

Chel, A., and G. Kaushik. 2011. "Renewable Energy for Sustainable Agriculture." *Agronomy for Sustainable Development* 31 (1): 91–118. https://doi.org/10.1051/agro/2010029.

Chen, Chi, Taejin Park, Xuhui Wang, Shilong Piao, Baodong Xu, Rajiv K. Chaturvedi, Richard Fuchs, et al. 2019. "China and India Lead in Greening of the World through Land-Use Management." *Nature Sustainability* 2: 122–9. https://doi.org/10.1038/s41893-019-0220-7.

Chidthaisong, A., N. Cha-un, B. Rossopa, C. Buddaboon, C. Kunuthai, P. Sriphirom, S. Towprayoon, T. Tokida, A. T. Padre, and K. Minamikawa. 2018. "Evaluating the Effects of Alternate Wetting and Drying (AWD) on Methane and Nitrous Oxide Emissions from a Paddy Field in Thailand." *Soil Science and Plant Nutrition* 64 (1): 31–38. https://doi.org/10.1080/00380768.2017.1399044.

Chiriac, Daniela, and Baysa Naran. 2020. *Examining the Climate Finance Gap for Small-Scale Agriculture.* San Francisco, CA: Climate Policy Initiative. https://www.climatepolicyinitiative.org/publication/climate-finance-small-scale-agriculture/.

Christiaensen, L., Z. Rutledge, and J. E. Taylor. 2021. "Viewpoint: The Future of Work in Agri-food." *Food Policy* 99:101963. https://doi.org/10.1016/j.foodpol.2020.101963.

Chun, Yuan, Guangyao Sheng, Cary T. Chiou, and Baoshan Xing. 2004. "Compositions and Sorptive Properties of Crop Residue-Derived Chars." *Environmental Science Technology* 38 (17): 4649–55. https://doi.org/10.1021/es035034w.

Clairand, J.-M., M. Briceño-León, G. Escrivá-Escrivá, and A. M. Pantaleo. 2020. "Review of Energy Efficiency Technologies in the Food Industry: Trends, Barriers, and Opportunities." *IEEE Access* 8: 48015–29. https://doi.org/10.1109/ACCESS.2020.2979077.

Clark, Michael A., Nina G. G. Domingo, Kimberly Colgan, Sumil K. Thakrar, David Tilman, John Lynch, Inés L. Azevedo, and Jason D. Hill. 2020. "Global Food System Emissions Could Preclude Achieving the 1.5° and 2°C Climate Change Targets." *Science* 370: 705–8. https://doi.org/10.1126/science.aba7357.

Clark, M., and D. Tilman, D. 2017. "Comparative Analysis of Environmental Impacts of Agricultural Production Systems, Agricultural Input Efficiency, and Food Choice." *Environmental Research Letters* 12 (6): 064016. https://doi.org/10.1088/1748-9326/aa6cd5.

Climate Watch. 2023. "Historical GHG Emissions: Global Historical Emissions" (web page). 2023. Accessed April 14, 2024. https://www.climatewatchdata.org/ghg-emissions.

Cold Hubs. n.d. "The Solution: Walk-In, Solar-Powered Cold Stations for 24/7 Storage and Preservation" (web page). Accessed April 14, 2024. https://www.coldhubs.com/.

Colen, L., P. C. Melo, Y. Abdul-Salam, D. Roberts, S. Mary, S. Gomez y Paloma. 2018. "Income Elasticities for Food, Calories and Nutrients across Africa: A Meta-analysis." *Food Policy* 77 (2018): 116-132. https://doi .org/10.1016/j.foodpol.2018.04.002.

Conti, Costanza, Giacomo Zanello, and Andy Hall. 2021. "Why Are Agri-food Systems Resistant to New Directions of Change? A Systematic Review." *Global Food Security* 31: 100576. https://doi.org/10.1016/j .gfs.2021.100576.

Costa Jr., C., E. Wollenberg, M. Benitez, R. Newman, N. Gardner, and F. Bellone. 2022. "Roadmap for Achieving Net-Zero Emissions in Global Food Systems by 2050." *Scientific Reports* 12 (1): 15064. https:// doi.org/10.1038/s41598-022-18601-1.

Crippa, M., E. Solazzo, D. Guizzardi, F. Monforti-Ferrario, F. N. Tubiello, and A. Leip. 2021."Food Systems Are Responsible for a Third of Global Anthropogenic GHG Emissions." *Nature Food* 2: 198–209. https:// doi.org/10.1038/s43016-021-00225-9.

Cui, Zhenling, Hongyan Zhang, Xinping Chen, Chaochun Zhang, Wenqi Ma, Chengdong Huang, Weifeng Zhang, et al. 2018. "Letter: Pursuing Sustainable Productivity with Millions of Smallholder Farmers." *Nature* 555: 363–6. https://doi.org/10.1038/nature25785.

Curtis, P. G., C. M. Slay, N. L. Harris, A. Tyukavina, and M. C. Hansen. 2018. "Classifying Drivers of Global Forest Loss." *Science* 361 (6407): 1108–11. https://doi.org/10.1126/science.aau3445.

Damania, Richard, Stephen Polasky, Mary Ruckelshaus, Jason Russ, Markus Amann, Rebecca Chaplin-Kramer, James Gerber, et al. 2023. *Nature's Frontiers: Achieving Sustainability, Efficiency, and Prosperity with Natural Capital.* Environment and Sustainable Development series. Washington, DC: World Bank. https://doi.org/10.1596/978-1-4648-1923-0.

De Boer, J., H. Schösler, and H. Aiking. 2014. "'Meatless Days' or 'Less but Better'? Exploring Strategies to Adapt Western Meat Consumption to Health and Sustainability Challenges." *Appetite* 76: 120–8. https://doi.org/10.1016/j.appet.2014.02.002.

Delacote, Philippe. 2009. "On the Sources of Consumer Boycotts Ineffectiveness." *Journal of Environment and Development* 18 (3): 306–22. https://doi.org/10.1177/1070496509338849.

Delgado, C., M. Rosegrant, H. Steinfeld, S. Ehui, and C. Courbois. 1999. "Livestock to 2020: The Next Food Rrevolution." Food, Agriculture, and the Environment Discussion Paper 28, International Food Policy Research Institute, Washington, DC. https://hdl.handle.net/10568/333.

DeValue, K., N. Takahashi, T. Woolnough, C. Merle, S. Fortuna, and A. Agostini. 2022. "Halting Deforestation from Agricultural Value Chains: The Role of Governments." Food and Agriculture Organization of the United Nations. https://www.fao.org/3/cc2262en/cc2262en.pdf.

Dooley, K., H. Keith, A. Larson, G. Catacora-Vargas, W. Carton, K. L. Christiansen, O. Enokenwa Baa, et al. 2022. *The 2022 Land Gap Report.* Melbourne, Australia: Land Gap Report. https://landgap.org/2022 /report.

Dubois, Olivier, Alessandro Flammini, Ana Kojakovic, Irini Maltsoglou, Manas Puri, and Luis Rincon. 2017. *Energy Access: Food and Agriculture.* Sustainable Energy for All (SEAR) Special Feature. Washington, DC: International Bank for Reconstruction and Development/World Bank. https://www.esmap.org /node/76477.

Dupraz, C., H. Marrou, G. Talbot, L. Dufour, A. Nogier, and Y. Ferard. 2011. "Combining Solar Photovoltaic Panels and Food Crops for Optimizing Land Use: Towards New Agrivoltaic Schemes." *Renewable Energy* 36 (10): 2725–32. https://doi.org/10.1016/j.renene.2011.03.005.

Eckstein, David, Veronika Kuenzel, and Lisa Schaefer. 2021. *Global Climate Risk Index*. Bonn: Germanwatch e.V. https://www.germanwatch.org/sites/default/files/Global%20Climate%20Risk%20Index%202021_2.pdf.

Ecosystem Marketplace Insights Team. 2023. "New Research: Carbon Credits Are Associated with Businesses Decarbonizing Faster" (article). Updated October 10, 2023. https://www.ecosystemmarketplace.com/articles/new-research-carbon-credits-are-associated-with-businesses-decarbonizing-faster/.

Eggleston, H. Simon, Leandro Buendia, Kyoko Miwa, Todd Ngara, and Kiyoto Tanabe, eds. 2006. *IPCC Guidelines for National Greenhouse Gas Inventories*. Vol. 5, *Waste*. Geneva: IPCC. https://www.ipcc-nggip.iges.or.jp/public/2006gl/vol5.html.

Elshurafa, Amro M., Hatem Alatawi, Salaheddine Soummane, and Frank A. Felder. 2021. "Assessing Effects of Renewable Deployment on Emissions in the Saudi Power Sector until 2040 Using Integer Optimization." *Electricity Journal* 34 (6): 106973. https://doi.org/10.1016/j.tej.2021.106973.

Energy 4 Impact. 2021. "Solar Irrigation Rwanda—Developing a New Market for Smallholder Farmers" (article). April 20, 2021. https://energy4impact.org/news/solar-irrigation-rwanda-%E2%80%93-developing-new-market-smallholder-farmers.

Erisman, Jan Willem, Mark A. Sutton, James Galloway, Zbigniew Klimont, and Wilfried Winiwarter 2008. "How a Century of Ammonia Synthesis Changed the World." *Nature Geoscience* 1: 636–9. https://doi.org/10.1038/ngeo325.

Escobar Carbonari, Daniel, Godefroy Grosjean, Peter Läderach, Nghia Tran Dai, Bjoern Ole Sander, Justin McKinley, Sebastian Leocadio, and Jeimar Tapasco. 2019. "Reviewing Vietnam's Nationally Determined Contribution: A New Perspective Using the Marginal Cost of Abatement." *Frontiers in Sustainable Food Systems* 3: 14. https://doi.org/10.3389/fsufs.2019.00014.

European Environment Agency. 2015. "Renewables Successfully Driving Down Carbon Emissions in Europe" (article). Updated January 13, 2017. https://www.eea.europa.eu/highlights/renewables-successfully-driving-down-carbon.

Fairbrother, Malcolm. 2013. "Rich People, Poor People, and Environmental Concern: Evidence across Nations and Time." *European Sociological Review* 29: 910–22. https://doi.org/10.1093/esr/jcs068.

FAO (Food and Agriculture Organization of the United Nations). 2011.*"Energy-Smart" Food for People and Climate*. Issue Paper. Rome: FAO. https://www.fao.org/3/i2454e/i2454e.pdf.

FAO (Food and Agriculture Organization of the United Nations). 2013. *Climate-Smart Agriculture Sourcebook*. Rome: FAO. https://www.fao.org/climate-smart-agriculture-sourcebook/en/.

FAO (Food and Agriculture Organization of the United Nations). 2015. *The Impact of Natural Hazards and Disasters on Agriculture and Food Security and Nutrition*. Rome: FAO. https://www.fao.org/3/i4434e/i4434e.pdf.

FAO (Food and Agriculture Organization of the United Nations). 2017a. "Climate-Smart Livestock Production Systems in Practice." In *CSA Sourcebook* (online version), Section B2-3.1. Rome: FAO. https://www.fao.org/climate-smart-agriculture-sourcebook/production-resources/module-b2-livestock/chapter-b2-3/en/.

FAO (Food and Agriculture Organization of the United Nations). 2017b. *The Future of Food and Agriculture: Trends and Challenges*. Rome. https://www.fao.org/3/i6583e/i6583e.pdf.

FAO (Food and Agriculture Organization of the United Nations). 2018. "The 10 Elements of Agroecology: Guiding the Transition to Sustainable Food and Agricultural Systems." FAO, Rome. https://www.fao.org/3/i9037en/i9037en.pdf.

FAO (Food and Agriculture Organization of the United Nations). 2019a. *Five Practical Actions towards Low-Carbon Livestock*. Rome: FAO. https://www.fao.org/documents/card/en/c/ca7089en/.

FAO (Food and Agriculture Organization of the United Nations). 2019b. *The State of Food and Agriculture 2019: Moving Forward on Food Loss and Waste Reduction.* Rome: FAO. https://www.fao.org/3/ca6030en /ca6030en.pdf.

FAO (Food and Agriculture Organization of the United Nations). 2020. *The State of Food and Agriculture 2020: Overcoming Water Challenges in Agriculture.* Rome: FAO. https://doi.org/10.4060/cb1447en.

FAO (Food and Agriculture Organization of the United Nations). 2021a. *The Impact of Disasters and Crises on Agriculture and Food Security: 2021.* Rome: FAO. https://doi.org/10.4060/cb3673en.

FAO (Food and Agriculture Organization of the United Nations). 2021b. *The State of the World's Land and Water Resources for Food and Agriculture: Systems at Breaking Point.* Synthesis Report 2021. Rome: FAO. https://doi.org/10.4060/cb7654en.

FAO (Food and Agriculture Organization of the United Nations). 2022a. "Black Soils Global Map." FAO, Rome. https://www.fao.org/3/cc0236en/cc0236en.pdf; https://www.fao.org/documents/card/en/c /cc0236en.

FAO (Food and Agriculture Organization of the United Nations). 2022b. "Catalyzing the Efficiency and Sustainability of Azerbaijan's Hazelnut Sector." Project UTF/AZE/016/AZE. FAO, Rome. https://www .fao.org/3/cb8762en/cb8762en.pdf.

FAO (Food and Agriculture Organization of the United Nations). 2022c. *Drivers and Triggers for Transformation.* Future of Food and Agriculture 3. Rome: FAO. https://doi.org/10.4060/cc0959en.

FAO (Food and Agriculture Organization of the United Nations). 2022d. *Global Soil Organic Carbon Sequestration Potential Map—GSOCseq v.1.1.* Technical Report. Rome: FAO. https://doi.org/10.4060 /cb9002en.

FAO (Food and Agriculture Organization of the United Nations). 2022e. "The State of the World's Forests 2022: Forest Pathways for Green Recovery and Building Inclusive, Resilient and Sustainable Economies." In Brief. FAO, Rome. https://doi.org/10.4060/cb9363en.

FAO (Food and Agriculture Organization of the United Nations). 2023a. "Global Livestock Environmental Assessment Model (GLEAM)" (web page). Accessed April 14, 2024. https://www.fao.org/gleam/en/.

FAO (Food and Agriculture Organization of the United Nations). 2023b. *Greenhouse Gas Emissions from Pre- and Post-agricultural Production Processes: Global, Regional and Country Trends, 1990–2020.* FAOSTAT Analytical Brief Series 65. Rome: FAO. https://doi.org/10.4060/cc5768en.

FAO (Food and Agriculture Organization of the United Nations). 2023c. "Integrated Production Systems." In *Climate Smart Agriculture Sourcebook.* Rome: FAO. https://www.fao.org/climate-smart-agriculture -sourcebook/production-resources/module-b5-integrated-production-systems/chapter-b5-1/en/.

FAO (Food and Agriculture Organization of the United Nations). 2023d. "Sustainability Pathways: Food Wastage Footprint" (web page). Accessed April 14, 2024. https://www.fao.org/nr/sustainability/food -loss-and-waste/en/#:~:text=Food%20loss%20refers%20to%20the,levels%2C%20mostly%20in%20 developed%20countries.

FAO (Food and Agriculture Organization of the United Nations), IFAD (International Fund for Agricultural Development), UNICEF (United Nations Children's Fund), WFP (World Food Programme), and WHO (World Health Organization). 2020. *The State of Food Security and Nutrition in the World 2020: Transforming Food Systems for Affordable Healthy Diets.* Rome: FAO. https://doi.org/10.4060/ca9692en.

FAO (Food and Agriculture Organization of the United Nations), IFAD (International Fund for Agricultural Development), UNICEF (United Nations Children's Fund), WFP (World Food Programme), and WHO (World Health Organization). 2021. *The State of Food Security and Nutrition in the World 2021: Transforming Food Systems for Food Security, Improved Nutrition and Affordable Healthy Diets for All.* Rome: FAO. https://doi.org/10.4060/cb4474en.

FAO (Food and Agriculture Organization of the United Nations), IFAD (International Fund for Agricultural Development), UNICEF (United Nations Children's Fund), WFP (World Food Programme), and WHO (World Health Organization). 2022. *The State of Food Security and Nutrition in the World 2022: Repurposing Food and Agricultural Policies to Make Healthy Diets More Affordable.* Rome: FAO. https://doi.org/10.4060/cc0639en.

FAO (Food and Agriculture Organization of the United Nations) and IRENA (International Renewable Energy Agency). 2021. *Renewable Energy for Agri-food Systems: Towards the Sustainable Development Goals and the Paris Agreement.* Rome: FAO and Abu Dhabi: IRENA. https://doi.org/10.4060/cb7433en.

FAO (Food and Agriculture Organization of the United Nations) and ITPS (Intergovernmental Technical Panel on Soils). 2021. "Soil Organic Carbon and Nitrogen: Reviewing the Challenges for Climate Change Mitigation and Adaptation in Agri-Food Systems." ITPS Soil Letters 2. Rome: FAO and ITPS. https://www.fao.org/documents/card/en/c/cb3965en.

FAOSTAT. 2023a. FAOSTAT, Food Balance Sheets 1990–2009 and 2010–20. Accessed April 12, 2024. https://www.fao.org/faostat/en/#data/FBSH.

FAOSTAT. 2023b. "Emission Intensities" (data set). Accessed April 14, 2024. https://www.fao.org/faostat/en/#data/EI.

FAOSTAT. 2023c. "Emissions Totals" (data set). Accessed April 12, 2024. https://www.fao.org/faostat/en/#data/Gt.

FAOSTAT. 2023d. "Apparent Intake" (data set). Accessed April 26, 2024. https://www.fao.org/faostat/en/#data/HCES.

FAOSTAT. 2023e. "Crops and livestock products" (data set). Accessed April 26, 2024. https://www.fao.org/faostat/en/#data/QCL.

FAOSTAT. 2023f. "Fertilizers by Product" (data set). Accessed April 26, 2024. https://www.fao.org/faostat/en/#data/RFB.

Farmer, Adam, Michael Breazeale, Jennifer L. Stevens, and Stacie F. Waites. 2017. "Eat Green, Get Lean: Promoting Sustainability Reduces Consumption." *Journal of Public Policy and Marketing* 36: 299–312. https://doi.org/10.1509/jppm.16.087.

Federative Republic of Brazil. 2022. "Federative Republic of Brazil: Paris Agreement; Nationally Determined Contribution." Communication to the United Nations Framework Convention on Climate Change Secretariat. https://unfccc.int/sites/default/files/NDC/2022-06/Updated%20-%20First%20NDC%20-%20FINAL%20-%20PDF.pdf.

Flammini, A., X. Pan, F. N. Tubiello, S. Y. Qiu, L. Rocha Souza, R. Quadrelli, S. Bracco, P. Benoit, and R. Sims. 2022. "Emissions of Greenhouse Gases from Energy Use in Agriculture, Forestry and Fisheries: 1970–2019." *Earth System Science Data* 14: 811–21. https://doi.org/10.5194/essd-14-811-2022.

Foley, Jonathan A., Navin Ramankutty, Kate A. Brauman, Emily S. Cassidy, James S. Gerber, Matt Johnston, Nathaniel D. Mueller, et al. 2011. "Solutions for a Cultivated Planet." *Nature* 478 (7369): 337–42. https://www.nature.com/articles/nature10452.

Fowler, D., C. E. Steadman, D. Stevenson, M. Coyle, R. M. Rees, U. M. Skiba, M. A. Sutton, et al. 2015. "Effects of Global Change during the 21st Century on the Nitrogen Cycle." *Atmospheric Chemistry and Physics* 15: 13849–93. https://acp.copernicus.org/articles/15/13849/2015/.

Frank, Stefan, Petr Havlik, Elke Stehfest, Hans van Meijl, Peter Witzke, Ignacio Pérez-Dominguez, Michiel van Diji, et al. 2019. "Agricultural Non-CO_2 Emission Reduction Potential in the Context of the 1.5°C Target." *Nature Climate Change* 9 (1): 66–72. https://pure.iiasa.ac.at/id/eprint/15632/1/Agricultural_nonCO2_mitigation_paper_v3_epure.pdf.

Frelih-Larsen, A., S. Ittner, S. Herb, J. Tarpey, E. J. Olesen, M. Graversgaard, L. Claessens, et al. 2020. "CIRCASA Deliverable D2.3: Synthesis Report on Knowledge Demands and Needs of Stakeholders." Recherche Data Gouv, V2. https://doi.org/10.15454/Q0XVVD.

Fresán, U., and J. Sabaté. 2019. "Vegetarian Diets: Planetary Health and Its Alignment with Human Health." *Advances in Nutrition* 10 (S4): 380–8. https://doi.org/10.1093/advances/nmz019.

Fukagawa, N. K., and L. H. Ziska. 2019. "Rice: Importance for Global Nutrition." Supplement, *Journal of Nutritional Science and Vitaminology* (Tokyo) 65: S2–S3. https://doi.org/10.3177/jnsv.65.S2.

Funke, F., L. Mattauch, I. van den Bijgaart, H. C. J. Godfray, C. Hepburn, D. Klenert, M. Springmann, and N. Treich. 2022. "Toward Optimal Meat Pricing: Is It Time to Tax Meat Consumption?" *Review of Environmental Economics and Policy* 16 (2): 219–40.

Fuss, Sabine, William F. Lamb, Max W. Callaghan, Jérôme Hilaire, Felix Creutzig, Thorben Amann, Tim Beringer, Wagner de Oliveira Garcia, Jens Hartmann, and Tarun Khanna. 2018. "Negative Emissions—Part 2: Costs, Potentials and Side Effects." *Environmental Research Letters* 13 (6): 063002. https://doi .org/10.1088/1748-9326/aabf9f.

Galimberti, Alessandro. 2021. "Behavioural Change Promotion toward Cleaner Cooking Solutions." Deutsche Gesellschaft für Internationale Zusammenarbeit (GIZ), Eschborn, Germany. https://endev .info/wp-content/uploads/2021/10/EnDev_Learning-and-Innovation-Agenda_Clean-Cooking _Behavioural-change-promotion-toward-cleaner-cooking-solutions.pdf.

Galimova, T., M. Ram, and C. Breyer. 2022. "Mitigation of Air Pollution and Corresponding Impacts during a Global Energy Transition towards 100% Renewable Energy System by 2050." *Energy Reports* 8: 14124–43. https://doi.org/10.1016/j.egyr.2022.10.343.

Gao, Y., and A. Cabrera Serrenho. 2023. "Greenhouse Gas Emissions from Nitrogen Fertilizers Could Be Reduced by Up to One-Fifth of Current Levels by 2050 with Combined Interventions." *Nature Food* 4: 170–78. https://doi.org/10.1038/s43016-023-00698-w.

Garnett, Tara, Sophie Mathewson, Philip Angelides, and Fiona Borthwick. 2015. *Policies and Actions to Shift Eating Patterns: What Works? A Review of the Evidence of the Effectiveness of Interventions Aimed at Shifting Diets in More Sustainable and Healthy Directions.* London: Food Climate Research Network and Chatham House. https://www.oxfordmartin.ox.ac.uk/publications/policies-and-actions-to-shift-eating -patterns-what-works/.

Garrett, R. D., S. Levy, K. M. Carlson, T. A. Gardner, J. Godar, J. Clapp, P. Dauvergne, et al. 2019. "Criteria for Effective Zero-Deforestation Commitments." *Global Environmental Change* 54: 135–47. https://doi .org/10.1016/j.gloenvcha.2018.11.003.

Gerber, P. J., B. Henderson, C. Opio, A. Mottet, and H. Steinfeld. 2013. *Tackling Climate Change through Livestock—A Global Assessment of Emissions and Mitigation Opportunities.* Rome: Food and Agriculture Organization of the United Nations. https://www.fao.org/3/i3437e/i3437e.pdf.

GGI Insights. 2023. "Energy Innovation: Catalyzing Affordable and Clean Energy Solutions." *GGI Insights* (blog), March 27. https://www.graygroupintl.com/blog/energy-innovation#:~:text=Innovation%20 plays%20a%20critical%20role,both%20the%20environment%20and%20society.

GIZ Programme on Conservation, Sustainable Use of Forest Biodiversity and Ecosystem Services in Viet Nam. 2022. "Impacts of the Logging Ban in Viet Nam." Policy brief, Programme on Conservation, Sustainable Use of Forest Biodiversity and Ecosystem Services in Viet Nam. https://snrd-asia.org/wp -content/uploads/2022/05/2022-05-18-Policy-brief-Impacts-of-the-logging-ban-in-Viet-Nam_EN.pdf.

GLOPAN (Global Panel on Agriculture and Food Systems for Nutrition). 2017. "Policy Actions to Support Enhanced Consumer Behavior for High-Quality Diets." Policy Brief 8, GLOPAN, London. https://www .glopan.org/sites/default/files/Downloads/GlobalPanelConsumerBehaviourBrief.pdf.

Godde, C. M., I. J. M. de Boer, , E. zu Ermgassen, M. Herrero, C. E. van Middelaar, A. Muller, E. Röös, C. Schader, P. Smith, H. H. E. van Zanten, and T. Garnett. 2020. "Soil Carbon Sequestration in Grazing Systems: Managing Expectations." *Climatic Change* 161: 385–391. https://doi.org/10.1007/s10584-020 -02673-x.

Gokarn, S., and T. S. Kuthambalayan. 2017. "Analysis of Challenges Inhibiting the Reduction of Waste in Food Supply Chain." *Journal of Cleaner Production* 168: 595–604. https://doi.org/10.1016/j .jclepro.2017.09.028.

Gollnhofer, Johanna F., Henri A. Weijo, and John W. Schouten. 2019. "Consumer Movements and Value Regimes: Fighting Food Waste in Germany by Building Alternative Object Pathways." *Journal of Consumer Research* 46 (3): 460–82. https://doi.org/10.1093/jcr/ucz004.

Gonocruz, Ruth Anne, Ren Nakamura, Kota Yoshino, Masaru Homma, Tetsuya Doi, Yoshikuni Yoshida, and Akira Tani. 2021. "Analysis of the Rice Yield under an Agrivoltaic System: A Case Study in Japan." *Environments* 8 (7): 65. https://doi.org/10.3390/environments8070065.

Gonzalez Fischer, Carlos, and Tara Garnett. 2016. *Plates, Pyramids and Planets: Developments in National Healthy and Sustainable Dietary Guidelines; A State of Play Assessment.* Rome: Food and Agriculture Organization of the United Nations and Food Climate Research Network at University of Oxford. https://www.fao.org/3/I5640E/i5640e.pdf.

Good Food Institute. 2022. *State of Global Policy: Public Investments in Alternative Proteins to Feed a Growing World*. Washington, DC: Good Food Institute. https://gfi.org/wp-content/uploads/2023/01/State_of_Global_Policy_Report_2022.pdf.

Graziose, M. M., and I. Y. H. Ang. 2019. "Factors Related to Fruit and Vegetable Consumption at Lunch among Elementary Students: A Scoping Review." *Preventing Chronic Disease* 15 (5). https://www.cdc.gov/pcd/issues/2018/17_0373.htm.

Green, Julia K., Sonia I. Seneviratne, Alexis M. Berg, Kirsten L. Findell, Stefan Hagemann, David M. Lawrence, and Pierre Gentine. 2019. "Large Influence of Soil Moisture on Long-Term Terrestrial Carbon Uptake." *Nature* 565: 476–79. https://doi.org/10.1038/s41586-018-0848-x.

Grunert, Klaus G. 2011. "Sustainability in the Food Sector: A Consumer Behaviour Perspective." *International Journal on Food System Dynamics* 2 (3): 207–18. https://doi.org/10.18461/ijfsd.v2i3.232.

Grunert, Klaus G., S. Hieke, and J. Wills. 2014. "Sustainability Labels on Food Products: Consumer Motivation, Understanding, and Use." *Food Policy* 44: 177–89. https://doi.org/10.1016/j.foodpol.2013.12.001.

Guha-Sapir, Debarati, Philippe Hoyois, and Regina Below. 2015. *Annual Disaster Statistical Review: The Numbers and Trends*. Brussels: Centre for Research on the Epidemiology of Disasters. http://www.cred.be/sites/default/files/ADSR_2014.pdf.

Hallegatte, Stephane, Mook Bangalore, Laura Bonzanigo, Marianne Fay, Tamaro Kane, Ulf Narloch, Julie Rozenberg, David Treguer, and Adrien Vogt-Schilb. 2016. *Shock Waves: Managing the Impacts of Climate Change on Poverty*. Climate Change and Development. Washington, DC: World Bank. http://hdl.handle.net/10986/22787.

Hanss, Daniel, and Gisela Böhm. 2013. "Promoting Purchases of Sustainable Groceries: An Intervention Study." *Journal of Environmental Psychology* 33: 53–67. https://doi.org/10.1016/j.jenvp.2012.10.002.

Hanusch, Marek, and Jon Strand. 2023. "How Much Should We Pay to Preserve the Amazon?" *Latin America and Caribbean* (blog), June 8, 2023. https://blogs.worldbank.org/latinamerica/how-much-should-we-pay-preserve-amazon.

Harring, Niklas. 2013. "Understanding the Effects of Corruption and Political Trust on Willingness to Make Economic Sacrifices for Environmental Protection in a Cross-National Perspective." *Social Science Quarterly* 94 (3): 660–71. https://doi.org/10.1111/j.1540-6237.2012.00904.x.

Harris, N. L., D. A. Gibbs, A. Baccini, R. A. Birdsey, S. de Bruin, M. Farina, L. Fatoyinbo, et al. 2021. "Global Maps of Twenty-First Century Forest Carbon Fluxes." *Nature Climate Change* 11: 234–40. https://doi.org/10.1038/s41558-020-00976-6.

Hartung, H., and L. Pluschke. 2018. "The Benefits and Risks of Solar-Powered Irrigation: A Global Overview." FAO and GIZ. Accessed April 12, 2024. https://www.fsnnetwork.org/resource/benefits-and-risks-solar-powered-irrigation.

Hassan, M. U., M. Aamer, A. Mahmood, M. I. Awan, L. Barbanti, M. F. Seleiman, G. Bakhsh, et al. 2022. "Management Strategies to Mitigate N2O Emissions in Agriculture." *Life (Basel)* 12 (3): 439. https://doi.org/10.3390/life12030439.

Hawkins, James, Gabriel Yesuf, Mink Zijlstra, George C. Schoneveld, and Mariana C. Rufina. 2021. "Feeding Efficiency Gains Can Increase the Greenhouse Gas Mitigation Potential of the Tanzanian Dairy Sector." *Scientific Reports* 11: 4190. https://doi.org/10.1038/s41598-021-83475-8.

Herrero, M., P. Havlík, H. Valin, A. Notenbaert, M. C. Rufino, P. K. Thornton, M. Blümmel, F. Weiss, D. Grace, and M. Obersteiner. 2013. "Biomass Use, Production, Feed Efficiencies, and Greenhouse Gas Emissions from Global Livestock Systems." *Proceedings of the National Academy of Sciences of the United States of America* 110 (52): 20888–93. https://doi.org/10.1073/pnas.1308149110.

Herrero, M., M. Hugas, U. Lele, A. Wirakartakusumah, and M. Torero. 2023. "A Shift to Healthy and Sustainable Consumption Patterns." In *Science and Innovations for Food Systems Transformation*, edited by J. von Braun, K. Afsana, L. O. Fresco, and M. H. A. Hassan. Cham, Switzerland: Springer. https://doi.org/10.1007/978-3-031-15703-5_5.

Hoeppe, Peter. 2016. "Trends in Weather-Related Disasters: Consequences for Insurers and Society." *Weather and Climate Extremes* 11: 70–79. https://doi.org/10.1016/j.wace.2015.10.002.

Hong Kong Waste Reduction Website. n.d. "Waste Reduction Programme: Source Separation of Domestic Waste" (web page). Accessed: April 14, 2024. https://www.wastereduction.gov.hk/en/household/source _detail.htm.

Huber, D. M. 2010. "Ag Chemical and Crop Nutrient Interactions—Current Update." In *Proceedings of the Fluid Fertilizer Forum*, Scottsdale, AZ, February 14–16. Manhattan, KS: Fluid Fertilizer Foundation. http://soilcursebuster.com/Huber_at_Fluid_Fert._2-10.pdf.

Iaconangelo, David. 2023. "Washington State Hits the Brakes on Landmark Gas Ban." *E&E News*, May 25, 2023. https://www.eenews.net/articles/washington-state-hits-the-brakes-on-landmark-gas-ban.

IEA (International Energy Agency). 2021a. *Ammonia Technology Roadmap: Towards More Sustainable Nitrogen Fertilizer Production*. Paris: IEA. https://www.iea.org/reports/ammonia-technology-roadmap.

IEA (International Energy Agency). 2021b. *Renewables 2021: Analysis and Forecasts to 2026*. Paris: IEA. https://www.iea.org/reports/renewables-2021.

IEA (International Energy Agency). 2022a. *Energy Efficiency 2022*. Paris: IEA. https://iea.blob.core.windows .net/assets/7741739e-8e7f-4afa-a77f-49dadd51cb52/EnergyEfficiency2022.pdf.

IEA (International Energy Agency). 2022b. *Global Methane Tracker 2022: Strategies to Reduce Emissions from Fossil Fuel Operations*. Paris: IEA. https://www.iea.org/reports/global-methane-tracker-2022/strategies -to-reduce-emissions-from-fossil-fuel-operations.

IEA (International Energy Agency). 2022c. "Overview." In *World Energy Employment* (online version). Paris: IEA. https://www.iea.org/reports/world-energy-employment/overview.

IEA (International Energy Agency). 2022d. *Renewables 2022: Renewable Electricity*. Paris: IEA. https://www .iea.org/reports/renewables-2022/renewable-electricity.

IEA (International Energy Agency). 2023a. "Executive Summary." In A Vision for Clean Cooking Access for All. Paris: IEA. https://www.iea.org/reports/a-vision-for-clean-cooking-access-for-all/executive -summary.

IEA (International Energy Agency). 2023b. *Global Methane Tracker 2023*. Paris: IEA. https://www.iea.org /reports/global-methane-tracker-2023.

IEA (International Energy Agency). n.d.-a. "Renewables." Accessed April 11, 2024. https://www.iea.org /energy-system/renewables.

IEA (International Energy Agency). n.d.-b. "Tracking the Impact of Fossil-Fuel Subsidies: Energy Subsidies" (web page). Accessed April 14, 2024. https://www.iea.org/topics/energy-subsidies.

IEA (International Energy Agency) and UNSD (United Nations Statistics Division). 2021. "UNSD: Energy Statistics Database." Accessed July 2023. DATA.UN.org, http://data.un.org/Explorer.aspx?d=EDATA.

IEA (International Energy Agency), IRENA (International Renewable Energy Agency), UNSD (United Nations Statistics Division), World Bank, and WHO (World Health Organization). 2022. *Tracking SDG 7: The Energy Progress Report*. Washington, DC: World Bank. https://trackingsdg7.esmap.org/data/files /download-documents/sdg7-report2022-full_report.pdf.

ILO (International Labour Organization). 2020. "ILO Modelled Estimates Database (ILOSTAT)" (database). Accessed April 14, 2024. https://ilostat.ilo.org/data/.

IMF (International Monetary Fund). 2022. "The Democratic Republic of the Congo." IMF Country Report 22/211, IMF, Washington, DC. https://www.imf.org/media/Files/Publications/CR/2022/English /1CODEA2022003.ashx.

Instituto Escolhas. 2020. "From Pasture to Plate: Subsidies and the Environmental Footprint of the Beef Industry in Brazil." São Paolo: Instituto Escolhas. https://www.escolhas.org/wp-content /uploads/2020/01/From-pasture-to-plate-subsidies-and-the-enviromental-footprint-EXECUTIVE -SUMARY.pdf.

International Fertilizer Association. 2022. "IFASTAT: Consumption" (web page). Accessed April 14, 2024. https://www.ifastat.org/databases/plant-nutrition.

International Trade Centre, n.d. "Trade Statistics" (database). Accessed December 2023. https://intracen.org/.

IPCC (Intergovernmental Panel on Climate Change). 2000. "Summary for Policymakers." In *IPCC Special Report: Land Use, Land Use Change, and Forestry.* Geneva: IPCC. https://archive.ipcc.ch/pdf/special-reports/spm/srl-en.pdf.

IPCC (Intergovernmental Panel on Climate Change). 2014. *Climate Change 2014: Synthesis Report; Contribution of Working Groups I, II and III to the Fifth Assessment Report of the Intergovernmental Panel on Climate Change.* Geneva: IPCC. https://www.ipcc.ch/report/ar5/syr/.

IPCC (Intergovernmental Panel on Climate Change). 2019. *Climate Change and Land: An IPCC Special Report on Climate Change, Desertification, Land Degradation, Sustainable Land Management, Food Security, and Greenhouse Gas Fluxes in Terrestrial Ecosystems.* https://www.ipcc.ch/site/assets/uploads/2019/11/SRCCL-Full-Report-Compiled-191128.pdf.

IPCC (Intergovernmental Panel on Climate Change). 2022a. *Climate Change 2022: Impacts, Adaptation and Vulnerability; Contribution of Working Group II to the Sixth Assessment Report of the Intergovernmental Panel on Climate Change* Cambridge: Cambridge University Press. https://doi.org/10.1017/9781009325844.

IPCC (Intergovernmental Panel on Climate Change). 2022b. *Climate Change and Land: IPCC Special Report on Climate Change, Desertification, Land Degradation, Sustainable Land Management, Food Security, and Greenhouse Gas Fluxes in Terrestrial Ecosystems.* Cambridge: Cambridge University Press. https://doi.org/10.1017/9781009157988.

IPCC (Intergovernmental Panel on Climate Change). 2022c. "Summary for Policymakers." In *Climate Change 2022: Mitigation of Climate Change. Contribution of Working Group III to the Sixth Assessment Report of the Intergovernmental Panel on Climate Change,* edited by P. R. Shukla, J. Skea, R. Slade, A. Al Khourdajie, R. van Diemen, D. McCollum, M. Pathak, et al., 6–51 Cambridge: Cambridge University Press. https://doi.org/10.1017/9781009157926.001.

IRENA (International Renewable Energy Agency). 2022. *Bioenergy for the Energy Transition: Ensuring Sustainability and Overcoming Barriers.* Abu Dhabi: IRENA. https://www.irena.org/-/media/Files/IRENA/Agency/Publication/2022/Aug/IRENA_Bioenergy_for_the_transition_2022.pdf.

IRENA (International Renewable Energy Agency). 2023. *Renewable Capacity Statistics 2023.* Abu Dhabi: IRENA. https://www.irena.org/Publications/2023/Mar/Renewable-capacity-statistics-2023.

IRENA (International Renewable Energy Agency) and ILO (International Labour Organization). 2022. *Renewable Energy and Jobs: Annual Review 2022.* Abu Dhabi and Geneva: IRENA and ILO. https://www.ilo.org/wcmsp5/groups/public/---dgreports/---dcomm/documents/publication/wcms_856649.pdf.

IRRI (International Rice Research Institute). 2013. "Rice Facts" (web page). Accessed August 24, 2023. http://www.knowledgebank.irri.org/training/fact-sheets.

Isenhour, Cindy. 2012. "On the Challenges of Signaling Ethics without the Stuff: Tales of Conspicuous Green Anti-consumption." In *Ethical Consumption: Social Value and Economic Practice*, edited by James G. Carrier and Peter G. Luetchford, 164–80. New York: Berghahn. https://www.researchgate.net/publication/285840416_On_the_challenges_of_signalling_ethics_without_the_stuff_Tales_of_conspicuous_green_anti-consumption.

Islam, S. M., Y. K. Gaihre, J. C. Biswas, U. Singh, M. Ahmed, J. Sanabria, and M. A. Saleque. 2018. "Nitrous Oxide and Nitric Oxide Emissions from Lowland Rice Cultivation with Urea Deep Placement and Alternate Wetting and Drying Irrigation." *Scientific Reports* 8: 17623. https://doi.org/10.1038/s41598-018-35939-7.

Jo, M. S., J. H. Shin, W. J. Kim, and J. W. Jeong. 2017. "Energy-Saving Benefits of Adiabatic Humidification in the Air Conditioning Systems of Semiconductor Cleanrooms." *Energies* 10 (11): 1774. https://doi.org/10.3390/en10111774.

Johal, G. S., and D. M. Huber. 2009. "Glyphosate Effects on Diseases of Plants." *European Journal of Agronomy* 31 (3): 144–52. https://doi.org/10.1016/j.eja.2009.04.004.

Jones, M. W., G. P. Peters, T. Gasser, R. M. Andrew, C. Schwingshackl, J. Gütschow, R. A. Houghton, P. Friedlingstein, J. Pongratz, and C. Le Quéré. 2023. "National Contributions to Climate Change Due to Historical Emissions of Carbon Dioxide, Methane, and Nitrous Oxide since 1850." *Scientific Data* 10: 155. https://doi.org/10.1038/s41597-023-02041-1.

Jones, N., J. R. A. Clark, and C. Malesios. 2015. "Social Capital and Willingness-to-Pay for Coastal Defenses in South-East England." *Ecological Economics* 119: 74–82. https://doi.org/10.1016/j.ecolecon.2015.07.023.

Kallbekken, S., and H. Sælen. 2013. "Nudging' Hotel Guests to Reduce Food Waste as a Win-Win Environmental Measure." *Economics Letters* 119 (3): 325–27. https://doi.org/10.1016/j.econlet .2013.03.019.

Kampschreur, M. J., H. Temmink, R. Kleerebezem, M. S. Jetten, and M. C. van Loosdrecht. 2009. "Nitrous Oxide Emission during Wastewater Treatment." *Water Research* 43 (17): 4093–103. https://doi.org /10.1016/j.watres.2009.03.001.

Kane, Daniel A., Mark A. Bradford, Emma Fuller, Emily E. Oldfield, and Stephen A. Wood. 2021. "Hydraulic Redistribution: A Driver of Dryland Forest Responses to Interannual Climate Variability." *Environmental Research Letters* 16 (4): 044018. https://doi.org/10.1088/1748-9326/abe492.

Karl, Kevin, and Francesco Tubiello. 2021. "Methods for Estimating Greenhouse Gas Emissions from Food Systems—Part II: Waste Disposal." FAO Statistics Working Paper 21/28, Food and Agriculture Organization of the United Nations, Rome. https://doi.org/10.4060/cb7028en.

Karwacka, M., A. Ciurzyńska, A. Lenart, and M. Janowicz. 2020. "Sustainable Development in the Agri-food Sector in Terms of the Carbon Footprint: A Review." *Sustainability* 12 (16). https://doi.org/10.3390 /su12166463.

Khatri-Chhetri, A., A. Wilkes, and C. Odhong. 2020. "Mitigation Options and Finance for Transition to Low-Emissions Dairy in Kenya." Consultative Group on International Agricultural Research (CGIAR) Research Program on Climate Change Agriculture and Food Security (CCAFS) Working Paper.

Kim, B. F., R. E. Santo, A. P. Scatterday, J. P. Fry, C. M. Synk, S. R. Cebron, M. M. Mekonnen, et al. 2020. "Country-Specific Dietary Shifts to Mitigate Climate and Water Crises." *Global Environmental Change* 62: 101926. https://doi.org/10.1016/j.gloenvcha.2019.05.010.

Kim, D. G., S. Saggar, and P. Roudier. 2012. "The Effect of Nitrification Inhibitors on Soil Ammonia Emissions in Nitrogen Managed Soils: A Meta-analysis." *Nutrient Cycling in Agroecosystems* 93: 51–64. https://doi.org/10.1007/s10705-012-9498-9.

Kjellstrom, Tord, Nicolas Maître, Catherine Saget, Matthias Otto, and Tahmina Karimova. 2019. *Working on a Warmer Planet: The Impact of Heat Stress on Labour Productivity and Decent Work.* Geneva: International Labour Office.

Koçak, B., A. I. Fernandez, and H. Paksoy. 2020. "Review on Sensible Thermal Energy Storage for Industrial Solar Applications and Sustainability Aspects." *Solar Energy* 209: 135–69. https://doi.org/10.1016/j .solener.2020.08.081.

Koerth, Jana, Nikoleta Jones, Athanasios T. Vafeidis, Panayiotis G. Dimitrakopoulos, Androniki Melliou, Evaggelia Chatzidimitriou, and Sotirios Koukoulas. 2013. "Household Adaptation and Intention to Adapt to Coastal Flooding in the Axios–Loudias–Aliakmonas National Park, Greece." *Ocean & Coastal Management* 82: 43–50. https://doi.org/10.1016/j.ocecoaman.2013.05.008.

Koistinen, L., E. Pouta, J. Keikkilä, S. Forsman-Hugg, J. Kotro, J. Mäkelä, and M. Niva. 2013. "The Impact of Fat Content, Production Methods and Carbon Footprint Information on Consumer Preferences for Minced Meat." Food Quality and Preference 29 (2): 126–36. https://www.sciencedirect.com/science /article/abs/pii/S0950329313000438.

Konisky, D. M., J. Milyo, and L. E. Richardson. 2008. "Environmental Policy Attitudes: Issues, Geographical Scale, and Political Trust." *Social Science Quarterly* 89 (5): 1066–85. https://doi.org/10.1111/j.1540-6237 .2008.00574.x.

Laborde, David, Abdullah Mamun, Will Martin, Valeria Piñeiro, and Rob Vos. 2021. "Agricultural Subsidies and Global Greenhouse Gas Emissions." *Nature Communications* 12: 2601. https://doi.org/10.1038 /s41467-021-22703-1.

Lagomarsino, A., A. E. Agnelli, B. Linquist, M. A. Adviento-Borbe, A. Agnelli, G. Gavina, S. Ravaglia, and R. M. Ferrara. 2016. "Alternate Wetting and Drying of Rice Reduced CH_4 Emissions but Triggered

N₂O Peaks in a Clayey Soil of Central Italy." *Pedosphere* 26: 533–48. https://doi.org/10.1016/S1002
-0160(15)60063-7.

Lal, Rattan. 2011. "Soil Carbon Sequestration." SOLAW Background Thematic Report TR04B, Food and
Agriculture Organization of the United Nations, Rome. https://www.fao.org/fileadmin/templates/solaw
/files/thematic_reports/TR_04b_web.pdf.

Lal, Rattan. 2018. "Digging Deeper: A Holistic Perspective of Factors Affecting Soil Organic Carbon
Sequestration in Agroecosystems." *Global Change Biology* 24 (8). https://doi.org/10.1111/gcb.14054.

Lal, Rattan, C. Monger, L. Nave, and P. Smith. 2021. "The Role of Soil in Regulation of Climate." *Philosophical
Transactions of the Royal Society* 376 (1834): 20210084. https://doi.org/10.1098/rstb.2021.0084.

Lambin, Eric F., Holly K. Gibbs, Robert Heilmayr, Kimberly M. Carlson, Leonardo C. Fleck, Rachael D.
Garrett, Yann le Polain de Waroux, et al. 2018. "The Role of Supply-Chain Initiatives in Reducing
Deforestation." *Nature Climate Change* 8 (2): 109–16. https://doi.org/10.1038/ s41558-017-0061-1.

Lassaletta, Luis, Gilles Billen, Bruna Grizzetti, Juliette Anglade, and Josette Garnier. 2014. "50 Year Trends
in Nitrogen Use Efficiency of World Cropping Systems: The Relationship between Yield and Nitrogen
Input to Cropland."" *Environmental Research Letters* 9 (10): 105011. https://doi.org/10.1088/1748
-9326/9/10/105011.

Latka, Catharina, Marijke Kuiper, Stefan Frank, Thomas Heckelei, Petr Havlik, Heinz-Peter Witzke, Adrian
Leip, et al. 2021. "Paying the Price for Environmentally Sustainable and Healthy EU Diets." *Global Food
Security* 28. https://doi.org/10.1016/j.gfs.2020.100437.

Leonard, T. 2008. "Review of 'Nudge: Improving Decisions about Health, Wealth, and Happiness' by Richard
H. Thaler and Cass R. Sunstein." *Constitutional Political Economy* 19 (4): 356–60. https://doi.org/10.1007
/s10602-008-9056-2.

Levesque, C. A., and J. E. Rahe. 1992. "Herbicide Interactions with Fungal Root Pathogens, with Special
Reference to Glyphosate." *Annual Review of Phytopathology* 30: 579–602. https://doi.org/10.1146
/annurev.py.30.090192.003051.

Li, Y. H., and R. Barker. 2004. "Increasing Water Productivity for Paddy Irrigation in China." *Paddy and
Water Environment* 2 (4): 187–93. https://doi.org/10.1007/s10333-004-0064-1.

Licina, D., and C. Sekhar. 2012. "Energy and Water Conservation from Air Handling Unit Condensate in Hot
and Humid Climates." *Energy and Buildings* 45: 257–63. https://doi.org/10.1016/j.enbuild.2011.11.016.

Ling, Changming., Yifei Wang, Chunhua Min, and Yuwen Zhang. 2018. "Economic Evaluation of Reverse
Osmosis Desalination System Coupled with Tidal Energy." *Frontiers in Energy* 12: 297–304. https://doi
.org/10.1007/s11708-017-0478-2.

Linquist, B. A., M. M. Anders, M. A. Adviento-Borbe, R. L. Chaney, L. L. Nalley, E. F. da Rosa, and C. van
Kessel. 2015. "Reducing Greenhouse Gas Emissions, Water Use, and Grain Arsenic Levels in Rice
Systems." *Global Change Biology* 21 (1): 407–17. https://doi.org/10.1111/gcb.12701.

Linquist, B. A., K. J. Van Groenigen, M. A. Adviento-Borbe, C. Pittelkow, and C. Van Kessel. 2012. "An
Agronomic Assessment of Greenhouse Gas Emissions from Major Cereal Crops." *Global Change Biology*
18 (1): 194–209. https://doi.org/10.1111/j.1365-2486.2011.02502.x.

Liu, Sean X. 2014. *Food and Agricultural Wastewater Utilization and Treatment.* New York: Wiley. https://
onlinelibrary.wiley.com/doi/book/10.1002/9781118353967.

Liu, X., A. Elgowainy, and M. Wang. 2020. "Life Cycle Energy Use and Greenhouse Gas Emissions of
Ammonia Production from Renewable Resources and Industrial bB-Products." *Green Chemistry*
22: 5751–61. https://pubs.rsc.org/en/content/articlelanding/2020/GC/D0GC02301A#!divCitation.

Lowder, Sarah K., Marco V. Sánchez, and Raffaele Bertini. 2021. "Which Farms Feed the World and Has
Farmland Become More Concentrated?" *World Development* 142: 105455. https://doi.org/10.1016/j
.worlddev.2021.105455.

Ludden, Geke D., and Laura H. de Ruijter. 2016. "Supporting Healthy Behavior: A Stages of Change
Perspective on Changing Snacking Habits of Children." In *Future Focused Thinking—DRS International
Conference 2016* (June 27–30, Brighton), edited by P. Lloyd and E. Bohemia, 1473–86. https://doi
.org/10.21606/drs.2016.303.

Luoto, Jill, and Katherine Grace Carman. 2014. "Behavioral Economics Guidelines with Applications for Health Interventions." Technical Note IDB-TN-66, Social Protection and Health Division, Inter-American Development Bank, Washington, DC. https://publications.iadb.org/en/behavioral-economics-guidelines-applications-health-interventions.

Ma, Jing, Yang Ji, Guangbin Zhang, Hua Xu, and Kazuyuki Yagi. 2013. "Timing of Midseason Aeration to Reduce CH_4 and N_2O Emissions from Double Rice Cultivation in China." *Soil Science and Plant Nutrition* 59 (1): 35–45. https://doi.org/10.1080/00380768.2012.730477.

Mahmod, Safa Senan, Azratul Madihah Azahar, Abdullah Amru Indera Luthfi, Peer Mohamed Abdul, Mohd Shahbudin Mastar, Nurina Anuar, Mohd Sobri Takriff, and Jamaliah M. D. Jahim. 2020. "Potential Utilisation of Dark-Fermented Palm Oil Mill Effluent in Continuous Production of Biomethane by Self-Granulated Mixed Culture." *Scientific Reports* 10: 9167. https://doi.org/10.1038/s41598-020-65702-w.

Mancino, Lisa, Joanne F. Guthrie, Michele Ver Ploeg, and Biing-Hwan Lin. 2018. "Nutritional Quality of Foods Acquired by Americans: Findings From USDA's National Household Food Acquisition and Purchase Survey." Economic Information Bulletin EIB-188, Economic Research Service, US Department of Agriculture, Washington, DC. https://www.ers.usda.gov/publications/pub-details/?pubid=87530.

Mani, A., S. Mullainathan, E. Shafir, and J. Zhao. 2013. "Poverty Impedes Cognitive Function." *Science* 341 (6149): 976–80.

Manik, S. M. N., G. Pengilley, G. Dean, B. Field, S. Shabala, and M. Zhou. 2019. "Soil and Crop Management Practices to Minimize the Impact of Waterlogging on Crop Productivity." *Frontiers in Plant Science* 10: 140. https://doi.org/10.3389/fpls.2019.00140.

Manuell, Roy. 2022. "COP27: Ghana, Switzerland Authorize First Emissions Transfer under Paris Agreement" (article). https://carbon-pulse.com/179842/.

Martins, M. L., S. S. Rodrigues, L. M. Cunha, and A. Rocha. 2020. "Factors Influencing Food Waste during Lunch of Fourth-Grade School Children." *Waste Management* 113: 439–46. https://doi.org/10.1016/j.wasman.2020.06.023.

Martzopoulou, A., V. Firfiris, and T. Kotsopoulos. 2020. "Application of Urban Passive Cooling Systems and Design Techniques in Livestock Buildings." *IOP Conference Series: Earth and Environmental Science* 410 (1): 12029. https://doi.org/10.1088/1755-1315/410/1/012029.

Mateo-Sagasta, Javier, Liqa Raschid-Sally, and A. Thebo. 2015. "Global Wastewater and Sludge Production, Treatment and Use." In *Wastewater: Economic Asset in an Urbanizing World*, edited by Pay Drechsel, Manzoor Qadir, and D. Wichelns, 15–38. Dordrecht, the Netherlands: Springer. https://doi.org/10.1007/978-94-017-9545-6_2.

McIsaac, G. F., M. B. David, G. Z. Gertner, and D. A. Goolsby. 2001. "Nitrate Flux in the Mississippi River." *Nature* 414 (6860): 166–67. https://doi.org/10.1038/35102672.

McKinsey & Company. 2020. *Agriculture and Climate Change: Reducing Emissions through Improved Farming Practices*. New York: McKinsey & Company. https://www.mckinsey.com/industries/agriculture/our-insights/reducing-agriculture-emissions-through-improved-farming-practices.

McKinsey & Company. 2023. *The Agricultural Transition: Building a Sustainable Future*. New York: McKinsey & Company. https://www.mckinsey.com/industries/agriculture/our-insights/the-agricultural-transition-building-a-sustainable-future.

Medora, Sabrina. 2023. "The Country's First Gas Stove Ban Has Been Overturned." *Food & Wine*, April 18, 2023. https://www.foodandwine.com/federal-court-overturns-berkeley-ca-gas-stove-ban-7482137#.

Menegat, S., A. Ledo, and R. Tirado. 2022. "Greenhouse Gas Emissions from Global Production and Use of Nitrogen Synthetic Fertilisers in Agriculture." *Scientific Reports* 12: 14490. https://doi.org/10.1038/s41598-022-18773-w.

Messer, Tiffany L., L. Trisha Moore, Natalie G. Nelson, Laurent M. Ahiablame, Eban Z. Bean, Chelsie Boles, Sonja L. Cook, Steven G. Hall, John McMaine, and Derek Alan Schlea. 2021. "Constructed Wetlands for Water Quality Improvement: A Synthesis on Nutrient Reduction from Agricultural Effluents." *Transactions of the ASABE* 64: 625–39. https://elibrary.asabe.org/abstract.asp?aid=52167.

Metzger, Jim 2017. "Solving Humidity Issues in Manufacturing Facilities" (article). July 7, 2017. https://www
.ien.com/operations/article/20867207/solving-humidity-issues-in-manufacturing-facilities.

Michalak, Anna M., Eric J. Anderson, Dmitry Beletsky, Steven Boland, Nathan S. Bosch, Thomas B.
Bridgeman, Justin D. Chaffin, et al. 2013. "Record-Setting Algal Bloom in Lake Erie Caused by
Agricultural and Meteorological Trends Consistent with Expected Future Conditions." *Proceedings of
the National Academy of Sciences* 110 (16): 6448–52. https://doi.org/10.1073/pnas.1216006110.

Millennium Challenge Corporation. 2022. "As-Samra Wastewater Treatment Plant Expansion Project"
(web page). Accessed October 15, 2022. https://www.mcc.gov/resources/story/section-jor-ccr-as-samra
-project.

Miller, Victoria, Julia Reedy, Frederick Cudhea, Jianyi Zhang, Peilin Shi, Josh Erndt-Marino, Jennifer
Coates, Renata Micha, Patrick Webb, and Dariush Mozaffarian. 2022. "Global, Regional, and National
Consumption of Animal-Source Foods between 1990 and 2018: Findings from the Global Dietary
Database." *Lancet Planetary Health* 6 (3): e243–e256. https://doi.org/10.1016/S2542-5196(21)00352-1.

Ministry of Agriculture and Farmers Welfare, Government of India. 2018. "National Mission for Sustainable
Agriculture" (web page). Accessed: [[date]]. https://nmsa.dac.gov.in/.

Ministry of New and Renewable Energy, Government of India. 2021. *MNRE Annual Report 2020–2021.*
New Delhi: Government of India. https://mnre.gov.in/annual-reports-2020-21-2/.

Mota dos Santos, A., C. F. Assunção da Silva, P. M. Almeida Jr., A. P. Rudke, and S. Nogueira de Melo.
2021. "Deforestation Drivers in the Brazilian Amazon: Assessing New Spatial Predictors." *Journal of
Environmental Management* 294: 113020. https://doi.org/10.1016/j.jenvman.2021.113020.

Mottet, Anne, Benjamin Henderson, Carolyn Opio, Alessandra Falcucci, Giuseppe Tempio, Silvia Silvestri,
Sabrina Chesterman, and Pierre J. Gerber 2017. "Climate Change Mitigation and Productivity Gains
in Livestock Supply Chains: Insights from Regional Case Studies." *Regional Environmental Change*
17: 129–41. https://doi.org/10.1007/s10113-016-0986-3.

Nabuurs, G-J., R. Mrabet, A. Abu Hatab, M. Bustamante, H. Clark, P. Havlík, J. House, et al. 2022.
"Agriculture, Forestry and Other Land Uses (AFOLU)." In *Climate Change 2022: Mitigation of Climate
Change; Contribution of Working Group III to the Sixth Assessment Report of the Intergovernmental
Panel on Climate Change,* edited by P. R. Shukla, J. Skea, R. Slade, A. Al Khourdajie, R. van Diemen,
D. McCollum, M. Pathak, et al., chap. 7. Cambridge, UK: Cambridge University Press. https://doi.org
/10.1017/9781009157926.009.

Naran, Baysa, Jake Connolly, Paul Rosane, Dharshan Wignarajah, and Githungo Wakaba. 2022. *Global
Landscape of Climate Finance: A Decade of Data; 2011–2020.* Washington, DC: Climate Policy Initiative.
https://www.climatepolicyinitiative.org/wp-content/uploads/2022/10/Global-Landscape-of-Climate
-Finance-A-Decade-of-Data.pdf.

Nayak, Dali, Eli Saetnan, Kun Cheng, Wen Wang, Frank Koslowski, Yan-Fen Cheng, Wei Yun Zhu, et al.
2015. "Management Opportunities to Mitigate Greenhouse Gas Emissions from Chinese Agriculture."
Agriculture, Ecosystems & Environment 209: 108–24. https://doi.org/10.1016/j.agee.2015.04.035.

Nelson, Gerald C. 2009. *Agriculture and Climate Change: An Agenda for Negotiation in Copenhagen.*
Washington, DC: International Food Policy Research Institute. https://www.ifpri.org/publication
/agriculture-and-climate-change-agenda-negotiation-copenhagen.

Nelson, K. M., B. O. Sander, B. T. Yen, S. Yadav, and A. Laborte. 2022. *Monitoring, Reporting, and Verification
System for Rice Production Aligned with Paris Agreement Transparency Guidelines.* Los Baños,
Phillipines: International Rice Research Institute.

Nguyen, Angela, and Michael J. Platow. 2021. "'I'll Eat Meat Because That's What We Do': The Role of
National Norms and National Social Identification on Meat Eating." *Appetite* 164: 105287. https://doi
.org/10.1016/j.appet.2021.105287.

Ni, X., and P. M. Groffman. 2018. "Declines in Methane Uptake in Forest Soils." *Proceedings of the National
Academy of Sciences* 115 (34): 8587–90. https://doi.org/10.1073/pnas.1807377115.

Niesseron, C., R. Glardon, N. Zufferey, and M. A. Jafari. 2020. "Energy Efficiency Optimisation in Supply
Chain Networks: Impact of Inventory Management." *International Journal of Supply Chain and
Inventory Management* 3 (2): 93–123. https://doi.org/10.1504/IJSCIM.2020.107237.

O'Neill, Brian, Maarten van Aalst, and Zelina Zaiton Ibrahim. 2022. "Key Risks across Sectors and Regions." In *Climate Change 2022: Impacts, Adaptation and Vulnerability; Contribution of Working Group II to the Sixth Assessment Report of the Intergovernmental Panel on Climate Change,* 2411–538. Cambridge: Cambridge University Press. https://doi.org/10.1017/9781009325844.025.

OECD (Organisation for Economic Co-operation and Development). 2017. *Improving Energy Efficiency in the Agro-Food Chain: Why Does Energy Efficiency in the Agro-Food Chain Matter?* Paris: OECD Publishing. https://doi.org/10.1787/9789264278530-en.

OECD (Organisation for Economic Co-operation and Development). 2021. "A Global Analysis of the Cost-Efficiency of Forest Carbon Sequestration." Working Paper 185, OECD, Paris. https://doi.org/10.1787/e4d45973-en.

OECD (Organisation for Economic Co-operation and Development). 2022. *Climate Finance Provided and Mobilised by Developed Countries in 2016–2020: Insights from Disaggregated Analysis.* Paris: OECD Publishing. https://doi.org/10.1787/286dae5d-en

OECD (Organisation for Economic Co-operation and Development) and FAO (Food and Agriculture Organization of the United Nations). 2021. *OECD-FAO Agricultural Outlook 2021–2030.* Paris: OECD Publishing. https://doi.org/10.1787/19428846-en.

Ollinaho, Ossi I., and Markus Kröger. 2021. "Agroforestry Transitions: The Good, the Bad and the Ugly." *Journal of Rural Studies* 82: 210–21. https://doi.org/10.1016/j.jrurstud.2021.01.016.

Ontl, T. A., and L. A. Schulte. 2012. "Soil Carbon Storage." *Nature Education Knowledge* 3 (10): 35. https://www.nature.com/scitable/knowledge/library/soil-carbon-storage-84223790/?_amp=true.

Ordway, Elsa M., Denis J. Sonwa, Patrice Levang, Fideline Mboringong, Ludovic Miaro III, Rosamond L. Naylor, and Raymond N. Nkongho. 2019. "Sustainable Development of the Palm Oil Sector in the Congo Basin: The Need for a Regional Strategy Involving Smallholders and Informal Markets." CIFOR Info Brief 255, Center for International Forestry Research, Bogor, Indonesia. https://doi.org/10.17528/cifor/007279.

Ortiz-Bobea, A., T. R. Ault, C. M. Carrillo, R. G. Chambers, and D. B. Lobell. 2021. "Anthropogenic Climate Change Has Slowed Global Agricultural Productivity Growth." *Nature Climate Change* 11: 306–12. https://doi.org/10.1038/s41558-021-01000-1.

Özkan, Ş., F. Teillard, B. Lindsay, H. Montgomery, A. Rota, P. Gerber, M. Dhingra, and A. Mottet. 2022. *The Role of Animal Health in National Climate Commitments.* Rome: Food and Agriculture Organization of the United Nations. https://doi.org/10.4060/cc0431en.

Pandey, S., S. Yadav, J. Hellin, J. Balié, H. Bhandari, A. Kumar, and M. K. Mondal. 2020. "Why Technologies Often Fail to Scale: Policy and Market Failures behind Limited Scaling of Alternate Wetting and Drying in Rice in Bangladesh." *Water* 12 (5): 1510. https://doi.org/10.3390/w12051510.

Pangestu, Mari Elka, and Axel van Trotsenburg. 2022. "Trade Restrictions Are Inflaming the Worst Food Crisis in a Decade." *Voices* (blog), July 6. https://blogs.worldbank.org/voices/trade-restrictions-are-inflaming-worst-food-crisis-decade.

Park, T., K. Londakova, I. Brennan, A. Schein, J. Reynolds, E. Whincup, E. Chan, M. Pelenur, and D. Halpern. 2023. *How to Build a Net Zero Society.* London: Behavioural Insights Team. https://www.bi.team/publications/how-to-build-a-net-zero-society/.

Pearson-Stuttard, Jonathan, Piotr Bandosz, Colin D. Rehm, Jose Penalvo, Laura Whitsel, Thomas Gaziano, Zach Conrad, et al. 2017. "Reducing US Cardiovascular Disease Burden and Disparities through National and Targeted Dietary Policies: A Modelling Study." *PLoS Medicine* 14 (6): e1002311. https://doi.org/10.1371/journal.pmed.1002311.

Pendrill, Florence, U. Martin Persson, Javier Godar, and Thomas Kastner. 2019. "Deforestation Displaced: Trade in Forest-Risk Commodities and the Prospects for a Global Forest Transition." *Environmental Research Letters* 14: 055003. https://doi.org/10.1088/1748-9326/ab0d41.

Peoples, M. B., H. Hauggaard-Nielsen, O. Huguenin-Elie, E. S. Jensen, E. Justes, and M. Williams. 2019. "The Contributions of Legumes to Reducing the Environmental Risk of Agricultural Production." In *Agroecosystem Diversity,* edited by G. Lemaire, P. C. D. F. Carvalho, S. Kronberg, and S. Recous, 123–43. New York: Academic Press. https://doi.org/10.1016/B978-0-12-811050-8.00008-X.

Perignon, M., F. Vieux, L. G. Soler, G. Masset, and N. Darmon. 2017. "Improving Diet Sustainability through Evolution of Food Choices: Review of Epidemiological Studies on the Environmental Impact of Diets." *Nutrition Reviews* 75 (1): 2–17. https://doi.org/10.1093/nutrit/nuw043.

Pink, Daniel H. 2012. *To Sell Is Human: The Surprising Truth about Moving Others.* New York: Riverhead.

Pont Omgeving. 2018. "Gas-Free New Construction from July 1, 2018: What Is the Change in the Law and What Are the Implications for Current New Construction Projects?" *News*, July 18, 2018. https://www.omgevingsweb.nl/nieuws/gasvrije-nieuwbouw-vanaf-1-juli-2018-wat-is-de-wetswijziging-en-wat-zijn-de-implicaties-voor-lopende-nieuwbouwprojecten/.

Poore, J., and T. Nemecek. 2018. "Reducing Food's Environmental Impacts through Producers and Consumers." *Science* 360 (6392): 987–92. https://doi.org/10.1126/science.aaq0216.

Popkin, B. M. and P. Gordon-Larsen. 2004. "The Nutrition Transition: Worldwide Obesity Dynamics and Their Determinants." *International Journal of Obesity* 28, S2–9. https://doi.org/10.1038/sj.ijo.0802804.

Popluga, D., K. Naglis-Liepa, A. Lenerts, and P. Rivza. 2017. "Marginal Abatement Cost Curve for Assessing Mitigation Potential of Latvian Agricultural Greenhouse Gas Emissions: Case Study of Crop Sector." *International Multidisciplinary Scientific GeoConference: SGEM* 17: 511–17. https://doi.org/10.5593/sgem2017/17/S07.065.

Pretty, J., C. Toulmin, and S. Williams. 2011. "Sustainable Intensification in African Agriculture." *International Journal of Agricultural Sustainability* 9 (1): 5–24. https://www.tandfonline.com/doi/pdf/10.3763/ijas.2010.0583.

Puri, M., L. Rincon, and I. Maltsoglou. 2021. *Renewable Energy for Agrifood Chains: Investing in Solar Energy in Rwanda.* Rome: Food and Agriculture Organization of the United Nations. https://doi.org/10.4060/cb6387en.

Qambrani, N. A., M. M. Rahman, S. Won, S. Shim, and C. Ra. 2017. "Biochar Properties and Eco-friendly Applications for Climate Change Mitigation, Waste Management, and Wastewater Treatment: A Review." *Renewable and Sustainable Energy Reviews* 79: 255–73. https://doi.org/10.1016/j.rser.2017.05.132.

Rabalais, Nancy N., R. Eugene Turner, and William J. Wiseman. 2002. "Gulf of Mexico Hypoxia, a.k.a. 'The Dead Zone.'" *Annual Review of Ecology and Systematics* 33: 235–63. http://www.jstor.org/stable/3069262.

Reis, T., and Y. Prada Moro. 2022. "Connecting Exports of Brazilian Soy to Deforestation" (article). December 7, 2022. https://trase.earth/insights/connecting-exports-of-brazilian-soy-to-deforestation.

Reis, T., zu Ermgassen, E., and Pereira, O. 2023. "Brazilian beef exports and deforestation". Stockholm Environment Institute. https://www.sei.org/features/trase-brazil-beef-exports-deforestation/

Reuters. 2023. "China's COFCO, Modern Farming Group Sign 'Deforestation Free' Soybean Deal." November 8, 2023. https://www.reuters.com/sustainability/land-use-biodiversity/chinas-cofco-modern-farming-group-sign-deforestation-free-soybean-deal-2023-11-08/.

Riahi, K., R. Schaeffer, J. Arango, K. Calvin, C. Guivarch, T. Hasegawa, K. Jiang, et al. 2022. "Mitigation Pathways Compatible with Long-Term Goals." In Intergovernmental Panel on Climate Change, *Climate Change 2022: Impacts, Adaptation and Vulnerability; Contribution of Working Group II to the Sixth Assessment Report of the Intergovernmental Panel on Climate Change.* Cambridge: Cambridge University Press. https://doi.org/10.1017/9781009157926.005.

Richardson, R., M. P. Prescott, and B. Ellison. 2021. "Impact of Plate Shape and Size on Individual Food Waste in a University Dining Hall." *Resources, Conservation and Recycling* 168: 105293. https://doi.org/10.1016/j.resconrec.2020.105293.

Rincón, Carlos Andrés, Amaury De Guardia, Annabelle Couvert, Isabelle Soutrel, Stevan Guezel, and Camille Le Serrec. 2019. "Odor Generation Patterns during Different Operational Composting Stages of Anaerobically Digested Sewage Sludge." *Waste Management* 95: 661–73. https://doi.org/10.1016/j.wasman.2019.07.006.

Ritchie, Hannah, Pablo Rosado, and Max Roser. 2022. "Environmental Impacts of Food Production" (article). Accessed April 14, 2024. https://ourworldindata.org/environmental-impacts-of-food.

Rodella, Aude-Sophie, Esha Zaveri, and François Bertone. 2023. "The Hidden Wealth of Nations: The Economics of Groundwater in Times of Climate Change." Washington, DC. Accessed April 12, 2024. https://openknowledge.worldbank.org/handle/10986/39917.

Röder, Mirjam, and Andrew Welfle. 2018. "Bioenergy." In *Managing Global Warming: An Interface of Technology and Human Issues*, edited by Trevor M. Letcher, 379–98. New York: Academic Press. https://doi.org/10.1016/B978-0-12-814104-5.00012-0.

Roe, S., C. Streck, R. Beach, J. Busch, M. Chapman, V. Daioglou, A. Deppermann, et al. 2021. "Land-Based Measures to Mitigate Climate Change: Potential and Feasibility by Country." *Global Change Biology* 27 (23): 6025–58. https://doi.org/10.1111/gcb.15873.

Rondoni, A., and S. Grasso. 2021. "Consumers Behavior towards Carbon Footprint Labels on Food: A Review of the Literature and Discussion of Industry Implications." *Journal of Cleaner Production* 301: 127031. https://doi.org/10.1016/j.jclepro.2021.127031.

Rouzi, Aihematijiang. 2022. "China Announces Plan to Reduce Emissions in Agriculture." Sino-German Agricultural Center, July 12, 2022. https://www.dcz-china.org/2022/07/12/china-announces-plan-to-reduce-emissions-in-agriculture/.

Roy, Diana. 2022. "In Brief: Deforestation of Brazil's Amazon Has Reached a Record High. What's Being Done?" (article). Council on Foreign Relations. Updated August 24, 2022. https://www.cfr.org/in-brief/deforestation-brazils-amazon-has-reached-record-high-whats-being-done.

Royal Society. 2020. "Ammonia: Zero-Carbon Fertiliser, Fuel and Energy Store." Policy briefing. Royal Society, London. https://royalsociety.org/-/media/policy/projects/green-ammonia/green-ammonia-policy-briefing.pdf.

Rozema, Eric R., Andrew C. VanderZaag, Jeff D. Wood, Aleksandra Drizo, Youbin Zheng, Ali Madani, and Robert J. Gordon. 2016. "Constructed Wetlands for Agricultural Wastewater Treatment in Northeastern North America: A Review." *Water* 8 (5): 173. https://doi.org/10.3390/w8050173.

Rud, J. J. P., and I. Trapeznikova. 2021. "Job Creation and Wages in Least Developed Countries: Evidence from Sub-Saharan Africa." *Economic Journal* 131 (635): 1331–64. https://doi.org/10.1093/ej/ueaa110.

Ruel, Marie T., and Jessica Fanzo. 2022. "Nutrition and Climate Change: Shifting to Sustainable Healthy Diets." In *2022 Global Food Policy Report: Climate Change and Food Systems*, 72–81. Washington, DC: International Food Policy Research Institute. https://ebrary.ifpri.org/utils/getfile/collection/p15738coll2/id/135889/filename/136101.pdf.

Ryan, John. 2021. "Seattle Bans Natural Gas in New Buildings." KUOW News and Stories, February 2, 2021. https://www.kuow.org/stories/seattle-bans-natural-gas-in-new-buildings.

Sander, Bjoern Ole, Reiner Wassmann, Leo Kris Palao, and Andrew Nelson. 2017. "Climate-Based Suitability Assessment for Alternate Wetting and Drying Water Management in the Philippines: A Novel Approach for Mapping Methane Mitigation Potential in Rice Production." *Carbon Management* 8 (4). https://www.tandfonline.com/doi/full/10.1080/17583004.2017.1362945.

Sanderman, Jonathan, Tomislav Hengl, and Gregory J. Fiske. 2017. "Soil Carbon Debt of 12,000 Years of Human Land Use." *Proceedings of the National Academy of Sciences* 114 (36): 9575–80. https://doi.org/10.1073/pnas.1706103114.

Sapkota, Tek B., Fahmida Khanam, Gokul Prasad Mathivanan, Sylvia Vetter, Sk. Ghulam Hussain, Anne-Laure Pilat, Sumona Shahrin, Md. Khaled Hossain, Nathu Ram Sarker, and Timothy J. Krupnik. 2021. "Quantifying Opportunities for Greenhouse Gas Emissions Mitigation Using Big Data from Smallholder Crop and Livestock Farmers across Bangladesh." *Science of the Total Environment* 786: 147344. https://doi.org/10.1016/j.scitotenv.2021.147344.

Sapkota, Tek B., I. Ortiz-Monasterio, K. Sonder, L. Wollenberg, M. B. Richards, J. C. Leyva, and M. A. Garcia. 2020. "Rapid Analysis of Country-Level Mitigation Potential from Agriculture, Forestry and Other Land Uses in Mexico." CCAFS Working Paper 309, CGIAR Research Program on Climate Change, Agriculture and Food Security (CCAFS), Wageningen, The Netherlands. https://ccafs.cgiar.org/resources/publications/rapid-analysis-country-level-mitigation-potential-agriculture-forestry.

Sapkota, Tek B., S. H. Vetter, M. Jat, S. Sirohi, P. B. Shirsath, R. Singh, and C. M. Stirling. 2019. "Cost-Effective Opportunities for Climate Change Mitigation in Indian Agriculture." *Science of the Total Environment* 655: 1342–54. https://doi.org/10.1016/j.scitotenv.2018.11.225.

Sartori, M., G. Philippidis, E. Ferrari, P. Borrelli, E. Lugato, L. Montanarella, and P. Panagos. 2019. "A Linkage between the Biophysical and the Economic: Assessing the Global Market Impacts of Soil Erosion." *Land Use Policy* 86: 299–312. https://doi.org/10.1016/j.landusepol.2019.05.014.

Schimel, J. 2000. "Rice, Microbes and Methane." *Nature* 403 (6768): 375, 377. https://doi.org/10.1038/35000325.

Schindler, David, Robert Hecky, and Gregory McCullough. 2012. "The Rapid Eutrophication of Lake Winnipeg: Greening under Global Change." *Journal of Great Lakes Research* 38: 6–13. https://doi.org/10.1016/j.jglr.2012.04.003.

Schösler, Hanna, Joop Boer, and Jan Boersema. 2013. "The Organic Food Philosophy: A Qualitative Exploration of the Practices, Values, and Beliefs of Dutch Organic Consumers within a Cultural-Historical Frame." *Journal of Agricultural and Environmental Ethics* 26: 439–60. https://doi.org/10.1007/s10806-012-9392-0.

Searchinger, Tim, and Tapan K. Adhya. 2015. "Wetting and Drying: Reducing Greenhouse Gas Emissions and Saving Water from Rice Production." Working Paper, Creating a Sustainable Food Future 8. World Resources Institute, Washington, DC. https://www.wri.org/research/wetting-and-drying-reducing-greenhouse-gas-emissions-and-saving-water-rice-production.

Searchinger, T., M. Herrero, X. Yan, J. Wang, P. Dumas, K. Beauchemin, and E. Kebreab. 2021. "Opportunities to Reduce Methane Emissions from Global Agriculture." https://searchinger.princeton.edu/sites/g/files/toruqf4701/files/methane_discussion_paper_nov_2021.pdf.

Serrano Fuentes, N., A. Rogers, and M. C. Portillo. 2019. "Social Network Influences and the Adoption of Obesity-Related Behaviors in Adults: A Critical Interpretative Synthesis Review." *BMC Public Health* 19: 1178. https://doi.org/10.1186/s12889-019-7467-9.

Setboonarng, S., and A. Markandya, eds. 2015. *Organic Agriculture and Post-2015 Development Goals: Building on the Comparative Advantage of Poor Farmers.* Tokyo: Asian Development Bank Institute. http://hdl.handle.net/11540/4411.

Sethi, C. K., S. K. Acharya, P. P. Patnaik, and A. Behera. 2021. "A Review on Solar Drying of Marine Applications." In *Current Advances in Mechanical Engineering: Lecture Notes in Mechanical Engineering,* edited by S. K. Acharya and D. P. Mishra, 271–81. Singapore: Springer. https://doi.org/10.1007/978-981-33-4795-3_26.

Seto, K. C., S. J. Davis, R. B. Mitchell, E.C. Stokes, G. Unruh, and D. Ürge-Vorsatz. 2016. "Carbon Lock-In: Types, Causes, and Policy Implications." *Annual Review of Environment and Resources* 41 (1): 425–52. https://www.annualreviews.org/doi/10.1146/annurev-environ-110615-085934.

Setyanto, Prihasto, Ali Pramono, Terry Ayu Adriany, Helena Lina Susilawati, Takeshi Tokida, Agnes T. Padre, and Kazunori Minamikawa. 2018. "Alternate Wetting and Drying Reduces Methane Emission from a Rice Paddy in Central Java, Indonesia without Yield Loss." *Soil Science and Plant Nutrition* 64 (1): 23–30. https://doi.org/10.1080/00380768.2017.1409600.

Shangguan, Siyi, Ashkan Afshin, Masha Shulkin, Wenjie Ma, Daniel Marsden, Jessica Smith, Michael Saheb-Kashaf, et al. 2019. "A Meta-analysis of Food Labeling Effects on Consumer Diet Behaviors and Industry Practices." *American Journal of Preventive Medicine* 56 (2): 300–14. http://www.ajpmonline.org/article/S0749379718323572/fulltext.

Simeone, Mariarosaria, and Debora Scarpato. 2020. "Sustainable Consumption: How Does Social Media Affect Food Choices?" *Journal of Cleaner Production* 277: 124036. https://doi.org/10.1016/j.jclepro.2020.124036.

Singh, A., A. K. Singh, S. Rawat, N. Pal, V. D. Rajput, T. Minkina, R. Sharma, N. P. Singh, and J. N. Tripathi. 2022. "Satellite-Based Quantification of Methane Emissions from Wetlands and Rice Paddies Ecosystems in North and Northeast India." *Hydrobiology* 1 (3): 317–30. https://doi.org/10.3390/hydrobiology1030023.

Slapø, H. B., and K. I. Karevold. 2019. "Simple Eco-labels to Nudge Customers toward the Most Environmentally Friendly Warm Dishes: An Empirical Study in a Cafeteria Setting." *Frontiers in Sustainable Food Systems* 3: 40. https://doi.org/10.3389/fsufs.2019.00040.

Smith, E. Keith, and Adam Mayer. 2018. "A Social Trap for the Climate? Collective Action, Trust, and Climate Change Risk Perception in 35 Countries." *Global Environmental Change* 49: 140–53. https://doi.org/10.1016/j.gloenvcha.2018.02.014.

Smith, Lawrence G., Guy J. D. Kirk, Philip J. Jones, and Adrian G. Williams. 2019. "The Greenhouse Gas Impacts of Converting Food Production in England and Wales to Organic Methods." *Nature Communications* 10: 4641. https://doi.org/10.1038/s41467-019-12622-7.

Song, G., H. M. Semakula, and P. Fullana-i-Palmer. 2019. "Shift from Feeding to Sustainably Nourishing Urban China: A Crossing-Disciplinary Methodology for Global Environment-Food-Health Nexus." *Science of the Total Environment* 647: 716–24. https://pubmed.ncbi.nlm.nih.gov/30092528/.

South Africa Department of Environmental Affairs. 2014. *South Africa's Greenhouse Gas (GHG) Mitigation Potential Analysis.* Pretoria: Department of Environmental Affairs. https://www.dffe.gov.za/sites/default /files/docs/mitigationreport.pdf.

Sova, C. A., G. Grosjean, T. Baedeker, T. N. Nguyen, M. Wallner, A. Jarvis, A. Nowak, C. Corner-Dolloff, E. Girvetz, P. Laderach, and M. Lizarazo. 2018. *Bringing the Concept of Climate-Smart Agriculture to Life: Insights from CSA Country Profiles across Africa, Asia, and Latin America.* Washington, DC: World Bank and International Centre for Tropical Agriculture.

Spears, Dean. 2011. "Economic Decision-Making in Poverty Depletes Behavioral Control." *BE Journal of Economic Analysis and Policy* 11 (1). https://doi.org/10.2202/1935-1682.2973.

Sperow, M. 2020. "What Might It Cost to Increase Soil Organic Carbon Using No-Till on U.S. Cropland?" *Carbon Balance and Management* 15: 26. https://doi.org/10.1186/s13021-020-00162-3.

Springmann, Marco, Michael Clark, Daniel Mason-D'Croz, Keith Weibe, Benjamin Leon Bodirsky, Luis Lassaletta, Wim de Vries, et al. 2018. "Options for Keeping the Food System within Environmental Limits." *Nature* 562: 519–25. https://doi.org/10.1038/s41586-018-0594-0.

Springmann, Marco, and F. Freund. 2022. "Options for Reforming Agricultural Subsidies from Health, Climate, and Economic Perspectives." *Nature Communications* 13: 82. https://doi.org/10.1038/s41467 -021-27645-2.

Springmann, Marco, H. Charles J. Godfray, Mike Rayner, and Peter Scarborough. 2016. "Analysis and Valuation of the Health and Climate Change Cobenefits of Dietary Change." *Proceedings of the National Academy of Sciences* 113 (15): 4146–51. https://doi.org/10.1073/pnas.1523119113.

Springmann, Marco, Daniel Mason-D'Croz, Sherman Robinson, Keith Wiebe, H. Charles J. Godfray, Mike Rayner, and Peter Scarborough. 2017. "Mitigation Potential and Global Health Impacts from Emissions Pricing of Food Commodities." *Nature Climate Change* 7 (1): 69–74. https://doi.org/10.1038 /nclimate3155. https://www.nature.com/articles/nclimate3155.

Sriphirom, Patikorn, Amnat Chidthaisong, Kazuyuki Yagi, Sudarut Tripetchkul, and Sirintornthep Towprayoon. 2020. "Evaluation of Biochar Applications Combined with Alternate Wetting and Drying (AWD) Water Management in Rice Field as a Methane Mitigation Option for Farmers' Adoption." *Soil Science and Plant Nutrition* 66 (1): 235–46. https://doi.org/10.1080/00380768.2019.1706431.

Stack, Liam. 2023. "New York to Ban Natural Gas, Including Stoves, in New Buildings." *New York Times,* April 28, 2023. https://www.nytimes.com/2023/04/28/nyregion/gas-stove-ban-ny.html.

Steensland, Aaron. 2022. *2022 Global Agricultural Productivity Report: Troublesome Trends and System Shocks,* edited by T. Thompson and J. Agnew. Blacksburg, VA: Virginia Tech College of Agriculture and Life Sciences. https://globalagriculturalproductivity.org/wp-content/uploads/2022/11/2022-GAP _Report_final_110922.pdf.

Steffen, Will, Katherine Richardson, Johan Rockström, Sarah E. Cornell, Ingo Fetzer, Elena M. Bennett, Reinette Biggs, et al. 2015. "Planetary Boundaries: Guiding Human Development on a Changing Planet." *Science* 347 (6223): 1259855. https://doi.org/10.1126/science.1259855.

Steg, Linda, and Charles Vlek. 2009. "Encouraging Pro-environmental Behavior: An Integrative Review and Research Agenda." *Journal of Environmental Psychology* 29 (3): 309–17. https://doi.org/10.1016/j .jenvp.2008.10.004.

Steinfeld, H., H. A. Mooney, F. Schneider, and L. E. Neville, eds. 2010. *Livestock in a Changing Landscape: Drivers, Consequences, and Responses.* Vol. 1. Centerport, NY: Island Press. https://hdl.handle.net /10568/16403.

Stewart, Naomi, ed. 2015. *The Value of Land: Prosperous Lands and Positive Rewards through Sustainable Land Management.* Bonn: ELD (Economics of Land Degradation) Initiative. www.eld-initiative.org.

Stewart, W. M., D. W. Dibb, A. E. Johnston, and T. J. Smyth. 2005. "The Contribution of Commercial Fertilizer Nutrients to Food Production." *Agronomy Journal* 97 (1): 1–6. https://doi.org/10.2134/agronj2005.0001.

Suman, S. 2018. "Evaluation and Impact Assessment of the Solar Irrigation Pumps Program in Andhra Pradesh and Chhattisgarh." Shri Shakti Alternative Energy Limited (SSAEL). https://www.ssael.co.in/images/Library/files/Solar-Pumps-Impact--SSAEL-Report.pdf.

SunCulture. 2023. "Life-Changing Technology for Everyday Challenges" (web page). Accessed April 14, 2023. https://sunculture.io/.

Sykes, Aladair J., Michael Macleod, Vera Eory, Robert M. Rees, Florian Payen, Vasilis Myrgiotis, Mathew Williams, et al. 2019. "Characterising the Biophysical, Economic, and Social Impacts of Soil Carbon Sequestration as a Greenhouse Gas Removal Technology." *Global Change Biology* 26 (3): 1085. https://doi.org/10.1111/gcb.14844.

Tate, Kevin R. 2015. "Soil Methane Oxidation and Land-Use Change—From Process to Mitigation." *Soil Biology and Biochemistry* 80: 260–72. https://doi.org/10.1016/j.soilbio.2014.10.010.

Taylor, Matthew. 2019. "Low-Carbon Heating to Replace Gas in New UK Homes after 2023." *Guardian*, March 13, 2019. https://www.theguardian.com/environment/2019/mar/13/hammond-says-gas-heating-will-be-replaced-by-low-carbon-systems.

Teng, Andrea M., Amanda C. Jones, Anja Mizdrak, Louise Signal, Murat Genç, and Nick Wilson. 2019. "Impact of Sugar-Sweetened Beverage Taxes on Purchases and Dietary Intake: Systematic Review and Meta-Analysis." *Obesity Reviews* 20 (9): 1187–204. https://doi.org/10.1111/obr.12868.

Terrer, C., R. P. Phillips, and B. A. Hungate. 2021. "A Trade-Off between Plant and Soil Carbon Storage under Elevated CO_2." *Nature* 591: 599–603. https://doi.org/10.1038/s41586-021-03306-8.

Thi, Ngoc Bao Dung, Gopalakrishnan Kumar, and Chiu-Yue Lin. 2015. "An Overview of Food Waste Management in Developing Countries: Current Status and Future Perspective." *Journal of Environmental Management* 157: 220–29. https://doi.org/10.1016/j.jenvman.2015.04.022.

Thornton, Philip, Yuling Chang, Ana Maria Loboguerrero, and Bruce Campbell. 2023. "Perspective: What Might It Cost to Reconfigure Food Systems?" *Global Food Security* 36:100669. https://doi.org/10.1016/j.gfs.2022.100669.

Thornton, P. K., and M. Herrero. 2010. "Potential for Reduced Methane and Carbon Dioxide Emissions from Livestock and Pasture Management in the Tropics." *Proceedings of the National Academy of Sciences of the United States of America* 107 (46): 19667–72. https://doi.org/10.1073/pnas.0912890107.

Thow, Anne Marie, Shauna M. Downs, Christopher Mayes, Helen Trevena, Temo Waqanivalu, and Jon Cawley. 2018. "Fiscal Policy to Improve Diets and Prevent Noncommunicable Diseases: From Recommendations to Action." *Bulletin of the World Health Organization* 96 (3): 201–10. https://doi.org/10.2471/BLT.17.195982.

Tilman, D., C. Balzer, J. Hill, and B. L. Befort. 2011. "Global Food Demand and the Sustainable Intensification of Agriculture." *Proceedings of the National Academy of Sciences* 108 (50): 20260–64. https://doi.org/10.1073/pnas.111643710.

Tobi, Rebecca C. A., Francesca Harris, Ritu Rana, Kerry A. Brown, Matthew Quaife, and Rosemary Green. 2019. "Sustainable Diet Dimensions: Comparing Consumer Preference for Nutrition, Environmental and Social Responsibility Food Labelling: A Systematic Review." *Sustainability* 11 (23): 6575. https://www.mdpi.com/2071-1050/11/23/6575/htm.

Tong, Dan, Qiang Zhang, Yixuan Zheng, Ken Caldeira, Christine Shearer, Chaopeng Hong, Yue Qin, and Steven J. Davis. 2019. "Letter: Committed Emissions from Existing Energy Infrastructure Jeopardize 1.5 °C Climate Target." *Nature* 572: 3737–7. https://www.nature.com/articles/s41586-019-1364-3.

Trang, Vu H., Katherine M. Nelson, Sabrina Rose, Arun Khatri-Chhetri, Eva K. Wollenberg, and Bjoern Ole Sander. "Rice cultivation ambition in the new and updated Nationally Determined Contributions: 2020-2021: Analysis of agricultural sub-sectors in countries' climate change strategies." Updated October 2022. CCAFS Info Note. Wageningen, The Netherlands: CGIAR Research Program on Climate Change, Agriculture and Food Security (CCAFS).

Trommsdorff, M., J. Kang, C. Reise, S. Schindele, G. Bopp, A. Ehmann, A. Weselek, P. Högy, and T. Obergfell. 2021. "Combining Food and Energy Production: Design of an Agrivoltaic System Applied in Arable and Vegetable Farming in Germany." *Renewable and Sustainable Energy Reviews* 140: 110694. https://www.sciencedirect.com/science/article/pii/S1364032120309783.

Tubiello, F., K. Karl, A. Flammini, J. Gutschow, G. Obli-Laryea, G. Conchedda, X. Pan, et al. 2022. "Pre- and Post-production Processes Increasingly Dominate Greenhouse Gas Emissions from Agri-food Systems." *Earth System Science Data* 14 (4): 1795–809. https://doi.org/10.5194/essd-14-1795-2022.

Tzilivakis, J., A. Green, D. Warner, K. McGeevor, and K. Lewis. 2012. "A Framework for Practical and Effective Eco-labelling of Food Products." *Sustainability Accounting, Management and Policy Journal* 3 (1): 50–73. https://doi.org/10.1108/20408021211223552.

UNCCD (United Nations Convention to Combat Desertification). 2022. *The Global Land Outlook.* 2nd ed. Bonn: UNCCD. https://www.unccd.int/sites/default/files/2022-04/UNCCD_GLO2_low-res_2.pdf.

UNCTAD (United Nations Conference on Trade and Development) and UNEP (United Nations Environment Programme). 2008. *Best Practices for Organic Policy: What Developing Country Governments Can Do to Promote the Organic Agriculture Sector.* Nairobi, Kenya: UNEP. https://wedocs.unep.org/bitstream/handle/20.500.11822/9557/UNCTAD_DITC_TED_2007_3.pdf?sequence=3&isAllowed=.

UNECE (United Nations Economic Commission for Europe). 2015. "Energy Efficiency: Getting More for Less." UNECE, Geneva. https://unece.org/fileadmin/DAM/energy/se/pdfs/Booklet_Dec2015/Booklet_Energy.Efficiency_Dec.2015.pdf.

UNEP (United Nations Environment Programme). 2021. *Food Waste Index Report 2021.* Nairobi: UNEP. https://www.unep.org/resources/report/unep-food-waste-index-report-2021.

UNEP (United Nations Environment Programme) and Climate and Clean Air Coalition. 2021. *Global Methane Assessment: Benefits and Costs of Mitigating Methane Emissions.* Nairobi: UNEP. https://wedocs.unep.org/bitstream/handle/20.500.11822/35917/GMA_ES.pdf.

UNESCO (United Nations Eduational, Scientific and Cultural Organization). 2020. *United Nations World Water Development Report 2020: Water and Climate Change.* Paris: UNESCO. https://unesdoc.unesco.org/ark:/48223/pf0000372985.

Ungerfeld, E. M. 2022. "Opportunities and Hurdles to the Adoption and Enhanced Efficacy of Feed Additives towards Pronounced Mitigation of Enteric Methane Emissions from Ruminant Livestock." *Methane* 1 (4): 262–85. https://doi.org/10.3390/methane1040021.

UN-Habitat (United Nations Human Settlements Programme) and WHO (World Health Organization). 2021. Progress on Wastewater Treatment—Global Status and Acceleration Needs for SDG Indicator 6.3.1. Geneva: UN-Habitat and WHO. https://unhabitat.org/sites/default/files/2021/08/sdg6_indicator_report_631_progress_on_wastewater_treatment_2021_english_pages.pdf.

United Nations. 2021. "Climate and Weather-Related Disasters Surge Five-Fold over 50 Years, but Early Warnings Save Lives: WMO Report." UN News, September 1, 2021. https://news.un.org/en/story/2021/09/1098662.

United Nations. 2022a. "Ghana Authorizes Transfer of Mitigation Outcomes to Switzerland." Press Release, November 14. https://ghana.un.org/en/207341-ghana-authorizes-transfer-mitigation-outcomes-switzerland.

United Nations. 2022b. "Horn of Africa: Extreme Drought Deepens Hunger in a Region Facing Conflict." *Africa Renewal,* November 20, 2022. https://www.un.org/africarenewal/magazine/november-2022/horn-africa-extreme-drought-deepens-hunger-region-facing-conflict.

United Nations Office for Disaster Risk Reduction. 2022. *Global Assessment Report on Disaster Risk Reduction 2022: Our World at Risk: Transforming Governance for a Resilient Future.* Geneva. Accessed April 12, 2024. https://www.undrr.org/media/79595/download?startDownload=true.

UNOCHA (United Nations Office for the Coordination of Humanitarian Affairs). 2022. "Horn of Africa Drought: Regional Humanitarian Overview and Call to Action." New York: UNOCHA. https://reliefweb.int/report/ethiopia/horn-africa-drought-regional-humanitarian-overview-call-action-revised-21-september-2022.

US EPA (United States Environmental Protection Agency). 2013. *Global Mitigation of Non-CO$_2$ Greenhouse Gases, 2010–2030*. EPA-430-R-13-011. Washington, DC: Office of Atmospheric Programs, United States Environmental Protection Agency. https://www.epa.gov/global-mitigation-non-co2-greenhouse-gases /global-mitigation-non-co2-ghgs-report-2010-2030.

US EPA (United States Environmental Protection Agency). 2023. "Indoor Air Quality (IAQ): Household Energy and Clean Air." Updated April 13, 2023. https://www.epa.gov/indoor-air-quality-iaq/household -energy-and-clean-air#:~:text=This%20represents%20about%202%25%20percent,6%20tons%20of%20 CO2%20annually.

Uwizeye, A., P. J. Gerber, C. I. Opio, G. Tempio, A. S. Mottet, H. P. S. Makkar, A. Falcucci, H. Steinfeld, and I. J. M. de Boer. 2019. "Nitrogen Flows in Global Pork Supply Chains and Potential Improvement from Feeding Swill to Pigs." *Resources, Conservation and Recycling* 146: 168–79. https://doi.org/10.1016/j .resconrec.2019.03.032.

Valin, H., P. Havlík, A. Mosnier, M. Herrero, E. Schmid, and M. Obersteiner. 2013. "Agricultural Productivity and Greenhouse Gas Emissions: Trade-Offs or Synergies between Mitigation and Food Security?" *Environmental Research Letters* 8 (3): 035019. https://doi.org/10.1088/1748-9326/8/3/035019.

Vallone, Simona, and Eric F. Lambin. 2023. "Public Policies and Vested Interests Preserve the Animal Farming Status Quo at the Expense of Animal Product Analogs." *One Earth* 6 (9), P1213–26. https://doi .org/10.1016/j.oneear.2023.07.013.

van Bodegom, Jan, Julia van Middelaar, and Nicole Metz. 2019. *"Circular Agriculture in Low- and Middle-Income Countries."* Discussion Paper, Food and Business Knowledge Platform, The Hague, the Netherlands. https://knowledge4food.net/wp-content/uploads/2020/03/191016_fbkp-circular -agriculture-lmics_discussionpaper.pdf.

Van Loo, Ellen J., Vincenzina Caputo, Rodolfo M. Nayga, and Wim Verbeke. 2014. "Consumers' Valuation of Sustainability Labels on Meat." *Food Policy* 49 (P1): 137–50. Accessed February 17, 2023. https://www .sciencedirect.com/science/article/abs/pii/S0306919214001092.

Verdone, M., and A. Seidl. 2017. "Time, Space, Place, and the Bonn Challenge Global Forest Restoration Target." *Restoration Ecology* 25 (6): 903–11. https://doi.org/10.1111/rec.12512.

Vermeir, Iris, and Wim Verbeke. 2006. "Sustainable Food Consumption: Exploring the Consumer 'Attitude-Behavioral Intention' Gap." *Journal of Agricultural and Environmental Ethics* 19: 169–94. https://doi .org/10.1007/s10806-005-5485-3.

Vermeir, Iris, Bert Weijters, Jan De Houwer, Maggie, Geuens, Hendrik Slabbinck, Adriaan Spruyt, Anneleen Van Kerckhove, Wendy Van Lippevelde, Hans De Steur, and Wim Verbeke. 2020. "Environmentally Sustainable Food Consumption: A Review and Research Agenda from a Goal-Directed Perspective." *Frontiers in Psychology* 11: 1603. https://www.frontiersin.org/articles/10.3389/fpsyg.2020.01603/full.

Verner, Dorte, Nanna Roos, Afton Halloran, Glenn Surabian, Edinaldo Tebaldi, Maximillian Ashwill, Saleema Vellani, and Yasuo Konishi. 2021. *Insect and Hydroponic Farming in Africa: The New Circular Food Economy*. Agriculture and Food Series. Washington, DC: World Bank. http://hdl.handle .net/10986/36401.

Vishnubhotla, Valli. 2024. "UK Gas Boiler Ban—In Effect from 2025 or 2035? Are Gas Boilers Being Phased Out?" *GreenMatch* (blog), March 25, 2024. https://www.greenmatch.co.uk/blog/gas-boiler-ban.

von Grebmer, Klaus, Jill Bernstein, Miriam Wiemers, Laura Reiner, Marilena Bachmeier, Asja Hanano, Olive Towey, Réiseal Ní Chéilleachair, Connell Foley, Seth Gitter, Grace Larocque, and Heidi Fritschel. 2022 Global Hunger Index: Food Systems Transformation and Local Governance. Bonn: Welthungerhilfe; and Dublin: Concern Worldwide, October 2022. https://www.globalhungerindex.org/pdf/en/2022.pdf.

Vourdoubas, Ioannis, and Olivier Dubois. 2016. "Energy and Agri-food Systems: Production and Consumption." In *Mediterra 2016: Zero Waste in the Mediterranean*, chap. 7. Paris: Presses de Sciences Po. http://www.ciheam.org/uploads/attachments/333/Mediterra2016_EN_BAT__1_.pdf.

Vranken, Liesbet, Tessa Avermaete, Dimitrios Petalios, and Erik Mathijs. 2014. "Curbing Global Meat Consumption: Emerging Evidence of a Second Nutrition Transition." *Environmental Science and Policy* 39: 95–106. https://doi.org/10.1016/j.envsci.2014.02.009.

Waldron, A., V. Adams, J. Allan, A. Arnell, J. P. Abrantes, G. Asner, S. Atkinson, et al. 2020. "Protecting 30 Percent of the Planet: Costs, Benefits and Economic Implications." Working paper. https://doi .org/10.13140/RG.2.2.19950.64327.

Wang, Cong, Jieyun Liu, Jianlin Shen, Dan Chen, Yong Li, Bingshen Jiang, and Jinshui Wu. 2018. "Effects of Biochar Amendment on Net Greenhouse Gas Emissions and Soil Fertility in a Double Rice Cropping System: A 4-Year Field Experiment." *Agriculture, Ecosystems & Environment* 262: 83–96. https://doi .org/10.1016/j.agee.2018.04.017.

Water Reuse Europe. 2018. *Review 2018*. Water Reuse Europe. https://www.water-reuse-europe.org/wp -content/uploads/2018/08/wre_review2018_final.pdf.

Wellesley, Laura, Catherine Happer, and Antony Froggatt. 2015. *Changing Climate, Changing Diets: Pathways to Lower Meat Consumption*. Chatham House Report. London: Chatham House. https://www .chathamhouse.org/2015/11/changing-climate-changing-diets-pathways-lower-meat-consumption.

Whitehair, Kelly J., Carol W. Shanklin, and Laura A. Brannon. 2013. "Written Messages Improve Edible Food Waste Behaviors in a University Dining Facility." *Journal of the Academy of Nutrition and Dietetics* 113 (1): 63–69. https://doi.org/10.1016/j.jand.2012.09.015.

WHO (World Health Organization). 2016. *Fiscal Policies for Diet and Prevention of Noncommunicable Diseases*. Technical Meeting Report, May 5–6, 2015, Geneva, Switzerland. Geneva: WHO. https://www .who.int/docs/default-source/obesity/fiscal-policies-for-diet-and-the-prevention-of-noncommunicable -diseases-0.pdf?sfvrsn=84ee20c_2.

WHO (World Health Organization). 2022a. "Household Air Pollution" (fact sheet). Updated December 15, 2023. https://www.who.int/news-room/fact-sheets/detail/household-air-pollution-and-health.

WHO (World Health Organization). 2022b. "Proportion of Population with Primary Reliance on Fuels/ Technologies for Cooking, by Fuel Type" (data). Accessed April 14, 2024. https://www.who.int/data/gho /data/indicators/indicator-details/GHO/gho-phe-primary-reliance-on-clean-fuels-and-technologies -proportion.

Wiatros-Motyka, Malgorzata. 2023. *Global Electricity Review 2023*. London: Ember. https://ember-climate .org/insights/research/global-electricity-review-2023/.

Wieben, E. 2019. *Priorities Related to Food Value Chains and the Agri-food Sector in the Nationally Determined Contributions (NDCs)*. Rome: Food and Agriculture Organization of the United Nations. https://www.fao.org/3/ca5740en/ca5740en.pdf.

Willer, Helga, Jan Trávníček, Claudia Meier, and Bernhard Schlatter, eds. 2021. *The World of Organic Agriculture: Statistics and Emerging Trends 2021*. Bonn: Research Institute of Organic Agriculture FiBL, Frick, and IFOAM—Organics International. https://www.organic-world.net/yearbook/yearbook-2021 .html.

Willett, Walter, Johan Rockström, Brent Loken, Marco Springmann, Tim Lang, Sonja Vermeulen, Tara Garnett, et al. 2019. "Food in the Anthropocene: The EAT–Lancet Commission on Healthy Diets from Sustainable Food Systems. *Lancet* 393 (10170): 447–92. https://doi.org/10.1016/S0140-6736(18)31788-4.

Williams, Portia Adade, Olivier Crespo, Mumuni Abu, and Nicholas Philip Simpson. 2018. "A Systematic Review of How Vulnerability of Smallholder Agricultural Systems to Changing Climate Is Assessed in Africa." *Environmental Research Letters* 13: 103004. https://iopscience.iop.org/article/10.1088/1748-9326 /aae026.

Winnick, M. J. 2021. "Stream Transport and Substrate Controls on Nitrous Oxide Yields from Hyporheic Zone Denitrification." *AGU Advances* 2: e2021AV000517. https://doi.org/10.1029/2021AV000517.

Wolff, F., N. Schönherr, and D. A. Heyen. 2017. "Effects and Success Factors of Sustainable Consumption Policy Instruments: A Comparative Assessment across Europe." *Journal of Environmental Policy and Planning* 19 (4): 457–72. https://doi.org/10.1080/1523908X.2016.1254035.

Wolosin, Michael. 2017. *Large-Scale Forestation for Climate Mitigation: Lessons from South Korea, China, and India*. San Francisco, CA: Climate and Land Use Alliance. https://www.climateandlandusealliance.org /wp-content/uploads/2017/10/arr-korea-china-india-main-paper.pdf.

World Bank. 2017. "Shadow Price of Carbon in Economic Analysis: Guidance Note." World Bank, Washington, DC. https://thedocs.worldbank.org/en/doc/911381516303509498-0020022018/original /2017ShadowPriceofCarbonGuidanceNoteFINALCLEARED.pdf.

World Bank. 2018. *Water Scarce Cities: Thriving in a Finite World*. World Bank: Washington, DC. http://hdl .handle.net/10986/29623.

World Bank. 2019a. "Bangladesh: Climate Smart Agriculture Investment Plan." World Bank, Washington, DC. https://openknowledge.worldbank.org/entities/publication/44341bb4-8d86-5ee5-ac68-f367e18ea060.

World Bank. 2019b. "Mali: Climate-Smart Agriculture Investment Plan." World Bank, Washington, DC. https://openknowledge.worldbank.org/entities/publication/d0abce47-05fa-5a93-a88e-b3683e7bcb78.

World Bank. 2019c. "Trees and Cows Offer Path to Recovery in Colombia" (feature story, July 8). https://www .worldbank.org/en/news/feature/2019/07/08/trees-and-cows-offer-path-to-recovery-in-colombia.

World Bank. 2019d. "Zambia: Climate-Smart Agriculture Investment Plan." World Bank, Washington, DC. https://openknowledge.worldbank.org/entities/publication/802ad03c-4b45-5c4a-bb14-a8bb0954864f.

World Bank. 2020a. *Addressing Food Loss and Waste: A Global Problem with Local Solutions*. Washington, DC: World Bank. http://hdl.handle.net/10986/34521.

World Bank. 2020b. *Taxes on Sugar-Sweetened Beverages: International Evidence and Experiences*. Washington, DC: World Bank. https://openknowledge.worldbank.org/handle/10986/33969.

World Bank. 2021a. "Climate-Smart Agriculture" (web page). Accessed April 14, 2024. https://www .worldbank.org/en/topic/climate-smart-agriculture.

World Bank. 2021b. *Soil Organic Carbon MRV Sourcebook for Agricultural Landscapes*. Washington, DC: World Bank. http://hdl.handle.net/10986/35923.

World Bank. 2022a. *State and Trends of Carbon Pricing 2022*. Washington, DC: World Bank. http://hdl .handle.net/10986/37455.

World Bank. 2022b. "World Bank Supports Pakistan to Increase Agricultural Resilience and Protect Small Farmers from Climate Change Impacts in Punjab." Press release, July 15. https://www.worldbank.org/en /news/press-release/2022/07/15/world-bank-supports-pakistan-to-increase-agricultural-resilience-and -protect-small-farmers-from-climate-change-impacts-i.

World Bank. 2023a. "Access to Clean Cooking Fuels and Technologies for Cooking (% of Population)" (web page). Accessed April 14, 2024. https://databank.worldbank.org/source/world-development-indicatorsc.

World Bank. 2023b. "Agriculture, Forestry, and Fishing, Value Added (% of GDP)" (data set). Accessed April 14, 2024. https://data.worldbank.org/indicator/NV.AGR.TOTL.ZS?locations=S4.

World Bank. 2023c. *The Development, Climate, and Nature Crisis: Solutions to End Poverty on a Livable Planet; Insights from World Bank Country Climate and Development Reports Covering 42 Economies*. Washington, DC: World Bank. http://hdl.handle.net/10986/40652.

World Bank. 2023d. "Indicators" (web page). Accessed April 14, 2024. https://data.worldbank.org/indicator.

World Bank. 2023e. "Livestock and Dairy Development Project" (article). Updated November 7, 2023. https://datahelpdesk.worldbank.org/knowledgebase/articles/378834-how-does-the-world-bank-classify -countries.

World Bank. 2023f. "World Bank Paris Alignment Method for Investment Project Financing." World Bank, Washington, DC. https://documents.worldbank.org/en/publication/documents-reports /documentdetail/099710403162331265/idu0782c88ff0c719041ed08b850a84f82eccaa4.

World Bank. n.d. "Data: World Bank Country and Lending Groups" (web page). Accessed April 14, 2024. https://datahelpdesk.worldbank.org/knowledgebase/articles/906519-world-bank-country-and-lending -groups.

World Bank Group. 2022. "Commodity Markets Outlook: The Impact of the War in Ukraine on Commodity Markets." April 2022. World Bank, Washington, DC. Accessed April 12, 2024. https://openknowledge .worldbank.org/server/api/core/bitstreams/da0196b9-6f9c-5d28-b77c-31a936d5098f/content.

WWAP (United Nations World Water Assessment Programme). 2017. *The United Nations World Water Development Report 2017—Wastewater: The Untapped Resource*. Paris: UNESCO. https://www.unesco.org/en/wwap/wwdr/2017.

Xu, X., P. Sharma, S. Shu, T.-S. Lin, P. Ciais, F. N. Tubiello, P. Smith, N. Campbell, and A. K. Jain. 2021. "Global Greenhouse Gas Emissions from Animal-Based Foods Are Twice Those of Plant-Based Foods." *Nature Food* 2: 724–32. https://doi.org/10.1038/s43016-021-00358-x.

Yahya, M., H. Fahmi, and R. Hasibuan. 2022. "Experimental Performance Analysis of a Pilot-Scale Biomass-Assisted Recirculating Mixed-Flow Dryer for Drying Paddy." *International Journal of Food Science* 2022: 4373292. https://doi.org/10.1155/2022/4373292.

Yontar, Emel. 2023. "Critical Success Factor Analysis of Blockchain Technology in Agri-food Supply Chain Management: A Circular Economy Perspective." *Journal of Environmental Management* 330: 117173. https://doi.org/10.1016/j.jenvman.2022.117173.

Yusuf, A. A., E. L. Roos, and J. M. Horridge. 2018. "Indonesia's Moratorium on Palm Oil Expansion from Natural Forests: Economy-Wide Impacts and the Role of International Transfers." *Asian Development Review* 35 (2): 85–112. https://doi.org/10.1162/adev_a_00115.

Zannakis, M., A. Wallin, and L.-O. Johansson. 2015. "Political Trust and Perceptions of the Quality of Institutional Arrangements—How Do They Influence the Public's Acceptance of Environmental Rules." *Environmental Policy and Governance* 25 (6): 424–38. https://doi.org/10.1002/eet.1676.

Zheng, Wei, Mingxin Guo, Teresa Chow, Douglas N. Bennett, and Nandakishore Rajagopalan. 2010. "Sorption Properties of Greenwaste Biochar for Two Triazine Pesticides." *Journal of Hazardous Materials* 181 (1–3): 121–26. https://doi.org/10.1016/j.jhazmat.2010.04.103.

Zomer, Robert J., D. A. Bossio, A. Trabucco, M. Noordwijk, and J. Xu. 2022. "Global Carbon Sequestration Potential of Agroforestry and Increased Tree Cover on Agricultural Land." *Circular Agricultural Systems* 2: 3. https://doi.org/10.48130/CAS-2022-0003.

Zomer, Robert J., Henry Neufeldt, Jianchu Xu, Antje Ahrends, Deborah Bossio, Antonio Trabucco, Meine van Noordwijk, and Mingcheng Wang 2016. "Global Tree Cover and Biomass Carbon on Agricultural Land: The Contribution of Agroforestry to Global and National Carbon Budgets." *Scientific Reports* 6 (1): 29987. https://doi.org/10.1038/srep29987.

zu Ermgassen, Erasmus K. H. J., Mairon G. Bastos Lima, Helen Bellfield, Adeline Dontenville, Toby Gardner, Javier Godar, Robert Heilmayr, et al. 2022. "Addressing Indirect Sourcing in Zero Deforestation Commodity Supply Chains." *Science Advances* 8 (17). https://doi.org/10.1126/sciadv.abn3132.

CHAPTER FOUR

The World Must Strengthen the Enabling Environment for the Agrifood System Transformation to Net Zero Emissions through Global and Country-Level Actions

The purpose of this chapter is to examine the need for building the world's enabling environment to transition the agrifood system to net zero emissions. The chapter is organized around the six "I"s of the enabling environment—namely, Investments, Incentives, Information, Innovation, Institutions, and Inclusion. The chapter looks at (1) Investments—and how stakeholders can fill the immense financing gap to achieve the Paris Agreement's goal of limiting this century's global temperature rise to 1.5°C. It finds there are many opportunities for scaling up climate finance, especially by targeting finance to those who can promote change, mitigating investment risks, creating accountability, and nurturing carbon markets. The chapter then looks at (2) Incentives—or the current state of agrifood system mitigation policy. It finds there are emerging policy areas that can accelerate the transformation of the agrifood system and opportunities to repurpose harmful subsidies toward climate-smart agriculture (CSA). The chapter continues with (3) Information—particularly the state of emissions monitoring systems or measurement, reporting, and verification (MRV) systems. It finds that these systems are still inadequate for tracking emissions reductions, but there are promising advances in these methods that could unlock the full potential of carbon markets. Next is (4) Innovation—the nascent agrifood mitigation technologies and opportunities to enhance research and development (R&D). It finds that many of these technologies are both effective and affordable and will continue to improve with greater R&D. The chapter then looks at (5) Institutions—the national and international institutions and frameworks that govern climate mitigation. It finds that these institutions are increasingly targeting agrifood systems in their climate commitments, but a faster shift is required in financing and action. The chapter concludes by looking at (6) Inclusion—the equity issues related to the agrifood system transition. It finds that stakeholders must pursue an equitable process that ensures procedural, restorative, and distributive justice and that ensures that certain groups are not left behind.

Investments: Governments and Businesses Can Remove Barriers to Agrifood Sector Climate Investments through Improved Targeting, De-risking, Accountability, and Carbon Markets

Several large economies have started embedding large investments in the agrifood system to catalyze economywide emissions reduction. For example, the US Inflation Reduction Act of 2022 commits approximately $20 billion to increase CSA practices among agricultural producers and forestland owners, with additional tax credits and grants to increase forest and soil conservation (Senate Democrats 2022). Under the European Green Deal's Farm to Fork strategy (2020), eco-schemes offer major funding streams to European farmers for boosting sustainable practices, including carbon farming, agroforestry, and mitigation-oriented practices within agroecology and animal husbandry (European Commission 2020b, 2021). Similarly, China launched its National Green Development Fund in 2021 and other financing mechanisms that funnel resources to lower-emission practices in agriculture and rural areas.

Sustainable private investments in agrifood systems have grown rapidly but still account for only a small share of assets under management. Sustainable investing, or impact investing, refers to investments that aim to achieve financial returns while creating long-term social and environmental benefits. Attention to social and environmental concerns in private investments has grown (Santos et al. 2022). Impact investing in particular has somewhat emphasized agrifood systems, with investments amounting to 9 percent of total assets under management in 2019, but this percentage is expected to increase (Santos et al. 2022). Sustainable investments such as environmental, social, and governance investing grew more than threefold between 2012 and 2018 in major markets globally, reaching $30 trillion (Santos et al. 2022).

That said, the shares of financing resources dedicated to climate change mitigation still do not match the scale of agrifood emissions. As chapter 2 discussed, only 4 percent of global climate finance is destined for the agrifood system, despite that system's generating nearly a third of all emissions. Likewise, only 5 percent of global support to agriculture encourages sustainable practices (Searchinger et al. 2020). Overall, $28 billion is allocated to environmental services, including land retirement or conservation. As such, governments and businesses must work together to remove the barriers to climate investments in the agrifood sector by targeting finance to those who can promote change, mitigating investment risks, creating accountability, and nurturing carbon markets.

Financing must target change agents

Private investment in the agrifood system should target change agents such as value chain actors and domestic financial service providers. Public support to producers for capital and on-farm services is often poorly targeted to beneficiaries (Searchinger et al. 2020; Tang et al. 2016). However, new business opportunities linked to food systems transformation may be worth $4.5 trillion a year by 2030 (FOLU 2020). Promising small and medium enterprises (SMEs) in CSA technologies need access to early-stage venture capital and angel investing to grow (Casey et al. 2021). That said, the high transaction costs of dealing with many small and dispersed producers and SMEs that often lack collateral, as well as with small investment sizes, pose challenges to investors and financial service providers (FSPs) (UN Secretary-General 2023; Wasafiri 2021; World Bank Group 2016). FSPs are financial institutions that provide services like loans, money transfers, and other financial options to consumers. The most typical of the service providers are banks, payment providers, insurers, receivables managers, intermediaries, and investment funds. These FSPs account for 85 percent of financing for agricultural SMEs in Sub-Saharan Africa and Southeast Asia (ISF Advisors 2022). FSPs are the first financing option for SMEs and small-scale producers, and have local knowledge of their client base. Commercial value chain actors such as traders, processors, or input providers could also finance the CSA actions of small-scale producers who do not have access to financial services and insurance products. These value chain actors already have well-established links with small-scale producers and offer them short-term loans, for example for agricultural inputs. However, value chain actors generally do not have the capability to offer medium- and longer-term financial solutions (Apampa et al. 2021). Moreover, these actors are often excluded from providing formal advisory and infrastructure support to smallholders (Casey et al. 2021). Improved targeting includes technical advice, contract flexibility, regular evaluations, cost-effective enrollment criteria, tailored payments to cover the costs of adopting proposed practices, and monitoring systems to ensure contract compliance (Guerrero 2021; OECD 2021).

Financial service providers often have limited capacity for appraising and managing the risks associated with financing CSA. Ideally, FSPs would include CSA-friendly offerings—such as longer maturities and flexible repayment schedules—as part of their financial products and services, but they lack the expertise and risk appetite to do so (FAO 2016; SAFIN 2022; World Bank Group 2016). As such, strengthening FSPs' appraisal and risk management capacities and developing CSA-targeted products is a strategic step for scaling climate finance. Helping FSPs adopt digital tools can improve their appraisal and risk management capacity and lower the costs of these services. Examples include credit scoring solutions for FSPs proposed by ADAPTA Earth, geomapping tools such as CropIn (supported by Palladium), or the Cool Farm Tool for tracking greenhouse gas (GHG) emissions and biodiversity impacts. Proper targeting should also include cost-effective enrollment criteria, tailored payments to cover the costs of adopting proposed practices, monitoring systems to ensure contract compliance, technical advice contract flexibility, and regular evaluations (Guerrero 2021; OECD 2021).

Governments must help de-risk agrifood system mitigation investing

Scaling up private investment in the agrifood system requires minimizing investment risks. Investors increasingly recognize climate risks as investment risks and account for these when shaping their portfolios, which improves the long-term profitability and growth of investments (UN Secretary-General 2023). That said, private sector investors need to embrace higher risk–return profiles and longer development lead times (Guarnaschelli, Limketkai, and Vandeputte 2018; Santos et al. 2022). Facilitating the private sector's risk acceptance for decarbonization projects requires (1) building a pipeline of bankable projects and (2) leveraging blended finance to de-risk private sector investments.

Increasing the pipeline of bankable projects would unlock financing for agrifood system decarbonization projects. A project is bankable when its risk–return profile meets investors' criteria and can secure financing, whether from public or private sources, to implement the project. However, the lack of a deep pipeline of bankable projects has held back mitigation financing levels, even in recent years of low to zero interest rates (Apampa et al. 2021; Millan, Limketkai, and Guarnaschelli 2020). Part of the problem is that investors find short-term loans with immediate returns appealing but shy away from offering medium- and longer-term financial solutions (Apampa et al. 2021), which are necessary for the food system transformation. This is especially true for loans to agri-SMEs, small-scale producers, microenterprises, and cooperatives that often lack the capacity or know-how to take advantage of financial services and insurance products (Casey et al. 2021). As such, building small-scale borrowers' capacity in business, technical, and financial literacy would enhance both the demand for climate finance and its likely success rate. Moreover, aggregating borrower assets and investments to raise ticket sizes can help attract investors and providing complementary risk mitigation instruments—such as insurance and guarantee schemes—can lower the cost of capital, which is often prohibitively high in agriculture.

Blended finance can facilitate SMEs' access to private finance for climate action by leveraging public finance to reduce credit risk (OECD 2021). Blended finance, as defined in chapter 2, is when public finance reduces the risks behind private investment; it can include a wide range of risk management instruments (see table 4.1). It is useful where there is a divergence between real and perceived risks and can transform near-bankable projects into bankable ones, increasing the availability of finance for these projects (Apampa et al. 2021). A review of agri-SMEs' early experiences with blended finance shows that grants, guarantees, and other risk-sharing instruments can make market ecosystems more inclusive, enhance SME liquidity through direct credit lines, and make investors more tolerant of longer-term loans (OECD 2021). Blended finance can also reduce the costs of emerging technologies. This is what happened with solar photovoltaic (PV) systems, whose costs declined by 64 percent, 69 percent, and 82 percent for residential, commercial, and utility-scale systems, respectively, between 2010 and 2019 (Timmer 2022).[1] Pairing blended finance with technical assistance can strengthen both finance provider and client capacity, improving the success rates of loans (OECD 2021). It can also improve monitoring and evaluation (M&E) capacity, which would help inform continued multistakeholder cooperation and refine approaches to ensure that financed projects innovate and achieve results, and that the public financing does not crowd out private finance (OECD 2021). Blended finance can also finance nascent technologies that have not reached maturity and are experiencing slow adoption (Santos et al. 2022). For example, the upfront costs of biomethane-based tractors or other low-carbon

TABLE 4.1 Potential Roles of Concessionary Finance Providers in Blended Finance Transactions

Role of development finance	Sample instruments	Additionality aspects
Identify and enable new financing structures	Grants, concessional loans	• Research to identify opportunities such as market research or concept testing with investors. • Design new investment structures.
Seed new structures: First (anchor) capital	Equity, debt	• Test new types of intermediation structures—for example, proof-of-concept funding and bringing financial instruments to scale. • Conduct and share professional due diligence. • Act as a transaction reference for other investors—for example, in syndications.
De-risk financing	Guarantees, first loss tranches, subordinated loans, risk-absorbing equity	• Change the risk–return calculation for private investors (perceived versus actual risk). • Reduce the intermediation cost of capital, thus improving investors' risks and returns.
De-risk technical support	Grants	• Provide grant funding alongside an investment—for example, technical assistance.
Remunerate nonfinancial development impacts	Grants, rebates	• Pay for additional, pre-agreed impact outcomes where appropriate—for example, through results-based financing.
Develop markets	Grants	• Conduct research on implementation successes. • Create investor dialogues and incentives—for example, on policy changes. • Develop systems to monitor financial and development impact, subsidize additional support, and harmonize data.

Source: Havemann 2019.

technologies can be prohibitively high for smallholders. However, green financing tools, such as the UK's Plug-in Car Grant (UK Government, n.d.), could subsidize low-emission technologies that are not yet profitable or prioritized by businesses.

Make investment recipients more accountable

Corporate commitments to provide green goods and services through private standards and certifications signal their growing interest in food system mitigation. Agrifood corporations have increased their carbon neutrality commitments, climate-related Voluntary Sustainability Standards (VSS), and climate certifications since the 2015 United Nations Climate Change Conference (COP21).[2] Climate-related VSS are private standards among companies to ensure that their goods and services contribute to climate adaptation and mitigation (Bissinger et al. 2020). A certification—attained through a third party's assessment of the climate impacts of a company's business operations, services, and products—helps consumers identify purchases that support climate causes. Standards, such as VSS, and certification schemes can fill information gaps in the market where consumers need information about a company's climate footprint or a product's "green nature." The proliferation[3] of corporate commitments, voluntary sustainability standards, and certificates signals a strong interest in markets playing a positive role in decarbonization.

However, corporate commitments lack consistent measurement and accountability systems, undermining their effectiveness. Corporate commitments are not homogeneous; different corporations adopt different objectives, typologies, and terminologies. For example, separate companies may pursue "net zero" while others pursue "zero carbon," "carbon neutrality," or "emissions reduction," although these are all different concepts (White, Hardisty, and Habib 2019). The same is true for VSS systems and certifications. Adding to the confusion, there are also different carbon footprint standards for organizations[4] and for products or services (Greenhouse Gas Protocol 2011). However, there is no single global reference system to measure emissions, and companies are not transparent about how they do this, leading to uneven implementation of corporate commitments (Santos et al. 2022). Many companies cite costs and the lack of a robust policy framework as barriers to consistently implementing their declared commitments (Acampora et al. 2023).

Strong regulatory practices and better climate-related disclosure by firms can improve corporate commitment accountability for agrifood system mitigation. Governments have taken important steps over the last two years to improve businesses' climate-related disclosures. The European Union (EU) launched the Corporate Sustainability Reporting Directive (CSRD) in January 2023. The CSRD introduced detailed sustainability reporting requirements for companies that operate in the EU. Under the CSRD, companies must disclose information about sustainability-related practices, including mitigation practices. The EU has also recently adopted the Taxonomy Regulation and the Sustainable Finance Disclosure Regulation to standardize accountability mechanisms. Moreover, EU governments continue to negotiate other related legislative and regulatory initiatives such as the Corporate Sustainability Due Diligence Directive and the EU green bond standard. In 2022, the US Securities and Exchange Commission proposed standardizing climate-related disclosures for investors. Likewise, in 2021, New Zealand's government passed legislation making climate-related disclosures mandatory for banks, insurers, investment managers, large publicly listed companies, and nonbank deposit takers. Another step toward greater accountability would be for banks, investors, and large-scale businesses to report climate-related risks and opportunities to the Task Force on Climate-related Financial Disclosures and to collaborate with the emerging Taskforce on Nature-related Financial Disclosure, both of which have improved knowledge and transparency on private sector emissions (UNEP 2023; UNFSS 2022).

Stronger private sector coordination mechanisms can help standardize and maximize corporate commitments to agrifood system mitigation. For example, the Glasgow Financial Alliance for Net Zero (GFANZ) can accelerate private sector "green" financing. GFANZ was launched in April 2021 by the UN Special Envoy on Climate, the COP26 presidency, and the United Nations Framework Convention on Climate Change (UNFCCC)-backed Race to Zero campaign to coordinate efforts among private sector actors to accelerate the transition to a net zero global economy. GFANZ's goals are to expand the number of net zero–committed financial institutions and establish a forum that brings together companies, civil society, experts, and climate scientists to address net zero challenges and ensure ambitious action.

There are opportunities to expand accountable financing mechanisms through results-based climate finance (RBCF). One example of RBCF is the World Bank's Scaling Climate Action by Lowering Emissions (SCALE) fund, an umbrella multipartner trust fund established to provide climate finance and incentivize low-carbon development through policy dialogue with governments and other stakeholders. SCALE pools funding from donor countries, the private sector, foundations, and others for programs to reduce GHG emissions. SCALE's funding target is to reach $5 billion through $50 million grants per project (Lawder 2022). Over the past decade, the World Bank has increasingly moved to RBCF mechanisms (IEG 2023).

Climate bonds are another innovative mechanism to generate agrifood system mitigation finance, but accountability issues constrain their adoption (IFPRI 2022). Climate bonds and green bonds are instruments that raise money for climate and environmental projects. In the rapidly growing private climate bond markets, which recorded an average growth rate of more than 50 percent in the last five years, sustainable agriculture has appeared with increasing frequency (Climate Bonds Initiative 2021). That said, there are still factors that dissuade investors from these bonds, such as issuers rarely providing details on the types of agricultural activities that the bond finances or on their climate-related benefits (Climate Bonds Initiative 2021). Furthermore, low-income countries (LICs) and middle-income countries (MICs) are not yet benefiting widely from innovations in private sustainability bonds. In fact, three-quarters of the total green bond volume in 2021, across various sectors, originated from high-income countries (HICs).

Incentivize finance with carbon markets

Carbon credits and carbon taxes offer opportunities to control the agrifood system's GHG emissions. Carbon credits, for example, can be purchased by governments and businesses in carbon markets to offset unavoidable emissions. In such a market, a country that is investing in activities that lead to traceable and credible reductions in emissions can earn carbon credits that they can sell on the open market. This is also known as an Emissions Trading System (ETS). These markets can either be mandatory, where participating organizations are required by law to participate in the market and to meet certain carbon reduction targets, or voluntary, where companies, governments, and other organizations can offset their carbon emissions on a voluntary basis—either to meet their own sustainability goals or to demonstrate their commitment to reducing their carbon footprint (CHOOOSE 2022). The EU's ETS is an example of a compliance carbon market because it requires large emitter companies to purchase carbon credits every year (European Commission, n.d.). Gold Standard is an example of a standard that facilitates exchange of carbon assets in a voluntary carbon market (VCM).[5] Carbon taxes or carbon pricing, by contrast, are government-determined price tags that organizations must pay for each ton of GHG they emit. Canada, for example, has one of the world's most ambitious carbon pricing programs—it taxes oil, gas, and coal use at \$15–\$38 per ton of carbon dioxide emitted (Plumer and Popovich 2019). The revenues from carbon credits and carbon taxes can then be used for development activities or low-emission practices, thereby creating a virtuous cycle in which emissions reduction payments finance further emissions reduction.

However, carbon credits and taxes are underutilized in the agrifood system and by smallholders. Almost a quarter of global GHG emissions are covered by the world's carbon markets or carbon pricing schemes, but few apply to nonenergy agricultural emissions (World Bank 2022c). For VCMs, the agrifood system (except for REDD+) accounts for only a small portion of volumes traded. This is a legacy of the Clean Development Mechanism (CDM)—the world's first carbon finance scheme established through the Kyoto Protocol in 1997—which largely excluded agriculture projects other than waste-to-energy livestock products. As such, VCMs may have unlocked as little as 0.5 percent of the annual cost-effective potential of nature-based solutions, including agricultural solutions (Climate Focus 2023, reference period 2021 through the third quarter of 2022). Moreover, the agriculture sector differs in its readiness to scale up carbon credits under VCMs or the Paris Agreement's market mechanisms. The forestry sector, in particular

REDD+, is the most prepared to scale up because of its ample experience in the VCM.[6] The livestock sector is the second most prepared because of the sector's experience in the CDM, particularly its CDM projects designed to capture methane from animal waste for energy. Smallholder farmers are also underrepresented in VCMs for various reasons, such as their lack of capacity, weak land tenure, difficulty measuring small-volume emissions reduction, and their changing household needs, which may alter their low-emission practices (TechnoServe 2022).

That said, VCMs offer growing opportunities for carbon finance. The VCM has grown considerably over the last five years, after slow growth since the 1990s (Streck, Dyck, and Trouwloon 2023; see also figure 4.1), to reach approximately $2 billion in 2022 (Shell and BCG 2023) with expectations of further growth to between $5 billion and $50 billion by 2030, depending on many factors (IETA 2022). Figure 4.1 shows that VCMs have been growing in both value and volumes of carbon credits. In 2022, the VCMs took a dip, with carbon offsets falling by 40 percent since 2021. Most analysts think this reduction is temporary and related to the regulatory and reputational uncertainty of carbon credits and their utility

FIGURE 4.1 **Voluntary Carbon Markets Have Been Growing in Both Value and Volume of Traded Carbon Credits**

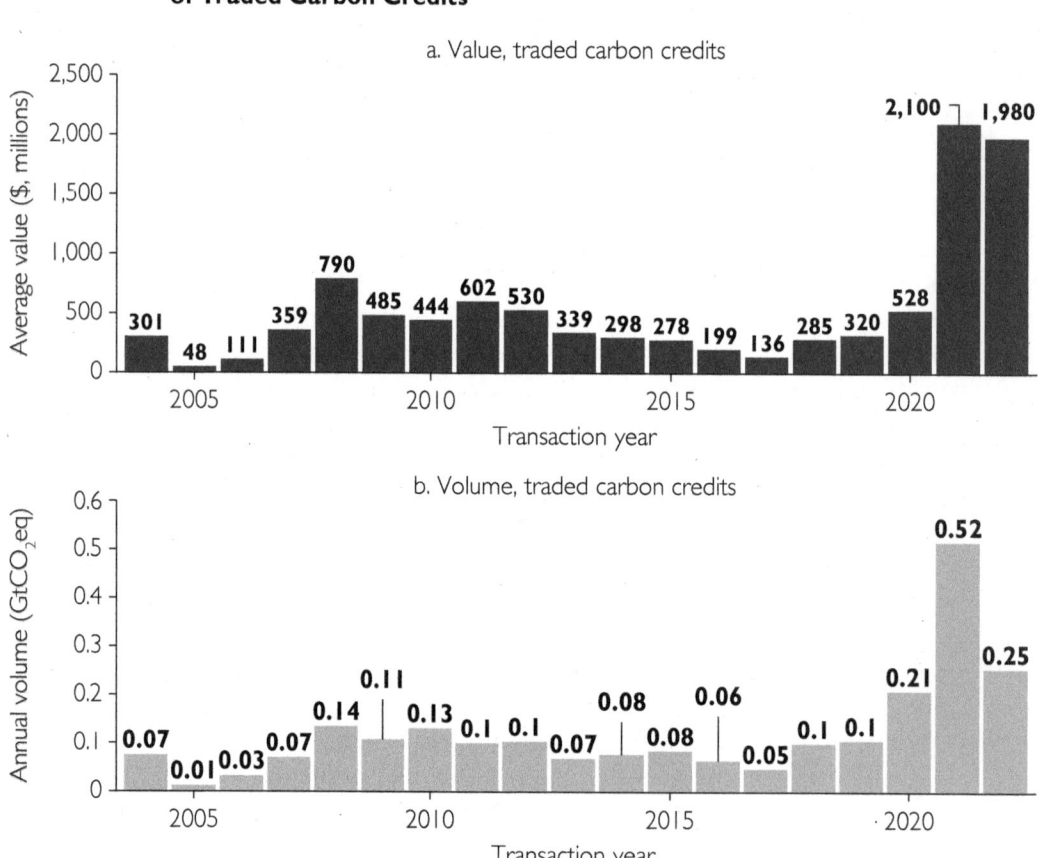

Source: Data from Ecosystem Marketplace Insights Team 2023.
Note: GtCO$_2$eq = gigatons of carbon dioxide equivalent.

Recipe for a Livable Planet

in realizing corporate net zero commitments. Within carbon markets, buyers have shown a growing preference for carbon removal schemes—from reforestation and agroforestry practices, among others—as opposed to carbon avoidance schemes such as REDD+ because of remaining uncertainty about how schemes will be standardized and regulated (ACMI 2022) and the absence of a universal agreement on the attributes of quality credits (Shell and BCG 2023). There is considerable potential for growth in carbon finance for agriculture, especially for carbon credit projects that produce co-benefits, such as community-based projects, nature-based solutions, and high-integrity projects, which have attracted higher carbon prices in the markets (Lou et al. 2022). Likewise, the expected increase in corporate commitments to net zero emissions is likely to contribute to future VCM growth.

However, VCMs and carbon pricing still suffer from several flaws. First, VCMs are subject to "carbon panics." This is what caused the CDM to collapse in 2012, when its credit price fell to a meager €0.5 per ton of CO_2, leading to a market panic and causing the pricing mechanism to break down completely (Kainou 2022). The CDM has since recovered to some extent, with support from key nations. However, the episode shows that VCMs are vulnerable to market crashes. Second, emissions exemptions undermine the value of carbon taxes. Some governments applied carbon taxes to upstream fuel use, for example from farm equipment use, which captures some agricultural and supply chain emissions. Then these same governments offered exemptions to agricultural businesses, thereby limiting the VCM's effectiveness. This was the case for carbon taxes in France, Japan, and Canada's British Columbia (World Bank 2023b). Third, carbon markets add complexity to already challenging agricultural sector operations (Henderson et al. 2021), which can entail diverse operations and purposes. Fourth, emissions reductions are difficult to monitor, report, and verify (World Bank 2022e). MRV is discussed in more detail later in this chapter.

The VCM can overcome these flaws and sustain its growth through greater transparency and carbon credit integrity. Sustainable growth of the VCM rests upon establishing mechanisms to ensure the integrity, or quality, of emissions reduction—in particular that they exceed business as usual scenarios. This is especially important given the increased scrutiny of voluntary credits' credibility and use in corporate decarbonization strategies (TSVCM 2021). Specialist rating companies, such as Sylvera, BeZero, and Calyx Global, independently assess the quality of carbon market projects and their related credits (see also Bloomberg NEF 2023). In March 2023, the Integrity Council for the Voluntary Carbon Market (ICVCM), an independent governing body for the VCM,[7] released assessment frameworks for "identifying high-integrity carbon credits that create real, verifiable climate impact, based on the latest science and best practice" (Integrity Council for the Voluntary Carbon Market 2022). The frameworks assess governance, sustainable development, and emissions impacts, including additionality and permanence. In this case, "high integrity" implies that credits that reduce the purchaser's footprint can be tracked and are only counted once. This is important because credits are currently registered in disparate, unconnected registry systems, which undermines trust in the VCM (Vives 2023). The World Bank is working with partners, including the International Emissions Trading Association (IETA), to enhance the transparency of carbon markets through the Climate Warehouse and through the Climate Action Data Trust. These are open-source metadata systems that use distributed ledger technology that links, aggregates, and harmonizes carbon credit data to avoid double counting, thereby enhancing trust in VCMs (IETA 2022). In addition to integrity concerns, VCMs lack the necessary liquidity for efficient trading, and credits are heterogeneous and not easily comparable—a constraint the assessment frameworks aim to address (Blaufelder et al. 2021). Moreover, VCM brokers and intermediaries often take large commissions in an opaque but booming market (Hodgson 2022). Linking carbon markets globally under Paris Agreement mechanisms can enhance their liquidity and integrity, but some of the operational details remain undefined as countries work out the details as part of continued UNFCCC negotiations.

Incentives: Policy Measures Are Emerging That Could Accelerate the Transformation to a Net Zero Agrifood System

Policy advances

Two decades ago, HICs pioneered the development of mitigation policies for the agrifood sector, a trend that continues. The EU's common agricultural policy (CAP) was initiated in 1962 and evolved in 2003 to being one of the world's first explicit climate change mitigation policies for agriculture (European Commission 2013). New Zealand enacted its Emissions Trading Scheme in 2008, which was one of the first national programs to include reporting of agricultural emissions—primarily methane and nitrous oxide—under a cap-and-trade system (Ministry for the Environment, New Zealand 2018). Other early examples of agriculture mitigation policies in HICs include (1) the United States' 2006 California Air Resources Board (CARB) Compliance Offset Program,[8] (2) Canada's 2007 Alberta Emission Offset System (AEOR 2019),[9] and (3) Australia's 2011 Carbon Farming Initiative (Department of Agriculture, Water, and the Environment, Government of Australia 2021) and 2014 Emissions Reduction Fund (figure 4.2).[10] More recently, the EU's CAP has evolved further and now commits 40 percent of its budget to climate mitigation

FIGURE 4.2 Greenhouse Gas Mitigation Policies in the Agrifood Sector Have Evolved Over the Past Two Decades and Will Continue to Evolve

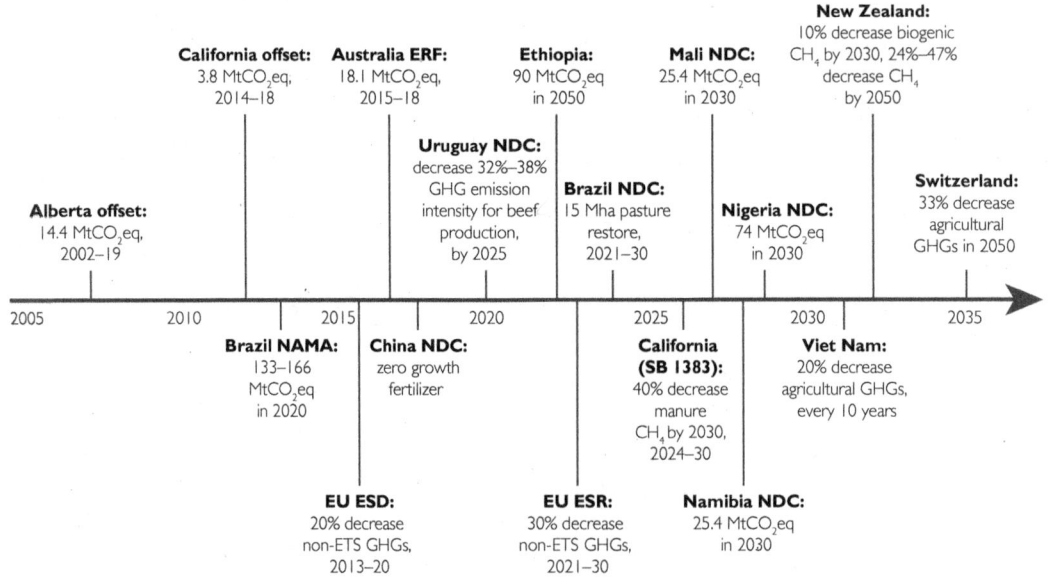

Source: Adapted from OECD 2019a.

Note: This nonexhaustive list of policies was selected in two steps. First, countries with ambitious emissions reduction targets in their Nationally Determined Contributions (NDCs) specific to agriculture were identified. Second, countries with mitigation policies that explicitly put a price on emissions or make substantial funds available for mitigation measures were selected. Emissions reductions from forestry and other land use were excluded. CH$_4$ = methane; ERF = emissions reduction fund; ESD = effort sharing decision; ESR = effort sharing regulation; ETS = Emissions Trading System; GHGs = greenhouse gases; Mha = millions of hectares; MtCo$_2$eq = megatons of carbon dioxide equipvalent; NAMA = Nationally Appropriate Mitigation Actions; SB = Senate Bill.

(European Commission 2020a). Likewise, in 2020, the UK announced its agricultural transition plan and followed it up in 2023 with its Sustainable Farming Incentive, which pays farmers for climate mitigation and environmental protection actions.

In recent years, several MICs began implementing large-scale mitigation programs that target agrifood emissions. Costa Rica had one of the earliest mitigation-related programs among MICs with its 1997 Payment for Environmental Services program. This program provided financial incentives to farmers and landowners to protect watersheds, maintain forest cover, and promote sustainable agricultural practices (Pagiola 2008). More recently, Brazil, China, and Viet Nam have launched large-scale agrifood emissions mitigation programs (figure 4.2). In Brazil, the government provides subsidized credit to farmers to restore 15 million hectares of degraded pastureland under the Low Carbon Emission in Agriculture program, now known as RenovAgro.[11] Notably, funding for RenovAgro grew from $1.35 billion in 2022–23 to $5.6 billion in 2023–24.[12] Concurrently, funding for Brazil's Plano Safra program grew by 26.8 percent between 2022–23 and 2023–24. The program provides low-interest loans to farmers to adopt sustainable agricultural practices (Ministry of Agriculture and Livestock, Brazil 2023). Meanwhile, in China, several programs recalibrate farmer incentives toward sustainable agriculture: (1) the Zero Growth of Chemical Fertilizer Use by 2020 to increase fertilizer use efficiency in grain production;[13] (2) the Grain for Green program, which provides cash and in-kind subsidies to farmers for converting fragile agricultural land into productive forests (Liu and Wu 2010); and (3) the Forest Ecosystem Benefit Compensation Fund, which provides payments and advisory services to protect natural forests in Inner Mongolia and Northeast China. In Viet Nam, the government is moving toward low-emission rice production (World Bank 2022d) by promoting alternate wetting and drying (AWD) irrigation at a large scale. It is estimated that the application of AWD results in an average net profit of $1,211 per hectare per year and GHG emissions reduction of 5.8 tons of carbon dioxide equivalent (tCO_2eq) per hectare per year (World Bank 2022b).

This movement toward agrifood sector mitigation is increasingly reflected in countries' Nationally Determined Contributions (NDCs). Currently, 147 out of 167 second-round NDCs include agriculture, forestry and other land use (AFOLU) or agrifood systems in their mitigation commitments. This represents an increase from 68 percent in first-round NDCs to 88 percent in second-round NDCs (figure 4.3) (Crumpler et al., forthcoming).[14] This is notable because prioritizing mitigation actions in NDCs allows countries to access financing for those actions more easily through the Green Climate Fund and other climate finance mechanisms. The quality of these commitments has also improved—between the first and second rounds, the share of NDCs with agriculture sector-specific GHG targets nearly doubled (from 20 percent to 38 percent) and the share with specific agriculture-related mitigation actions increased from 63 percent to 78 percent (Crumpler et al. 2021). Most mitigation commitments are in traditional agricultural activities. For example, two-thirds of mitigation contributions are committed to forest-related carbon sequestration actions, including afforestation, reforestation, and sustainable forest management; more than half are committed to managing cropland systems, including increased cover crops, reduced tillage, and on-farm energy efficiency and bioenergy production; and almost half are committed to managing livestock and grasslands systems, including improved feeding practices and pasture restoration (figure 4.4). That said, countries have also shifted toward a broader agrifood system approach in their NDCs. For instance, the share of NDCs committed to energy efficiency in broader agrifood systems increased from 41 percent to 52 percent, waste reuse increased from

FIGURE 4.3 Agrifood Mitigation Has Become a Stronger Component of Nationally Determined Contributions

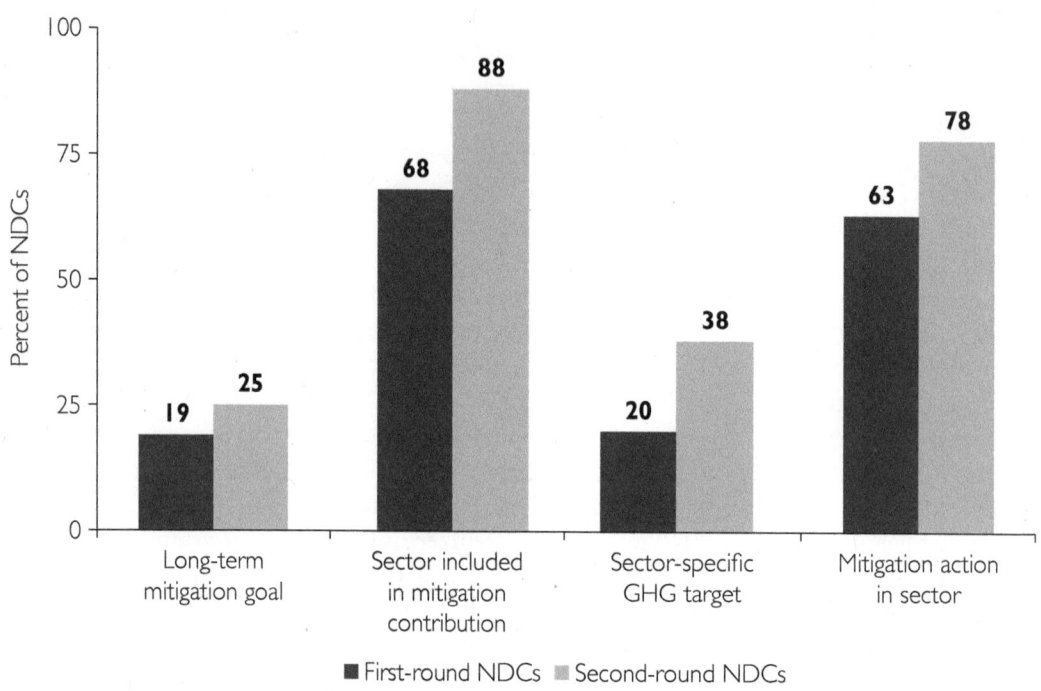

Source: World Bank based on data and original analysis carried out by the Food and Agriculture Organization for this report.
Note: Figure compares NDC mitigation contributions to the agrifood sector in first-round and second-round NDCs. GHG = greenhouse gas; NDCs = Nationally Determined Contributions.

15 percent to 19 percent, and sustainable fisheries and aquaculture systems increased from 2 percent to 10 percent between the first and second rounds.

These expanded NDC commitments are not matched by on-the-ground implementation. Most NDC commitments are conditional on international support. For example, 92 percent of MIC NDC commitments toward economywide emissions reduction that cover the AFOLU sector are fully or partially conditional on international support. This share is 100 percent for LICs, but only 54 percent for HICs (figure 4.5). These shares do not change much for direct commitments to the AFOLU sector, with 92 percent of MIC, 91 percent of LIC, and 75 percent of HIC NDC commitments being fully or partially conditional on international support. However, international financial support for climate action has been underwhelming (OECD 2022b, 2022c). The net result is that most NDC commitments on agrifood system mitigation remain only promises that will not be fulfilled until the international community accelerates climate financing in the sector. Negotiations around climate financing are discussed more thoroughly in the Institutions section of this chapter.

Policy coherence

Implementation of agrifood system mitigation commitments is hindered by a lack of national policy coherence across sectors and within the agrifood sector. Therefore, disconnected, uncoordinated responses act as a barrier to transforming the agrifood system. Within countries, there are often contradictory development goals. For example, the simultaneous

172   Recipe for a Livable Planet

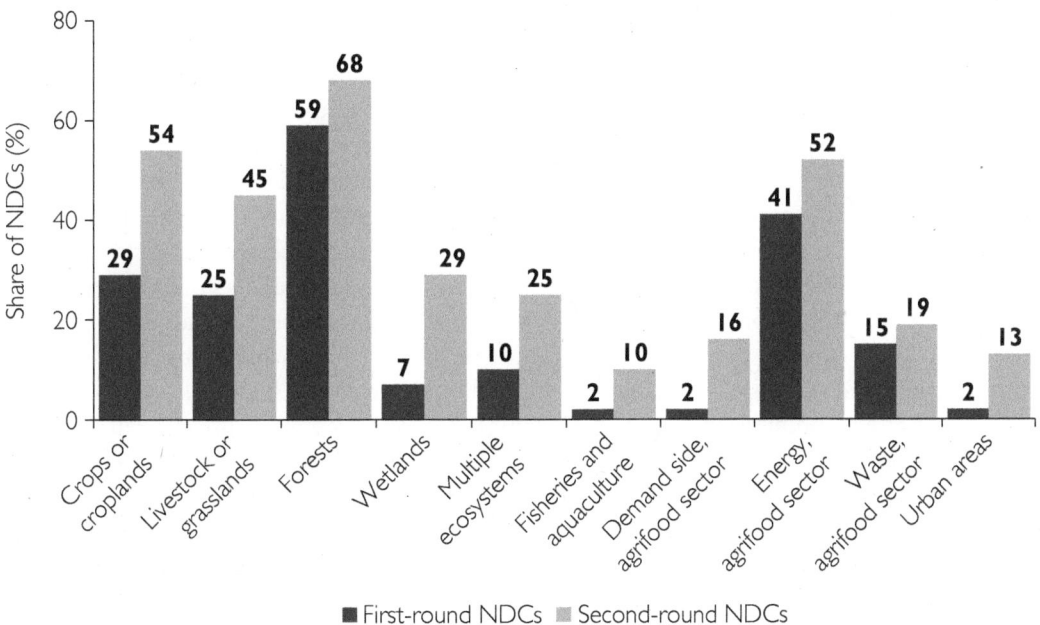

FIGURE 4.4 Agrifood System Mitigation Practices Are Being More Frequently Promoted in Nationally Determined Contributions

Source: Data from and original analysis carried out by the Food and Agriculture Organization for this report.
Note: Figure shows coverage of agrifood system mitigation contributions by sector in first- and second-round NDCs. NDCs = Nationally Determined Contributions.

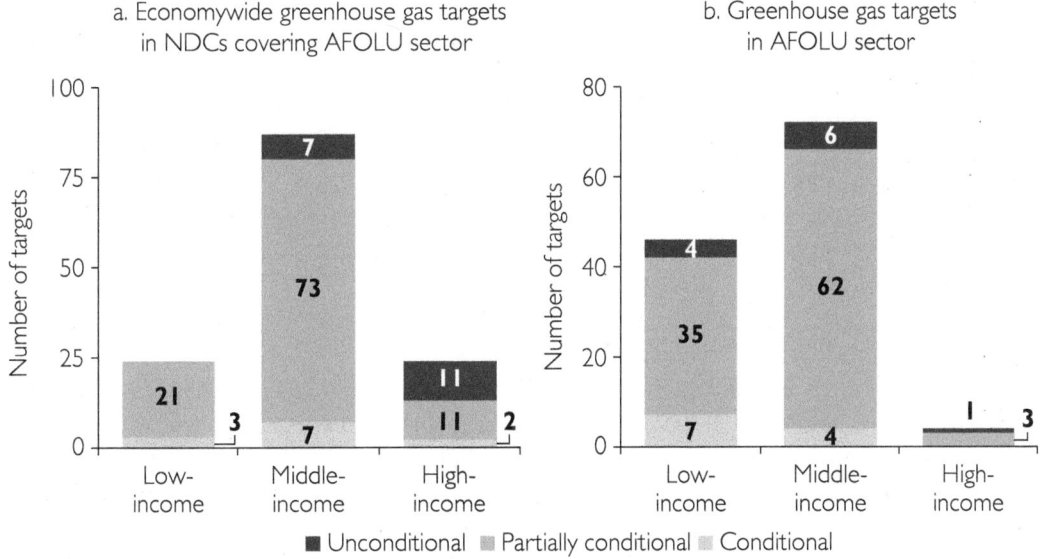

FIGURE 4.5 Emissions Reduction Targets of Low- and Middle-Income Countries Related to Their Agrifood Systems Are Conditional on International Support

Source: Data from and original analysis carried out by the Food and Agriculture Organization for this report.
Note: AFOLU = agriculture, forestry, and other land use; NDCs = Nationally Determined Contributions.

Enabling Environment for Agrifood System Transformation

pursuit of agricultural expansion—usually for food security—and emissions reduction presents potential trade-offs. This is especially true in heavily forested countries like Brazil, the Democratic Republic of Congo, Guyana, and Indonesia, where agricultural expansion requires more land, risking deforestation. This lack of economywide policy coherence can lead to funding shortfalls in implementing national climate commitments. For example, at the global level, governments allocated $7 trillion in 2022 to subsidize the cost of fossil fuels for consumers and businesses (Black et al. 2023). This is equivalent to 7.1 percent of global gross domestic product (GDP). At the same time, HICs that committed $100 billion annually for climate action under the Paris Climate Agreement have not been able to meet this target (OECD 2022b, 2022c). There are also incoherent policies within a country's agrifood sector. For example, the Colombian government has stated its ambition to "green" agriculture, but this represented only 1.2 percent of its total sector spending in 2021. At the same time, over 80 percent of its agriculture support is provided through distortive instruments, such as market price support and variable input subsidies, which tend to negatively affect the environment.[15] In other cases, countries may support mitigation at certain stages of the agrifood system value chain but not at others. For example, Estonia and Latvia support organic agriculture but do not market it as such. Consequently, organic milk in the Baltics, which is produced with lower emissions than conventional dairy in the US (Aguirre-Villegas et al. 2022), is not differentiated from cheaper milk products produced with higher emissions (OECD 2019b).

Effective climate policy must be implemented across jurisdictions and stakeholders. Reducing agrifood system emissions is a public good that requires collective action from many actors and institutions. In general, coalitions across jurisdictions can increase legitimacy and bargaining power; improve policy outcomes (Donahue, Weil, and Zeckhauser 2010); and achieve adaptive planning, collaborative action, and reflective monitoring (Brouwer and Woodhill 2019). For example, the BioCarbon Fund Initiative for Sustainable Forest Landscapes facilitated a multistakeholder coalition to implement comprehensive land use plans across large jurisdictions. This initiative balanced agricultural production, conservation, and restoration across Colombia, introduced agroforestry and silvo-pastoral systems across degraded areas in Mexico, and boosted climate resilience across jurisdictions in Ethiopia.[16] These coalitions shared several elements, including capacity building; digital collaboration tools; financial solutions (by blending public, private, and philanthropic resources); and problem-solving networks that convene leaders, academics, practitioners, businesses, and civil society actors (see, for instance, EcoAgriculture Partners, n.d.). Generally, climate programs that engage a diverse range of stakeholders are more successful in achieving their goals than those that do not (Kusters et al. 2018; Novick et al. 2023).

Policy distortions: subsidies and trade policy

Many policies, such as agricultural subsidies and trade barriers, damage the environment and contribute to higher GHG emissions. Many countries use negative market price support policies such as export restrictions to keep domestic food prices low, but this penalizes farmers. This is particularly true in LICs where price disincentives are higher than price incentives, making net support to agrifood systems –$1.2 billion. By contrast, MICs' net support is positive because price incentives ($230 billion) are higher than price disincentives (–$111 billion) and in HICs there is almost no implicit taxation of farming activities; these countries' support tends to have low or moderate negative environmental externalities. To compensate where there are negative market price support policies, governments then provide subsidies to farmers for variable farm inputs such as seeds and fertilizers. In many countries, fertilizer subsidies are some of the largest expenditures in government budgets. For instance, India spent approximately $28 billion on fertilizer subsidies in 2022–23 (Chaganti Singh and Ohri 2023; Tarique and Zafar 2023). A recent meta-analysis found that input subsidy programs can increase yields and farmers' incomes but often result in the inefficient use of resources and negative environmental outcomes (World Bank 2023c). For example, water subsidies in Pakistan for expanded irrigation have led to water overconsumption and ultimately to drought vulnerability. Also in Pakistan, energy subsidies, particularly for fuel or electricity, directly contribute to increased emissions (IMF 2022). Similarly, nitrogen fertilizer subsidies lead to their overapplication in South Asia (Kishore, Alvi, and Krupnik 2021) and countries like the Arab Republic of Egypt (Kurdi et al. 2020). As a consequence, crops cannot absorb all the fertilizer, which then leaks into water supplies, or fertilizer is broken down by soil microbes, releasing nitrous oxide—a potent GHG. Globally, inefficient input subsidies have reduced freshwater supplies and increased aquatic nitrogen pollution by up to 17 percent over the past 30 years (Damania et al. 2023).

Repurposing subsidies toward agrifood system mitigation and productivity growth can deliver emissions reduction and multiple other benefits. A recent World Bank report shows that repurposing $70 billion of the world's approximately $638 billion in annual agriculture support (Gautam et al. 2022; Voegele 2023) toward emissions reductions and improved productivity will boost crop production by 16 percent and livestock production by 11 percent. This would increase national incomes by 1.6 percent, reduce the cost of healthy diets by 18 percent, and decrease overall agricultural emissions by 40 percent compared to business as usual 2020–40 levels (see figure 4.6) (Gautam et al. 2022).

FIGURE 4.6 Repurposing Domestic Support for Sectors Can Reduce Agrifood Emissions and Increase Agricultural Production

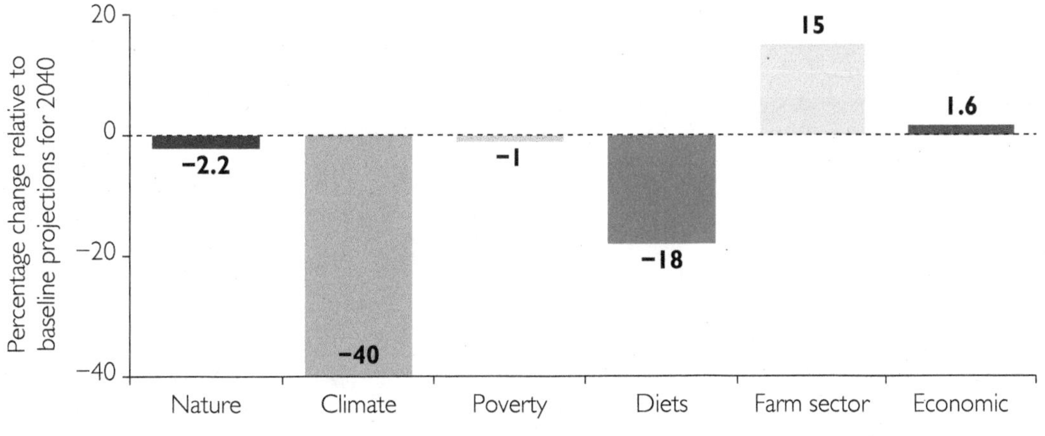

Source: Gautam et al. 2022.
Note: Figure shows the global Implications of repurposing domestic support by depicting the percentage change in agrifood system emissions and production relative to baseline projections for 2040. Nature = agricultural land, % change 2040; Climate = reduction in emissions from agriculture and land use, % change 2040; Poverty = poverty at purchasing power parity $1.90, % change 2040; Diets = healthy food prices, % change 2040; Farm sector = agricultural production volume, % change 2040; Economic = real national income, % change 2040.

Given this potential win–win–win scenario, governments should repurpose their support for policies with potentially high climate impacts—such as input and output subsidies or price disincentives—toward policies and activities with moderate or no environmental impacts—such as public goods and services, green technology subsidies, or decoupled payments (figure. 4.7). This would accelerate the adoption of mitigation options among smallholders, who are often constrained by inadequate access to credit for financing large upfront costs associated with switching to low-emission production technologies and practices.

That said, repurposing subsidies also entails some risks. Rapid repurposing can also contribute to negative short-term impacts for certain stakeholders. For example, removing distortive subsidies in countries with lower agricultural emissions intensity could reduce their competitiveness and induce agricultural production to shift to countries with higher emissions intensity, thereby leading to a net increase in global emissions (Guerrero et al. 2022; Laborde et al. 2021). Likewise, repurposing resources toward green technologies will fundamentally transform economies, leaving some workers from the previous economic structure with lower incomes or without work (see the Inclusion subsection on distributive justice for more on potential job losses) (Gautam et al. 2022; Guerrero et al. 2022). Similarly, repurposing resources could also increase food prices by lowering input use and converting agriculture land to natural land. As a result, many repurposing initiatives aimed at removing or reducing popular subsidies for fuel or food have been met with widespread resistance from the public or entrenched interests. This means that repurposing can be a highly political endeavor without simple solutions in certain cases that require proper communication and evidence-based decision-making. More generally, mitigating the short-term risks also requires technical solutions such as

FIGURE 4.7 Repurposing Agrifood Policies Requires Transitioning from Policies with High Impacts on Climate to Those with Low Impacts on Climate

High impacts
- Price incentives (positive and negative)
- Payments based on variable inputs and outputs
- Support to fossil fuels
- Payments for vessels and gear
- Expenditures for access to foreign waters

Moderate/low impacts
- Research and development
- Education, extension services, and training
- Payments for green technologies, ecosystem services, and CSA practices
- Energy efficiency in the value chain
- Educational campaigns for sustainable diets
- Food waste reduction

Source: Original figure for this publication.
Note: CSA = climate-smart agriculture.

strengthening land use regulations to protect forests and other natural areas with high carbon stocks, improving land titling and agriculture land property rights, establishing job training programs for farmers (Gautam et al. 2022), and strengthening social protection mechanisms for vulnerable farmers and consumers.

Similarly, there is a risk that hastily removing trade barriers could increase GHG emissions. Agriculture trade policy can play a key role in reducing the adverse impacts of climate change on food prices, undernourishment, and calorie intake (Baldos and Hertel 2015; Cui et al. 2018; Guerrero et al. 2022; Janssens et al. 2020). However, global computable general equilibrium simulations show that removing trade barriers in food products can increase GHG emissions as well. This is because lower food prices would lead to increased demand for food, which contributes to higher agricultural production and emissions (Gautam et al. 2022). Furthermore, livestock production is less emissions intensive in HICs but is highly dependent on imported grains and feed from MICs and LICs (Herrero et al. 2013). Therefore, removing trade barriers would increase GHG emissions by inducing deforestation in Latin American and Asian MICs that have a comparative advantage in grain and feed and also host rich carbon sinks (Guerrero et al. 2022; Laborde et al. 2021). Under these scenarios, it is conceivable that removing trade barriers could induce greater agricultural production and emissions in MICs and LICs.

Mitigation-related trade policies must be applied fairly and carefully designed to avoid harming poor countries. The EU's Carbon Border Adjustment Mechanism (CBAM) and deforestation regulation (EUDR) can be effective climate mitigation policies. The CBAM imposes tariffs on carbon-intensive imports to equalize the price of carbon between domestic and foreign firms. This policy incentivizes trading partners with less stringent climate policies to enact mitigation policies in order to access the EU market (World Bank, forthcoming). However, assessments of the CBAM suggest that it would reduce exports to the EU from large MICs—like Brazil, China, Egypt, India, the Russian Federation, and Ukraine—and from HICs—Australia, Japan, the Republic of Korea, New Zealand, and the United States (Xiaobei, Fan, and Jun 2022). Notably, the largest losses are projected to be incurred by Mozambique due to large economic footprint of its carbon-intensive exports of aluminum, iron, and steel (Xiaobei et al. 2022). Currently, the CBAM does not include agricultural products (Devarajan et al. 2022) but it will, and when it does it will likely reduce food exports from China, Egypt, India, Russia, and Türkiye, among others, translating to large drops in GDP in those countries (figure 4.8) (Devarajan et al. 2022; Xiaobei, Fan, and Jun 2022). Notably, the largest losses are projected to be incurred by Mozambique due to large economic footprint of its carbon-intensive exports of aluminum, iron, and steel (Xiaobei et al. 2022). With such high stakes, it is important that the CBAM and the EUDR (which is meant to ensure deforestation-free supply chains) take precautions against unintended consequences. For example, the CBAM takes into account the effective carbon price that a domestic producer may have already paid before entering the EU to prevent double charging and to ensure equity (Brenton et al. 2024). Similarly, both mechanisms should provide technical assistance and capacity building to strengthen MICs' and LICs' carbon and deforestation MRV systems and the ability of smallholders to comply with new regulations (Zhunusova et al. 2022).

FIGURE 4.8 An Expanded Carbon Border Adjustment Mechanism Will Lead to Dramatic Losses in GDP in Countries with High-Emitting Export Sectors

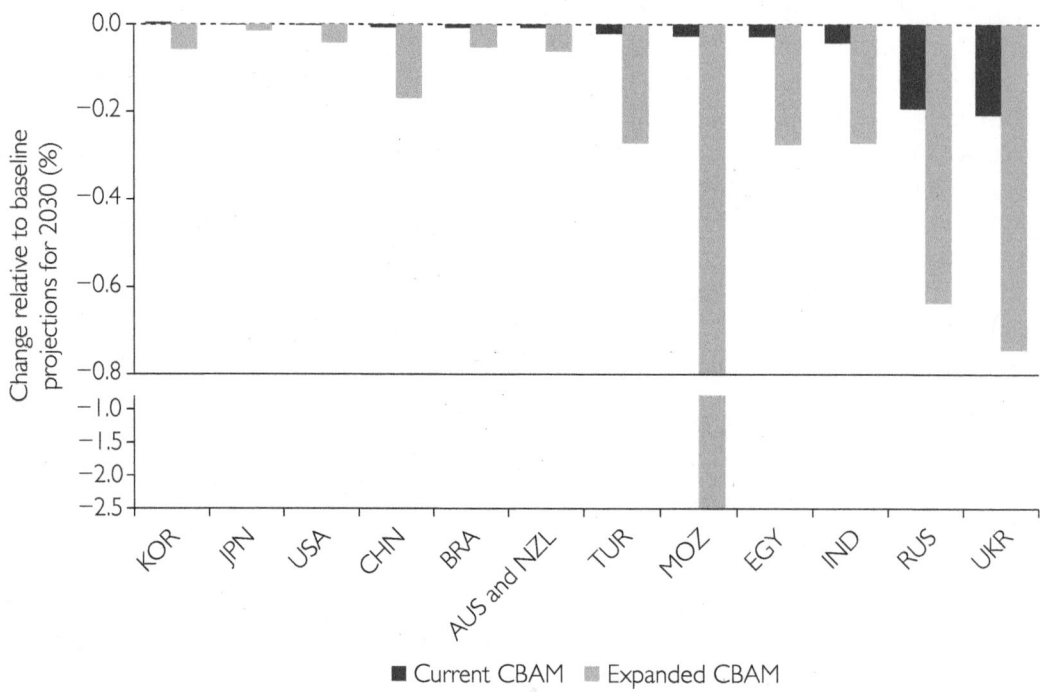

■ Current CBAM ▨ Expanded CBAM

Source: Xiaobei, Fan, and Jun 2022.
Note: Figure shows the impacts of the current Carbon Border Adjustment Mechanism (CBAM) (includes no agricultural products) and expanded CBAM (includes agricultural products) on countries' gross domestic product (GDP) as a percentage change from the baseline projections for 2030. AUS = Australia; BRA = Brazil; CHN = China; EGY = Egypt, Arab Rep.; INDIA = IND; JPN = Japan; KOR = Rep. Korea; MOZ = Mozambique; NZL = New Zealand; RUS = Russian Federation; TUR = Türkiye; UKR = Ukraine; USA = United States.

Policy for all GHGs

Carbon dioxide emissions receive much more policy attention than those of methane or nitrous oxide. As a result, products with high CO_2 emissions like coal, iron, steel, minerals, and pharmaceutical products are considered the most emissions intensive and thereby are the most targeted by climate mitigation policies. In fact, when only CO_2 emissions are considered, only two agrifood products are among the top 10 of the most emissions-intensive exports, defined as the products that require the most emissions to generate a dollar in export value (figure 4.9, panel a). This would help explain the relatively limited climate policy attention that agrifood system commodities have received historically. However, when accounting for the three major GHGs—CO_2, methane (CH_4), and nitrous oxide (N_2O)—agrifood products dominate the list of most emissions-intensive exports, comprising 8 of the top 10 products (figure 4.9, panel b). For example, a dollar of cattle exports leads to GHG emissions—largely methane—almost four times higher than mineral products, and 60 times higher than pharmaceutical products. By contrast, nitrous oxide is the main driver of GHG emissions intensity for cereals, oil seeds, and sugar. This has important policy ramifications because climate mitigation policies focused on CO_2 emissions—including carbon taxes and the EU's CBAM—risk shifting consumer demand toward methane-intensive livestock and rice production, especially in LICs and MICs where agrifood systems comprise a large share of domestic production and exports (World Bank, forthcoming). Some countries are aware of the need to target methane and nitrous

FIGURE 4.9 Agrifood Products Become the Most Emissions-Intensive Export Sectors When Mitigation Policy Takes into Account Not Just Carbon Dioxide, but Also Methane and Nitrous Oxide Emissions

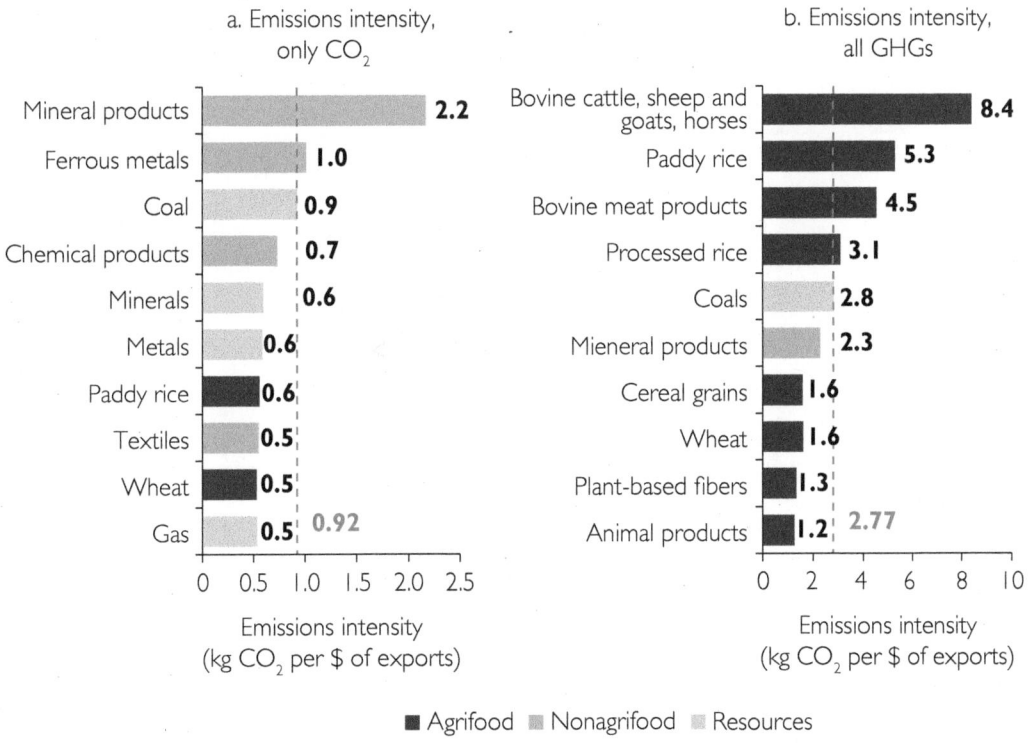

Source: Data from Brenton et al. 2024.
Note: The dashed orange line corresponds to the emissions intensity for coal and is included as a benchmark for the comparison with other products. CO_2 = carbon dioxide; GHGs = greenhouse gases; kg = kilogram.

oxide along with carbon dioxide in carbon pricing policies. For example, New Zealand's legally binding Climate Change Response (Zero Carbon) Amendment Act 2019 targets a 47 percent reduction in methane emissions by 2050 and net zero nitrous oxide emissions by the same year (OECD 2022d).

Climate mitigation policies that target all GHGs will reduce the export competitiveness of emissions-intensive countries, offering new opportunities for developing countries. Climate mitigation policies are expected to benefit products and activities that use clean energy while leaving products and activities that rely on fossil fuels less competitive (Mercure et al. 2018; Rempel and Gupta 2021). A recent World Bank simulation shows that climate mitigation scenarios will decrease the leading global exports and replace them with exports of lower emissions intensities (Brenton et al. 2024). For example, global exports of grains and oil seeds are projected to decline by 4.8 percent in 2050 under the most ambitious mitigation scenario, with the largest declines in Brazil (−1.80 percent), the rest of Latin America (−1.44 percent), and the EU (−1.06 percent). In the case of Brazil, grains and oil seeds exports will see the largest drop because their CO_2 emissions intensity (1.53 kilograms [kg] per $) is higher than the average CO_2 emissions intensity of other Brazilian exports (1.11 kg per $). On the other hand, Sub-Saharan Africa will increase its global grains and oil seeds exports because it requires fewer emissions to produce them there (figure 4.10). Likewise, some of the world's biggest meat exporters from 2015 to 2019—Brazil (beef and chicken) and the

FIGURE 4.10 **Most Countries' Grain Exports Would Become Much Less Competitive If Greenhouse Gas Emissions Were Properly Priced, but Sub-Saharan Africa's Low-Emission Grain Industry Would Benefit**

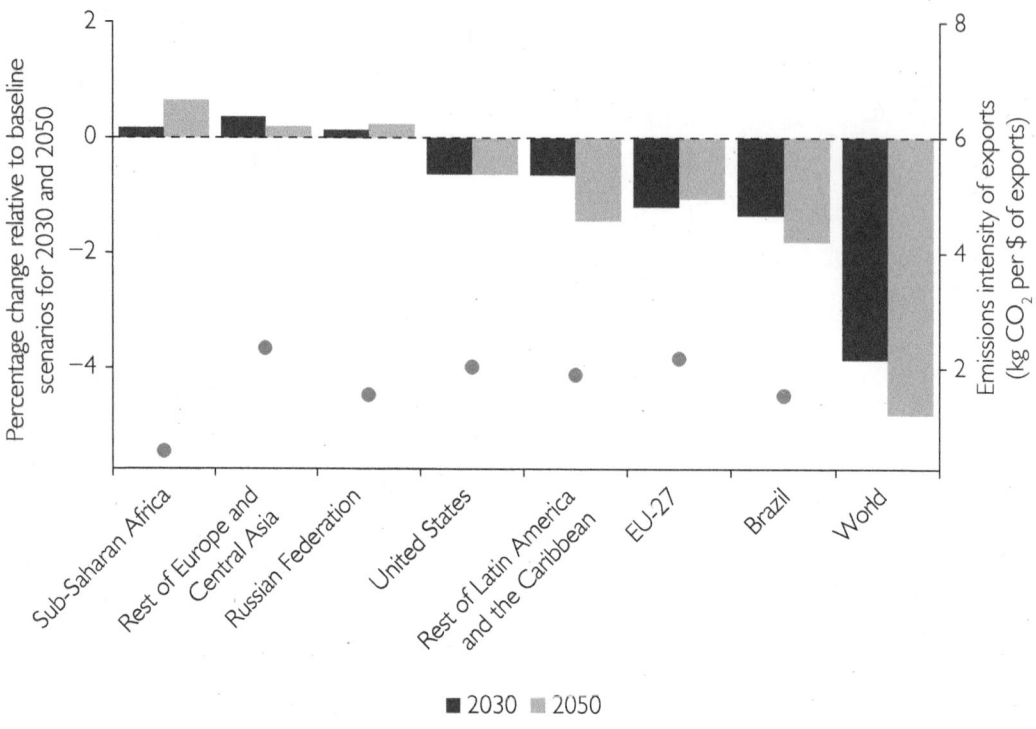

■ 2030 ■ 2050

Source: Data from Brenton et al. 2024.

Note: Figure shows the percentage change in grain and oil seed exports from the baseline projections for 2030 and 2050 (left axis) and the carbon dioxide (CO$_2$) emissions intensity of exports (right axis, ●). Carbon dioxide emissions intensity is for 2014. "Rest of Europe and Central Asia" refers to the region minus the Russian Federation and the EU-27; "Rest of Latin America and the Caribbean" refers to the region minus Brazil; CO$_2$ = carbon dioxide; EU-27 = the 27 countries that make up the European Union.

United States (pork)—do not have the lowest carbon footprints (figure 4.11). In fact, the emissions intensity of Brazil's beef production—after accounting for deforestation and land use change—is more than 50 percent higher than that of Australia's beef production and almost 2.5 times greater than that of the US (respectively, the second- and third-largest exporters). Russia and the US are the top two wheat exporters but also have the highest emissions intensities, with the use of synthetic fertilizer accounting for one-third of US wheat emissions and 10 percent of Russia's wheat emissions (Blaustein-Rejto 2023). Mitigation policies that target all three GHGs would reduce the comparative advantage for each of these countries.

Information: Improving GHG Monitoring Can Unlock Climate Finance

The measurement, reporting, and verification of GHG emissions is a complex and often inaccurate process. Agriculture emissions and carbon sequestration are not typically measured directly; instead, farmers use approximate models to estimate GHG emissions based on emissions averages for similar land uses or numbers of cattle, for example (Toman et al. 2022). A 2017 study demonstrated this point by showing that 119 of 140 developing

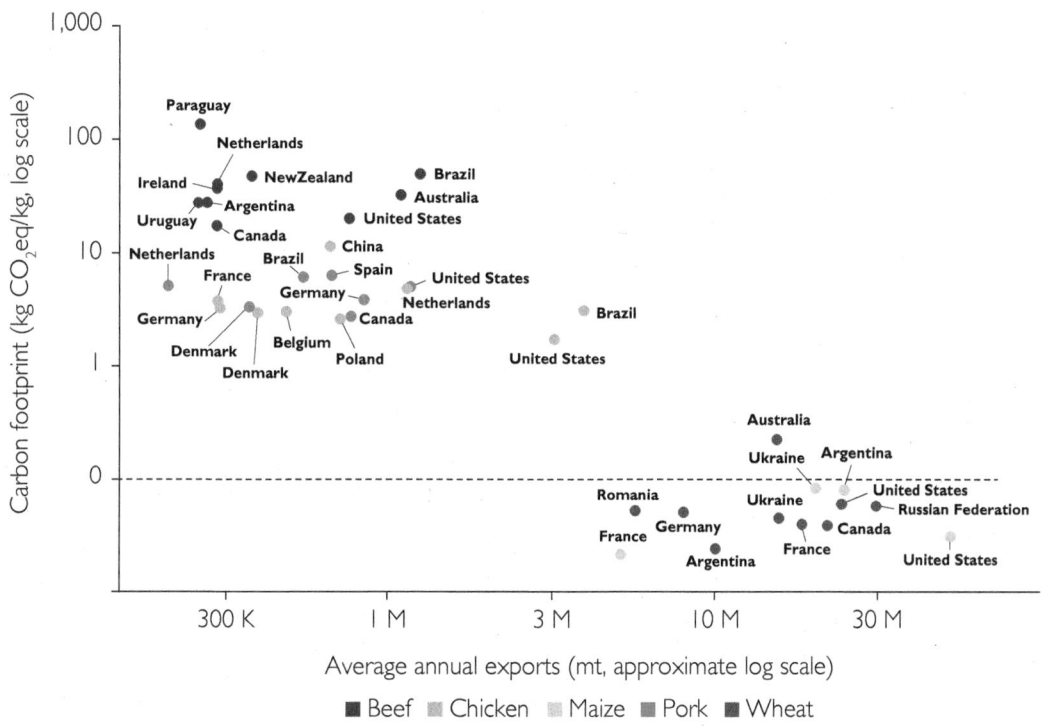

Source: Data from Blaustein-Rejto 2023.
Note: CO_2eq = carbon dioxide equivalent; K = thousand; kg = kilogram; M = million; mt = metric ton.

countries used fixed regional averages for emissions per head of livestock (Wilkes et al. 2017). The main output from these estimates is an approximate carbon footprint, or carbon balance, which is the emissions difference between implementing a mitigation strategy or not over a given period—usually 20 years or the time period assumed for carbon stocks to come to equilibrium (IPCC 2019a). Operators then use these carbon balances to derive an average of annual GHG emissions reduction. Formulaic measurements of emissions are needed because it is costly and challenging to directly measure the farm-level carbon content in soils or the amount of methane released by a particular head of cattle. In addition, climate conditions and other specific factors can be very different from one farm or microclimate to the next, often rendering these estimations inaccurate. Moreover, MRV systems must separately estimate the amount of GHG emissions reduced, avoided, and removed, and each MRV system may calculate these differently, so their calculations can vary greatly. For example, the scientific community has already developed dozens of GHG accounting tools for just the AFOLU component of the agrifood sector, and most of them serve a specific purpose such as informing food value chains, evaluating mitigation projects, sustainably managing land, or measuring the carbon footprint of a commodity (see reviews by Colomb et al. 2013; Toudert et al. 2018). MRV is especially challenging in low- and middle-income countries where the available data and methods are not suitable for reliably estimating GHG emissions (FAO 2019).

MRV is important at the farm level, national level, and international level. Farm-level operators, for example, must demonstrate if they have, in fact, reduced GHG emissions in order to access carbon markets or to verify they have maintained GHG levels below carbon tax limits. National decision-makers must also verify their GHG emissions reductions to assess progress against their NDC commitments. For example, the Paris Agreement's Enhanced Transparency Framework (ETF) requires parties and stakeholders to report on the different GHG milestones for the global warming potential of different GHGs in all sectors every two to five years.[17] At the international level, it is also necessary to estimate the impact of climate actions to determine progress toward achieving the Paris Agreement's emissions goals. This means estimating and reporting on national policies and their impact on GHG emissions reductions and carbon removal in tCO_2eq on a yearly basis over a long-term timescale—for example, until 2050.

More general monitoring frameworks are also important for tracking environmental impacts and project performance. MRV is specifically tailored to tracking GHG emissions, but in general robust monitoring and evaluation of policy implementation and project performance facilitates the food system transition. M&E frameworks are particularly important for tracking environmental impacts, such as air or water pollution from agricultural activities (Xepapadeas 1995). For example, the Danish government's M&E facilitated implementation of a policy package—which included market-based approaches, voluntary agreements, and command and control policies (Dalgaard et al. 2014)—to increase production and reduce water contamination from agriculture. These M&E systems set environmental targets, such as on waterway nutrient concentrations, and adopted processes to monitor them (OECD 2019c; Tan and Mudgal 2013). The M&E allowed the government to adapt its policy implementation based on continuous reporting.

Several constraints are holding back the development of robust MRV systems. A recent survey (UNFCCC 2019a) carried out by the UNFCCC's Consultative Group of Experts has revealed several constraints to developing national MRV systems. Most notably, these include limited dedicated budgets, data availability, technical capacity among practitioners, infrastructure to monitor emissions, and the aforementioned difficulties in accurately measuring GHGs. That said, a growing number of international organizations—including the World Bank, the UN Food and Agriculture Organization (FAO, n.d.), the UN Development Programme (UNDP), other UN agencies (the UN Environment Programme Copenhagen Climate Centre; UNFCCC GHG Help Desk), and other specialized institutions (for example, the Initiative for Climate Action Transparency, Partnership on Transparency in the Paris Agreement, and NDC Partnership)—are helping countries build MRV capacity to implement the Paris Agreement's ETF, which guides countries on reporting their GHG emissions, NDC progress, and other factors (WRI 2024). For example, the FAO's Nationally Determined Contribution Expert Tool provides 30-year estimates of annual and cumulated carbon removal and GHG reductions from climate actions in the AFOLU sector. Likewise, the FAO's Adaptation, Biodiversity and Carbon Mapping Tool is a geospatial tool that uses Google Earth to assess the environmental impact of NDCs, National Adaptation Plans, and other national policies (Schiettecatte et al. 2022). The Sustainable Rice Platform (SRP)—established by the United Nations Environment Programme (UNEP), the International Rice Research Institute (IRRI), and private companies like Olam and Mars—is using AtSource, a business-to-business sustainable sourcing platform, to monitor rice production's carbon footprint and expects that increased transparency will encourage sustainable consumer purchasing behavior.[18] A Singaporean climate tech venture is using smart carbon measurement platforms to minimize measurement inaccuracies (Olam 2022). It has measured over 230 million metric tons of GHG emissions across multiple sectors, including agriculture, in over 15 countries.

There are three main technologies that assist practitioners in measuring agricultural emissions. These include (1) remote sensing technologies, (2) ground-based sensors, and (3) ecosystem carbon flux measurements (Dhakhwa et al. 2021). Remote sensing technologies use satellite or airborne sensors to monitor the physical characteristics of an area by measuring its reflected and emitted radiation. These technologies should be accompanied by ground truthing (directly verifying the satellite images from the field) and have benefited from improved instrument calibration, atmospheric corrections, and machine learning. Measuring soil carbon and monitoring land management practices such as tillage and cover cropping through remote sensing technologies enable frequent, cost-effective monitoring. For example, Rabobank's Acorn program (Acorn, n.d.) supplements ground truthing with remote sensing to measure, certify, and monetize the biomass growth of planted trees and turn them into carbon removal units (CRUs). These units, after independent verification (Plan Vivo, n.d.), are then sold by Rabobank to the VCM. To date, the program covers 97,337 hectares, has generated 132,990 CRUs, and supports 65,487 farmers in adopting agroforestry practices. Similarly, agriculturalists deploy portable ground-based sensors in their fields to measure the soil's carbon content and other parameters of soil health. Likewise, ecosystem carbon flux measurements use a mass balance equation to estimate net ecosystem carbon storage. In the forestry sector, innovative digital approaches and increased data availability have enabled more frequent carbon stock monitoring; decreased the time needed to generate estimates from months to weeks; decreased the uncertainty of estimates; standardized estimates to make them comparable at different scales; and provided spatially explicit estimates (Forest Carbon Partnership Facility 2019).

Emerging digital technologies offer new opportunities to improve MRV. Digital technologies enable faster and easier access to information for all players in the agrifood value chain. This information flow incentivizes farmers to adopt production tools and systems that can mitigate climate change, contribute to environmental sustainability, and optimize productivity (Schroeder, Lampietti, and Elabed 2021). These digital solutions include the following:

Sensor technologies track data elements along the supply chain. These technologies should not be confused with remote sensing or portable field-based sensors discussed earlier. Sensor technologies have automated data collection capabilities that can track data elements in real time, such as the origin or use of water in the supply chain. These technologies assist end-to-end traceability of value chain products or inputs (World Economic Forum 2019).

- **Digital monitoring platforms** can measure the environmental impacts of various stages along the value chain. For example, these platforms can measure the carbon footprint of transporting produce from farms to stores by tracking the transport's speed, position, fuel usage, and other factors (Bilali and Allahyari 2018). These technologies have brought down off-farm MRV costs (Schroeder, Lampietti, and Elabed 2021) and assist online grocers and food delivery services in calculating their emissions (AP News 2023; Lerner and Filler 2022), and disclosing that information to conscious consumers or regulatory bodies (AP News 2023).
- **Blockchain and distributed ledger technologies** provide a secure and efficient way to record, store, and share supply chain data (World Economic Forum 2019). These technologies store "blocks" of transactional data across a shared network—allowing different users to access it simultaneously—and require every node of the network to verify and validate a new block before adding it to the network. As such, they also increase

the efficiency and transparency of the agricultural supply chain by decentralizing the food tracing process. This prevents users from tampering with or misusing data (Schroeder, Lampietti, and Elabed 2021). An improved information flow along the agrifood value chain can allow producers to reduce food waste by up to 30 million tons annually (World Economic Forum 2018) by offloading surplus or imperfect produce (Schroeder, Lampietti, and Elabed 2021). Blockchain-enabled contracts facilitate interactions among various players in the supply chain by cutting out intermediary roles (Hall 2017).

- **Artificial intelligence (AI)** technologies could lower information-related transaction costs and facilitate carbon tracking. AI technologies could calculate emissions reduction in real time using remote sensing data (Zhang et al. 2023), hyperspectral imaging (Wang et al. 2022), or raw portable sensor data (Linaza et al. 2021). With the proper raw inputs, AI models could analyze forest carbon projects or mitigation actions for both large-scale and smallholder operations. AI's potential application in agrifood system emissions reduction is still largely unknown.

These technologies can reduce MRV costs, but currently these costs remain high, particularly for small-scale users. Emissions measurement costs tend to vary depending on their purpose, geography, and value chain coverage. That said, verification costs are embedded in the fee structure of third-party verifiers and are well known. For example, establishing an MRV system sophisticated enough to track the supply chain emissions for carbon markets can range from $150,000 to $350,000,[19] which may be cost prohibitive for SMEs. This undermines an opportunity for smallholder farmers because MRV-type schemes in the energy sector have worked well in low-capacity contexts. For example, the Standardized Crediting Framework (Ci-Dev 2022), developed and supported by the Carbon Initiative for Development (Ci-Dev), is a streamlined, country-owned emissions reduction crediting framework that has been successfully piloted in Rwanda and Senegal for energy access programs. Fortunately, the development of good MRV practices (primarily through REDD+) and the adoption of the technologies described previously have driven down the cost of emissions measurement and enabled many countries to tap into carbon payments for large jurisdictions (Nesha et al. 2022). For example, in the forest and land use sector, satellite data allows users to more cheaply estimate carbon stocks across large areas. Moreover, lowering the costs of MRV of GHG emissions and soil organic carbon at different spatial scales holds untapped potential and could unleash opportunities in accessing carbon markets and developing consumer trust (IFPRI 2022).

Governments and the private sector can work together to drive down the costs of digital technologies and increase their uptake. The private sector leads in developing many of these technologies but cannot act alone, and the public sector also has a role to play (Schroeder, Lampietti, and Elabed 2021). Governments can enact policies around digital infrastructure that ensure strong rural connectivity, nondigital investments to power digital equipment, and digitization of public information systems. In Estonia, for example, mobile farm management applications found success when the government implemented an electronic identification and verification system. Farmers could easily access their state support funds while spending less time on paperwork and compliance reporting to payment agencies (Schroeder, Lampietti, and Elabed 2021). In Nigeria, the government provided fertilizer subsidies through e-vouchers sent to electronic wallets on mobile phones. The policy registered 12 million farmers in three years, increased the proportion of farmers that benefited from the policy from 11 percent to 92 percent, and created $192 million in government savings. That said, poor mobile connectivity in rural areas caused registration and validation delays, highlighting the need for wider investments in digital infrastructure (Schroeder, Lampietti, and Elabed 2021). Also, as digital technologies make data more available, there is a greater risk of acquiring inaccurate, manipulated, or falsifiable food chain information. To prevent this, private companies can provide raw data for open data sets and digital platforms, and the public sector can enforce regulatory measures to police data usage and data protection. This was the case in Indonesia's Rice Crop Manager project—a digital agriculture management platform that calculates appropriate nutrient and fertilizer application rates to reach target rice yields. IRRI and other Asian partners used an algorithm that relied on the private sector's raw data to calculate these rates, thereby boosting rice production in an environmentally sustainable manner (International Rice Research Institute 2023).

Innovation: Innovative Practices for Reducing Agrifood Emissions Are Expanding and Becoming Cost-Effective, While More Research and Development Can Continue This Trend

Nascent, innovative mitigation technologies could greatly reduce emissions in the agrifood system

There are emerging technologies that can curtail methane emissions from enteric fermentation. Among these, chemical inhibitors have reached the most advanced stage, and can reduce methane emissions by up to 36 percent for dairy cows (Pitta et al. 2022) and 70 percent for beef cattle (McGinn et al. 2019). This technology is expected to be commercially available in some countries by 2024, but further research is required on these chemicals' long-term mitigation impacts and the public's acceptance of them. As such, obstacles remain before chemical inhibitors are approved and administered on pasture systems (Nabuurs et al. 2022). Other emerging technologies to reduce methane emissions include feed additives that derive from red seaweed. Tests show that these additives can reduce methane emissions by up to 55 percent in dairy cattle (Stefenoni et al. 2021) and 98 percent in beef cattle (Kinley et al. 2020). So far, the market share for methane-reducing feed additives from seaweed is small, at only $47 million in 2022, but it is projected to grow by 57 percent with a market potential of $306 million by 2030 (World Bank 2023d). That said, there are still questions about the safety, palatability, scalability, and environmental implications of these additives. Other means for reducing methane emissions include injecting livestock with vaccines that target methane-producing microorganisms and breeding low-emission cattle. But these technologies are still in their early development stages and require much more research and testing (Nabuurs et al. 2022).

Technologies like cellular fermentation and plant-based protein can provide low-emission alternatives to meat. These methods can benefit animal welfare while reducing land, water, and nutrient consumption for livestock (IPCC 2022). A 2019 study (Fresán et al. 2019) reported that plant-based meats had mean GHG intensities of 0.21–0.23 kg CO_2 equivalent per 20 g of protein, which is much lower than red meat intensity. A literature review (Santo et al. 2020) on the GHG footprint of plant-based protein substitutes concluded that the median footprint was smaller than animal-based proteins and emitted 34 percent less than farmed fish, 43 percent less than poultry, 63 percent less than pig meat, 72 percent less than crustaceans, 87 percent less than dairy herds, and 93 percent less than beef herds (figure 4.12). Similarly, microbial or single-cell protein can be derived from the cellular fermentation of algae, fungi, or bacteria. These proteins are already being produced for human or animal consumption (Leger et al. 2021).

FIGURE 4.12 Cradle-to-Processing Greenhouse Gas Footprints per 100 Grams of Protein

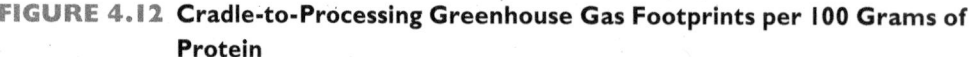

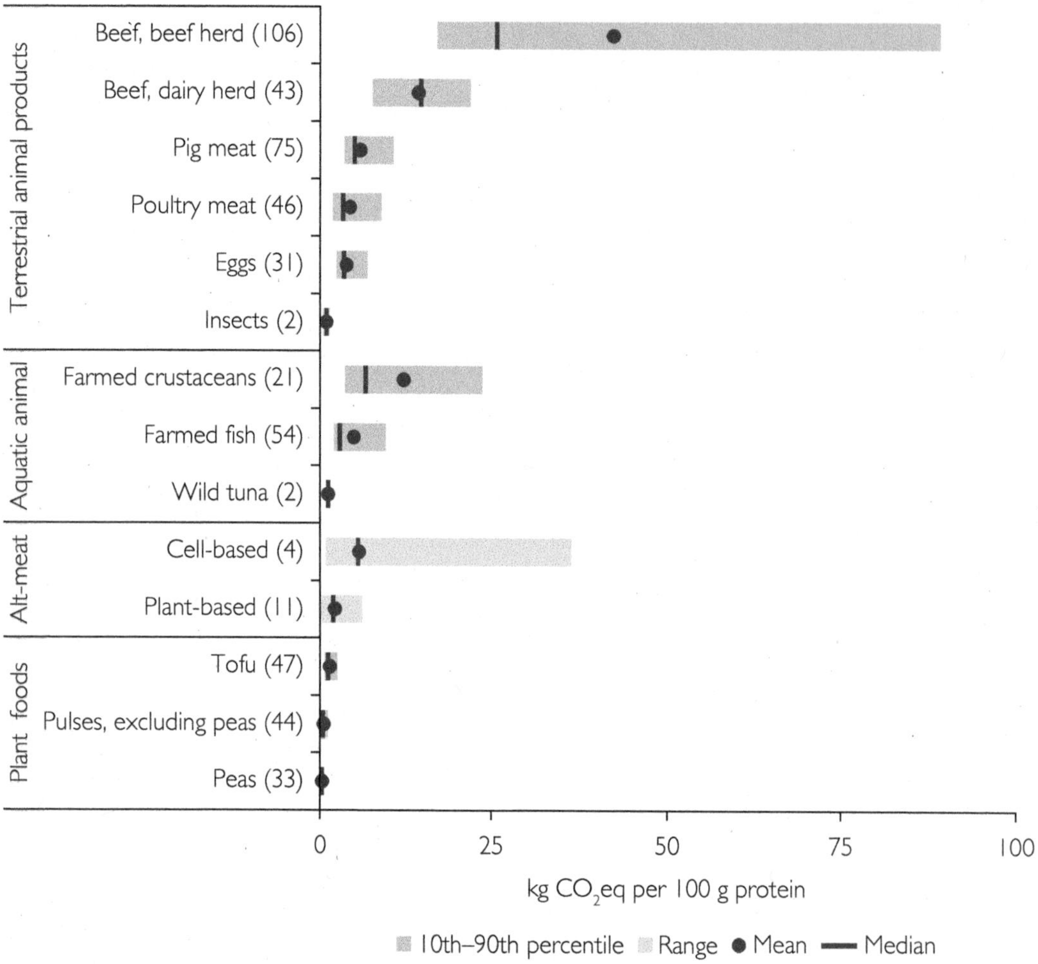

Source: Santo et al. 2020.
Note: Figure shows that plant-based meats and foods have significantly lower greenhouse gas footprints than red meat. Number of observations appears in parentheses. CO_2eq = carbon dioxide equivalent; g = gram; kg = kilogram.

Lab-grown protein, or cultured meat, could transform protein consumption practices, but its impacts on emissions are still relatively unknown. These innovative products are still in their early stages and their development is contingent on continued investments, technological growth, regulatory endorsements, and consumer approval. An analysis of laboratory-scale cultured meat production indicates that its carbon footprint largely depends on what energy source it uses during manufacturing (Sinke et al. 2023). However, there have not yet been any assessments of its emissions potential from large-scale production (Van Eenennaam and Werth 2021). Indeed, only a few countries have approved the sale of cultivated meat because of its many technical, ethical, and political challenges (Wood et al. 2023). Cultured meat also still has questions about its safety and health consequences (FAO and WHO 2019). That said, the cultured meat market is expected to grow by 44 percent annually, reaching a $3.4 billion market share by 2030 (Biotech Forecasts 2022). Other market forecasts range from $517 million (GlobeNewswire 2022) to $25 billion (Brennan et al. 2021) by 2030.

Other protein sources, such as algae, bivalves, and insects, have GHG reduction capabilities and offer important co-benefits. Algae and bivalves, including oysters, can provide food while purifying water systems. Proper management that considers spatial and temporal factors can maintain positive environmental biochemistry benefits. These considerations also help mitigate potential risks like toxin buildup, uncontrolled proliferation, and other adverse effects on ecosystems. Specifically, oysters remove excess nitrogen by stimulating denitrification, encourage efficient nutrient recycling, and likely have a negligible GHG footprint (Ray and Fulweiler 2021). Additionally, there are proposals to develop macroalgae aquaculture for marine biomass carbon dioxide removal, either by sinking cultured macroalgae into deep sea regions or using marine algae for biochar (Correia et al. 2020). Still, more research is needed on the duration of carbon capture and any potential side effects. Furthermore, Biofloc, a sustainable aquaculture system that utilizes microorganisms to enhance water quality and aquatic animal health, has emerged as a climate-smart aquaculture technology that sequesters carbon (Mana et al. 2016; Ogello et al. 2021). Likewise, insects present a viable protein source for both direct human consumption and as livestock feed. As a World Bank study (Verner et al. 2021) reported, the market for insect-based proteins is expected to grow at a compound annual growth rate of 24 percent, achieving an estimated value of $8 billion by 2030. Addressing concerns like food safety, adhering to regulatory frameworks, and enhancing consumer acceptance can assure future progress in this area. Proteins from insects, bivalves, and cultured meat tend to have relatively small carbon footprints (0.3–3.1 kg CO_2eq per 100 g protein). In contrast, algae like chlorella and spirulina require more energy, leading to higher emissions (11–13 kg CO_2eq per 100 g protein). For comparison, milk, eggs, and tuna have mean values ranging from 1.2 to 5.4 kg CO_2eq per 100 g protein (Babiker et al. 2022).

Scientists are also exploring the capacity of crop roots to sequester carbon. They aim to develop crops—like corn, wheat, and barley—that can absorb CO_2 by analyzing the roots' genetic traits (Mulhollem 2021). If successful and widely adopted, carbon sequestration from plant roots could sequester up to 746 million metric tons of CO_2 per year in US soils. However, these projections remain speculative, and further developing this technology would require $40–$50 million in annual funding until 2039 (Breakthrough Institute 2023). Such innovations in gene editing could also increase agricultural productivity and land use efficiency, but they must first navigate challenges related to biosafety, public acceptance, and regulatory clearances.

Indoor farming methods can lead to environmental benefits and reduce GHG emissions. These methods, including hydroponic farming, require little land, pesticides, or fertilizer (FAO 2021b). The FAO examined the GHG emissions of different agricultural products and found that lettuce cultivation in vertical farming, for example, exhibited a broad range of GHG emissions—from 0.16 to 25 kg CO_2eq per kg of lettuce produced, compared to 0.5 kg CO_2eq per kg of lettuce in open-air farming. This variance depends on the production method and the type of energy the system relies upon. A system run on clean energy would presumably be less emissions intensive than one powered by fossil fuels, and it would not require the same land and water resources as conventional agriculture (Verner et al. 2021).

There are a number of innovative methods for fertilizer production that could reduce fertilizer's GHG emissions. For example, enhanced efficiency fertilizers (EEFs) are designed to increase nutrient availability and reduce nutrient losses. They provide a controlled or gradual release of nutrients, thereby optimizing nutrient uptake by plants and minimizing potential negative environmental impacts and GHG emissions. EEFs can reduce on-farm nitrous oxide emissions by up to 27 percent. The cost-effectiveness of EFFs and their broader ecological effects, for example on aquatic ecosystems, require further research (Breakthrough Institute 2023). Scientists are also exploring the possibility of producing ammonia with a lower carbon footprint. Potential methods include electrochemical nitrogen reduction reaction and renewable energy-powered electrolysis. These methods can theoretically be scaled down for on-site, on-demand ammonia production on farms, reducing both the economic and environmental costs of storing or transporting fertilizers. Pilot projects, like wind-to-ammonia plants in Minnesota, show promise and suggest that "green" ammonia could be produced on a large scale (Ornes 2021).

Precision machinery could transform agriculture by reducing its emissions footprint and enhancing farmers' decision-making processes (Schroeder, Lampietti, and Elabed 2021). Precision agriculture refers to the use of satellite navigation (GPS), remote sensing, and on-ground sensors to collect site-specific data, which is then analyzed to guide planting, fertilization, pest control, and irrigation decisions for maximizing agricultural productivity while minimizing resource waste and environmental impacts. These sophisticated machines log agricultural management practices and capture data on nitrous oxide emissions, soil carbon sequestration, and other emissions data. Such detailed recordkeeping links production activities with their specific emissions and environmental impacts (Peterson 2023; Schroeder, Lampietti, and Elabed 2021). Empowered by sensors and AI-based analytics, precision technology can ensure the judicious use of fertilizers, herbicides, and pesticides, paving the way for innovative sustainable farming practices that minimize labor, emissions, and environmental damage.

Some of these technologies are already providing viable near-term solutions that are cost-effective. Near term refers to 2030 and, as noted in chapter 3, these measures are cost-effective at $100/tCO_2$eq or less. For example, installing N_2O-abating catalysts in nitric acid plants or producing ammonia from water electrolysis rather than from fossil fuel feedstock for nitrogen fertilizer production could contribute at least 300 megatons of carbon dioxide equivalent ($MtCO_2$eq) annually to the world's mitigation potential. Based on conservative estimates, plant-based proteins and lab-based meat have a 30–90 percent lower GHG emissions intensity than animal-sourced foods and could add 300 $MtCO_2$eq or more to the annual emissions reduction potential in the near term. On a farm, powering agricultural machinery with low-emission electricity sources has already become cost-negative while preventing 167 $MtCO_2$eq of emissions per year. Likewise, energy efficiency measures, coupled with the uptake of renewables, could save 330 $MtCO_2$eq per year and cut today's on-farm electricity and energy use emissions in half. For livestock, a 10 percent increase in feed digestibility could reduce 120 $MtCO_2$eq per year of enteric fermentation emissions, especially in pasture management systems in low- and middle-income countries. Also, if feed additive costs become commercially viable in the near term and are applied more widely to industrial livestock systems, its use would save an additional 380 $MtCO_2$eq per year in livestock-related methane emissions. In the post-production phase, converting cold chains and cooling to renewable energy sources could cost-effectively mitigate over 400 $MtCO_2$eq per year. The combined emissions reduction potential of these additional measures is an estimated 2,000 $MtCO_2$eq (2 gigatons CO_2eq) per year.

Research and development can drive future agrifood system mitigation technologies

Investing in R&D in the agrifood sector can improve productivity, reduce emissions, and generate other co-benefits. R&D can sustain the technological transformation of the agrifood system through novel and innovative solutions (Conti, Zanello, and Hall 2021; UNFCCC Technology Executive Committee 2017), which are sparse in the agrifood system compared to other sectors (Testa et al. 2022). R&D investment that focuses on emerging low-carbon technologies can reduce these technologies' costs and make them competitive with fossil fuel options (Bosetti et al. 2009). The causal link from R&D spending to accumulated knowledge and subsequently to productivity growth is well established (Alston et al. 2011). However, it is less well established that increasing R&D spending would reduce food system emissions, though several studies have started to show this (see, for instance, Adetutu and Ajayi 2020; Fragkiadakis, Fragkos, and Paroussos 2020; Verdolini et al. 2018). A recent analysis by the Breakthrough Institute (Baldos and Blaustein-Rejto 2021) suggests that increasing R&D investments in agriculture in the United States between 2020 and 2030, would increase US crop productivity, thereby increasing US exports and the country's international agriculture competitiveness. The analysis shows that doubling US agriculture R&D spending—equivalent to a 7 percent annual increase from 2020 to 2030—would cut global crop prices by nine percentage points, reduce cropland use by over 16 million hectares, and reduce GHG emissions by 100 million tCO$_2$eq per year by 2050 compared to business as usual. This exemplifies how productivity improvements in one country also provide global benefits. Another study shows that R&D is a cost-efficient mechanism to improve total factor productivity (outputs per unit of input) in crop and livestock production, which would reduce input-related emissions (Valin et al. 2013).

R&D spending on agrifood sector innovations has been minimal, even though the rates of return for such investments are high. Global investments in agricultural R&D totaled $56 billion in 2011. Public investments in agricultural R&D were $42.4 billion, with developing countries, LICs and most MICs, accounting for 53 percent of this amount. This investment was equivalent to 0.52 percent of agricultural GDP or $26 per farm worker in those countries. In HICs, this investment was much higher, equivalent to 3.25 percent of agricultural GDP, or $1,300 per farm worker (Fuglie et al. 2020). China spent the most on agricultural R&D, followed by the EU, the United States, India, and Brazil. Indeed, China's public spending on agricultural R&D surged fivefold from 2002 to 2019, growing from $1.3 billion to $6.6 billion, while the United States' spending decreased by about one-third over the same period (Plastina and Townsend 2023). The private sector's expenditures on agricultural R&D rose by a factor of three, to about $6 billion, between 1970 and 2013. As a result, private sector expenditures on agricultural R&D accounted for nearly 60 percent of total agricultural R&D expenditures in 2013. According to IEA estimates, public R&D spending on energy-related industries grew by 10 percent in 2022—to nearly $44 billion—with 80 percent devoted to developing clean energy sources. Private companies have also increased their total R&D spending for low-emitting energy technologies by around 40 percent and, overall, private R&D spending in the energy sector is growing faster than public R&D spending (IEA 2020). Fewer data are available on agrifood R&D spending (Heisey and Fuglie 2018), but one study suggests that from 1960 to 2011, governments in HICs invested more in agrifood sector R&D than did MICs (Pardey et al. 2016). But more recently, MICs have led the way (Heisey and Fuglie 2018). The limited investment in agrifood sector R&D is surprising given that the returns from R&D expenditures are high for both developing and developed countries: a one percentage increase in R&D investment yields an internal rate of return of 46 percent in developed countries and 43 percent in developing countries (Alston et al. 2000).

Investing in research and innovation can make even more agrifood mitigation options cost-effective. As noted earlier, several on-farm mitigation options have high cost-effectiveness potential with comparable marginal abatement costs (MACs) to widely deployed mitigation options in the energy and transport sectors. For example, limiting the overapplication of fertilizer is a cost-saving mitigation option both globally (McKinsey & Company 2023) and in major agrifood producing countries like Bangladesh (Sapkota et al. 2021), China (Nayak et al. 2015), and India (Sapkota et al. 2019). Its cost-effective mitigation potential is comparable to popular technologies like solar PV, electric vehicles, and heat pumps (Environmental Defense Fund 2021). Likewise, improving rice paddy water management is a low-cost mitigation option, in the $0–$60 per tCO_2eq range, which is comparable to onshore and offshore wind generation (Environmental Defense Fund 2021). Conversely, there are mitigation options that are technically feasible but not cost-effective (above $100 per tCO_2eq), making them ripe for innovation. For example, enteric fermentation represents 17.6 percent of agrifood emissions but options for reducing it currently have relatively low technical and cost-effective potential (figure 4.13) (Roe et al. 2021). As such, investing in effective technologies like chemical inhibitors (discussed earlier in this section) could make them more cost-effective. Similarly, alternative proteins from plants, insects, cultivated meat, or microbial fermentation could potentially lower emissions from animal-sourced foods (Mukherji et al. 2023). In these cases, policy incentives, public and private sector innovation, and large-scale deployment could accelerate R&D, generate economies of scale, and lower the financial costs of adoption. In fact, this is precisely what led to massive cost reductions in key climate technologies like solar PV panels (a reduction of 85 percent between 2009 and 2019) (NREL 2021) and lithium-ion batteries used in electric vehicles (a reduction of 89 percent between 2008 and 2022) (US Department of Energy 2023).

Public-private partnerships (PPPs) can be a particularly strong mechanism for driving R&D and technological innovations in the agrifood sector. The Paris Agreement calls for "collaborative approaches" to enhance and produce climate-related technologies.[20] There are many examples of PPPs expanding low-emission solutions. For example, the World Bank's Hydrogen for Development Partnership project has helped PPPs develop green hydrogen technologies in the agrifood system to sustainably produce ammonia (Kane and Gil 2022). In Morocco, an African Development Bank project developed PPPs that provided solar PV rooftop panels to rural Moroccans (AfDB 2024). In Uganda, the government leveraged a €90 million grant to generate up to $500 million in private investments for renewable energy generation projects (UNFCCC, n.d.-b). The public sector can also set fiscal and regulatory incentives to encourage private sector investments in R&D and innovation (OECD 2015). For example, the UK government provided £100 million to generate carbon dioxide removal technology (Department for Business, Energy and Industrial Strategy and Department for Energy Security and Net Zero, United Kingdom 2022). Similarly, the US government provided $100 million for a global competition to develop and demonstrate carbon dioxide removal technologies (XPRIZE, n.d.). In China, the government increased its public expenditure in agriculture R&D to $4.1 billion, making it the world's largest public investor in agricultural R&D. This reversed a policy that lasted until the mid-1990s of implicitly taxing agriculture to keep urban food prices low. Most of this R&D focuses on developing biotechnology and digital technology[21] to reduce fertilizer and pesticide use and promote low-carbon and circular economies (IFPRI 2022). There are also examples of nongovernment collaborations developing funds to reduce costs for carbon removal. For example, the NextGen Facility (South Pole 2021), a partnership between the South Pole member governments and several multinational corporations, is worth $925 million.

FIGURE 4.13 Innovation in Mitigation Technologies Targeting Enteric Fermentation Will Have a Large Impact on Reductions in Agrifood Emissions

a. Agrifood system emissions by system component

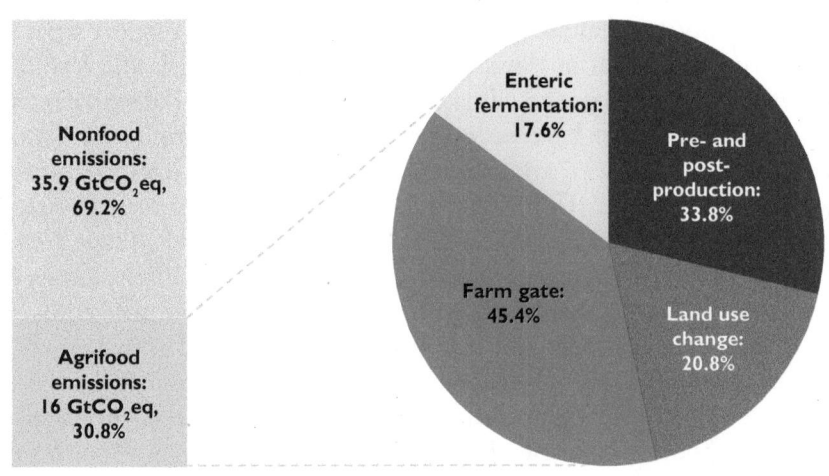

b. Technical and cost-effective mitigation potential

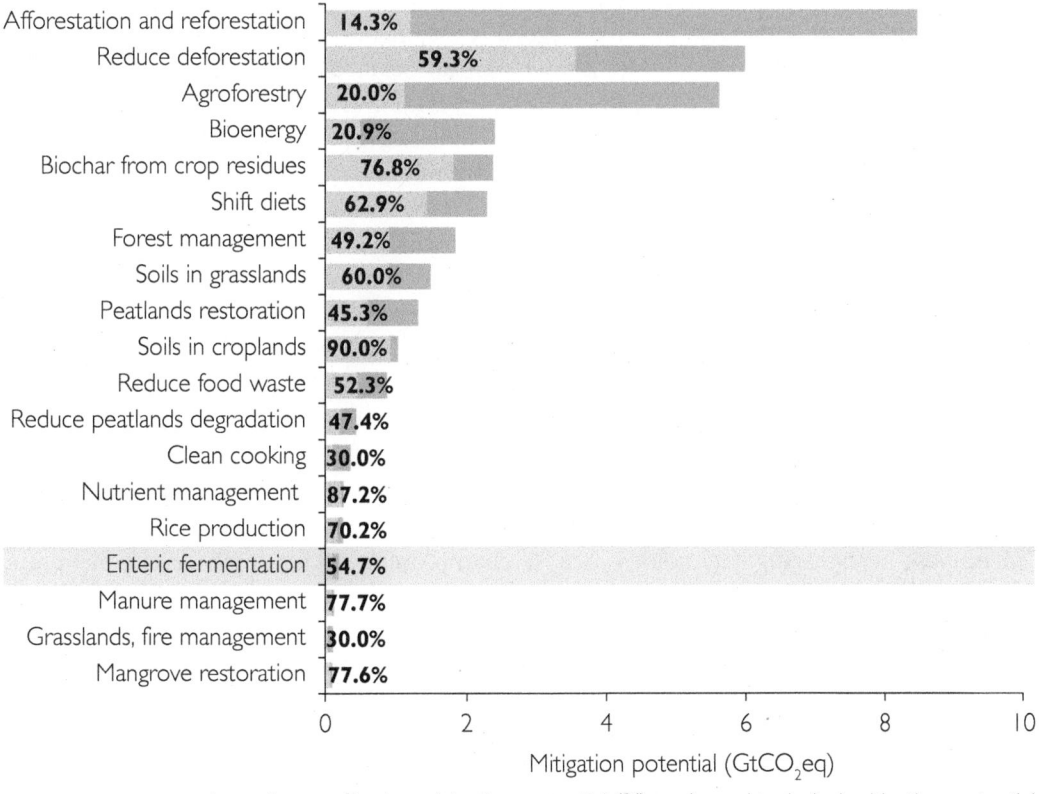

■ Annual cost-effective mitigation potential (%)   ■ Annual technical mitigation potential

Source: World Bank based on data from FAOSTAT 2023a and Roe et al. 2021.
Note: GtCO₂eq = gigatons of carbon dioxide equivalent.

Institutions: Climate Institutions Need to Rapidly Shift Focus to Mitigation through the Agrifood System

International frameworks

The global institutional landscape supporting climate action in the agrifood system is complex and operates at various levels. On the international stage, the UNFCCC's secretariat facilitates the global response to climate change. This includes intergovernmental climate change negotiations, which have led to landmark agreements on climate change mitigation, like the Kyoto Protocol in 1997 and the Paris Agreement in 2015. It also maintains the registry for each country's NDCs (UNFCCC, n.d.-a). The Intergovernmental Panel on Climate Change (IPCC) is the UN's technical arm for assessing global climate trends, providing the scientific basis for governments to take climate action. Other UN agencies like the FAO and the UNEP provide governments with technical support in mitigating or adapting to climate change, especially as it relates to the food system and the natural environment. In this institutional landscape, multilateral development banks (MDBs) like the World Bank, or bilateral donors like the US or German government aid agencies, provide both technical and financial support to countries for climate action. Intergovernmental groupings like the G20 and OECD have also committed to reducing agrifood system emissions.[22] Likewise, several coalitions of private financial institutions have aligned with the Paris Agreement. As of March 2022, at least 547 financial institutions, representing $129 trillion in assets under management, have announced net zero targets. These major coalitions include the Net Zero Asset Owner Alliance, GFANZ, Net Zero Financial Service Providers Alliance, and Net Zero Investment Consultants Initiative (Solomon 2022). These governments, businesses, and multilateral financial institutions all have complementary roles in creating the enabling environment for agrifood sector climate action (figure 4.14).

There are international frameworks to aid developing countries in acquiring technologies and knowledge to address climate change challenges. For example, one of UNFCCC's mandates is to promote and facilitate environmentally sound technology transfers to these nations, ensuring effective climate change mitigation and adaptation. This technology transfer is orchestrated through the UNFCCC Technology Mechanism, encompassing two pivotal bodies: the Climate Technology Centre and Network (CTCN) and the Technology Executive Committee (TEC). The CTCN serves as the operational facet of the UNFCCC Technology Mechanism, offering technical assistance and aiding developing nations in pinpointing, accessing, and deploying climate-centric technologies. In contrast, the TEC shoulders the task of delivering policy advice on technology dimensions, with roles that encompass recognizing technology needs, championing technology development and transfer, and guiding the realization of technology projects in the developing world. The financial mechanism, inclusive of entities like the Green Climate Fund (GCF), Global Environment Facility (GEF), and the Least Developed Countries Fund, bolsters technology transfer by ensuring ample financial backing to developing countries for various support avenues, prominently the technology transfer initiative (as detailed in the GEF and GCF reports presented during the last Conference of the Parties (COP). International development organizations also have a role in filling technological knowledge gaps and convening stakeholders. They are specially positioned to learn from implementation successes and failures and share that knowledge with stakeholders.[23] Some knowledge transfer mechanisms include the International Fund for Agricultural Development Smallholder and Agri-SME Finance and Investment Network [24] and the joint MDB-sponsored Finance in Common Summits.

FIGURE 4.14 Governments, Businesses, Civil Society Groups, and International Organizations All Have Roles to Play in Scaling Climate Action

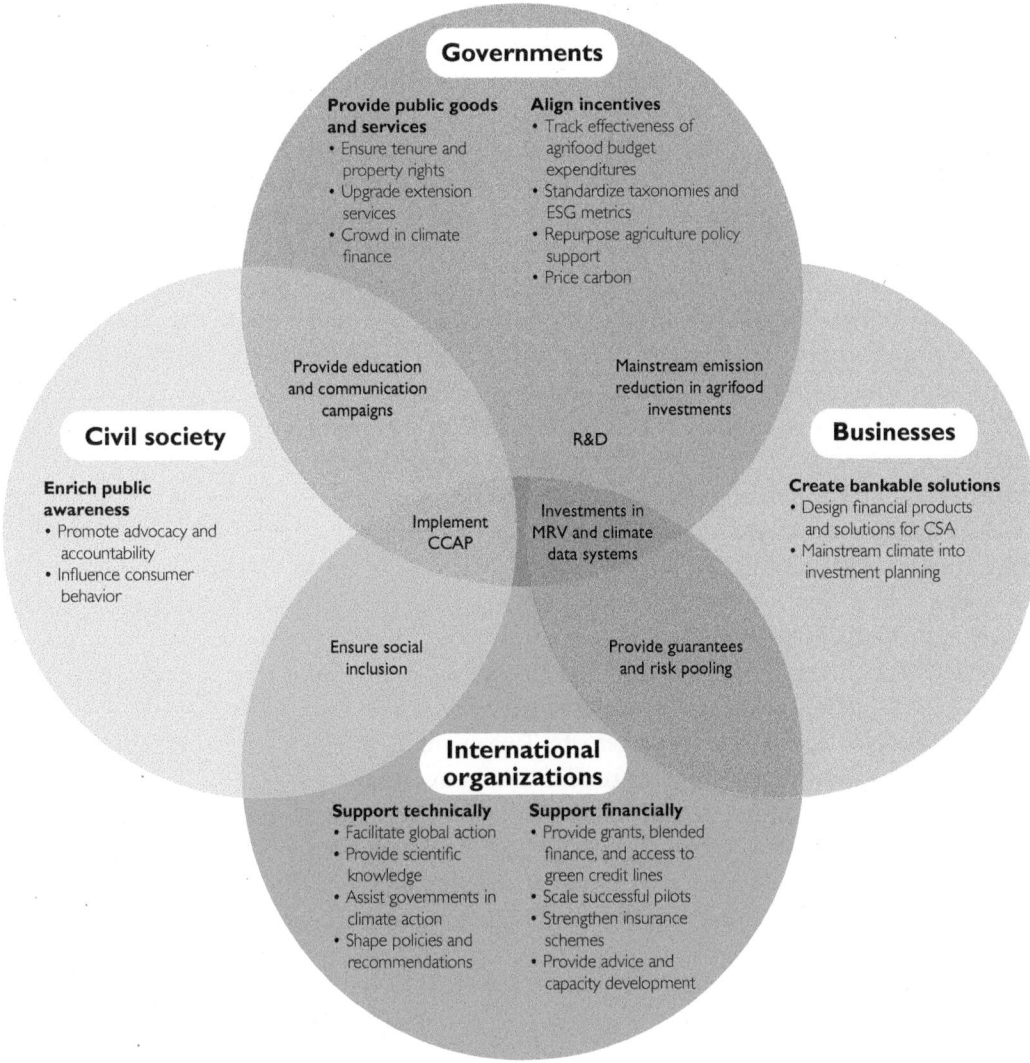

Governments

Provide public goods and services
• Ensure tenure and property rights
• Upgrade extension services
• Crowd in climate finance

Align incentives
• Track effectiveness of agrifood budget expenditures
• Standardize taxonomies and ESG metrics
• Repurpose agriculture policy support
• Price carbon

Provide education and communication campaigns

Mainstream emission reduction in agrifood investments

R&D

Civil society

Enrich public awareness
• Promote advocacy and accountability
• Influence consumer behavior

Implement CCAP

Investments in MRV and climate data systems

Businesses

Create bankable solutions
• Design financial products and solutions for CSA
• Mainstream climate into investment planning

Ensure social inclusion

Provide guarantees and risk pooling

International organizations

Support technically
• Facilitate global action
• Provide scientific knowledge
• Assist governments in climate action
• Shape policies and recommendations

Support financially
• Provide grants, blended finance, and access to green credit lines
• Scale successful pilots
• Strengthen insurance schemes
• Provide advice and capacity development

Source: Original figure for this publication.
Note: CCAP = Climate Change Action Plan; CSA = climate-smart agriculture; ESG = environmental, social, and governance; MRV = measurement, reporting, and verification; R&D = research and development.

The UNFCCC's mechanisms to transfer climate finance to developing countries continue to evolve. The UNFCCC established the GCF and the GEF to transfer climate and environmental finance to developing countries well before the Paris Agreement. Both funds support CSA investments in mitigation and adaptation, with GCF projects tending to have a broader scope within forest and land use–related sectors and GEF tending to have more targeted projects. The GEF's[25] current funding cycle (2022–26) allocates $5.3 billion to help LICs and MICs shift toward net zero GHG emissions and climate-resilient development, including through sustainable agrifood value chains.[26] The Kyoto Protocol established the CDM as a carbon offset mechanism geared toward HICs. That is, it allows industrialized economies to meet their emissions reduction targets by investing in mitigation projects in LICs and MICs. However, the CDM has rarely been used to finance agrifood system mitigation projects due to certain technical and political challenges in doing so (Dinar, Aapris, and Larson 2011). The UNFCCC also has a joint implementation mechanism, which is similar to the CDM but between countries from the same income group (UNFCCC, n.d.-c). Going forward, the UNFCCC, through Article 6 of the Paris Agreement, is moving toward Internationally Transferred Mitigation Outcomes, a tradeable carbon asset class. These combine financing arrangements between countries with market-based approaches that involve private parties, such as private financiers of emissions-reducing activities or private buyers of carbon credits. These mechanisms are meant to move emissions reduction efforts to where they are most cost-effective.

MDBs, national development finance institutions, and regional climate finance funds also facilitate financial transfers for climate action. Among these, MDBs represent significant sources of public climate financing, reaching a record of nearly $100 billion in 2022, an all-time high. Of this amount, $38 billion was for mitigation finance for MICs and LICs, but only $2.3 billion of this was allocated to mitigation in the AFOLU and fisheries sector. Incidentally, MDBs, mainly the European Investment Bank, provide HICs with nearly the same amount ($36.3 billion) for mitigation finance (Bennett 2023). To help track mitigation finance across lending institutions, a group of development banks developed the Common Principles for Climate Mitigation Finance Tracking in October 2021. National development finance institutions also play an important role, having provided $5.7 billion in public climate finance for agrifood systems, with 91 percent of this targeting mitigation projects.[27] There are also dedicated climate finance funds for donors to fund agrifood system mitigation efforts. Two examples are the BioCarbon Fund and the Amazon Fund (Sadler 2016). There are also risk management and risk pooling mechanisms that help countries gather resources to respond in the case of natural disasters. These mechanisms include the World Bank's Global Shield, the African Union's African Risk Capacity, and the Caribbean governments' long-standing Caribbean Catastrophe Risk Insurance Facility Segregated Portfolio Company, among others.

National institutions

National and subnational institutions often lack coherence, making coordinated action in reducing agrifood system emissions difficult. At the national level, policymakers on agrifood system climate action are frequently fragmented across various public institutions. For example, agrifood mitigation policy may involve officials from ministries of finance, planning, agriculture, environment, and climate change. This fragmentation makes it difficult to align economy and sector-wide policies. Some governments have attempted to bridge these institutional silos. For example, Zambia created an Interim Inter-Ministerial Secretariat for Climate Change (England et al. 2018) that involves "climate champions" from all relevant ministries (Antwi-Agyei, Dougill, and Stringer 2017). The lack of coherence is also evident among nonpublic institutions. For example, producer associations operate at different scales; some are geared toward smallholders and others toward large agribusinesses. Likewise, these associations tend to focus on specific products rather than the agrifood system as a whole. This segmented approach can foster institutional competitiveness and undermine institutional collaboration, as shown by preliminary results from the World Farmers' Organisation's global producer consultations (World Farmers' Organisation 2023). At the subnational level, the ability to offer comprehensive solutions for lower agrifood emissions is even more constrained because of an added level of division among different administrative areas. As discussed in the policy incentives section of this chapter, green jurisdictions—where subnational jurisdictions come together around climate action—can mitigate many subnational divisions. EAT Cities (EAT 2022) and the Milan Urban Food Policy Pact (2020) are two such examples. However, in many cases these jurisdictions are also fragmented or focus on competing or parallel issues. Further complicating subnational policy coherence are human resource capacity gaps at all levels (Khan, Gao, and Abid 2020).

Climate negotiations

Countries have engaged in contentious negotiations for decades over how HICs can financially support climate mitigation in MICs and LICs. These negotiations have mainly taken place within the UNFCCC and its subsequent agreements. At the heart of these negotiations is the principle of "common but differentiated responsibilities and respective capabilities." This principle recognizes that all countries have a shared obligation to address global warming, but that developed nations have a greater responsibility because they "acknowledge the responsibility that they bear in the international pursuit of sustainable development in view of the pressures their societies place on the global environment and of the technologies and financial resources they command."[28]

High-income countries pledged to mobilize $100 billion annually by 2020 to support developing nations in their climate actions at COP15 in 2009. The goal was further recognized in the Cancun Agreements at COP16 and reiterated and extended to 2025 at COP21 in Paris in 2015 (UNFCCC 2015). As a result, in 2020, the UNFCCC's initial target year for the $100 billion goal, developed countries provided $83.3 billion in total climate finance. This was a 4 percent increase from 2019, but still $16.7 billion short of the goal (OECD 2022a). Of the $83.3 billion, nearly half went to the energy and transport sectors, and 8 percent went to "agriculture, forestry, and fishing." Besides the amount, countries also discussed the form that the financial assistance should take, whether as grants, loans, or investments, and how these funds should be distributed and used. Questions about transparency, accountability, and effectiveness of the funds added further layers of complexity to the negotiations (UNFCCC 2022). In conclusion, there is a broad consensus on the need for financial cooperation to address climate change, but the specifics about who pays, how much, and in what form remain ongoing challenges in global climate negotiations.

Agrifood mitigation has only recently become a major part of climate negotiations (Rioux et al. 2023). The original text of UNFCCC appealed to parties to address emissions from diverse sectors, notably highlighting agriculture and forestry (United Nations 1992). Agriculture's vulnerability to climate variations was readily acknowledged, with the convention emphasizing the threat climate change poses to food security. However, a dedicated discussion focusing on the intersection of climate change and agriculture was not initiated until a decade after the UNFCCC's establishment (Drieux et al. 2019). Another 15 years would elapse before the Koronivia joint work on agriculture (KJWA) was introduced at COP23, emphasizing the sector's potential in climate responses (Sarku, Tauzie, and Whitfield 2023). Yet KJWA primarily underscored vulnerability and adaptation, with a limited focus on mitigation (Rioux et al. 2023). Notably, KJWA did not consider losses and damage from climate change, a highly contentious and politically sensitive matter (Sarku, Tauzie, and Whitfield 2023). Also, KJWA's scope was limited to agriculture and did not follow a broader food systems approach. During COP27 in Sharm el Sheikh, parties agreed to establish a new four-year work program on agriculture and food security (Wirkowski 2023).

Most developing countries have not adequately defined the financing needs for agrifood system adaptation and mitigation goals in their NDCs. According to an FAO working paper (Crumpler et al. 2021), 92 percent of NDCs outline qualitative financial needs, but only half explicitly state the monetary values they need to accomplish their NDCs. A mere 22 percent of NDCs differentiate between domestic and international financing. Furthermore, only 35 percent discern between adaptation and mitigation financing needs, with an even smaller fraction (18 percent) estimating costs for agricultural sector initiatives. That said, a striking 77 percent of countries highlight their need for technology development and transfer. Interestingly, nearly half of these technological demands pertain to agriculture, while the remainder focuses on resilient infrastructure and natural resources management. Meanwhile, 71 percent of countries say they require greater capacity for planning and implementing their NDCs. Over half of these capacity demands center on the agricultural sector, underscoring deficiencies in research, technical proficiency, educational outreach, institutional coordination, and financial mobilization.

Recent climate negotiations on agrifood systems have encountered several hurdles, but at the time of this writing there are signs of progress. At the forefront of challenges is the inadequate climate finance allocated for agriculture and food, leading to appeals from LICs and MICs for increased international support (Buto et al. 2023; Galbiati and Bernoux 2022). As noted earlier in this chapter, a significant portion of NDC targets linked to agriculture are conditional upon this international assistance. Moreover, many low- and middle-income countries express concern that ambitious mitigation action, like adopting carbon pricing for agriculture, might jeopardize food security and disproportionately burden smallholder farmers, issues that were discussed in chapter 2. The Bonn Climate Change Conference in June 2023 was particularly indicative of these challenges, with parties failing to reach a consensus on establishing a dedicated agricultural mechanism under the UNFCCC and being divided over adopting a comprehensive food systems strategy (World Farmers' Organisation 2020) versus a restricted agricultural focus (Chakamba 2022). Consequently, the conference in Bonn concluded without agreement, and discussions on these issues were postponed until COP28 in Dubai in December 2023 (UNFCCC SBI 2023). At COP28, a full day was dedicated to agrifood issues for the first time. One hundred and fifty countries, including some of the largest food producers and emitters—including Brazil, China, and the United States—signed a declaration on climate action that promotes a "shift from higher GHG emitting practices to more sustainable production and consumption" under Objective 5, and affirms the intention to integrate food and agriculture into NDCs.[29] However, COP28 did not lead to a declaration to integrate agrifood system mitigation into formal UNFCCC processes and negotiated texts. That said, the momentum generated at COP27 and COP28, coupled with the growing recognition of agrifood systems in NDCs, provides hope that these issues will assume the prominent role they deserve in climate negotiations. However, to maintain this momentum, HICs will need to step up their financial backing to ensure that countries fulfill their conditional NDC targets.

Multilateral development banks

MDBs and bilateral donors are positioning themselves to lead in climate action, but still lag in agrifood transformation. MDBs have been discussing reforms to increase climate investments since at least the early 2000s (Saxena et al. 2023). These efforts have gained momentum in recent years, as shareholders increasingly demand a global response to climate change. As such, in June 2021, the World Bank announced a new Climate Change

Action Plan 2021–2025 (World Bank Group 2021) with a target to allocate 35 percent of total World Bank financing to climate change. That same year, the Asian Development Bank raised its cumulative 2019–30 Climate Finance Ambition to $100 billion (ADB 2021). Similarly, the European Investment Bank pledged in 2019 to align all of its financing with Paris Agreement goals and to provide €1 trillion in cumulative climate and environmental sustainability investments by 2030 (EIB 2023). Bilateral donors are another source of climate finance for developing countries. For example, the French Development Agency, the German Agency for International Cooperation, and the Japan International Cooperation Agency have spent billions of dollars on climate change activities (Minister for Europe and Foreign Affairs, France Diplomacy 2022). They have also focused to a smaller extent on agrifood system climate action, providing $1.2 billion in total annual agrifood climate finance in 2019–20 (Chiriac, Vishnumolakala, and Rosane 2023). However, most agriculture-related climate support from donors is for adaptation and resilience building and still lacks explicit emissions reduction targets in the agrifood sector.

The World Bank, specifically the International Bank of Reconstruction and Development (IBRD), has steadily increased its climate financing in agriculture over the last decade. The World Bank's Agriculture and Food Global Practice (AGF GP) financing increased from nearly $2 billion to $5.9 billion between fiscal year (FY) 2013 and FY23. The AGF GP's climate co-benefits financing, which is the share of a project's financing that contributes to climate change mitigation or adaptation, has steadily increased (from $326 million in FY13 to $3 billion in FY23, with mitigation financing now accounting for $1.35 billion, or 45 percent of climate co-benefit financing.[30] This represents 23 percent of the AGF GP's overall financing, a nearly sixfold increase from 4 percent in FY13 (figure 4.15). AGF GP's climate co-benefits peaked at 59 percent, or $2.9 billion, in FY21 because of a surge in

FIGURE 4.15 **Both Climate and Mitigation Finance Have Grown Steadily in the World Bank's Agriculture and Food Portfolio, FY13–23**

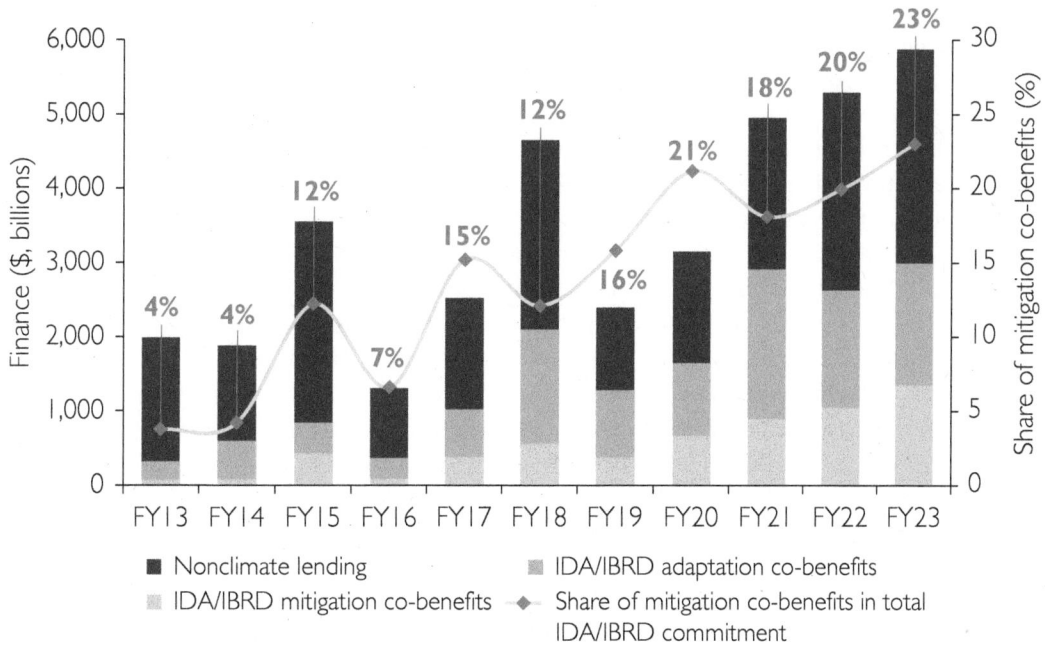

Source: Original figure for this publication.
Note: FY = fiscal year; IBRD = International Bank for Reconstruction and Development; IDA = International Development Association.

COVID-19 financing before leveling at 51 percent, or $3 billion, in FY23 as a share of the total International Development Association (IDA)/IBRD commitment. AGF GP's active project portfolio[31] has delivered an estimated $14 billion in ex ante climate financing (measured by climate co-benefits).[32] This accounted for half of its $28.05 billion in total commitments as of September 2023. Mitigation's share within AGF GP's active portfolio's climate financing was 36 percent, or $4.9 billion, compared to 64 percent for adaptation.

The World Bank's knowledge products help governments reduce their emissions, including those from their agrifood systems. Notable recent contributions are the World Bank's Country Climate and Development Reports (CCDRs), which were mandated by its 2021–2025 Climate Change Action Plan. CCDRs take a cross-cutting and whole-of-economy approach to analyzing a country's climate pathway, thereby advancing World Bank policy dialogues with country clients. These diagnostics help countries prioritize the most effective actions they can take to reduce GHG emissions and build climate resilience. The CCDRs do not exclusively focus on the agrifood system but have prioritized it for some countries. For example, the Viet Nam CCDR recommends repurposing public expenditure in agriculture to adopt lower-emitting crop varieties and production technologies, particularly for rice. The China CCDR recommends repurposing subsidies for expanding low-carbon land use, cutting food loss and waste, and increasing trade and food supply efficiency. The Brazil CCDR makes "curbing illegal deforestation and boosting agricultural productivity" one of its three climate-related sectoral priorities. Other CCDRs prioritize agrifood systems as entry points for adaptation actions. These include Bangladesh, Morocco, Peru, the Philippines, and the Sahel. As of this writing, the World Bank has published 31 CCDRs. The World Bank also produces CSA country profiles, which summarize a country's agricultural challenges and CSA options and inform World Bank investments. To date, the World Bank has published 36 country profiles (World Bank 2019). Similarly, the World Bank publishes CSA Investment Plans (CSAIPs), which identify climate-smart investments and policies for governments. So far, there are CSAIPs for 14 countries that have identified potential CSA investments of more than $2.5 billion and that could benefit over 80 million people (World Bank Group 2021).

The International Finance Corporation (IFC) is supporting the agrifood transition through private sector investments, partnerships, and advisory services. In FY17, using the World Bank's definition, IFC became the first private sector financial institution to develop a private sector–oriented approach to CSA. This led to a rapid increase in IFC's agricultural investments, from around 5 percent of its total investments before FY17 to 35 percent by FY22. Likewise, IFC's committed portfolio in agribusiness and forestry reached $4 billion by the end of FY23, supporting 247 projects.[33] This sector's advisory services promote climate-smart farming practices, certification schemes, and low-emission products and approaches. IFC's new CSA strategy under the World Bank's Climate Change Action Plan (2021–2025) focuses on improving productivity through precision farming and conservation agriculture; making livestock production more sustainable and productive; and reducing post-harvest losses in supply chains through improved logistics and distribution, appropriate packaging, modern storage facilities, and cold chains to reduce waste (World Bank Group 2021). Specifically, IFC supports clients who are committed to sustainability in the agrifood sector. For example, Nespresso and Mondelēz International are two of IFC's decades-long anchor clients. These partnerships strengthen community-level climate resilience by sharing regenerative farming practices and providing inclusive economic opportunities for smallholder farmers (Nestlé Nespresso 2022). Other IFC clients include Campbells, Hershey's, and Kellogg's, all of which are reducing supply chain emissions.

IFC has also made notable efforts to decarbonize the rice and livestock sectors in developing regions. In 2022, the IFC published its Practices for Sustainable Investment in Private Sector Livestock Operations and worked with FAO and the Carbon Trust to develop the Global Livestock Environmental Assessment Model, an online GHG calculator specific to the livestock sector. For example, in Zambia, IFC's client, Zambeef, expects to abate 14,000 tCO_2eq per year. In India, IFC works with a large global food commodity company to train smallholder rice farmers in climate-smart sustainable rice cultivation practices. These practices are expected to increase farmer revenues by $600 per hectare while reducing annual water use by over 450 cubic meters per hectare of rice produced. Likewise, in Côte d'Ivoire, IFC supports a large input provider's efforts to improve the land and water use capacity of 11,000 rice farmers and to increase the nutrient efficiency of their lands. The project hopes to improve rice yields by 20 percent.

Inclusion: Governments and Civil Society Must Work Together to Ensure the Agrifood System Transformation Is Equitable, Inclusive, and Just

A just agrifood system transition requires adopting adaptation and mitigation options that protect vulnerable groups, particularly during the food system transition period. A just transition in the agrifood system means reducing emissions while ensuring jobs, good health, livelihoods, and food security to those who cultivate, produce, process, and consume the world's food across different spatial and temporal scales (Baldock and Buckwell 2022; Tribaldos and Kortetmäki 2022). However, previous food system transformations have led to adverse health, social, economic, and environmental impacts (Tribaldos and Kortetmäki 2022). For example, there is a risk that CSA programs could disproportionately benefit large-scale actors at the expense of poor and marginalized smallholder farmers (Karlsson et al. 2017). Further, poorly targeted mitigation policies could also risk raising food prices, which accounts for a larger share of household budgets for poor people than for the well-off. Chapter 2 shows that these food prices may eventually decline, but the unequal burden-sharing in the short term could create a perception of unfairness and provoke a social or political backlash (Harvey 2023). Therefore, mitigation programs such as carbon payment schemes should be designed to directly benefit smallholder farmers and agri-SMEs—the food system actors that bear the cost and risk of adopting CSA technologies and practices. Climate-resilient development pathways can also reduce risks for vulnerable populations. The IPCC describes climate-resilient development pathways (CRDPs) as "development trajectories that integrate adaptation and mitigation" to reduce poverty, build resilience, enhance equality, and protect the environment (Schipper et al. 2022). There is evidence that CRDPs, such as agroecological approaches and diversified agroforestry systems, can achieve these goals simultaneously (Sinclair et al. 2019), but CRDPs have never been adopted at scale, so evidence on their ultimate effectiveness remains limited (Iiyama et al. 2018). Overall, a just agrifood system transition away from emissions-intensive practices should include procedural justice, distributive justice, and restorative justice (Tribaldos and Kortetmäki 2022). Each of these is explored next.

The transformation must ensure procedural justice

Ensuring procedural justice, or process legitimacy, requires ample stakeholder engagement. Engaging stakeholders draws on their expertise and accounts for their needs while ensuring that decision-making processes are democratic and accountable

(Tschersich and Kok 2022). Examples from countries transitioning away from coal energy demonstrate the benefits of stakeholder engagement and the pitfalls of failing to do it. For example, in Ukraine and in the United Kingdom, the coal transition lacked stakeholder engagement and as a result, reforms were either blocked (as in Ukraine) or beset by protracted conflicts between the government and unions or mine workers (as in the UK) (Stanley et al. 2018). By contrast, in Romania, government representatives engaged mine workers and community representatives to build local acceptance for mine closures by addressing the needs of workers, their families, and mining communities. Likewise, citizen "juries" and "assemblies" in France, Ireland, the United Kingdom, and the United States[34] helped convene stakeholders to deliberate on the potential risks of transitioning away from the coal sector and eventually informed emerging government policies. The World Bank and other development organizations have ample experience in local and community-led development. In one such example from Kenya, the World Bank–supported Financing Locally Led Climate Action Program is helping the most vulnerable communities work with governments and civil society to develop socially inclusive climate solutions. In Belize, the Belizean government established an Indigenous Peoples Desk and an indigenous technical team to oversee and strengthen stakeholder engagement in developing the REDD+ emissions reduction program (World Bank 2023a). These unique structures received ongoing feedback from Belize's indigenous peoples and informed project and program implementation (REDD+ Belize 2022). Such mechanisms can be replicated in other settings and among other marginalized groups and, when accompanied by grievance redress mechanisms (Carbon Brief 2021), can ensure that decision-makers are held accountable for delivering a just transition.

Assessing the potential risks and equity impacts of the agrifood transition, including mitigation actions, can contribute to the transition's procedural justice. There are several proven approaches to assessing these risks and impact. For example, poverty and social impact analyses (PSIAs) (World Bank 2003) explore the social and distributional impacts of policy reforms and program implementation, particularly on marginalized groups. Likewise, strategic environmental and social assessments (SESAs) are useful in bringing together analytical and participatory approaches to systematically analyze social and environmental risks from policies or programs (World Bank 2023e). Both of these analytical tools identify risks and risk mitigation measures to ensure that the food transition does not exacerbate inequality or the vulnerability of marginalized populations. Behavioral science can also inform these assessments by contemplating cultural and historical constraints within vulnerable social groups and by focusing on adapting behaviors rather than radically changing them (Heimlich and Ardoin 2008). Ethnography and human-centered design are methodologies that behavioral scientists use to understand the behavioral barriers to adopting sustainable practices and to design interventions based on people's real experiences (World Bank 2022a). For example, the Mind, Behavior and Development Unit at the World Bank has applied exploratory fieldwork in Mozambique and Nepal to diagnose and understand the behavioral bottlenecks affecting women's participation in productive activities (World Bank 2022a).

The transformation must ensure distributive justice, especially in agrifood system employment

Benefit sharing mechanisms can ensure distributive justice and the equitable distribution of benefits from food system transformations. Benefit sharing distributes the benefits and burdens from the transition equitably among those affected, ensuring that no one is left behind. For instance, the benefits of modern irrigation systems should be shared by all farmers, not only higher earning farmers or businesses that can afford upfront capital investments (Izzi 2021). Similarly, CSA measures that conserve natural resources, such as forests and fisheries, need to consider the potentially outsized impacts on the users of those resources, such as forest communities and artisanal fisheries (Bennett and Dearden 2014; Holmes and Cavanagh 2016). Lessons on benefit sharing can be drawn from countries implementing Forest Carbon Partnership Facility REDD+ programs. Following more than a decade of REDD+ readiness and implementation actions to reduce deforestation and forest degradation, many forested countries are now starting the results-based payments phase. However, before receiving these payments, each country must prepare a benefit sharing plan (BSP). These plans lay out the basic strategies by which funds will be distributed. The objective is to distribute these funds equitably, while also maximizing emissions reduction (Forest Carbon Partnership Facility, n.d.). BSPs are designed in close collaboration with public and private sector actors and forest-dependent communities. A review of BSPs in REDD+ projects highlighted the importance of encouraging and ensuring the inclusion of women, indigenous peoples, and other marginalized groups (World Bank 2019). The review also highlighted the importance of improving land tenure security, since land ownership determines a person's eligibility to participate in benefit sharing (World Bank 2019). This is particularly important for indigenous peoples because land and resource ownership increase climate resilience, food sovereignty, and food security and preserve indigenous peoples' cultural identity (FAO and Alliance of Biodiversity International and CIAT 2021). Stable land tenure is also a global public good that encourages landowners to protect forests and biodiversity (Walker et al. 2020) and mitigate climate change (IPCC 2019b). In relation to food systems transformation, benefit sharing arrangements could compensate farmers or indigenous peoples for traditional practices like seed exchanges that maintain native species diversity and ensure stable and ecologically sustainable food supplies (FAO and Alliance of Biodiversity International and CIAT 2021).

Agrifood system mitigation can accelerate the transition of farm work to higher quality nonfarm jobs, while still increasing food production. Currently, most agrifood system labor is in MICs, amounting to about 900 million agrifood sector workers across 108 countries. On average this is over 8 million agrifood sector workers per country. In LICs, there is upward of 130 million workers across 28 countries, or about 4.5 million workers per country. In HICs, there are only about 75 million agrifood sector workers across 77 countries, or fewer than a million workers per country (figure 4.16). That said, the highest share of on-farm work is in LICs, at over 90 percent, and the highest share of off-farm work is in HICs, at 74 percent. This reflects a well-established pattern of structural transformation: agricultural work declines as a share of employment, as per capita country incomes rise (Morris et al. 2020). International Model for Policy Analysis of Agricultural Commodities and Trade (IMPACT) macroeconomic simulations to 2050 project that under the business-as-usual scenario, every major global region will likely see reductions in agricultural employment even without mitigation action (figure 4.17). Figure 4.17 also shows that the movement of labor out of agriculture will likely be accelerated if the world adopts a comprehensive set of mitigation practices, including investments in agricultural R&D, water use efficiency, no-till agriculture, and a greener

FIGURE 4.16 **Most Employment in the Agrifood Sector Is in Middle-Income Countries, and Both Low- and Middle-Income Countries Have Large Shares of Workers Working on Farms**

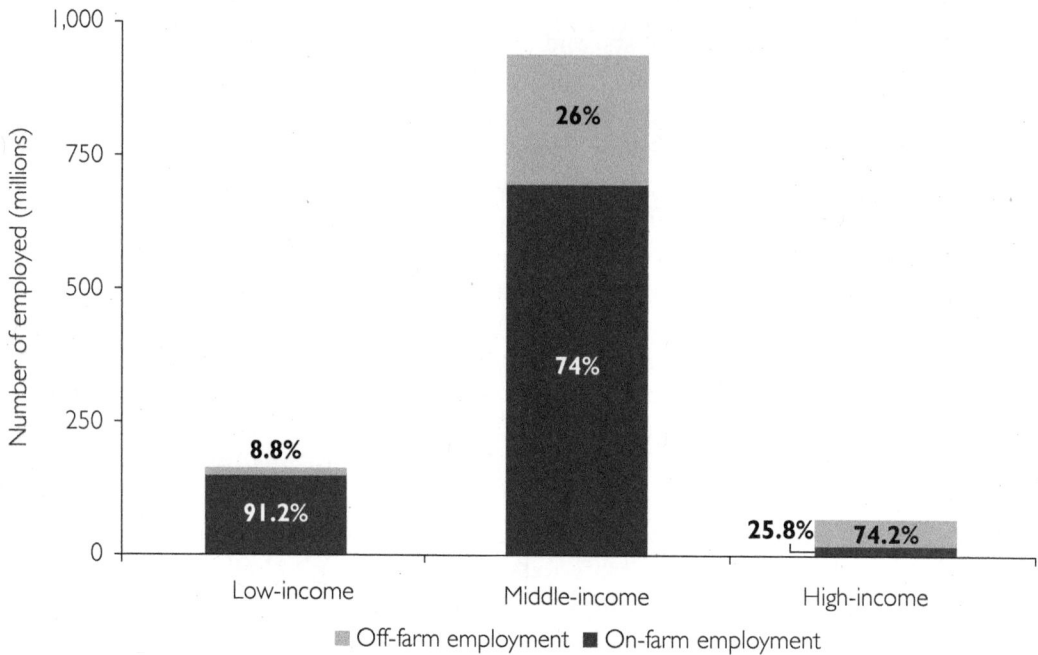

Source: Data from Nico and Christiaensen 2023.

market infrastructure. Overall, this comprehensive scenario would simultaneously raise global agricultural production by 11.5 percent and reduce agricultural employment by 4.3 percent, leading to 101 million fewer on-farm workers relative to business as usual. The largest projected declines in agricultural employment would be in South Asia (at 22.4 percent) and Sub-Saharan Africa (at 21.9 percent), reflecting the large shares of farm employment in those regions (figure 4.17). However, the comprehensive mitigation scenario would likely create a double benefit of (1) increasing higher-quality off-farm employment, with some jobs moving to agrifood manufacturing and services, and (2) increasing agrifood production, especially if accompanied by investments in value chain development (Nico and Christiaensen 2023).

Some agriculture workers are likely to transition to work in emerging jobs in a low-emission agrifood system. The agrifood system transformation will likely create new types of high-value jobs in the agricultural sector or add value to traditional livelihoods. For example, sustainable forest management, long practiced by forest communities, would be more valuable under a low-emission development pathway by promoting mitigation objectives while providing long-term livelihoods to local communities and enhancing their resilience to climate risks (Turnhout et al. 2017). Likewise, as shown in chapter 2, adopting CSA practices in areas with low agricultural mechanization, such as parts of Sub-Saharan Africa, will increase demand for on-farm labor. Similarly, reducing GHG

FIGURE 4.17 Employment Is Moving Out of Agriculture with or without Climate Change and Mitigation Policies

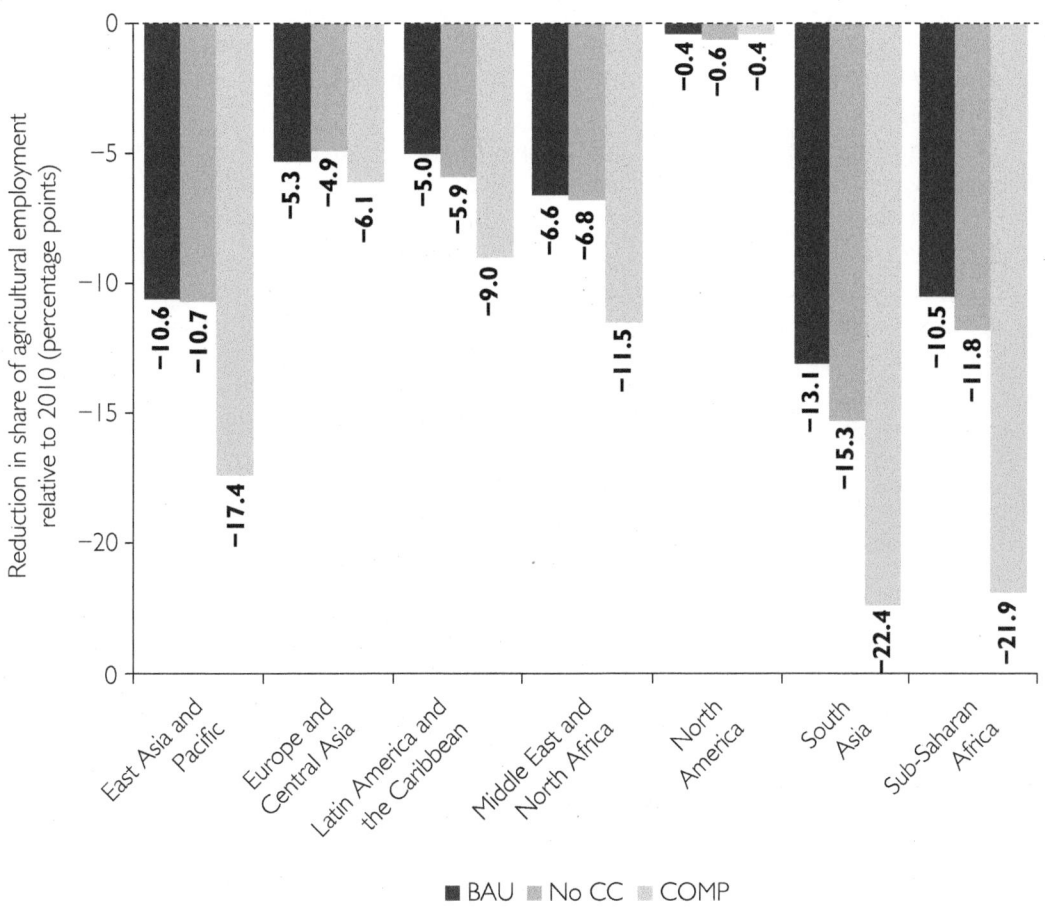

Source: Data from original analysis carried out by the Food and Agriculture Organization for this report.
Note: Figure shows by region the reductions by 2050 of agricultural employment under a business-as-usual (BAU) scenario, a scenario without climate change (No CC), and a scenario with a comprehensive package of agrifood system mitigation investments (COMP).

emissions from agriculture is often achieved by sustainable intensification technologies, which are innovations that increase agricultural productivity and have positive social and environmental impacts. The increased productivity could also reduce current needs for on-farm labor, notably self-employed and wage labor. However, this low-carbon transition will also create stable, higher-paying jobs in agrifood manufacturing and services, which tend to expand as agricultural productivity and production grow (Christiaensen, Rutledge, and Taylor 2021; Fuglie et al. 2020). Significantly, the transition to a low-emission agrifood system is also likely to generate a skills gap for farm workers. For example, shifting rice production from conventional transplanting to direct seeding or machine transplanting (Gartaula et al. 2020) reduces the need for field labor, and adopting precision agriculture requires new labor skills that the current labor force may not have (Rotz et al. 2019). The Canadian government is currently investing in climate-smart and precision technologies that "will contribute to Canada's place as a world leader in agricultural clean technology" (Agriculture and Agri-Food Canada

2018), but appropriate education and lifelong training will be required to avail those jobs (Rotz et al. 2019). That said, there is a high likelihood that current agricultural workers will be able to transition into other jobs within the broader agrifood system, including emerging higher-skill jobs (Townsend et al. 2017). However, workers transitioning into dissimilar labor sectors require more time and this entails higher costs for training and networking.

Governments can help agricultural workers transition to higher quality agrifood sector jobs by investing in skills and capacity and bolstering mobility assistance. This requires (1) boosting agricultural extension, advisory services (Azzarri and Nico 2022), and farmer training (Rotz et al. 2019), (2) facilitating the adoption of CSA technologies and practices (Nico and Christiaensen 2023), and (3) reinforcing social protection programs to assist labor migrants in this transition. The tangible impact of capacity-building initiatives is exemplified by a study in northwest Bangladesh, where a targeted training program for rural households, when paired with a stipend or internship, led to a significant uptick in rural worker employment in urban garment factories (Shonchoy, Raihan, and Fujii 2017). Even a developed country like Canada, with its well-developed system of high school and post-secondary education for preparing youth to enter the workforce, acknowledges that the country lacks proper skills development support for workers in their productive years (Advisory Council on Economic Growth, Government of Canada 2017). In response, the Canadian government established the Future Skills Centre to research future skill needs and test new approaches to skills development. It is committed to ensuring that government policies meet the evolving needs of employers and job seekers (Employment and Social Development Canada 2023). Several studies argue that investing in training and skills development, especially for marginalized demographics like smallholder farmers, is a pathway to a more inclusive workforce (Rotz et al. 2019). Social protection strategies that diminish barriers to geographic mobility can also facilitate workers to transition to off-farm employment. These strategies include ensuring safe transportation options (Cheema et al. 2020), implementing legal and streamlined money transfer mechanisms (Batista and Vicente 2020), promoting jobs in high-value sectors (Townsend et al. 2017) and climate-smart agriculture (World Bank 2015), and providing information on safe work-related migration practices (Strohmaier et al. 2016).

The informal jobs sector can buffer the agriculture sector from job losses and food insecurity and assist with short-term job placement. From a macro level, diversified economies are most likely to absorb surplus labor, while income subsidies and safety nets can help ease the transition. The informal job sector would also play an important role during any agrifood system transition. For example, in developing countries, informal midstream businesses—including traders, transporters, and street vendors—help maintain affordable food supplies for low-income households (Termeer et al. 2022). Studies have shown that implementing mitigation policies alone can harm food security at times when food demand is increasing (Hasegawa et al. 2018; Springmann et al. 2017). In Cape Town, South Africa, during the COVID-19 pandemic and related lockdowns, the informal food sector acted as a buffer for food supply disruptions by distributing food aid, starting urban farming, and engaging in regenerative environmental practices (Kushitor, Alimohammadi, and Currie 2022). That said, promoting informal sectors contributes to other negative outcomes, such as poor working conditions, higher rates of poverty and exclusion, and limited access to knowledge, technology, social services, and productive assets (Termeer et al. 2022). Other complementary actions such as investing in R&D to increase food output (Fuglie et al. 2022), reallocating carbon credits or tax revenues to improve health and nutrition (Fujimori et al. 2018), or repurposing agricultural investments toward food security safety nets or direct farmer payments (Gautam et al. 2022) can reduce the adverse effects that mitigation policies can have on food security.

The transformation must ensure restorative justice

Supporting groups that historically have not benefited from the agrifood system, such as smallholder farmers, will help ensure the transformation's restorative justice. The transformation of agrifood systems creates an opportunity to redress preexisting social inequalities by empowering marginalized groups to access new opportunities in the agrifood system. These marginalized groups include women, ethnic minorities, nomadic and pastoralist groups, or geographically isolated or smallholder farms (Ortiz Valverde, Mesias, and Peris-Blanes 2022). The history of agrifood systems shows that they are riddled with perverse and costly policies such as public food price support, production subsidies, import controls, export subsidies, proposed technologies mismatched to the needs and capacities of small-scale farmers, and the inaccurate accounting of food system externalities. All of these issues distort food costs and prices and subsequently production decisions; they tend to benefit large landholders and agroprocessors, not smallholder farmers.[35] Moreover, just as the current food system exacerbates social inequalities, so too can policies to advance low-emission development pathways in agriculture if they are not responsive to the needs and priorities of those most vulnerable (Eriksen et al. 2021; Hasegawa et al. 2018; Markkanen and Anger-Kraavi 2019; Schipper 2022). In coastal Bangladesh, for example, the introduction of shrimp aquaculture as an adaptive response to rising sea levels and salt water intrusion has benefited local elites involved in commercial shrimp production but has dispossessed smallholder rice farmers of their productive land and agrarian livelihoods (Paprocki 2018). In Madagascar, REDD+ projects impact smallholders and forest communities, but the compensation for REDD+ impacts continues to favor local elites, despite social safeguards (Poudyal et al. 2016). However, experience shows that there are ways to preserve the restorative justice in a food system transformation. In Bolivia, for example, smallholder farmers improved their bargaining power in output markets, which are typically controlled by intermediaries and large agroprocessors (Jacobi, Rist, and Altieri 2017). Literature also shows that smallholders must have well-functioning farmer's networks and co-learning platforms that are supported by local and national governments and civil society organizations (HLPE 2019).

Governments should partner with impacted communities and local governments to ensure that the food system transformation delivers local social empowerment. Local partnerships can maintain support among those who are concerned they will be unfairly impacted by agrifood mitigation practices. Moreover, local communities and indigenous people are the best-placed stewards of natural ecosystems, biodiversity conservation, and low-emission land management practices. For example, there are between 200 and 500 million pastoralists globally (IPCC 2019c) who ensure food security in regions where crops are difficult to cultivate. In the Sahel, pastoralists supply 65 percent of the meat and 70 percent of the milk sold on local markets (FAO 2023) while protecting soil fertility and biodiversity (FAO 2021; Mekuyie, Jordaan, and Melka 2018). Studies from West Africa

BOX 4.1 Agrifood Emissions In-Depth: Ethiopia

Ethiopia's rich pastoralist history and cultural reverence for cattle help make it a major low-income country (LIC) emitter of agrifood system greenhouse gases. Ethiopia is the second largest agrifood system emitter among LICs and among the top 20 agrifood system emitters in the world (FAOSTAT 2023b). Ninety-four percent of Ethiopia's greenhouse gas emissions come from its agrifood system (FAOSTAT 2023b), with livestock-related emissions, from enteric fermentation and manure, accounting for two-thirds of its agrifood system emissions. This is because Ethiopia has the largest livestock population in Africa. There are several reasons for this (Mekuriaw and Harris-Coble 2021). First, livestock is a critical source of income for a large share of Ethiopia's population (Behnke and Metaferia 2011) and is a symbol of wealth and status within the country's large pastoralist populations (Coppock 1994). Second, cattle hold important traditional and cultural significance among certain segments of Ethiopian society, for example, among the Oromo (Abbas 2012) and Sidama people (Molvaer 1995). Unfortunately for the planet, Ethiopia's beef production is extremely GHG intensive, emitting close to 200 kg of carbon dioxide equivalent (CO_2eq) per kilogram of beef. In comparison, beef produced in the United States emits around 13 kg CO_2eq per kilogram. On the positive side, this means that Ethiopians have great potential to reduce its livestock emissions by simply enhancing livestock productivity. They can do this by improving feed quality, supplementing feeds, improving livestock health management, and switching to more productive animal breeds. These measures would increase livestock productivity by up to 225 percent, while reducing emission intensity by as much as 65 percent and generating important economic returns (FAO and New Zealand Agricultural Greenhouse Gas Research Centre 2017). However, Ethiopia's nationally determined contributions are not that ambitious in this regard, aiming simply to maintain the current agriculture-related emissions levels while increasing output. That said, the country's Long-Term Low Emission and Climate Resilient Development Strategy does prioritize reducing agrifood sector emissions.

FIGURE B4.1.1 Ethiopia's Agrifood System Emissions, 1990–92 and 2018–20

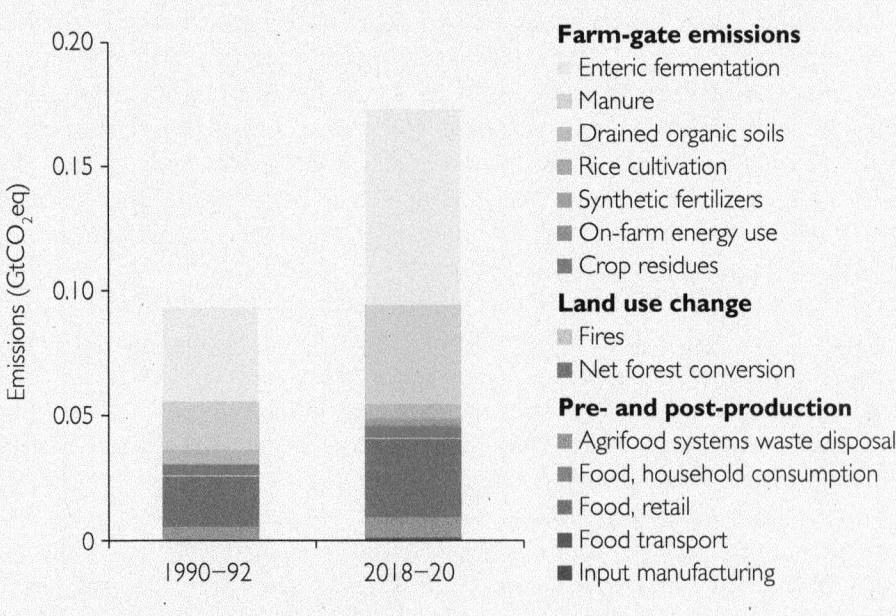

Source: World Bank based on data from FAOSTAT (2023a).
Note: GtCO₂eq = gigatons of carbon dioxide equivalent.

show that local farmer partnerships (Reij, Tappan, and Smale 2009) reversed tree cover and diversity losses while increasing soil carbon, crop yields, and household incomes (Bayala et al. 2020; Garrity et al. 2010; Haglund et al. 2011). The World Bank's Financing Locally Led Climate Action Program in Kenya builds partnerships between citizens and local governments to assess climate risks and identify socially inclusive mitigation and adaptation solutions (Arnold and Soikan 2021). Through this process, local partnerships identified 100 public goods investments that reached more than 500,000 beneficiaries, mostly women. Local partnerships are especially valuable when they tap into local knowledge. For example, many studies from Africa demonstrate how farmers use traditional knowledge to adapt to and mitigate climate change impacts (Reij and Waters-Bayer 2014). As such, recovering the knowledge of indigenous farmers and native communities, where it still survives, and applying it to the food system transformation would yield emissions benefits while building local ownership for low-emission practices (Borras, Franco, and Nam 2020). Box 4.1 presents an example of an African country dealing with GHG emissions from agrifood.

Notes

1. In Morocco, the African Development Bank's Ouarzazate Project developed public-private partnerships to meet rural energy needs by providing solar photovoltaic rooftop panels to rural Moroccans. The project will double Morocco's power generation capacity and develop 2,000 megawatts (MW) of solar capacity by 2020 (see Gardiner et al. 2015). In Uganda, a public-private partnership leverages a €90 million grant to generate up to $500 million in private investments for renewable energy generation projects (see UNFCCC, n.d.-b).

2. VSS are private, market-based mechanisms designed to address development challenges by defining responsible practices that can be monitored for adherence and serve as a basis for certifying a product or process (Morgan 2023).

3. The Standards Map App, hosted by the International Trade Center (ITC, n.d.), lists 185 standards linked thematically to carbon, almost 100 of which are for the agriculture sector.

4. ISO 14064, GHG Protocol Corporate Standard, GHG Protocol Value Chain Standard.

5. Gold Standard (https://www.goldstandard.org/).

6. Recent controversies have called into question the rigor of some of the standards and methodologies in ensuring achievement of real emissions reduction (see, for instance, "N4C Weekly Brief: Jan. 17–23," at Nature4Climate 2024). It is important to note, however, that additionality concerns have also been raised for projects in other sectors, notably renewable energy (see the November 8, 2022, issue of Bloomberg Green magazine [https://www.bloomberg.com/magazine/green/green_22_07]).

7. The ICVCM was launched by the Taskforce on Scaling Voluntary Carbon Markets (TSVCM), a private sector-led initiative working to establish high-integrity voluntary carbon markets that can scale effectively and efficiently to help meet the goals of the Paris Agreement.

8. The CARB Compliance Offset Program (CARB 2019) is narrower in scope, including only protocols for measures to reduce methane from livestock manure and rice production. Policy action was substantially augmented with the state of California Senate Bill 1383 on Climate Short-Lived Pollutants (2016), which sets a target of cutting dairy and livestock manure methane by 40 percent from 2013 levels by 2030 (equal to a reduction of about 12 $MtCO_2$eq per year in 2030) (Lee and Sumner 2018).

9. The Albert Emission Offset System (AEOS) offsets are purchased using private funds, with the majority from increased soil carbon sequestration as a result of reduced and zero tillage. These AEOS offsets also include new uses of the Anaerobic Decomposition of Agricultural Materials protocol and the Reducing Emissions from Fed Cattle protocols (AEOR 2019).

10. The Emissions Reduction Fund is notable for its relatively large government budget and the scale of its emissions reductions, the overwhelming share of which have come from vegetation projects that enhance or protect carbon stocks, mostly on farmland (OECD 2019c).

11. In its 2015 Nationally Determined Contribution submission under the Paris Agreement, Brazil pledged to strengthen its Low Carbon Emission Agriculture program, including actions to restore an additional 15 million hectares of degraded pastureland (OECD 2019a; UNFCCC 2019b).

12. RenovAgro can finance sustainable practices, such as the recovery of degraded areas and pastures, integrated crop-livestock-forestry systems, conservation practices, and the management and protection of natural resources. It can also finance organic agriculture, recomposition of permanent preservation areas or legal reserves, development of systems for generating renewable energy, and other sustainable practices that culminate in low emissions of GHGs.

13. In 2015, China's Ministry of Agriculture and Rural Affairs issued the *Zero Growth Action Plan for Fertilizer Use by 2020* and the Implementation Opinions of the Ministry of Agriculture on *Fighting the Battle against Agricultural Surface Source Pollution*, proposing the implementation of fertilizer reduction and efficiency actions. They proposed the goal of "one control, two reductions, and three basic" in 2020. The "two reductions" refer to "reducing the use of chemical fertilizers and pesticides and implementing zero-growth action on chemical fertilizers and pesticides" (Chen, Pu, and Zhong 2022, 3).

14. "First-round NDCs" refers to Intended NDCs and NDCs submitted by parties to the UNFCCC as of July 29, 2016 (cutoff date corresponds to FAO's 2016 count (Strohmaier et al. 2016). "Second-round NDCs" refers to the latest NDCs submitted by parties to the UNFCCC as of June 30, 2023 (cutoff date corresponds to the FAO [forthcoming] Global Update Publication and represents an update to the 2021 edition [Crumpler et al. 2021]. This includes new or updated NDCs as well as initial NDCs (if new or updated NDCs were not submitted).

15. Authors' analysis.

16. Details on countries in BioCarbon Fund ISFL (2021).

17. See UNFCCC Decisions 18/CMA1 and 5/CMA3 (UNFCCC 2018, 2023).

18. The SRP had 16 founding members, such as Olam, Mars, and the German Development Agency (GIZ), as reported by Eco-Business (2020). In 2019, the SRP became an independent entity and currently has more than 100 member organizations and 500,000 farmers participating in 25 projects across 21 countries.

19. According to key informant interviews.

20. In accordance with Article 10, Paragraph 5, of the Paris Agreement.

21. Committed to carbon neutrality by 2060, China also expanded its Store Grains (Food) in Land (SGiL) and Store Grains (Food) in Technology (SGiT) programs, making large-scale investments in "high-standard farmland" with drought and flood resilience, water-saving practices, high yields, and soil improvement.

22. Recent examples including the Deccan High-Level Principles in 2023 (G20 2023) and the Organisation for Economic Co-operation and Development's Declaration on Transformative Solutions for Sustainable Agriculture and Food Systems, adopted in 2022 (OECD 2022e).

23. Partly based on Casey et al. (2021).

24. Sustainable Agriculture Finance Network (https://safinetwork.org/).

25. GEF also manages the Least Developed Countries Fund and the Special Climate Change Fund.

26. The GEF-8 strategy focuses explicitly on sustainable, regenerative, nature-positive production systems and supports efficient value and supply chains covering food crops, commercial commodities, livestock, and aquaculture (GEF Secretariat 2023).

27. Approximately 91 percent of funds from national development finance institutions were directed to East Asia and Pacific, particularly China, where they supported afforestation, reforestation, and biosphere conservation efforts through project-level market-rate debt (Chiriac, Vishnumolakala, and Rosane 2023).

28. Principle 7 of the 1992 Rio Declaration on Environment and Development, in UN General Assembly (1992).

29. Objective 5 of the COP28 UAE Declaration on Sustainable Agriculture, Resilient Food Systems and Climate Action refers to a "shift from higher GHG emitting practices to more sustainable production and consumption" (https://www.cop28.com/en/food-and-agriculture).

30. This increase reflects growing AGF GP financing, surges in World Bank financing during emergency responses (for example, COVID-19 and the global food and nutrition security crisis), the establishment of the joint MDB climate finance tracking methodology, and periodic updates to this assessment.

31. "Active portfolio" refers to the total of 154 agriculture and food operations (IBRD/IDA) that are approved by the World Bank Boards of Directors, effective, or ongoing (under implementation) covering FY11–23. The portfolio analysis does not include exclusively trust-funded projects, given the absence of climate finance data on trust-funded projects.

32. Climate co-benefits (CCBs) refer to the share of financing dedicated to climate change adaptation or mitigation by the World Bank's own accounts (IDA/IBRD). While commonly referred as climate finance, the World Bank uses "climate co-benefits" to make a distinction between such financing and dedicated climate finance coming from funds such as the Climate Investment Funds, the GCF, and the Adaptation Fund. The calculation for CCBs is based on the joint MDB methodologies for tracking climate finance in adaptation and mitigation (published in the annual Joint Report on Multilateral Development Banks' Climate Finance; see MDBs 2020). The methodologies are refined regularly. For instance, a new methodology for climate mitigation finance has been updated and has been informing mitigation tracking since 2021/22. CCBs measure climate inputs ex ante and inform how much finance supports climate action in investment operations.

33. This portfolio's activities fall under four broad sectors: (1) Primary Production and Commodity Processing (42 percent of portfolio); (2) Sustainable Protein (27 percent); (3) Forestry and Wood Products (24 percent); and (4) Packaged Food and Beverages (6 percent). Financing instruments in this portfolio are predominantly loans/quasi-loans (84 percent), followed by equities/quasi-equities (16 percent) and guarantees/risk management (1 percent).

34. Citizen Convention on Climate Change, France (https://www.conventioncitoyennepourleclimat.fr/en/); Climate Assembly UK (https://www.climateassembly.uk/); Department of the Environment, Climate and Communications, Government of Ireland (https://www.gov.ie/en/organisation/department-of-the-environment-climate-and-communications/).

   Rural Climate Dialogues in Minnesota (2014–16) (see Center for New Democratic Processes 2023) used citizen's juries to develop community resilience proposals, several of which were adopted by county and state policymakers and implemented through community resilience plans. The New York Rising Community Reconstruction Program (2013–present) (see Homes and Community Renewal, New York State, n.d.) is a participatory recovery and resiliency imitative established to provide assistance to New York communities severely damaged by Superstorm Sandy, Hurricane Irene, and Tropical Storm Lee. The program provides federal support to planning and implementing community-developed recovery and resiliency projects in 124 communities across New York (each receiving at least $3 million) (Center for New Democratic Processes 2023).

35. The vast resources used in the monocropping of sugarcane, corn, and soy are prime examples.

References

Abbas, H. 2012. "Cultural Significance and Community Importance of Irreecha Festival." *Science, Technology and Arts Research Journal* 1 (3): 31–8.

Acampora, Alessia, Luca Ruini, Giovanni Mattia, Carlo Alberto Pratesi, and Maria Claudia Lucchetti. 2023. "Towards Carbon Neutrality in the Agri-food Sector: Drivers and Barriers." *Resources, Conservation and Recycling* 189. https://doi.org/10.1016/j.resconrec.2022.106755.

ACMI (Africa Carbon Markets Initiative. 2022). "Roadmap Report: Harnessing Carbon Markets for Africa." Global Energy Alliance for People and Planet, Sustainable Energy for All, and United Nations Economic Comission for Africa, November 2022. https://www.seforall.org/system/files/2022-11/ACMI_Roadmap_Report_Nov_16.pdf.

Acorn (Agriforestry CRUs for the Organic Restoration of Nature). n.d. "About Us" (web page). Accessed April 8, 2024. https://acorn.rabobank.com/en/about-us/.

ADB (Asian Development Bank). 2021. "ADB Raises 2019–2030 Climate Finance Ambition to $100 Billion." News release, October 13. https://www.adb.org/news/adb-raises-2019-2030-climate-finance-ambition-100-billion.

Adetutu, Morakinyo O., and Victor Ajayi. 2020. "The Impact of Domestic and Foreign R&D on Agricultural Productivity in Sub-Saharan Africa." *World Development* 125. https://doi.org/10.1016/j.worlddev.2019.104690.

Advisory Council on Economic Growth, Government of Canada. 2017. "Learning Nation: Equipping Canada's Workforce with Skills for the Future." Government of Canada, Ottawa, ON. https://www.budget.canada.ca/aceg-ccce/pdf/learning-nation-eng.pdf.

AEOR (Alberta Emission Offset Registry). 2019. "About" (web page). Accessed April 8, 2024. https://alberta.csaregistries.ca/GHGR_Listing/AEOR_About.aspx.

AfDB (African Development Bank Group). 2024. "Data Portal: Morocco—Ouarzazate Solar Complex Project—Phase II (NOORo II and NOORo III Power Plants" (web page). Updated March 29, 2024. https://projectsportal.afdb.org/dataportal/VProject/show/P-MA-FF0-002.

Agriculture and Agri-Food Canada. 2018. "Government of Canada Launches Agricultural Clean Technology Program." News release, March 19. https://www.canada.ca/en/agriculture-agri-food/news/2018/03/government-of-canada-launches-agricultural-clean-technology-program.html.

Aguirre-Villegas, H. A., R. A. Larson, N. Rakobitsch, M. A. Wattiaux, and E. Silva. 2022. "Farm Level Environmental Assessment of Organic Dairy Systems in the U.S.C." *Journal of Cleaner Production* 363: 132390. https://doi.org/10.1016/j.jclepro.2022.132390.

Alston, J. M., M. A. Andersen, J. S. James, and P. G. Pardey. 2011. "The Economic Returns to U.S. Public Agricultural Research." *American Journal of Agricultural Economics* 93 (5): 1257–77. https://doi.org/10.1093/ajae/aar044.

Alston, J. M., M. C. Marra, P. G. Pardey, and T. J. Wyatt. 2000. "Research Returns Redux: A Meta-analysis of the Returns to Agricultural R&D." *Australian Journal of Agricultural and Resource Economics* 44 (2): 185–215. https://doi.org/10.1111/1467-8489.00108.

Antwi-Agyei, Philip, Andrew J. Dougill, and Lindsay C. Stringer. 2017. "Assessing Coherence between Sector Policies and Climate Compatible Development: Opportunities for Triple Wins." *Sustainability* 9 (11): 2130. https://doi.org/10.3390/su9112130.

AP (Associated Press) News. 2023. "CES 2023: Companies Tout Environmental Tech Innovations" (article). January 9, 2023. https://apnews.com/article/CES-2023-las-vegas-technology-sustainability-climate-31d2663e9e47b6e18f99d87afc311338.

Apampa, A., C. Clubb, B. E. Cosgrove, G. Gambarelli, H. Loth, R. Newman, V. Rodriguez Osuna, J. Oudelaar, and A. Tasse. 2021. "Scaling Up Critical Finance for Sustainable Food Systems through Blended Finance." CCAFS Discussion Paper, CGIAR Research Program on Climate Change, Agriculture and Food Security (CCAFS), CGIAR, Montpellier, France. https://financeincommon.org/sites/default/files/2021-11/Scaling%20up%20critical%20finance%20for%20sustainable%20food%20systems%20through%20blended%20finance.pdf.

Arnold, Margaret, and Nicholas Soikan. 2021. "Kenya Moves to Locally Led Climate Action." *Nasikiliza* (blog), October 27. https://blogs.worldbank.org/nasikiliza/kenya-moves-locally-led-climate-action.

Azzarri, C., and G. Nico. 2022. "Sex-Disaggregated Agricultural Extension and Weather Variability in Africa South of the Sahara." *World Development* 155: 105897.

Babiker, M., G. Berndes, K. Blok, B. Cohen, A. Cowie, O. Geden, V. Ginzburg, et al. 2022. "Cross-Sectoral Perspectives." In *Climate Change 2022: Mitigation of Climate Change. Contribution of Working Group III to the Sixth Assessment Report of the Intergovernmental Panel on Climate Change,* chap. 12. Cambridge: Cambridge University. https://doi.org/10.1017/9781009157926.005.

Baldock, D., and A. Buckwell. 2022. *Just Transition in the EU Agriculture and Land Use Sector.* Brussels: Institute for European Environmental Policy. https://ieep.eu/publications/just-transition-in-the-eu-agriculture-and-land-use-sector.

Baldos, Uris, and Dana Blaustein-Rejto. 2021. *Investing in Public R&D for a Competitive and Sustainable US Agriculture.* Oakland, CA: Breakthrough Institute. https://s3.us-east-2.amazonaws.com/uploads.thebreakthrough.org/Uris-Memo_Fine.pdf.

Baldos, Uris, and Thomas Hertel. 2015. "The Role of International Trade in Managing Food Security Risks from Climate Change." *Food Security* 7: 275–90. https://doi.org/10.1007/s12571-015-0435-z.

Batista, C., and P. C. Vicente. 2020. "Improving Access to Savings through Mobile Money: Experimental Evidence from African Smallholder Farmers." *World Development* 129: 104905. https://doi.org/10.1016/j.worlddev.2020.104905.

Bayala, J., J. Sanou, H. R. Bazié, A. Coe, A. Kalinganire, and F. L. Sinclair. 2020. "Regenerated Trees in Farmers' Fields Increase Soil Carbon across the Sahel." *Agroforestry Systems* 94 (2): 401–15. https://doi.org/10.1007/s10457-019-00403-6.

Behnke, R., and F. Metaferia. 2011. "The Contribution of Livestock to the Ethiopian Economy—Part II." IGAD Livestock Policy Initiative Working Paper 02-11, Intergovernmental Authority on Development, Addis Ababa, Ethiopia.

Bennett, Nathan James, and Philip Dearden. 2014. "Why Local People Do Not Support Conservation: Community Perceptions of Marine Protected Area Livelihood Impacts, Governance and Management in Thailand." *Marine Policy* 44: 107–16. https://doi.org/10.1016/j.marpol.2013.08.017.

Bennett, Vanora. 2023. "Multilateral Development Banks Deliver Record Climate Finance—Report." European Bank for Reconstruction and Development, October 12. https://www.ebrd.com/news/2023/multilateral-development-banks-deliver-record-climate-finance-report.html.

Bilali, H. E., and M. S. Allahyari. 2018. "Transition towards Sustainability in Agriculture and Food Systems: Role of Information and Communication Technologies." *Information Processing in Agriculture* 5 (4): 456–64. https://doi.org/10.1016/j.inpa.2018.06.006.

BioCarbon Fund ISFL (Initiative for Sustainable Forest Landscapes). 2021. *2021 Annual Report.* Washington, DC: World Bank. https://www.biocarbonfund-isfl.org/sites/default/files/2021-10/ISFL%202021%20Annual%20Report_Web_120dpi_Sprds.pdf.

Biotech Forecasts. 2022. *Cultured Meat Market—Global Market Analysis and Industry Forecast: 2022–2023.* https://www.biotechforecasts.com/cultured-meat-market.

Bissinger, K., C. Brandi, S. Cabrera de Leicht, M. Fiorini, P. Schleifer, S. Fernandez de Cordova, and N. Ahmed. 2020. *Linking Voluntary Standards to Sustainable Development Goals.* Geneva: International Trade Centre. https://hdl.handle.net/11245.1/971c9382-f054-47f0-b286-17ff76059013.

Black, Simon, Antung A. Liu, Ian Parry, and Nate Vernon. 2023. "IMF Fossil Fuel Subsidies Data: 2023 Update." Working Paper 23/169, International Monetary Fund, Washington, DC. https://www.imf.org/en/Publications/WP/Issues/2023/08/22/IMF-Fossil-Fuel-Subsidies-Data-2023-Update-537281.

Blaufelder, Christopher, Cindy Levy, Peter Mannion, and Dickon Pinner. 2021. "A Blueprint for Scaling Voluntary Carbon Markets to Meet the Climate Challenge." *McKinsey Sustainability Deep Blue,* January 29. https://www.mckinsey.com/capabilities/sustainability/our-insights/a-blueprint-for-scaling-voluntary-carbon-markets-to-meet-the-climate-challenge.

Blaustein-Rejto, Dan. 2023. "How to Cut Emissions through Agricultural Trade" (article). Accessed April 8, 2024. https://thebreakthrough.org/issues/food-agriculture-environment/how-to-cut-emissions-through-agricultural-trade.

Bloomberg NEF. 2023. "Five Need-to-Knows About the Future of Voluntary Carbon Offset Markets" (web page). January 26, 2023." Accessed April 8, 2024. https://about.bnef.com/blog/five-need-to-knows-about-the-future-of-voluntary-carbon-offset-markets/.

Borras, S. M. Jr., J. C. Franco, and Z. Nam. 2020. "Climate Change and Land: Insights from Myanmar." *World Development* 129. https://doi.org/10.1016/j.worlddev.2019.104864.

Bosetti, Valentina, Carlo Carraro, Romain Duval, Alessandra Sgobbi, and Massimo Tavoni. 2009. "The Role of R&D and Technology Diffusion in Climate Change Mitigation: New Perspectives Using the WITCH Model." Unpublished manuscript, Stanford University, Stanford, CA. http://stanford.edu/dept/france-stanford/Conferences/Climate/Carraro.pdf.

Breakthrough Institute. 2023. *From Lab to Farm: Assessing Federal R&D Funding for Agricultural Climate Mitigation.* Oakland, CA: Breakthrough Institute.

Brennan, Tom, Joshua Katz, Yossi Quint, and Boyd Spencer, eds. 2021. *Cultivated Meat: Out of the Lab, Into the Frying Pan.* New York: McKinsey & Company. https://www.mckinsey.com/industries/agriculture/our-insights/cultivated-meat-out-of-the-lab-into-the-frying-pan.

Brenton, P., V. Chemutai, M. Maliszewska, and I. Sikora. 2024. *Trade and the Climate Change: Policy Considerations for Developing Countries.* Washington, DC: World Bank.

Brouwer, H., and J. Woodhill. 2019. *The MSP Guide: How to Design and Facilitate Multi-stakeholder Partnerships.* 3rd ed. Rugby, UK: Practical Action Publishing. https://edepot.wur.nl/543151.

Buto, O., G. M. Galbiati, N. Alekseeva, and M. Bernoux. 2023. *Climate-Related Development Finance in the Agriculture and Land Use Sector between 2000–2019—Special Update.* Rome: Food and Agriculture Organization of the United Nations.

CARB (California Air Resources Board). 2019. "Compliance Offset Program" (web page). Accessed April 8, 2024. https://ww2.arb.ca.gov/our-work/programs/compliance-offset-program.

Carbon Brief. 2021. "Climate Justice: The Challenge of Achieving a 'Just Transition' in Agriculture" (article). October 6. https://www.carbonbrief.org/climate-justice-the-challenge-of-achieving-a-just-transition-in-agriculture/.

Casey, Jonathan, Alexander Bisaro, Alvaro Valverde, Marlon Martinez, and Martin Rokitzki. 2021. *Private Finance Investment Opportunities in Climate-Smart Agriculture Technologies.* Peniciuk, Scotland: Commercial Agriculture for Smallholders and Agribusiness Programme, Foreign, Commonwealth and Development Office. https://www.casaprogramme.com/wp-content/uploads/2021/10/Private-finance-investment-opportunities-in-climate-smart-agriculture-technologies.pdf.

Center for New Democratic Processes. 2023. "Rural Climate Dialogues" (project page). Accessed April 8, 2024. https://www.cndp.us/rural-climate-dialogues/.

Chaganti Singh, Sarita, and Nikunj Ohri. 2023. "India Aims for $17 Bln Cut in Food, Fertiliser Subsidies in 2023/24—Sources." *Reuters*, January 3. https://www.reuters.com/markets/asia/india-aims-17-bln-cut-food-fertiliser-subsidies-202324-sources-2023-01-03/.

Chakamba, R. 2022. "Inside Development: COP 27; Some G77 Countries Oppose Widening Climate Agriculture Pact" (article), Devex. November 15. https://www.devex.com/news/exclusive-some-g77-countries-oppose-widening-climate-agriculture-pact-104439.

Cheema, A., A. I. Khwaja, M. F. Naseer, and J. N. Shapiro. 2020. "Glass Walls: Experimental Evidence on Access Constraints Faced by Women." Working Paper, Princeton University, Princeton, NJ. https://khwaja.scholar.harvard.edu/files/asimkhwaja/files/glass_walls_020222.pdf.

Chen, X., M. Pu, and Y. Zhong. 2022. "Evaluating China Food's Fertilizer Reduction and Efficiency Initiative Using a Double Stochastic Meta-Frontier Method." *International Journal of Environmental Research and Public Health* 19 (12). https://doi.org/10.3390/ijerph19127342.

Chiriac, Daniela, Harsha Vishnumolakala, and Paul Rosane. 2023. *Landscape of Climate Finance for Agrifood Systems.* San Francisco, CA: Climate Policy Initiative. https://www.climatepolicyinitiative.org/publication/landscape-of-climate-finance-for-agrifood-systems/.

CHOOOSE. 2022. "Compliance Carbon Markets vs Voluntary Carbon Markets" (article). September 4, 2022. https://www.chooose.today/insights/compliance-carbon-markets-vs-voluntary-carbon-markets?utm_source=insights&utm_medium=website&utm_campaign=climate-glossary.

Christiaensen, L., Z. Rutledge, and J. E. Taylor. 2021. "Viewpoint: The Future of Work in Agri-food." *Food Policy* 99: 101963. https://doi.org/10.1016/j.foodpol.2020.101963.

Ci-Dev (Carbon Initiative for Development). 2022. "The Standardized Crediting Framework." World Bank, Washington, DC https://www.ci-dev.org/standardized-crediting-framework.

Climate Bonds Initiative. 2021. *Sustainable Debt: Global State of the Market 2021.* London: Climate Bonds Initiative. https://www.climatebonds.net/files/reports/cbi_global_sotm_2021_02h_0.pdf.

Climate Focus. 2023. "2022 Overview Voluntary Carbon Market (VCM)." https://climatefocus.com/wp-content/uploads/2023/01/VCM-Dashboard-2022-Overview-1.pdf.

Colomb, Vincent, Ophélie Touchemoulin, Louis Bockel, Jean-Luc Chotte, Sarah Martin, Marianne Tinlot, and Martial Bernoux. 2013. "Selection of Appropriate Calculators for Landscape-Scale Greenhouse Gas Assessment for Agriculture and Forestry." *Environmental Research Letters* 8 (1): 015029. https://doi.org/10.1088/1748-9326/8/1/015029.

Conti, Costanza, Giacomo Zanello, and Andy Hall. 2021. "Why Are Agri-food Systems Resistant to New Directions of Change? A Systematic Review." *Global Food Security* 31: 100576. https://doi.org/10.1016/j.gfs.2021.100576.

Coppock, D. L. 1994. *The Borana Plateau of Southern Ethiopia: Synthesis of Pastoral Research, Development, and Change, 1980–91*. Addis Ababa, Ethiopia: International Livestock Centre for Africa.

Correia, Marta, Isabel Costa Azevedo, Helena Peres, Rui Magalhães, Aires Oliva-Teles, Cristina Marisa Ribiero Almeida, and Laura Guimarães. 2020. "Integrated Multi-trophic Aquaculture: A Laboratory and Hands-On Experimental Activity to Promote Environmental Sustainability Awareness and Value of Aquaculture Product." *Frontiers in Marine Science* 7. https://doi.org/10.3389/fmars.2020.00156.

Crumpler, K., R. Abi Khalil, E. Tanganelli, N. Rai, L. Roffredi, A. Meybeck, V. Umulisa, J. Wolf, and M. Bernoux. 2021. "Global Update Report—Agriculture, Forestry and Fisheries in the Nationally Determined Contributions." Environment and Natural Resources Management Working Paper 91, Food and Agriculture Organization of the United Nations, Rome. https://doi.org/10.4060/cb7442en.

Crumpler, K., C. Angioni, P. Prosperi, L. Roffredi, M. Salvatore, E. Tanganelli, V. Umulisa, A. Wybieralska, I. Brierley, N. Rai, G. Dahlet, G. Bhalla, M. Knowles, J. Wolf, and M. Bernoux. Forthcoming. *Agrifood Systems in Nationally Determined Contributions: Global Analysis*. Rome: Food and Agriculture Organization of the United Nations (FAO).

Cui, Zhenling, Hongyan Zhang, Xinping Chen, Chaochun Zhang, Wenqi Ma, Chengdong Huang, Weifeng Zhang, et al. 2018. "Letter: Pursuing Sustainable Productivity with Millions of Smallholder Farmers." *Nature* 555: 363–6. https://doi.org/10.1038/nature25785.

Dalgaard, Tommy, Birgitte Hansen, Berit Hasler, Ole Hertel, Nicholas J. Hutchings, Brian H. Jacobsen, Lars Stoumann Jensen, et al. 2014. "Policies for Agricultural Nitrogen Management—Trends, Challenges and Prospects for Improved Efficiency in Denmark." *Environmental Research Letters* 9 (11): https://doi.org/10.1088/1748-9326/9/11/115002.

Damania, Richard, Esteban Balseca, Charlotte de Fontaubert, Joshua Gill, Kichan Kim, Jun Rentschler, Jason Russ, and Esha Zaveri. 2023. *Detox Development: Repurposing Environmentally Harmful Subsidies*. Washington, DC: World Bank. https://doi.org/10.1596/978-1-4648-1916-2.

Department for Business, Energy and Industrial Strategy and Department for Energy Security and Net Zero, United Kingdom. 2022. "Projects Selected for Phase 1 of the Direct Air Capture and Greenhouse Gas Removal Programme" (web page). Updated July 8, 2022. https://www.gov.uk/government/publications/direct-air-capture-and-other-greenhouse-gas-removal-technologies-competition/projects-selected-for-phase-1-of-the-direct-air-capture-and-greenhouse-gas-removal-programme.

Department of Agriculture, Water, and the Environment, Government of Australia. 2021. "Carbon Credits (Carbon Farming Initiative) Act 2011." No. 101, 2011 (including amendments). Accessed April 8, 2024. https://www.legislation.gov.au/C2011A00101/2020-09-06/text.

Devarajan, Shanta, Delfin S. Go, Sherman Robinson, and Karen Thierfelder. 2022. "The Role of Trade Policy in Climate Mitigation: Carbon Border Adjustment Mechanism (CBAM)." Paper presented at the Global Trade Analysis Project's 25th Annual Conference on Global Economic Analysis, June 8–10 (virtual). https://ageconsearch.umn.edu/record/333494/.

Dhakhwa, Timila, Nkulumo Zinyengere, Bethany Joy Linton, Erick C. M. Fernandes, Chandra Shekhar Sinha, Timothy R. H. Pearson, Blanca Bernal, Sophia Simon, and Meyru Bhanti. 2021. *Soil Organic Carbon MRV Sourcebook for Agricultural Landscapes*. Washington, DC: World Bank Group. http://documents.worldbank.org/curated/en/948041625049766862/Soil-Organic-Carbon-MRV-Sourcebook-for-Agricultural-Landscapes.

Dinar, Ariel, Frisbie J. Aapris, and Donald F. Larson. 2011. "Agriculture and the Clean Development Mechanism." Policy Research Working Paper 5621, World Bank, Washington, DC.

Donahue, John D., Frank A. Weil, and Richard J. Zeckhauser. 2010. "Who's Afraid of Central Park? Modeling Collaborative Governance." *Public Manager* [Association for Talent Development] 39 (3): 56–60.

Drieux, E., M. St-Louis, J. Schlickenrieder, and M. Bernoux. 2019. *State of the Koronivia Joint Work on Agriculture: Boosting Koronivia*. Rome: FAO. https://www.fao.org/documents/card/en/c/ca6910en.

EAT. 2022. "EAT Cities." EAT, Oslo. https://eatforum.org/content/uploads/2022/05/EAT-Cities-2022.pdf.

EcoAgriculture Partners. n.d. "Our Work" (web page). Accessed April 8, 2024. https://ecoagriculture.org/how-we-work/strategic-partnerships/. https://ecoagriculture.org/our-work.

Eco-Business. 2020. "Industry Spotlight: The Race against Time to Cut Rice's Carbon Footprint." News, March 17. https://www.eco-business.com/news/the-race-against-time-to-cut-rices-carbon-footprint/.

Ecosystem Marketplace Insights Team. 2023. "New Research: Carbon Credits Are Associated with Businesses Decarbonizing Faster" (article). Updated October 10, 2023. https://www.ecosystemmarketplace.com /articles/new-research-carbon-credits-are-associated-with-businesses-decarbonizing-faster/.

EIB (European Investment Bank). 2023. *Climate Bank Roadmap, 2021–2025*. Luxembourg: EIB. https://www .eib.org/en/projects/topics/climate-action/cbr.

Employment and Social Development Canada. 2023. "Future Skills: Preparing Canadians for Jobs of the Future" (web page). Updated October 16, 2023. https://www.canada.ca/en/employment-social -development/programs/future-skills.html.

England, Matthew I., Andrew J. Dougill, Lindsay C. Stringer, Katharine E. Vincent, Joanna Pardoe, Felix K. Kalaba, David D. Mkwambisi, Emilinah Namaganda, and Stavros Afionis. 2018. "Climate Change Adaptation and Cross-Sectoral Policy Coherence in Southern Africa." *Regional Environmental Change* 18: 2059–71. https://doi.org/10.1007/s10113-018-1283-0.

Environmental Defense Fund. 2021. "A Revamped Cost Curve for Reaching Net-Zero Emissions: How to Find the Most Cost-Effective Ways to Cut Carbon" (web page). August 26, 2021. https://www.edf.org/revamped-cost -curve-reaching-net-zero-emissions#:~:text=Technologies:%20At%20modest%20costs%2C%20clean%20 electricity%20measures,energy%20tax%20credits%2C%20could%20drive%20these%20reductions.

Eriksen, Siri, E. Lisa F. Schipper, Morgan Scoville-Simonds, Katharine Vincent, Hans Nicolai Adam, Nick Brooks, Brian Harding, et al. 2021. "Adaptation Interventions and Their Effect on Vulnerability in Developing Countries: Help, Hindrance or Irrelevance?" *World Development* 141: 105383. https://doi .org/10.1016/j.worlddev.2020.105383.

European Commission. 2013. "Overview of CAP Reform 2014–2020." Agricultural Policy Perspectives Brief No. 5, European Commisssion, Brussels.

European Commission. 2020a. "Factsheet: How the Future CAP Will Contribute to the EU Green Deal" (web page). Accessed April 8, 2024. https://ec.europa.eu/commission/presscorner/detail/en /fs_20_910.

European Commission. 2020b. "Farm to Fork Strategy: For a Fair, Healthy, and Environmentally-Friendly Food System." European Commission, Brussels. https://food.ec.europa.eu.mcas.ms/system/files/2020-05 /f2f_action-plan_2020_strategy-info_en.pdf?McasCtx=4&McasTsid=20892.

European Commission. 2021. "List of Potential Agricultural Practices That Eco-Schemes Could Support" (factsheet). European Commission, Brussels. https://agriculture.ec.europa.eu.mcas.ms/system /files/2021-01/factsheet-agri-practices-under-ecoscheme_en_0.pdf?McasCtx=4&McasTsid=20892.

European Commission. n.d. "EU Emissions Trading System (EU ETS)" (web page). Accessed April 8, 2024. https://climate.ec.europa.eu/eu-action/eu-emissions-trading-system-eu-ets_en.

FAO (Food and Agriculture Organization of the United Nations). 2016. "Intended Nationally Determined Contributions: Global Analysis Key Findings." FAO, Rome. https://www.fao.org/3 /i6573e/i6573e.pdf.

FAO (Food and Agriculture Organization of the United Nations). 2019. *Five Practical Actions towards Low-Carbon Livestock*. Rome: FAO. https://www.fao.org/documents/card/en/c/ca7089en/.

FAO (Food and Agriculture Organization of the United Nations). 2021. *Unlocking the Potential of Protected Agriculture in the Countries of the Gulf Cooperation Council: Saving Water and Improving Nutrition*. Cairo: FAO. https://doi.org/10.4060/cb4070en.

FAO (Food and Agriculture Organization of the United Nations). 2023. "Pastoralist Knowledge Hub" (web page). Accessed April 8, 2024. https://www.fao.org/pastoralist-knowledge-hub/en/.

FAO (Food and Agriculture Organization of the United Nations). Forthcoming. "Global Update Publication." FAO, Rome.

FAO (Food and Agriculture Organization of the United Nations. n.d. "Climate Change Knowledge Hub:" (web page). Accessed April 15, 2024. https://www.fao.org/climate-change/knowledge-hub/en.

FAO (Food and Agriculture Organization of the United Nations) and Alliance of Biodiversity International and CIAT (International Center for Tropical Agriculture). 2021. *Indigenous Peoples' Food Systems: Insights on Sustainability and Resilience in the Front Line of Climate Change*. Rome: FAO. https://doi .org/10.4060/cb5131en.

FAO (Food and Agriculture Organization of the United Nations) and New Zealand Agricultural Greenhouse Gas Research Centre. 2017. *Supporting Low Emissions Development in the Ethiopian Dairy Cattle Sector—Reducing Enteric Methane for Food Security and Livelihoods*. Rome: FAO.

FAO (Food and Agriculture Organization of the United Nations) and WHO (World Health Organization). 2019. "Sustainable Healthy Diets: Guiding Principles." Issue paper. FAO and WHO, Rome. http://www.fao.org/3/ca6640en/CA6640EN.pdf.

FAOSTAT. 2023a. "Emission Intensities" (database). Accessed April 8, 2024. https://www.fao.org/faostat/en/#data/EI.

FAOSTAT. 2023b. "Emissions Totals" (database) Accessed April 8, 2023. https://www.fao.org/faostat/en/#data/GT.

FOLU (Food and Land Use Coalition). 2020. "Food and Land Use Transformation Pyramid" (web page). 2020. https://www.foodandlandusecoalition.org/interactive-pyramid/#:~:text=The%20Food%20and%20Land%20Use,all%20while%20unlocking%20%244.5%20trillion.

Forest Carbon Partnership Facility. 2019. "Policy Paths towards Second-Generation Measurement, Reporting and Verification (MRV 2.0." Policy Brief, Forest Carbon Partnership Facility, Washington, DC. https://www.forestcarbonpartnership.org/sites/fcp/files/policy_brief_r5.pdf.

Forest Carbon Partnership Facility. n.d. "REDD+ Benefit Sharing" (web page). Accessed April 8, 2024. https://www.forestcarbonpartnership.org/redd-benefit-sharing.

Fragkiadakis, Kostas, Panagiotis Fragkos, and Leonidas Paroussos. 2020. "Low-Carbon R&D Can Boost EU Growth and Competitiveness." In "Energy Systems Analysis and Modeling towards Decarbonization," special issue, *Energies* 13 (19): 5236. https://doi.org/10.3390/en13195236.

Fresán, U., M. A. Mejia, W. J. Craig, K. Jaceldo-Siegl, and J. Sabaté. 2019. "Meat Analogs from Different Protein Sources: A Comparison of Their Sustainability and Nutritional Content." *Sustainability* 11 (12): 3231. https://doi.org/10.3390/su11123231.

Fuglie, Keith, Madhur Gautam, Aparajita Goyal, and William F. Maloney. 2020. *Harvesting Prosperity: Technology and Productivity Growth in Agriculture*. Washington, DC: World Bank. https://doi.org/10.1596/978-1-4648-1393-1.

Fuglie, Keith, Srabashi Ray, Uris Lantz C. Baldos, and Thomas W. Hertel. 2022. "The R&D Cost of Climate Mitigation in Agriculture." *Applied Economic Perspectives and Policy* 44 (4): 1955–74. https://doi.org/10.1002/aepp.13245.

Fujimori, S., T. Hasegawa, J. Rogelj, X. Su, P. Havlik, V. Krey, K. Takahashi, and K. Riahi. 2018. "Inclusive Climate Change Mitigation and Food Security Policy under 1.5°C Climate Goal." *Environmental Research Letters* 13 (7): 074033.

G20 (Group of Twenty). 2023. "Annex to G20 Agriculture Ministers' Outcome Document and Chair's Summary: Deccan High Level Principles on Food Security and Nutrition 2023." G20, India. https://g7g20-documents.org/database/document/2023-g20-india-sherpa-track-agricultural-ministers-ministers-annex-annex-to-g20-agriculture-ministers-outcome-document-and-chairs-summary-deccan-high-level-principles-on-food-security-and-nutrition-2023.

Galbiati, G. M., and M. Bernoux. 2022. "Climate-Related Finance in the Agriculture and Land Use Sector between 2000 and 2020: Brief Update." Food and Agriculture Organization of the United Nations, Rome. https://doi.org/10.4060/cc3651en.

Gardiner, Ann, Matthieu Bardout, Francesca Grossi, and Sandrine Dixson-Declève. 2015. *Public-Private Partnerships for Climate Finance*. Copenhagen: Nordic Council of Ministers. https://norden.diva-portal.org/smash/get/diva2:915864/FULLTEXT01.pdf.

Garrity, D. P., F. K. Akinnifesi, O. C. Ajayi, S. G. Weldesemayat, J. G. Mowo, A. Kalinganire, M. Larwanou, and J. Bayala. 2010. "Evergreen Agriculture: A Robust Approach to Sustainable Food Security in Africa." *Food Security* 2 (3): 197–214. https://doi.org/10.1007/s12571-010-0070-7.

Gartaula, H., T. B. Sapkota, A. Khatri-Chhetri, G. Prasad, and L. Badstue. 2020. "Gendered Impacts of Greenhouse Gas Mitigation Options for Rice Cultivation in India." *Climatic Change* 163 (2): 1045–63. https://doi.org/10.1007/s10584-020-02941-w.

Gautam, Madhur, David Laborde, Abdullah Mamun, Will Martin, Valeria Pineiro, and Rob Vos. 2022. *Repurposing Agricultural Policies and Support: Options to Transform Agriculture and Food Systems to Better Serve the Health of People, Economies, and the Planet*. Washington, DC: World Bank. http://hdl.handle.net/10986/36875.

GEF (Global Environment Facility) Secretariat. 2023. *GEF-8 Corporate Scorecard—June 2023*. Washington, DC: GEF. https://www.thegef.org/newsroom/publications/gef-8-corporate-scorecard-june-2023.

GlobeNewswire. 2022. "Cultured Meat Market to Reach US$ 517 Million by 2030—Exclusive Report by Acumen Research & Consulting." *GlobeNewswire*, June 14, 2022. https://www.globenewswire.com/en/news-release/2022/06/14/2462113/0/en/Cultured-Meat-Market-to-Reach-US-517-Million-by-2030-Exclusive-Report-By-Acumen-Research-Consulting.html.

Greenhouse Gas Protocol. 2011. *Product Life Cycle Accounting and Reporting Standard*. Washington, DC: World Resources Institute and Geneva: World Business Council for Sustainable Development. https://ghgprotocol.org/sites/default/files/standards/Product-Life-Cycle-Accounting-Reporting-Standard_041613.pdf.

Guarnaschelli, Serena, Benhan Limketkai, and Pauline Vandeputte. 2018. "Financing Sustainable Land Use: Unlocking Business Opportunities in Sustainable Land Use with Blended Finance." KOIS Invest, Brussels. https://koisinvest.com/wp-content/uploads/2020/04/Financing-sustainable-land-use-report.pdf.

Guerrero, Santiago, Ben Henderson, Hugo Valin, Charlotte Janssens, Petr Havlik, and Amanda Palazzo. 2022. "The Impacts of Agricultural Trade and Support Policy Reform on Climate Change Adaptation and Environmental Performance: A Model-Based Analysis." OECD Food, Agriculture and Fisheries Papers 180, OECD Publishing, Paris. https://doi.org/10.1787/520dd70d-en.

Guerrero, Santiago. 2021. "Characterising Agri-Environmental Policies: Towards Measuring Their Progress." OECD Food, Agriculture and Fisheries Papers 155. OECD Publishing, Paris. https://www.econbiz.de/Record/characterising-agri-environmental-policies-towards-measuring-their-progress-guerrero-santiago/10012630113.

Haglund, E., J. Ndjeunga, L. Snook, and D. Pasternak. 2011. "Dry Land Tree Management for Improved Household Livelihoods: Farmer Managed Natural Regeneration in Niger." *Journal of Environmental Management* 92 (7): 1696–705. https://doi.org/10.1016/j.jenvman.2011.01.027.

Hall, Julien. 2017. "AgriDigital Pioneers Blockchain Use with First Farmer-Buyer Agriculture Settlement." *Insight Blog,* February 2. https://www.spglobal.com/commodityinsights/en/market-insights/blogs/agriculture/020217-agridigital-pioneers-blockchain-use-with-first-farmer-buyer-agriculture-settlement.

Harvey, Fiona. 2023. "Ban Private Jets to Address Climate Crisis, Says Thomas Piketty." *Guardian*, November 22. https://www.theguardian.com/environment/2023/nov/22/ban-private-jets-to-address-climate-crisis-says-thomas-piketty?CMP=oth_b-aplnews_d-1.

Hasegawa, Tomoko, Shinichiro Fujimori, Petr Havlík, Hugo Valin, Benjamin Leon Bodirsky, Jonathan C. Doelman, Thomas Fellmann, et al. 2018. "Risk of Increased Food Insecurity under Stringent Global Climate Change Mitigation Policy." *Nature Climate Change* 8: 699–703. https://doi.org/10.1038/s41558-018-0230-x.

Havemann, Tanja. 2019. "Landscape Report Blended Finance for Agriculture." Working paper, Smallholder and Agri-SME Finance and Investment Network (SAFIN), Rome. https://safinetwork.org.mcas.ms/wp-content/uploads/2019/12/Landscape-report_BF4A_SAFIN.pdf?McasCtx=4&McasTsid=20892.

Heimlich, J. E., and N. M. Ardoin. 2008. "Understanding Behavior to Understand Behavior Change: A Literature Review." *Environmental Education Research* 14 (3): 215–37. https://doi.org/10.1080/13504620802148881.

Heisey, Paul W., and Keith O. Fuglie. 2018. "Public Agricultural R&D in High-Income Countries: Old and New Roles in a New Funding Environment." *Global Food Security* 17: 92–102. https://doi.org/10.1016/j.gfs.2018.03.008.

Henderson, Ben, Stefan Frank, Petr Havlik, and Hugo Valin. 2021. "Policy Strategies and Challenges for Climate Change Mitigation in the Agriculture, Forestry and Other Land Use (AFOLU) Sector." OECD Food, Agriculture and Fisheries Papers 149, OECD Publishing, Paris. https://doi.org/10.1787/47b3493b-en.

Herrero, M., P. Havlík, H. Valin, A. Notenbaert, M. C. Rufino, P. K. Thornton, M. Blümmel, F. Weiss, D. Grace, and M. Obersteiner. 2013. "Biomass Use, Production, Feed Efficiencies, and Greenhouse Gas Emissions from Global Livestock Systems." *Proceedings of the National Academy of Sciences of the United States of America* 110 (52): 20888–93. https://doi.org/10.1073/pnas.1308149110.

HLPE (High Level Panel of Experts on Food Security and Nutrition). 2019. *Agroecological and Other Innovative Approaches for Sustainable Agriculture and Food Systems That Enhance Food Security and Nutrition*. Rome: Food and Agriculture Organization of the United Nations. http://www.fao.org/3/ca5602en/ca5602en.pdf.

Hodgson, Camilla. 2022. "Surge of Investment into Carbon Credits Creates Boom Time for Brokers." *Financial Times*, May 2. https://www.ft.com/content/739a5517-4de6-43f7-ae47-1ce8d4774d50.

Holmes, George, and Connor J. Cavanagh. 2016. "A Review of the Social Impacts of Neoliberal Conservation: Formations, Inequalities, Contestations." *Geoforum* 75: 199–209. https://doi.org/10.1016/j.geoforum.2016.07.014.

Homes and Community Renewal, New York State. n.d. "Resilient Homes and Communities Programs" (web page). Accessed April 8, 2024. https://hcr.ny.gov/resilient-homes-and-communities?utm_medium=301&utm_source=stormrecovery.ny.gov.

IEA (International Energy Agency). 2020. *Clean Energy Innovation*. Paris: IEA. https://www.iea.org/reports/clean-energy-innovation/global-status-of-clean-energy-innovation-in-2020.

IEG (Independent Evaluation Group). 2023. *Morocco Country Program Evaluation (2023)*. Washington, DC: IEG.

IETA (International Emissions Trading Association). 2022. "Greenhouse Gas Market Report 2022." IETA, Geneva, Switzerland. https://ieta.b-cdn.net/wp-content/uploads/2023/09/IETA_GHGMarketReport_2022.pdf.

IFPRI (International Food Policy Research Institute). 2022. *2022 Global Food Policy Report: Climate Change and Food Systems*. Washington, DC: International Food Policy Research Institute. https://doi.org/10.2499/9780896294257.

Iiyama, Miyuki, Athanase Mukuralinda, Jean Damascene Ndayambaje, Bernard S. Musana, Alain Ndoli, Jeremias G. Mowo, Dennis Garrity, Stephen Ling, and Vicky Ruganzu. 2018. "Addressing the Paradox—The Divergence between Smallholders' Preference and Actual Adoption of Agricultural Innovations." *International Journal of Agricultural Sustainability* 16 (6): 472–85. https://doi.org/10.1080/14735903.2018.1539384.

IMF (International Monetary Fund). 2022. "The Democratic Republic of the Congo." IMF Country Report 22/211, IMF, Washington, DC. https://www.imf.org//media/Files/Publications/CR/2022/English/1CODEA2022003.ashx.

Integrity Council for the Voluntary Carbon Market. 2022. "The Core Carbon Principles, Plus the Program-Level Assessment Framework and Assessment Procedure" (web page). Accessed April 8, 2024. https://icvcm.org/the-core-carbon-principles/.

International Rice Research Institute. 2023. "IRRI Engages with Indonesian Govt, Leading Telecom Company for Rice Crop Manager Project." News, December 13. https://www.irri.org/news-and-events/news/irrl-engages-indonesian-govt-leading-telecom-company-rice-crop-manager-project.

IPCC (Intergovernmental Panel on Climate Change). 2019a. "2019 Refinement: Glossary." In *2019 Refinement to the 2006 IPCC Guidelines for National Greenhouse Gas Inventories*, Vol. 4, *Agriculture, Forestry Land Use*, edited by E. Calvo Buendia, K. Tanabe, A. Kranjc, J. Baasansuren, M. Fukuda, S. Ngarize, et al., chap. 2. Geneva: IPCC. https://www.ipcc-nggip.iges.or.jp/public/2019rf/pdf/4_Volume4/19R_V4_Ch02_Generic%20Methods.pdf

IPCC (Intergovernmental Panel on Climate Change). 2019b. *Climate Change and Land: An IPCC Special Report on Climate Change, Desertification, Land Degradation, Sustainable Land Management, Food Security, and Greenhouse Gas Fluxes in Terrestrial Ecosystems*. https://www.ipcc.ch/site/assets/uploads/2019/11/SRCCL-Full-Report-Compiled-191128.pdf.

IPCC (Intergovernmental Panel on Climate Change). 2019c. "Food Security." In *Climate Change and Land: An IPCC Special Report on Climate Change, Desertification, Land Degradation, Sustainable Land Management, Food Security, and Greenhouse Gas Fluxes in Terrestrial Ecosystems*, chap. 5. Cambridge: Cambridge University Press. https://doi.org/10.1017/9781009157988.007.

IPCC (Intergovernmental Panel on Climate Change). 2022. *Climate Change and Land: IPCC Special Report on Climate Change, Desertification, Land Degradation, Sustainable Land Management, Food Security, and Greenhouse Gas Fluxes in Terrestrial Ecosystems*. Cambridge: Cambridge University Press. https://doi.org/10.1017/9781009157988.

ISF Advisors. 2022. *The State of the Agri-SME Sector—Bridging the Finance Gap.* London: Commercial Agriculture for Smallholders and Agribusiness. https://isfadvisors.org/wp-content/uploads/2022/04/ISF_AgriSME-Finance-state-of-the-sector-report.pdf.

ITC (International Trade Centre). n.d. "Standards Map App" (web page). Accessed April 8, 2024. https://www.standardsmap.org/en/identify.

Izzi, Gabriella. 2021. "Farmer-Led Irrigation: The What, Why, and How-to Guide." *Water Blog*, March 22. https://blogs.worldbank.org/water/farmer-led-irrigation-what-why-and-how-guide.

Jacobi, J., S. Rist, and M. A. Altieri. 2017. "Incentives and Disincentives for Diversified Agroforestry Systems from Different Actors' Perspectives in Bolivia." *International Journal of Agricultural Sustainability* 15 (4): 365–79. https://doi.org/10.1080/14735903.2017.1332140.

Janssens, Charlotte, Petr Havlik, Tamás Krisztin, Justin Baker, Stefan Frank, Tomoko Hasegawa, David Leclère, et al. 2020. "Global Hunger and Climate Change Adaptation through International Trade." *Nature Climate Change* 10 (9): 829–35. https://doi.org/10.1038/s41558-020-0847-4.

Kainou, Kazunari. 2022. "Collapse of the Clean Development Mechanism Scheme under the Kyoto Protocol and Its Spillover: Consequences of 'Carbon Panic.'" VoxEU column, March 16, 2022. https://cepr.org/voxeu/columns/collapse-clean-development-mechanism-scheme-under-kyoto-protocol-and-its-spillover.

Kane, Michael Kobina, and Stephanie Gil. 2022. "Green Hydrogen: A Key Investment for the Energy Transition." *Getting Infrastructure Finance Right* (blog), June 23. https://blogs.worldbank.org/ppps/green-hydrogen-key-investment-energy-transition.

Karlsson, L., A. Nightingale, L. O. Naess, and J. Thompson. 2017. "'Triple Wins' or 'Triple Faults'? Analyzing Policy Discourses on Climate-Smart Agriculture (CSA)." CCAFS Working Paper. 197, CGIAR Research Program on Climate Change, Agriculture and Food Security, Copenhagen.

Khan, N. A., Q. Gao, and M. Abid. 2020. "Public Institutions' Capacities Regarding Climate Change Adaptation and Risk Management Support in Agriculture: The Case of Punjab Province, Pakistan." *Scientific Reports* 10 (1): 14111. https://doi.org/10.1038/s41598-020-71011-z.

Kinley, R. D., G. Martinez-Fernandez, M. K. Matthews, R. de Nys, M. Magnusson, and N. W. Tomkins. 2020. "Mitigating the Carbon Footprint and Improving Productivity of Ruminant Livestock Agriculture Using a Red Seaweed." *Journal of Cleaner Production* 259: 120836. https://doi.org/10.1016/j.jclepro.2020.120836.

Kishore, Avinash, Muzna Alvi, and Timothy J. Krupnik. 2021. "Development of Balanced Nutrient Management Innovations in South Asia: Perspectives from Bangladesh, India, Nepal, and Sri Lanka." *Global Food Security* 28. https://doi.org/10.1016/j.gfs.2020.100464.

Kurdi, Sikandra, Mai Mahmoud, Kibrom A. Abay, and Clemens Breisinger. 2020. "Too Much of a Good Thing? Evidence That Fertilizer Subsidies Lead to Overapplication in Egypt." MENA RP Working Paper 27, International Food Policy Research Institute, Washington, DC. https://doi.org/10.2499/p15738coll2.133652.

Kushitor, S. B., S. Alimohammadi, and P. Currie. 2022. "Narrative Explorations of the Role of the Informal Food Sector in Food Flows and Sustainable Transitions during the COVID-19 Lockdown." *PLOS Sustainability and Transformation* 1 (12): e0000038. https://doi.org/10.1371/journal.pstr.0000038.

Kusters, Koen, Louise Buck, Maartje de Graaf, Peter Minang, Cora van Oosten, and Roderick Zagt. 2018. "Participatory Planning, Monitoring and Evaluation of Multi-Stakeholder Platforms in Integrated Landscape Initiatives." *Environmental Management* 62: 170–81. https://doi.org/10.1007/s00267-017-0847-y.

Laborde, David, Abdullah Mamun, Will Martin, Valeria Piñeiro, and Rob Vos. 2021. "Agricultural Subsidies and Global Greenhouse Gas Emissions." *Nature Communications* 12: 2601. https://doi.org/10.1038/s41467-021-22703-1.

Lawder, David. 2022. "World Bank to Launch New Trust Fund for Emissions Reduction Grants." Reuters, October 10. https://www.reuters.com/business/sustainable-business/world-bank-launch-new-trust-fund-emissions-reduction-grants-2022-10-11/.

Lee, Hyunok, and Daniel A. Sumner. 2018. "Dependence on Policy Revenue Poses Risks for Investments in Dairy Digesters." *UC Agriculture & Natural Resources* 72 (4). https://doi.org/10.3733/ca.2018a0037.

Leger, Dorian, Silvio Matassa, Elad Noor, and Arren Bar-Even. 2021. "Photovoltaic-Driven Microbial Protein Production Can Use Land and Sunlight More Efficiently than Conventional Crops." *Proceedings of the National Academy of Sciences* 118 (26): e2015025118. https://doi.org/10.1073/pnas.2015025118.

Lerner, Anna, and Alison Filler. 2022. "Climate Collective: Emerging Digital MRV Tools Shape a New Climate Information Ecosystem." *Medium*, November 23. https://medium.com/@ClimateCollective/emerging-digital-mrv-tools-shape-a-new-climate-information-ecosystem-1e266df28f80.

Linaza, Maria Teresa, Jorge Posada, Jürgen Bund, Peter Eisert, Marco Quartulli, Jürgen Döllner, Alain Pagani, et al. 2021. "Data-Driven Artificial Intelligence Applications for Sustainable Precision Agriculture." *Agronomy* 11 (6): 1227.

Liu, C., and B. Wu. 2010. "'Grain for Green Programme' in China: Policy Making and Implementation." Briefing Series 60, China Policy Institute, University of Nottingham, Nottingham, UK. https://www.nottingham.ac.uk/iaps/documents/cpi/briefings/briefing-60-reforestation.pdf.

Lou, Jiehong, Nathan Hultman, Anand Patwardhan, and Yueming Lucy Qiu. 2022. "Integrating Sustainability into Climate Finance by Quantifying the Co-benefits and Market Impact of Carbon Projects." *Communications Earth & Environment* 3: 137. https://doi.org/10.1038/s43247-022-00468-9.

Mana, Hidayah, Julia H. Z. Moh, Nor Azman Kasan, Suhaimi Suratman, and Mhd Ikhwanuddin. 2016. "Study on Carbon Sinks by Classified Biofloc Phytoplankton from Marine Shrimp Pond Water." *AACL Bioflux* 9 (4): 845–53. https://www.researchgate.net/publication/321487515_Study_on_carbon_sinks_by_classified_biofloc_phytoplankton_from_marine_shrimp_pond_water.

Markkanen, Sanna, and Annela Anger-Kraavi. 2019. "Social Impacts of Climate Change Mitigation Policies and Their Implications for Inequality." *Climate Policy* 19 (7): 827–44. https://doi.org/10.1080/14693062.2019.1596873.

McGinn, S. M., T. K. Flesch, K. A. Beauchemin, A. Shreck, and M. Kindermann. 2019. "Micrometeorological Methods for Measuring Methane Emission Reduction at Beef Cattle Feedlots: Evaluation of 3-Nitrooxypropanol Feed Additive." *Journal of Environmental Quality* 48 (5): 1454–61. https://doi.org/10.2134/jeq2018.11.0412.

McKinsey & Company. 2023. *The Agricultural Transition: Building a Sustainable Future*. New York: McKinsey & Company. https://www.mckinsey.com/industries/agriculture/our-insights/the-agricultural-transition-building-a-sustainable-future.

MDBs (Multilateral Development Banks). August 2020. *2019 Joint Report on Multilateral Development Banks' Climate Finance*. London: European Bank for Reconstruction and Development. https://thedocs.worldbank.org/en/doc/999311596711498678-0020022020/original/1257jointreportonmdbsclimatefinance2019final.pdf.

Mekuriaw, Zeleke, and Lacey Harris-Coble. 2021. *Ethiopia's Livestock Systems: Overview and Areas of Inquiry*. Gainesville, FL: Feed the Future Innovation Lab for Livestock Systems.

Mekuyie, Muluken, Andries Jordaan, and Yoseph Melka. 2018. "Understanding Resilience of Pastoralists to Climate Change and Variability in the Southern Afar Region, Ethiopia." *Climate Risk Management* 20: 64–77. https://doi.org/10.1016/j.crm.2018.02.004.

Mercure, J-F., H. Pollitt, J. E. Viñuales, N. R. Edwards, P. B. Holden, U. Chewpreecha, P. Salas, I. Sognnaes, A. Lam, and F. Knobloch. 2018. "Macroeconomic Impact of Stranded Fossil Fuel Assets." *Nature Climate Change* 8: 588–93. https://doi.org/10.1038/s41558-018-0182-1.

Milan Urban Food Policy Pact. 2020. "Milan Urban Food Policy Pact" (web page). Accessed April 8, 2024. https://www.milanurbanfoodpolicypact.org/the-milan-pact/.

Millan, Alberto, Benhan Limketkai, and Serena Guarnaschelli. 2020. "Financing the Transformation of Food Systems under a Changing Climate." CGIAR Research Program on Climate Change, Agriculture and Food Security (CCAFS), KOIS Invest, Wageningen, the Netherlands. https://cgspace.cgiar.org/server/api/core/bitstreams/70043f85-8577-4320-b475-a1dc6d057551/content.

Minister for Europe and Foreign Affairs, France Diplomacy. 2022. "Climate Finance in Developing Countries: France Passes the €6 Billion Mark and Exceeds Its Commitments." News, November 9. https://www.diplomatie.gouv.fr/en/french-foreign-policy/climate-and-environment/news/article/climate-finance-in-developing-countries-france-passes-the-eur6-billion-mark-and.

Ministry for the Environment, New Zealand. 2018. "About the New Zealand Emissions Trading Scheme" (web page). Accessed April 8, 2024. https://environment.govt.nz/what-government-is-doing/areas-of-work/climate-change/ets/about-nz-ets/.

Ministry of Agriculture and Livestock, Brazil. 2023. "Plano Safra 2023/2024 Encourages Sustainability and Has 13 Investment Programs." Rural Credit, July 14. https://www.gov.br/agricultura/pt-br/assuntos/noticias/plano-safra-2023-2024-incentiva-sustentabilidade-e-conta-com-13-programas-para-custeio-comercializacao-e-investimentos.

Molvaer, R. K. 1995. *Socialization and Social Control in Ethiopia*. Otto, NY: Harrassowitz Verlag.

Morgan, M. 2023. *CGIAR-ISEAL Scoping Study: State of Gender Integration among ISEAL Community Members in the Agri-food Sector*. Rome: Alliance of Biodiversity International and the International Center for Tropical Agriculture.https://hdl.handle.net/10568/129728.

Morris, Michael, Ashwini Rekha Sebastian, Viviana Maria Eugenia Perego, John D. Nash, Eugenio Diaz-Bonilla, Valeria Pineiro, David Laborde, et al. 2020. *Future Foodscapes: Re-imagining Agriculture in Latin America and the Caribbean*. Washington, DC: World Bank Group. http://documents.worldbank.org/curated/en/942381591906970569/Future-Foodscapes-Re-imagining-Agriculture-in-Latin-America-and-the-Caribbean.

Mukherji, A., C. Arndt, J. Arango, F. Flintan, J. Derera, W. Francesconi, S. Jones, et al. 2023. *Achieving Agricultural Breakthrough: A Deep Dive into Seven Technological Areas*. Montpellier, France: CGIAR. https://hdl.handle.net/10568/131852.

Mulhollem, Jeff. 2021. "Newly Discovered Trait Helps Plants Grow Deeper Roots in Dry, Compacted Soils." Research, February 1. https://www.psu.edu/news/research/story/newly-discovered-trait-helps-plants-grow-deeper-roots-dry-compacted-soils/.

Nabuurs, G.-J., R. Mrabet, A. Abu Hatab, M. Bustamante, H. Clark, P. Havlík, J. House, et al. 2022. "Agriculture, Forestry and Other Land Uses (AFOLU)." In *Climate Change 2022: Mitigation of Climate Change; Contribution of Working Group III to the Sixth Assessment Report of the Intergovernmental Panel on Climate Change,* edited by P. R. Shukla, J. Skea, R. Slade, A. Al Khourdajie, R. van Diemen, D. McCollum, M. Pathak, et al., chap. 7. Cambridge: Cambridge University Press. https://doi.org/10.1017/9781009157926.009.

Nature4Climate. 2024. "N4C Weekly Brief: Jan 17-23." Accessed April 8, 2024. https://nature4climate.org/n4c-weekly-brief-jan-17-23/.

Nayak, Dali, Eli Saetnan, Kun Cheng, Wen Wang, Frank Koslowski, Yan-Fen Cheng, Wei Yun Zhu, et al. 2015. "Management Opportunities to Mitigate Greenhouse Gas Emissions from Chinese Agriculture." *Agriculture, Ecosystems & Environment* 209: 108–24. https://doi.org/10.1016/j.agee.2015.04.035.

Nesha, Karimon, Martin Herold, Veronique De Sy, Sytze de Bruin, Arnan Araza, Natalia Málaga, Javier G. P. Gamarra, et al. 2022. "Exploring Characteristics of National Forest Inventories for Integration with Global Space-Based Forest Biomass Data." *Science of the Total Environment* 850: 157788. https://doi.org/10.1016/j.scitotenv.2022.157788.

Nestlé Nespresso. 2022. "Nespresso and IFC Join Forces to Boost Climate Resilience, Improve Opportunities for Women and Enable More Prosperous Livelihoods for Coffee Farmers in Zimbabwe and Uganda" (article). October 21. https://nestle-nespresso.com/nespresso-and-ifc-join-forces-boost-climate-resilience.

Nico, Gianluigi, and Luc Christiaensen. 2023. "Jobs, Food and Greening: Exploring Implications of the Green Transition for Jobs in the Agri-Food System." World Bank Jobs Working Paper 75, World Bank, Washington, DC. http://hdl.handle.net/10986/39819.

Novick, B., J. Crouch, A. Ahmad, M. Rodiansyah, S. M. Kartikawati, N. Sudaryanti, N. Sagita, and A. E. Miller. 2023. "Understanding the Interactions between Human Well-Being and Environmental Outcomes through a Community-Led Integrated Landscape Initiative in Indonesia." *Environmental Development* 45: 100791.

NREL (National Renewable Energy Laboratory). 2021. "Documenting a Decade of Cost Declines for PV Systems." News, February 10. https://www.nrel.gov/news/program/2021/documenting-a-decade-of-cost-declines-for-pv-systems.html.

OECD (Organisation for Economic Co-operation and Development). 2015. *Aligning Policies for a Low-Carbon Economy*. Paris: OECD Publishing. https://doi.org/10.1787/9789264233294-en.

OECD (Organisation for Economic Co-operation and Development). 2019a. *Enhancing Climate Change Mitigation through Agriculture*. Paris: OECD Publishing. https://doi.org/10.1787/e9a79226-en.

OECD (Organisation for Economic Co-operation and Development). 2019b. "Policy Coherence in Food and Agriculture." In *Innovation, Productivity and Sustainability in Food and Agriculture: Main Findings from Country Reviews and Policy Lessons*. Paris: OECD Publishing. https://www.oecd-ilibrary.org/sites/f13335a7-en/index.html?itemId=/content/component/f13335a7-en.

OECD (Organisation for Economic Co-operation and Development). 2019c. *Trends and Drivers of Agri-environmental Performance in OECD Countries*. Paris: OECD Publishing. https://doi.org/10.1787/b59b1142-en.

OECD (Organisation for Economic Co-operation and Development). 2021. "Good Blended Finance Practices Can Scale Up Finance for Agri-SMEs." OECD Development Co-operation Directorate, Paris. Accessed April 8, 2024. https://www.oecd.org/dac/financing-sustainable-development/blended-finance-principles/documents/Blended-Finance-in-Agriculture.pdf.

OECD (Organisation for Economic Co-operation and Development). 2022a. "Climate Finance and the USD 100 Billion Goal: Climate Finance Provided and Mobilised by Developed Countries in 2013–2020." OECD, Paris. https://www.oecd.org/climate-change/finance-usd-100-billion-goal/aggregate-trends-of-climate-finance-provided-and-mobilised-by-developed-countries-in-2013-2020.pdf.

OECD (Organisation for Economic Co-operation and Development). 2022b. "Climate Finance and the USD 100 Billion Goal: Spotlight; Aggregate Trends for 2013–21" (web page.) Accessed April 8, 2024. https://www.oecd.org/climate-change/finance-usd-100-billion-goal/.

OECD (Organisation for Economic Co-operation and Development). 2022c. *Climate Finance Provided and Mobilised by Developed Countries in 2016–2020: Insights from Disaggregated Analysis*. Paris: OECD Publishing. https://doi.org/10.1787/286dae5d-en.

OECD (Organisation for Economic Co-operation and Development). 2022d. "In Practice: New Zealand's Plans for Agricultural Emissions Pricing" (web page). Accessed April 8, 2024. https://www.oecd.org/climate-action/ipac/practices/new-zealand-s-plans-for-agricultural-emissions-pricing-d4f4245c/.

OECD (Organisation for Economic Co-operation and Development). 2022e. "OECD Agriculture Ministerial Declaration on 'Transformative Solutions for Sustainable Agriculture and Food Systems.'" I/A item note, OECD, Brussels.

Ogello, E. O., N. O. Outa, K. O. Obiero, D. N. Kyule, and J. M. Munguti. 2021. "The Prospects of Biofloc Technology (BFT) for Sustainable Aquaculture Development." *Scientific African* 14. https://doi.org/10.1016/j.sciaf.2021.e01053.

Olam. 2022. "Olam Launches Climate-Tech Venture Terrascope to Enable Enterprises to Achieve Their Net Zero Ambitions." Press release, June 9. https://www.olamgroup.com/news/all-news/press-release/olam-launches-climate-tech-venture-terrascope-to-enable-enterprises-to-achieve-their-net-zero-ambitions.html.

Ornes, Stephen. 2021. "Green Ammonia Could Produce Climate-Friendly Ways to Store Energy and Fertilize Farms." *Proceedings of the National Academy of Sciences* 118 (49): e2119584118. https://doi.org/10.1073/pnas.2119584118.

Ortiz Valverde, Rosalba, Pablo Aránguiz Mesías, and Jordi Peris-Blanes. 2022. "Just Transitions through Agroecological Innovations in Family Farming in Guatemala: Enablers and Barriers towards Gender Equality." *Environmental Innovation and Societal Transitions* 45: 228–45. https://doi.org/10.1016/j.eist.2022.11.002.

Pagiola, S. 2008. *Payments for Environmental Services in Costa Rica*. Washington, DC: World Bank.

Paprocki, Kasia. 2018. "Threatening Dystopias: Development and Adaptation Regimes in Bangladesh." *Annals of the American Association of Geographers* 108 (4): 955–73. https://doi.org/10.1080/24694452.2017.1406330.

Pardey, Philip G., Connie Chan-Kang, Stephen P. Dehmer, and Jason M. Beddow. 2016. "Agricultural R&D Is On the Move." *Nature* 537: 301–3. https://doi.org/10.1038/537301a.

Peterson, Brittany. 2023. "CES 2023: Companies Tout Environmental Tech Innovations." *AP News*, January 9. https://apnews.com/article/ces-2023-las-vegas-technology-sustainability-climate-31d2663e9e47b6e18f99d87afc311338.

Pitta, Dipti W., Nagaraju Indugu, Audino Melgar, Alexander Hristov, Krishna Challa, Bonnie Vecchiarelli, Meagan Hennessy, et al. 2022. "The Effect of 3-Nitrooxypropanol, a Potent Methane Inhibitor, on Ruminal Microbial Gene Expression Profiles in Dairy Cows." *Microbiome* 10: 146. https://doi.org/10.1186/s40168-022-01341-9.

Plan Vivo. n.d. "ACORN" (web page). Accessed April 8, 2024. https://www.planvivo.org/acorn/.

Plastina, Alejandro, and Terry Townsend. 2023. "World Spending on Agricultural Research and Development." *Agricultural Policy Review* [Center for Agricultural and Rural Development, Iowa State University] (Winter). www.card.iastate.edu/ag_policy_review/article/?a=152.

Plumer, Brad, and Nadja Popovich. 2019. "These Countries Have Prices on Carbon. Are They Working?" *New York Times*, April 2. https://www.nytimes.com/interactive/2019/04/02/climate/pricing-carbon-emissions.html#:~:text=Canada%20currently%20has%20one%20of,%2438%20per%20ton%20by%202022.

Poudyal, Mahesh, Bruno S. Ramamonjisoa, Neal Hockley, O. Sarobidy Rakotonarivo, James M. Gibbons, Rina Mandimbiniaina, Alexandra Rasoamanana, and Julia P. G. Jones. 2016. "Can REDD+ Social Safeguards Reach the 'Right' People? Lessons from Madagascar." *Global Environmental Change* 37: 31–42. https://doi.org/10.1016/j.gloenvcha.2016.01.004.

Ray, N. E., and R. W. Fulweiler. 2021. "Meta-analysis of Oyster Impacts on Coastal Biogeochemistry." *Nature Sustainability* 4: 261–69. https://doi.org/10.1038/s41893-020-00644-9.

REDD+ Belize. 2022. "REDD+ Readiness Package." National Climate Change Office, Belmopan, Belize. https://www.forestcarbonpartnership.org/system/files/documents/redd_belize_readiness_package_final.pdf.

Reij, Chris, and Ann Waters-Bayer, eds. 2014. *Farmer Innovation in Africa: A Source of Inspiration for Agricultural Development*. Abingdon-on-Thames, UK: Routledge.

Reij, Chris., G. Gray Tappan, and Melinda Smale. 2009. *Agroenvironmental Transformation in the Sahel: Another Kind of "Green Revolution."* Report 914. Sioux Falls, SD: Earth Resources Observation and Science Center, US Geological Survey. https://www.usgs.gov/publications/agroenvironmental-transformation-sahel-another-kind-green-revolution

Rempel, Arthur, and Joyeeta Gupta. 2021. "Fossil Fuels, Stranded Assets and COVID-19: Imagining an Inclusive and Transformative Recovery." *World Development* 146 (C). https://doi.org/10.1016/j.worlddev.2021.105608.

Rioux, J., I. Vasileiou, S. Burgos, J. Wolf, E. Drieux, L. Kagure, and M. Bernoux. 2023. "Outcomes and Lessons Learned from the Koronivia UNFCCC Negotiations on Agriculture and Food Security, and the Way Forward after COP 27: Brief Note." Food and Agriculture Organization of the United Nations, Rome. https://doi.org/10.4060/cc5739en.

Roe, S., C. Streck, R. Beach, J. Busch, M. Chapman, V. Daioglou, A. Deppermann, et al. 2021. "Land-Based Measures to Mitigate Climate Change: Potential and Feasibility by Country." *Global Change Biology* 27 (23): 6025–58. https://doi.org/10.1111/gcb.15873.

Rotz, S., E. Gravely, I. Mosby, E. Duncan, E. Finnis, M. Horgan, J. LeBlanc, et al. 2019. "Automated Pastures and the Digital Divide: How Agricultural Technologies Are Shaping Labor and Rural Communities." *Journal of Rural Studies* 68: 112–22. https://doi.org/10.1016/j.jrurstud.2019.01.023.

Sadler, Marc Peter. 2016. "Making Climate Finance Work in Agriculture." Discussion Paper, World Bank, Washington, DC. http://documents.worldbank.org/curated/en/986961467721999165/Making-climate-finance-work-in-agriculture.

SAFIN (Smallholder and Agri-SME Finance and Investment Network). 2022. *"Annual Progress Report 2022." International Fund for Agricultural Development, Rome.* https://www.ifad.org/documents/38714170/47669864/safin-ar-2022.pdf/f667449e-224c-6a14-5ed8-c4e247754eaf?t=1686640304465.

Santo, Raychel E., Brent F. Kim, Sarah E. Goldman, Jan Dutkiewicz, Erin M. B. Biehl, Martin W. Bloem, Roni A. Neff, and Keeve E. Nachman. 2020. "Considering Plant-Based Meat Substitutes and Cell-Based Meats: A Public Health and Food Systems Perspective." *Frontiers in Sustainable Food Systems* 4: 1–23. https://doi.org/10.3389/fsufs.2020.00134.

Santos, N., J. Monzini Taccone di Sitizano, E. Pedersen, and E. Borgomeo. 2022. *Investing in Carbon Neutrality—Utopia or the New Green Wave? Challenges and Opportunities for Agrifood Systems.* Rome: Food and Agriculture Organization of the United Nations. https://doi.org/10.4060/cc0011en.

Sapkota, Tek B., Fahmida Khanam, Gokul Prasad Mathivanan, Sylvia Vetter, Sk. Ghulam Hussain, Anne-Laure Pilat, Sumona Shahrin, Md. Khaled Hossain, Nathu Ram Sarker, and Timothy J. Krupnik. 2021. "Quantifying Opportunities for Greenhouse Gas Emissions Mitigation Using Big Data from Smallholder Crop and Livestock Farmers across Bangladesh." *Science of the Total Environment* 786: 147344. https://doi.org/10.1016/j.scitotenv.2021.147344.

Sapkota, Tek B., Sylvia H. Vetter, M. L. Jat, Smita Sirohi, Paresh B. Shirsath, Rajbir Singh, Hanuman S. Jat, Pete Smith, Jon Hillier, and Clare M. Stirling. 2019. "Cost-Effective Opportunities for Climate Change Mitigation in Indian Agriculture." *Science of the Total Environment* 655: 1342–54. https://doi.org/10.1016/j.scitotenv.2018.11.225.

Sarku, R., M. Tauzie, and S. Whitfield. 2023. "Making a Case for Just Agricultural Transformation in the UNFCCC: An Analysis of Justice in the Koronivia Joint Work on Agriculture." *Frontiers in Sustainable Food Systems* 6. https://doi.org/10.3389/fsufs.2022.1033152.

Saxena, Riya, Weiting Li, Sabina Flandrick, Lila Holzman, and Benjamin Bartle. 2023. "Private Finance Is Coming off the Sidelines on MDB Reform" (article). RMI, July 10. https://rmi.org/private-finance-is-coming-off-the-sidelines-on-mdb-reform/#:~:text=The%20MDB%20reform%20agenda%20involves,private%20capital%20for%20climate%20investments.

Schiettecatte, L.-S., P. Audebert, V. Umulisa, D. Dionisio, and M. Bernoux. 2022. "The Nationally Determined Contribution Expert Tool (NEXT): A Comprehensive Greenhouse Gas Accounting Tool to Support Annual Environmental Impact Assessment over a 30-Year Time Series in the Agriculture, Forestry and Other Land Use Sector." *Frontiers in Climate* 4: 906142. https://doi.org/10.3389/fclim.2022.906142.

Schipper, E. L. F. 2022. "Catching Maladaptation before It Happens." *Nature Climate Change* 12: 617–18. https://doi.org/10.1038/s41558-022-01409-2.

Schipper, E.L.F., A. Revi, B.L. Preston, E.R. Carr, S.H. Eriksen, L.R. Fernandez-Carril, B.C. Glavovic, N.J.M. Hilmi, D. Ley, R. Mukerji, M.S. Muylaert de Araujo, R. Perez, S.K. Rose, and P.K. Singh. 2022. "Climate Resilient Development Pathways." In: Climate Change 2022: Impacts, Adaptation and Vulnerability. Contribution of Working Group II to the Sixth Assessment Report of the Intergovernmental Panel on Climate Change. H.-O. Pörtner, D.C. Roberts, M. Tignor, E.S. Poloczanska, K. Mintenbeck, A. Alegría, M. Craig, S. Langsdorf, S. Löschke, V. Möller, A. Okem, B. Rama (eds.). Cambridge: Cambridge University Press. pp. 2655–2807, doi:10.1017/9781009325844.027.

Schroeder, Kateryna, Julian Lampietti, and Ghada Elabed. 2021. *What's Cooking: Digital Transformation of the Agrifood System.* Agriculture and Food Series. Washington, DC: World Bank. http://hdl.handle.net/10986/35216.

Searchinger, Timothy D., Chris Malins, Patrice Dumas, David Baldock, Joe Glauber, Thomas Jayne, Jikun Huang, and Paswel Marenya. 2020. *Revising Public Agricultural Support to Mitigate Climate Change.* Development Knowledge and Learning. Washington, DC: World Bank. https://documents1.worldbank.org/curated/en/773701588657353273/pdf/Development-Knowledge-and-Learning-Revising-Public-Agricultural-Support-to-Mitigate-Climate-Change.pdf.

Senate Democrats. 2022. "Summary of the Energy Security and Climate Change Investments in the Inflation Reduction Act of 2022." https://www.democrats.senate.gov/imo/media/doc/summary_of_the_energy_security_and_climate_change_investments_in_the_inflation_reduction_act_of_2022.pdf.

Shell and BCG (Boston Consulting Group). 2023. "The Voluntary Carbon Market: 2022 Insights and Trends." Shell, London. https://www.shell.com/shellenergy/othersolutions/carbonmarketreports.html.

Shonchoy, A. S., S. Raihan, and T. Fujii. 2017. "Reducing Extreme Poverty through Skill Training for Industry Job Placement." GMLIC Policy Brief 9, Gender, Growth and Labour Markets in Low-Income Countries, Foreign, Commonwealth & Development Office, London. https://www.gov.uk/research-for-development-outputs/reducing-extreme-poverty-through-skill-training-for-industry-job-placement-policy-brief-no-9.

Sinclair, Fergus, Alexander Wezel, Cheikh Mbow, Susan Chomba, Valentina Robiglio, and Rhett Harrison. 2019. "The Contribution of Agroecological Approaches to Realizing Climate-Resilient Agriculture." Background paper, Global Commission on Adaptation, Rotterdam and Washington, DC. https://gca.org/wp-content/uploads/2020/12/TheContributionsOfAgroecologicalApproaches.pdf.

Sinke, Pelle, Elliot Swartz, Hermes Sanctorum, Coen van der Giesen, and Ingrid Odegard. 2023. "Ex-Ante Life Cycle Assessment of Commercial-Scale Cultivated Meat Production in 2030." *International Journal of Life Cycle Assessment* 28: 234–54. https://doi.org/10.1007/s11367-022-02128-8.

Solomon, Matthew. 2022. "Private Financial Institutions' Paris Alignment Commitments: 2022 Update." Climate Policy Initiative, San Francisco, CA. https://www.climatepolicyinitiative.org/wp-content /uploads/2022/06/Private-Financial-Institutions-Paris-Alignment-Commitments-l-2022-Update.pdf.

South Pole. 2021. "South Pole Announces Development of New Facility to Scale Up the Next Generation of Carbon Removals Together with Mitsubishi Corporation." News, May 7. https://www.southpole.com /news/south-pole-announces-development-of-new-facility-to-scale-up-the-next-generation-of-carbon -removals-together-with-mitsubishi-corporation.

Springmann, Marco, Daniel Mason-D'Croz, Sherman Robinson, Keith Wiebe, H. Charles J. Godfray, Mike Rayner, and Peter Scarborough. 2017. "Mitigation Potential and Global Health Impacts from Emissions Pricing of Food Commodities." *Nature Climate Change* 7 (1): 69–74. https://doi.org/10.1038 /nclimate3155. https://www.nature.com/articles/nclimate3155.

Stanley, Michael C., John E. Strongman, Rachel Bernice Perks, Helen Ba Thanh Nguyen, Wendy Cunningham, -Achim Daniel Schmillen, and Michael Stephen McCormick. 2018. "Managing Coal Mine Closure: Achieving a Just Transition for All." Working Paper 130659, World Bank Group, Washington, DC. http://documents.worldbank.org/curated/en/484541544643269894/Managing-Coal -Mine-Closure-Achieving-a-Just-Transition-for-All.

State of California. 2016. Senate Bill 1383 on Climate Short-Lived Pollutants. http://www.leginfo.ca.gov /pub/15-16/bill/sen/sb_1351-1400/sb_1383_bill_20160919_chaptered.htm.

Stefenoni, H. A., S. E. Räisänen, S. F. Cueva, D. E. Wasson, C. F. A. Lage, A. Melgar, M. E. Fetter, et al. 2021. "Effects of the Macroalga Asparagopsis Taxiformis and Oregano Leaves on Methane Emission, Rumen Fermentation, and Lactational Performance of Dairy Cows." *Journal of Dairy Science* 104 (4): 4157–73. https://doi.org/10.3168/jds.2020-19686.

Streck, Charlotte, Melaina Dyck, and Danick Trouwloon. 2023. *The Voluntary Carbon Market Explained.* Updated ed. Amsterdam: Climate Focus. https://vcmprimer.files.wordpress.com/2023/01/20230118_vcm -explained_all-chapters_compressed_final.pdf.

Strohmaier, R., J. Rioux, A. Seggel, A. Meybeck, M. Bernoux, M. Salvatore, J. Miranda, and A. Agostini. 2016. "The Agriculture Sectors in the Intended Nationally Determined Contributions: Analysis." Environment and Natural Resources Management Working Paper 62, Food and Agriculture Organization of the United Nations, Rome.

Tan, Adrian R., and Shailendra Mudgal. 2013. "Reducing Fertiliser Use in Denmark." DYNAMIX Policy Mix Evaluation. Berlin: DYNAMIX. http://dynamix-project.eu/sites/default/files/Fertilisers_Denmark.pdf.

Tang, Kai, Marit E. Kragt, Atakelty Hailu, and Chunbo Ma. 2016. "Carbon Farming Economics: What Have We Learned?" *Journal of Environmental Management* 172: 49–57. https://doi.org/10.1016/j .jenvman.2016.02.008.

Tarique, Md., and Shadman Zafar. 2023. "Is India's Fertilizer Subsidy Poorly Targeted?" *Business Today,* July 12. https://www.businesstoday.in/opinion/columns/story/is-indias-fertilizer-subsidy-poorly-targeted -389372-2023-07-12.

TechnoServe. 2022. *2022 Annual Report.* Arlington, VA: TechnoServe. https://www.technoserve.org/2022 -annual-report/.

Termeer, Emma, Siemen van Berkum, Youri Dijkxhoorn, and Bart de Steenhuijsen Piters. 2022. "Unpacking the Informal Midstream: How the Informal Economy Can and Should Contribute to Enhanced Food System Outcomes." Policy Paper 2022-106, Wageningen Economic Research, Wageningen, the Netherlands. https://edepot.wur.nl/576754.

Testa, Stefania, Kristian Roed Nielsen, Steen Vallentin, and Federica Ciccullo. 2022. "Sustainability-Oriented Innovation in the Agri-food System: Current Issues and the Road Ahead." *Technological Forecasting and Social Change* 179. https://doi.org/10.1016/j.techfore.2022.121653.

Timmer, John. 2022. "US Installs Record Solar Capacity as Prices Keep Falling." Ars Technica, September 21. https://arstechnica.com/science/2022/09/us-installs-record-solar-capacity-as-prices-keep-falling/.

Toman, M. J. Baker, R. Beach, H. Feng, E. McLellan, and E. Joiner. 2022. "Policies to Increase Mitigation of Agricultural Greenhouse Gas Emissions." Issues Brief 22-10, Resources for the Future, Washington, DC. https://media.rff.org/documents/IB_22-10.pdf.

Toudert, Anass, Ademola Braimoh, Martial Bernoux, Maylina St-Louis, Manar Abdelmagied, Louis Bockel, Adriana Ignaciuk, and Yuxuan Zhao. 2018. "Greenhouse Gas Accounting for Sustainable Land Management: Quick Guidance for Users." World Bank, Washington, DC. http://documents.worldbank .org/curated/en/553171544165496697/Greenhouse-Gas-Accounting-for-Sustainable-Land-Management -Quick-Guidance-for-Users.

Townsend, Robert, Rui Manuel Benfica, Ashesh Prasann, Maria Lee, and Parmesh Shah. 2017. *Future of Food: Shaping the Food System to Deliver Jobs*. Washington, DC: World Bank Group. http://documents .worldbank.org/curated/en/406511492528621198/Future-of-food-shaping-the-food-system-to-deliver-jobs.

Tribaldos, Theresa, and Teea Kortetmäki. 2022. "Just Transition Principles and Criteria for Food Systems and Beyond." *Environmental Innovation and Societal Transitions* 43: 244–56. https://doi.org/10.1016/j .eist.2022.04.005.

Tschersich, Julia, and Kristiaan P. W. Kok. 2022. "Deepening Democracy for the Governance toward Just Transitions in Agri-food Systems." *Environmental Innovation and Societal Transitions* 43: 358–74. https://doi.org/10.1016/j.eist.2022.04.012.

TSVCM (Taskforce on Scaling Voluntary Carbon Markets). 2021. *Task Force on Scaling Voluntary Carbon Markets: Final Report*. https://www.iif.com/Portals/1/Files/TSVCM_Report.pdf.

Turnhout, Esther, Aarti Gupta, Janice Weatherley-Singh, Marjanneke J. Vijge, Jessica de Koning, Ingrid J. Visseren-Hamakers, Martin Herold, and Markus Lederer. 2017. "Envisioning REDD+ in a Post-Paris Era: Between Evolving Expectations and Current Practice." *WIREs Climate Change* 8 (1): e425. https:// doi.org/10.1002/wcc.425.

UK Government. n.d. "Low-Emission Vehicles Eligible for a Plug-In Grant" (web page). Accessed April 8, 2024. https://www.gov.uk/plug-in-vehicle-grants.

UN (United Nations) General Assembly. 1992. "Report of the United Nations Conference on Environment and Development (Rio de Janeiro, 3–14 June 1992), Annex I: Rio Declaration on Environment and Development." A/CONF.151/26 (Vol. I), August 12. URL: https://www.un.org/en/development/desa /population/migration/generalassembly/docs/globalcompact/A_CONF.151_26_Vol.I_Declaration.pdf.

UN Secretary-General. 2023. "Making Food Systems Work for People and Planet: UN Food Systems Summit +2." Report of the Secretary-General. United Nations, New York. https://www .unfoodsystemshub.org/docs/unfoodsystemslibraries/stocktaking-moment/un-secretary-general /unfss2-secretary-general-report.pdf.

UNEP (United Nations Environment Programme). 2023. "Annual Report 2022." UNEP, Nairobi, Kenya. https://www.unep.org/resources/annual-report-2022.

UNFCCC (United Nations Framework Convention on Climate Change). 2015. "The Paris Agreement." UNFCCC, Bonn. https://unfccc.int/process-and-meetings/the-paris-agreement/the-paris-agreement.

UNFCCC (United Nations Framework Convention on Climate Change). 2018. "Modalities, Procedures and Guidelines for the Transparency Framework for Action and Support Referred to in Article 13 of the Paris Agreement, 18/CMA.1." Decision 18/CMA.1, December 2, 2018. https://unfccc.int/resource /tet/0/00mpg.pdf.

UNFCCC (United Nations Framework Convention on Climate Change). 2019a. "Institutionalizing Data Management System: 2nd CGE Pilot Informal Forum." Capacity-Building Hub, December 5. https:// unfccc.int/sites/default/files/resource/2nd%20CGE%20informal%20forum_CGE.pdf.

UNFCCC (United Nations Framework Convention on Climate Change). 2019b. *Report of the Conference of the Parties Serving as the Meeting of the Parties to the Paris Agreement on the Third Part of Its First Session, Held in Katowice from 2 to 15 December 2018. Addendum 2. Part Two: Action Taken by the Conference of the Parties Serving as the Meeting of the Parties to the Paris Agreement*. FCCC/PA /CMA/2018/3/Add.2. Bonn: UNFCCC. https://unfccc.int/documents/193408.

UNFCCC (United Nations Framework Convention on Climate Change). 2022. "UNFCCC Standing Committee on Finance." https://unfccc.int/sites/default/files/resource/J0156_UNFCCC%20100BN%20 2022%20Report_Book_v3.2.pdf.

UNFCCC (United Nations Framework Convention on Climate Change). 2023. "Operationalization of the New Funding Arrangements, including a Fund, for Responding to Loss and Damage Referred to in Paragraphs 2–3 of Decisions 2/CP.27 and 2/CMA.4." Decision 5/CMA.5, November 30, 2023. https:// unfccc.int/decisions?f%5B0%5D=body%3A4099.

UNFCCC (United Nations Framework Convention on Climate Change). n.d.-a. "About the Secretariat" (web page). Accessed April 8, 2024. https://unfccc.int/about-us/about-the-secretariat.

UNFCCC (United Nations Framework Convention on Climate Change), n.d.-b. "GET FiT Uganda" (web page). Accessed March 26, 2023. https://unfccc.int/climate-action/momentum-for-change/activity-database/get-fit-uganda.

UNFCCC (United Nations Framework Convention on Climate Change). n.d.-c. "Mechanisms under the Kyoto Protocol: Joint Implementation" (web page). Accessed April 8, 2024. https://unfccc.int/process/the-kyoto-protocol/mechanisms/joint-implementation.

UNFCCC SBI (United Nations Framework Convention on Climate Change Subsidiary Body for Implementation). 2023. "Sharm el-Sheikh Joint Work on Implementation of Climate Action on Agriculture and Food Security: Draft Conclusions Proposed by the Chairs." UNFCCC, Bonn. https://unfccc.intdocuments/629501.

UNFCCC Technology Executive Committee. 2017. "Enhancing Financing for the Research, Development, and Demonstration of Climate Technologies." Technology Executive Committee Working Paper, United Nations Framework Convention on Climate Change, Bonn. https://unfccc.int/ttclear/docs/TEC_RDD%20finance_FINAL.pdf.

UNFSS (United Nations Forum on Sustainability Standards). 2022. "Voluntary Sustainability Standards Sustainability Agenda and Developing Countries: Opportunities and Challenges. 5th Flagship Report of the United Nations Forum on Sustainability Standards." https://unfss.org/wp-content/uploads/2022/10UNFSS-5th-Report_14Oct2022_rev.pdf.

United Nations. 1992. "United Nations Framework Convention on Climate Change." United Nations, New York. https://unfccc.int/files/essential_background/background_publications_htmlpdf/application/pdf/conveng.pdf.

US Department of Energy. 2023. "Electric Vehicle Battery Pack Costs in 2022 Are Nearly 90 percent Lower Than in 2008, According to DOE Estimates." Fact of the Week 1272, January 9. https://www.energy.gov/eerevehicles/articles/fotw-1272-january-9-2023-electric-vehicle-battery-pack-costs-2022-are-nearly.

Valin, H., P. Havlík, A. Mosnier, M. Herrero, E. Schmid, and M. Obersteiner. 2013. "Agricultural Productivity and Greenhouse Gas Emissions: Trade-Offs or Synergies between Mitigation and Food Security?" *Environmental Research Letters* 8 (3): 035019. https://doi.org/10.1088/1748-9326/8/3/035019.

Van Eenennaam, A. L., and S. J. Werth. 2021. "Animal Board Invited Review: Animal Agriculture and Alternative Meats—Learning from Past Science Communication Failures." *Animal* 15 (10). https://doi.org/10.1017/S1751731121000725.

Verdolini, E., L. D. Anadón, E. Baker, V. Bosetti, and L. A. Reis. 2018. "Future Prospects for Energy Technologies: Insights from Expert Elicitations." *Review of Environmental Economics and Policy* 12 (1): 133–53. https://doi.org/10.1093/reep/rex028.

Verner, Dorte, Nanna Roos, Afton Halloran, Glenn Surabian, Edinaldo Tebaldi, Maximillian Ashwill, Saleema Vellani, and Yasuo Konishi. 2021. *Insect and Hydroponic Farming in Africa: The New Circular Food Economy.* Agriculture and Food Series. Washington, DC: World Bank. http://hdl.handle.net/10986/36401.

Vives, Gemma Torres. 2023. "Why Data Infrastructure Is Key for a Transparent Carbon Market." *Climate Action Data Trust Blog*, August 3. https://climateactiondata.org/why-data-infrastructure-is-key-for-a-transparent-carbon-market/.

Voegele, Juergen. 2023. "Transforming Our Food Systems for Healthy People, Environment, and Economies." *Voices* (blog), January 17. https://blogs.worldbank.org/voices/transforming-our-food-systems-healthy-people-environment-and-economies.

Walker, Wayne S., Seth R. Gorelik, Alessandro Baccini, Jose Luis Aragon-Osejo, Carmen Josse, Chris Meyer, Marcia N. Macedo, et al. 2020. "The Role of Forest Conversion, Degradation, and Disturbance in the Carbon Dynamics of Amazon Indigenous Territories and Protected Areas." *Proceedings of the National Academy of Sciences* 117 (6): 3015–25. https://doi.org/10.1073/pnas.1913321117.

Wang, Sheng, Kaiyu Guan, Chenhui Zhang, DoKyoung Lee, Andrew J. Margenot, Yufeng Ge, Jian Peng, Wang Zhou, Qu Zhou, and Yizhi Huang. 2022. "Using Soil Library Hyperspectral Reflectance and Machine Learning to Predict Soil Organic Carbon: Assessing Potential of Airborne and Spaceborne Optical Soil Sensing." *Remote Sensing of Environment* 271: 112914. https://doi.org/10.1016/j.rse.2022.112914.

Wasafiri. 2021. "A Small Business Agenda for the UN Food Systems Summit." July. United Nations, Washington, DC. https://www.un.org/sites/un2.un.org/files/2021/07/unfss-small_business_agenda.pdf.

White, K., D. J. Hardisty, and R. Habib. 2019. "The Elusive Green Consumer." *Harvard Business Review*, July–August. https://hbr.org/2019/07/the-elusive-green-consumer.

Wilkes, A., A. Reisinger, E. Wollenberg, and S. van Dijk. 2017. *Measurement, Reporting and Verification of Livestock GHG Emissions by Developing Countries in the UNFCCC: Current Practices and Opportunities for Improvement.* CCAFS Report 17. Wageningen, the Netherlands: CGIAR Research Program on Climate Change, Agriculture and Food Security (CCAFS) and Global Research Alliance for Agricultural Greenhouse Gases (GRA). https://hdl.handle.net/10568/89335.

Wirkowski, K. 2023. "COP27: Growing Roles for Agriculture and Food Security." *IICA Blog,* February 2. https://blog.iica.int/en/blog/cop27-growing-roles-agriculture-and-food-security.

Wood, Paul, Lieven Thorrez, Jean-François Hocquette, Declan Troy, and Mohammed Gagaoua. 2023. "Cellular Agriculture: Current Gaps between Facts and Claims Regarding 'Cell-Based Meat.'" *Animal Frontiers* 13 (2): 68–74. https://doi.org/10.1093/af/vfac092.

World Bank. 2003. "A User's Guide to Poverty and Social Impact Analysis." Working Paper 30405, World Bank, Washington, DC. http://documents.worldbank.org/curated/en/278581468779694160/A-users-guide-to-poverty-and-social-impact-analysis.

World Bank. 2015. *Future of Food: Shaping a Climate-Smart Global Food System.* Washington, DC: World Bank. https://openknowledge.worldbank.org/handle/10986/22927.

World Bank. 2019. "Climate Smart Agriculture Investment Plans: Bringing CSA to Life" (web page). Accessed April 5, 2024. https://www.worldbank.org/en/topic/agriculture/publication/climate-smart-agriculture-investment-plans-bringing-climate-smart-agriculture-to-life

World Bank. 2022a. "Behavioral Sciences Approach to Empowering Women in Forest Landscape: Diagnostics Toolkit." World Bank, Washington, DC. https://hdl.handle.net/10986/37777.

World Bank. 2022b. "Spearheading Vietnam's Green Agricultural Transformation: Moving to Low-Carbon Rice." World Bank, Washington, DC. https://documents.worldbank.org/en/publication/documents-reports/documentdetail/099735109222222315/p17448205335130730bb7e0a6e231e1f667.

World Bank. 2022c. *State and Trends of Carbon Pricing 2022.* Washington, DC: World Bank. http://hdl.handle.net/10986/37455.

World Bank. 2022d. "Transition to Low-Carbon Rice Will Help Vietnam Meet Its Emission Target While Maintaining Competitiveness Edge." Press Release, September 24. https://www.worldbank.org/en/news/press-release/2022/09/24/transition-to-low-carbon-rice-will-help-vietnam-meet-its-emission-target-while-maintaining-competitiveness-edge.

World Bank. 2022e. "What You Need to Know About the Measurement, Reporting, and Verification (MRV) of Carbon Credits" (feature story, July 7). https://www.worldbank.org/en/news/feature/2022/07/27/what-you-need-to-know-about-the-measurement-reporting-and-verification-mrv-of-carbon-credits.

World Bank. 2023a. "Belize FCPF REDD Readiness Preparation: Development Objective" (web page). Accessed April 8, 2024. https://projects.worldbank.org/en/projects-operations/project-detail/P152415.

World Bank. 2023b. "Carbon Pricing Dashboard" (web page). Accessed January 27, 2023. https://carbonpricingdashboard.worldbank.org.

World Bank. 2023c. "The Effect of Agricultural Input Subsidies on Productivity: A Meta-analysis." Policy Research Working Paper 10399, World Bank, Washington, DC. https://openknowledge.worldbank.org/server/api/core/bitstreams/e9774ae9-3fe5-41d7-83ab-297a0f239dd4/content.

World Bank. 2023d. *Global Seaweed: New and Emerging Markets Report, 2023.* Washington, DC: World Bank. http://hdl.handle.net/10986/40187.

World Bank. 2023e. "Guidance Note for Borrowers: ESS1 Assessment and Management of Environmental and Social Risks and Impacts Guidance Note." Environmental & Social Framework for IPF Operations, World Bank, Washington, DC. https://documents1.worldbank.org/curated/en/142691530216729197/ESF-Guidance-Note-1-Assessment-and-Management-of-Environmental-and-Social-Risks-and-Impacts-English.pdf.

World Bank. Forthcoming. *Trade and Climate Change: Policy Considerations for Developing Countries.* Washington, DC: World Bank.

World Bank Group. 2016. *Enabling the Business of Agriculture 2016: Comparing Regulatory Good Practices.* Washington, DC: World Bank. https://doi.org/10.1596/978-1-4648-0772-5.

World Bank Group. 2021. *World Bank Group Climate Change Action Plan 2021–2025: Supporting Green, Resilient, and Inclusive Development.* Washington, DC: World Bank. http://hdl.handle.net/10986/35799.

World Economic Forum. 2018. *Innovation with a Purpose: The Role of Technology Innovation in Accelerating Food Systems Transformation.* Geneva: World Economic Forum. https://www.weforum.org/reports/innovation-with-a-purpose-the-role-of-technology-innovation-in-accelerating-food-systems-transformation.

World Economic Forum. 2019. "Top 10 Emerging Technologies 2019." Insight report. World Econoic Forum, Geneva. https://www3.weforum.org/docs/WEF_Top_10_Emerging_Technologies_2019_Report.pdf.

World Farmers' Organisation. 2020. *The Farmers' Route to Sustainable Food Systems.* Policy Paper on Sustainable Food Systems, World Farmers' Organisation, Rome. https://www.wfo-oma.org/wp-content/uploads/2020/07/WFO-Policy-Paper-on-Sustainable-Food-Systems_approved-by-the-WFO-2020-GA_EN.pdf.

World Farmers' Organisation. 2023. "Climate-Smart Agriculture: First Global Producers' Consultation." World Farmers' Organisation, Rome. https://www.wfo-oma.org/wp-content/uploads/2023/11/AG-MISSION-REPORT-CSA-2023.pdf.

WRI (World Resources Institute). 2024. "Navigating the Paris Rulebook: Enhanced Transparency Framework" (web page). Accessed April 8, 2024. https://www.wri.org/paris-rulebook/enhanced-transparency-framework.

Xepapadeas, A. 1995. "Observability and Choice of Instrument Mix in the Control of Externalities." *Journal of Public Economics* 56 (3): 485–98. https://doi.org/10.1016/0047-2727(94)01441-P.

Xiaobei, He, Zhai Fan, and Ma Jun. 2022. "The Global Impact of a Carbon Border Adjustment Mechanism: A Quantitative Assessment." Working paper, Task Force on Climate, Development and the International Monetary Fund. https://www.bu.edu/gdp/files/2022/03/TF-WP-001-FIN.pdf.

XPRIZE. n.d. "$100M prize for carbon removal" (web page). Accessed April 8,2024. https://www.xprize.org/prizes/carbonremoval.

Zhang, Siwei, Ma Jun, Xiaohu Zhang, and Cui Guo. 2023. "Atmospheric Remote Sensing for Anthropogenic Methane Emissions: Applications and Research Opportunities." *Science of the Total Environment* 893: 164701. https://doi.org/10.1016/j.scitotenv.2023.164701.

Zhunusova, E., V. Ahimbisibwe, A. Sadeghi, T. Toledo-Aceves, G. Kabwe, and S. Günter. 2022. "Potential Impacts of the Proposed EU Regulation on Deforestation-Free Supply Chains on Smallholders, Indigenous Peoples, and Local Communities in Producer Countries outside the EU." *Forest Policy and Economics* 143: 102817. https://doi.org/10.1016/j.forpol.2022.102817.

CHAPTER FIVE

The Recipe Is Doable

The global agrifood system is a major contributor to climate change and requires a deep and broad transformation. This system generates nearly one-third of global greenhouse gas (GHG) emissions, causing disastrous consequences for the planet and societies. These escalating emissions imperil the Paris Agreement's 1.5°C global heating limit, necessitating urgent mitigation measures and a fundamental change in how the world produces and consumes food. Agrifood emissions are highly concentrated within the top 20 global emitters, which mostly are middle-income countries (MICs). These top emitters generate about two-thirds of all agrifood system emissions, and this share is growing. Low-income countries (LICs), by contrast, have contributed the least to global emissions but bear the brunt of their negative consequences. High-income countries (HICs) have shaped the emissions-intensive way that food is produced and consumed, a way emulated by MICs, and increasingly by some LICs, to the detriment of the planet.

The agrifood system's transformation to net zero, if not done carefully, can generate trade-offs and potential costs—but the costs of inaction are even higher. The agrifood system must deliver many benefits at once. It must feed and nourish the global population while providing jobs and economic opportunities, all without damaging the planet or contributing to global heating. If the work is not done correctly, focusing on one element could come at the cost of another element. For example, applying agrifood system mitigation practices could potentially lead to lower agricultural production and higher food prices, much like higher food production led to land degradation and high emissions in the first place. The current food system causes trillions of dollars in negative externalities every year and has pushed the planet past two-thirds of its operating boundaries, exceeding the biosphere's integrity and water loss limits, among others. Moreover, an agrifood system transformation will likely encounter political and cultural headwinds from agricultural producers—who are often already struggling—and consumers who will need to make behavioral changes. However, the costs of inaction are much greater as climate change continues to have disastrous consequences for the planet, its people, and its food supplies.

The agrifood system can simultaneously feed and protect the planet, contribute to economic growth, *and* reduce GHG emissions. Multiple macroeconomic simulations show that there is no inherent trade-off between climate mitigation and food security. As outlined in chapter 2, adopting climate-smart practices could increase cropland, livestock, and forestry incomes by approximately $329 billion annually and increase global food production by enough to feed the world until 2050, without losses in biodiversity or carbon storage capacity (Damania et al. 2023). Further, $70 billion of the world's approximately $638 billion in annual agriculture support (Gautam et al. 2022; Voegele 2023) can be repurposed toward agrifood system mitigation and productivity growth to deliver a 40 percent reduction in agricultural emissions while increasing crop production by 16 percent and livestock production by 11 percent by 2040 (Gautam et al. 2022). Modeling shows that adopting a comprehensive set of mitigation practices in the agrifood sector by 2050—including investments in no-till agriculture, water use efficiency, and agricultural research and development (R&D)—would raise global agricultural production by 11.5 percent relative to the agrifood system's current path. This would accelerate national income growth and the ongoing transition of employment away from agriculture toward higher-quality off-farm employment in virtually all countries, especially if accompanied by investments in value chain development and job skills training (Nico and Christiaensen 2023).

This chapter offers a recipe for achieving net zero emissions and meeting the climate targets set in the Paris Agreement. The recipe provides solutions that can cost-effectively reduce agrifood emissions while maintaining global food security, economic growth, and marginal group equality. This recipe prescribes solutions for each country income category—high-, middle-, and low-income—to harness the potential to tackle its greatest concentrations of agrifood systems emissions, as outlined in chapter 3. These solutions will allow countries to quickly and cheaply diminish or prevent agrifood GHGs from reaching the atmosphere by focusing their efforts on the biggest emissions sources and the most cost-effective mitigation options. These approaches are not mutually exclusive, and all countries should aim to reduce all emissions sources. That said, countries have shared, but differentiated, opportunities to combat climate change through the agrifood system—and transformative pathways are available in every country. The recipe also illuminates a path for creating an enabling environment for the agrifood system's transformation around the six "I"s examined in chapter 4—investments, incentives, information, innovation, institutions, and inclusion. Collaborative efforts among governments, businesses, citizens, and international organizations to bolster these "I"s will further accelerate the agrifood system's transformation, giving the world its best chance to reach net zero and meet the Paris Agreement emissions targets.

Guiding Country Action

High-income countries should lead the way

They can do this by curbing energy emissions, aiding developing nations in their shift to low-emissions development pathways, and reducing the demand for high-emissions foods.

Expanding clean energy. Most post-food production emissions come from energy with the largest share in HICs. Activities such as retail and transport become more emissions intensive as food chains become longer and more complex, or require refrigerated transport.

Likewise, as households become wealthier, household food consumption emissions, mostly from kitchen appliance energy needs, become elevated. On-farm and land use practices also consume lots of energy. As such, governments should incentivize energy efficiency and clean energy sources to wean the agrifood system from its dependence on fossil fuel energy. Deploying renewables in the agrifood sector leads to other positive outcomes as well, such as reduced pollution and diversified, high-quality employment. Favorable policies and declining costs can spur the agrifood industry's continued adoption of renewable energy.

Supporting MICs and LICs with finance and technologies. Rich countries have the means to support less wealthy, emerging economies in the transition to low-emitting agrifood systems. One of the primary ways is through financial support. Moreover, many HICs are at the forefront of technological advancements, such as feed additives that reduce ruminant livestock emissions. As such, HICs can leverage their expertise to transfer advanced technologies to LICs and MICs, empowering those countries to adopt low-emissions practices. However, this support needs to go beyond just finance and technology and encompass policy support, capacity building, collaborative projects, and trade and investments. International institutions, such as the United Nations Framework Convention on Climate Change (UNFCCC), can facilitate these transfers, and bilateral and multilateral donors can also contribute through finance, knowledge, and climate diplomacy.

Reducing demand for high-emissions foods. As global populations become wealthier, they consume more emissions-intensive foods, such as meat and dairy. Demand for these foods in HICs and, increasingly, in MICs, leads to nearly two-thirds of total agrifood emissions. Indeed, excluding animal-derived food products from diets would halve global agrifood GHG emissions. There are several approaches that can feasibly and affordably do this. Simply shifting to alternative sources of animal protein can reduce emissions while providing the same nutritional value. For example, poultry causes only about 10 percent of the emissions generated by beef. Such changes can also reduce the health burdens of high-emitting foods, which also tend to be less nutritious. However, government subsidies for fossil fuels and certain food sectors, along with free environmental inputs such as land and water, make the cost of meat and dairy 20–60 percent cheaper than it otherwise would be. Therefore, simply removing these subsidies and fully costing environmental externalities would make low-emissions alternatives more competitive and desirable among consumers. Public policies and private sector decisions can also promote dietary changes by influencing the consumer behaviors that dictate people's food consumption patterns—for instance, through health guidelines, food labeling, food waste levies, and education campaigns, among others. In addition, governments and businesses can promote R&D and innovation in new technologies that provide healthy and low-emissions choices to consumers.

Middle-income countries have an outsized role to play

These countries generate two-thirds of global agrifood emissions and could curb most of them by focusing on sustainable land use—in particular, the reduction of deforestation—lowering methane emissions from rice and livestock production, harnessing the potential of soils to sequester carbon, and shifting to cleaner, more efficient, and circular approaches to the agrifood system's pre- and post-production activities.

Reducing forest loss and ecosystem degradation. Agricultural commodity production has a massive global emissions footprint. One-quarter to one-third of permanent forest loss is linked to the production of seven agricultural commodities, including cattle and high-value tree crops such as palm oil and cocoa. And much of the commodity-linked forest conversion is highly concentrated in a few MICs with extensive forests. A shift to more sustainable land use in MICs could reduce one-third of global agrifood emissions cost-effectively. The largest share of global cost-effective agrifood mitigation options comes from the conservation, improved management, and restoration of forests and other ecosystems, especially in tropical regions. Using cost-effective land use mitigation measures could avoid 5 gigatons of carbon dioxide equivalent ($GtCO_2eq$) of emissions per year in MICs alone (6.5 $GtCO_2eq$ globally). In response, a growing number of commodity producers in those countries have introduced programs to reduce their deforestation footprint. Despite significant progress in some countries, the loss of globally vital forests and other ecosystems (such as peatlands) continues to be stubbornly high and growing. Greater progress is hampered by insufficiently strong regulations, policies, and incentives to reduce the rate of forest loss, as well as a lack of transparency about the sources of many agricultural commodities.

Curbing livestock emissions. One-quarter of MICs' agrifood emissions comes from livestock, stemming from growing consumer demand for more animal-source foods from mostly affluent, urban populations. As mentioned, demand-side measures, such as dietary changes, have the greatest technical and cost-effective potential to reduce livestock emissions, but there are many supply-side solutions as well. For example, halving food waste by 2050, from 12 percent to 6 percent, would reduce livestock emissions by about 500 million tons of CO_2eq. Also, improving productivity and resource use efficiency can cut livestock emissions by up to 30 percent. This is especially true in MICs, which generate 50 percent more emissions per kilogram of protein produced than do HICs. Similarly, there are modern innovations that can further reduce livestock-related GHG emissions. For instance, breeding cattle for low enteric fermentation or modifying animal diets or feed additives shows promising results in reducing methane emissions. Likewise, biogas digesters, which convert methane and CO_2 into energy, can supplement energy costs and capture up to 80 percent of the methane from manure that would otherwise be emitted into the atmosphere.

Curbing rice emissions. Rice production is a significant source of global methane emissions, with virtually all originating in Asian MICs. In fact, 16 percent of agricultural methane emissions, or 1.5 percent of total anthropogenic GHG emissions, come from rice production. There are several on-farm practices that can cost-effectively reduce those emissions. For example, intermittent water application methods reduce GHG emissions by 15–45 percent compared to continuously flooding rice paddies, which is still widely practiced. Aerobic rice cultivation, which eliminates the methane produced by bacteria in waterlogged soils, holds great potential for emissions cuts, but it can also reduce yields. Governments should apply policy and financing incentives to promote low-emission rice practices. For instance, governments could redirect rice subsidies that incentivize flooding or invest in the R&D of higher-yielding aerobic rice varieties, which farmers increasingly use as cash crops.

Harnessing soil sequestration. Unsustainable land management practices, including intensive and repetitive tillage, have released large amounts of soil carbon into the atmosphere and reduced soil organic carbon in croplands and grazed grasslands by up to 75 percent. In addition, conventional agriculture's soil management practices, which often overuse nitrogen fertilizers, cause harmful nitrous oxide emissions. By contrast, restoring and sustainably managing soils reduce GHG emissions while boosting soil fertility and productivity. Soils have the technical potential to sequester 2–5 billion tons of carbon per year, 40 percent of which comes from protecting existing soil organic carbon and 60 percent from restoring depleted soils. Around half of the soil organic carbon sequestration potential would cost less than $100 per ton of CO_2eq, amounting to an additional billion tons of solid carbon stored in soils. Twelve of the 15 countries with the highest soil organic carbon sequestration potential are MICs.

Making pre- and post-production processes less emissions intensive. These processes make up 35 percent of MICs' agrifood emissions. Much of these come from fertilizer production and use, food waste, and household food consumption. MICs consume 80 percent of the world's fertilizer, which generates GHG emissions through its production and application. A combination of interventions could reduce nitrogen fertilizer production emissions by up to 84 percent. Likewise, shifting from coal and natural gas to renewable energy to generate hydrogen for ammonia production would eliminate 75 percent of fertilizer production-related emissions. Improving soil fertility through carbon sequestration (as previously described) also reduces fertilizer demand, and thus the associated emissions. Food loss and waste represent avoidable emissions across the entire food chain. Agrifood waste disposal in MICs generates 1 $GtCO_2eq$ year, roughly four times the amount generated in HICs and LICs. Digital solutions can help match food supply and demand, thereby reducing this unnecessary waste. Also, circular practices on farms and along value chains can reuse food waste for productive purposes. Likewise, some agrifood wastewater management practices can mitigate emissions and reduce the energy needs for treating it. Household food consumption is the second-largest emissions category within pre- and post-production emissions behind waste disposal, with three-quarters of these emissions coming from MICs. Household consumption emissions come from the electricity needed to power stoves and kitchen appliances. One solution is to transition to "clean" cooking using electric appliances. The private sector could also help deliver many of these solutions to industry, municipalities, or households, but doing so would require the right enabling environment, as will be discussed.

Low-income countries can bypass the high-emissions development path taken by HICs and MICs for a greener, more competitive development path. LICs have an opportunity to make smart choices now that will benefit them in the long term by avoiding the high-emissions pathways that are costly to reverse later. They should prioritize and monetize the protection and restoration of carbon-rich forests and other ecosystems, improve agrifood systems' efficiency, and promote climate-smart practices, thereby achieving a triple win of increased productivity, climate resilience, and reduced emissions.

Protecting ecosystems. Eleven percent of global GHG emissions come from deforestation. In LICs, forest conversion to farmland makes up nearly half of agrifood system emissions. Moreover, the vast tracts of standing forests in some LICs mean that the potential for further deforestation is also high. As such, avoiding permanent forest loss, improving ecosystem management, and restoring forests and other ecosystems—such as degraded peatlands or grasslands—are among the most cost-effective measures to avoid emissions. Similarly, adding trees to production systems, through agroforestry or silvo-pastoral systems, can sequester carbon and contribute to more-efficient and productive land use. As in MICs, commodity demand in LICs is the driving force behind these ecosystem losses. Therefore, governments and businesses should fulfill their commitments to make agricultural commodity value chains more sustainable and productive. This could potentially benefit LICs, which currently have a relatively low market share of these commodities but tend to produce them with fewer emissions. Furthermore, emerging economies are beginning to monetize their forest cover and agrifood emissions reductions through carbon credits and emissions trading, yet there is still significant untapped potential for LICs and some MICs to become carbon sinks and ecosystem service providers.

Improving efficiency and productivity. Most LICs and MICs are fulfilling less than half of their agricultural output potential, whereas HICs are fulfilling 70 percent of theirs. More-efficient land use could preserve vital natural systems and sequester an additional 85 $GtCO_2eq$ without any adverse economic impacts. Agriculture value added in LICs is only $210 per hectare, whereas it is five times that in MICs at $1,100 per hectare, meaning there is room to dramatically improve agricultural productivity, farmer incomes, and food security in LICs. This requires changing LICs' agricultural practices, providing adequate financing, removing distortive policies, and investing in innovative practices. LICs could also orient their agrifood systems to deliver healthy, organic, or circular foods to emerging retail markets, which can increase their competitiveness and create market opportunities.

Adopting climate-smart practices. Climate-smart agricultural (CSA) practices reduce emissions, boost resilience, and contribute to economic development. These practices represent a wide range of approaches, and there are over 1,700 such systems under implementation today. These practices can generate high rates of economic returns, with examples in this report showing returns ranging from 27 percent to 126 percent. Moreover, CSA practices are a cost-effective way to reduce emissions. Such practices go hand-in-hand with low-carbon energy adoption through solar power, bioenergy, and others. These energy sources not only reduce energy costs and emissions but also generate social benefits in LICs through higher incomes or rural electrification. In fact, renewable energy generation is often more viable than fossil fuel–based sources in off-grid rural areas. Further, these communities can export electricity surpluses to nearby grids, stimulating local economic development.

Solutions are available now that could eliminate most agrifood system emissions by 2050 at an affordable price tag. Figure 5.1 shows that HICs, MICs, and LICs have the shared cost-effective mitigation potential to eliminate all 16 gigatons of the agrifood system's annual emissions. Broken down, table 5.1 shows that land use mitigation actions to protect carbon-rich ecosystems could cost-effectively reduce emissions of 6.5 $GtCO_2eq$ per year. This represents 31 percent of the cost-effective mitigation potential in HICs, 47 percent in MICs, and 65 percent in LICs. On-farm mitigation measures to reduce rice and livestock emissions, increase soil sequestration, and recycle farm biomass for energy can cost-effectively reduce emissions by 5.8 $GtCO_2eq$ per year. This represents 52 percent of the cost-efficient mitigation potential in HICs, 39 percent in MICs, and 28 percent in LICs. Pre- and post-production mitigation measures such as dietary changes, reduced food waste, and cleaner household cooking could cost-effectively reduce emissions by nearly 2 $GtCO_2eq$ per year. This represents 17 percent of the cost-effective mitigation potential in HICs, 14 percent in MICs, and 7 percent in LICs. In total, these available cost-effective measures would reduce 14.4 gigatons of the 16 gigatons of annual CO_2eq from the agrifood system.

FIGURE 5.1 By 2050, Cost-Effective Mitigation Action in the Agrifood System Transformation Can Reduce Greenhouse Gases by Over 16 Gigatons a Year, Achieving Net Zero Emissions

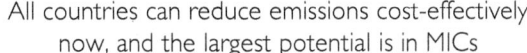

All countries can reduce emissions cost-effectively
now, and the largest potential is in MICs

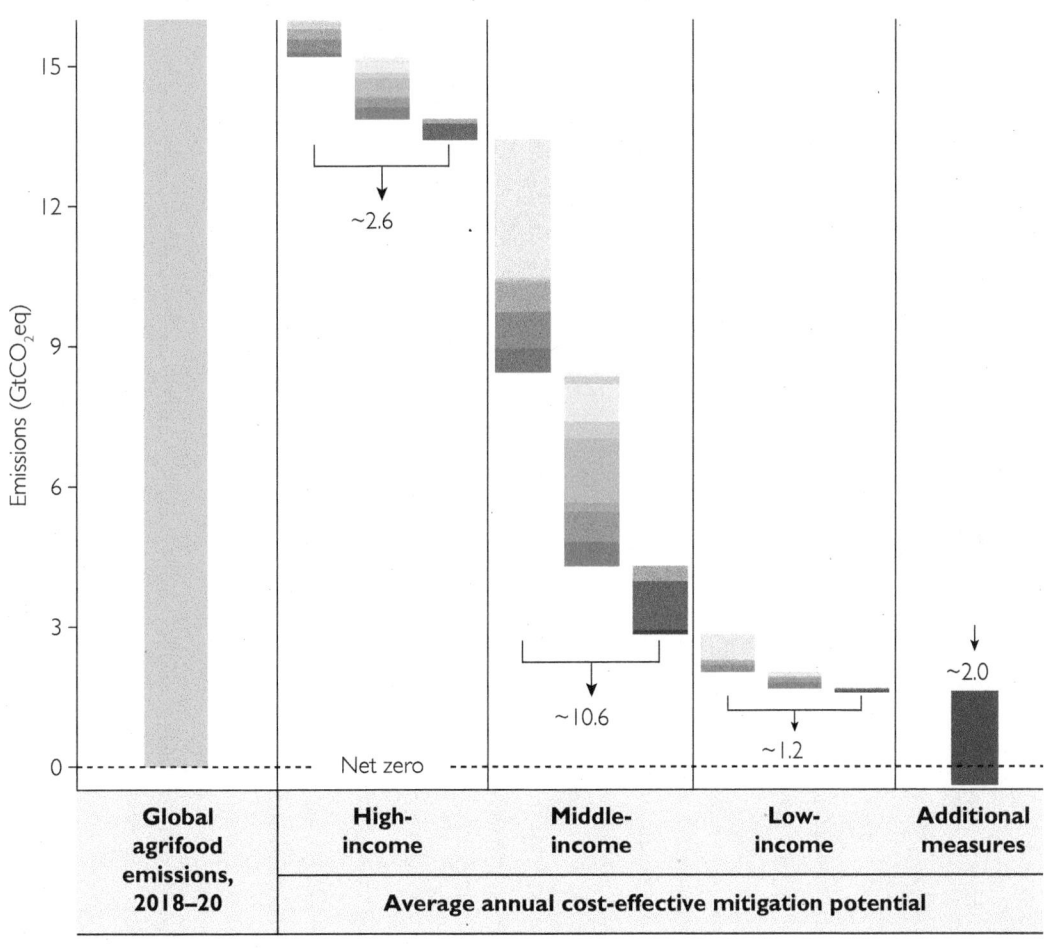

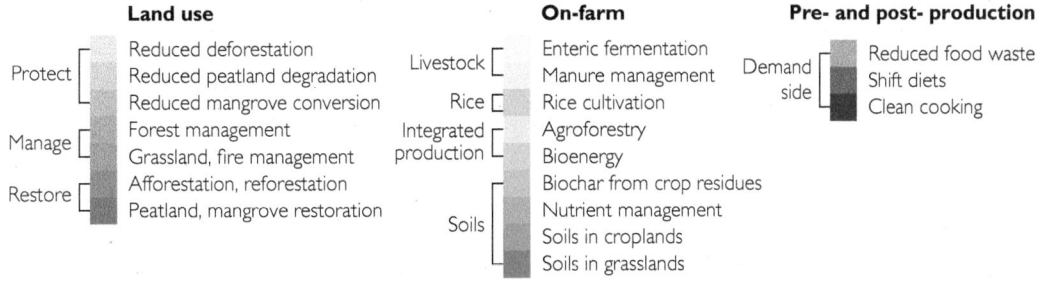

Source: World Bank based on data from Roe et al. 2021 and World Bank 2024.

Note: This figure shows by country income group the cost-effective annual mitigation potential for reducing emissions from land use, on-farm, and pre- and post-production process. Additional measures include technologies and innovations that can deliver cost-effective emissions reductions by 2030. These include: nitrous oxide abatement in fertilizer production; plant-based proteins; low-emission energy sources for on-farm machinery; improved on-farm energy-efficiency; improved livestock feed digestibility and feed additives; and increased use of renewable energy in cold chains. Details on these measures are described in chapter 4. Average annual mitigation potential for land-based mitigation measures for high-, middle-, and low-income countries are based on 2020–50 scenarios. GtCO$_2$eq = gigatons of carbon dioxide equivalent; HICs = high-income countries; LICs = low-income countries; MICs = middle-income countries.

TABLE 5.1 The Recipe for Reducing Agrifood Sector GHGs to Net Zero by 2050 through Concerted but Differentiated Efforts across Countries

Agrifood system component	Priority area	Mitigation measure and practice	Cost-effective mitigation potential (< $100/tCO$_2$eq)					
			MtCO$_2$eq/year			Share (%)		
			HICs	MICs	LICs	HICs	MICs	LICs
Land use	Ecosystems	Reduced deforestation	46	2,958	559	1.8	28.0	45.0
		Improved forest management	217	612	74	8.5	5.8	6.0
		Afforestation and reforestation	288	778	142	11.2	7.3	11.4
		Reduced mangrove conversion/restoration	7	62	3	0.3	0.6	0.2
		Reduced peatland degradation/conversion	140	56	9	5.5	0.5	0.7
		Restoration of peatland	83	508	2	3.2	4.8	0.1
		Grassland/savanna fire management	2	12	17	0.1	0.1	1.4
		Subtotal, by income group	**783**	**4,986**	**806**	**30.6**	**47.1**	**64.8**
		Subtotal, all countries		**6,573**		**n.a.**	**n.a.**	**n.a.**
On-farm	Livestock	Productivity enhancement	25	64	9	1.0	0.6	0.7
		Manure management	64	28	0	2.5	0.3	0.1
	Rice	Improved rice cultivation	6	161	4	0.2	1.5	0.3
	Integrated production systems	Agroforestry	245	797	79	9.5	7.5	6.4
		Bioenergy with carbon capture and storage	121	366	12	4.7	3.5	1.0
	Soil	Nutrient management	38	183	2	1.7	1.7	0.1
		Biochar from crop residues	399	1,380	36	15.5	13.0	2.9
		Increased soil organic carbon in croplands	190	649	83	7.4	6.1	6.6
		Increased soil organic carbon in grasslands	249	514	129	9.8	5.0	10.3
		Subtotal, by income group	**1,337**	**4,142**	**354**	**52.1**	**39.2**	**28.4**
		Subtotal, all countries		**5,833**		**n.a.**	**n.a.**	**n.a.**

(table continued next page)

TABLE 5.1 The Recipe for Reducing Agrifood Sector GHGs to Net Zero by 2050 through Concerted but Differentiated Efforts across Countries (Continued)

Agrifood system component	Priority area	Mitigation measure and practice	Cost-effective mitigation potential (< $100/tCO₂eq)					
			MtCO₂eq/year			Share (%)		
			All country income groups			*By country income group*		
			HICs	MICs	LICs	HICs	MICs	LICs
		Emerging mitigation technologies						
	Livestock	Feed additives		380			n.a.	
	Livestock	Improved feed digestibility		120			n.a.	
	Energy	Electrified farm machinery		167			n.a.	
	Energy	Renewable energy, energy efficiency		330			n.a.	
		Subtotal, all on-farm measures		6,830			n.a.	
			HICs	MICs	LICs	HICs	MICs	LICs
Pre- and post-production	Diet	Dietary change	337	1043	53	13.1	9.8	4.3
	Food waste	Reduced food waste	107	330	15	4.2	3.1	1.2
	Household consumption	Clean cookstoves	1	88	16	n.a.	0.8	1.3
		Subtotal, by income group	445	1,461	84	17.3	13.7	6.8
		Subtotal, all countries		1,990			n.a.	
		Emerging mitigation technologies — *All country income groups*				*By country income group*		
	Inputs	Low GHG fertilizer production		300			n.a.	
	Energy	Green cold chain		400			n.a.	
	Diets	Alternative proteins		300			n.a.	
		Subtotal, all pre- and post-production measures		2,990			n.a.	

	HICs	MICs	LICs
Total agrifood system, by HICs, MICs, LICs	2,565	10,589	1,244
Total agrifood system, additional measures, all income groups		1,995	
Total agrifood system, all measures, all countries		16,393	

Sources: Roe et al. 2021 and Becken et al. 2011; Cerutti et al. 2023; Gao and Cabrera Serrenho 2023; IEA et al. 2020; McKinsey & Company 2023; Morach et al. 2022; Mukherji et al. 2023; Ripple et al. 2014; Royal Society 2020; Smith et al. 2007; Thornton and Herrero 2010; World Bank based on Ungerfeld 2022; and World Bank based on Xu et al. 2021.

Note: The measures in the table have a combined annual emissions reduction potential of 16.4 gigatons of carbon dioxide equivalent per year and were estimated for the 2020–50 period. All measures are cost-effective and can be implemented for $100 per ton of CO_2 equivalent per year or less. CO_2 = carbon dioxide; GHG = greenhouse gas; HICs = high-income countries; LICs = low-income countries; MICs = middle-income countries; MtCO₂eq = megatons of carbon dioxide equivalent; n.a. = not applicable; tCO₂eq = tons of carbon dioxide equivalent.

Emerging mitigation technologies will help the agrifood system reach net zero emissions, keeping the Paris Agreement's climate targets for midcentury within reach. As discussed in chapter 4 and shown in table 5.1, there are emerging on-farm and pre- and post-production innovations that will be available by 2030 that would cost-effectively save an additional 2 $GtCO_2eq$ per year. Taken together, the study team has calculated that available and soon-to-be-available cost-effective mitigation options could affordably save 16.4 $GtCO_2eq$ per year, bringing agrifood systems to net zero emissions. To put that into perspective, this would have a higher impact than eliminating all GHG emissions from global electricity and heat production (14 $GtCO_2eq$) and is about four times the European Union's economywide annual emissions (3.5 $GtCO_2eq$).[1] Moreover, the estimated costs of mitigating the agrifood system's climate impact are just a fraction—roughly one-tenth—of global energy investments for 2023 and less than 5 percent of global fossil fuel subsidies, which reached $7.1 trillion in 2022 (Black et al. 2023).

Building the Enabling Environment

Empowering countries to take these actions at scale requires a conducive enabling environment, both globally and within countries. Governments, businesses, consumers, and international organizations must work together to (1) generate investments and create incentives through policy, (2) improve information and innovation to drive the agrifood system's transformation into the future, and (3) leverage institutions to facilitate these opportunities while ensuring the inclusion of stakeholders and marginalized groups (figure 5.2).

Generating investments and policy incentives

Investments. The implementation of the most urgent short-term agrifood mitigation policy actions by 2030 requires an average of $260 billion in financing per year. This amount would reduce the world's agrifood system GHG emissions by 8 $GtCO_2eq$ in 2030, equivalent to half of current agrifood emissions and about 15 percent of the economywide emissions projected for that year. This emission reduction is roughly half the world's annual cost-effective mitigation potential until 2050 (figure 5.1). However, the agrifood system receives just $28.5 billion in total climate finance and only $14.4 billion in total mitigation finance. As such, annual investments will need to increase by at least 14 times to reduce current food system emissions by half by 2030. At the same time, scaling up private investment in the food system requires targeting financial service providers and minimizing investment risks in low-emitting CSA practices, especially in emerging small-scale green initiatives. Public resources can minimize these risks through blended finance. Meanwhile, concessional finance providers can offer loans, grants, guarantees, or equity investments to finance elements of the agrifood system's transformation. Corporate commitments, through private standards and certifications, signal a growing private sector interest in agrifood system mitigation. Carbon pricing instruments offer further opportunities to control the agrifood system's GHG emissions. However, all of this requires robust accountability and regulatory systems.

Incentives. Policy reforms can incentivize the uptake of agrifood system mitigation practices. They can redirect harmful agricultural subsidies to emissions-reducing activities

FIGURE 5.2 The Recipe for Creating an Enabling Environment Allows Countries in All Income Groups to Contribute to Transforming Agrifood Systems to Achieve Net Zero Emissions

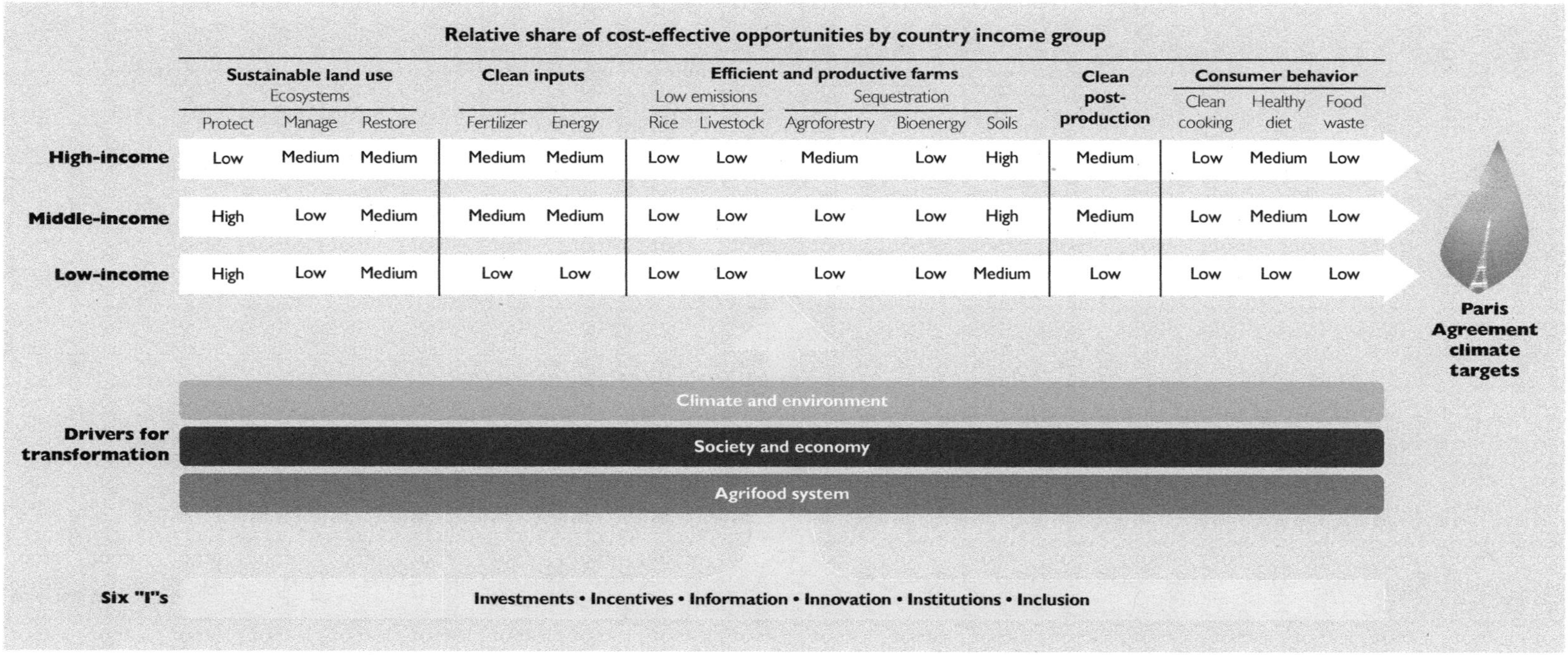

Relative share of cost-effective opportunities by country income group

	Sustainable land use – Ecosystems			Clean inputs		Efficient and productive farms – Low emissions		Sequestration			Clean post-production	Consumer behavior		
	Protect	Manage	Restore	Fertilizer	Energy	Rice	Livestock	Agroforestry	Bioenergy	Soils		Clean cooking	Healthy diet	Food waste
High-income	Low	Medium	Medium	Medium	Medium	Low	Low	Medium	Low	High	Medium	Low	Medium	Low
Middle-income	High	Low	Medium	Medium	Medium	Low	Low	Low	Low	High	Medium	Low	Medium	Low
Low-income	High	Low	Medium	Low	Low	Low	Low	Low	Low	Medium	Low	Low	Low	Low

Paris Agreement climate targets

Climate and environment

Society and economy

Agrifood system

Drivers for transformation

Six "I"s — Investments • Incentives • Information • Innovation • Institutions • Inclusion

Source: Original figure for this publication.

Note: Figure summarizes the distribution of cost-effective mitigation potential by income group across 14 key areas of intervention related to sustainable land use, clean inputs, efficient and productive farms, clean post-production, and consumer behavior (top part of the table). The relative share of cost-effective mitigation potential is indicated as follows: low: <8 percent, medium: 8–16 percent, high: >16 percent.

and remove trade barriers. This and other repurposing could cover about one-third of the total finance needed for the agrifood system's transformation. Moreover, climate mitigation policies that properly target all GHGs, including methane in the agricultural sector, will boost the competitiveness of countries that can produce lower-emitting commodities. However, for any policy to be effectively implemented, it must be clear and coherent across sectors, regions, and the agrifood system.

Improving information and pursuing innovation

Information. Improving methods to measure GHG emissions across the agrifood system makes investments and policy incentives work. Such measurement, reporting, and verification (MRV) of emissions reductions keeps the focus on results at all levels, from the farm to international markets, and unlocks climate finance by making recipients accountable and by verifying carbon market compliance. New advances in sensor technologies and digital data processing make MRV more accurate, information more accessible, and processes more transparent. Governments and the private sector can work together to drive down the costs of these technologies and increase their uptake. Stakeholders, whether in the public or private sector, can leverage the better information to direct investments to where they are most effective. For example, country-specific marginal abatement cost information can guide policies and strategic investments in agrifood system emissions reductions.

Innovation. Governments in all countries can support nascent, innovative mitigation technologies that accelerate emission reductions in the agrifood system. For example, plant-based proteins can make dietary change more acceptable, and feed additives can make livestock production less harmful. Likewise, indoor farming and precision machinery generate fewer emissions and reduce input or externality costs. Research and development are effective at driving agrifood system mitigation innovation, but funding for them has been incommensurate with the challenge despite high rates of return. These rates of return make public-private partnerships a particularly strong mechanism for driving R&D and technological innovations in the agrifood sector. Adequate investment in R&D, along with technology transfers from HICs, can bring down the costs of mitigation technologies in LICs and MICs, especially for emissions sources that are currently more costly to abate, such as rice or livestock production. Lower costs would allow countries to harness more of the technical mitigation potential of low-emissions practices. Similarly, innovation can expand the reach of renewable energy to all stages of the agrifood system by bringing down costs and raising functionality.

Leveraging institutions and ensuring inclusion

Institutions. Governments, businesses, international organizations, and civil society organizations must work together through the international institutional architecture to bridge the north–south divide for trade, climate, and development. These institutions and frameworks are necessary for mobilizing investments, incentives, information, and innovation. These frameworks can transfer finance and technologies from HICs to MICs and LICs, as agreed to through the UNFCCC's Conference of the Parties. National institutions also play a role in establishing legal or regulatory systems. However, all of these overlapping frameworks, policies, and institutions must operate coherently or risk establishing counteracting incentives. For example, some countries promote agricultural expansion on the one hand while making mitigation pledges on the other. In recent years, multilateral development banks have assumed a more central function in the agrifood system's transformation as financers, conveners, and knowledge generators.

Recipe for a Livable Planet

Inclusion. Governments and civil society must work together to ensure that the agrifood system's transformation is equitable, inclusive, and just. They can do this by bolstering jobs, good health, livelihoods, and food security during the transformation. Ensuring procedural justice through ample stakeholder engagement can improve the social accountability of policies and practices. It can also assess and mitigate the potential risks for affected communities. Establishing distributive justice through benefit-sharing mechanisms can ensure that the agrifood system's benefits are equitably distributed. As part of this, governments can facilitate the ongoing structural diversification of developing economies away from agriculture. They can also provide skills training and mobility support to make sure that current agrifood system workers are not left behind in the transition. Ensuring restorative justice can empower those who have not benefited from the agrifood system in the past, such as smallholder farmers, in the new low-emissions agrifood system. To do so, governments should partner with affected communities and local governments to redress preexisting social inequalities and empower marginalized groups.

Moving Forward

This recipe lists the required ingredients for transforming the global agrifood system to net zero emissions. In 2023, parties to the Paris Agreement performed the first global stock-taking of its progress toward meeting climate targets. The result is sobering. In 2023, the planet was warmer than it had ever been since the advent of agriculture roughly 10,000 years ago (IPCC 2023). Moreover, financing and technical progress in emissions reduction have been stymied by many factors. As a result, reducing agrifood system emissions is more urgent than ever. As such, all of the mitigation and enabling actions described and promoted in chapters 3 and 4 should be implemented immediately and concurrently by all countries. This report has mapped out the areas of greatest mitigation potential for different country income groups—HICs, MICs, and LICs—to focus their efforts first. The study team determined these opportunities based on the potential emissions reductions and relative costs of those actions. Put simply, the recommendations guide countries toward agrifood system mitigation efforts that have the most bang for the buck. Consequently, this should be a country-driven approach in which HICs, the World Bank, and other bilateral or multilateral donors play a key role in providing the knowledge and finance to enable public and private national actors to contribute to this transformation. These donors facilitate and provide much-needed finance from concessional, private, or blended sources. They provide essential information to stakeholders and generate the political will and incentives for global climate action.

More immediately, the World Bank and its development partners can build off this report to fill remaining knowledge gaps and carry out similar analyses at the country level. As noted in chapter 1, *Recipe for a Livable Planet* is one of the first comprehensive global strategic road maps on climate change mitigation for the agrifood system. Its purpose is to raise awareness of the role that the agrifood system must play in the world's climate change mitigation efforts. To complete the picture and guide action at the country level, there are important knowledge gaps to be filled, including the following:

1. **Comprehensive global mitigation data:** Globally, there are still basic data missing on the technical potential and cost-effectiveness of agrifood system mitigation options. These include data on the one-third of agrifood system emissions generated by pre- and post-production processes and data for certain on-farm measures, like increasing productivity.

2. **Country-level analysis:** This report presents the global recipe for an agrifood system transformation based on average emissions and common opportunities across country income groups. However, agrifood systems are highly diverse across countries, even within the same income categories. This report has highlighted some of these differences in the country boxes and country marginal abatement cost curve (MACC) examples. It will be necessary to carry out similar analyses of emissions sources and mitigation opportunities for individual countries to achieve progress on the ground.

3. **Marginal abatement cost curves:** An important part of these country-level analyses should be the collection and analysis of agrifood marginal abatement cost data, which are currently lacking for the vast majority of countries. The World Bank and its partners could establish a global database of such MACC data to guide donors' mitigation investments.

The conditions are in place to accelerate the agrifood transformation; the solutions are available and affordable. The transformation can build on food system successes from the past three decades, during which agricultural producers have increased their production through improved resource use efficiency and better technologies and practices. Likewise, there are promising trends that can accelerate the agrifood system's transformation. These include innovative technologies, a more involved private sector, increased consumer awareness, and powerful digital tools. Moreover, the study team finds no inherent trade-off between climate action and income or food security. Through the correct action, the world can reduce agrifood system emissions while growing economies and feeding more people. Most important from a practical standpoint is that the transformation is currently affordable and will eventually be profitable. As the report shows, the agrifood sector's mitigation options are more cost-effective than options in any other sector. As a result, estimated agrifood system mitigation costs are only about a 10th of what is projected to be invested in energy globally in 2023 (IEA 2023). Moreover, this transformation will quickly become profitable once the world stops underpricing harmful fossil fuels, which amounted to a staggering annual subsidy of $7.1 trillion in 2022 (Black et al. 2023). Once this happens, low-emitting products and countries will propel the global economy.

Note

1. World Bank calculations using data from FAOSTAT, IEA, and the European Environment Agency, averaged over 2018–20.

References

Becken, K., D. de Graaf, C. Elsner, G. Hoffmann, F. Krüger, K. Martens, W. Plehn, and R. Sartorius. 2011. *Avoiding Fluorinated Greenhouse Gases: Prospects for Phasing Out.* German Federal Environment Agency, Dessau-Rosslau. https://www.umweltbundesamt.de/sites/default/files/medien/publikation /long/3977.pdf.

Black, Simon, Antung A. Liu, Ian Parry, and Nate Vernon. 2023. "IMF Fossil Fuel Subsidies Data: 2023 Update." Working Paper 23/169, International Monetary Fund, Washington, DC. https://www.imf.org /en/Publications/WP/Issues/2023/08/22/IMF-Fossil-Fuel-Subsidies-Data-2023-Update-537281.

Cerutti, N., W. F. Lamb, M. Crippa, A. Leip, E. Solazzo, F. N. Tubiello, and J. C. Minx. 2023. "Food System Emissions: A Review of Trends, Drivers, and Policy Approaches, 1990–2018." *Environmental Research Letters* 18 (7): 074030. https://doi.org/10.1088/1748-9326/acddfd.

Damania, Richard, Stephen Polasky, Mary Ruckelshaus, Jason Russ, Markus Amann, Rebecca Chaplin-Kramer, James Gerber, et al. 2023. *Nature's Frontiers: Achieving Sustainability, Efficiency, and Prosperity with Natural Capital*. Environment and Sustainable Development series. Washington, DC: World Bank. https://doi.org/10.1596/978-1-4648-1923-0.

Gao, Y., and A. Cabrera Serrenho. 2023. "Greenhouse Gas Emissions from Nitrogen Fertilizers Could Be Reduced by up to One-Fifth of Current Levels by 2050 with Combined Interventions." *Nature Food* 4: 170–78. https://doi.org/10.1038/s43016-023-00698-w.

Gautam, Madhur, David Laborde, Abdullah Mamun, Will Martin, Valeria Pineiro, and Rob Vos. 2022. *Repurposing Agricultural Policies and Support: Options to Transform Agriculture and Food Systems to Better Serve the Health of People, Economies, and the Planet*. Washington, DC: World Bank. http://hdl.handle.net/10986/36875.

IEA (International Energy Agency). 2023. *World Energy Investment 2023*. IEA, Paris. https://www.iea.org/reports/world-energy-investment-2023.

IEA (International Energy Agency), IRENA (International Renewable Energy Agency), UNSD (United Nations Statistics Division), World Bank, and WHO (World Health Organization). 2020. *Tracking SDG 7: The Energy Progress Report*. Washington, DC: World Bank. https://www.irena.org/Publications/2023/Jun/Tracking-SDG7-2023.

IPCC (Intergovernmental Panel on Climate Change). 2023. *Climate Change 2023: Synthesis Report; Contribution of Working Groups I, II and III to the Sixth Assessment Report of the Intergovernmental Panel on Climate Change,* edited by H. Lee and J. Romero. Geneva: IPCC. https://doi.org/10.59327/IPCC/AR6-9789291691647.

McKinsey & Company. 2023. "The Agricultural Transition: Building a Sustainable Future." https://www.mckinsey.com/industries/agriculture/our-insights/the-agricultural-transition-building-a-sustainable-future.

Morach B., M. Clausen, J. Rogg, M. Brigl, U. Schulze, N. Dehnert, M. Hepp, V. Yang, T. Kurth, E. von Koeller et al. 2022. "The Untapped Climate Opportunity in Alternative Proteins." Food for Thought report, BCG (Boston Consulting Group). https://www.bcg.com/publications/2022/combating-climate-crisis-with-alternative-protein.

Mukherji, A., C. Arndt, J. Arango, F. Flintan, J. Derera, W. Francesconi, S. Jones, A. M. Loboguerrero, D. Merrey, J. Mockshell, M. Quintero, D. G. Mulat, C. Ringler, L. Ronchi, M. Sanchez, T. Sapkota, and S. Thilsted. 2023. *Achieving Agricultural Breakthrough: A Deep Dive into Seven Technological Areas*. Montpellier, France: CGIAR System Organization. https://hdl.handle.net/10568/131852.

Nico, Gianluigi, and Luc Christiaensen. 2023. "Jobs, Food and Greening: Exploring Implications of the Green Transition for Jobs in the Agri-Food System." World Bank Jobs Working Paper 75, World Bank, Washington, DC. http://hdl.handle.net/10986/39819.

Ripple, W., P. Smith, H. Haberl, S. A. Montzka, C. McAlpine, and D. H. Boucher. 2014. "Ruminants, Climate Change and Climate Policy." Nature Climate Change 4: 2–5. https://doi.org/10.1038/nclimate2081.

Roe, S., C. Streck, R. Beach, J. Busch, M. Chapman, V. Daioglou, A. Deppermann, et al. 2021. "Land-Based Measures to Mitigate Climate Change: Potential and Feasibility by Country." *Global Change Biology* 27 (23): 6025–58. https://doi.org/10.1111/gcb.15873.

Royal Society. 2020. "Ammonia: Zero-Carbon Fertiliser, Fuel and Energy Store." Policy briefing, Royal Society, London. https://royalsociety.org/-/media/policy/projects/green-ammonia/green-ammonia-policy-briefing.pdf.

Smith, P., D. Martino, Z. Cai, D. Gwary, H. Janzen, P. Kumar, B. McCarl, S. Ogle, F. O'Mara, C. Rice, et al. 2007. "Greenhouse Gas Mitigation in Agriculture." *Philosophical Transactions of the Royal Society B: Biological Sciences* 363 (1492): 789–813. https://doi.org/10.1098/rstb.2007.2184.

Thornton, P. K., and M. Herrero. 2010. "Potential for Reduced Methane and Carbon Dioxide Emissions from Livestock and Pasture Management in the Tropics." *Proceedings of the National Academy of Sciences* 107 (46): 19667–72. https://doi.org/10.1073/pnas.0912890107.

Ungerfeld, E. M. 2022. "Opportunities and Hurdles to the Adoption and Enhanced Efficacy of Feed Additives towards Pronounced Mitigation of Enteric Methane Emissions from Ruminant Livestock." *Methane* 1 (4): 262–85. https://doi.org/10.3390/methane1040021.

Voegele, Juergen. 2023. "Transforming Our Food Systems for Healthy People, Environment, and Economies." *Voices* (blog), January 17. https://blogs.worldbank.org/voices/transforming-our-food-systems-healthy-people-environment-and-economies.

World Bank. 2024. "Indicators" (web page). Accessed April 14, 2024. https://data.worldbank.org/indicator.

Xu, X., P. Sharma, S. Shu, T.-S. Lin, P. Ciais, F. N. Tubiello, P. Smith, N. Campbell, and A. K. Jain. 2021. "Global Greenhouse Gas Emissions from Animal-Based Foods Are Twice Those of Plant-Based Foods." *Nature Food* 2: 724–32. https://doi.org/10.1038/s43016-021-00358-x.

APPENDIX A

Agrifood Emissions Profiles of High-, Middle-, and Low-Income Countries and Economies

TABLE A.1 Average Annual Agrifood Emissions, Share of Total Emissions, and Per Capita Emissions in High-Income Countries and Economies, 2018–20

Country or economy	Agrifood emissions, all gases (MtCO₂eq)				Share of total emissions (%)	Per capita emissions (tCO₂eq/ person)
	FG[a]	LU[a]	PPP[a]	Agrifood emissions total		
Andorra	0.0	0.0	0.1	0.1	22.1	1.5
Antigua and Barbuda	0.1	0.0	0.1	0.2	28.5	1.9
Aruba	0.0	0.0	0.3	0.3	28.1	2.6
Australia	143.2	1.5	52.1	196.8	33.0	7.8
Austria	8.8	0.2	8.0	17.0	18.5	1.9
Bahamas, The	0.1	0.0	0.6	0.8	32.1	1.9
Bahrain	0.1	0.0	3.7	3.8	6.7	2.6
Barbados	0.1	0.0	0.4	0.5	34.3	1.8
Belgium	11.9	0.0	11.8	23.7	18.0	2.1
Bermuda	0.0	0.0	0.0	0.1	—	0.8
British Virgin Islands	0.0	0.0	0.0	0.0	9.6	0.6

(table continued next page)

245

TABLE A.1 Average Annual Agrifood Emissions, Share of Total Emissions, and Per Capita Emissions in High-Income Countries and Economies, 2018–20 *(Continued)*

Country or economy	Agrifood emissions, all gases (MtCO$_2$eq)				Share of total emissions (%)	Per capita emissions (tCO$_2$eq/ person)
	FG[a]	LU[a]	PPP[a]	Agrifood emissions total		
Brunei Darussalam	0.3	0.1	1.1	1.5	9.0	3.5
Canada	118.3	96.1	70.7	285.2	34.4	7.6
Cayman Islands	0.0	0.0	0.1	0.1	—	1.6
Chile	13.2	0.0	19.1	32.3	53.4	1.7
Croatia	3.4	0.5	4.4	8.2	38.4	2.0
Cyprus	0.5	0.0	1.1	1.7	20.2	1.4
Czechia	8.0	1.0	12.1	21.1	18.2	2.0
Denmark	14.4	2.3	4.4	21.0	44.7	3.6
Estonia	7.7	0.0	1.6	9.4	33.4	7.1
Faroe Islands	0.6	0.0	0.0	0.6	206.6	12.4
Finland	21.3	0.0	5.3	26.5	31.1	4.8
France	91.5	0.0	81.4	172.9	45.0	2.6
French Polynesia	0.1	0.0	0.1	0.1	356.4	0.5
Germany	95.8	0.0	88.0	183.8	23.4	2.2
Gibraltar	0.0	0.0	0.1	0.1	—	3.6
Greece	8.9	0.0	13.9	22.8	27.9	2.1
Greenland	0.2	0.0	0.0	0.2	—	3.6
Guam	0.0	0.0	0.0	0.0	—	0.0
Hong Kong SAR, China	0.0	0.0	11.6	11.6	26.2	1.6
Hungary	15.2	0.4	10.7	26.3	36.3	2.7
Iceland	2.0	0.0	0.5	2.4	44.1	6.8
Ireland	35.6	0.0	5.4	41.0	56.9	8.3
Isle of Man	0.0	0.0	0.0	0.0	201.9	0.6
Israel	2.6	0.1	14.5	17.2	19.2	1.9
Italy	41.0	0.0	83.7	124.7	31.8	2.1
Japan	37.8	1.7	116.4	156.0	12.2	1.2
Korea, Republic of	19.0	2.8	70.8	92.5	14.0	1.8
Kuwait	0.5	0.0	11.0	11.5	7.7	2.6
Latvia	8.6	0.6	1.3	10.5	76.4	5.5
Liechtenstein	0.0	0.0	0.0	0.0	6.9	0.3
Lithuania	15.3	0.7	6.5	22.5	68.5	8.0
Luxembourg	0.7	0.0	0.9	1.6	16.2	2.6
Macao SAR, China	0.0	0.0	0.3	0.4	15.6	0.6
Malta	0.1	0.0	0.5	0.6	22.2	1.3

(table continued next page)

TABLE A.I Average Annual Agrifood Emissions, Share of Total Emissions, and Per Capita Emissions in High-Income Countries and Economies, 2018–20 (Continued)

Country or economy	Agrifood emissions, all gases (MtCO₂eq)				Share of total emissions (%)	Per capita emissions (tCO₂eq/ person)
	FGᵃ	LUᵃ	PPPᵃ	Agrifood emissions total		
Monaco	0.0	0.0	0.0	0.0	6.0	0.2
Nauru	0.0	0.0	0.0	0.0	20.5	1.0
Netherlands	33.4	0.0	26.6	60.1	28.2	3.5
New Caledonia	0.3	0.0	0.2	0.5	173.4	1.7
New Zealand	47.0	1.8	6.5	55.3	69.7	11.1
Northern Marianas Islands	0.0	0.9	0.0	0.9	95.8	18.6
Norway	11.3	0.0	2.9	14.2	20.7	2.7
Oman	1.8	0.0	9.4	11.3	9.7	2.5
Panama	4.3	3.8	3.9	12.1	57.5	2.9
Poland	76.7	0.0	59.8	136.5	32.5	3.6
Portugal	8.6	0.0	10.1	18.6	20.2	1.8
Puerto Rico	0.9	0.0	3.8	4.7	—	1.5
Qatar	1.6	0.0	9.5	11.1	5.4	4.0
Romania	18.1	5.1	15.1	38.3	43.9	2.0
San Marino	0.0	0.0	0.0	0.0	6.3	0.3
Saudi Arabia	6.7	0.0	54.6	61.4	8.1	1.7
Seychelles	0.0	0.0	0.1	0.1	21.9	1.1
Singapore	0.0	0.0	5.2	5.3	8.9	0.9
Slovak Republic	2.8	0.0	3.8	6.7	15.4	1.2
Slovenia	2.1	1.2	1.8	5.1	27.4	2.4
Spain	48.8	0.8	39.5	89.1	28.5	1.9
St. Kitts and Nevis	0.0	0.0	0.0	0.1	17.6	1.1
Sweden	18.9	23.8	4.0	46.7	88.2	4.5
Switzerland	7.0	0.5	8.9	16.4	38.8	1.9
Taiwan, China	6.1	0.0	30.7	36.8	11.8	1.6
Trinidad and Tobago	0.4	0.1	17.4	17.9	26.8	11.8
Turks and Caicos Islands	0.0	0.0	0.0	0.0	19.0	1.1
United Arab Emirates	2.1	0.0	16.6	18.8	7.7	2.0
United Kingdom	79.5	0.0	49.5	129.0	28.2	1.9
United States	481.4	59.7	478.4	1,019.5	16.7	3.1
Uruguay	28.3	0.0	2.5	30.8	74.6	9.0
Virgin Islands (US)	0.0	0.0	0.2	0.2	—	1.6

Source: FAOSTAT 2023.

Note: Negligible emissions are marked with —. MtCO₂eq = megatons of carbon dioxide equivalent; tCO₂eq = tons of carbon dioxide equivalent.

a. FG = farm gate; LU = land use and land use change; PPP = pre- and post-production.

TABLE A.2 Average Annual Agrifood Emissions, Share of Total Emissions, and Per Capita Emissions in Middle-Income Countries and Economies, 2018–20

Country or economy	Agrifood emissions, all gases (MtCO$_2$eq)				Share of total emissions (%)	Per capita emissions (tCO$_2$eq/ person)
	FG[a]	LU[a]	PPP[a]	Agrifood emissions total		
Albania	3.3	0.0	1.5	4.8	52.6	1.7
Algeria	12.9	0.6	46.3	59.8	21.4	1.4
American Samoa	0.0	0.0	0.1	0.1	—	1.8
Angola	34.7	48.5	4.8	88.0	57.6	2.7
Argentina	155.7	55.0	49.5	260.1	65.2	5.8
Armenia	1.9	0.0	1.5	3.5	32.8	1.2
Azerbaijan	9.0	0.5	7.3	16.7	28.7	1.7
Bangladesh	111.3	0.1	25.5	136.9	55.1	0.8
Belarus	68.1	0.0	17.5	85.6	75.9	9.1
Belize	0.6	5.1	0.4	6.1	92.8	15.7
Benin	5.9	10.8	2.3	19.1	67.0	1.6
Bhutan	0.5	0.0	0.2	0.7	41.5	0.9
Bolivia	30.8	75.1	7.9	113.7	59.0	9.7
Bosnia and Herzegovina	2.8	0.0	3.3	6.2	21.3	1.8
Botswana	5.3	40.5	1.4	47.2	87.0	18.9
Brazil	552.3	666.0	166.7	1,385.0	84.9	6.5
Bulgaria	7.0	3.2	4.8	15.0	59.8	2.2
Cabo Verde	0.1	0.0	0.2	0.3	32.8	0.5
Cambodia	22.9	33.2	4.1	60.1	76.2	3.7
Cameroon	14.8	34.1	3.4	52.3	69.3	2.0
China	788.1	0.0	1,388.2	2,176.3	17.0	1.5
Colombia	72.5	83.0	32.0	187.5	63.5	3.7
Comoros	0.3	0.1	0.1	0.5	50.6	0.6
Congo, Republic of	6.0	7.3	0.7	14.1	42.1	2.5
Costa Rica	4.6	0.0	2.9	7.6	86.4	1.5
Côte d'Ivoire	9.0	23.7	8.0	40.7	70.4	1.6
Cuba	13.8	0.0	6.5	20.4	49.4	1.8
Djibouti	0.8	0.0	0.3	1.0	55.9	0.9
Dominica	0.0	0.0	0.0	0.1	36.6	1.2
Dominican Republic	10.0	0.6	10.5	21.2	54.5	1.9
Ecuador	13.7	26.0	10.7	50.5	52.9	2.9
Egypt, Arab Rep.	27.2	0.2	62.6	89.9	26.1	0.9
El Salvador	2.3	1.1	3.1	6.6	51.1	1.0
Equatorial Guinea	0.1	3.8	0.4	4.3	20.0	2.8
Eswatini	1.1	0.3	1.1	2.5	110.9	2.1
Fiji	0.6	0.0	0.4	1.0	99.9	1.1
Gabon	1.1	5.7	0.6	7.4	31.0	3.3
Georgia	2.1	0.0	3.1	5.1	34.8	1.4

(table continued next page)

Country or economy	Agrifood emissions, all gases (MtCO₂eq)				Share of total emissions (%)	Per capita emissions (tCO₂eq/person)
	FG[a]	LU[a]	PPP[a]	Agrifood emissions total		
Ghana	11.5	0.1	6.9	18.5	99.7	0.6
Grenada	0.0	0.0	0.1	0.1	32.6	1.0
Guatemala	11.1	4.6	6.2	21.8	51.1	1.3
Guyana	5.8	9.8	0.5	16.1	89.6	20.3
Haiti	4.7	0.6	6.5	11.8	72.4	1.1
Honduras	7.4	6.0	4.1	17.5	60.7	1.8
India	773.2	0.6	510.7	1,284.5	34.1	0.9
Indonesia	398.3	451.0	153.8	1,003.2	57.2	3.7
Iran, Islamic Rep.	48.6	0.0	83.2	131.8	13.0	1.5
Iraq	8.2	0.5	21.0	29.6	7.4	0.7
Jamaica	2.8	0.0	2.3	5.1	52.6	1.8
Jordan	1.6	0.0	6.9	8.5	30.6	0.8
Kazakhstan	30.8	0.0	23.9	54.7	15.2	3.0
Kenya	51.5	0.0	8.4	59.8	70.7	1.2
Kiribati	0.0	0.0	0.0	0.0	27.4	0.2
Kyrgyz Republic	5.8	0.0	1.5	7.4	43.0	1.1
Lao PDR	10.7	14.5	2.9	28.0	61.2	3.9
Lebanon	1.0	0.0	6.0	7.0	29.1	1.2
Lesotho	1.3	0.0	0.5	1.8	37.9	0.8
Libya	3.0	0.0	8.3	11.3	16.7	1.7
Malaysia	45.5	37.2	39.7	122.4	30.1	3.7
Maldives	0.1	0.0	0.3	0.3	18.9	0.7
Marshall Islands	0.0	0.0	0.0	0.0	13.9	0.6
Mauritania	10.3	0.7	0.9	11.9	82.8	2.7
Mauritius	0.1	0.0	1.6	1.7	30.4	1.4
Mexico	112.0	15.4	108.4	235.8	29.8	1.9
Micronesia, Fed. Sts.	0.1	0.0	0.0	0.1	46.5	0.8
Mongolia	53.3	0.2	4.6	58.1	52.6	18.0
Montenegro	0.5	0.0	0.6	1.1	23.5	1.7
Morocco	18.2	0.0	26.3	44.5	43.7	1.2
Myanmar	109.1	95.2	12.2	216.5	84.5	4.1
Namibia	8.1	10.6	0.5	19.2	82.9	7.8
Nepal	30.8	0.7	5.2	36.7	68.8	1.3
Nicaragua	12.0	20.6	2.9	35.5	89.7	5.3
Nigeria	86.4	46.5	42.3	175.2	36.5	0.9
North Macedonia	1.3	0.0	1.9	3.2	31.4	1.5
Pakistan	204.9	7.0	56.1	268.0	48.9	1.2

(table continued next page)

Agrifood Emissions Profiles of High-, Middle-, and Low-Income Countries and Economies **249**

TABLE A.2 Average Annual Agrifood Emissions, Share of Total Emissions, and Per Capita Emissions in Middle-Income Countries and Economies, 2018–20 (Continued)

Country or economy	Agrifood emissions, all gases (MtCO$_2$eq)				Share of total emissions (%)	Per capita emissions (tCO$_2$eq/person)
	FG[a]	LU[a]	PPP[a]	Agrifood emissions total		
Palau	0.0	0.0	0.0	0.0	10.2	1.8
Papua New Guinea	24.4	11.5	0.8	36.8	70.7	3.9
Paraguay	32.7	48.2	3.1	84.1	93.7	12.9
Peru	28.0	93.0	16.4	137.4	71.4	4.2
Philippines	66.7	0.0	36.7	103.4	40.5	0.9
Moldova	2.1	0.0	3.5	5.6	57.4	2.1
Russian Federation	170.5	34.5	230.1	435.1	21.4	3.0
Samoa	0.2	0.1	0.0	0.3	48.9	1.5
São Tomé and Príncipe	0.0	0.2	0.0	0.3	65.7	1.3
Senegal	13.2	4.0	4.5	21.7	66.7	1.4
Serbia	6.7	6.6	8.1	21.5	26.7	3.1
Solomon Islands	0.1	0.2	0.1	0.5	1.0	0.7
South Africa	38.0	6.7	45.2	89.9	14.6	1.5
Sri Lanka	7.7	0.6	6.1	14.4	36.2	0.7
St. Lucia	0.0	0.0	0.2	0.2	66.7	1.3
St. Vincent and the Grenadines	0.0	0.0	0.1	0.1	33.8	1.1
Suriname	1.6	8.6	0.4	10.6	79.6	17.6
Tajikistan	7.0	0.0	1.9	8.9	54.1	0.9
Tanzania	65.3	63.5	17.2	146.0	88.6	2.4
Türkiye	65.0	0.0	75.1	140.1	25.8	1.7
Thailand	81.8	14.3	81.7	177.9	39.1	2.5
Timor-Leste	1.1	0.5	0.4	2.0	30.7	1.5
Tonga	0.1	0.0	0.0	0.1	36.9	1.1
Tunisia	5.9	0.0	10.2	16.1	46.7	1.3
Turkmenistan	11.9	0.0	7.7	19.7	14.2	3.2
Tuvalu	0.0	0.0	0.0	0.0	74.6	1.6
Ukraine	54.7	1.4	42.0	98.1	35.4	2.2
Uzbekistan	37.0	0.0	25.8	62.8	31.9	1.9
Vanuatu	0.3	0.0	0.1	0.4	69.6	1.4
Venezuela, RB	42.3	40.4	16.7	99.4	42.8	3.4
Viet Nam	83.2	0.3	62.8	146.3	37.8	1.5
West Bank and Gaza	0.3	0.0	4.4	4.8	—	0.9
Zimbabwe	11.4	10.7	2.9	24.9	21.5	1.6

Source: FAOSTAT 2023.
Note: Negligible emissions are marked with —. MtCO$_2$eq = megatons of carbon dioxide equivalent; tCO$_2$eq = tons of carbon dioxide equivalent.
a. FG = farm gate; LU = land use and land use change; PPP = pre- and post-production.

TABLE A.3 Average Annual Agrifood Emissions, Share of Total Emissions, and Per Capita Emissions in Low-Income Countries and Economies, 2018–20

Country or economy	Agrifood emissions, all gases, (MtCO$_2$eq)				Share of total emissions	Per capita emissions (tCO$_2$eq/ person)
	FG[a]	LU[a]	PPP[a]	Agrifood emissions total		
Afghanistan	15.6	0.0	6.2	21.8	68.7	0.6
Burundi	5.8	0.0	1.6	7.4	80.1	0.6
Burkina Faso	24.4	6.5	3.6	34.5	57.0	1.6
Central African Republic	17.8	34.5	0.9	53.2	96.6	10.2
Chad	77.5	24.5	2.1	104.1	95.5	6.5
Congo, Democratic Republic of	27.5	630.0	10.0	667.5	95.2	7.4
Eritrea	4.8	0.7	0.1	5.6	72.1	1.6
Ethiopia	132.0	31.5	9.3	172.9	81.0	1.5
Gambia, The	1.3	0.5	0.3	2.2	70.2	0.9
Guinea	22.3	11.5	1.7	35.5	84.0	2.8
Guinea Bissau	2.0	1.7	0.4	4.1	82.0	2.1
Korea, Democratic People's Republic of	7.0	3.1	2.8	12.9	21.7	0.5
Liberia	0.6	13.8	0.7	15.1	82.9	3.0
Madagascar	28.7	5.0	3.7	37.3	79.0	1.4
Malawi	9.0	7.4	1.3	17.7	77.3	0.9
Mali	36.9	0.1	2.3	39.3	86.3	1.9
Mozambique	19.5	58.9	3.6	81.9	69.0	2.7
Niger	33.0	1.3	2.9	37.2	88.8	1.6
Rwanda	5.2	0.0	3.3	8.5	96.4	0.7
Sierra Leone	3.8	3.5	0.8	8.1	73.0	1.0
Somalia	23.8	17.4	1.2	42.4	86.3	2.7
South Sudan	57.8	1.7	1.8	61.3	90.2	5.8
Sudan	79.5	21.0	8.4	108.9	78.2	2.5
Syrian Arab Republic	6.5	0.3	9.2	16.0	31.8	0.8
Togo	3.2	1.2	1.9	6.3	53.2	0.8
Uganda	34.7	10.5	11.7	56.9	90.6	1.3
Yemen, Rep.	8.3	0.0	8.6	16.9	47.2	0.5
Zambia	36.8	40.3	2.6	79.8	84.0	4.3

Source: FAOSTAT 2023.
Note: MtCO$_2$eq = megatons of carbon dioxide equivalent; tCO$_2$eq = tons of carbon dioxide equivalent.
a. FG = farm gate; LU = land use and land use change; PPP = pre- and post-production.

Reference

FAOSTAT. 2023. FAOSTAT (database). Accessed April 11, 2024. https://www.fao.org/faostat/en/#data.

Co-benefits of Mitigation Measures and Low-Cost Mitigation Options for Selected Countries

TABLE B.1 Co-benefits of AFOLU and Demand-Side Mitigation Measures

Mitigation measure	Resilience and adaptation	Food security	Biodiversity	Air	Socioeconomic (income and livelihoods)	Soil fertility	Water	Improved animal welfare
Forests and other ecosystems								
Reduce deforestation	Yes	Yes	Yes	Yes	Yes	Yes	Yes	No
Reduce mangrove conversion	Yes	Yes	Yes	Yes	Yes	Yes	Yes	No
Reduce peatland degradation and conversion	Yes	Yes	Yes	Yes	Yes	Yes	Yes	No
Improve forest management	Yes	Yes	Yes	Yes	Yes	Yes	Yes	No

(table continued next page)

TABLE B.1 Co-benefits of AFOLU and Demand-Side Mitigation Measures *(Continued)*

Mitigation measure	Resilience and adaptation	Food security	Biodiversity	Air	Socioeconomic (income and livelihoods)	Soil fertility	Water	Improved animal welfare
Grassland fire management	Yes	Yes	Yes	Yes	Yes	Yes	No	No
Afforestation and reforestation	Yes	Yes	Yes	Yes	Yes	Yes	Yes	No
Mangrove restoration	Yes	Yes	Yes	Yes	Yes	Yes	Yes	No
Peatland restoration	Yes	No	Yes	Yes	Yes	Yes	Yes	No
Agriculture								
Enteric fermentation	No	Yes	No	Yes	No	No	No	Yes
Manure management	Yes	Yes	No	Yes	Yes	Yes	Yes	No
Nutrient management	Yes	Yes	No	Yes	Yes	Yes	Yes	No
Improved rice cultivation	Yes	Yes	No	Yes	Yes	Yes	Yes	No
Agroforestry	Yes	Yes	Yes	Yes	Yes	Yes	Yes	No
Biochar from crop residues	Yes	Yes	Yes	Yes	Yes	Yes	Yes	No
Soil organic carbon in croplands	Yes	Yes	Yes	Yes	No	Yes	Yes	No
Soil organic carbon in grasslands	Yes	Yes	Yes	Yes	No	Yes	Yes	No
Bioenergy								
Bioenergy with carbon capture and storage	No	No	No	Yes	Yes	Yes	Yes	No
Demand side								
Increase clean cookstoves	Yes	No	Yes	Yes	No	Yes	No	No
Reduce food waste	No	Yes	Yes	Yes	Yes	No	No	No
Shift to sustainable healthy diets	No	Yes	Yes	Yes	Yes	No	No	No

Source: World Bank based on data from Roe et al. 2021.
Note: AFOLU = agriculture, forestry, and other land use.

TABLE B.2 Cost-Saving and Low-Cost Mitigation Options in Selected MICs and LICs, by Sector

Country	Sector coverage (reference date)	Cost-saving mitigation options (<$0/tCO$_2$eq)	Low-cost mitigation options ($0–$100/tCO$_2$eq)	Source
Bangladesh	Agriculture (2030)	• Nutrient management (crops) • Zero tillage (crops) • Rice water management (crops)	• Short duration varieties (rice)	Sapkota et al. 2021
China	Agriculture (2020)	• Probiotics addition to the diet (livestock) • Animal breeding (livestock) • Fertilizer best management practices (wheat and maize)—right time and placement • Ionophores addition to the diet (livestock) • Fertilizer best management practices (crops)—right time and placement • Conservation tillage for upland crops (crops) • Fertilizer best management practices—right rate (crops) • Tea saponins addition to the diet (livestock) • Anaerobic digestion of manure (livestock)	• Reduction of stocking rate, medium grazing intensity (livestock) • Enhanced-efficiency fertilizers (crops) • Grazing prohibition for 35 percent of grazed grasslands (livestock) • Reduction of stocking rate, light grazing intensity (livestock) • Fertilizer and water best management in rice paddies (crops)	Nayak et al. 2015
India	Agriculture (2030)	• Green fodder supplement (livestock) • Vermicompost (crops) • Improved diet management of small ruminants (livestock) • Molasses urea products (livestock) • Laser land leveling (crops) • Biogas (livestock) • Increased concentrate feeding (livestock) • Efficient fertilizer use (crops) • Zero tillage (crops) • Improved diet, pigs (livestock) • Rice water management (crops)	• Eliminate residue burning (crops)	Sapkota et al. 2019

(table continued next page)

TABLE B.2 Cost-Saving and Low-Cost Mitigation Options in Selected MICs and LICs, by Sector *(Continued)*

Country	Sector coverage (reference date)	Cost-saving mitigation options (<$0/tCO$_2$eq)	Low-cost mitigation options ($0–$100/tCO$_2$eq)	Source
Kenya	Dairy (2030)	• Improved feed with different types of fodder (feed management) • Artificial insemination with improved breed • Loss minimization in cooling centers (food loss and waste) • Loss minimization in collection centers (food loss and waste)	• Biogas plant (manure management) • Improving energy use efficiency through retrofitting dairy plant	Khatri-Chhetri, Wilkes, and Odhong 2020
Latvia	Crops (2030)	• Minimum tillage • Precision application of nitrogen, phosphorus, and potassium	• Fertilization planning • Nitrogen fixation • Liming acid soils	Popluga et al. 2017
Mexico	AFOLU (2030)	• Nitrogen use efficiency • Laser land leveling • Conservation agriculture	• Stop residue burning • National Protected Areas management • Increase in carbon stocks • Zero deforestation • Biodigester, pig	Sapkota et al. 2020
Nigeria	AFOLU (2035)	• Annuals and conservation agriculture • Perennials • Livestock and pasturelands improvement • Sustainable rice intensification • Agroforestry and non-forest land use changes	• Avoided deforestation	Cervigni, Dvorak, and Rogers 2013
South Africa	AFOLU (2030)	• Expanding plantations • Treatment of livestock waste • Biochar addition to cropland	• Rural tree planting (thickets) • Urban tree planting • Restoration of mesic grasslands	Department of Environmental Affairs, South Africa 2014

(table continued next page)

TABLE B.2 Cost-Saving and Low-Cost Mitigation Options in Selected MICs and LICs, by Sector *(Continued)*

Country	Sector coverage (reference date)	Cost-saving mitigation options (<$0/tCO$_2$eq)	Low-cost mitigation options ($0–$100/tCO$_2$eq)	Source
Viet Nam	AFOLU (2030)	• Intercropping coffee and avocado (agroforestry) • Intercropping coffee and durian (agroforestry) • Feeding dairy cows with total mixed ration • Beef diet supplement • Replace rice with shrimp farming (land use change) • Replace urea with ammonium sulphate in sugarcane fields • Rubber planted in bare land (land use change) • Alternate wetting and drying in Mekong Delta 1 • Alternate wetting and drying in Mekong Delta 2 • Alternate wetting and drying in Red River Delta 1 • Replace urea with ammonium sulphate in maize fields • Alternate wetting and drying in Red River Delta 2 • Compost from pigs • Acacia plantation in bare land (land use change)	• Rainforest protection 1 (prevent degradation to commercial forestry) • Biogas from waste in pig farms • Rainforest restoration 2 (in degraded land) • Forest restoration 2 (in degraded land) • Low tillage • Rainforest restoration 1 (in bare land) • Rainforest protection 2 • Forest restoration 1 (in bare land) • Bamboo restoration 2 (in degraded land) • Bamboo restoration 1 (in bare land) • Rice straw (integrated crop management) • Coffee and cassia (agroforestry) • Forest protection 1 (prevent conversion to crops) • Mangrove protection • Bamboo protection (prevent conversion to crops) • Rainforest restoration 3 in current commercial forestry (acacia) • Forest restoration 3 in agricultural crops (cassava, maize) • Maize residues (not burning; integrated crop management)	Escobar Carbonari et al. 2019

Source: World Bank.
Note: AFOLU = agriculture, forestry, and other land use; LICs = low-income countries; MICs= middle-income countries; tCO$_2$eq = tons of carbon dioxide equivalent.

References

Cervigni, Raffaello, Irina Dvorak, and John Allen Rogers. 2013. *Assessing Low-Carbon Development in Nigeria: An Analysis of Four Sectors.* Washington, DC: World Bank. https://doi.org/10.1596/978-0-8213 -9973-6.

Department of Environmental Affairs, South Africa. 2014. *South Africa's Greenhouse Gas (GHG) Mitigation Potential Analysis.* Pretoria: Department of Environmental Affairs. https://www.dffe.gov.za/sites/default /files/docs/mitigationreport.pdf.

Escobar Carbonari, Daniel, Godefroy Grosjean, Peter Läderach, Nghia Tran Dai, Bjoern Ole Sander, Justin McKinley, Sebastian Leocadio, and Jeimar Tapasco. 2019. "Reviewing Vietnam's Nationally Determined Contribution: A New Perspective Using the Marginal Cost of Abatement." *Frontiers in Sustainable Food Systems* 3: 14. https://doi.org/10.3389/fsufs.2019.00014.

Khatri-Chhetri, A., A. Wilkes, and C. Odhong. 2020. "Mitigation Options and Finance for Transition to Low-Emissions Dairy in Kenya." Consultative Group on International Agricultural Research (CGIAR) Research Program on Climate Change Agriculture and Food Security (CCAFS) Working Paper, CCAFS, Wageningen, the Netherlands.

Nayak, Dali, Eli Saetnan, Kun Cheng, Wen Wang, Frank Koslowski, Yan-Fen Cheng, Wei Yun Zhu, et al. 2015. "Management Opportunities to Mitigate Greenhouse Gas Emissions from Chinese Agriculture." *Agriculture, Ecosystems and Environment* 209: 108–24. https://doi.org/10.1016/j.agee.2015.04.035.

Popluga, D., K. Naglis-Liepa, A. Lenerts, and P. Rivza. 2017. "Marginal Abatement Cost Curve for Assessing Mitigation Potential of Latvian Agricultural Greenhouse Gas Emissions: Case Study of Crop Sector." *International Multidisciplinary Scientific GeoConference: SGEM* 17: 511–17. https://doi.org/10.5593 /sgem2017/17/S07.065.

Roe, S., C. Streck, R. Beach, J. Busch, M. Chapman, V. Daioglou, A. Deppermann, et al. 2021. "Land-Based Measures to Mitigate Climate Change: Potential and Feasibility by Country." *Global Change Biology* 27 (23): 6025–58. https://doi.org/10.1111/gcb.15873.

Sapkota, Tek B., Fahmida Khanam, Gokul Prasad Mathivanan, Sylvia Vetter, Sk. Ghulam Hussain, Anne-Laure Pilat, Sumona Shahrin, Md. Khaled Hossain, Nathu Ram Sarker, and Timothy J. Krupnik. 2021. "Quantifying Opportunities for Greenhouse Gas Emissions Mitigation Using Big Data from Smallholder Crop and Livestock Farmers across Bangladesh." *Science of the Total Environment* 786: 147344. https://doi.org/10.1016/j.scitotenv.2021.147344.

Sapkota, Tek B., I. Ortiz-Monasterio, K. Sonder, L. Wollenberg, M. B. Richards, J. C. Leyva, and M. A. Garcia. 2020. "Rapid Analysis of Country-Level Mitigation Potential from Agriculture, Forestry and Other Land Uses in Mexico." CCAFS Working Paper 309, CGIAR Research Program on Climate Change, Agriculture and Food Security (CCAFS), Wageningen, the Netherlands. https://ccafs.cgiar.org /resources/publications/rapid-analysis-country-level-mitigation-potential-agriculture-forestry.

Sapkota, Tek B., Sylvia H. Vetter, M. L. Jat, Smita Sirohi, Paresh B. Shirsath, Rajbir Singh, Hanuman S. Jat, Pete Smith, Jon Hillier, and Clare M. Stirling. 2019. "Cost-Effective Opportunities for Climate Change Mitigation in Indian Agriculture." *Science of the Total Environment* 655: 1342–54. https://doi .org/10.1016/j.scitotenv.2018.11.225.